Logic

AN EMPHASIS ON CRITICAL THINKING
AND INFORMAL LOGIC

Logic

Fourth Edition

AN EMPHASIS ON CRITICAL THINKING
AND INFORMAL LOGIC

Stan Baronett

New York   Oxford
Oxford University Press

Oxford University Press is a department of the University of Oxford. It furthers
the University's objective of excellence in research, scholarship, and education by
publishing worldwide. Oxford is a registered trade mark of Oxford University Press
in the UK and certain other countries.

Published in the United States of America by Oxford University Press
198 Madison Avenue, New York, NY 10016, United States of America.

For titles covered by Section 112 of the US Higher Education
Opportunity Act, please visit www.oup.com/us/he for the latest
information about pricing and alternate formats.

Library of Congress Cataloging-in-Publication Data

Names: Baronett, Stan, author.
Title: Logic : an emphasis on critical thinking and informal logic / Stan
  Baronett.
Description: Fourth edition. | New York : Oxford University Press, 2018. |
  Does not include all chapters from the main book—publisher's comments.
Identifiers: LCCN 2018003152 (print) | LCCN 2018017894 (ebook) | ISBN
  9780190691882 (Ebook) | ISBN 9780190691875 (pbk.)
Subjects: LCSH: Logic
Classification: LCC BC108 (ebook) | LCC BC108 .B26 2018d (print) | DDC
  160—dc23
LC record available at https://lccn.loc.gov/2018003152

9 8 7 6 5 4 3 2 1
Printed by LSC Communications, United States of America

Brief Contents

Contents

Part IV Inductive Logic

Instructors interested in providing students with an opportunity for further analysis can refer them to Online Chapter 15, located on the companion website at www.oup.com/us/baronett.

Preface

This is the *Logic: An Emphasis on Critical Thinking and Informal Logic* alternate edition. It was created for instructors who want to present the core skills of a typical critical thinking course. The text offers topics such as distinguishing arguments from non-arguments, diagramming arguments, informal fallacies, and a five-chapter part on inductive logic that includes detailed discussions of analogical, legal, moral, statistical, and scientific reasoning.

Today's logic students want to see the relevance of logic to their lives. They need motivation to read a logic textbook and do the exercises. Logic and critical thinking instructors want their students to read the textbook and to practice the skills being taught. They want their students to come away with the ability to recognize and evaluate arguments, an understanding of formal and informal logic, and a lasting sense of why they matter. These concerns meet head-on in the classroom. This textbook is designed to help alleviate these concerns.

THE CONTINUING STORY

The focus of the fourth edition has been on fine-tuning an already student-friendly and comprehensive introduction to logic book. To that effect, several passages have been reworked with an eye toward more clarity and precision. The goal has been to define, explain, and illustrate those key logical concepts that require an in-depth understanding based on the many possible applications of those concepts. The idea is to provide as much information as possible regarding key concepts so students are well equipped to tackle the exercise sets.

The driving force behind writing the fourth edition has been the continuing effort to make logic **relevant, interesting, and accessible to today's students**, without sacrificing the coverage that instructors demand and expect. An introduction to logic is often a student's only exposure to rigorous thinking and symbolism. It should prepare them for reasoning in their lives and careers. It must balance careful coverage of abstract reasoning with **clear, accessible explanations and vivid everyday examples**.

This book was written to meet all those challenges. **Relevant examples provide a bridge between formal reasoning and practical applications of logic, thereby connecting logic to students' lives and future careers.** Each chapter opens with a discussion of an everyday example, often taken directly from contemporary events, to pose the problem and set the narrative tone. This provides an immediate connection between logic and real-world issues, motivating the need for logic as a tool to help with the deluge of information available today.

The challenge of any introduction to logic textbook is to connect logic to students' lives. Yet existing texts can and should do more to reinforce and improve the basic skills of reasoning we all rely on in daily life. Relevant, real-life examples are essential to making logic accessible to students, especially when they mesh seamlessly with the technical material. To accomplish this, quotes and passages from modern and classic sources illustrate the relevance of logic through some of the perennial problems that impact everyone's lives. Examples concerning the workplace, careers, sports, politics, movies, music, TV, novels, new inventions, gadgets, cell phones, transportation, newspapers, magazines, computers, speeches, science, religion, superstition, gambling, drugs, war, abortion, euthanasia, capital punishment, the role of government, taxes, military spending, and unemployment are used **to show how arguments, and thus the role of logic, can be found in nearly every aspect of life**. The examples were chosen to be interesting, thought-provoking, and relevant to students, and the writing style was crafted to engage students by connecting logic to their lives.

AN INCLUSIVE TEXT

The fourteen chapters are designed to provide a comprehensive logic textbook, but also one that can be tailored to individual courses and their needs. The result is a full five chapters on deductive logic, but also a uniquely applied five-chapter part on inductive logic. Here separate chapters on analogical arguments, legal arguments, moral arguments, statistical arguments, and scientific arguments allow students to apply the logical skills learned in the earlier parts of the book. As with previous editions, explanations and examples have been created to facilitate student comprehension, and to show students that the logical skills they are learning do in fact have practical, real-world application. The material also provides more resources to help students when they do the exercise sets.

Since each chapter has been developed to provide maximum flexibility to instructors, some sections can be skipped in lecture without loss of continuity. In addition, those wishing for a briefer text can choose a text tailored to their course. They may choose to emphasize or omit certain chapters on formal logic or critical reasoning, and they may choose a selection of the five applied chapters to reflect their and their students' interests.

ALTERNATE FORMATS AND CUSTOM EDITIONS

Because every course and professor is unique, *Logic*, Fourth Edition, is available in a variety of formats to fit any course structure or student budget.

The full text can be purchased in numerous formats:

- Print, ISBN: 9780190691714
- Loose leaf, ISBN: 9780190691738
- eBook, ISBN: 9780190691745

Additionally, Dashboard, the book's optional online homework system, includes a full interactive version of the text that can be assigned alongside or in place of the print text. Please see the Instructor and Student Resources section of the preface for more information on Dashboard.

For those who do not wish to assign the complete text, Alternate and Custom Editions are available in print and digital format. Each Alternate Edition comes with answers to problems, a full glossary, and an index. Please see the ISBN information below:

Logic: Concise Edition
> Chapters 1, 3, 4, 5, 6, 7, 8
> Order the print version using ISBN: 9780190691837
> The eBook version is available from numerous eBook vendors. Look for
> eBook ISBN: 9780190691844.

Logic: An Emphasis on Critical Thinking and Informal Logic
> Chapters 1, 2, 3, 4, 10, 11, 12, 13, 14
> Order the print version using ISBN: 9780190691875
> The eBook version is available from numerous eBook vendors. Look for
> eBook ISBN: 9780190691882.

Logic: An Emphasis on Formal Logic
> Chapters 1, 4, 5, 6, 7, 8, 9
> Order the print version using ISBN: 9780190691851
> The eBook version is available from numerous eBook vendors. Look for
> eBook ISBN: 9780190691868.

It is also possible to create a customized textbook by choosing the specific chapters necessary for a course. For more information on Alternate and Custom Editions, please contact your Oxford University Press sales representative, call 1-800-280-0280 for details, or see the insert at the beginning of the Instructor's Edition of this book.

NEW TO THE FOURTH EDITION

Since student response to previous editions has been very positive, careful attention has been given to retain the style of presentation and the voice of the previous editions. Every change is designed to preserve the delicate balance of rigor with the text's overriding goal of relevance, accessibility, and student interest.

General changes: There are many new or modified exercises intended to keep students focused on applying the logical principles in each section. The overriding goal has always been to provide exercises that are challenging, interesting, thought-provoking, and relevant.

Chapter 1: Four new illustrations were added: First, in section 1F, a new table and accompanying explanation illustrates the various connections between premises, conclusions, validity, and soundness in deductive arguments. The second and third new illustrations and accompanying explanations flesh out the various connections between premises, conclusions, strength, and cogency in inductive arguments in section 1G. The fourth new illustration, in section 1H, offers an end-of-chapter summary regarding statements and arguments. A discussion of the difference between what is stated and what is implied by statements in everyday conversation has been added to section 1A.

In section 1E, the definitions of deductive and inductive arguments now incorporate the role of the inferential claim. In section 1G, the definitions of strong and weak inductive arguments emphasize the probable truth of the conclusion *following from* the truth of the premises. This emphasis leads to the discussion of an inductive argument in which premises that are irrelevant to the conclusion fail to provide any probabilistic support for the conclusion, resulting in a weak argument. Finally, the "principle of charity" discussion has been expanded to stress its role in the search for truth.

Chapter 2: Two new reference boxes were added to help students with exercise sets 2C and 2D. Several new examples have been added to the discussion of operational definitions. The discussions of *value judgments, cognitive meaning,* and *emotive meaning* have been reworked to offer more clarity.

Chapter 3: Additional explanation and examples of dependent premises, independent premises, and diagramming techniques associated with extended arguments are provided. A new key term has been added: A simple diagram consists of a single premise and a single conclusion. Finally, several new exercises have been added.

Chapter 4: Several definitions of key terms have been revised. The revisions bring out additional aspects of the concepts involved, thereby making it easier for students to apply the definitions to the exercise sets. The revised terms include *informal fallacies, tu quoque, appeal to the people,* and *rigid application of a generalization.*

Chapter 5: The terms "distributed" and "undistributed" have been clarified for categorical statements. A new set of exercises has been added to Exercises 5E to give students more practice in analyzing immediate inferences under the modern interpretation. The discussion of existential import in 5C has been modified to clarify its use in both the modern and traditional interpretations of universal propositions. Also, the discussion of the traditional square of opposition in 5F has been rewritten to clarify the understanding and application of existential import and the "assumption of existence" for universal propositions. A new set of exercises has been added to Exercises 5F to give students more practice in analyzing immediate inferences under the traditional interpretation. The directions for Exercise set 5G have been rewritten to offer more guidance to students.

Chapter 7: The concept of a *well-formed formula* has been reworked to offer more clarity and precision for students, and to help with the related exercises. The discussions of *inclusive disjunction* and *exclusive disjunction* have been clarified. Several exercises in 7A have been moved to a later exercise set where students have additional information to apply to the exercises. The concept of a *truth-functional proposition* has been clarified. The concept of *negation* has been expanded. The concept of a *tautology* has been revised. The question of whether or not a set of statements is consistent has been expanded to reveal its practical applications.

Chapter 8: A new discussion illustrates how natural deduction proofs allow for creativity by showing how more than one correct proof is possible for a given problem. This is coupled with examples of questions that naturally arise when students start creating their own proofs. The discussion of *misapplications of distribution* has been expanded along with new examples.

Chapter 9: The discussions of *universal generalization* and *existential generalization* have been expanded and clarified by the addition of new examples. The *change of quantifier* section now has additional examples to help facilitate understanding the four logical equivalences. The *identity rules* have been modified to include special symbols that are more in line with the way the inference rules for predicate logic are presented. Additional examples further illustrate each identity rule.

Chapter 12: Additional discussion of the role that logic plays in moral reasoning is presented, especially in the analysis, evaluation, and construction of moral arguments.

Three new *Profiles in Logic* have been added: Rudolf Carnap in Chapter 2; Francis Bacon in Chapter 4; and G. E. Moore in Chapter 12.

New Appendix: Many instructors have asked for material that directly applies the logical skills introduced in the book to the Law School Admission Test (LSAT). In a new appendix to the book, LSAT-type questions are presented and analyzed by reference to specific logical reasoning techniques that occur in *Logic*. This new section offers an in-depth look at the skills and techniques needed to do well on the LSAT *logical reasoning* questions. By working through the study guide, students can readily see that what they learn in *Logic* has direct application to the LSAT.

New Interactive eBook within Dashboard: An interactive eBook now appears within Dashboard, our online homework platform. Marginal icons in the text alert students to related exercises, video tutorials, and other study materials within Dashboard.

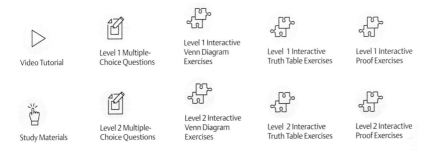

These icons serve as live links in the interactive eBook, instantly connecting Dashboard users with available resources.

SPECIAL FEATURES

The features that instructors found most useful in the third edition have been retained:

- Each chapter opens with a *preview*, beginning with real-life examples and outlining the questions to be addressed. It thus serves both as motivation and overview, and wherever possible it explicitly bridges both formal and informal logic to real life. For example, Chapter 1 starts with the deluge of information facing students today, to show the very need for a course in logic or critical thinking.
- Marginal definitions of key terms are provided for quick reference. Key terms appear in boldface when they are first introduced.

- The use of reference boxes has been expanded, since they have proven useful to both students and instructors. They capture material that is spread out over a number of pages in one place for easy reference.
- *Profiles in Logic* are short sketches of logicians, philosophers, mathematicians, and others associated with logic. The men and women in these sketches range in time from Aristotle and the Stoics to Christine Ladd-Franklin, the early ENIAC programmers, and others in the past century.
- Bulleted summaries are provided at the end of each chapter, as well as a list of key terms.
- The *Exercises* include a solution to the first problem in each set. Explanations are also provided where additional clarity is needed. This provides a model for students to follow, so they can see what is expected of their answers. In addition, approximately 25% of the exercises have answers provided at the back of the book.
- End-of-chapter *Logic Challenge* problems are included for each chapter. These are the kind of puzzles—like the problem of the hats, the truth teller and the liar, and the scale and the coins—that have long kept people thinking. They end chapters on a fun note, not to mention with a reminder that the challenges of logic are always lurking in plain English.
- A full glossary and index are located at the end of the book.

STUDENT AND INSTRUCTOR RESOURCES

A rich set of supplemental resources is available to support teaching and learning in this course. These supplements include Instructor Resources on the **Oxford University Press Ancillary Resource Center (ARC)** at www.oup-arc.com/access/baronett4e; intuitive, auto-graded assessments and other student resources on **Dashboard** by Oxford University Press, at www.oup.com/us/dashboard; a free **Companion Website** for students available at www.oup-arc.com/access/baronett4e; and downloadable **Learning Management System Cartridges**.

The **ARC** site at www.oup-arc.com/access/baronett4e houses a wealth of **Instructor Resources**:

- A customizable, auto-graded **Computerized Test Bank** of roughly 1500 multiple-choice and true/false questions.
- An **Instructor's Manual**, which includes the following:
  - ▷ A traditional "Pencil-and-Paper" version of the Test Bank, containing the same 1500 questions as the Computerized Test Bank, but converted for use in hard-copy exams and homework assignments, including some open-ended questions that allow students to develop extended analysis, such as drawing Venn diagrams, completing truth tables, and doing proofs.
  - ▷ A list of the 1500 questions from the Computerized Test Bank (in their closed-ended, multiple-choice and true/false format).
  - ▷ Complete answers to every set of exercises in the book—around 2800 exercises in total—including extended explanations for many of the questions that often require additional discussion and clarification.

▷ Complete answers and extended explanations for every end-of-chapter "Logic Challenge."

▷ Bulleted Chapter Summaries, which allow the instructor to scan the important aspects of each chapter quickly and to anticipate section discussions.

▷ A list of the boldfaced Key Terms from each chapter of the book.

- **PowerPoint-based Lecture Outlines** for each chapter, to assist the instructor in leading classroom discussion.
- **Online Chapter 15**, "Analyzing a Long Essay."

The Instructor's Manual and Test Bank are also available in printed format.

Dashboard at www.oup.com/us/dashboard contains a wealth of **Student Resources** and connects students and instructors in an intuitive, integrated, mobile device–friendly format:

- Chapter Learning Objectives adapted from the book's chapter headings.
- Level-One and Level-Two Quizzes with a total of around 2500 questions, auto-graded and linked to the Learning Objectives for easy instructor analysis of each student's topic-specific strengths and weaknesses. Each question set is preceded by a short recap of the material pertaining to the questions.
- **A Proof-Checking Module for solving symbolic proofs that allows students to enter proof solutions, check their validity, and receive feedback, both by line and as a whole, as well as Venn Diagram and Truth Table Creation Modules, all feeding automatically into a gradebook that offers instructors the chance to view students' individual attempts.**
- A full interactive eBook version of the text now appears within Dashboard. Marginal icons in the text alert students to related exercises, video tutorials, and other study materials within Dashboard.

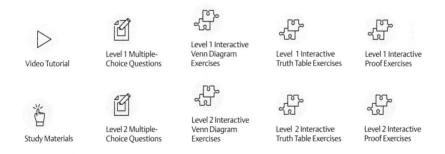

When students click on these icons from within the interactive eBook, they are instantly connected with available resources.

- Quiz Creation Capability for instructors who wish to create original quizzes in multiple-choice, true/false, multiple-select, long-answer, short-answer, ordering, or matching question formats, including customizable answer feedback and hints.
- A built-in, color-coded Gradebook that allows instructors to quickly and easily monitor student progress from virtually any device.

- Video Tutorials that work through specific example questions, bringing key concepts to life and guiding students on how to approach various problem types.
- Interactive Flashcards of Key Terms and their definitions from the book.
- A Glossary of Key Terms and their definitions from the book.
- Chapter Guides for reading that help students to think broadly and comparatively about the new ideas they encounter.
- Tipsheets that help students to understand the particularly complicated ideas presented in each chapter.
- Online Chapter 15, "Analyzing a Long Essay."
- Tools for student communication, reference, and planning, such as messaging and spaces for course outlines and syllabi.

Access to **Dashboard** can be packaged with *Logic* at a discount, stocked separately by your college bookstore, or purchased directly at www.oup.com/us/dashboard. For information about bundling Dashboard in a money-saving package with the print text, please contact your Oxford University Press sales representative or call 1-800-280-0280.

The free **Companion Website** at www.oup-arc.com/access/baronett4e contains supplemental **Student Resources**:

- Level-One and Level-Two Student Self-Quizzes, containing roughly 1500 multiple-choice and true/false questions. The "Pre-Chapter" quizzes feature questions taken from and answered in the book itself, while the "Post-Chapter" quizzes are unique to the Student Resources and give students a chance to review what they encountered in each chapter. Each question set is preceded by a short recap of the material pertaining to the questions.
- Interactive Flashcards of Key Terms and their definitions from the book.
- Video Tutorials that work through specific example questions, bringing key concepts to life and guiding students on how to approach various problem types.
- Chapter Guides for reading that help students to think broadly and comparatively about the new ideas they encounter.
- Tipsheets that help students to understand the particularly complicated ideas presented in each chapter.
- Online Chapter 15, "Analyzing a Long Essay."

The Instructor Resources from the ARC and the Student Resources from the Companion Website are also available in **Course Cartridges** for virtually any Learning Management System used in colleges and universities.

To find out more information or to order a printed Instructor's Manual, Dashboard access, or a Course Cartridge for your Learning Management System, please contact your Oxford University Press representative at 1-800-280-0280.

ACKNOWLEDGMENTS

For their very helpful suggestions throughout the writing process, I would like to thank the following reviewers:

- Mohamad Al-Hakim, Florida Gulf Coast University
- Guy Axtell, Radford University
- Ida Baltikauskas, Century College
- Joshua Beattie, California State University–East Bay
- Luisa Benton, Richland College
- Michael Boring, Estrella Mountain Community College
- Daniel Brunson, Morgan State University
- Julia R. Bursten, University of Kentucky
- Jeremy Byrd, Tarrant County College
- Bernardo Cantens, Moravian College
- John Casey, Northeastern Illinois University
- Darron Chapman, University of Louisville
- Eric Chelstrom, Minnesota State University, Moorhead
- Lynnette Chen, Humboldt State University
- Kevin DeLapp, Converse College
- Tobyn DeMarco, Bergen Community College
- William Devlin, Bridgewater State University
- Ian Duckles, Mesa College
- David Lyle Dyas, Los Angeles Mission College
- David Elliot, University of Regina
- Thompson M. Faller, University of Portland
- Craig Fox, California State University, Pennsylvania
- Matthew Frise, Baylor University
- Dimitria Electra Gatzia, University of Akron
- Cara Gillis, Pierce College
- David Gilboa, University of Wisconsin, Oshkosh
- Nathaniel Goldberg, Washington and Lee University
- Michael Goodman, Humboldt State University
- John Grey, Michigan State University
- Mary Gwin, San Diego Mesa College
- Matthew Hallgarth, Tarleton State University

- Anthony Hanson, De AnzaCollege
- Merle Harton, Jr., Everglades University
- John Helsel, University of Colorado, Boulder
- Will Heusser, Cypress College
- Ryan Hickerson, Western Oregon University
- Charles Hogg, Grand Valley State University
- Jeremy D. Hovda, Katholieke Universiteit Leuven
- Debby D. Hutchins, Gonzaga University
- Brian Huth, Kent State University
- Daniel Jacobson, University of Michigan–Ann Arbor
- William S. Jamison, University of Alaska Anchorage
- Benjamin C. Jantzen, Virginia Polytechnic Institute & State University
- Gary James Jason, California State University, Fullerton
- William M. Kallfelz, Mississippi State University
- Robert Larmer, University of New Brunswick
- Lory Lemke, University of Minnesota–Morris
- Court Lewis, Owensboro Community and Technical College
- David Liebesman, Boston University
- Brandon C. Look, University of Kentucky
- Ian D. MacKinnon, University of Akron
- Erik Meade, Southern Illinois University Edwardsville
- Alexander Miller, Piedmont Technical College
- James Moore, Georgia Perimeter College
- Allyson Mount, Keene State College
- Nathaniel Nicol, Washington State University
- Rosibel O'Brien-Cruz, Harold Washington College
- Joseph B. Onyango Okello, Asbury Theological Seminary
- Stephen Russell Orr, Solano Community College

- Lawrence Pasternack, Oklahoma State University
- James Pearson, Bridgewater State University
- Christian Perring, Dowling College
- Adam C. Podlaskowski, Fairmont State University
- Michael Potts, Methodist University
- Mark Reed, Tarrant County College
- Greg Rich, Fayetteville State University
- Miles Rind, Boston College
- Linda Rollin, Colorado State University
- Marcus Rossberg, University of Connecticut
- Frank X. Ryan, Kent State University
- Eric Saidel, George Washington University
- Kelly Salsbery, Stephen F. Austin State University
- David Sanson, Illinois State University
- Stephanie Semler, Virginia Polytechnic Institute & State University
- Robert Shanab, University of Nevada–Las Vegas
- David Shier, Washington State University
- Aeon J. Skoble, Bridgewater State University
- Nancy Slonneger- Hancock, Northern Kentucky University
- Basil Smith, Saddleback College
- Joshua Smith, Central Michigan University
- Paula Smithka, University of Southern Mississippi
- Deborah Hansen Soles, Wichita State University
- Charles Stein, St. Mary's College of Maryland
- David Stern, University of Iowa
- Tim Sundell, University of Kentucky
- Eric Swanson, University of Michigan, Ann Arbor
- Matthew Talbert, West Virginia University
- Erin Tarver, Emory University
- James Taylor, College of New Jersey
- Ramon Tello, Shasta College
- Joia Lewis Turner, St. Paul College
- Patricia Turrisi, University of North Carolina–Wilmington
- Michael Ventimiglia, Sacred Heart University
- Mark C. Vopat, Youngstown State University
- Reginald Williams, Bakersfield College
- Mia Wood, Pierce College
- Kiriake Xerohemona, Florida International University
- Jeffrey Zents, South Texas College

Many thanks also to the staff at Oxford University Press, Robert Miller, executive editor; Maegan Sherlock, development editor; Alyssa Palazzo, associate editor; Barbara Mathieu, senior production editor, and Michele Laseau, art director, for their work on the book. The *Profiles in Logic* portraits were drawn by Katie Klasmeier.

PART I

SETTING THE STAGE

Chapter 1

What Logic Studies

A. Statements and Arguments
B. Recognizing Arguments
C. Arguments and Explanations
D. Truth and Logic
E. Deductive and Inductive Arguments
F. Deductive Arguments: Validity and Soundness
G. Inductive Arguments: Strength and Cogency
H. Reconstructing Arguments

Study Materials

We live in the Information Age. The Internet provides access to millions of books and articles from around the world. Websites, blogs, and online forums contain instant commentary about events, and cell phones allow mobile access to breaking stories and worldwide communication. Cable television provides local and world news 24 hours a day. Some of the information is simply entertaining. However, we also find stories that are important to our lives. In fact, they may do more than just supply facts. They may make us want to nod in agreement or express disbelief. For example, suppose you read the following:

> The Senate recently held hearings on for-profit colleges, investigating charges that the schools rake in federal loan money, while failing to adequately educate students. Critics point to deceptive sales tactics, fraudulent loan applications, high drop-out rates, and even higher tuitions. In response, the Department of Education has proposed a "gainful employment" rule, which would cut financing to for-profit colleges that graduate (or fail) students with thousands of dollars of debt and no prospect of salaries high enough to pay them off.
>
> Jeremy Dehn, "Degrees of Debt"

If the information in this passage is accurate, then government decisions might affect thousands of people. On reading this, you would probably search for related material, to determine whether the information is correct. However, you would be concerned for more than just accuracy. You would also be asking what it means for you. Are the critics correct? Are the new rules justified, and do they address the criticism? Further research on the topic might help answer your questions.

Other types of information contain different claims. For example, in 2005, California passed a law prohibiting the sale of violent video games to minors. The law applied to games (a) in which the range of options available to a player includes killing, maiming, dismembering, or sexually assaulting an image of a human being, (b) that are offensive to prevailing standards in the community, and (c) that lack serious literary, artistic, political, or scientific value for minors. Representatives for the video game industry argued that the law was unconstitutional. The case went to the Supreme Court, where the decision was 7-2 in favor of overturning the law. Here is an excerpt of the Court's decision:

> Like protected books, plays, and movies, video games communicate ideas through familiar literary devices and features distinctive to the medium. And the basic principles of freedom of speech do not vary with a new and different communication medium. The most basic principle—that government lacks the power to restrict expression because of its message, ideas, subject matter, or content—is subject to a few limited exceptions for historically unprotected speech, such as obscenity, incitement, and fighting words. But a legislature cannot create new categories of unprotected speech simply by weighing the value of a particular category against its social costs and then punishing it if it fails the test. Therefore, video games qualify for First Amendment protection.
>
> Adapted from *California v. Entertainment Merchants Association*

The information in this passage contains an argument. An **argument** is a group of **statements** (sentences that are either true or false) in which the conclusion is claimed to follow from the premise(s). A **premise** is the information intended to provide support for the **conclusion** (the main point of an argument). An argument can have one or more premises, but only one conclusion. In the foregoing example, the conclusion is "video games qualify for First Amendment protection." The premises are the first four sentences of the passage.

It is quite common for people to concentrate on the individual statements in an argument and investigate whether they are true or false. Since people want to know things, the actual truth or falsity of statements is important; but it is not the only important question. Equally important is the question "Assuming the premises are true, do they support the conclusion?" This question offers a glimpse of the role of logic. **Logic** is the systematic use of methods and principles to analyze, evaluate, and construct arguments.

Arguments can be simple, but they can also be quite complex. In the argument regarding video games and the First Amendment, the premises and conclusion are not difficult to recognize. However, this is not always the case. Here is an example of a complex piece of reasoning taken from the novel *Catch-22*, by Joseph Heller:

> There was only one catch and that was Catch-22, which specified that a concern for one's own safety in the face of dangers that were real and immediate was the process of a rational mind. Orr was crazy and could be grounded. All he had to do was ask; and as soon as he did, he would no longer be crazy and

Argument A group of statements in which the conclusion is claimed to follow from the premise(s).

Statement A sentence that is either true or false.

Premise The information intended to provide support for a conclusion.

Conclusion The statement that is claimed to follow from the premises of an argument; the main point of an argument.

Logic The systematic use of methods and principles to analyze, evaluate and construct arguments.

would have to fly more missions. Orr would be crazy to fly more missions and sane if he didn't, but if he was sane he had to fly them. If he flew them he was crazy and didn't have to; but if he didn't want to he was sane and had to. Yossarian was moved very deeply by the absolute simplicity of this clause of Catch-22 and let out a respectful whistle.

This passage cleverly illustrates complex reasoning. Once you know how to tease apart its premises and conclusions, you may find yourself as impressed as Yossarian.

Logic investigates the level of correctness of the reasoning found in arguments. There are many times when we need to evaluate information. Although everyone reasons, few stop to think about reasoning. Logic provides the skills needed to identify other people's arguments, putting you in a position to offer coherent and precise analysis of those arguments. Learning logical skills enables you to subject your own arguments to that same analysis, thereby anticipating challenges and criticism. Logic can help, and this book will show you how. It introduces the tools of logical analysis and presents practical applications of logic.

A. STATEMENTS AND ARGUMENTS

The terms "sentence," "statement," and "proposition" are related, but distinct. Logicians use the term "statement" to refer to a specific kind of sentence in a particular language—a *declarative sentence*. As the name indicates, we declare, assert, claim, or affirm that something is the case. In this sense every statement is either true or false, and these two possibilities are called **truth values**. For example, the statement "Water freezes at 32° F" is in English, and it is true. Translated into other languages we get the following statements:

Truth value Every statement is either true or false; these two possibilities are called *truth values*.

El agua se congela a 32° F.
  (Spanish)
Wasser gefriert bei 32° F. (German)
Pānī 32 ḍigrī ēpha mēṁ freezes.
  (Hindi)
L'eau gèle à 32° F. (French)

Nu'ó'c đóng băng ó' 32° F.
  (Vietnamese)
Tubig freezes sa 32° F. (Filipino)
Air membeku pada 32° F. (Malay)
Maji hunganda yapitapo nyuzi joto
  32° F. (Swahili)

The foregoing list contains eight *sentences* in eight different languages that certainly look different and, if spoken, definitely sound different. Since the eight sentences are all declarative sentences, they are all *statements*. However, the eight statements all *make the same claim*, and it is in that sense that logicians use the term "proposition." In other words, a **proposition** is the information content imparted by a statement, or, simply put, its meaning. Since each of the eight statements makes the same claim, they all have the same truth value.

Proposition The information content imparted by a statement, or, simply put, its meaning.

Although we are able to connect basic logic to ordinary language, we will not always be able to capture all the various conversational contexts, intricacies, and nuances of ordinary language. Since some statements in everyday conversation can communicate more than their informational contents, there can be a difference between what is *stated* and what is *implied*. For example, suppose you ask a stranger on the street, "Where can I get something to eat?" The stranger might reply, "There is a restaurant around the corner." The speaker *implies* that you can get something to eat at the restaurant, but the stranger did not explicitly say that. However, this does not affect the truth value of the stranger's statement: If there is a restaurant around the corner, then the statement is true; if there is not a restaurant around the corner, then the statement is false.

It is not necessary for us to know the truth value of a proposition to recognize that it must be either true or false. For example, the statement "There is a diamond ring buried fifty feet under my house" is either true or false regardless of whether or not anyone ever looks there. The same holds for the statement "Abraham Lincoln sneezed four times on his 21st birthday." We can accept that this statement must be true or false, although it is unlikely that we will ever know its truth value.

Many sentences do not have truth values. Here are some examples:

What time is it? (Question)
Clean your room now. (Command)
Please clean your room. (Request)
Let's do lunch tomorrow. (Proposal)

None of these sentences make an assertion or claim, so they are neither true nor false. Quite often we must rely on context to decide whether a sentence is being used as a statement. For example, in the song "Visions of Johanna," Bob Dylan wrote: "The ghost of 'lectricity howls in the bones of her face." Given its use of imagery, we probably should not interpret Dylan as making a claim that is either true or false. The term **inference** is used by logicians to refer to the *reasoning process* that is expressed by an argument. The act or process of reasoning from premises to a conclusion is sometimes referred to as *drawing an inference*. Arguments are created in order to establish support for a claim, and the premises are supposed to provide good reasons for accepting the conclusion.

Inference A term used by logicians to refer to the reasoning process that is expressed by an argument.

Arguments can be found in almost every part of human activity. Of course, when we use the term in a logical setting, we do not mean the kinds of verbal disputes that can get highly emotional and even violent. Logical analysis of arguments relies on rational use of language and reasoning skills. It is organized, is well thought out, and appeals to relevant reasons and justification.

Arguments arise when we expect people to know what they are talking about. Car mechanics, plumbers, carpenters, electricians, engineers, computer programmers, accountants, nurses, office workers, and managers all use arguments regularly. Arguments are used to convince others to buy, repair, or upgrade a product. Arguments can be found in political debates, and in ethical and moral disputes. Although it is common to witness the emotional type of arguments when fans discuss sports, for example, nevertheless there can be logical arguments even in that setting. For example, if fans use statistics and historical data to support their position, they can create rational and logical arguments.

B. RECOGNIZING ARGUMENTS

Studying logic enables us to master many important skills. It helps us to recognize and identify arguments correctly, in either written or oral form. In real life, arguments are rarely found in nice neat packages. We often have to dig them out, like prospectors searching for gold. We might find the premises and conclusions occurring in any order in an argument. In addition, we often encounter incomplete arguments, so we must be able to recognize arguments even if they are not completely spelled out.

An argument offers reasons in support of a conclusion. However, not all groups of sentences are arguments. A series of sentences that express *beliefs* or *opinions*, by themselves, do not constitute an argument. For example, suppose someone says the following:

> I wish the government would do something about the unemployment situation. It makes me angry to see some CEOs of large corporations getting huge bonuses while at the same time the corporation is laying off workers.

The sentences certainly let us know how the person feels. However, none of the sentences seem to offer any support for a conclusion. In addition, none of the sentences seem to be a conclusion. Of course it sometimes happens that opinions are meant to act as premises of an argument. For example, suppose someone says the following:

> I don't like movies that rely on computer-generated graphics to take the place of intelligent dialogue, interesting characters, and an intricate plot. After watching the ads on TV, I have the feeling that the new movie *Bad Blood and Good Vibes* is not very good. Therefore, I predict that it will not win any Academy Awards.

Although the first two sentences express opinions and feelings, they are offered as reasons in support of the last sentence, which is the conclusion.

Many newspaper articles are good sources of information. They are often written specifically to answer the five key points of reporting: *who, what, where, when,* and *why*. A well-written article can provide details and key points, but it need not conclude anything. Reporters sometimes simply provide information, with no intention of giving reasons in support of a conclusion. On the other hand, the editorial page of newspapers can be a good source of arguments. Editorials generally provide extensive information as *premises*, meant to support a position strongly held by the editor. The editorial page usually contains letters to the editor. Although these pieces are often highly emotional responses to social problems, some of them do contain arguments.

When people write or speak, it is not always clear that they are trying to conclude something. Written material can be quite difficult to analyze because we are generally not in a position to question the author for clarification. We cannot always be certain that what we think are the conclusion and premises are, in fact, what the author had intended. Yet we can, and should, attempt to provide justification for our interpretation. If we are speaking with someone, at least we can stop the conversation and seek clarification. When we share a common language and have similar sets of background knowledge and experiences, then we can recognize arguments when they occur by calling on those shared properties.

Since every argument must have a conclusion, it sometimes helps if we try to identify that first. Our shared language provides **conclusion indicators**—useful words that nearly all of us call on when we wish to conclude something. For example, we often use the word "therefore" to indicate our main point. Here are other words or phrases to help recognize a conclusion:

Conclusion indicators
Words and phrases that indicate the presence of a conclusion (the statement claimed to follow from premises).

CONCLUSION INDICATORS

Therefore	Consequently	It proves that
Thus	In conclusion	It suggests that
So	It follows that	It implies that
Hence	We can infer that	We can conclude that

We can see them at work in the following examples:

1. Salaries are up. Unemployment is down. People are happy. *Therefore*, re-elect me.
2. Salaries are down. Unemployment is up. People are not happy. *Consequently*, we should throw the governor out of office.
3. The book was boring. The movie based on the book was boring. The author of both the book and the screenplay is Horst Patoot. *It follows that* he is a lousy writer.

Although conclusion indicators can help us to identify arguments, they are not always available to us, as in this example:

> We should boycott that company. They have been found guilty of producing widgets that they knew were faulty, and that caused numerous injuries.

If you are not sure which sentence is the conclusion, you can simply place the word "therefore" in front of each of them to see which works best. In this case, the first sentence seems to be the point of the argument, and the second sentence seems to offer reasons in support of the conclusion. In other words, *because* the company has been found guilty of producing widgets that they knew were faulty, and that caused numerous injuries, *therefore* we should boycott the company.

In addition to identifying the conclusion, our analysis also helped reveal the premise. As with "because" in this example, a **premise indicator** distinguishes the premise from the conclusion. Here are other words or phrases that can help in recognizing an argument:

Premise indicators
Words and phrases that help us recognize arguments by indicating the presence of premises (statements being offered in support of a conclusion).

PREMISE INDICATORS

Because	Assuming that	As indicated by
Since	As shown by	Seeing that
Given that	For the reason(s) that	It follows from

When premise and conclusion indicators are not present, you can still apply some simple strategies to identify the parts of an argument. First, to help locate the conclusion, try placing the word "therefore" in front of the statements. Second, to help locate the premise or premises, try placing the word "because" in front of the statements.

In some cases you will have to read a passage a few times in order to determine whether an argument is presented. You should keep a few basic ideas in mind as you read. For one thing, at least one of the statements in the passage has to provide a reason or evidence for some other statement; in other words, it must be a premise. Second, there must be a claim that the premise supports or implies a conclusion. If a passage *expresses a reasoning process*—that the conclusion follows from the premises—then we say that it makes an **inferential claim**. The inferential claim is an objective feature of an argument, and it can be *explicit* or *implicit*. Explicit inferential claims can often be identified by the premise and conclusion indicator words and phrases discussed earlier (e.g., "because" and "therefore"). On the other hand, while implicit inferential claims do not have explicit indicator words, they still contain an inferential relationship between the premises and the conclusion. In these cases we follow the advice given earlier by supplying the words "therefore" or "because" to the statements in the passage in order to help reveal the inferential claim that is implicit.

Of course, determining whether a given passage in ordinary language contains an argument takes practice. Even the presence of an indicator word may not by itself mean that the passage contains an argument:

> He climbed the fence, threaded his stealthy way through the plants, till he stood under that window; he looked up at it long, and with emotion; then he laid him down on the ground under it, disposing himself upon his back, with his hands clasped upon his breast and holding his poor wilted flower. And *thus* he would die—out in the cold world, with no shelter over his homeless head, no friendly hand to wipe the death-damps from his brow, no loving face to bend pityingly over him when the great agony came. Mark Twain, *Tom Sawyer*

In this passage the word "thus" (my italics) is not being used as a conclusion indicator. It simply indicates the manner in which the character would die. Here is another example:

> The modern cell phone was invented during the 1970s by an engineer working for the Motorola Corporation. However, the communications technologies that made cell phones possible had been under development *since* the late 1940s. Eventually, the ability to make and receive calls with a mobile telephone handset revolutionized the world of personal communications, with the technology still evolving in the early 21st century. Tom Streissguth, "How Were Cell Phones Invented?"

Although the passage contains the word "since" (my italics), it is not being used as a premise indicator. Instead, it is used to indicate the period during which communications technology was developing.

We pointed out that *beliefs* or *opinions* by themselves do not constitute an argument. For example, the following passage simply *reports* information, without expressing a reasoning process:

Inferential claim If a passage expresses a reasoning process—that the conclusion follows from the premises—then we say that it makes an inferential claim.

> Approximately 2,000 red-winged blackbirds fell dead from the sky in a central Arkansas town. The birds had fallen over a 1-mile area, and an aerial survey indicated that no other dead birds were found outside of that area. Wildlife officials will examine the birds to try to figure out what caused the mysterious event.   "Why Did 2,000 Dead Birds Fall From Sky?" Associated Press

The statements in the passage provide information about an ongoing situation, but no conclusion is put forward, and none of the statements are offered as premises.

A noninferential passage can occur when someone provides *advice* or words of wisdom. Someone may recommend that you act in a certain way, or someone may give you advice to help you make a decision. Yet if no evidence is presented to support the advice, then no inferential claim is made. Here are a few simple examples:

> In three words I can sum up everything I've learned about life: it goes on.
> Robert Frost, as quoted in *The Harper Book of Quotations* by Robert I. Fitzhenry

> People spend a lifetime searching for happiness; looking for peace. They chase idle dreams, addictions, religions, even other people, hoping to fill the emptiness that plagues them. The irony is the only place they ever needed to search was within.
> Ramona L. Anderson, as quoted in *Wisdom for the Soul* by Larry Chang

The passages may influence our thinking or get us to reevaluate our beliefs, but they are noninferential. The same applies to *warnings*, a special kind of advice that cautions us to avoid certain situations:

- Dangerous currents. No lifeguard on duty.
- All items left unattended will be removed.
- Unauthorized cars will be towed at owner's expense.

The truth value of these statements can be open to investigation, but there is no argument. No evidence is provided to support the statements, so the warnings, however important they may be, are not inferential.

Sometimes a passage contains *unsupported* or *loosely associated statements* that elaborate on a topic but do not make an inferential claim:

> Coaching takes time, it takes involvement, it takes understanding and patience.   Byron and Catherine Pulsifer, "Challenges in Adopting a Coaching Style"

> Our ability to respect others is the true mark of our humanity. Respect for other people is the essence of human rights.   Daisaku Ikeda, "Words of Wisdom"

The passages lack an inferential claim. The statements in the passages may elaborate a point, but they do not support a conclusion.

Some passages contain information that illustrates how something is done, or what something means, or even how to do a calculation. An *illustration* may be informative without making an inferential claim:

> To lose one pound of fat, you must burn approximately 3500 calories over and above what you already burn doing daily activities. That sounds like a lot of calories and you certainly wouldn't want to try to burn 3500 calories in one

day. However, by taking it step-by-step, you can determine just what you need to do each day to burn or cut out those extra calories.

Paige Waehner, "How to Lose Weight: The Basics of Weight Loss"

The passage provides information about calories, fat, and weight loss. It illustrates what is required in order to lose one pound of fat, but it does not make an inferential claim. For another example, a passage may define a technical term:

> In order to measure the performance of one investment relative to another you can calculate the "Return on Investment (ROI)." Quite simply, *ROI* is based on returns over a certain time period (e.g., one year) and it is expressed as a percentage. Here's an example that illustrates how to perform the calculation: A 25% annual ROI would mean that a $100 investment returns $25 in one year. Thus, in one year the total investment becomes $125.

"How to Calculate a Return on an Investment," eHow, Inc.

The passage defines "Return on Investment" and illustrates how to do a simple calculation. However, even though the word "thus" occurs at the beginning of the last statement, it is not a conclusion indicator in this context.

A passage might combine several of the things we have been describing—a report, an illustration, and an example—which makes it more challenging to decide whether it's an argument. Let's examine the following passage:

> Last year, more people died from selfies than shark attacks. And many more have been injured by taking their own picture. We're obsessed with proving that we *had* experiences, rather than appreciating them as they occur. We cannot admire a breathtaking mountain without inserting ourselves into the scenery. We're not living in the moment; we're making sure we can demonstrate we *had* the moment to everyone we know (and don't know). Selfies are killing our experiences.

Adapted from Faith Salie, "Death by Selfie," CBS Interactive Inc.

The passage provides information about the dangers posed from taking selfies. It also describes how the proliferation of selfies has changed the way we experience life. Although the passage does not contain a conclusion indicator word or phrase, the sentence "Selfies are killing our experiences" can be used as the basis for interpreting the passage as expressing an implicit inferential claim.

There is one more topic regarding noninferential passages that needs to be explored—the role of *explanations*. That discussion will be presented in the next section.

EXERCISES 1B

Level 1 Multiple-
Choice Questions

I. Pick out the premises and conclusions in the following arguments. (A complete answer to the first problem in each exercise section is given as a model for you to follow. The problems marked with a star are answered in the back of the book.)

1. Exercise helps strengthen your cardiovascular system. It also lowers your cholesterol, increases the blood flow to the brain, and enables you to think longer. Thus, there is no reason for you not to start exercising regularly.

Level 2 Multiple-Choice Questions

Answer:

Premises:

    (a) Exercise helps strengthen your cardiovascular system.

    (b) It (exercise) also lowers your cholesterol.

    (c) (Exercise) increases the blood flow to the brain.

    (d) (Exercise) enables you to think longer.

Conclusion: There is no reason for you not to start exercising regularly. The indicator word "Thus" helps identify the conclusion. The other statements are offered in support of this claim.

2. If you start a strenuous exercise regimen before you know if your body is ready, you can cause serious damage. Therefore, you should always have a physical checkup before you start a rigid exercise program.

3. Since television commercials help pay the cost of programming, and because I can always turn off the sound of the commercials, go to the bathroom, or get something to eat or drink, it follows that commercials are not such a bad thing.

4. Since television commercials disrupt the flow of programs, and given that any disruption impedes the continuity of a show, consequently we can safely say that commercials are a bad thing.

5. We should never take our friends for granted. True friends are there when we need them. They suffer with us when we fail, and they are happy when we succeed.

6. They say that "absence makes the heart grow fonder," so my teachers should really love me, since I have been absent for the last 2 weeks.

7. I think, therefore I am.
        René Descartes

8. I believe that humans will evolve into androids, because we will eventually be able to replace all organic body parts with artificial parts. In addition, we will be able to live virtually forever by simply replacing the parts when they wear out or become defective.

9. At one time Gary Kasparov had the highest ranking of any chess grand master in history. However, he was beaten in a chess tournament by a computer program called Deep Blue, so the computer program should be given a ranking higher than Kasparov.

10. It is true that $1 + 4 = 5$, and it is also true that $2 + 3 = 5$. Thus, we can conclude with certainty that $(1 + 4) = (2 + 3)$.

11. The digital camera on sale today at Cameras Galore has 5.0 megapixels and costs $200. The digital camera on sale at Camera Warehouse has 4.0 megapixels and

Video Tutorial

it costs $150. You said that you did not want to spend over $175 for a camera, so you should buy the one at Camera Warehouse.

12. You should buy the digital camera at Cameras Galore. After all, you did say that you wanted the most megapixels you can get for up to $200. The digital camera on sale today at Cameras Galore has 5.0 megapixels and costs $200. But the digital camera on sale at Camera Warehouse has only 4.0 megapixels and it costs $150.

 13. The world will end on August 6, 2045. I know this because my guru said it would, and so far everything she predicted has happened exactly as she said it would.

14. Fast-food products contain high levels of cholesterol. They also contain high levels of sodium, fat, and trans fatty acids. These things are bad for your health. I am going to stop eating in fast-food places.

15. You should eat more vegetables. They contain low levels of cholesterol. They also contain low levels of sodium, fat, and trans fatty acids. High levels of those things are bad for your health.

Level 1 Multiple-Choice Questions

II. Determine whether the following passages contain arguments. Explain your answers.

1. Our company has paid the highest dividends of any Fortune 500 company for the last 5 consecutive years. In addition, we have not had one labor dispute. Our stock is up 25% in the last quarter.

Level 2 Multiple-Choice Questions

Answer: Not an argument. The three propositions can be used to support some other claim, but together they simply form a set of propositions with no obvious premise or conclusion.

2. Our cars have the highest resale value on the market. Customer loyalty is at an all-time high. I can give you a good deal on a new car today. You should really buy one of our cars.

3. I hate the new music played today. You can't even find a station on either AM or FM that plays decent music anymore. The movies are no better. They are just high-priced commercials for ridiculous products, designed to dupe unsuspecting, unintelligent, unthinking, unenlightened consumers.

4. We are going to have a recession. For 100 years, anytime the stock market has lost at least 20% of its value from its highest point in any fiscal year, there has been a recession. The current stock market has lost 22% of its value during the last fiscal year.

Video Tutorial

5. She doesn't eat pork, chicken, beef, mutton, veal, venison, turkey, or fish. It follows that she must be a vegetarian.

6. Income tax revenues help pay for many important social programs, and without that money some programs would have to be eliminated. If this happens, many

adults and children will suffer needlessly. That is why everyone, individuals and corporations, should not cheat on their income taxes.

7. The cost of electronic items, such as televisions, computers, and cell phones, goes down every year. In addition, the quality of the electronic products goes up every year. More and more people throughout the world will soon be able to afford at least one of those items.

8. There is biological evidence that the genetic characteristics for nonviolence have been selected over time by the species, and the height and weight of humans have increased over the centuries.

★ 9. He didn't create this situation of fear; he merely exploited it—and rather successfully.
Edward R. Murrow, "See It Now," CBS, March 9, 1954

10. In Italy, for thirty years under the Borgias, they had warfare, terror, murder and bloodshed, but they produced Michelangelo, Leonardo da Vinci and the Renaissance. In Switzerland, they had brotherly love, they had five hundred years of democracy and peace—and what did that produce? The cuckoo clock.
Orson Welles as Harry Lime in *The Third Man*

11. All living things (plants, animals, humans) have the ability to absorb nourishment, to grow, and to propagate. All "living creatures" (animals and humans) have in addition the ability to perceive the world around them and to move about. Moreover, all humans have the ability to think, or otherwise to order their perceptions into various categories and classes. So there are in reality no sharp boundaries in the natural world.
Jostein Gaarder, *Sophie's World*

12. *Veidt*: Will you expose me, undoing the peace millions died for? Kill me, risking subsequent investigation? Morally you're in checkmate.
Jon: Logically, I'm afraid he's right. Exposing this plot, we destroy any chance of peace, dooming Earth to worse destruction. On Mars, you demonstrated life's value. If we would preserve life here, we must remain silent.
Alan Moore and Dave Gibbons, *Watchmen*

★ 13. The officer shook his head, perplexed. The handprint on the wall had not been made by the librarian himself; there hadn't been blood on his hands. Besides, the print did not match his, and it was a strange print, the whorls of the fingers unusually worn. It would have been easy to match, except that they'd never recorded one like it.
Elizabeth Kostrova, *The Historian*

14. Johnny wondered if the weather would affect his plans. He worried that all the little fuses and wires he had prepared might have become damp during the night. Who could have thought of rain at this time of year? He felt a sudden shiver of doubt. It was too late now. All was set in motion. If he was to become the most famous man in the valley he had to carry on regardless. He would not fail.
Tash Aw, *The Harmony Silk Factory*

15. It may be no accident that sexual life forms dominate our planet. True, bacteria account for the largest number of individuals, and the greatest biomass. But by any reasonable measures of species diversity, or individual complexity, size, or intelligence, sexual species are paramount. And of the life forms that reproduce sexually, the ones whose reproduction is mediated by mate choice show the greatest biodiversity and the greatest complexity. Without sexual selection, evolution seems limited to the very small, the transient, the parasitic, the bacterial, and the brainless. For this reason, I think that sexual selection may be evolution's most creative force. Geoffrey Miller, *The Mating Mind*

16. Sue hesitated; and then impulsively told the woman that her husband and herself had been unhappy in their first marriages, after which, terrified at the thought of a second irrevocable union, and lest the conditions of the contract should kill their love, yet wishing to be together, they had literally not found the courage to repeat it, though they had attempted it two or three times. Therefore, though in her own sense of the words she was a married woman, in the landlady's sense she was not. Thomas Hardy, *Jude the Obscure*

⭐ 17. [A] distinction should be made between whether human life has a purpose and whether one's individual life is purposeful. Human life could have been created for a purpose, yet an individual's life could be devoid of purposes or meaning. Conversely, human life could have been unintended, yet an individual's life could be purposeful. Brooke Alan Trisel, "Intended and Unintended Life"

18. In 1995, a program called Chinook won a man vs. machine world checkers championship. In 1997, Garry Kasparov, probably the best (human) chess player of all time, lost a match to an IBM computer called Deep Blue. In 2007, checkers was "solved," mathematically ensuring that no human would ever again beat the best machine. In 2011, Ken Jennings and Brad Rutter were routed on "Jeopardy!" by another IBM creation, Watson. And last March, a human champion of Go, Lee Sedol, fell to a Google program in devastating and bewildering fashion. Oliver Roeder, "The Machines Are Coming for Poker," *FiveThirtyEight*

19. I don't know when children stop dreaming. But I do know when hope starts leaking away, because I've seen it happen. Over the years, I have spent a lot of time talking with school children of all ages. And I have seen the cloud of resignation move across their eyes as they travel through school without making any real progress. They know they are slipping through the net into the huge underclass that our society seems willing to tolerate. We must educate our children. And if we do, I believe that will be enough.
Alan Page, Minnesota Supreme Court Justice, NFL Hall of Fame Induction Speech

20. To me the similarities between the *Titanic* and *Challenger* tragedies are uncanny. Both disasters could have been prevented if those in charge had heeded the warnings of those who knew. In both cases, materials failed due to thermal effects. For the *Titanic*, the steel of her hull was below its ductile-to-brittle

transition temperature; and for the *Challenger,* the rubber of the O-rings lost pliability in sub-freezing temperatures. And both tragedies provoked a world-wide discussion about the appropriate role for technology.

Mark E. Eberhart, *Why Things Break*

21. Project Gutenberg eBooks are often created from several printed editions, all of which are confirmed as Public Domain in the U.S. unless a copyright notice is included. Thus, we do not necessarily keep eBooks in compliance with any particular paper edition. Project Gutenberg website

22. Lab tests conducted by a team of Korean researchers revealed that when bacteria are exposed to the standard over-the-counter antibacterial ingredient known as triclosan for hours at a time, the antiseptic formulation is a more potent killer than plain soap. The problem: People wash their hands for a matter of seconds, not hours. And in real-world tests, the research team found no evidence to suggest that normal hand-washing with antibacterial soap does any more to clean the hands than plain soap.

Alan Mozes, "Which Works Better, Plain Soap or Antibacterial?" *HealthDay*

23. We are intelligent beings: intelligent beings cannot have been formed by a crude, blind, insensible being: there is certainly some difference between the ideas of Newton and the dung of a mule. Newton's intelligence, therefore, came from another intelligence. Voltaire, *Philosophical Dictionary*

24. Churches are block-booking seats for *March of the Penguins,* which is apparently a "condemnation of gay marriage" and puts forward the case for "intelligent design," i.e., Creationism. To be honest, this is good news. If American Christians want to go public on the fact that they're now morally guided by penguins, at least we know where we all stand. Caitlin Moran, "Penguins Lead Way"

25. Authoritarian governments are identified by ready government access to information about the activities of citizens and by extensive limitations on the ability of citizens to obtain information about the government. In contrast, democratic governments are marked by significant restrictions on the ability of government to acquire information about its citizens and by ready access by citizens to information about the activities of government.

Robert G. Vaughn, "Transparency—The Mechanisms"

26. *Charlie Brown:* Why would they ban Miss Sweetstory's book?
Linus: I can't believe it. I just can't believe it!
Charlie Brown: Maybe there are some things in her book that we don't understand.
Sally: In that case, they should also ban my Math book!

Charles M. Schulz, *Peanuts*

27. According to the American Academy of Arts and Sciences' recently completed Lincoln Project report, between 2008 and 2013, states reduced financial

support to top public research universities by close to 30 percent. Many state legislators seem to be ignoring public opinion as they essentially starve some of the best universities—those that educate about two-thirds of American college students. [This amounts] to a pillaging of the country's greatest state universities. And that pillaging is not a matter of necessity, as many elected officials would insist—it's a matter of choice. The consequence of such policy choices is that tuition will go up and access for kids from poorer families will go down.

Adapted from Jonathan R. Cole, "The Pillaging of America's State Universities," *The Atlantic*

28. The '80s debaters tended to forget that the teaching of vernacular literature is quite a recent development in the long history of the university. (The same could be said about the relatively recent invention of art history or music as an academic research discipline.) So it is not surprising that, in such a short time, we have not yet settled on the right or commonly agreed upon way to go about it.

Robert Pippin, "In Defense of Naïve Reading"

29. The greatest tragedy in mankind's entire history may be the hijacking of morality by religion.

Arthur C. Clarke, *Collected Essays*

30. Jokes of the proper kind, properly told, can do more to enlighten questions of politics, philosophy, and literature than any number of dull arguments.

Isaac Asimov, *Treasury of Humor*

31. The aim of argument, or of discussion, should not be victory, but progress.

Joseph Joubert, *Pensées*

32. Whenever I hear anyone arguing for slavery, I feel a strong impulse to see it tried on him personally.

Abraham Lincoln, Speech to 14th Indiana regiment, March 17, 1865

33. The most important thing in an argument, next to being right, is to leave an escape hatch for your opponent, so that he can gracefully swing over to your side without too much apparent loss of face.

Sydney J. Harris, as quoted in *Journeys 7*

34. The logic of the world is prior to all truth and falsehood.

Ludwig Wittgenstein, *Notebooks 1914–1916*

35. I am aware that the assumed instinctive belief in God has been used by many persons as an argument for His existence. But this is a rash argument, as we should thus be compelled to believe in the existence of many cruel and malignant spirits, only a little more powerful than man; for the belief in them is far more general than in a beneficent Deity.

Charles Darwin, *The Descent of Man*

36. [T]he essential act of the Party is to use conscious deception while retaining the firmness of purpose that goes with complete honesty. To tell deliberate lies while genuinely believing in them, to forget any fact that has become inconvenient, and then, when it becomes necessary again, to draw it back from oblivion for just so long as it is needed, to deny the existence of objective reality and all

the while to take account of the reality which one denies—all this is indispensably necessary. George Orwell, *1984*

⭐ 37. For nothing requires a greater effort of thought than arguments to justify the rule of nonthought. I experienced it with my own eyes and ears after the war, when intellectuals and artists rushed like a herd of cattle into the Communist Party, which soon proceeded to liquidate them systematically and with great pleasure. You are doing the same. You are the brilliant ally of your own gravediggers. Milan Kundera, *Immortality*

38. When you plant lettuce, if it does not grow well, you don't blame the lettuce. You look for reasons it is not doing well. It may need fertilizer, or more water, or less sun. You never blame the lettuce. Yet if we have problems with our friends or our family, we blame the other person. But if we know how to take care of them, they will grow well, like the lettuce. Blaming has no positive effect at all, nor does trying to persuade using reason and argument. That is my experience. If you understand, and you show that you understand, you can love, and the situation will change. Thich Nhât Hanh, *Peace Is Every Step*

39. Your friends praise your abilities to the skies, submit to you in argument, and seem to have the greatest deference for you; but, though they may ask it, you never find them following your advice upon their own affairs; nor allowing you to manage your own, without thinking that you should follow theirs. Thus, in fact, they all think themselves wiser than you, whatever they may say. Viscount William Lamb Melbourne, *Lord Melbourne's Papers*

40. Violence and lawlessness spread across London . . . property and vehicles have been set on fire in several areas, some burning out of control. One reporter pointed out that in Clapham where the shopping area had been picked clean, the only shop left unlooted and untouched was the book shop. Martin Fletcher, "Riots Reveal London's Two Disparate Worlds," *NBC News*

⭐ 41. The most perfidious way of harming a cause consists of defending it deliberately with faulty arguments. Friedrich Nietzsche, *The Gay Science*

42. I've put in so many enigmas and puzzles that it will keep the professors busy for centuries arguing over what I meant, and that's the only way of insuring one's immortality. James Joyce, as quoted in *James Joyce* by Richard Ellmann

43. The Keynesian argument that if the private sector lacks confidence to spend, the government should spend is not wrong. But Keynes did not spell out where the government should spend. Nor did he envisage that lobbyists can influence government spending to be wasteful. Hence, every prophet can be used by his or her successors to prove their own points of view. This is religion, not science. Andrew Sheng, "Economics Is a Religion, Not a Science"

44. All true wisdom is found on T-shirts. I wear T-shirts, so I must be wise.

45. The National Biosafety Board has approved the release of genetically modified mosquitoes for field testing. This particular type of mosquito can spread the dengue fever and yellow fever viruses. Clinical trial at the laboratory level was successful and the biosafety committee has approved it for testing in a controlled environment. The males would be genetically modified and when mated with female mosquitoes in the environment, it is hoped the killer genes would cause the larvae to die. The regional director cautioned that care be taken in introducing a new species to the environment.

Newspaper article, "Field Testing Approved for Genetically Modified Mosquitoes"

46. It may not always be immediately apparent to frustrated investors—they wish management would be more frugal and focus more on the stock price—but there's usually some calculated logic underlying Google's unconventional strategy. Google's brain trust—founders Larry Page and Sergey Brin, along with CEO Eric Schmidt—clearly think differently than most corporate leaders, and may eventually encourage more companies to take risks that might not pay off for years, if ever. Page and Brin warned potential investors when they laid out their iconoclastic approach to business before Google sold its stock in an initial public offering. "Our long-term focus may simply be the wrong business strategy," they warned. "Competitors may be rewarded for short-term tactics and grow stronger as a result. As potential investors, you should consider the risks around our long-term focus."

Michael Liedtke, "Calculated Risks? Making Sense of Google's Seemingly Kooky Concepts"

47. Tribalism is about familiarity within the known entity. It's not about hatred of others, it's about comfort within your own, with a natural reluctance to expend the energy and time to break across the barriers and understand another group. Most of what we're quick to label racism isn't really racism. Racism is premeditated, an organized class distinction based on believed superiority and inferiority of different races. That "ism" suffix makes racism a system, just like capitalism or socialism. Racism is used to justify exclusion and persecution based on skin color, things that rarely come into play in today's NBA.

J. A. Adande, "LeBron James, Race and the NBA"

48. Kedah Health Department employees who smoke will not be eligible for the annual excellence performance awards even if they do well in their work. The Director said, "Thirty percent or 3,900 of our 13,000 department personnel are smokers. As staff representing a health department, they should act as role models. Thus, I hope that they will quit smoking."

Embun Majid, "Health Department Snuffs Out Excellence Awards for Smokers"

49. Even though testing in horse racing is far superior in many respects to testing in human athletics, the concern remains among horse racing fans and industry participants that medication is being used illegally.

Dr. Scott Palmer, "Working in the Light of Day"

50. I stated above that I am among those who reject the notion that a full-fledged human soul comes into being the moment that a human sperm joins a human ovum to form a human zygote. By contrast, I believe that a human soul—and, by the way, it is my aim in this book to make clear what I mean by this slippery, shifting word, often rife with religious connotations, but here not having any—comes slowly into being over the course of years of development. It may sound crass to put it this way, but I would like to suggest, at least metaphorically, a numerical scale of "degrees of souledness." We can initially imagine it as running from 0 to 100, and the units of this scale can be called, just for the fun of it, "hunekers." Thus you and I, dear reader, both possess 100 hunekers of souledness, or thereabouts.   Douglas Hofstadter, *I Am a Strange Loop*

C. ARGUMENTS AND EXPLANATIONS

We saw that, in some contexts, words such as "since" or "thus" are not used as premise or conclusion indicators. In much the same way, the word "because" is often placed in front of an **explanation**, which provides reasons for why or how an event occurred. To see the difference between an *argument* and an *explanation*, imagine that a student's cell phone starts ringing and disturbs everyone's concentration during an exam. After class, one of the students might complain:

> *Because* you failed to turn off your cell phone before entering the classroom, I think it is safe to say that your behavior shows that you are self-centered, inconsiderate, and rude.

The speaker concludes that the cell phone owner's lack of consideration reveals character flaws—"self-centered, inconsiderate, and rude." In this setting, the word "because" is used to indicate that evidence is being offered in support of a conclusion; so we have an argument.

Now, as it happens, the student whose cell phone started ringing responds using the word "because" too:

> I forgot to turn off my cell phone *because* I was almost in a car accident on my way to take the exam this morning, and I was completely distracted thinking about what happened.

In this setting, however, the word "because" is used to indicate an *explanation*. This speaker does not dispute the fact that her cell phone went off during the exam; rather, she is attempting to explain *why* it happened.

Here are two more examples to consider:

A. Because you started lifting weights without first getting a physical checkup, you will probably injure your back.

B. Your back injury occurred because you lifted weights without first getting a physical checkup.

The first passage contains an inferential claim. In this context the word "because" indicates that a statement is used as support for the conclusion "you will probably

Explanation An explanation provides reasons for why or how an event occurred. By themselves, explanations are not arguments; however, they can form part of an argument.

injure your back." The premise uses the accepted fact that the person has started lifting weights, so the premise is not in dispute. Since the person has not yet injured his or her back (and might not in the future), the conclusion can turn out to be either true or false.

However, in the second passage the word "because" is not used to indicate support for a conclusion. From the context it appears that the back injury is not in dispute, so what the passage contains is an explanation for the back injury. The explanation may be correct, or it might be incorrect, but in either case there is no argument in the second passage.

Let's work through another example. Suppose your car does not start. A friend might say, "Your car doesn't start *because* you have a dead battery." If you thought that the word "because" is acting as a premise indicator ("you have a dead battery"), then the conclusion would be, "Your car doesn't start." The problem with treating this example as an argument is that the alleged conclusion is not in doubt; it has already been established as true. We generally construct arguments in order to provide good reasons (premises) to support a proposition (the conclusion) *whose truth is in question*. But in this example you do not need any reasons to believe that your car doesn't start: You already know that. In general, explanations do not function directly as premises in an argument if they explain an already accepted fact.

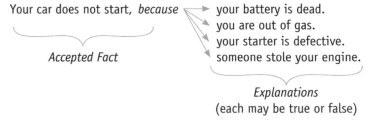

However, explanations can also be used to construct arguments—the goal being to *test* the explanation, to see if it is correct. Chapter 14 further develops the relationships between explanations, experiments, and predictions.

EXERCISES 1C

Level 1 Multiple-Choice Questions

Level 2 Multiple-Choice Questions

Determine whether each of the following passages contains an *argument* or an *explanation*. Explain your answer.

1. Clare must have found a better job; that's why she didn't come to work today.
Answer: Explanation. It is a fact that she did not come to work today; so an explanation is being offered.

2. In platonic love there can be no tragedy, because in that love all is clear and pure.
                                                                    Leo Tolstoy, *Anna Karenina*

3. In the nation's public policy, we too often allow ideology and political maneuvering to render facts moot, especially when those facts support inconvenient

truths such as global climate change. . . . From public education to health care, we focus more on the politics of changing public policy than the efficacy and morality of making the changes. Consequently, our nation, a house divided, struggles to stand.

Jeff Rivers, "From Sports to Politics to Life, We Must Face Our Truths,
Problems and All," The Undefeated

4. The job of arguing with the umpire belongs to the manager, because it won't hurt the team if he gets thrown out of the game.

Earl Weaver, as quoted in Home Plate by Brenda Berstler

⭐ 5. Computers now write some 1 billion business press releases every year. Everything from tax returns to legal forms can be completed by machines. Clearly, artificial intelligence and robotics will eliminate many semi-skilled professions.

John Wasik, "How College Students Can Make Better Career Choices," Moneywatch

6. People generally quarrel because they cannot argue.

Gilbert K. Chesterton, The Collected Works of G. K. Chesterton

7. An independent candidate will never win the presidency of the United States. This is because the two-party system of Democrats and Republicans is too powerful to let a third party get any wide base of support among the American voting public.

8. That God cannot lie is no advantage to your argument, because it is no proof that priests cannot, or that the Bible does not.

Thomas Paine, The Life and Works of Thomas Paine

⭐ 9. Because it is limited in characters, texting discourages thoughtful discussion or any level of detail.

Adapted from Daniel J Levitin, "Why the Modern World Is Bad for Your Brain," The Guardian

10. There has been an overall decrease in violence among humans worldwide throughout recorded history. Some biologists claim that this is because the genetic characteristics for nonviolence have been selected over time by the species.

11. Project Gutenberg is synonymous with the free distribution of electronic works in formats readable by the widest variety of computers including obsolete, old, middle-aged and new computers. It exists because of the efforts of hundreds of volunteers and donations from people in all walks of life.

From Project Gutenberg website

12. Since there is biological evidence that the genetic characteristics for nonviolence have been selected over time by the species, we should see an overall decrease in violence among humans worldwide in the coming centuries.

⭐ 13. To make Windows Phone 7 a success, Microsoft has to win over not just phone manufacturers and phone companies, but software developers. The iPhone and Android are popular in part because of the tens of thousands of tiny applications, or "apps," made by outside software developers.

Newspaper article, "Microsoft Bets Big on New Phone Software"

14. Presently I began to detect a most evil and searching odor stealing about on the frozen air. This depressed my spirits still more, because of course I attributed it to my poor departed friend.   Mark Twain, *How to Tell a Story, and Other Essays*

15. While it is true that science cannot decide questions of value, that is because they cannot be intellectually decided at all, and lie outside the realm of truth and falsehood. Whatever knowledge is attainable, must be attained by scientific methods; and what science cannot discover, mankind cannot know.

    Bertrand Russell, *Religion and Science*

16. "You must understand," said he, "it's not love. I've been in love, but it's not that. It's not my feeling, but a sort of force outside me has taken possession of me. I went away, you see, because I made up my mind that it could never be, you understand, as a happiness that does not come on earth; but I've struggled with myself, I see there's no living without it. And it must be settled."

    Leo Tolstoy, *Anna Karenina*

★ 17. Years ago I used to think sometimes of making a lecturing trip through the antipodes and the borders of the Orient, but always gave up the idea, partly because of the great length of the journey and partly because my wife could not well manage to go with me.   Mark Twain, *How to Tell a Story, and Other Essays*

18. Briefly, Cosmic Consciousness, according to Bucke, is a higher form of consciousness that is slowly but surely coming to the entire human race through the process of evolution. The mystics and religious leaders of the past were simply ahead of their time. Bucke believes that Cosmic Consciousness is the real source of all the world's religions. He did not believe that the cosmic state is necessarily infallible. Like the development of any faculty, it takes a long time to become perfected. And so, just because Cosmic Consciousness is the root of religious beliefs, it doesn't follow that the beliefs are necessarily correct.

    Raymond Smullyan, *Some Interesting Memories: A Paradoxical Life*

19. It's nothing or everything, Culum. If you're prepared to be second-best, go topside now. What I'm trying to make you understand is that to be *the* Tai-Pan of The Noble House you have to be prepared to exist alone, to be hated, to have some aim of immortal value, and to be ready to sacrifice anyone you're not sure of. Because you're my son I'm offering you today, untried, a chance at supreme power in Asia. Thus a power to do almost anything on earth.

    James Clavell, *Tai-Pan*

20. All the big corporations depreciate their possessions, and you can, too, provided you use them for business purposes. For example, if you subscribe to the *Wall Street Journal*, a business-related newspaper, you can deduct the cost of your house, because, in the words of U.S. Supreme Court Chief Justice Warren Burger in a landmark 1979 tax decision: "Where else are you going to read the paper? Outside? What if it rains?"   Dave Barry, "Sweating Out Taxes"

D. TRUTH AND LOGIC

Determination of the truth value of a statement is distinct from analysis of the logic of an argument. **Truth value analysis** determines whether the information in the premises is accurate, correct, or true. **Logical analysis** determines the strength with which the premises support the conclusion. If you are not aware of the difference between the truth value of statements and the logic of an argument, then confusion can arise. Suppose you hear that the book you are now reading weighs 2000 pounds. If you are like most people, you immediately know the statement to be false. Your decision happens so fast you could not stop it if you tried. This shows that one part of our mind is constantly analyzing information for truth value. We must recognize that our minds are constantly working on two different levels, and we must learn to keep those levels separate. In order to evaluate the logic of an argument, we must often temporarily ignore the truth values—not because they are unimportant, but simply because an analysis of the logic requires us to focus on an entirely different question. We must learn to not be distracted by trying to determine the truth value of the statements—just as when we close our eyes to concentrate on hearing something.

Of course it is important that our statements be true. However, a thorough analysis of arguments requires an active separation of the truth value from the logic. Think of what happens when children begin learning addition. For example, an elementary school teacher gave two cookies to each student at the beginning of the class. "Okay Sam," she said, "you have two cookies, and Sophie has two cookies. How many cookies do you have together?" At that point Sam started to cry. The teacher thought that Sam was embarrassed because he didn't know the answer. In fact, Sam had already eaten his two cookies. His reaction was based on knowing that the teacher's statement that he had two cookies was false, so perhaps he thought he would be in trouble for having eaten the cookies. It is easy to forget that it often takes time to learn to think abstractly.

Truth value analysis Determines if the information in the premises is accurate, correct, or true.

Logical analysis Determines the strength with which the premises support the conclusion.

E. DEDUCTIVE AND INDUCTIVE ARGUMENTS

Logical analysis of an argument is concerned with determining the *strength of the inferential claim*—the claim that the conclusion follows from the premises. We start with a working definition of two main classes of arguments: deductive and inductive.

A **deductive argument** is one in which the inferential claim is that the conclusion *follows necessarily* from the premises. In other words, under the *assumption* that the premises are true it is *impossible* for the conclusion to be false.

An **inductive argument** is one in which the inferential claim is that the conclusion is *probably true* if the premises are true. In other words, under the *assumption* that the premises are true it is *improbable* for the conclusion to be false.

Deductive argument An argument in which the inferential claim is that the conclusion follows *necessarily* from the premises. In other words, under the *assumption* that the premises are true it is *impossible* for the conclusion to be false.

Inductive argument An argument in which the inferential claim is that the conclusion is *probably true* if the premises are true. In other words, under the *assumption* that the premises are true it is *improbable* for the conclusion to be false.

To help identify arguments as either deductive or inductive, one thing we can do is look for key words or phrases. For example, the words "necessarily," "certainty," "definitely," and "absolutely" suggest a deductive argument:

A. Jupiter is a planet in our solar system. Every planet in our solar system is smaller than the Sun. Therefore, it follows necessarily that Jupiter is smaller than the Sun.

The indicator word "necessarily" suggests that the argument can be classified as deductive.

On the other hand, the words "probably," "likely," "unlikely," "improbable," "plausible," and "implausible" suggest inductive arguments:

B. Some parts of the United States have had severe winters for the last 10 years. The *Farmer's Almanac* predicts another cold winter next year. Therefore, probably some parts of the United States will have a severe winter next year.

The indicator word "probably" suggests that the argument can be classified as inductive. Of course we have to remember that specific indicator words or phrases may not always occur in ordinary language. In addition, although a passage may contain an indicator word or phrase, the person using the phrase may be misusing the term. In some instances people overstate their case, while in other instances they may not be aware of the distinction between deductive arguments and inductive arguments, so they might use terms indiscriminately. However, looking for indicator words can help in understanding an argument by letting you see how the information is arranged.

Another factor to consider when determining whether an argument is deductive or inductive is the strength of the inferential connection between the premises and the conclusion. In other words, if the conclusion does follow *necessarily* from premises that are assumed to be true, then the argument is clearly deductive. Here is an example:

C. All vegetables contain vitamin C. Spinach is a vegetable. Therefore, spinach contains vitamin C.

Assuming the premises are true, the conclusion is necessarily true. In other words, if we assume that it is true that all vegetables contain vitamin C, and if we also assume that it is true that spinach is a vegetable, then it is impossible for spinach not to contain vitamin C. Therefore, this argument can be classified as deductive. Notice once again the importance of disregarding the truth value of the premises at this point in our analysis. We are *not* claiming that the premises are in fact true. Instead, we are claiming that *under the assumption that the premises are true* it is impossible for the conclusion to be false.

There is another result of examining the actual strength of the inferential connection between the premises and the conclusion. If we determine that the conclusion of an argument follows probably from premises that are assumed to be true, then it is often best to consider the argument as inductive. Here is an example:

D. The majority of plasma TVs last for 5 years. Chris just bought a new plasma TV. Therefore, Chris's new plasma TV will last 5 years.

Let's examine argument D. Under the assumption that the premises are true, the conclusion is highly likely to be true; however, it is possible that it is false. In other words, if we assume that it is true that the vast majority of plasma TVs last for 5 years, and if we also assume that it is true that Chris just bought a new plasma TV, then it is probable that Chris's new plasma TV will last 5 years. Therefore, this argument can be classified as inductive. Again, we are disregarding the truth value of the premises. We are not claiming that the premises are in fact true. Instead, we are claiming that *under the assumption that the premises are true*, it is probable that the conclusion is true. Therefore, argument D can be classified as inductive.

Inductive arguments amplify the scope of the information in the premises. For example, the first premise in example D provides information about plasma TVs, but it does not make a claim about every plasma TV. Nor does it make a claim about any specific TV (including Chris's TV); instead, it only states something about the majority of plasma TVs. It is in this sense that we say that the conclusion regarding Chris's TV goes beyond the information in the premises; hence it is possible that the conclusion is false even under the assumption that the premises are true.

However, this does not take away from the value of strong inductive arguments. In fact, we rely on them nearly every day. For most practical purposes, we do not have sufficient knowledge of the world to make the conclusions of our arguments necessarily true, so we rely on evidence and experience to make many decisions. That's why knowing the likelihood of something happening can assist our rational decision making. Inductive arguments play a crucial role in our lives.

There are many kinds of inductive arguments, such as *analogical arguments, statistical arguments, causal arguments, legal arguments, moral arguments,* and *scientific arguments.* (More on these kinds of inductive arguments can be found in Part IV of this book.) Analogical arguments are based on the idea that when two things share some relevant characteristics, they probably share other characteristics as well. Here is an example:

I previously owned two Ford station wagons. They both got good gas mileage, both needed few repairs, and both had a high resale value. I just bought a new Ford station wagon, so it will get good gas mileage, need few repairs, and have a high resale value.

Statistical arguments are based on our ability to generalize. When we observe a pattern, we often create an argument that uses a statistical regularity:

In a survey of 1000 university students in the United States, 80% said that they expect to make more money in their lives than their parents. Therefore, the vast majority of all university students expect to make more money in their lives than their parents.

Causal arguments are arguments based on knowledge of either causes or effects. For example, a team of medical scientists may conduct experiments to determine if a new drug (the potential cause) will have a desired effect on a particular disease. In a different setting, a forensic expert might do a series of tests to determine the cause of a person's death. Causal arguments can even be found in everyday occurrences. For example, someone might say the following:

> The lamp in my room does not work. I changed the light bulb, but it still did not work. I moved the lamp to another room just in case the wall outlet was defective, but the lamp still did not work. So, it must be the wiring in the lamp that is defective.

We defined a deductive argument as one in which it is claimed that the conclusion follows necessarily from the premises. If we look once again at example C, then we can see that the conclusion does not amplify or expand the scope of the information in the premises. The first premise provides information about *every* vegetable, and the second premise states that spinach is a vegetable. Therefore, under the assumption that the premises are true, the conclusion does not go beyond what is already contained in the premises.

It should not be surprising that deductive arguments can be found in mathematics and geometry. Even simple arithmetical calculations are deductive. For example, if you assume that you can save $50 a week, then you can conclude that after 1 year (52 weeks) you will have saved $2600. When we encounter an argument that is based on mathematics, we can consider it to be deductive.

Earlier we said that many statistical arguments can be classified as inductive. Of course, there are statistical calculations that are purely mathematical in nature; in those cases, the calculations are deductive. However, when the conclusion goes beyond what is provided by the premises, the statistical argument is inductive, like our survey of 1000 university students. Since the conclusion stated something about all university students, it went beyond the scope of the premises.

Classifying arguments into different types will allow you to apply the specific evaluation techniques that will be introduced in this book. Your ability to classify an argument as deductive or inductive will continue to grow as you have the opportunity to analyze many different arguments.

EXERCISES 1E

Level 1 Multiple-
Choice Questions

Level 2 Multiple-
Choice Questions

The following exercises are intended to apply your understanding of the difference between deductive and inductive arguments. Determine whether the following arguments are best classified as being deductive or inductive. Explain your answers.

1. Every insect has six legs. What's crawling on me is an insect. So what's crawling on me has six legs.

Answer: Deductive. The first premise says something definite about every insect. The second premise says that an insect is crawling on me. If both premises are assumed to be true, then the conclusion is necessarily true.

2. Most insects have six legs. What's crawling on me is an insect. Therefore, what's crawling on me probably has six legs.

3. The exam's range of A scores is 90–100. I got a 98 on the exam. It follows necessarily that I got an A on the exam.

4. The exam's range of A scores is 90–100. I got an A on the exam, thus I got a 98 on the exam.

⭑ 5. All fires need oxygen. There is no oxygen in that room. So there is no fire in that room.

6. Some fires need no oxygen. There is no oxygen in that room. So there is no fire in that room.

7. Carly tossed a coin ten times, and in each case it came up heads. I have a feeling that it is a trick coin. I predict the next toss will be heads.

8. Carly tossed a coin ten times, and in each case it came up heads. The law of averages says that this cannot go on indefinitely. I predict the next toss will be tails.

⭑ 9. All elements with atomic weights greater than 64 are metals. Z is an element with an atomic weight of 79. Therefore, Z is a metal.

10. The majority of elements with atomic weights greater than 64 are metals. Z is an element with an atomic weight of 79. Therefore, Z is probably a metal.

11. Antibiotics have no effect on viruses. You have a disease that is caused by a virus. You are taking the antibiotic Q. Thus the antibiotic you are taking will have no effect on your disease.

12. Some antibiotics are effective for treating certain bacterial infections. You have a bacterial infection. You are taking the antibiotic Q. Thus the antibiotic you are taking will be effective in treating your bacterial infection.

Video Tutorial

⭑13. Anyone over 21 years of age can legally play the slot machines in Las Vegas. Sam is 33 years old. Sam can legally play the slot machines in Las Vegas.

14. Anyone over 21 years of age can legally play the slot machines in Las Vegas, unless they are a convicted felon. Sam is 33 years old. Sam can legally play the slot machines in Las Vegas.

15. Every orange has seeds. I am eating an orange, so I am eating something with seeds.

16. Most fruit have seeds. I am eating an orange. All oranges are fruit, so I am eating something with seeds.

⭑ 17. Most Doberman dogs bark a lot. My cousin just got a Doberman dog. Therefore, my cousin's Doberman dog will probably bark a lot.

18. The vast majority of a survey of 600 people who identified themselves as being very religious reported that they were against capital punishment. It is safe to say that the vast majority of all Americans think the same way.

19. Last week, when my car would not start, Mom took me to get a new battery. As soon as I installed it, my car started right up. So my old battery was probably defective.

20. No car battery that has at least one defective cell can be repaired. Your car battery has at least one defective cell, so it cannot be repaired.

★ 21. It's our job to make college basketball players realize that getting an education is something that's important, because life after basketball is a real long time.

Larry Brown, Southern Methodist University basketball coach

22. Many women who used to be full-time mothers are discovering that outside work gives them friends, challenges, variety, money, independence; it makes them feel better about themselves, and therefore lets them be better parents.

Wendy Coppedge Sanford, *Ourselves and Our Children*

23. If the NBA Finals rock, then the NBA thrives. If the NBA Finals are filled with stars, then the NBA Finals rock. If the Heat make the NBA Finals, then the NBA Finals will be filled with stars. Therefore, if the Heat make the NBA Finals, then the NBA thrives.   Dan Wheeler, adapted from "Rick Reilly's Mailbag," ESPN.com

24. Even when people think they're multitasking, what they are really doing is switching between tasks, not doing them simultaneously. And constant exposure to multiple devices at the same time isn't making people any better at it. "The more stuff you have, the less you are able to focus on individual things. There is very limited bandwidth for conscious thought," said Earl Miller, professor of neuroscience at MIT.

Keith Wagstaff, "The 'Smart Life': How Connected Cars,
Clothes and Homes Could Fry Your Brain," NBC News

★ 25. Studies indicate that when you have been forced to wait at the end of the line throughout your childhood, you tend to jump at the opportunity to be first when you grow up. So, if your last name begins with a letter near the end of the alphabet you're more likely to have a twitchy finger anxious to hit the buy button, whether for clothes or concert tickets.

"How Your Last Name Affects Shopping Decisions," Today.com

26. Senate Majority Leader Harry Reid said that he thinks the Washington Redskins football team will change the name. Reid accused Redskins owner Daniel Snyder of hiding behind tradition in retaining his team's name. "It is untoward of Daniel Snyder to try to hide behind tradition," Reid said. "Tradition? What tradition? A tradition of racism is all that name leaves in its wake. Mr. Snyder knows that in sports the only tradition that matters is winning, so I urge Daniel Snyder to do what's morally right and remove this degrading term from the league by changing his team's name."   Interview with Harry Reid in *The Washington Post*

27. "The policies the United States has had for the last 41 years have become irrelevant," said Morris Panner, a former counternarcotics prosecutor in New York and at the American Embassy in Colombia, who is now an adviser at Harvard's Kennedy School of Government. "The United States was worried about shipments of cocaine and heroin for years, but whether those policies worked or not doesn't matter because they are now worried about Americans using prescription drugs."

> Damien Cave and Michael S. Schmidt, "Rise in Pill Abuse
> Forces New Look at U.S. Drug Fight," *The New York Times*

28. The decision by this Administration to try terrorists in civilian court was the wrong one from day one, and yesterday's acquittal on 284 of 285 charges against Ghailani is further proof it has no overarching strategy to prosecute the War on Terror and keep America safe. It's time for the Administration to reverse course, and commit to keeping Khalid Sheikh Mohammed and other Gitmo detainees outside the United States and to try them in military courts.

> John Boehner, Speaker of the United States House of Representatives

⭐ 29. The Supreme Court sided with the video game industry today, declaring a victor in the six-year legal match between the industry and the California lawmakers who wanted to make it a crime for anyone in the state to sell extremely violent games to kids. . . . Writing for a plurality of justices, Justice Scalia said California's arguments "would fare better if there were a longstanding tradition in this country of specially restricting children's access to depictions of violence, but there is none." He cited numerous examples of violence in literature. "Reading Dante is unquestionably more cultured and intellectually edifying than playing 'Mortal Kombat.' But these cultural and intellectual differences are not constitutional." "[Therefore, t]he basic principles of freedom of speech . . . do not vary with a new and different communication medium," Scalia wrote in the Court's opinion, citing an earlier speech case.

> Stephen Totilo, "1st Amendment Beats Ban in Video Game Battle," MSNBC.MSN.com

30. The belief in God has often been advanced as not only the greatest, but the most complete of all the distinctions between man and the lower animals. It is however impossible, as we have seen, to maintain that this belief is innate or instinctive in man. On the other hand a belief in all-pervading spiritual agencies seems to be universal; and apparently follows from a considerable advance in man's reason, and from a still greater advance in his faculties of imagination, curiosity and wonder. I am aware that the assumed instinctive belief in God has been used by many persons as an argument for His existence. But this is a rash argument, as we should thus be compelled to believe in the existence of many cruel and malignant spirits, only a little more powerful than man; for the belief in them is far more general than in a beneficent Deity. The idea of a universal and beneficent Creator does not seem to arise in the mind of man, until he has been elevated by long-continued culture.

> Charles Darwin, *The Descent of Man*

F. DEDUCTIVE ARGUMENTS: VALIDITY AND SOUNDNESS

Logical analysis of a deductive argument is concerned with determining whether the conclusion follows necessarily from the premises. Placed in the form of a question, logical analysis of a deductive argument asks the following: "Assuming the premises are true, is it possible for the conclusion to be false?" Answering this question will provide us with some key terms with which we can dig deeper into deductive arguments.

A **valid deductive argument** is one in which, assuming the premises are true, it is *impossible* for the conclusion to be false. In other words, the conclusion follows necessarily from the premises. On the other hand, an **invalid deductive argument** is one in which, assuming the premises are true, it is *possible* for the conclusion to be false. In other words, the conclusion *does not* follow necessarily from the premises.

Determining the validity or the invalidity of an argument rests on logical analysis. We rely on the assumption that the premises are true in order to determine whether the conclusion necessarily follows. However, truth value does have a role in the overall analysis of deductive arguments. The determination that a deductive argument is valid rests on the *assumption* that the premises are true. A valid deductive argument can have premises or a conclusion whose actual truth value is false. Combining logical analysis with truth value analysis provides us with two more definitions. First, when logical analysis shows that a deductive argument is valid, and when truth value analysis of the premises shows that they are all true, then the argument is **sound**. However, if the deductive argument is invalid, or if at least one of the premises is false, then the argument is **unsound**.

To determine whether a deductive argument is valid or invalid, we apply logical analysis by assuming the premises are true. If logical analysis determines that the argument is valid, then we apply truth value analysis in order to determine whether the argument is sound or unsound. The following flow chart illustrates the process:

Valid deductive argument An argument in which, assuming the premises are true, it is *impossible* for the conclusion to be false. In other words, the conclusion follows necessarily from the premises.

Invalid deductive argument An argument in which, assuming the premises are true, it is *possible* for the conclusion to be false. In other words, the conclusion does not follow necessarily from the premises.

Sound argument A deductive argument is sound when the argument is valid, and the premises are true.

Unsound argument A deductive argument is unsound when the argument is invalid, or when at least one of the premises is false.

DEDUCTIVE ARGUMENT

If the premises are assumed to be true, then is it impossible for the conclusion to be false?

Yes → Valid

No → Invalid → Unsound

Valid → *Are all the premises true?*

Yes → Sound

No → Unsound

The flow chart illustrates an important point: A *valid* argument is one where it is impossible for the conclusion to be false, *assuming* the premises are true. And since a *sound* argument is one where the premises *are true*, we know that every sound argument's conclusion is true.

Argument Form

It is easy to confuse the question of the truth value of statements with the logical question of what follows from the statements. To keep the two questions clear and distinct when you analyze arguments, it can help to think about logical possibilities. To illustrate this idea, we start with a brief table listing the logical possibilities available in deductive arguments:

DEDUCTIVE ARGUMENTS			
Premises	Conclusion	Validity	Soundness
1. True	True	Valid or invalid	Sound or unsound
2. True	False	Invalid	Unsound
3. At least one is false	True	Valid or invalid	Unsound
4. At least one is false	False	Valid or invalid	Unsound

Line 2 states that a deductive argument with true premises and a false conclusion is invalid and unsound. This is a straightforward result of the previous section's discussion, so it should be easy to understand. However, lines 1, 3, and 4 can cause some confusion, so we will work slowly through them.

First, notice that under the column "Validity," deductive arguments that have the characteristics listed in lines 1, 3, and 4 are said to be *either* valid or invalid. Second, under the column "Soundness," deductive arguments that have the characteristics listed in both lines 3 and 4 are said to be unsound, but those in line 1 can be *either* sound or unsound.

Let's look at lines 3 and 4. Since both lines refer to deductive arguments that have "at least one false premise," the arguments are automatically unsound. In contrast, the deductive arguments referred to in line 1 have true premises, and since they can be *either* valid or invalid, they can be *either* sound or unsound. At this point, we are simply listing the logical possibilities. We now need to flesh out those possibilities to see how we can make the final determinations. For that we need to further explore the *logical analysis* and *truth value analysis* of some arguments.

Let's begin by looking at two arguments:

A. All dogs are cats. All cats are snakes. Therefore, all dogs are snakes.
B. No mammals are beagles. No mammals are dogs. Therefore, no beagles are dogs.

Each premise and conclusion in examples A and B relates two *classes* of objects (also called *groups* or *categories*). For example, the first premise of argument A refers to the *class of dogs* and the *class of cats*. The first premise of argument B refers to the *class of mammals* and the *class of beagles*. (Statements and arguments that use class terms are the subject of *categorical logic*, which is explored in Chapters 5 and 6.)

It should be easy to determine that all the premises and the conclusions in both A and B are false. However, since we want to focus on the *logical question of validity*, we do not want to get bogged down in truth value analysis. We need to reveal the *argument form*, which is the structure of the argument, not its content. In categorical logic, an **argument form** is an arrangement of logical vocabulary and letters that stand for class terms such that a uniform substitution of class terms for the letters results in an argument. In other words, an argument is valid or invalid based on its logical form, not on its subject matter.

To get started, we need to separate the *logical vocabulary* from the *nonlogical vocabulary* in the individual statements. For example, the first premise of argument A contains the logical vocabulary words "all," and "are," while the nonlogical vocabulary consists of the class terms "dogs" and "cats." In contrast, the first premise of argument B contains the logical vocabulary words "no," and "are," while the nonlogical vocabulary consists of the class terms "mammals" and "beagles."

We can use letters to stand for the nonlogical terms "dogs" and "cats" while keeping the logical vocabulary ("all" and "are") intact to reveal the statement form of the first premise. In categorical logic, a **statement form** is an arrangement of logical vocabulary and letters that stand for class terms such that a uniform substitution of class terms for the letters results in a statement. For example, if we let D = *dogs*, and C = *cats*, then the statement form is the following: "All D are C." We can extend the technique to reveal the *argument forms* of A and B, which we will then label FA and FB. Here are the letters we will use: Let D = *dogs*, C = *cats*, S = *snakes*, M = *mammals*, and B = *beagles*.

FA. All D are C.
All C are S.
All D are S.

FB. No M are B.
No M are D.
No B are D.

Notice that we introduced a horizontal line to separate the premises from the conclusion. This technique allows us to eliminate the word "Therefore." We know that an argument is constructed entirely of statements, and we know that each of the premises and the conclusion have two possible truth values (true or false). Recall that a valid argument is a deductive argument in which, assuming the premises are true, it is *impossible* for the conclusion to be false. An invalid argument is a deductive argument in which, assuming the premises are true, it is *possible* for the conclusion to be false.

We used the letters D, C, S, M, and B to stand for *dogs, cats, snakes, mammals,* and *beagles*. However, we can substitute *any* class or group term we wish for those letters, *as long as we keep the argument form intact.* A **substitution instance** of a *statement* occurs when a uniform substitution of class terms for the letters results in a statement. A substitution instance of an *argument* occurs when a uniform substitution of class terms for the letters results in an argument. For example, if we now let D = *Android phones*, C = *popular products*, and S = *inexpensive items*, we get the following substitution instance for argument form FA:

Argument form In categorical logic, an argument form is an arrangement of logical vocabulary and letters that stand for class terms such that a uniform substitution of class terms for the letters results in an argument.

Statement form In categorical logic, a statement form is an arrangement of logical vocabulary and letters that stand for class terms such that a uniform substitution of class terms for the letters results in a statement.

Substitution instance In categorical logic, a substitution instance of a *statement* occurs when a uniform substitution of class terms for the letters results in a statement. A *substitution instance* of an *argument* occurs when a uniform substitution of class terms for the letters results in an argument.

All Android phones are popular products.
<u>All popular products are inexpensive items.</u>
All Android phones are inexpensive items.

What we want to do is determine whether it is *possible* that either argument form FA or argument form FB, or both, can have true premises and a false conclusion. In order to make our task as easy as possible, we will use examples in which the truth value of the premises and conclusions are obvious to nearly everyone. For example, most people find it easier to determine the truth value of the statement "All beagles are dogs," than it is for the statement "All bivalves are mollusks." The following table supplies substitution instances for both FA and FB:

Argument Form FA—VALID	Argument Form FB —INVALID
1. *True* All beagles are dogs. *True* <u>All dogs are mammals.</u> *True* All beagles are mammals. **SOUND**	1. *True* No dogs are snakes. *True* <u>No dogs are cats.</u> *True* No snakes are cats. **UNSOUND**
2. *True* *True* None exist *False*	2. *True* No cats are beagles. *True* <u>No cats are dogs.</u> *False* No beagles are dogs. **UNSOUND**
3. *True* All beagles are mammals. *False* <u>All mammals are dogs.</u> *True* All beagles are dogs. **UNSOUND**	3. *True* No beagles are cats. *False* <u>No beagles are dogs.</u> *True* No cats are dogs. **UNSOUND**
4. *True* All dogs are mammals. *False* <u>All mammals are snakes.</u> *False* All dogs are snakes. **UNSOUND**	4. *True* No cats are dogs. *False* <u>No cats are mammals.</u> *False* No dogs are mammals. **UNSOUND**
5. *False* All dogs are cats. *True* <u>All cats are mammals.</u> *True* All dogs are mammals. **UNSOUND**	5. *False* No beagles are dogs. *True* <u>No beagles are cats.</u> *True* No dogs are cats. **UNSOUND**
6. *False* All cats are beagles. *True* <u>All beagles are dogs.</u> *False* All cats are dogs. **UNSOUND**	6. *False* No cats are mammals. *True* <u>No cats are dogs.</u> *False* No mammals are dogs. **UNSOUND**
7. *False* All beagles are cats. *False* <u>All cats are dogs.</u> *True* All beagles are dogs. **UNSOUND**	7. *False* No mammals are cats. *False* <u>No mammals are dogs.</u> *True* No cats are dogs. **UNSOUND**
8. *False* All dogs are cats. *False* <u>All cats are snakes.</u> *False* All dogs are snakes. **UNSOUND**	8. *False* No mammals are beagles. *False* <u>No mammals are dogs.</u> *False* No beagles are dogs. **UNSOUND**

No matter what we substitute into the form FA it is logically impossible for a false conclusion to follow from true premises. In other words, form FA can result in arguments that correspond to every combination of truth values in the table, *except number 2*. On the other hand, it is logically possible to substitute into form FB and get a false conclusion following from true premises. Form FB can result in arguments that correspond to every combination in the table, *including number 2*.

Even though the actual truth value of the original statements in both argument A and argument B were the same (false premises and a false conclusion), argument A is valid, but argument B is invalid. It is important to remember that when we evaluate arguments, we must always distinguish truth value analysis from the logical analysis.

Counterexamples

The overall analysis of a deductive argument requires two things: logical analysis and truth value analysis. Based on logical analysis deductive arguments are either valid or invalid. When we add the results of truth value analysis, deductive arguments are either sound or unsound. Most people have more experience in evaluating the truth value than the logic of an argument, simply because our formal education is heavily devoted to what is known to be true. A large part of education is the teaching of facts.

The difference between logical analysis and truth value analysis can be illustrated by the role of **counterexamples**. A counterexample to a *statement* is evidence that shows the statement is false, and it concerns truth value analysis. Suppose someone says, "No human is taller than eight feet." If we are able to find a human who is taller than eight feet, then we have evidence that the statement is false. The evidence can be considered to be a counterexample to the statement "No human is taller than eight feet."

Statements that use the words "never," "always," or the phrase "every time" are often subject to simple counterexamples. Here are some examples of statements and counterexamples:

> Statement: "I never get to stay home from school."
> Counterexample: "You stay home from school when you are sick and when we go on vacation."
> Statement: "He always gets to go first."
> Counterexample: "You went first when we rode on the roller coaster at the park last week."
> Statement: "The phone rings every time I'm taking a shower."
> Counterexample: "But you took a shower last night and the phone didn't ring."

A counterexample to an *argument* plays a different role. It shows that the premises assumed to be true do not make the conclusion necessarily true. A single counterexample to a deductive argument is enough to show that the argument is invalid. This should not be surprising. If you recall, every deductive argument is either valid or invalid. Therefore, it is not necessary to find more than one counterexample to a

Counterexample A counterexample to a statement is evidence that shows the statement is false. A counterexample to an argument shows the possibility that premises assumed to be true do not make the conclusion necessarily true. A single counterexample to a deductive argument is enough to show that the argument is invalid.

deductive argument because there are no degrees of invalidity. In other words, deductive arguments cannot be classified as *partially valid* or *semi-valid*.

Let's consider the following deductive argument:

C. All bomohs are scam artists.
All grifters are scam artists.
All bomohs are grifters.

You do not need to know what either a bomoh or a grifter or a scam artist is in order to determine if the argument is valid or invalid. Whatever those things are we can begin by thinking about the argument in a logical way. The argument relates two things (bomohs and grifters) to a third thing (scam artists). Now even if we assume that every bomoh and every grifter is a scam artist, is it necessarily true that every bomoh is a grifter? The first step of the analysis is to reveal the argument form. Let's substitute letters for the terms in order to reveal the form: B = *bomohs*, S = *scam artists*, and G = *grifters*.

FC. All B are S.
All G are S.
All B are G.

The second step is to substitute three terms for the letters, such that the substitution instance will be a counterexample. Let's try the following: B = *beagles*, S = *mammals*, and G = *dogs*.

D. All beagles are mammals.
All dogs are mammals.
All beagles are dogs.

Truth value analysis shows that the premises and the conclusion are true, so this substitution instance is not a counterexample. At this point it can help to change our strategy, so that our thinking does not get stuck in a loop. Repeating the same approach to a problem may cause us to miss other possibilities. We might fail to see alternative paths because our minds are locked into one way of analysis. Sometimes, however, the light bulb goes on, and we instantly see the answer (the *Aha!* experience). A puzzle illustrates how this can happen.

Imagine that you are given a knife and are told to cut a cake (with no icing) into two equal pieces with one slice. You must always cut the cake in straight lines; you cannot stop a cut halfway through the cake and resume it at another place; and you cannot touch the cake in any other way. This is easily accomplished as follows:

Once you have successfully cut the cake into two equal pieces, you are then asked to cut the cake into four equal pieces with one more slice. You should be able to do this quite easily:

At this point, you are now asked to cut the cake into eight equal parts with just one more slice. Remember the rules: You must cut the cake in straight lines; you cannot start a cut in one place and resume it somewhere else; and you cannot touch the cake in any other way. Can you do it? Do you think it is impossible?

Before reading further, you should have struggled with the problem for a while in order to experience fully the possibility of attacking the problem in only one way. The puzzle, as stated, has set your mind thinking in one direction by imagining the cake as a two-dimensional object. But the cake is a three-dimensional object. It can be cut in half through its middle, leaving four pieces on top and four on the bottom, all equal to each other.

If our search for a counterexample starts with the premises, then we start by making the premises true and then seeing if the conclusion turned out to be false. Although it is generally easier to think of things that would make the premises true, we could get stuck in a loop.

However, there is a way to shorten the amount of time needed to find a counterexample, and that is to analyze an argument from the bottom up. This technique temporarily ignores the premises and instead concentrates on the conclusion. For our current example, the conclusion is "All B are G." Since we are searching for a counterexample, we must substitute terms that make the conclusion false. It helps to choose simple terms that will make the conclusion obviously false. For example, let's try the following substitutions: B = *men*, G = *women*.

> All men are S.
> <u>All women are S.</u>
> All men are women.

The conclusion is clearly false. Now if we can substitute a term for the "S" in the premises, and have the premises be true, then this will produce a counterexample. But before we simply start randomly trying different terms, we should think of what we are trying to accomplish. We need to substitute something for the "S" such that both premises are true. That means that we have to think of something that both men and women have in common. Well, since every man and every woman is a human being, we can try that and see what happens.

> **E.** All men are human beings.
> <u>All women are human beings.</u>
> All men are women.

The premises of this argument are true and the conclusion is false, so we have created a counterexample. The counterexample shows that the argument is invalid.

Let's look at another example:

G. All bomohs are scam artists.
All scam artists are grifters.
All bomohs are grifters.

Here we have switched the order of the terms in the second premise. Once again, the first step is to reveal the argument form. Let's substitute the same letters we used earlier for the terms in order to reveal the form: B = *bomohs*, S = *scam artists*, and G = *grifters*.

FG. All B are S.
All S are G.
All B are G.

This has the same general argument form that we encountered in example FA:

FA. All D are C.
All C are S.
All D are S.

Since we already said that FA is a valid form, FG is valid as well. However, let's work through the argument using the bottom-up technique for additional practice. We can use the same substitutions as before: B = *men*, S = *human beings*, and G = *women*.

All men are human beings.
All human beings are women.
All men are women.

The conclusion is false and the first premise is true. However, the second premise is false. Therefore, this particular substitution instance is not a counterexample. At this point we can take another look at the form of argument FG. If we assume that every B is an S (premise 1), and every S is a G (premise 2), then it seems to follow that every B must be a G. However, we might want to try another substitution instance. Let's use these: B = *women*, S = *human beings*, and G = *mammals*.

All women are human beings.
All human beings are mammals.
All women are mammals.

The premises are true, but so is the conclusion. This particular substitution instance is also not a counterexample. This brings up an interesting point. The counterexample method can be effectively used to show that an argument is invalid, but it cannot show that an argument is valid. If you think about this, it begins to make sense. Invalid arguments have counterexamples, but valid arguments do not.

In order to create a counterexample it helps to use simple terms with which you are familiar. This helps ensure that the truth value of the statements you create are generally well known to everyone. If you noticed, we used terms such as *men, women, cats,* and *dogs*. Although counterexamples are a good way to identify invalid arguments, they are sometimes difficult to create. If we are unable to create a counterexample, then this by itself does not show that the argument is valid; instead it might be that we just failed to find a counterexample. (Part III introduces additional techniques of logical analysis that are capable of showing validity.)

Since many real-life arguments do not fall easily into a form like the examples we have been examining, we sometimes have to be creative in finding a counterexample. For example, consider this argument:

> Every student in my daughter's psychology class has at least a 3.0 average. But all the students in her calculus class have at least a 2.0 average. So it has to be that every single student in my daughter's psychology class has a higher average than every single student in my daughter's calculus class.

The first two statements are premises, and the third statement is the conclusion. Another way to create a counterexample to an argument is to construct a *model* that shows the possibility of true premises and a false conclusion.

Suppose that a particular student from the psychology class has a 3.2 average. This possibility would make the first premise true. Now suppose that a particular student from the calculus class has a 3.6 average. This is possible because the claim in the second premise is that the students have at least a 2.0 average. In this case, the second premise is true, too, but the conclusion is false. We have created a counterexample that shows the argument is invalid.

So far, we have been using letters to represent class terms (for example, we let D = *dogs*). We can now expand this technique to different types of statements. Let's compare the following two examples:

H. All *pizza toppings* are *delicious morsels*.
I. If *Sherry lives in Los Angeles*, then *Sherry lives in California*.

In example H, the two italicized words are *class terms*, which *by themselves* are neither true nor false. However, the two italicized parts of example I are *statements* that are either true or false (we can call them *simple statements*). In addition, example I contains the logical vocabulary words "if" and "then." Example I is a good illustration of how a *sentence* in English can contain *multiple simple statements*. Taken as a whole, example I is a *compound statement* and it, too, is either true or false.

We can use letters to represent the simple statements in example I while we keep the logical vocabulary in place. For example, if we let *L* = *Sherry lives in Los Angeles*, and *C* = *Sherry lives in California*, then we get the following for example I: If *L*, then *C*.

This technique can be applied to certain kinds of arguments. For example:

Argument J:	**Argument Form:**
If Sherry lives in Los Angeles, then Sherry lives in California.	**If *L*, then *C*.**
Sherry lives in California.	*C*.
Sherry lives in Los Angeles.	*L*.

The first premise, "If Sherry lives in Los Angeles, then Sherry lives in California," is an example of a *conditional statement*. The simple statement that follows the word "if" is referred to as the *antecedent*. The other simple statement, which follows the word "then," is referred to as the *consequent*. At this stage, the most important thing to recognize is that a conditional statement *does not assert* that either the antecedent or the consequent is true. What is asserted is that *if* the antecedent is true, *then* the consequent is true.

Given this understanding of a conditional statement, let's analyze argument J. We can start by assuming that the first premise is true. Why? Because it *does not assert* that Sherry actually lives in Los Angeles, it just asserts that *if* she lives in Los Angeles, then she lives in California. Next, let's assume that the second premise is also true, that Sherry lives in California. We can now ask: Is the conclusion necessarily true? No, because it is *possible* that Sherry lives in San Francisco. Thus, argument J is invalid.

The *argument form* for argument J is referred to as the *fallacy of affirming the consequent*. It is a *formal fallacy*, a logical error that occurs in the form of an argument. Formal fallacies are restricted to *deductive* arguments. (Formal fallacies are also discussed in Chapters 6–8.) In contrast to this, *informal fallacies* are mistakes in reasoning that occur in ordinary language. (Informal fallacies are discussed in Chapter 4.)

Let's look at another argument:

Argument K:	**Argument Form:**
If Sherry lives in Los Angeles, then Sherry lives in California.	If *L*, then *C*.
<u>Sherry lives in Los Angeles.</u>	<u>*L*.</u>
Sherry lives in California.	*C*.

Relying on our understanding of a conditional statement, we can analyze argument K. As we saw with argument J, we can start by assuming that the first premise is true. Now, *if* the second premise is true, then the conclusion is *necessarily true*. Thus, argument K is valid. The *argument form* for argument K is referred to as *modus ponens*. In order to fully appreciate this result, we need to understand that since argument K is valid, no counterexample exists. This is an important claim, and we will try to explain it with the apparatus we currently have.

Recall that we were able to create a counterexample to argument J by recognizing that even if both premises were true, it is possible that the conclusion is false (that Sherry lives in San Francisco). Let's try that with argument K. As before, we can assume that the first premise is true. Now if we assume that the second premise is true, then the conclusion follows necessarily. (You can learn about different methods for demonstrating validity, as well as other methods for showing invalidity, in Part III, "Formal Logic.")

Let's look at a few more examples:

Argument M:	**Argument Form:**
If Sherry lives in Los Angeles, then Sherry lives in California.	If *L*, then *C*.
<u>Sherry does not live in Los Angeles.</u>	**It is not the case that *L*.**
Sherry does not live in California.	**It is not the case that *C*.**

We have been using the letter "*L*" to represent the simple statement "Sherry lives in Los Angeles." In order to represent the statement "Sherry does *not* live in Los Angeles," we place the phrase "It is not the case that" in front of the letter "*L*." Similarly, we have been using the letter "*C*" to represent the simple statement "Sherry lives in California." In order to represent the statement "Sherry does *not* live in California," we place the phrase "It is not the case that" in front of the letter "*C*."

Let's analyze argument M. We can start by assuming that the two premises are true. Is the conclusion necessarily true? No, because it is possible that Sherry lives in San Francisco. Thus, argument M is invalid. The *argument form* for argument M is referred to as the *fallacy of denying the antecedent*, and it is a *formal fallacy*.

Here is another example:

Argument N:	**Argument Form:**
If Sherry lives in Los Angeles, then Sherry lives in California.	**If *L*, then *C*.**
<u>Sherry does not live in California.</u>	**<u>It is not the case that *C*.</u>**
Sherry does not live in Los Angeles.	**It is not the case that *L*.**

Let's analyze argument N. We can start by assuming that the premises are true. Given this, the conclusion is necessarily true. Thus, argument N is valid. The *argument form* for argument N is referred to as *modus tollens*. Since argument N is valid, no counterexample exists.

We will look at two more examples.

Argument P:	**Argument Form:**
If Sherry lives in Los Angeles, then Sherry lives in California.	**If *L*, then *C*.**
<u>If Sherry lives in California, then Sherry lives in the United States.</u>	**<u>If *C*, then *U*.</u>**
If Sherry lives in Los Angeles, then Sherry lives in the United States.	**If *L*, then *U*.**

Let's analyze argument P. We start by assuming that the premises are true. Given this, the conclusion is necessarily true. Thus, argument P is valid. The *argument form* for argument P is referred to as *hypothetical syllogism*. Since argument P is valid, no counterexample exists.

Our last example is the following:

Argument Q:	**Argument Form:**
Sherry lives in Los Angeles or Sherry lives in San Francisco.	**L or S.**
<u>Sherry does not live in Los Angeles.</u>	**<u>It is not the case that *L*.</u>**
Sherry lives in San Francisco.	**S.**

Let's analyze argument Q. The first premise is a compound statement that contains two simple statements ("Sherry lives in Los Angeles" and "Sherry lives in San Francisco"). It also contains the logical vocabulary word "or." This kind of compound statement is called a *disjunction*, and the two nonlogical parts are called *disjuncts*. When we assert a disjunction, we claim that at least one of the two disjuncts is true. In other words, the only way a disjunction is false is if both disjuncts are false.

We can start our analysis by assuming that the first premise is true. Given this assumption, one of the disjuncts must be true. Now, *if* the second premise is true, then it eliminates the first disjunct in the first premise. Therefore, the conclusion is *necessarily true*. Thus, argument Q is valid. The *argument form* for argument Q is referred to as *disjunctive syllogism*. Since argument Q is valid, no counterexample exists.

There are other methods of translating arguments to reveal the form, as we will see in Part III. For now, though, you can use your practical knowledge of counterexamples to help analyze arguments.

Summary of Deductive Arguments

Valid argument: A deductive argument in which, assuming the premises are true, it is *impossible* for the conclusion to be false.

Invalid argument: A deductive argument in which, assuming the premises are true, it is *possible* for the conclusion to be false.

Sound argument: A deductive argument is sound when both of the following requirements are met:
1. The argument is valid (logical analysis).
2. All the premises are true (truth value analysis).

Unsound argument: A deductive argument is unsound if either or both of the following conditions hold:
1. The argument is invalid (logical analysis).
2. The argument has at least one false premise (truth value analysis).

EXERCISES 1F

I. Create a counterexample or model to show that the following deductive arguments are invalid.

1. All towers less than 200 years old are skyscrapers. All buildings made of steel are skyscrapers. Therefore, all buildings made of steel are towers less than 200 years old.

Answer: If we let T = *towers less than 200 years old*, S = *skyscrapers*, and B = *buildings made of steel*, then the argument form is the following:

All T are S.
All B are S.
All B are T.

Level 1 Multiple-
Choice Questions

Level 2 Multiple-
Choice Questions

The following substitutions create a counterexample: Let T = *cats*, S = *mammals*, and B = *dogs*.

> All cats are mammals.
> <u>All dogs are mammals.</u>
> All dogs are cats.

Both premises are true, and the conclusion is false. Therefore, the counterexample shows that the argument is invalid.

2. No skyscrapers are buildings made of steel. No skyscrapers are towers less than 200 years old. Therefore, no buildings made of steel are towers less than 200 years old.

3. All Phi Beta Kappa members are seniors in college. All Phi Beta Kappa members are liberal arts majors. Therefore, all liberal arts majors are seniors in college.

4. No Phi Beta Kappa members are seniors in college. No Phi Beta Kappa members are liberal arts majors. Therefore, no liberal arts majors are seniors in college.

Video Tutorial

5. All computers are electronic devices. All things that require an AC adapter are electronic devices. Therefore, all computers are things that require an AC adapter.

6. No computers are electronic devices. No electronic devices are things that require an AC adapter. Therefore, no computers are things that require an AC adapter.

7. All skateboards are items made of wood. All items made of wood are flammable objects. Therefore, all flammable objects are skateboards.

8. No skateboards are items made of wood. No items made of wood are flammable objects. Therefore, no flammable objects are skateboards.

9. No unicorns are immortal creatures. No centaurs are immortal creatures. It follows that no unicorns are centaurs.

10. Book A has more than 200 pages. Book B has more than 500 pages. Therefore, book B has more pages than book A.

11. Book A has more than 200 pages. Book B has more than 500 pages. Therefore, book A has more pages than book B.

12. Barney was born before 1989. Hazel was born before 1959. Thus, Hazel was born before Barney.

13. Fidelix was born before 1990. Gil was born before 1991. Thus, Fidelix was born before Gil.

14. Maegan spent ⅓ of her yearly income on her car. Alyssa spent ½ of her yearly income on her car. Therefore, Alyssa spent more money on her car than Maegan.

15. Michelle spent ½ of her yearly income on her car. Kaitlin spent ⅓ of her yearly income on her car. Therefore, Kaitlin spent more money on her car than Michelle.

16. All psychiatrists are people with medical degrees. All people who can prescribe drugs are people with medical degrees. Therefore, all psychiatrists are people who can prescribe drugs.

17. All strawberries are fruit. All strawberries are plants. It follows that all fruit are plants.

18. All members of the U.S. Congress are citizens of the United States. All people under 21 years of age are citizens of the United States. Therefore, no people under 21 years of age are members of the U.S. Congress.

19. All humans are things that contain carbon. All inanimate objects are things that contain carbon. Therefore, all humans are inanimate objects.

20. No coal mines are dangerous areas to work. All dangerous areas to work are places inspected by federal agencies. Therefore, no coal mines are places inspected by federal agencies.

II. First, reveal the argument form of the following deductive arguments. Second, label it as either the *fallacy of affirming the consequent, modus ponens, the fallacy of denying the antecedent, modus tollens, hypothetical syllogism,* or *disjunctive syllogism.* Third, create a counterexample for each of the invalid argument forms.

Level 1 Multiple-Choice Questions

Level 2 Multiple-Choice Questions

1. If Sam goes to the meeting, then Joe will stay home. Sam is not going to the meeting. Therefore, Joe will not stay home.
Answer: If we let *S = Sam goes to the meeting,* and *J = Joe will stay home,* then the argument form is the following:

> If *S*, then *J*.
> It is not the case that *S*.
> It is not the case that *J*.

Fallacy of denying the antecedent. The argument is invalid.

Since this is an invalid argument form, we can try to create a counterexample. We can make the letters "*S*" and "*J*" stand for *any statements that we wish.* All we need to do is create a scenario where both premises are true and the conclusion is false. Suppose that we make *S = my mom ate an apple,* and *J = my mom ate a fruit.* In addition, suppose that my mom actually ate an orange instead of an apple. Under these assumptions, the first premise would still be true (recall that the conditional statement *does not assert* that she ate an apple; it asserts only that *if* she ate an apple, then she ate a fruit). Since we assumed that she ate an orange, the second premise is also true. However, the conclusion is false because she did eat a fruit.

2. Either you take a cut in pay or we will lay you off. You did not take a cut in pay. Thus, we will lay you off.

3. If today is your birthday, then you received presents. You received presents. So, today is your birthday.

4. If animals have rights, then animals can vote. Animals have rights. Therefore, animals can vote.

⭐ 5. If birds can swim, then birds are aquatic animals. Birds are not aquatic animals. Thus, birds cannot swim.

6. If bananas are fruit, then bananas are plants. If bananas are plants, then bananas use photosynthesis. So, if bananas are fruit, then bananas use photosynthesis.

7. If Mary stayed home from work, then her car is in the garage. Mary's car is in the garage. Therefore, Mary stayed home from work.

8. If animals have rights, then animals can vote. Animals do not have rights. Thus, animals cannot vote.

⭐ 9. Either you are lost or you are confused. You are not lost. Therefore, you are confused.

10. If Linda went swimming, then she is at the lake. Linda is not at the lake. Thus, Linda did not go swimming.

11. If your motorcycle is burning oil, then it is wasting energy. If your motorcycle is wasting energy, then it is polluting the air. So, if your motorcycle is burning oil, then it is polluting the air.

12. If Jane Blythe is a secret agent, then she is licensed to carry a gun. Jane Blythe is not a secret agent, so she is not licensed to carry a gun.

⭐ 13. If I can save $1000, then I can buy a car. I can save $1000. Thus, I can buy a car.

14. If you graduated, then you got a high-paying job. You got a high-paying job, so you graduated.

15. Either you completed the coursework or you failed the course. You did not complete your coursework. Therefore, you failed the course.

G. INDUCTIVE ARGUMENTS: STRENGTH AND COGENCY

Often our arguments are not expected to achieve validity. As we shall see, the results of analysis of inductive arguments are not all-or-nothing. If you recall, deductive arguments can be valid, invalid, sound, or unsound. In addition, one deductive argument cannot be more valid (or invalid) than another deductive argument. In contrast to this, one inductive argument can be classified as *stronger* or *weaker* than another inductive argument. We can compare them by how likely their respective conclusions are true, under the assumption that the premises are true. Recall that an inductive argument is one in which the inferential claim is that the conclusion is *probably true* if the premises are true. In other words, under the *assumption* that the premises are true it is *improbable* for the conclusion to be false.

A **strong inductive argument** is such that if the premises are *assumed* to be true, then the conclusion is *probably true*. Let's look at a simple example:

> Most cars in the United States use gasoline. Therefore, my aunt's new car probably uses gasoline.

If we *assume* that the premise is true, then the conclusion is *probably* true. The important thing to consider is that the premise offers direct and relevant support, so we can say that the *probable truth* of the conclusion *follows from* the truth of the premise.

In contrast, a **weak inductive argument** is an argument such that either (a) if the premises are *assumed* to be true, then the conclusion is *probably not true,* or (b) a probably true conclusion *does not follow from the premises.*

Let's look at a simple example of (a):

> Most cars in the United States use gasoline. Therefore, my aunt's new car probably is electric.

If we *assume* that the premise is true, then the conclusion is probably not true. Thus, the argument is weak. Notice that we are *not* claiming that the conclusion is false; we are claiming only that is *unlikely to be true,* assuming the premise is true.

The other way an inductive argument can be weak is (b) a probably true conclusion *does not follow from the premises.* This typically occurs when premises that are *irrelevant* to the conclusion do not provide any probabilistic support for the conclusion. In these cases, *even though the conclusion is probably true,* the argument is weak. Here is a simple example:

> You need a valid driver's license to legally drive an automobile. Therefore, for the near future most new automobiles will use gasoline.

There is no direct, relevant connection between the premise and the conclusion. Although the conclusion is probably true, that probability is *not* based on the assumption that the premise is true. Since the conclusion is probably true *independently of the premise,* the argument is weak. The important consideration in evaluating the strength or weakness of an inductive argument is the probabilistic support the premises give to the conclusion.

When we add truth value analysis to the results of the logical analysis, we get two additional classifications. An inductive argument is **cogent** when the argument is strong and the premises are true. On the other hand, an inductive argument is **uncogent** if either or both of the following conditions hold: The argument is weak, or the argument has at least one false premise. The following flow chart illustrates the process:

Strong inductive argument An argument such that if the premises are *assumed* to be true, then the conclusion is *probably* true. In other words, the probable truth of the conclusion *follows from* the truth of the premises.

Weak inductive argument An argument such that either (a) if the premises are *assumed* to be true, then the conclusion is *probably not true,* or (b) a probably true conclusion *does not follow from the premises.*

Cogent argument An inductive argument is cogent when the argument is strong and the premises are true.

Uncogent argument An inductive argument is uncogent if either or both of the following conditions hold: The argument is weak, or the argument has at least one false premise.

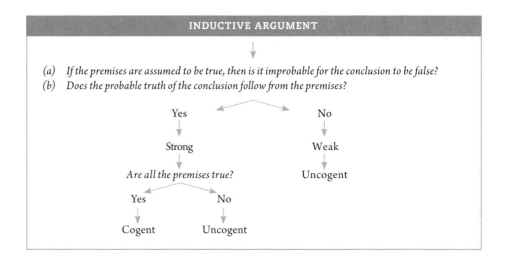

Since it is easy to confuse the question of the truth value of statements with the logical question of what follows from those statements, it is important to keep the two questions separate when you analyze arguments. To help, we start with a brief table listing the logical possibilities available in inductive arguments:

INDUCTIVE ARGUMENTS			
Premises	**Conclusion**	**Strength**	**Cogency**
1. True	Probably true	Strong or weak	Cogent or uncogent
2. True	Probably false	Weak	Uncogent
3. At least one false	Probably true	Strong or weak	Uncogent
4. At least one false	Probably false	Strong or weak	Uncogent

Line 2 states that an inductive argument with true premises and a false conclusion is weak and uncogent. This is a straightforward result of the previous discussion. On the other hand, lines 1, 3, and 4 may need additional explanation.

Notice that under the column "Strength," inductive arguments that have the characteristics listed in lines 1, 3, and 4 are said to be either strong or weak. Under the column "Cogency," inductive arguments that have the characteristics listed in both lines 3 and 4 are said to be uncogent, but those in line 1 can be either cogent or uncogent.

Let's look at lines 3 and 4. Since both lines refer to inductive arguments that have at least one false premise, the arguments are automatically uncogent. In contrast, the inductive arguments referred to in line 1 have true premises, and since they can be either strong or weak, they can be either cogent or uncogent. At this point, we are simply listing the logical possibilities. We now need to flesh out those possibilities to see how we can make the final determinations. Here are some examples:

Premise/Conclusion	Strong	Weak
True premise	Most cars use gasoline.	A few cars are antiques.
Probably true conclusion	Therefore, probably my cousin's car uses gasoline. COGENT	Therefore, probably my cousin's car uses gasoline. UNCOGENT
True premise		A few cars are antiques.
Probably false conclusion	None exist	Therefore, probably my cousin's car is an antique. UNCOGENT
False premise	Most new cars cost over $100,000.	Most cars are antiques.
Probably true conclusion	Therefore, probably your new Ferrari costs over $100,000. UNCOGENT	Therefore, probably your car uses gasoline. UNCOGENT
False premise	Most cars are antiques.	Most cars are hybrids.
Probably false conclusion	Therefore, probably your car is an antique. UNCOGENT	Therefore, probably your car is a Ferrari. UNCOGENT

Techniques of Analysis

Let's start with an analysis of an inductive argument:

> Most National Basketball Association most valuable players (MVPs) are at <u>least six feet tall.</u>
> The next National Basketball Association MVP will be at least six feet tall.

The logical analysis begins by assuming that the premise is true. The key for applying the logical analysis in this example is the term "most." Under the assumption that the premise is true, the conclusion is probably true; therefore, the argument is strong. Turning now to the truth value analysis, research shows that the premise is true. Therefore, the argument is both strong and cogent.

Let's now analyze a pair of inductive arguments at the same time. Imagine that you have the following information: An opaque jar contains exactly 100 marbles. There are 99 blue marbles and 1 red marble in the jar. Next, you are told that someone has reached into the jar and picked 1 marble, and you and a friend guess what color it is. You choose blue and your friend chooses red. We can use this case to create two inductive arguments:

A. An opaque jar contains exactly 100 marbles.
There are 99 blue marbles in the jar.
<u>There is 1 red marble in the jar.</u>
The marble picked is blue.

B. An opaque jar contains exactly 100 marbles.
There are 99 blue marbles in the jar.
<u>There is 1 red marble in the jar.</u>
The marble picked is red.

Using the definitions for inductive arguments, a logical analysis shows that argument A is strong and argument B is weak. Based on the assumption that the premises are true we can calculate that the conclusion of argument A has a 99/100 chance of being true, while the conclusion of argument B has only a 1/100 chance of being true. Given this, we can say that argument A is much stronger than argument B.

Now suppose we are shown the actual marble that was picked and it is red. Is this a counterexample to argument A that would make argument A weak? And would this result suddenly render argument B strong? The answer to both questions is *No*. We determined that the premises, *if they are assumed to be true*, make the conclusion of argument A *probably true*. On the other hand, the premises, *if they are assumed to be true*, make the conclusion of argument B *not probably true*. Therefore, the single result of a red marble does not change our mind.

However, at some point new evidence can become a factor in our overall assessment. We turn now to that discussion.

The Role of New Information

In order to advance the discussion, we will continue our analysis of arguments A and B from the end of the previous section. Suppose that the red marble is returned to the jar, the jar is shaken, and a *second* pick yields a red marble again. Since we are assuming that there is only 1 red marble in the jar, the probability of this happening is $1/100 \times 1/100 = 1/10,000$—which is very small, *but not impossible*. In fact, in a very long series of picks, we would eventually expect this to happen. But now suppose that the *next five picks* all result in a red marble, and each time the red marble is returned and the jar shaken. The probability is now 1/100 multiplied by itself seven times (that is, the original two picks plus five more). Faced with the new evidence, we may need to explain why we are getting these unexpected results.

We still assume that the premises are true; this is how we are coming up with the probabilities. But at some point the actual results may cause us to *question the truth of the original premises*. Although we were told that the jar contained 99 blue marbles and 1 red marble, we might start doubting this. In fact, we might even doubt that there are any blue ones at all, or if there are 100 marbles. It could even be that this is a scam; the person picking the marble palms a red one and never really puts it back. In other words, we might start doubting the truth of any or all of the premises.

As this example shows, determining whether an inductive argument is strong or weak is not an all-or-nothing thing. Also, a single counterexample does not have the same effect on an inductive argument that it has on a deductive argument. The goals of inductive and deductive arguments are simply different.

Another interesting point to consider regarding inductive arguments is that by adding an additional premise or premises to a weak inductive argument, we can often create a new argument that is strong. For example, consider the following argument:

> There are green and black socks in the box. Thus, a sock picked at random will probably be green.

Since we do not know how many socks of each color are in the box, the premise *does not* make the conclusion highly likely to be true; thus it is a weak argument. However, suppose we are given some new information:

> There are green and black socks in the box. *Eight of the socks are green and two are black*. Thus, a sock picked at random will probably be green.

Based on the new information, there is an 8/10 chance of picking a green sock. Since the conclusion is now highly likely to be true, the addition makes this a strong argument.

On the other hand, it is also possible that new information will affect a strong inductive argument such that the added premises create a new, weak argument. For example, consider the following argument:

> I just drank a bottle of Sunrise Spring Mineral Water. Since it has been shown that most bottled water is safe, I can conclude, with some confidence, that the water was safe.

Assuming the premises are true, this is a strong argument. However, suppose we pick up the newspaper and read an article reporting the following:

> Happy Sunshine Manufacturing Corporation has announced that it is recalling all of its Sunrise Spring Mineral Water due to a suspected contamination at one of its bottling facilities. Anyone having purchased this product is advised to return it to the store of purchase for a full refund.

When added as additional premises, this new information makes the original conclusion unlikely to be true; thus its addition creates a weak argument.

Of course, not all additional information will affect an inductive argument. For example, if new information is added as a premise, *but it is irrelevant to the conclusion*, then it has no effect on the strength of the argument.

As we saw earlier, there are many types of inductive arguments. In Part IV ("Inductive Logic") we introduce techniques of analysis for several types of inductive arguments.

Summary of Inductive Arguments

Strong inductive argument: An argument such that if the premises are *assumed* to be true, then the conclusion is *probably* true. In other words, the probable truth of the conclusion *follows from* the truth of the premises.

Weak inductive argument: An argument such that either (a) if the premises are *assumed* to be true, then the conclusion is *probably not true,* or (b) a probably true conclusion *does not follow from the premises.*

Cogent argument: An inductive argument is cogent when both of the following requirements are met:
1. The argument is strong (logical analysis).
2. All the premises are true (truth value analysis).

Uncogent argument: An inductive argument is uncogent if either or both of the following conditions hold:
1. The argument is weak (logical analysis).
2. The argument has at least one false premise (truth value analysis).

EXERCISES 1G

Level 1 Multiple-
Choice Questions

Level 2 Multiple-
Choice Questions

Video Tutorial

I. Determine whether the following inductive arguments are *strong* or *weak.*

1. Most insects have six legs. What's crawling on me is an insect. So what's crawling on me has six legs.

Answer: Strong. If we assume the premises are true, then the conclusion is probably true.

2. The exam's range of A scores is 90–100. I got an A on the exam, thus I got a 98 on the exam.

3. The exam's range of A scores is 90–100; B scores are 80–89; C scores are 70–79; D scores are 60–69; and F scores are 0–59. I did not get a 98 on the exam. Therefore, I probably did not get an A on the exam.

4. Shane tossed a coin ten times, and in each case it came up heads. Therefore, the next toss will be tails.

⭐ 5. Shane tossed a coin ten times, and in each case it came up heads. Therefore, the next toss will be heads.

6. Most elements with atomic weights greater than 64 are metals. Z is an element with an atomic weight of 79. Therefore, Z is a metal.

7. Most elements with atomic weights greater than 64 are metals. Z is an element with an atomic weight less than 64. Therefore, Z is a metal.

8. Most antibiotics are effective for treating bacterial infections. You have a bacterial infection. You are taking the antibiotic Q. Thus, the antibiotic you are taking will be effective in treating your bacterial infection.

⭐ 9. Most fruit have seeds. I am eating an orange, so I am eating something with seeds.

10. Most Doberman dogs bark a lot. My cousin just got a Doberman dog. Therefore, my cousin's Doberman dog will probably bark a lot.

II. **The following exercises are designed to get you to evaluate the strength of inductive arguments as the result of adding new information. You will be given an inductive argument; then additional information will be provided. Determine whether the new information *strengthens* or *weakens* the original argument. Evaluate each piece of new information independently of the others. Here is the argument:**

Level 1 Multiple-
Choice Questions

Level 2 Multiple-
Choice Questions

<u>**The lamp in your room does not work.**</u>
The light bulb is defective.

1. The ceiling light works.

Answer: Strengthens the argument. If the ceiling light works, then there is electricity available in the room.

2. The lamp is plugged into the wall socket correctly.

3. Your radio is working, and it is connected to the same outlet as the lamp.

4. The ceiling light does not work.

5. The lamp is not plugged into the wall socket correctly.

6. Your radio is not working, and it is connected to the same outlet as the lamp.

7. You replace the light bulb, and the lamp now works.

8. You replace the light bulb, and the lamp does not work.

9. Every other electrical fixture in the room works.

10. No electrical fixture in the room works.

Apply the same kind of analysis to the next inductive argument. Evaluate the new information to decide if that particular piece of information *strengthens* or *weakens* the argument. Treat each new piece of information independently of the others.

<u>**Your car won't start.**</u>
Your battery is dead.

11. The headlights don't work.

Answer: Strengthens the argument. Headlights draw their power from the battery; therefore, this new evidence strengthens the argument.

12. The headlights do work.

13. The battery is 5 years old.

14. The battery is 3 months old.

15. The horn works.

16. The horn does not work.

17. The battery terminal clamps are loose.

18. The battery terminal clamps are tight.

19. When you jump-start the car, it starts.

20. When you jump-start the car, it does not start.

H. RECONSTRUCTING ARGUMENTS

People often take shortcuts when creating arguments. Someone might intentionally leave out important information because he or she thinks that the missing information is already understood. In such instances, we need to reconstruct the argument by filling in the missing information. For example, someone might say the following:

> The novel I just bought is by Judy Prince, so I'm sure I'm going to like it.

Even if the speaker is not someone you know well, you can probably supply the missing premise:

> The novel I just bought is by Judy Prince [and I liked every novel of hers that I have read so far], so I'm sure I'm going to like it.

Enthymemes
Arguments with missing premises, missing conclusions, or both.

Notice that we placed brackets around the missing premise in order to indicate that the additional statement was not part of the original argument. Arguments with missing premises, missing conclusions, or both are called **enthymemes**. (The term derives from two roots: "en," meaning *in*, and "thymos," which refers to the mind, literally meaning, *to keep in the mind*.) The missing information is therefore *implied*. Enthymemes are context-driven. Our recognition and subsequent reconstruction of the argument depends on the setting in which the information appears. However, sometimes we are expected to supply missing information with which we are not necessarily familiar. For example, suppose someone says this:

> I have a Cadillac; therefore, I don't have to spend much on maintenance.

The assumption is that we will supply something like the following:

> I have a Cadillac [and Cadillacs require very little maintenance]; therefore, I don't have to spend much on maintenance.

Advertisements can be effective when they have missing conclusions. A billboard once displayed the following message:

> Banks lend money. We're a bank.

The advertisers were clever enough to know that most people would easily fill in the conclusion: "We lend money." Some clever ads say very little but imply a lot. The visual is created in order for you to mindlessly fill in the missing conclusion: "If I buy this product, then I will experience what is being depicted." (Of course, nobody falls for this.)

What we choose to supply as a missing premise or conclusion can affect the subsequent evaluation of the argument. For example, suppose someone says the following:

> Bill Gateway is rich; it follows that he cheats on his taxes.

We can fill in the missing premise in these two ways:

(1) Bill Gateway is rich; [and since all rich people cheat on their taxes] it follows that he cheats on his taxes.
(2) Bill Gateway is rich; [and since most rich people cheat on their taxes] it follows that he cheats on his taxes.

Because the term "rich" is vague, we need to define it for purposes of analysis. We can arbitrarily stipulate that "rich" means any individual whose income exceeds $250,000 a year. In addition, we can stipulate that "most" means at least 70%.

Let's apply logical analysis first. Reconstruction (1) makes the argument deductive, and assuming the premises are true, it is valid. Reconstruction (2) makes the argument inductive, and assuming the premises are true, it is a strong argument. Now let's apply truth value analysis. In reconstruction (1), the added premise, "all rich people cheat on their taxes," is false if even one rich person does not cheat on his or her taxes. It seems likely that at least one rich person has not cheated. Thus, the argument is valid, but probably unsound.

For reconstruction (2), the truth value of the added premise, "most rich people cheat on their taxes," is not so obvious. While many people probably have strong feelings regarding the truth or falsity of this added premise, objective evidence is necessary to decide the issue. For example, if the Internal Revenue Service (IRS) published a report stating that approximately 70% of all "rich" people (using our stipulated definition of the term) who have been audited have been found to cheat on their taxes, then this could be used as objective evidence to show the premise is true. If so, the argument is cogent. However, if the IRS published a report stating that only around 15% of all "rich" people who have been audited have been found to cheat on their taxes, then this could be used as objective evidence to show the premise is false. If so, we would classify the argument as uncogent, because at least one premise is false.

Given both analyses, we should choose the reconstructed argument that *gives the benefit of the doubt to* the person presenting the argument. In this case, reconstructing the argument as inductive is the better choice. This process is referred to as the **principle of charity**. The principle is based on a sense of fairness and an open mind. Since we expect other people to interpret and analyze our arguments in the most reasonable way, we should do the same. This principle also stresses the *concern for truth*. Reconstructing a reasonable argument *raises* the possibility that we will arrive at the truth and learn something. Reconstructing an illogical argument *reduces* the possibility that we will arrive at the truth and learn something.

Principle of charity
We should choose the reconstructed argument that gives the benefit of the doubt to the person presenting the argument.

Suppose someone says the following:

Expanding educational opportunities for all Americans will require our elected representatives to allocate more tax money for education than is currently available. Without this additional funding we will not be able to compete in a fast-changing world, and our economy and standard of living will suffer. No one wants that to happen.

Based on the information given, the speaker probably wants us to conclude something like the following:

We should allocate more tax money for education than is currently available.

If we accept the premises as *true*, then this is a strong argument. However, we can question the accuracy of the premises. For example, we can ask whether there are other ways to expand educational opportunities without raising taxes. We can also ask whether our economy and standard of living will suffer, as stated in the argument. Answering these questions will serve to help us learn something about the important issues raised by the argument.

In contrast, someone who fails to apply the principle of charity might conclude the following:

We have to cut military spending.

This results in a weak argument since nothing in the premises directly supports the cutting of military spending. However, this reconstruction avoids the possibility of a reasonable argument that deserves serious evaluation.

There is another important aspect to deductive arguments that we should investigate. It is often quite easy to add a premise to an invalid argument, thereby creating a new valid argument. For example, consider the following:

Frank committed a murder. Therefore, Frank committed a felony.

The argument is invalid. It requires an added premise to make it valid, as the following reconstruction shows:

Frank committed a murder. [Every murder is a felony.] Therefore, Frank committed a felony.

If we add a premise to make an argument valid, then we must make sure that the new premise does not create an unsound argument. For example:

Frank committed a felony. Therefore, Frank committed a murder.

This is an invalid argument. It can be made valid by adding a new premise:

Frank committed a felony. [Every felony is a murder.] Therefore, Frank committed a murder.

This is a valid argument. However, not every felony is a murder (selling illegal drugs is a felony). Thus, the new premise is false, and the argument is unsound. Therefore we must be careful to add premises that not only logically support the conclusion, but that are also true.

Additional premises can affect a deductive argument, but only in one way. As we saw, it is possible to add premises to an invalid argument and create a new valid argument. However, the opposite result cannot happen. Since the original premises of a valid argument provide the necessary support to ensure that the argument is valid, no additional premise(s) can affect that outcome.

As we saw with enthymemes, context can influence our recognition and reconstruction of arguments, which is why interpretations of statements and arguments must be justified. Since it is easy to take a statement out of context and give it any interpretation we please, we often need the original context to help us settle disagreements. The more we know about the setting in which the statements and arguments were made, the people involved, and the issues at hand, the more accurate our interpretations, analyses, and evaluations will be.

Of course, not all uses of language are transparent. For instance, people often speak *rhetorically*; that is, the language they employ may be implying things that are not explicitly said. We must be careful when we interpret this kind of language, and we need to justify our reconstructions of arguments.

Although arguments are constructed out of statements, sometimes a premise or conclusion is disguised as a question. A *rhetorical question* guides and persuades the reader or the listener. Here is an example:

> Using rhetorical questions in speeches is a great way to keep the audience involved. Don't you think those kinds of questions would keep your attention?
>
> Bo Scott Bennett, *Year to Success*

The passage engages us in a dialogue, but the writer is clever enough to persuade us to accept his intended answer. Suppose someone says the following:

> You have not saved any money, you have only a part-time job, and at your age car insurance will cost you at least $2000 a year. Do you really think you can afford a car?

Although the last sentence poses a question, it should be clear from the context that the speaker's intention is to assert a conclusion: "You can't afford a car." So the rhetorical question is really a statement disguised in the form of a question. We can reconstruct the argument as follows:

> You have not saved any money. You have only a part-time job. At your age car insurance will cost you at least $2000 a year. [Therefore, you can't afford a car.]

Since we changed the rhetorical question into a statement, we placed it in brackets. In some arguments, both a premise and a conclusion appear as rhetorical questions. For example, suppose a disgruntled teenager says the following:

> I do my share of work around this house. Don't I deserve to get something in return? Why shouldn't I be allowed to go to the Weaknotes concert today?

The speaker is using two rhetorical questions for dramatic effect. Our reconstruction should reveal the assertions implied by the speaker, as follows:

> I do my share of work around this house. [I deserve to get something in return.] [Thus, I should be allowed to go to the Weaknotes concert today.]

The reconstruction gives us a clearer understanding of the argument. Here is another example of a rhetorical question appearing as part of an argument:

> Why do you waste your time worrying about your death? It won't happen during your lifetime.

Here is the reconstructed argument:

> [Your death won't happen during your lifetime. So, stop wasting your time worrying about it.]

There are other aspects of rhetorical language. For instance, suppose you tell a friend that you are trying to lose twenty-five pounds. Your friend might say the following:

> If you were really serious about losing weight, then you would not be eating that large pepperoni pizza all by yourself.

From the context, it should be clear that the speaker is observing you eating a pizza, so that fact is not in dispute. The observation is then used as the basis to imply a conclusion. In this example, the consequent of the conditional statement contains the intended premise, while the antecedent contains the intended conclusion. Here is the reconstructed argument:

> [You are eating that large pepperoni pizza all by yourself. Therefore, you are not really serious about losing weight.]

A conditional statement that is used to imply an argument is called a *rhetorical conditional*. We must take care to reconstruct a conditional statement as an argument only when we are reasonably sure that the conditional is being used rhetorically. A correct reconstruction of a conditional statement as an argument requires an understanding of the context in which the conditional appears.

A rhetorical conditional can even occur in the form of a question. Depending on the context, a rhetorical conditional can be reconstructed in different ways. For example, suppose we encounter this statement:

> If you truly care about your children, then why are you neglecting them?

If the speaker happens to be a close friend or relative whose intent is to change someone's behavior, the argument might be reconstructed as follows:

> [I know you care about your children. So, you have to stop neglecting them.]

On the other hand, if the speaker is a social worker who has observed repeated instances of child neglect, the argument might be reconstructed differently:

> [You repeatedly neglect your children. Therefore, you do not truly care for them.]

In this case, the social worker may be using the rhetorical conditional as part of a more extended justification for removing the children from a negligent parent.

The next example adds a new dimension to our discussion of rhetorical conditionals. Suppose a parent says this to a child:

> If you are smart, and I know you are, then you will do the right thing.

It is possible to reconstruct the argument and yet retain a conditional as a premise. We might want to allow the phrase "I know you are" to play a key role in our reconstruction. If so, the argument can be displayed as follows:

[If you are smart, then you will do the right thing. I know that you are smart. Thus, you will do the right thing.]

Alternatively, we might reconstruct the argument by eliminating the conditional aspect. If we interpret the phrase "I know you are" as directly asserting the antecedent, then we can place emphasis on the purely rhetorical nature of the conditional. The new reconstruction might look like this:

[You are smart; therefore, you will do the right thing.]

Whichever way we decide to reconstruct an argument, we should be prepared to justify our reconstruction by reference to the context in which it originally occurred.

Finally, it is important to remember that (1) *arguments are neither true nor false*, and (2) *statements are neither valid nor invalid nor strong nor weak*. The following chart illustrates these two points.

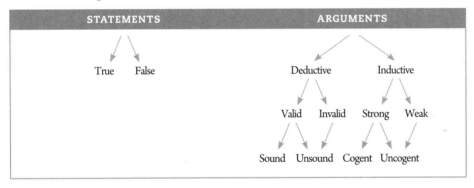

EXERCISES 1H

I. For each of the following enthymemes, supply either the missing premise(s) or the missing conclusion. Apply the *principle of charity* to your reconstructions. Evaluate the resulting arguments, and explain your answers.

Level 1 Multiple-Choice Questions

1. I am talking to a human; therefore, I am talking to a mammal.

Answer:

Reconstruction 1: Missing premise: *All humans are mammals.*

This makes the argument deductively valid. Since the added premise is true, if the first premise is true, then it is a sound argument.

Level 2 Multiple-Choice Questions

Reconstruction 2: Missing premise: *The vast majority of humans are mammals.*

This makes the argument inductively strong. But since we know that all humans are mammals, this reconstruction would not be the best choice.

2. I am talking to a mammal; therefore, I am talking to a human.

3. Shane owns a Honda, so it must be a motorcycle.

4. Shane owns a motorcycle, so it must be a Honda.

5. I have a headache. I just took two aspirins. Aspirins relieve headaches.

6. The office laser printer can print twenty pages a minute in black and white or ten pages a minute in color. It took 1 minute to print John's ten-page report on the office laser printer.

7. Viola just had a big lasagna dinner, so I know she is very happy now.

8. Since Viola just had a big lasagna dinner, it follows that she will soon be looking for the antacid tablets.

9. Jill has a viral infection. She decided to take some penicillin. But she doesn't realize that penicillin has no effect on viruses.

10. Jill has a bacterial infection. She decided to take some penicillin. Penicillin can be effective when treating bacteria.

11. Frances must be an honest person, because she is an educated person.

12. There are ten marbles in the jar; nine red and one blue. I picked, at random, one of the marbles from the jar.

Video Tutorial

13. Jamillah is a safe driver, so her insurance rates are low.

14. Wilma has an expensive camera, therefore she takes perfect pictures.

15. Shane is a well-prepared and diligent student. Teachers respect students who are well prepared and diligent.

16. Perform at your best when your best is required. Your best is required every day.

    Adapted from John Wooden's *Pyramid of Success*

17. Most of us today live in cities and spend far less time outside in green, natural spaces than people did several generations ago. Various studies have found that urban dwellers with little access to green spaces have a higher incidence of psychological problems than people living near parks. But city dwellers who visit natural environments have lower levels of stress hormones immediately afterward than people who have not recently been outside.

    Gretchen Reynolds, "How Walking in Nature Changes the Brain," *The New York Times*

18. When drunk in excess, alcohol damages nearly all organ systems. It is also connected to higher death rates and is involved in a greater percentage of crime than most other drugs, including heroin. But the problem is that "alcohol is too embedded in our culture and it won't go away," said Leslie King, an adviser to the European Monitoring Centre for Drugs.

    Adapted from "Alcohol More Lethal than Heroin, Cocaine," Associated Press

19. Some 80,000 Western-trained Chinese scientists have returned to work in the pharmaceutical and health-care industries in China since the mid-1980s. In addition to the accelerated return of Chinese scientists, the Chinese government and private industry have instituted a surge in investment in research and development in the above mentioned fields.

Adapted from the article "China as Innovator," Straits Times

20. There are some things in our society and some things in our world of which I'm proud to be maladjusted, and I call upon all men of goodwill to be maladjusted to these things until the good society is realized. I must honestly say to you that I never intend to adjust myself to racial segregation and discrimination. I never intend to adjust myself to religious bigotry. I never intend to adjust myself to economic conditions that will take necessities from the many to give luxuries to the few, and leave millions of God's children smothering in an airtight cage of poverty in the midst of an affluent society.

Martin Luther King, Jr., 1963 speech

II. Reconstruct arguments based on your understanding and interpretation of the *rhetorical* aspect of the passages that follow. In each case be prepared to offer justification for your reconstruction and interpretation.

1. You already ate more than your fair share of our limited food supply; do you really want more?

Answer:

<u>You already ate more than your fair share of our limited food supply.</u>
[You do not really want more.]

The rhetorical force behind the assertion "You already ate *more* than your *fair share* of our *limited* food supply" (added emphasis) seems to be indicating that the conclusion should be negative in tone.

2. Capital punishment sometimes leads to the execution of innocent humans. As a society we cannot continue to perform such brutal acts of inhumanity. Isn't it time to change the existing laws?

3. You are not happy at your job, so why not quit?

4. If he is being accused of taking steroids now, then why has he hit approximately the same number of home runs each year since he first started playing professional baseball?

5. If you are correct that he has not taken steroids, then how can you explain his suddenly gaining forty pounds of muscle and doubling his average home run total?

6. If the United States cannot find the number one terrorist on the list, then it cannot ever hope to eliminate the large number of cells of anonymous terrorists.

7. If you want to get in shape, then why do you sit around the house all day doing nothing?

8. If the Catholic Church really believes in the equality of women, then why aren't there any women priests?

9. If she committed suicide by shooting herself, then why is there no trace of gunpowder on her hands?

10. If U.S. international policy is not to be a nation builder, then we wouldn't keep overthrowing governments we don't like and installing puppet leaders.

11. If you want to be financially secure in your retirement years, then why don't you have a retirement counselor?

12. You hate getting prank phone calls, so why don't you get an unlisted phone number?

13. If you want to get rich quick, then why don't you buy more lottery tickets?

14. Does any wrong-headed decision suddenly become right when defended with religious conviction? In this age, don't we know better? If my God told me to poke the elderly with sharp sticks, would that make it morally acceptable to others? *Rick Reilly, "Wrestling with Conviction"*

15. Now I know I'm fighting an uphill battle in some sense. If someone willingly chooses to be illogical, how do you argue with them? Through logic? Clearly you cannot, because they don't subscribe to this. If someone maintains that the world is 6,000 years old and that any evidence otherwise is just a trick by God to make us think the world is older, how do I argue against this? *Tony Piro, interview at "This Week in Webcomics"*

Study Materials

Summary

- Argument: A group of statements of which one (the conclusion) is claimed to follow from the others (the premises).
- Statement: A sentence that is either true or false.
- Premise(s): The information intended to provide support for a conclusion.
- Logic is the systematic use of methods and principles to analyze, evaluate, and construct arguments.
- Every statement is either true or false; these two possibilities are called "truth values."
- Proposition: The information content imparted by a statement, or, simply put, its meaning.
- Inference: The term used by logicians to refer to the reasoning process that is expressed by an argument.

- In order to help recognize arguments, we rely on premise indicator words and phrases, and conclusion indicator words and phrases.
- If a passage expresses a reasoning process—that the conclusion follows from the premises—then we say that it makes an inferential claim.
- If a passage does not express a reasoning process (explicit or implicit), then it does not make an inferential claim (it is a noninferential passage).
- Explanation: Provides reasons for why or how an event occurred. By themselves, explanations are not arguments; however, they can form part of an argument.
- Truth value analysis determines if the information in the premises is accurate, correct, or true.
- Logical analysis determines the strength with which the premises support the conclusion.
- Deductive argument: An argument in which the inferential claim is that the conclusion follows *necessarily* from the premises. In other words, under the *assumption* that the premises are true it is *impossible* for the conclusion to be false.
- Inductive argument: An argument in which the inferential claim is that the conclusion is *probably true* if the premises are true. In other words, under the *assumption* that the premises are true it is *improbable* for the conclusion to be false. In other words, the *probable truth* of the conclusion *follows from* the premises.
- Valid deductive argument: An argument in which, assuming the premises are true, it is *impossible* for the conclusion to be false. In other words, the conclusion follows necessarily from the premises.
- Invalid deductive argument: An argument in which, assuming the premises are true, it is *possible* for the conclusion to be false. In other words, the conclusion does not follow necessarily from the premises.
- When logical analysis shows that a deductive argument is valid, and when truth value analysis of the premises shows that they are all true, then the argument is sound.
- If a deductive argument is invalid, or if at least one of the premises is false (truth value analysis), then the argument is unsound.
- In categorical logic, an argument form is an arrangement of logical vocabulary and letters that stand for class terms such that a uniform substitution of class terms for the letters results in an argument.
- In categorical logic, a statement form is an arrangement of logical vocabulary and letters that stand for class terms such that a uniform substitution of class terms for the letters results in a statement.
- A substitution instance of a *statement* occurs when a uniform substitution of class terms for the letters results in a statement. A substitution instance of an *argument* occurs when a uniform substitution of class terms for the letters results in an argument.

- A counterexample to a statement is evidence that shows the statement is false, and it concerns truth value analysis. A counterexample to an argument shows the possibility that premises assumed to be true do not make the conclusion necessarily true. A single counterexample to a deductive argument is enough to show that an argument is invalid.
- Conditional statement: In English, the word "if" typically precedes the antecedent of a conditional statement, and the word "then" typically precedes the consequent.
- Fallacy of affirming the consequent: An invalid argument form; it is a formal fallacy.
- *Modus ponens*: A valid argument form.
- Fallacy of denying the antecedent: An invalid argument form; it is a formal fallacy.
- *Modus tollens*: A valid argument form.
- Hypothetical syllogism: A valid argument form.
- Disjunction: A compound statement that has two distinct statements, called disjuncts, connected by the word "or."
- Disjunctive syllogism: A valid argument form.
- Strong inductive argument: An argument such that if the premises are assumed to be true, then the conclusion is probably true. In other words, the probable truth of the conclusion follows from the truth of the premises.
- Weak inductive argument: An argument such that either (a) if the premises are *assumed* to be true, then the conclusion is *probably not true,* or (b) a probably true conclusion *does not follow from the premises.*
- An inductive argument is cogent when the argument is strong and the premises are true. An inductive argument is uncogent when either or both of the following conditions hold: the argument is weak, or the argument has at least one false premise.
- Enthymemes: Arguments with missing premises, missing conclusions, or both.
- Principle of charity: We should choose the reconstructed argument that gives the benefit of the doubt to the person presenting the argument.
- Rhetorical language: When we speak or write for dramatic or exaggerated effect. When the language we employ may be implying things that are not explicitly said.
- Rhetorical question: Occurs when a statement is disguised in the form of a question.
- Rhetorical conditional: A conditional statement that is used to imply an argument.

KEY TERMS

argument   3
argument form   32
cogent argument   45
conclusion   3
conclusion indicators   7
counterexample   34
deductive argument   23
enthymemes   52
explanation   19
inductive argument   23
inference   5
inferential claim   8

invalid deductive
   argument   30
logic   3
logical analysis   23
premise   3
premise indicators   7
principle of charity   53
proposition   4
sound argument   30
statement   3
statement form   32

strong inductive
   argument   45
substitution instance   32
truth value   4
truth value analysis   23
uncogent argument   45
unsound argument   30
valid deductive
   argument   30
weak inductive
   argument   45

LOGIC CHALLENGE: THE PROBLEM OF THE HATS

Scientists, philosophers, mathematicians, detectives, logicians, and physicians all face logical problems. How do they go about solving them? For insights, try your own hand at a challenge, the *problem of the hats*. Once you are given the facts of the case, be aware of how you attack the problem, how you take it apart, what you place emphasis on, your avenues of pursuit, and plausible conjectures. The answer requires "seeing" a key move.

Here is the challenge: A teacher comes to class with a box and shows the contents of the box to the students. It contains three white hats, two red hats, and nothing else. There happen to be only three students in this class, and the teacher tells them that he is going to blindfold each one and then place one of the five hats on each of their heads. The remaining two hats will then be placed back in the box, so no one can see them once the blindfolds are removed. If anyone can tell what color hat they have on their heads, then the teacher will give that student an A. But the students are not allowed to guess: They must be able to *prove* they have that color hat.

The teacher removes the blindfold from the first student, who is now able to see the color of the hats on the other two students—but not his own. The first student looks carefully at the other two hats, thinks silently for a while, and says he does not know the color of his hat. The teacher then removes the blindfold from the second student. He, too, looks at the hats on the other two students, thinks for a while, and says he does not know the color of his hat. (As before, this student does *not* say aloud the color of the hats he sees on the other two students' heads.) Now, just as the teacher is about to remove the blindfold from the third student, she says that she knows exactly the color of the hat on her head. In fact, she doesn't even need to see the hats of the other two students to know this.

Can you see how she did it? No information is being held back, no tricks are being played, and no word games are used. All the information necessary to solve the problem is contained in its description. There are three possibilities for you to consider. Which is correct?

1. She cannot possibly know what color hat she has on her head.
2. She has a red hat and can prove it.
3. She has a white hat and can prove it.

PART II

INFORMAL LOGIC

Chapter 2

Language Matters

Study Materials

Words are powerful. They can incite riots and move people to revolt, or they can create calm and soothe those in pain. They take on the aura of "magic words," like secret spells, or they can harm others by their very meaning, such as racial or religious slurs. Words can also fail us. Visiting someone in a hospital or attending a funeral is uncomfortable if we don't know what to say. Even asking for a date can be a frightening experience. We imagine that there are perfect sentences, and if we were lucky enough to utter them, then the person of our dreams would fall in love.

Skill and practice are essential in order to use language effectively—and so are clear, unambiguous, and precise definitions. Most words have multiple meanings, which helps explain why communication can misfire. Hearing or reading something in context can help, and in conversation we can often ask for clarification. But misunderstandings can have serious consequences, and a choice between two meanings of a single word can affect the course of history.

> A Japanese word, *mokusatsu*, may have changed all our lives. It has two meanings: (1) to ignore, (2) to refrain from comment. The release of a press statement using the second meaning in July 1945 might have ended the war then. The Emperor was ready to end it, and had the power to do so. The cabinet was preparing to accede to the Potsdam ultimatum of the Allies—surrender or be crushed—but wanted a little more time to discuss the terms. A press release was prepared announcing a policy of *mokusatsu*, with the *no comment* implication. But it got on the foreign wires with the *ignore* implication through a mix-up in translation: "The cabinet *ignores* the demand to surrender." To recall the release would have entailed an unthinkable loss of face. Had the intended meaning been publicized, the cabinet might have backed up the Emperor's decision to surrender. In which event, there might have been no

atomic bombs over Hiroshima and Nagasaki, no Russian armies in Manchuria, no Korean war to follow. The lives of tens of thousands of Japanese and American boys might have been saved. One word, misinterpreted.

Stuart Chase, *Power of Words*

Definitions play an important part in analyzing statements and arguments because terms often have numerous meanings. They do, in fact, in the title of this chapter. In "Language Matters," the word "matters" has two legitimate interpretations. It can refer to the subject of the chapter—*the use of language*—or it can refer to the significance of that subject. As we'll see, language is an important topic for the study of logic.

Ambiguity can serve a purpose, just as in the chapter title, and it can also be a great source for jokes. A *double entendre* can be funny when we recognize that a key word has both a common meaning and a risqué or suggestive one. However, when it comes to arguments, *vague*, *ambiguous*, or *imprecise* terms can reduce the clarity of statements and get in the way of our understanding of an argument.

A term is *vague* whenever there is no clear or distinct meaning that is attached to it. For example, the phrases "a rich person," "a fair price," and "natural preservatives" remain vague until we are given precise information regarding their intended meaning. In some cases, vagueness occurs because a term is relative to a given situation. For example, you might be considered rich in one country, but not in another. Here is another statement that uses a vague term: "The amount of nuclear waste material in the United States is quite small." What counts as "quite small"? Would the nuclear waste material fit in a tractor trailer, or would it fill up a football stadium? Descriptions like these can clarify a term's meaning.

A term is *ambiguous* if it has several meanings (each of which can be clear and distinct). For example, in the statement "He just bought a light suit," the term "light" might mean either the color of the suit or the weight of the material. We normally rely on context to alert us to which meaning is intended. For example, the terms "left" and "right" are ambiguous unless we are told which direction we are facing. In the following three examples, the term "premises" has multiple distinct meanings, but each is used in a way that eliminates ambiguity:

A. "Premises" means statements that are offered in support of a conclusion.
B. "These premises are off-limits" means that only police authorities are permitted to enter.
C. In a bill of equity case, "premises" means the preliminary or explanatory statements or facts of a document, as in a deed.

In each instance, the term "premises" was defined in a way that eliminates ambiguity, vagueness, and imprecision. Throughout this chapter, we will illustrate how language is used, along with methods that are available to clarify the words in statements and arguments. We hope you gain an appreciation of the relationship between language and logic.

A. INTENSION AND EXTENSION

Clarifying the meaning of statements requires a close look at the meaning of the terms. A **term** is either a single word or a group of words that can be the subject of a statement. A term can be a common name, a proper name, or even a descriptive phrase:

Term A single word or a group of words that can be the subject of a statement; it can be a common name, a proper name, or even a descriptive phrase.

Common Names	Proper Names	Descriptive Phrases
plant	Cleopatra	registered voters
building	Los Angeles	purple flowers
car	Mars	the director of *Inception*
mammal	Moby Dick	military personnel
money	Michael Jordan	Nobel Prize winners

In this section, we look closely at two kinds of meaning: *intension* and *extension*. First, however, we need to be sure we know what we mean by using a term.

Terms, Use, and Mention

Not all words are terms. Generally speaking, prepositions, adverbs, some adjectives, conjunctions, and ungrammatical phrases are not considered to be terms, because they are not the subject of a statement. Here are some examples:

Prepositions	Adverbs	Conjunctions
in, on, by, since	*quickly, very happily, easily*	*and, but, because, however*

Certain Adjectives	Ungrammatical Phrase
good, wise, another, rotten	*a heavily into pothole thus*

We can also distinguish the *use* of a word from the *mention* of a word. This distinction is helpful because it introduces a method that helps clarify some written language. Three sentences can help illustrate the difference:

- John is my brother.
- "John" is a four-letter word.
- "John" means a toilet or bathroom.

The first statement *uses* the word "John" as the subject. (Notice that the term does not appear in quotes in that statement.) Thus we say that the first statement *uses* the word "John" (without quotes) to refer to a person. However, in the second example it is not the term itself that is the subject. Instead, it is the term that appears within quotation marks that is the subject. We say that it is being *mentioned*. In other words, the subject of the first statement is a *person*, while the subject of the second statement is the *word* that appears within quotation marks. The subject of the third sentence is also the word appearing within quotation marks.

Earlier we described conjunctions, such as the word "because," as not being terms. However, "because" can still be the subject of a statement when it is enclosed in quotes and is being mentioned. Consider the following two examples:

A. The word "because" is a good premise indicator.
B. I will vote for her because she has outlined a clear strategy for economic recovery.

In the first example the word "because" (appearing in quotes) is being *mentioned*; the quoted word is the subject of the statement. However, in the second example the word "because" (appearing without quotes) is being *used*; it is not a subject.

Two Kinds of Meaning

Two kinds of meaning are associated with terms. The first is the **intension** of a term, which is specified by listing the properties or attributes that the term connotes—in other words, its *sense*. For example, to specify the intensional meaning of the term "automobile," you might provide a partial list of properties: passenger vehicle; powered by an engine; used for traveling on roads and highways. (Do not confuse the term "intension" with "intention." *Intension* is the connotation (sense) of a term, whereas *intention* is a mental determination, the intent or purpose of an action.)

The second kind of meaning associated with a term is the **extension**—the **class** or collection of objects to which the term applies. In other words, what the term denotes (its *reference*).

The term "automobile" and its meanings

Intension *(connotation):*
The properties:
passenger vehicle; powered by an engine; used for traveling on roads and highways.

Extension *(denotation):*
The class members:
all the cars in the world.

Some terms have intension but no extension. For example, the term "centaur" connotes the following properties: a creature that has a man's head, torso, and arms, but the body and legs of a horse. However, the term "centaur" has no extension; it denotes an **empty class**, or one that has zero members. We get the same result for all fictional terms. This illustrates an important general rule: *Extension is determined by intension.* To see what effect intension has on extension, take a simple example:

water; ocean; Pacific Ocean

This sequence of terms has **increasing intension**, meaning that each term after the first connotes more attributes than the previous term. Simply put, the series of terms displays an increase in specific attributes. On the other hand, the sequence of terms has **decreasing extension**, meaning that each term after the first denotes a

---

Intension The intension of a term is specified by listing the properties or attributes that the term connotes—in other words, its sense.

Extension The class or collection of objects to which the term applies. In other words, what the term denotes (its reference).

Class A group of objects.

Empty class A class that has zero members.

Increasing intension A sequence of terms in which each term after the first connotes more attributes than the previous term.

Decreasing extension A sequence of terms in which each term after the first denotes a set of objects with fewer members than the previous term.

set of objects with fewer members than the previous term. The extension of the term "water" is all the water in the world; the extension of the term "ocean" is the five recognized oceans (Arctic, Atlantic, Indian, Pacific, and the Southern or Antarctic Ocean); the extension of the term "Pacific Ocean" is one specific ocean.

Let's look at another example:

banana; fruit; food; commodity

Decreasing intension
A sequence of terms in which each term after the first connotes fewer attributes than the previous term.

Increasing extension
A sequence of terms in which each term after the first denotes a set of objects with more members than the previous term.

This sequence of terms has **decreasing intension**, meaning that each term after the first connotes fewer attributes than the previous term. In other words, the series of terms displays a decrease in specific attributes. However, the sequence of terms has **increasing extension**; each term after the first denotes a set of objects with more members than the previous term. The extension of the term "banana" is all the bananas in the world; the extension of the term "fruit" includes all types of fruit (including bananas); the extension of the term "food" is all kinds of food (including fruit); and finally, the extension of the term "commodity" is any kind of product or article of trade or commerce (including food).

Generally speaking, we will find the following to be the case:

- A series of terms that has *increasing intension* has *decreasing extension*.
- A series of terms that has *decreasing intension* has *increasing extension*.

Of course, these general rules have some exceptions. If a term denotes an empty class, then a series of terms with increasing (or decreasing) intension will not affect the extension (it will remain empty). Here is an example:

leprechaun; leprechaun with red hair; leprechaun with red hair and a green hat

The series of terms regarding leprechauns displays increasing intension, but each term in the sequence denotes an empty class. Another exception to the general rule is when the series of terms has increasing intension but the extension, while not empty, nevertheless remains the same throughout the series. Here is an example:

living horse; living horse with DNA; living horse with DNA and a central nervous system

The series of terms displays increasing intension, but all the terms in the series have the same (non-empty) extension.

Proper Names

One further point needs to be clarified. Since proper names, such as "Cleopatra," can refer to different people, they require a slightly different type of analysis. One way to think about a proper name is that it is simply a shorthand way of describing a person. The descriptions we attach to proper names are, therefore, a special kind of intension, and again will determine the extension of the term. Here is an example:

After Julius Caesar's assassination, Cleopatra, the Queen of Egypt who died in 30 BCE, aligned with Mark Antony instead of Caesar's son Augustus.

Since there are typically many different descriptions that can be used to identify the denotation of a proper name, context and a familiarity with their descriptions can help clear up any confusion. Here is another example that uses the term "Cleopatra":

> Cleopatra, the Los Angeles-based record company, recently announced that it signed Huw Lloyd-Langton to a long-term record deal.

Once again, the description attached to the proper name is used to clarify the intended denotation. Whereas the proper name "Cleopatra" denotes a person in the first example, it denotes a record company in the second example. These examples illustrate how relevant descriptions can be used to help determine the extension of a proper name.

The next two sections will explore some specific techniques used to produce definitions. We will begin by describing four intensional definition techniques—*synonymous definitions, word origin definitions, operational definitions,* and *definition by genus and difference.* This will be followed by an examination of three extensional definition techniques—*ostensive definitions, enumerative definitions,* and *definition by subclass.*

EXERCISES 2A

I. List some of the properties connoted by the following terms.

1. athlete

Answer: strong, fast, agile, stamina, skilled, competitor

2. country
3. animal
4. game
⭐ 5. president
6. mammal
7. book
8. planet
⭐ 9. plant
10. teacher
11. computer
12. city

Level 1 Multiple-Choice Questions

Level 2 Multiple-Choice Questions

II. Name three things denoted by the following terms.

1. athlete

Answer: Tiger Woods, Shaquille O'Neal, Tom Brady

2. magazine
3. movie
4. U.S. senator
⭐ 5. philosopher
6. novelist
7. Nobel Prize winner
8. jazz musician
⭐ 9. lake
10. extinct animal

III. Name all the things denoted by the following terms.

1. capital city of California
Answer: Sacramento

2. Nobel Prize winner in two different science fields

3. Earth continent

4. first person to step on the Moon

5. Seven Wonders of the Ancient World

6. person who won the most Best Actress Academy Awards

7. tallest mountain on Earth

8. planet in our solar system

9. month with 31 days

10. first person to fly solo across the Atlantic Ocean

IV. The following will require you to apply your knowledge of intension and extension to a sequence of terms.

Put the following series of terms in the order of *increasing intension*.

1. mammal, animal, pediatrician, physician, human
Answer: animal, mammal, human, physician, pediatrician

2. American sports car, Corvette, car, sports car, vehicle

3. shrub, Portland rose, plant, perennial, rose

Put the following series of terms in the order of *increasing extension*.

4. polygon, equilateral triangle, isosceles triangle, convex polygon, triangle

5. robin, animal, thrush, flying animal, bird

6. skyscraper, office building, building, New York City skyscraper, Empire State Building

Put the following series of terms in the order of *decreasing intension*.

7. Usain Bolt, human, track and field athlete, athlete, Olympic Gold Medal winner

8. printing, book, 20th-century fictional book, *The Grapes of Wrath*, fictional book

9. chilled dessert, dessert, Jell-O, food, Cherry Jell-O

Put the following series of terms in the order of *decreasing extension*.

10. *In the Heat of the Night*, dramas, entertainment, Sidney Poitier movies, movies

11. painting, Vincent van Gogh's *Still Life with Flowers*, still life, art, 19th-century still life

12. human, *Apollo 11* crew member, pilot, Neil Armstrong, astronaut

Video Tutorial

B. USING INTENSIONAL DEFINITIONS

Part of the analysis of statements and arguments is evaluating the clarity of the terms involved. We saw earlier that the term "matters" can convey two meanings, as in the chapter title. In that setting the ambiguity is not out of place. However, when it comes to arguments, ambiguity should be eliminated. Much of ordinary language contains ambiguous or imprecise political terms, such as "liberal" and "conservative." Typically, statements containing these political labels suffer from being unclear. Consider the following argument:

> My opponent for governor is a liberal, so you should vote against her.

Since we have no idea what the speaker means by the term "liberal," our understanding of the argument is hindered—precisely because of the lack of clarity. An important requirement for a good argument, then, is that all the terms have an acceptable, clear, and unambiguous meaning. This is also a simple but crucial requirement for all communication; its strict adherence would eliminate many confusions and controversies. Problems related to unclear terms can lead to difficulty in determining the truth content of individual statements. In turn, these individual statement problems sometimes lead to *informal fallacies* (the subject of Chapter 4).

A **definition** assigns a meaning to a word, phrase, or symbol. Logicians use the term **definiendum** to refer to that which is being defined, and the term **definiens** to refer to that which does the defining. For example, if you look in a dictionary for the definition of the term "book" (the definiendum), you might find the following partial entry: "a printed work of fiction or nonfiction" (the definiens). In one sense then, what the definiens does is provide an alternative symbolism that has the same meaning as the definiendum. It is in this manner that we say that the definition has assigned a meaning to the definiendum. Here are some examples:

Definition A definition assigns a meaning to a word, phrase, or symbol.

Definiendum Refers to that which is being defined.

Definiens Refers to that which does the defining.

DEFINITIONS

Definiendum	Definiens
e-book	short for "electronic book"; any book published in digital form
dog-eat-dog world	ruthless competition; looking out for your own self-interest
shaman	a person claiming to use magic to cure diseases or predict the future

An **intensional** (connotative) **definition** assigns a meaning to a term by listing the properties or attributes shared by all the objects that are denoted by the term. We will examine some of the different techniques that are used for intensional definitions.

Intensional definition Assigns a meaning to a term by listing the properties or attributes shared by all the objects that are denoted by the term.

Synonymous Definitions

As the name indicates, a **synonymous definition** assigns a meaning to a term by providing another term with the same meaning; in other words, by providing a synonym. This can be a very simple and effective technique to convey the meaning of a term, as

Synonymous definition Assigns a meaning to a term by providing another term with the same meaning; in other words, by providing a synonym.

long as the synonym is readily understood. Here are a few examples of synonymous definitions:

- "Honest" means trustworthy.
- "Attorney" means lawyer.
- "Feckless" means irresponsible.
- "Adversity" means misfortune.

Since many words cannot be defined accurately by a synonym, this technique has its limitations. For example, someone might try defining "obscene" as "indecent," "offensive," or "depraved." But this word cannot be easily captured by a mere synonym, partly because of the moral and legal issues connected with its use. The Supreme Court has wrestled with trying to define the term "obscene" for legal purposes. In the case of *Miller v. California* (1973), a decision to adopt a definition had five justices in agreement. The majority opinion stated that there were three basic guidelines: "(a) whether 'the average person, applying contemporary community standards' would find that the work, taken as a whole, appeals to the prurient interest; (b) whether the work depicts or describes, in a patently offensive way, sexual conduct specifically defined by the applicable state law; and (c) whether the work, taken as a whole, lacks serious literary, artistic, political, or scientific value." Four justices dissented.

As you can see, these "guidelines" are filled with terms that need to be defined. "Average person," "contemporary community standards," "prurient interest," "sexual conduct," and "serious literary, artistic, political, or scientific value" all need to be clarified.

Word Origin Definitions

Word origin definition
Assigns a meaning to a term by investigating its origin. The study of the history, development, and sources of words is called *etymology*.

A **word origin definition** assigns a meaning to a term by investigating its origin. Since most ordinary English words originated in older languages, such as Latin, Greek, and Arabic, we can often trace the current meaning back to its original sources to see how it has changed through time. The study of the history, development, and sources of words is called *etymology*. For example, the word "etymology" itself comes from the Greek word "etymologia," which combines two root words—"etymo," meaning *true sense*, and "logos," meaning *word*. The suffix "-logy" has another common meaning—*the study of*. Although the term "etymology" originally meant *the true sense of a word*, it now means *the study of the origin of words*. The importance of investigating the origin of words is expressed by the following quote:

The older a word, the deeper it reaches.   Ludwig Wittgenstein, *Notebooks*

Knowing the origin of a word can sometimes illustrate why the term was chosen. Here is one example:

"Malaria" means an infectious disease characterized by recurring attacks of chills and fever. The term derives from the Italian "mala," meaning bad, and "aria," meaning air. The term was used because of the mistaken belief that the disease was caused by the bad air in swampy districts. It was only during the 1890s that experiments revealed that the disease was caused by mosquitoes.

Many familiar terms use the common suffix "-logy." For example, "psychology" is now defined as the science or study of human and animal behavior. The term is derived from two Greek words: "psyche," meaning *soul*, and "logia," meaning *the study of*. The term "biology" is now defined as the science or study of living organisms. The term is derived from two Greek words: "bios," meaning *life*, and "logia," meaning *the study of*. Here is one more example of a word origin definition:

> "Philosophy" means love of wisdom. It derives from the Greek word "philoso-phia," which is a combination of the two root words "philo," meaning *loving*, and "sophia," meaning *wisdom or knowledge*.

Word origin definitions have a practical value as well. Anyone who has watched the National Spelling Bee will recognize the common strategy of not only asking for the definition of a word, but also asking for the language of origin of a word. Contestants who have studied the root words of a given language can use that knowledge to break down a complex word into its component parts. This can help them decide which prefix or suffix to try when piecing together the spelling of a word.

Operational Definitions

An **operational definition** defines a term by specifying a measurement procedure. For example, academic achievement is very important for many people in the field of education, including teachers, administrators, test developers, and students. An operational definition of "academic achievement" might use grade point average (GPA) as a measuring procedure. This measuring device is *quantitative* because it provides us with a range of numerical values. In most colleges, the range is from 4.0 to 0.0, with the highest (4.0) for all A's, to the lowest (0.0) for all F's.

> **Operational definition** Defines a term by specifying a measurement procedure.

An alternative operational definition for "academic achievement" might use letters of recommendation written by teachers. This measuring device is quite different from a GPA; it is *qualitative* because its range of values is open-ended. Letters of recommendation may state the grades you received, as well as an assessment of your position relative to other students (for example, the top 10% of the class). It might also mention other important factors, such as your ability to write original essays, self-discipline, willingness to help other students, the ability to ask relevant questions and grasp abstract material, and the prospects for graduate work, to name a few.

We could rank each student in order, from those with the strongest letters of recommendation to those with the weakest. This would not be easy because we are not dealing with a straightforward quantitative method. For example, the terms "strongest" and "weakest" need to be defined. For the same reason, if we then compare two sets of student rankings for the same student body, we might be surprised to see a large variation. The two lists might not match up very well at all. Therefore, the kind of operational definition we give to a term may affect the strength of the argument in which it plays a part.

Here are a few more examples:

- "Aggression" means the number of behaviors that result in verbal threats or physical harm.
- Isaac Newton's definition of "force" is mass times acceleration.
- For some economists, "recession" means two consecutive quarters of falling GDP (gross domestic product).

Many terms denote phenomena that can be observed only indirectly, such as radioactivity. We cannot see radioactivity. We do, however, have powerful ways of measuring it, as with a Geiger counter, an instrument designed to detect radioactive particles. As in this example, we need some empirical means of measuring or performing experiments on many phenomena in order to obtain objective evidence about them. Scientists can study electrons and other subatomic particles only indirectly, in a device called a "cloud chamber," which is a sealed container containing alcohol vapor. The

PROFILES IN LOGIC
Rudolf Carnap

Rudolf Carnap (1891–1970) was born in Germany but later became a U.S. citizen. At university, Carnap studied both physics and philosophy, which he applied to his research and allowed him to make important contributions to several areas of philosophy, including the philosophy of language. Carnap argued that because much of ordinary language is ambiguous, many philosophical problems can be resolved by a logical analysis of language, which, for Carnap, meant *formal* languages that incorporate the rules of logic and mathematics. Since formal languages offer precise meanings to statements, ambiguity is eliminated.

To help in this analysis, Carnap developed a *verifiability principle*, according to which a *statement* is meaningful only if it is verifiable; in other words, all terms must be reducible by means of definitions to observational language. A *term* is meaningful relative to a specific theory given in a specific language. Although Carnap admitted that some theoretical terms are not reducible to observational terms, their meaning is acquired by direct connection to other terms that are observational terms. Furthermore, *observational terms* get their meaning by *operational definitions*, which are governed by how scientists actually apply them. Over time, Carnap's position was criticized by other philosophers who showed problems with Carnap's attempt to connect theoretical terms with direct empirical observations. Carnap modified his position and held that there is an *indirect connection* to observations.

A driving force guiding Carnap's work is captured in this statement: "The function of logical analysis is to analyze all knowledge, all assertions of science and of everyday life, in order to make clear the sense of each such assertion and the connections between them."

electrons traveling through the chamber condense the vapor, much like the vapor trails you see in the sky behind a jet airplane. In each of these examples, we are offered strong evidence that these terms denote something that can be physically observed, albeit indirectly.

Since many terms require extraordinary evidence to convince us that they denote actual existing objects, researchers must develop strong methods of gathering indirect evidence. To help us determine if a term truly refers to objects that we can observe only indirectly, we rely on measurement, prediction, and explanation.

First, if a claim uses a term to denote a part of the physical world (however invisible it might be to our five senses), the person asserting the claim must be able to provide strong, credible evidence to back it up. This has been accomplished by devices that can detect and measure what we cannot directly observe. For example, scientists have developed barometers, thermometers, Geiger counters, cloud chambers, and cyclotrons, to name just a few inventions, in order to gather evidence. Second, these measuring devices must allow the accurate prediction of future experimental results. Finally, we must be able to explain how and why the events occur as they do. In other words, the explanations require a theoretical framework or model, as we explore in detail in Chapter 14.

Definition by Genus and Difference

We saw that an intensional definition specifies the attributes that a term connotes, and in this way it determines the class denoted by the term. Any class that has members can be divided into smaller classes called *subclasses*. For example, the class of fruit has many subclasses, such as cherries, strawberries, and apples. And each of those subclasses can be further divided. For example, the subclass of apples has several subclasses of its own, such as McIntosh, Rome, and Granny Smith. We refer to any class of objects that is being divided as the *genus* and the subclasses as *species*. (You can think of the "genus" as *general*, and the "species" as *specific*.)

The terms "genus" and "species" have a slightly different meaning in logic than they do in biology. Biological classifications are ways to relate all life in a hierarchy, sometimes referred to as the *tree of life*. For example, humans, whales, dolphins, wolves, and dogs are all members of the class *mammals*. However, humans belong to the order (subclass) *primates*; whales and dolphins belong to the order *cetacea*; wolves and dogs both belong to the order *canidae*.

Logic uses the terms "genus" and "species" in a more flexible way, so classes and subclasses do not need to remain in a rigid hierarchy. A person can be placed in many different classes and subclasses, which do not need to have a sense of higher or lower. It is possible for a person to be a mother, daughter, sister, cousin, aunt, professor, scientist, Pulitzer Prize winner, and skier. In fact, it is possible for a class to be a genus relative to one species, and yet that same class can be a species relative to a different genus. For example, the class of siblings is a genus in relation to the species sister. But the class of siblings happens to be a species in relation to the genus offspring. For our purposes, a *genus* is simply any class that is larger than any of its subclasses (*species*).

We can distinguish the different species (subclasses) of a genus by listing the attribute(s) that indicates the *difference* (or specific difference) between each species. For example, consider the genus *offspring* and two species, *son* and *daughter*. When we qualify the genus offspring by adding the term "male" we supply the difference. The combination of a term denoting the genus (in this example "offspring") with a term that connotes a specific difference (in this example "male") creates the meaning of the term that denotes the species. Here are five examples that illustrate the complete process:

DEFINIENDUM		DEFINIENS	
Species		**Difference + Genus**	
"Mother"	means	female	parent
"Bachelor"	means	unmarried	adult male
"Igloo"	means	snow	house
"Triangle"	means	three-sided	polygon
"Gelding"	means	castrated	male horse

PROFILES IN LOGIC
Ludwig Wittgenstein

What would you do if you wrote a book in which you thought you had answered all philosophical questions? Give away the substantial fortune that you inherited? Go teach primary school in a small village? That's exactly what Ludwig Wittgenstein did.

Ludwig Wittgenstein (1889–1951) came from one of the wealthiest families in Vienna. He served in the Austrian army during World War I, and during his time as a prisoner of war he began writing what came to be known as *Tractatus Logico-Philosophicus*, one of the most influential books of the last century. In it, Wittgenstein applied recent advances in logic to traditional philosophical questions—and declared them over and done. As he wrote in the preface, "I am, therefore, of the opinion that the problems have in essentials been finally solved."

The *Tractatus* is a difficult book, subject to many interpretations. Wittgenstein himself said, "I should not like my writing to spare other people the trouble of thinking." For him, the limits of thought are established by clarifying the limits of language: "What we cannot speak about we must pass over in silence."

But Wittgenstein did return to philosophy. He gave lectures to small groups of students, many of whom went on to become influential philosophers themselves. He also wrote a substantial amount of his thoughts in a series of notebooks. Although he withheld publishing anything else during his lifetime, his *Philosophical Investigations* became enormously influential. Despite Wittgenstein's best efforts, philosophical questions are still being asked.

As the examples illustrate, a **definition by genus and difference** assigns a meaning to a term (the *species*) by establishing a *genus* and combining it with the attribute (the specific *difference*) that distinguishes the members of that species.

C. USING EXTENSIONAL DEFINITIONS

We will now examine some of the different techniques that are used for extensional definitions. An **extensional** (denotative) **definition** assigns meaning to a term by indicating the class members denoted by the term. We will describe three ways of assigning meaning by extensional definitions—*ostensive definitions, enumerative definitions*, and *definitions by subclass*.

Ostensive Definitions

An **ostensive definition** involves demonstrating the term—for example, by pointing to a member of the class that the term denotes. (The word "ostensive" comes from the Latin word "ostendere," which means *to show*.) Suppose a car mechanic tells you that you need a new alternator, but you have never seen one. The mechanic could provide an ostensive definition by either pointing to the alternator (if it is still attached to the engine) or letting you see the alternator (if it has been detached from the engine). The act of showing someone an object is the basis for most ostensive definitions in everyday life.

Ostensive definitions are used to introduce children to many terms by showing some examples of what the term denotes. Children are often introduced to words by repeatedly connecting a word to pictures of the objects denoted by the term. Ostensive definitions are also used to teach a foreign language by pointing to an object and repeating a word. An ostensive definition is called for whenever you hold an object or point to it and ask, "What is this called?" The answer to the question will be a term associated with that class of objects.

Ostensive definitions require nonverbal behavior—pointing, gesturing, drawing a picture, or showing a photograph. Ostensive definitions show what an object looks like, but they do not provide synonyms or redefine the term by giving alternate meanings. Ostensive definitions are used typically when only a small number of the members of a class are available; this sets limitations on their effectiveness. For example, it is possible that a child who has learned the term "deer" through an ostensive definition will then point to a moose and say "deer." Similarly, when we point to an object, it is not always apparent what we are emphasizing. Is it the shape of the object, its color, or the material out of which it is made? Although ostensive definitions provide some information regarding the extension of a term, they do not provide information regarding the intension of a term.

Enumerative Definitions

Enumerative definition
Assigns a meaning to
a term by naming the
individual members of
the class denoted by the
term.

An **enumerative definition** assigns a meaning to a term by naming the individual members of the class denoted by the term. Here are a few examples:

- "New England" means Connecticut, Maine, Massachusetts, New Hampshire, Rhode Island, and Vermont.
- "The Knights of the Round Table" means the group that includes Sir Galahad, Sir Lancelot, and Sir Gawain, among others.

The first example illustrates a complete enumeration of the members of the class that the term "New England" denotes because every member of the class is included in the definition. The second example, however, provides only a partial enumeration of the members of the class denoted (many members of the class are left out of the definition).

Both partial and complete enumerations can be useful; the context in which the definition occurs provides direction as to which type is appropriate. For example, a complete enumeration of all the members of the class of stars is impractical since there are hundreds of billions of stars in our galaxy alone. However, a complete enumeration of the members of the class of U.S. senators who voted for (or against) a particular bill is something that would be easy to compile and may be important for deciding future elections.

Definition by Subclass

Definition by subclass
Assigns a meaning
to a term by naming
subclasses (species) of
the class denoted by the
term.

A **definition by subclass** assigns a meaning to a term by naming subclasses (*species*) of the class denoted by the term. (This differs from an enumerative definition where individual members were named.) A definition by subclass can be partial or complete (it is complete only when the subclasses named include the entire extension). Here are a few examples:

- "Music" means rock, blues, jazz, hip-hop, country, classical, and so forth.
- "Movie genre" means comedy, action, drama, film noir, romance, horror, along with others.
- "Coal" means lignite, subbituminous, bituminous, and anthracite.

The subclasses named in the first definition, when taken together, do not include all the members of the class, so it is a partial definition. The same is true of the second definition. However, the subclasses named in the third definition, when taken together, do include all the members of the class, and therefore is a complete definition.

As we saw with enumerative definitions, both partial and complete definitions by subclass can be useful. Once again, the context in which the definition occurs can provide a direction as to which type is appropriate. For example, a complete definition by subclass of all the species of insects is impractical. After all, there are more than a million species, with probably a lot more yet to be discovered. However, a complete definition by subclass of the members of the class of coal might be useful in determining how much of each type exists and its potential as future sources of energy.

DEFINITIONAL TECHNIQUES

Synonymous definition Assigns a meaning to a term by providing another term with the same meaning; in other words, by providing a synonym.

Word origin definition Assigns a meaning to a term by investigating its origin. The study of the history, development, and sources of words is called *etymology*.

Operational definition Defines a term by specifying a measurement procedure.

Definition by genus and difference Assigns a meaning to a term (the species) by establishing a genus and combining it with the attribute that distinguishes the members of that species.

Ostensive definition Involves demonstrating the term—for example, by pointing to a member of the class that the term denotes.

Enumerative definition Assigns a meaning to a term by naming the individual members of the class denoted by the term.

Definition by subclass Assigns a meaning to a term by naming subclasses (species) of the class denoted by the term.

EXERCISES 2C

Determine whether the following are synonymous definitions, word origin (etymological) definitions, operational definitions, definitions by genus and difference, ostensive (demonstrative) definitions, enumerative definitions, or definitions by subclass.

1. "Felony" means murder, rape, and arson, among other things.
Answer: Subclass

2. "Dentist" is a term derived from the Latin word "dens," meaning *tooth*.

3. "Typhoon" means a tropical hurricane that occurs in Asia and the Pacific Ocean.

4. See that big green thing in front of you? That's an oak tree.

⭐ 5. "Hat" means headgear.

6. "Intelligence" means the score a person receives on the Stanford-Binet I.Q. Test.

7. "Country" means something such as the United States, Mexico, Italy, Indonesia, or Japan.

8. "Epistemology" is a term derived from the Greek word "episteme," meaning *knowledge,* and the suffix "-ology," meaning *the study of.*

Level 1 Multiple-Choice Questions

Level 2 Multiple-Choice Questions

Video Tutorial

9. "Natural language" means something such as English, Spanish, French, Chinese, or Hindi.

10. Look where I'm pointing; that's your car's alternator.

11. "Novice" means beginner.

12. "Piano" means a musical stringed instrument set in a vertical or horizontal frame, played by depressing keys that cause hammers to strike the strings and produce audible vibrations.

13. "Virus" means chicken pox, smallpox, measles, polio, and the like.

14. "Atmospheric pressure" means the reading found on a barometer.

15. The plant next to the shed is a bougainvillea.

16. "Abode" means residence.

17. "Construction equipment" means bulldozer, crane, pile driver, dredger, grader, and the like.

18. "Metaphysics" comes from the Greek words "meta," meaning *after*, and "physika," meaning *natural things*. The name was used by Andronicus of Rhodes in 70 BCE simply as a reference to the books written by Aristotle that happened to be placed in order after his works on physics. It has since come to mean the study of first principles and is even used by some to refer to any investigation that is outside the physical realm.

19. "Biomass" means organic materials used as renewable energy sources, such as wood, crops, and waste.
   Clean-energy-ideas.com

20. "Element" means something such as hydrogen, helium, carbon, or oxygen.

21. There is a question that some people use to summarize the concerns of medieval scholars: "How many angels can dance on the head of a pin?" Wendell Johnson is credited with offering this answer: "Bring me a pin, and some angels, and we'll soon find out."

22. "Goods and services" means (in the area of trademarks) chemicals, machinery, hand tools, advertising, transportation, storage, to name only a few.
   Adapted from About.com

23. "Laborer" means worker.

24. If I know that someone means to explain a color-word to me, then "That is called 'sepia'" will help me to understand the word.
   Ludwig Wittgenstein, *Philosophical Investigations*

25. "Rock opera" means something such as *Quadrophenia*, *The Wall*, *The Rise and Fall of Ziggy Stardust and the Spiders from Mars*, or *Operation: Mindcrime*.

26. The popular definition of tragedy is heavy drama in which everyone is killed in the last act; comedy being light drama in which everyone is married in the last act. George Bernard Shaw, "Tolstoy: Tragedian or Comedian?"

27. "Logic" can be defined as the study of the methods of reasoning and the evaluation of arguments. The term is derived from the Greek word "logikos," which means *pertaining to speaking or reasoning.* In turn, the word "logikos" was derived from the word "logos," which means *word, idea,* or *reason.*

28. To find the length of an object, we have to perform certain physical operations. The concept of length is therefore fixed when the operations by which length is measured are fixed: that is, the concept of length involves as much as and nothing more than the set of operations by which length is determined.
Percy W. Bridgman, *The Logic of Modern Physics*

29. She showed me what the word "pungent" meant by holding a durian under my nose and letting me smell it.

30. "Patent classification system" means Class 2 Apparel; Class 7 Compound tools; Class 14 Bridges, and many others. Adapted from the U.S. Patent Office

31. The most common way to find out whether you're overweight or obese is to figure out your body mass index (BMI). BMI is an estimate of body fat, and it's a good gauge of your risk for diseases that occur with more body fat. The overweight group is anyone with a BMI over 25.
U.S. Department of Health and Human Services

32. "President of the United States" means someone such as George Washington, Abraham Lincoln, Franklin D. Roosevelt, or John F. Kennedy.

33. "Salary" means wages.

34. "O.K." means acceptable or agreeable (also spelled *okay*). It is a facetious phonetic spelling of *oll korrect* which was meant to represent *all correct.* It was first used in Boston in 1839, then used in 1840 by Democrat partisans of Martin Van Buren during his election, who allegedly named their organization the *O.K. Club* in allusion to the initials of "Old Kinderhook," Van Buren's nickname, derived from his birthplace Kinderhook, New York.
Adapted from *The Random House Dictionary*

35. White lies are at the other end of the spectrum of deception from lies in a serious crisis. They are the most common and the most trivial forms that duplicity can take. The fact that they are so common provides their protective coloring. And their very triviality, when compared to more threatening lies, makes it seem unnecessary or even absurd to condemn them. Some consider all well-intentioned lies, however momentous, to be white; I shall adhere to the narrower usage: a white lie, in this sense, is a falsehood not meant to injure anyone, and of little moral import. Sissela Bok, *Lying: Moral Choice in Public and Private Life*

D. APPLYING DEFINITIONS

The techniques used so far also apply to how definitions can be used in ordinary language. However, many examples found in newspapers, magazines, novels, and other sources do not typically follow the format used in this chapter. In fact, they often make a point of the ambiguity that our techniques so far are designed to avoid.

Generally speaking, many everyday sources do not use quotation marks to indicate that a term is being defined. In addition, by convention some writers use quotation marks differently from how they were introduced in this chapter. For example, an author might use quotation marks to emphasize that a word is being used sarcastically:

That was certainly a "beautiful" dress she had on tonight.

Or a writer might use scare quotes around a phrase to indicate irony. In spoken language, we may even use our hands to mimic the appearance of written scare quotes—the gesture referred to as "air quotes."

Later in this chapter, we introduce techniques that can help clarify statements and arguments in ordinary language. These techniques, such as paraphrasing, will incorporate ideas that you have learned thus far, such as intension, extension, and definitions. For now, though, we need to look more closely at definitions from sources as they typically appear.

Stipulative Definitions

Stipulative definition
Introduces a new meaning to a term or symbol.

Stipulations help avoid mistakes in interpretation by specifying precise points of reference or measuring devices. A **stipulative definition** does more: It introduces an entirely new meaning. When the new meaning applies to a familiar term or symbol, confusion can easily occur. For example, if a child says, "These pants are tight!" his or her parent might naturally think the following: "I will take them back and get you a larger size." From the child's perspective, the parent is woefully out of touch. The child then enlightens the parent by exclaiming, "You don't get it. *Tight* means *cool!*"

People using a new term for the first time establish the meaning. Yet the term and its meanings can still be modified by others for their own purposes. For example, when Apple introduced the iPod, it coined a new word and at the same time provided a stipulative definition: a portable digital audio player with the capacity to store thousands of audio files. Since that time, Apple has introduced even more new words with stipulative definitions. For example, you can now get many different types of iPhones: iPhone 6, iPhone 7, iPhone 8, and iPhone X. Whenever scientists discover new things about the world, they may create new terms or symbols, along with new definitions, or they may use old terms but provide new stipulative definitions. For example, Nobel Prize laureate Murray Gell-Mann coined the term "quark" to refer to the elementary particles that combine to make up protons, neutrons, and other subatomic particles. The six kinds of quarks make a great illustration of the arbitrary nature of stipulative definitions. Physicists refer to them as having six "flavors": *up, down, charm, strange, top*, and *bottom*. Of course, the playful nature of these names also shows the importance of having easy-to-remember terms if we are to communicate at all.

In addition to intensional definition techniques, stipulative definitions can also use all three types of extensional definitions of a term. For example, a speaker can assign the new meaning of a term by pointing to an object denoted by the term (an ostensive definition). On the other hand, an enumerative definition may be offered, identifying individual members either partially or completely. Finally, a definition by subclass may be given (again, either partial or complete).

Stipulative definitions are proposals to create a new term or to use an old term in a new way. The proposals can be accepted, rejected, modified, or even ignored. However, there are some drawbacks to excessive stipulations of a term. If the meaning of a term is stretched so that it denotes nearly anything, then the term loses its informative value. For example, if everything is "tall," then the term provides no information. Another example, "awesome," means something that inspires a sense of wonder or reverence. But this colloquial meaning can easily mean anything that is great or excellent. In an interview (adapted slightly here), a U.S. Olympic Gold Medal winner managed to apply it to everything from a *game* and his *teammates* to *feelings*, a *crowd*, *opponents*, and an *experience*:

The game was awesome.	My teammates were awesome.
It felt awesome.	The crowd was awesome.
The other team was awesome.	The whole experience was awesome.

At some point the term "awesome" loses its informative power, and it winds up having no more meaning than "Wow!"

Since stipulative definitions are specific but arbitrary, care must be taken when introducing them in an argument. The possibility of confusion can compound mistakes in interpretation, analysis, understanding, and the evaluation of an argument containing stipulated terms. That is why all terms in a good argument are clearly understood or expressly defined, given the context in which the argument occurs. For example, the most modern meaning of the word "mouse" began as a stipulative definition among computer users. Given the widespread acceptance of the new meaning and the reference of the term, and the hundreds of millions of computer users around the world, the directive "Move the mouse to position the cursor at the beginning of the word you want to delete" would rarely be understood as telling you to manipulate a small rodent.

Lexical Definitions

Like the definition of a mouse as a device to position the cursor, over time a stipulative definition can go from use by a small group of people to widespread acceptance. At this point the term is included among *lexical definitions*.

A **lexical definition** is a definition based on the common use of a word, term, or symbol. The definitions found in dictionaries provide the common meanings of terms and are examples of lexical definitions. "Lexical" means the common vocabulary of a

Lexical definition A definition based on the common use of a word, term, or symbol.

given language as determined by the actual use in a community of speakers and writers. Unlike stipulative definitions, a lexical definition is useful if it accurately reports the way a term is commonly used; otherwise it is not very useful.

Since most terms have multiple meanings, we often rely on lexical definitions to clear up any ambiguity that can lead to a misunderstanding. For example, a lexical definition of "career" might include "a way of making a living" or "a paid occupation"; but it can also mean the general progress of a part of life, such as "my career as a student." A lexical definition of "ornament" might be "a decorative object." However, the term "ornament" can be used to indicate an inanimate object (such as a piece of jewelry), or it can be used to indicate an attractive person who accompanies someone to a function.

The lexical definitions found in many dictionaries often use all four types of intensional definitions. First, a lexical definition might provide information regarding the intension of a term by genus and difference. For example, a dictionary might provide the following information for the term "puppy": *genus*—dog; *difference*—very young. Second, since lexical definitions sometimes offer synonyms as part of the definition, they facilitate the creation of new sentences using alternative words for the term being defined. Third, lexical definitions found in dictionaries typically supply the etymology of a term. And finally, a lexical definition might provide an operational definition.

In addition to intensional definitions, many dictionaries often use all three types of extensional definition techniques. First, they might provide an ostensive definition by an illustration or a picture of the objects denoted by the term. Second, an enumerative definition may identify the individual members (again, either partial or complete). Third, a dictionary may supply a definition by subclass.

When we consult a lexical definition, we have the opportunity to clear up any ambiguity—and we should, whenever we encounter ambiguity in statements and arguments. We rely on lexical definitions to provide accurate guidelines to correct and incorrect usage as determined by a community using a common language.

Functional Definitions

Functional definition
Specifies the purpose or use of the objects denoted by the term.

A **functional definition** specifies the *purpose* or *use* of the objects denoted by the term. For example, a functional definition of the term "cup" can be "a small open container used to hold liquid or solids." Although cups are used mostly for liquids (e.g., coffee, tea, juice, or water), they are also used in cooking (e.g., a cup of sugar or flour). Since a functional definition concentrates on specifying how something is used, it often omits any mention of the material out of which the object is composed. For example, a cup can be made of glass, plastic, cardboard, wood, and many other materials, as long as it performs its function correctly. In fact, you can always *cup your hands* temporarily to hold water.

We use functional definitions to define the normal use of objects that have been created or designed for specific purposes. For example, if you have your car inspected, you might be told that you need a new alternator. If you have no idea what an alternator does, you can ask the mechanic. She probably will tell you that the alternator supplies electrical power throughout the car. Also, the alternator is necessary to recharge the battery after you start the car, since power is temporarily taken from the battery. This intensional definition does not tell you what an alternator looks like. Still, it provides an adequate description of the function of an alternator. Of course, if you ask to see an alternator, the mechanic can point to it in the engine compartment or show you one that is not already connected to an engine. In fact, a functional definition of many simple objects, unlike an alternator, can be given by extension. For example, the best way to illustrate the function of a saw, a hammer, or a doorstopper is to see the tool in action.

Precising Definitions

A **precising definition** reduces the vagueness and ambiguity of a term by providing a sharp focus, often a technical meaning, for a term. Precising definitions can be found in settings that require very distinct and specific meanings of terms, such as law, science, medicine, or manufacturing.

A legal setting might rely on a precise definition of what constitutes a "dangerous weapon" or "illegal drug." A different legal situation might rely on a precising definition of "burglary": *the breaking and unwarranted entry into the dwelling place of another person with the intention of committing a felony.* Law enforcement officers can use this definition in meeting the requirements for arresting a suspect. At a trial, debate over technical matters internal to the definition may continue as well. For example, the word "breaking" seems to imply the use of force. Nevertheless, some states have interpreted it loosely to include any fraudulent entry—for example, telling the person at the door that you are from the gas company and are there to check for leaks. (Notice the similarity of the words "intension" and "intention." As we saw, "intension" refers to the meaning of a term, while "intention," in a legal setting, means what a person has set his or her mind to doing.)

In science, terms such as "energy," "momentum," and "mass" must have precise definitions. A scientific definition of "energy" includes some discussion of how "*matter can do work by its mass, electric charge,* or *motion.*" The italicized terms would themselves need precising definitions to convey a complete understanding.

Medical settings also rely on precise definitions. Doctors must often make ethical decisions regarding the status of a critically ill patient. And that can require a precise determination of when a human being is dead. Although this is a highly controversial topic, nevertheless there have been attempts to offer precise definitions of the term "dead" as it pertains to humans. (You can imagine a similar debate over the definition of when human life begins.) Here is one example:

> The National Conference of Commissioners on Uniform State Laws in 1980 formulated the Uniform Determination of Death Act. It states that: "An individual who has sustained either (1) irreversible cessation of circulatory and

Precising definition
Reduces the vagueness and ambiguity of a term by providing a sharp focus, often a technical meaning, for a term.

respiratory functions, or (2) irreversible cessation of all functions of the entire brain, including the brain stem, is dead. A determination of death must be made in accordance with accepted medical standards." This definition was approved by the American Medical Association in 1980 and by the American Bar Association in 1981.   MedicineNet, Inc.

This precising definition is an operational definition. It specifies medical procedures that are to be used to determine if the term "dead" applies. Precising definitions are used in many other areas as well. For example, the U.S. Census Bureau has crafted a precising definition of "poverty" based on family income. The definition was used in 2010 to determine the poverty rate in the United States.

Size of family unit: 1 person—$11,136; 2 people—$14,220; 3 people—$17,378 (the list continues at roughly $3000–$4000 increments per added person).

The Census Bureau also provides the method that they used to calculate the different thresholds:

The preliminary estimates of the weighted average poverty thresholds for 2010 are calculated by multiplying the 2009 weighted average thresholds by a factor of 1.016403, the ratio of the average annual Consumer Price Index for All Consumers (CPI-U) for 2010 to the average annual CPI-U for 2009.

Once again, we can see that this kind of precising definition is an operational definition. It establishes the meaning of the term "poverty" by specifying monetary thresholds that will be used to determine the number of households in each category, and thus the overall poverty rate in the United States in the year 2010.

As the examples illustrate, precising definitions clarify meaning by eliminating vagueness and ambiguity. Extensional definitions are not useful as precising definitions, because they do not eliminate the potential for vagueness. That is because intension determines extension—and not the other way around.

Since precising definitions are not simply arbitrary assignments of meanings, they differ from stipulative definitions. A stipulative definition can be a way of hiding your intended meaning from those not in your small group. When used this way, a stipulative definition is meant to exclude others from understanding what you mean. In contrast, a precising definition is meant to include as many people as possible by focusing on legitimate, useful, accurate, clear, and direct meaning.

Theoretical Definitions

Theoretical definition
Assigns a meaning to a term by providing an understanding of how the term fits into a general theory.

A **theoretical definition** assigns a meaning by providing an understanding of how the term fits into a general theory. Take some illustrations from science. For example, the term "inheritance" can mean *the estate that passes to an heir,* or it can mean *the characteristics transmitted from parents to their offspring.* The second meaning concerns biology and has been the subject of both theoretical and experimental research for centuries. One of the first modern biological theories of inheritance was formulated by Gregor Mendel in the 19th century. It illustrates the role of theoretical definitions:

- "Factor" means the hereditary unit in which a characteristic (trait) is transmitted from one generation to the next.
- "The first principle of inheritance" means that each individual inherits two factors, one from each parent.
- "The second principle of inheritance" means that the factors are inherited randomly from each parent.
- If two traits are inherited that cannot both be displayed, then the trait that is displayed is called "dominant" and the other is called "recessive."

Mendel's theoretical definitions clearly provide intensional meanings for terms. But the terms could just as well have denoted classes with zero extension. Mendel himself could not know for sure until he began his experiments. In fact, we now use the term "allele" in place of Mendel's term "factor," and the resulting pair of alleles (one from each parent) is now called a "gene." This illustrates an important connection between theoretical definitions and precising definitions. If a theory is successful, then scientists can develop precise definitions for many of the concepts suggested by the theory (e.g., the modern precising definitions of "gene"). The resulting precising definitions (using operational techniques) then pave the way for additional specific ways to measure the objects, which in turn open up new avenues for testing.

Not all theoretical definitions stand the test of time. For example, the term "phlogiston" was originally defined as "the element or particles that exist in a physical body and which are released during combustion." Part of the reasoning behind theorizing that such an element existed was that most material gives off heat and smoke during combustion, so something has to be released into the atmosphere. Also, it was known that if you place a candle in an enclosed space, then the candle soon stops burning. The phlogiston theory explained this by claiming that phlogiston saturates the enclosed space until no more room is available for the release of new particles. This sounds entirely plausible. However, you probably have never heard of phlogiston because we now know that the term denotes an empty class; there is no phlogiston. The discovery of oxygen signaled the end of the phlogiston theory. The candle goes out in an enclosed space not because phlogiston fills the space, but rather because fires need oxygen and all the available oxygen has been used up.

Scientific theories can be understood as *sets of abstract theoretical definitions*. For example, Isaac Newton's definition of the term "gravity" is "an attractive force between bodies that have mass." One of the component terms in this definition is "force," which itself needs defining. Newton's definition of "force" is contained in his three laws of motion. (The first law is "Every object in a state of uniform motion tends to remain in that state of motion unless an external force is applied to it.") Newton's theory is, therefore, the complete set of related theoretical definitions.

A close look at theoretical definitions reveals their main purpose—to provide a way of imagining consequences that can be experimentally tested. It is in this capacity that theoretical definitions can be fruitful. In other words, a theoretical definition can only plant a seed in our imagination. But a precising definition is created in order to be directly applied. Precising definitions offer direct procedures and criteria for determining whether something falls under a certain category. (Who, for example, meets the criteria that define "poverty"?) Theoretical definitions do not function that way. They do not provide a means of direct application. In fact, some highly abstract theories cannot be tested because the technical apparatus has not yet been invented. It took many decades to invent the necessary machinery required to test much of quantum theory. More recently, some physicists, including Stephen Hawking, believe that M-theory will be the final "theory of everything." As of now, however, M-theory remains purely theoretical.

If a theoretical definition is fruitful, then scientists can gain knowledge of how a particular part of the world works. They can attain varying degrees of usefulness or they can be completely useless, as many theories have proven to be. Therefore, we can speak of a theoretical definition as being like an abstract tool. And just as many tools turned out to have no significant utility and were soon discarded, the same fate has befallen many theories. This is why experimentation is so important in helping us learn about the world. What experiments and testing do is to provide the means of determining the success, failure, or limitations of a theory. We can learn from success, but also from failure. (Chapter 14 returns to how theories are tested.)

Persuasive Definitions

Persuasive definition
Assigns a meaning to a term with the direct purpose of influencing attitudes or opinions.

A **persuasive definition** assigns a meaning to a term with the direct purpose of influencing attitudes or opinions. The goal is to persuade the listener or reader to adopt either a favorable or unfavorable response toward whatever is denoted by the term. We will discuss two types of persuasive definitions, those that use *emotional language*, and those that use *figurative language*.

Let's start with a few examples that illustrate opposite sides of a contentious issue:

- "National health care" means that the government decides whether you live or die.
- "National health care" means that we get the same medical care that greedy politicians get.

Both definitions fail to offer specific information about the actual policies behind the health-care program. Instead, each definition is crafted to influence a specific attitude and arouse a particular emotional response toward the issue.

Let's look at another example.

> Life seems to be an experience in ascending and descending. You think you're beginning to live for a single aim—for self-development, or the discovery of cosmic truths—when all you're really doing is to move from place to place as if devoted primarily to real estate.   Margaret Anderson, *The Fiery Fountains*

The writer is presenting a persuasive definition. It is meant to get us to see that our so-called progress through life may not be as wonderful as it might appear. It offers an alternative vision of life that might cause us to rethink our attitude toward our goals and dreams.

We might come across a persuasive definition that is very subtle, especially if the writer is very gifted and creative. Although the definition might be hidden inside the passage, it can be quite powerful. Here is an example:

> I thought if war did not include killing, I'd like to see one every year.
>
> Maya Angelou, *Gather Together in My Name*

The author presents an interesting way of defining the term "war." Angelou's way of presenting the issue is meant to get us to realize that, among other things, wars cause death; and she believes that should be enough to persuade us to abandon the practice.

A persuasive definition might be offered as a way to *reinforce* or *change* an opinion. Political speeches are often laced with persuasive definitions that are meant either to create a positive attitude toward a position (or group) or else to disparage the opposing position (or group). However, some debates concern the definition of "politics" itself:

> Politics is the art of the possible.   Otto Von Bismarck, *Complete Works*, vol. 7

> Politics is not the art of the possible. It consists in choosing between the disastrous and the unpalatable.   John Kenneth Galbraith, *Letter to President Kennedy*

Von Bismarck's definition is meant to place the practice of politics in a positive light. The word "art" suggests that politics is something that skilled artisans can perfect in order to create beneficial results through negotiation. In contrast, Galbraith's definition casts politics in a negative light by contradicting Von Bismarck's claim and elaborates directly on the shortcomings of politics.

The overall goal of a persuasive definition is not to provide direct or accurate information regarding the intension or extension of a term, but instead to influence our thinking about an issue. This is why persuasive definitions are used extensively in politics. Given this, it is not surprising to find that people who rely on a persuasive definition are rarely interested in whether the definition is accurate; they are concerned simply with the definition's effectiveness as persuasion.

Figurative definitions offer metaphors in place of the attributes normally given through an intensional meaning. They function differently than an informative definition, which provides accurate information regarding how a term is normally used. Consider this definition of "accordion":

> Accordion: An instrument in harmony with the sentiments of an assassin.
>
> Ambrose Bierce, *The Devil's Dictionary*

Bierce's definition relies on your being familiar with the way an accordion looks and sounds. It is humorous only if you already understand the lexical definition:

> "Accordion" means a portable wind instrument having a large bellows for forcing air through small metal reeds, a keyboard for the right hand, and buttons for sounding single bass notes or chords for the left hand.
>
> *The Random House Dictionary*

Here is another definition that uses both figurative and emotional language.

Religion is the sigh of the oppressed creature, the heart of a heartless world, and the soul of soulless conditions. It is the opium of the people.

Karl Marx, *A Contribution to the Critique of Hegel's Philosophy of Right*

The terms "sigh," "oppressed," "heartless," and "soulless" are emotionally charged. And the term "opium" is used figuratively; it is meant to evoke a hopeless addiction to the "drug" of religion.

Persuasive definitions are often used in arguments. However, a persuasive definition that relies solely on an emotional response, or uses figurative language, does not offer a good, objective reason as support for a conclusion. (This is discussed further in Chapter 4, "Informal Fallacies.")

TYPES OF DEFINITIONS

Stipulative definition Introduces a new meaning to a term or symbol.
Lexical definition A definition based on the common use of a word, term, or symbol.
Functional definition Specifies the purpose or use of the objects denoted by the term.
Precising definition Reduces the vagueness and ambiguity of a term by providing a sharp focus, often a technical meaning, for a term.
Theoretical definition Assigns a meaning to a term by providing an understanding of how the term fits into a general theory.
Persuasive definition Assigns a meaning to a term with the direct purpose of influencing attitudes or opinions.

EXERCISES 2D

Level 1 Multiple-
Choice Questions

Level 2 Multiple-
Choice Questions

Determine whether the following definitions are stipulative, lexical, precising, theoretical, functional, or persuasive.

1. "Mouse" means a small rodent, or a device for moving the cursor across a computer monitor.

Answer: Lexical

2. Properly speaking, history is nothing but the crimes and misfortunes of the human race.
   Pierre Bayle, "Manicheans"

3. "Horn" means a device on a moving vehicle used to get the attention of people and animals. *Functional or Lexical*

4. "n00b" means a novice gamer or a newcomer to video games. *Stipulative*

decided what it means

⭐ 5. "Momentum" means the impetus of an object in motion.

6. But if you want to be free, you've got to be a prisoner. It's the condition of freedom—true freedom.
   Aldous Huxley, *Eyeless in Gaza*

7. "Water molecule" means two atoms of hydrogen and one atom of oxygen.

8. "Scissors" means a device used to cut material or paper. *Functional or Lexical*

9. "Love" means a strong attraction, devotion, or attachment to a person.

10. "Area of a triangle" means ½ base × height.

11. From now on, "late" means anytime after 10:30 PM.

12. "Freedom" is just another word for nothing left to lose.

From the song "Me and Bobby McGee"

13. "Right to privacy" means the control of access to undocumented personal information.

14. "Barometer" means an instrument that measures atmospheric pressure.

15. "Purr" means a low, murmuring sound expressive of satisfaction.

16. "E-cigarettes" means plastic and metal devices that heat a liquid nicotine solution in a disposable cartridge.

Adapted from the Associated Press

17. "No" means no.

18. No one is more dangerous than he who imagines himself pure in heart: for his purity, by definition, is unassailable.

James Baldwin, *Nobody Knows My Name*

19. "Substance" means the fundamental constituent of existence.

20. "Science" means the systematic knowledge gained through observation and experiment.

21. A "derivative" is the rate of change of a function at a specific value of x.

Lawrence Spector, "The Math Page"

22. Definition of a classic: a book everyone is assumed to have read and often thinks they have.

Alan Bennett, *Independent*

23. "Semantics" means the study of the meaning or the interpretation of words and sentences in a language.

24. The difference between gratitude and attribution is not negligible; one displays humility, the other hubris. It seems like a basic tenet of Christianity to give glory to God, quite another to pronounce that God was giving glory to *you*.

Tim Keown, ESPN

25. "Fraud" is the intentional use of deceit, a trick or some dishonest means to deprive another of his/her/its money, property or a legal right. Law.com

26. "Grue" is the property of an object that makes it appear green if observed before some future time t, and blue if observed afterward.

Nelson Goodman, *The New Riddle of Induction*

27. Freedom is nothing else but a chance to be better.

Albert Camus, *Resistance, Rebellion, and Death*

28. "Biofuel" means fuel produced from renewable biomass material, commonly used as an alternative, cleaner fuel source. Clean-energy-ideas.com

▷

Video Tutorial

29. [I]f you want a stronger version of "good," what sense is there in having a whole string of vague useless words like "excellent" and "splendid" and all the rest of them? "Plusgood" covers the meaning, or "doubleplusgood" if you want something stronger still. Of course we use those forms already, but in the final version of Newspeak there'll be nothing else.

George Orwell, *1984*

30. A colorimeter is a machine that measures the way an object either reflects or transmits light across the visible spectrum, and records the values which correlate with the way the human eye sees color.

Technical Definition, Sample 1, quoted at www.engl.nie.edu

31. A Coffee Dialogue:
Customer: I'll have a small coffee.
Salesperson: I'm sorry; we only have *Tall, Grande, Venti*, or our newest size, *Trenta*.
Customer: What's the smallest?
Salesperson: That would be *Tall*.
Customer: So "Tall" means small?
Salesperson: In a manner of speaking.

32. "Alternator" means a device used for producing electrical current.

33. "Microscope" means an instrument invented to magnify objects too small to be seen under normal conditions.

34. It's a rare parent who can see his or her child clearly and objectively. At a school board meeting I attended . . . the only definition of a gifted child on which everyone in the audience could agree was "mine."

Jane Adams, *I'm Still Your Mother*

35. "Malaria" means the disease caused by the bite of an anopheles mosquito infected with any of four protozoans of the genus *Plasmodium*.

Collins Dictionary

36. Psycho-analysis pretends to investigate the Unconscious. The Unconscious by definition is what you are not conscious of. But the Analysts already know what's in it—they should, because they put it all in beforehand.

Saul Bellow, *The Dean's December*

37. "Syntax" means the study of the grammatical rules of a language.

38. There are two words in the English language that the sports world just can't seem to get right. The first is "ironic," which often gets confused with "coincidental." The second is "redemption," which often gets confused with "The guy who got in trouble in the offseason is playing really well now."

LZ Granderson, "Ben Roethlisberger's Redemption"

39. Absolute, True, and Mathematical Time, of itself, and from its own nature flows equably without regard to anything external, and by another name is called Duration.

Isaac Newton, *Principia*

40. History for multiculturalists is not a succession of dissolving texts, but a tense tangle of past actions that have reshaped the landscape, distributed the nation's wealth, established boundaries, engendered prejudices, and unleashed energies.

    Joyce Appleby, "Recovering America's Historic Diversity"

⭐ 41. Virus and spyware definitions are files that Security Essentials uses to identify malicious or potentially unwanted software on your computer.

    Microsoft Security Essentials

42. A jerk, then, is a man (or woman) who is utterly unable to see himself as he appears to others. He has no grace, he is tactless without meaning to be, he is a bore even to his best friends, he is an egotist without charm. All of us are egotists to some extent, but most of us—unlike the jerk—are perfectly and horribly aware of it when we make asses of ourselves. The jerk never knows.

    Sydney J. Harris, "A Definition of a Jerk"

43. "Life" means the property or quality that distinguishes living organisms from dead organisms and inanimate matter, manifested in functions such as metabolism, growth, reproduction, and response to stimuli or adaptation to the environment originating from within the organism.

    The American Heritage Dictionary of the English Language

44. An electronic message is "spam" if (A) the recipient's personal identity and context are irrelevant because the message is equally applicable to many other potential recipients; and (B) the recipient has not verifiably granted deliberate, explicit, and still-revocable permission for it to be sent.

    The Spamhaus Project Ltd.

⭐ 45. Religion can be defined as a system of beliefs and practices by means of which a group of people struggles with the ultimate problems of human life. It expresses their refusal to capitulate to death, to give up in the face of frustration, to allow hostility to tear apart their human aspirations.

    J. Milton Yinger, *The Scientific Study of Religion*

46. "Dementia" is the significant loss of intellectual abilities such as memory capacity, severe enough to interfere with social or occupational functioning. The criteria for diagnosis of dementia include impairment of attention, orientation, memory, judgment, language, motor and spatial skills, and function.

    Adapted from Medterms.com

47. The effect is further enhanced because human lips are "everted," meaning that they purse outward. This trait sets us apart from other members of the animal kingdom. Unlike other primates, the soft, fleshy surface of our lips remains exposed, making their shape and composition intensely alluring.

    Sheril Kirshenbaum, *The Science of Kissing*

48. Challenged with a 100 million euro ($133 million) deficit, one western German
     city has introduced a day tax on prostitutes to help whittle down its budget gap.
     The new "pleasure tax" requires prostitutes in Dortmund to purchase a 6 euro
     "day ticket" for each day they work, or face a potential fine. Such taxes are not
     unusual in Germany where prostitution is legal and sex workers must pay tax
     on their income. Cologne introduced a 150 euro "pleasure tax" on sex workers
     in 2004 and later added a 6 euro day tax option for part-time prostitutes.

     Reuters

★ 49. There was a time when "universe" meant "all there is." Everything. The whole
     shebang. The notion of more than one universe, more than one everything,
     would seemingly be a contradiction in terms. Yet a range of theoretical devel-
     opments has gradually qualified the interpretation of "universe." To a physicist,
     the word's meaning now largely depends on context. Sometimes "universe" still
     connotes absolutely everything.   Brian Greene, *The Hidden Reality*

50. Civil disobedience is a moral weapon in the fight for justice. But how can dis-
     obedience ever be moral? Well I guess that depends on one's definition of the
     words. In 1919, in India, ten thousand people gathered in Amritsar to protest
     the tyranny of British rule. General Reginald Dyer trapped them in a courtyard
     and ordered his troops to fire into the crowd for ten minutes. Three hundred
     seventy-nine died—men, women, children, shot down in cold blood. Dyer said
     he had taught them "a moral lesson." Gandhi and his followers responded not
     with violence, but with an organized campaign of noncooperation. Govern-
     ment buildings were occupied. Streets were blocked with people who refused
     to rise, even when beaten by police. Gandhi was arrested. But the British were
     soon forced to release him. He called it a "moral victory." The definition of
     moral: Dyer's "lesson" or Gandhi's victory. You choose.

     James Farmer, Jr., "Resolved: Civil Disobedience Is a Moral Weapon in the Fight for Justice"

E. GUIDELINES FOR INFORMATIVE DEFINITIONS

Ordinary language relies heavily on lexical definitions. Conversations between
friends and relatives assume, for the most part, a common agreement on the everyday meaning of words. If a misunderstanding occurs because a term is ambiguous or
vague, then the people involved can often clarify the intended meaning. A conversation among coworkers can be informal, regarding non-work-related topics, or it can
include technical terms that rely on precise definitions (e.g., a medical procedure to
be performed).

   Since definitions are used in a variety of settings and for many different purposes,
there is no single rule to which every definition must conform. For example, definitions used in poetry, novels, music, or jokes often use metaphors. They do not have

to be truthful, informative, or even accurate in order to be effective. However, if our goal is to impart correct and accurate information, then our definitions should follow definite guidelines. Also, if definitions are to play a role in arguments, then ambiguity, vagueness, and any other source of imprecision need to be eliminated. Fortunately, eight guidelines can make the construction of informative definitions easier.

1. An informative definition should use quotation marks appropriately.
We have already offered a few examples from written sources that did not use quotation marks around a term being defined. However, definitions that are meant to be informative should follow the pattern used in this chapter. Here is an example:

> Life is the sum of the forces that resist death.
>
> Gustav Eckstein, *The Body Has a Head*

This can be easily changed to match the format we have used:

> "Life" means the sum of the forces that resist death.

Here are a few more examples:

- A Sicilian pizza is made with a thick crust.
- "Sicilian pizza" means a pizza made with a thick crust.
- A dune buggy is a small open vehicle with low-pressure tires for riding on sandy beaches.
- "Dune buggy" means a small open vehicle with low-pressure tires for riding on sandy beaches.

In each instance, the ordinary language sentence was rewritten in order to place the definiendum within quotation marks. This lets the reader know that the term is being mentioned (the quoted term is the subject).

2. An informative definition should include the essential meaning of a term.
If a definition is to impart information, then it should include the fundamental attributes associated with the objects denoted by the term. The essential properties are what distinguish the objects being referred to from other things. Consider the following example.

> "Television" means plasma, LCD, or LED.

Although the definition does provide extensional meaning through subclasses, it does not give any information about the essential properties of a television (intensional meaning). The next example provides an intensional meaning of the term.

> "Television" means a device for receiving electrical signals and converting them into moving images and sound.

There are many other objects that require a functional definition to provide the essential meaning (e.g., pneumatic jackhammer, computer, and cyclotron). However, an essential definition of "child" would not include a functional definition because we do not define humans by specifying that they serve any distinct purpose.

3. An informative definition should not be too broad or too narrow.

Definitions that are too broad will allow things to be included that should be excluded. For example:

> "Horse" means a large animal that humans often ride.

The definition is too broad. It allows camels and elephants to be included, since they both fit the definition provided. Here is another example of the same term:

> "Horse" means a stallion.

This definition is too narrow. It eliminates females and the young of both sexes. Once again, if a definition is to provide accurate information, then it needs to be such that it includes all and only those objects that are correctly associated with the term's denotation. The following example illustrates this point.

> "Horse" means a quadruped belonging to the same family as zebras and donkeys; individuals typically have a long mane along the back of the neck; a few of the many breeds are appaloosa, mustang, and thoroughbred.

4. An informative definition should not be circular.

In order for a definition to be informative, it must provide substantial material that enlarges our understanding of a term. Some ordinary language definitions fail because they define a term by using the term itself.

> "Addict" means someone who is addicted to a drug.

The definition is circular because it uses the term "addict" as part of the definition. If you do not know already what the term "addict" means, then the proposed definition is not informative. Here are a few more examples:

- "Chemist" means someone who studies chemistry.
- "Length" means how long something is.

Both of these definitions are circular because they assume as part of the definition the very thing they are meant to define. The following are examples of how the three examples can be rewritten to eliminate circularity:

- "Addict" means someone who is physiologically or psychologically dependent on a substance or activity; some examples of addiction are drug, alcohol, and gambling.
- "Chemist" means someone who studies the properties, composition, reactions, and transformations of elementary substances; inorganic chemistry studies all compounds except those containing carbon; organic chemistry is the study of substances found in living organisms.
- "Length" means the extent of something when measured from end to end (also called "linear," meaning *represented by a line*); some common measuring devices for length are centimeters, inches, feet, yards, and meters.

Since the definition of "length" included measuring devices, it illustrates how an operational definition can help clarify the meaning of certain terms.

5. An informative definition should be affirmative and not negative.

We can convey some meaning by contrasting the objects denoted by a term with other objects. For example:

> "Honest" means someone who is not a cheat.

Yet such a definition fails to provide intensional meaning. A definition should make sure to include relevant properties normally associated with the objects it denotes, like this:

> "Honest" means someone who is trustworthy and reliable in their intentions and actions.

Let's look at another negative definition.

> "Normal" means someone who is not insane.

It can be rewritten as follows:

> "Normal" means conforming to a certain standard or convention; in medicine, it refers to someone free from disease; in psychiatry or psychology, it refers to someone free from any mental disorders.

Of course there are exceptions to this rule; in ordinary language situations, a negative definition can be quite adequate to the task. Here are a few simple examples.

- "Dead" means no longer living.
- "Bald tire" means a tire that does not have any tread.

The context in which the definition is used should provide a guide to the appropriateness of a negative definition.

6. An informative definition should not use ambiguous or vague language.

We have seen how ambiguity and vagueness can make a definition less effective and how we can avoid those mistakes. Ambiguity arises when a definition can be reasonably interpreted in more than one way. Here is an example:

> "Fanatic" means true believer.

The term "true believer" can mean a person with deep, genuine, and sincere beliefs. However, it can also mean a person whose belief is simply true. The first interpretation emphasizes the sincerity of the belief; the second interpretation emphasizes the truth value of the belief. The definition does not provide a sufficient context to eliminate the ambiguity.

Vagueness results from a definition that fails to delineate precisely what objects are denoted by a term. For example:

> "Capitalism" means the economic system whereby individuals control the wealth.

The term "individuals" is vague in this definition. Does it refer only to individuals, or are small companies and large corporations included? Does the term "wealth" include property as well as money? What role, if any, does a government have in the economic system defined? The definition is not very informative because it leaves too many unanswered questions.

7. An informative definition should not use emotionally charged or figurative language.

Definitions that rely on emotionally charged language generally fail to provide the essential attributes that are required for intensional meaning. The next example illustrates this point:

> To establish justice in a sinful world is the whole sad duty of the political order.
> Reinhold Niebuhr, On Politics

The definition uses the words "sinful" and "sad" to establish an emotional response in the reader. The definition may be effective for its intended purpose, but it does not provide either intensional or extensional meaning for the term "political order."

Let's look at another example:

> Ask any die-hard what conservatism is; he'll tell you that it's true socialism.
> Aldous Huxley, Eyeless in Gaza

The definition contains the term "die-hard," which is usually associated with a person who holds stubbornly to a position; it is intended to elicit an emotional response. Also, the term "true" in this setting is used to assert that there is only one correct interpretation of the terms involved.

Figurative definitions offer metaphors in place of the essential attributes normally given through an intensional meaning. Consider this example:

> Art is a fruit that grows in man, like a fruit on a plant, or a child in its mother's womb.
> Jean Arp, "Art Is a Fruit"

The use of figurative language is intended to be evocative and poetic; it is not intended to be informative. Therefore, it functions differently from a lexical definition.

8. An informative definition should include a context whenever necessary.

Many common words have more than one meaning. In order to avoid misunderstanding, it sometimes helps to provide the context, often in parentheses:

- "Bank" means (in geography) the dry land bordering a stream or river.
- "Bank" means (in flying) an aircraft's angle of inclination during a turn.
- "Bank" means (in finance) a business involved in saving and lending people's money.
- "Bank" means (in pool or billiards) a cue shot that strikes a side or end cushion.

Once again, the setting in which the definition occurs should provide you with clues regarding whether or not you should include an explicit reference to a context.

EXERCISES 2E

Analyze the following passages using the *Guidelines for Informative Definitions*. Explain why you think that one, more than one, or none of the guidelines are applicable to each passage.

1. Reality is that which, when you stop believing in it, doesn't go away.

   Philip K. Dick, *How to Build a Universe That Doesn't Fall Apart Two Days Later*

Answer: The definition uses irony to make its point, so it does not attempt to be informative by providing a lexical or precising definition. However, we can add quotation marks (using Guideline 1): "Reality" means that which, when you stop believing in it, doesn't go away.

2. One definition of man is "an intelligence served by organs."

   Ralph Waldo Emerson, "Works and Days"

3. "Politician" means an elected official who likes to spend other people's money.

4. The definition of the individual was: a multitude of one million divided by one million.

   Arthur Koestler, *Darkness at Noon*

⭐ 5. It is from the womb of art that criticism was born.

   Charles Baudelaire, "Salon of 1846"

6. A philanthropist is a man whose charity increases directly as the square of the distance.

   George Eliot, *Middlemarch*

7. I guess the definition of a lunatic is a man surrounded by them.

   Ezra Pound, Quoted in *Charles Olson and Ezra Pound*

8. Retaliation is related to nature and instinct, not to law. Law, by definition, cannot obey the same rules as nature.

   Albert Camus, *Resistance, Rebellion and Death*

⭐ 9. Grade point average (GPA) means the number determined by dividing the total grade points achieved by the number of credits earned.

10. It is the greatest happiness of the greatest number that is the measure of right and wrong.

    Jeremy Bentham, *Fragment of Government*

11. Tall means anyone who can eat peanuts off my head.

12. To be "conscious" means not simply to be, but to be reported, known, to have awareness of one's being added to that being.

    William James, "How Two Minds Can Know the Same Thing"

⭐ 13. To say the word Romanticism is to say modern art—that is, intimacy, spirituality, color, aspiration towards the infinite, expressed by every means available to the arts.

    Charles Baudelaire, "Salon of 1846"

14. Journalists write news stories based on the material, and then provide a link to the supporting documentation to prove our stories are true.

    Charlie Savage, "U.S. Tries to Build Case for Conspiracy by WikiLeaks"

Level 1 Multiple-Choice Questions

Level 2 Multiple-Choice Questions

Video Tutorial

15. The human mind is so complex and things are so tangled up with each other that, to explain a blade of straw, one would have to take to pieces an entire universe.... A definition is a sack of flour compressed into a thimble.

Rémy De Gourmont, "Glory and the Idea of Immortality"

16. If a thousand men were not to pay their tax-bills this year, that would not be as violent and bloody a measure as it would be to pay them and enable the State to commit violence and shed innocent blood. This is, in fact, the definition of a peaceable revolution, if any such is possible.

Henry David Thoreau, *On the Duty of Civil Disobedience*

★ 17. Whereas Smith noted that renegotiations or extensions of rookie contracts were "banned" until after the third year, a management official said the proposal "allows" for those renegotiations or extensions after the third year.

Chris Mortensen and Adam Schefter, "Sources: Sides Could Talk This Week"

18. By intuition is meant the kind of intellectual sympathy by which one places oneself within an object in order to coincide with what is unique in it and consequently inexpressible. Analysis, on the contrary, is the operation which reduces the object to elements already known, that is, to elements common both to it and other objects.

Henri Bergson, *An Introduction to Metaphysics*

19. The needs of a society determine its ethics, and in the Black American ghettos the hero is that man who is offered only the crumbs from his country's table but by ingenuity and courage is able to take for himself a Lucullan feast.

Maya Angelou, *I Know Why the Caged Bird Sings*

20. Physics is experience, arranged in economical order.

Ernst Mach, "The Economical Nature of Physics"

F. COGNITIVE AND EMOTIVE MEANING

We saw in Chapter 1 that sentences can be used for a variety of reasons, such as asking a question, providing information, making a request, or giving an order. Language also serves as a vehicle for expressing feelings through songs, poetry, stories, proverbs, jokes, and even lies. We will focus on two functions of language—to convey information and to express emotion.

Cognitive meaning
Language that is used to convey information has cognitive meaning.

Emotive meaning
Language that is used to express emotion or feelings has emotive meaning.

Language that is used to convey information has **cognitive meaning**, while language that is used to express emotion or feelings has **emotive meaning**. Consider two examples:

A. It's already 7:00. He is late for the appointment.
B. It's already 7:00. He is late for the appointment. I am fed up with his nonsense; he is completely untrustworthy, self-centered, and useless.

The two statements in A convey information, so they both have cognitive meaning. Although the first two statements in B convey information, the third statement is more complex. The phrase "I am fed up with his nonsense" has emotive meaning, and the terms "completely untrustworthy, self-centered, and useless" are value judgments. A **value judgment** is a claim that a particular human action or object has some degree of importance, worth, or desirability. However, the claim that the person referred to in B is "completely untrustworthy, self-centered, and useless" has terms that are vague and that need to be clearly defined. In addition, we are provided with no evidence to support the claim, other than that the person was once late for an appointment. Therefore, the value claim and the cognitive meaning are obscured by the emotive language.

Let's look at two more examples:

> A stem cell is an unspecialized cell found in fetuses, embryos, and some adult body tissues that has the potential to develop into specialized cells or divide into other stem cells. Stem cells from fetuses or embryos can develop into any type of differentiated cells, while those found in mature tissues develop only into specific cells. Stem cells can potentially be used to replace tissue damaged or destroyed by disease or injury, but the use of embryonic stem cells for this purpose is controversial.   *The American Heritage Science Dictionary*

> [This] would allow scientists to create an embryonic clone for the purposes of extracting the stem cells from that embryo, a procedure that will cause the embryo's immediate demise. The stem cells may then be used for experimental treatments on another human being with a disease. Let's see, creating a human being for the purposes of killing that person for another human being's health, sounds an awfully lot like cannibalism, only worse. . . . [T]he procedure would not merely use tissue from human embryos, it would destroy them. That's like saying removing someone's heart is just using their tissue.
> C. Ben Mitchell, "Biotech Cannibalism"

The first passage provides a definition of the term "stem cells" (an unspecialized cell) and also provides information regarding its sources (fetuses, embryos, and some adult body tissues). There is also information regarding the potential uses of the different kinds of stem cells. The passage illustrates an extended use of cognitive meaning.

The second passage also has examples of cognitive meaning—for example, "The stem cells may then be used for experimental treatments on another human being with a disease." However, it also has examples of emotive meaning—for example, "the embryo's immediate demise," and "sounds an awfully lot like cannibalism, only worse." There is even sarcasm laced with emotion: "That's like saying removing someone's heart is just using their tissue."

These two passages again illustrate that statements can contain both cognitive and emotive meaning. Look again at "[This] would allow scientists to create an embryonic clone for the purposes of extracting the stem cells from that embryo, a procedure that will cause the embryo's immediate demise." The first part of the sentence has cognitive meaning, and the second part contains both cognitive and emotive meaning. However, the emotional force of the language can sometimes make it difficult to

Value judgment A claim that a particular human action or object has some degree of importance, worth, or desirability.

distinguish or extract the cognitive meaning. We can extract the cognitive meaning of the phrase "a procedure that will cause the embryo's immediate demise" by looking closely at certain key words. The term "embryo" can be defined as the stage of development (in humans) up to the second month in the womb. The term "fetus" can be defined as the stage of development (in humans) occurring after the second month in the womb. We can replace the term "demise" with the more neutral term "death." The cognitive meaning can then be distinguished by paraphrasing the original: "a procedure that causes the death of the embryo."

There is another important use of emotive language in the second passage. The author first uses the term "embryo" but then switches to the term "human": "Let's see, creating a human being for the purposes of killing that person." The author has maneuvered the reader from "the embryo's immediate demise" to "killing that person." Since it is controversial whether an embryo is a *person*, the author is unjustified in simply substituting the term "person" for "embryo." (The terms are not synonymous.)

Since we want to focus on the informational content of the statements in an argument, emotionally charged language interferes with analysis. The emotive meaning of a statement can sometimes override and obscure the cognitive meaning and any value judgments that are made. Also, a vague claim can hide behind the emotionally charged language with the result that the evidence needed to support the claim is overlooked. (Chapter 12 offers a detailed discussion of value judgments.)

EXERCISES 2F

Level 1 Multiple-
Choice Questions

Level 2 Multiple-
Choice Questions

Determine whether the following passages contain phrases expressing cognitive meaning, emotive meaning, or both. Explain your answers.

1. Americans gave nearly $300 billion to charities last year, a 1% increase when adjusted for inflation.

Answer: Cognitive meaning. The passage provides information regarding the percentage of increase in charitable contributions.

2. Gambling is for suckers. As P. T. Barnum said, "There's a sucker born every minute." State lotteries bleed hard-earned money from those least able to afford it. The corrupt officials who voted to allow those obscene games should be sent to jail. I'll be happy to turn the key and lock them up.

3. The two new integrated resorts and casinos in Singapore have each generated over $100 million in profits per month since they opened. At this rate they will each be able to pay off their start-up costs in 5 years.

4. The independent assessment committee was satisfied that adequate measures were taken by the local authorities to meet all foreseeable contingencies.

5. The Great Pyramid of Giza is the only thing that still exists among the Seven Wonders of the Ancient World.

6. The powers-that-be were ridiculously unprepared for the huge crowd last night. The resulting chaos caused immense suffering and put precious lives in extreme peril. Some heads should roll over this tragedy.

7. At some point, if you don't want to worry about teams in minor markets, don't put teams in minor markets, or don't leave teams in minor markets if they're truly minor. Socialism, communism, whatever you want to call it, is never the answer.

Hank Steinbrenner, co-owner of the New York Yankees, quoted in the Associated Press

8. It is the business of thought to define things, to find the boundaries; thought, indeed, is a ceaseless process of definition.

Vance Palmer, in *Intimate Portraits*, ed. H. P. Heseltine

★ 9. As much as we want to keep everybody, we've already made these guys very, very rich, and I don't feel we owe anybody anything monetarily. Some of these players are wealthier than their bosses.   Hank Steinbrenner, quoted at CBSSports.com

10. It brings us one step closer to the brink of war, because I don't think the North would seek war by intention, but war by accident, something spiraling out of control has always been my fear.   Peter Beck, quoted at Guardian.co.uk

Video Tutorial

11. The utopian male concept which is the premise of male pornography is this—since manhood is established and confirmed over and against the brutalized bodies of women, men need not aggress against each other; in other words, women absorb male aggression so that men are safe from it.

Andrea Dworkin, *The Root Cause*

12. By contrast with history, evolution is an unconscious process. Another, and perhaps a better way of putting it would be to say that evolution is a natural process, history a human one. . . . Insofar as we treat man as a part of nature—for instance in a biological survey of evolution—we are precisely not treating him as a historical being. As a historically developing being, he is set over against nature, both as a knower and as a doer.   Owen Barfield, *History, Guilt, and Habit*

★13. The man who can roust the excitement and the enthusiasm of the coordination of the players is the one who will come through, the one that can bring their team to that high expectation of unity, solidarity and togetherness and performing above and beyond the call of duty, he will be the big, big winner Sunday.   Don King, boxing promoter, quoted at ESPN.go.com

14. Ah, California, my home sweet home. Did anyone catch the California Horse Racing Board's meeting the other day, during which the commissioners were asked to choose between bald-faced corporatism and open-handed charity? Okay, maybe it wasn't as simple as that, but contrary conclusions are hard to draw.   Jay Hovdey, *Daily Racing Form*

15. Choosing the wrong policy can have consequences. For example, when comparing breast cancer treatment coverage under three California policies, the study found that a patient would spend nearly $4,000 for a typical treatment under one policy or as much as $38,000 under another even though both policies had similar deductibles and out-of-pocket limits.

Susan Jaffe, "Speak Plain English, Health Insurers Told," *Kaiser Health News*

G. FACTUAL AND VERBAL DISPUTES

Factual dispute Occurs when people disagree on a matter that involves facts.

A **factual dispute** occurs when people disagree on a matter that involves facts. For example, one person might claim that Benjamin Franklin must have been a U.S. president because his picture is on the $100 bill, while another person claims that Franklin was not a U.S. president. This dispute can be resolved by consulting historical or biographical sources. Here is another example of a factual dispute:

- Our state legislature should pass a law authorizing capital punishment because it is an effective deterrent to violent crime.
- Our state legislature should not pass a law authorizing capital punishment because it has not been shown to be an effective deterrent to violent crime.

The dispute concerns the factual question of whether or not capital punishment is an effective deterrent to violent crime. Each side in the dispute needs to provide relevant scientific evidence in support of its position.

A factual dispute can involve emotional language. It occurs when people agree on certain facts and terms but express their feelings toward the facts in different ways. For example:

- Executing violent criminals is morally acceptable because those people are worthless and commit despicable acts against peace-loving, innocent humans.
- Executing violent criminals is morally unacceptable because even though those people are as bad as you say, we should open our hearts, and learn to love and forgive.

The disputants seem to agree on the terms "worthless," "despicable acts," and "peace-loving." However, their emotional responses to these terms differ, as do their value judgments regarding how we should act toward violent criminals.

Verbal dispute Occurs when a vague or ambiguous term results in a linguistic misunderstanding.

A **verbal dispute** occurs when a vague or ambiguous term results in a linguistic misunderstanding. In other words, statements that are thought to be about the objects denoted by certain key terms instead involve a dispute about the terms themselves. These kinds of disputes are resolved not by investigating the facts, but by an investigation of the definitions. Suppose someone is a "small bookmaker." Is his occupation illegal? Since the term "bookmaker" can mean either "a person who makes books" or "a person who accepts illegal wagers on sporting events" (often referred to as a "bookie"), the dispute hinges on an ambiguity arising from an unclear context. Disputes of this nature are easily cleared up once the correct meaning is identified.

However, there are more complicated kinds of verbal disputes. A term might be used when there is some overall agreement on its intension, but disagreement as to its extension. For example, some disputes have involved the question of whether a certain belief system qualifies as a "religion." Legal, governmental, and moral issues are all involved. A religion that is recognized by the government has certain privileges, such as being exempt from paying taxes. The disputes can sometimes be resolved by clarifying the intension of the term (which will further determine the extension), so that the court can make a decision. However, deciding the legal question will not necessarily satisfy everyone, because religious issues often evoke emotional responses.

Sometimes the parties involved cannot agree on a definition. Although most governments condemn acts of terrorism, we often hear that "one person's terrorist is another person's freedom fighter." In more formal language, a United Nations report in 2010 stated that "some delegations pointed out the necessity to distinguish between acts of terrorism and the legitimate struggle of people in the exercise of their right to self-determination."

In a report to the United Nations General Assembly, the Secretary-General offered this definition:

> Any action constitutes terrorism if it is intended to cause death or serious bodily harm to civilians or non-combatants with the purpose of intimidating a population or compelling a Government or an international organization to do or abstain from doing any act.
>
> *In Larger Freedom: Towards Development, Security and Human Rights for All*, March 21, 2005

The United Nations has still not adopted a definition of "terrorism." The contentious issues involving the term "terrorism" are not merely verbal. However, even if a verbal agreement could be reached, the emotive meaning, political divisions, and value judgments that get attached to the term still need to be settled.

EXERCISES 2G

Determine whether the following disputes are factual, verbal, or some combination of the two. Also, point out any emotional language that might be involved.

1. A: Drinking one glass of red wine a day has been linked with a lower risk of heart disease.

    B: Excessive alcohol consumption has been linked to liver disease.

    Answer: Verbal dispute. Person A talks about the effects of "drinking one glass of red wine a day," while person B talks about the effects of "excessive alcohol consumption." The dispute is not about the facts related to their respective claims.

2. A: All humans are created equal.

    B: That can't be. We all have a unique DNA profile.

Level 1 Multiple-Choice Questions

Level 2 Multiple-Choice Questions

3.   A: You were fired because of your poor work performance.
     B: I was fired because the supervisor didn't like me.

4.   A: My parents are in heaven.
     B: There is no heaven.

Video Tutorial

★ 5.   A: The capital city of Korea is Seoul.
       B: You are wrong. The capital city of Korea is Pyongyang.

6.   A: There is a higher incidence of child leukemia near nuclear power plants com-
        pared to the rest of the United States.
     B: Nuclear power plants provide the best opportunity to free ourselves from oil
        dependency.

7.   A: Here, have a martini.
     B: It's not a martini because it was not made with dry vermouth.
     A: But a martini doesn't have to be made with dry vermouth.

8.   A: This is my new car.
     B: That's not new. It's at least 5 years old.

★ 9.   A: Don't ask her whether you should take the job or not—make your own
          decision.
       B: I am making my own decision—I have decided to ask her what I should do.

10.   A: Sales will increase if we upgrade customer service because customers will
         feel that we care about their satisfaction.
      B: I disagree. Sales will decrease if we upgrade customer service because it will
         make it too easy for customers to return products after they used them for a
         while.

11.   A: Our business is booming. Total sales are up 13% over last year.
      B: Our business is not booming. Profit is down 3% from last year.

12.   A: Did you see his last movie? What an actor; he's a genius.
      B: I read somewhere that his I.Q. is only 110, so he's definitely not in the genius
         range.

★ 13.   A: I don't think, I know.
        B: I don't think you know either.

14.   A: The contract proposal offered by the company is reasonable.
      B: The contract proposal is just their way of further exploiting the working
         class.

15. A: No radio station east of the Mississippi can use the letter "K" as its first call letter.

    B: Oh really; then what about KDKA? It's in Pittsburgh, Pennsylvania.

16. A: The proposed tax hike is too high. The individuals who invest their hard-earned money in businesses that provide all the jobs are being robbed of that which is their sacred right to keep. The government is like a thief who steals rather than works. Taxes are immoral because they take what rightfully belongs to someone and give it to those too lazy or not talented enough to compete. We should be able to do whatever we want with what we earn instead of being subjected to onerous taxation spiraling out of control. The government wants higher and higher taxes the way an addict tries to satisfy an insatiable desire.

    B: The proposed tax hike is not too high. In fact, it is not enough. The rich people in this country are getting away with murder when it comes to paying their fair share. Big corporations need to fleece the public to ensure obscene profits for their shareholders, who then turn around and purchase luxury items that flaunt their wealth with lifestyles that rival the most decadent periods in human history.

★ 17. Some years ago, being with a camping party in the mountains, I returned from a solitary ramble to find every one engaged in a ferocious metaphysical dispute. The corpus of the dispute was a squirrel—a live squirrel supposed to be clinging to one side of a tree-trunk; while over against the tree's opposite side a human being was imagined to stand. This human witness tries to get sight of the squirrel by moving rapidly round the tree, but no matter how fast he goes, the squirrel moves as fast in the opposite direction, and always keeps the tree between himself and the man, so that never a glimpse of him is caught. The resultant metaphysical problem now is this: *Does the man go round the squirrel or not?* He goes round the tree, sure enough, and the squirrel is on the tree; but does he go round the squirrel? In the unlimited leisure of the wilderness, discussion had been worn threadbare. Every one had taken sides, and was obstinate; and the numbers on both sides were even.   William James, *What Pragmatism Means*

18. In his System of Nature, A.D. 1776, Linnaeus declares, "I hereby separate the whales from the fish.". . . The grounds upon which Linnaeus would fain have banished the whales from the waters, he states as follows: "On account of their warm bilocular heart, their lungs, their movable eyelids, their hollow ears."…I take the good old fashioned ground that the whale is a fish, and call upon holy Jonah to back me. This fundamental thing settled, the next point is, in what internal respect does the whale differ from other fish. Above, Linnaeus has given you those items. But in brief, they are these: lungs and warm blood; whereas, all other fish are lungless and cold blooded.   Herman Melville, *Moby Dick*

19. *M:* An argument isn't just contradiction.
A: It can be.
M: No it can't. An argument is a connected series of statements intended to establish a proposition.
A: No it isn't.
M: Yes it is! It's not just contradiction.
A: Look, if I argue with you, I must take up a contrary position.
M: Yes, but that's not just saying "No it isn't."
A: Yes it is!
M: No it isn't!
A: Yes it is!
M: Argument is an intellectual process. Contradiction is just the automatic gainsaying of any statement the other person makes. *(short pause)*
A: No it isn't.
M: It is.
A: Not at all.
                                                        Monty Python, "The Argument Sketch"

20. A: In 1982, 82 percent of college graduates read novels or poems for pleasure; two decades later, only 67 percent did. And more than 40 percent of Americans under 44 did not read a single book—fiction or nonfiction—over the course of a year. The proportion of 17-year-olds who read nothing (unless required to do so for school) more than doubled between 1984 and 2004. This time period, of course, encompasses the rise of personal computers, Web surfing and video games.   Susan Jacoby, "The Dumbing of America"

B: Susan Jacoby presents a compelling, though perhaps naïve and myopic, view of intellectualism and the persistence of literature in the 21st century. Like so many nervous academics of our age, Jacoby provides a view compounded by urgent pollster data, alarming statistics, and factoids heralding in the age of ignorance at the hands of the digital revolution. A concern about whether young people are wasting their minds has been intermittently fashionable throughout history. If Jacoby contends that "video" is eroding our intellect, I encourage her to immerse herself in the story of Wikipedia. This is a place where today's youth, in phenomenal numbers, are helping professors and graduate students to build a repository of living knowledge from all corners of this planet. This is not a project for the next decade or the century. It is a project for all time.
                    Jimmy Wales, the founder of Wikipedia, "We're Smarter than You Think"

Study Materials

Summary

- Term: A single word or a group of words that can be the subject of a statement; it can be a common name, a proper name, or even a descriptive phrase.
- Clarifying the meaning of a statement requires a close look at the meaning of the terms involved. Vague, ambiguous, or imprecise terms can reduce the clarity of individual statements and arguments.

- Intension: The intension of a term is specified by listing the properties or attributes that the term connotes—in other words, its sense.
- Class: A group of objects.
- Extension: The class or collection of objects to which the term applies. In other words, what the term denotes (its reference).
- A sequence of terms can have increasing intension, decreasing intension, increasing extension, or decreasing extension.
- Empty class: A class that has zero members.
- A definition assigns a meaning to a word, phrase, or symbol. Logicians use the term "definiendum" to refer to that which is being defined, and the term "definiens" to that which does the defining.
- Intensional definition: Assigns a meaning to a term by listing the properties or attributes shared by all the objects that are denoted by the term.
- Synonymous definition: Assigns a meaning to a term by providing another term with the same meaning; in other words, by providing a synonym.
- Word origin definition: A meaning can be assigned to a term by investigating its origin. The study of the history, development, and sources of words is called *etymology*.
- Operational definition: Defines a term by specifying a measurement procedure.
- Definition by genus and difference: Assigns a meaning to a term (the species) by establishing a genus and combining it with the attribute that distinguishes the members of that species.
- Extensional definition: Assigns meaning to a term by indicating the class members denoted by the term.
- Ostensive definition: Involves demonstrating the term—for example, by pointing to a member of the class that the term denotes.
- Enumerative definition: Assigns meaning to a term by naming the individual members of the class denoted by the term.
- Definition by subclass: Assigns meaning to a term by naming subclasses (species) of the class denoted by the term.
- Stipulative definition: Introduces a new meaning to a term or symbol.
- Lexical definition: A definition based on the common use of a word, term, or symbol.
- Functional definition: Specifies the purpose or use of the objects denoted by the term.
- Precising definition: Reduces the vagueness and ambiguity of a term by providing a sharp focus, often a technical meaning, for a term.
- Theoretical definition: Assigns a meaning to a term by providing an understanding of how the term fits into a general theory.
- Persuasive definition: Assigns a meaning to a term with the direct purpose of influencing attitudes or opinions.
- There are eight guidelines that are meant to facilitate the construction of informative definitions.

- Cognitive meaning: Language that is used to convey information.
- Emotive meaning: Language that is used to express emotion or feelings.
- Value judgment: A claim that a particular human action or object has some degree of importance, worth, or desirability.
- Factual dispute: Occurs when people disagree on a matter which involves facts.
- Verbal dispute: Occurs when a vague or ambiguous term results in a linguistic misunderstanding.

KEY TERMS

LOGIC CHALLENGE: THE PATH

A person walks up a mountain path in Tibet to visit a monastery in order to gain enlightenment. She starts out on her journey at 7:00 AM and arrives at the monastery 8 hours later. A monk hands her a note and tells her not to read it until she returns to the bottom of the mountain. The next morning she starts down the path at 7:00 AM. She is anxious to read the note, and since she is able to walk downhill very fast, she arrives at the bottom in 4 hours. She opens the note and reads the following:

> On your journey down the path you passed one spot at the exact same time that you passed it when you went up the path.

Is the note correct? Explain your answer.

Chapter 3

Diagramming Arguments

A. *The Basics of Diagramming Arguments*
B. *Diagramming Extended Arguments*

Study Materials

A diagram of an argument, like a road map, is a visual tool. It offers a graphic depiction of the argument's structure, and it allows us to follow a path from point A (the premises) to point B (the conclusion). It highlights connections—the connections between the statements that make up the argument. It takes a passage and extracts all the premises, numbers them, and then connects them to the conclusion. You can consult the numbers as you make those connections in the passage yourself.

Maps are especially helpful for long trips, and diagrams are especially useful for extended arguments. If you are on a road trip, you might find that you can get to your destination by several different routes, each through a different city. Similarly, an argument might contain premises that work independently of each other in support of the conclusion. On the other hand, when tracing a route on a map, you might find there is only one way to get where you want to go, and the route takes you through several stops along the way. In the same way, you might need all the premises of an argument, because they work together to support the conclusion.

A road map might show that you cannot get to your destination—or at least not easily, because some roads are not yet completed. In the same manner, some arguments are missing a premise or a conclusion, either intentionally or unintentionally. In those cases, we need to add the missing information based on our overall understanding. If we add a missing premise, then we are building a bridge, to connect the existing premises to the conclusion. If we add a missing conclusion, then we are providing a final destination. Of course, our diagram will have to distinguish the information we are given from what we have added to complete the argument. This chapter applies diagramming to both simple and extended arguments.

A. THE BASICS OF DIAGRAMMING ARGUMENTS

Once we have located an argument, we can create a diagram—a map of the premises and conclusion. There are a few basic techniques for creating diagrams, and they can be used as building blocks for diagramming extended arguments. For example, suppose you read this simple argument: "You do not take care of your dog. Therefore, you will not be able to accept the responsibility of owning a car." The first step in creating a diagram is to number the statements as they appear (disregarding, at this point, whether they are premises or conclusions).

> [1] You do not take care of your dog. Therefore, [2] you will not be able to accept the responsibility of owning a car.

The passage contains the conclusion indicator "therefore," so we can determine that statement 2 is the conclusion. The next step is to diagram the argument by connecting the premise to the conclusion with an arrow:

$$1$$
$$\downarrow$$
$$2$$

Simple diagram A diagram consisting of a single premise and a single conclusion.

The result is a **simple diagram** consisting of a single premise and a single conclusion. When there is more than one premise, the premises may act independently in support of the conclusion. **Independent premises** are such that the falsity of one does not nullify the support the others give to the conclusion. We can illustrate this by adding other premises to our example:

Independent premises Premises are independent when the falsity of one would not nullify any support the others would give to the conclusion.

> [1] You will not be able to accept the responsibility of owning a car because [2] you do not take care of your dog, [3] you don't clean your room, and [4] you do not handle your money responsibly.

Independent premises can be captured in a **convergent diagram**. Here is the convergent diagram for our example:

Convergent diagram A diagram that reveals the occurrence of independent premises.

Each of the three premises has its own arrow, because each premise offers independent support for the conclusion. In other words, each premise, by itself, offers a reason to accept the conclusion. Even if one or two of the premises are shown to be false, at least one arrow would remain.

Dependent premises Premises are dependent when they work together to support a conclusion. In other words, the falsity of one dependent premise weakens the support that the other dependent premises give to the conclusion.

There are other ways that premises can act to support a conclusion. **Dependent premises** work together to support a conclusion. In other words, the falsity of one dependent premise weakens the support that the other dependent premises give to the conclusion. For example:

> [1] Lead was found in the paint in that apartment building. [2] Lead poisoning can occur in children who ingest small amounts of lead over a long period of time. Thus, [3] the children living in those apartments should be tested for lead poisoning.

The conclusion, "the children living in those apartments should be tested for lead poisoning," is supported by the two premises *working together*. Each premise depends on the other to offer strong support for the conclusion. Premise 1 tells us that lead was found in the paint in the building, which, *by itself*, doesn't seem to strongly support the conclusion. Similarly, although premise 2 tells us that lead poisoning can occur in children who ingest small amounts of lead over a long period of time, premise 2, *by itself*, doesn't seem to strongly support the conclusion. However, when the two premises are *linked together* their joint information combines to support the conclusion. This is illustrated by the following diagram:

The diagram links premise 1 and premise 2 to show that they work together to support the conclusion. Dependent premises create a **linked diagram**. Notice the difference between a linked diagram and a convergent diagram in which each *independent* premise has its own arrow connecting it to the conclusion.

Linked diagram A diagram that reveals the occurrence of dependent premises.

Let's look at another example:

> [1] The movie version of *The Lord of the Rings* used some of the original dialogue from the books, [2] it used the language Tolkien invented, [3] it used the characters he created, [4] it kept the overall plot, and [5] the settings were the same as in the books. Therefore, [6] the movie trilogy *The Lord of the Rings* captured most of the spirit of the original books.

Here premises 1 through 5 are linked to support the conclusion, that the movies captured most of the spirit of the original books.

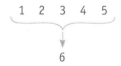

It is also possible that one premise supports more than one conclusion. Consider this argument:

> [1] The new movie *Son of Avatar* will be the highest grossing movie in history. Therefore, [2] it is sure to win multiple Academy Awards, and [3] some of the actors will be among the highest paid in the industry. We can also conclude that [4] the director will get to do anything he wants in the near future.

In this passage, one premise is being used to support three separate conclusions, resulting in a **divergent diagram**:

Divergent diagram A diagram that shows a single premise supporting independent conclusions.

Finally, some passages contain a series of arguments, in which a conclusion from one argument becomes a premise in the next one. For example:

¹ The government just cut taxes and ² put a freeze on the minimum wage.
³ This combination is sure to create higher unemployment. Of course, ⁴ that will lead to a drop in gross domestic sales. ⁵ This will surely cause a recession.

Serial diagram A diagram that shows that a conclusion from one argument is a premise in a second argument.

This results in a **serial diagram**:

Statements 1 and 2 are linked (conjoined) to support 3, which is an intermediate conclusion. Statement 3 then is a premise for statement 4, which is another intermediate conclusion. Finally, 4 is a premise for 5, the conclusion of the argument.

B. DIAGRAMMING EXTENDED ARGUMENTS

Extended arguments can require diagrams that combine two of our diagramming techniques, as in this example:

¹ Asbestos has been found in many of the recently built homes and apartments in this city. ² Asbestos has been found to cause cancer in humans. Also, ³ high levels of arsenic have been found in the city's drinking water supply. ⁴ Arsenic has been found to cause cancer in humans. Thus, ⁵ we can expect to see a rise in the cancer rate in the coming years.

Statement 1 tells us that asbestos has been found in many of the recently built homes and apartments in this city, which by itself doesn't strongly support the conclusion. On the other hand, statement 2 tells us that asbestos has been found to cause cancer in humans, which again by itself doesn't strongly support the conclusion. By working together, they offer stronger support than each individually. Upon close examination, statements 3 and 4 work similarly to 1 and 2. Our diagram will reflect this analysis.

As the diagram shows, 1 and 2 work together, so they are dependent premises that form a linked diagram when connected to 5 by way of an arrow. Likewise, 3 and 4 work together, so they, too, are dependent premises that form a linked diagram when connected to 5 by way of a separate arrow. Finally, the two arrows indicate the presence of a convergent diagram.

Extended arguments often require diagrams that combine more than two of our diagramming techniques, as in this example:

> [1] My working overtime each day for the next three weeks, and [2] my coming in on weekends, [3] will guarantee that I will finish the report early. Of course, [4] it is also possible that working a normal 40-hour week will lead to the same result. Therefore, [5] finishing the report early will lead to a bigger paycheck. [6] It could also lead to a promotion.

> [A] The arrow from 1 and 2 to 3 indicates the presence of a linked diagram (dependent premises).
> [B] The two arrows, one from 1 and 2 to 3, and the other from 4 to 3, indicate the presence of a convergent diagram (independent premises).
> [C] The two arrows, one leading from 3 to 5, and the other from 3 to 6, indicate the presence of a divergent diagram.
> [D] The entire diagram reveals the presence of a serial diagram.

Finally, if we add or change material from a passage, then our diagram has to reflect that change. We place the new statement in brackets to distinguish it from the given information. Here is an example:

> [1] The idea that space and time may form a closed surface without boundary also has profound implications for the role of God in the affairs of the universe. [2] So long as the universe had a beginning, we could suppose it had a creator. But [3] if the universe is really completely self-contained, having no boundary or edge, it would have neither beginning nor end; [4] it would simply be. What place, then, for a creator?   Stephen W. Hawking, *A Brief History of Time*

The final sentence of the passage is a rhetorical question that we can rewrite as a numbered statement:

> [5] [There is no place for a creator.]

We can now diagram the argument.

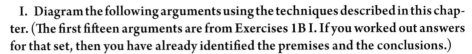

EXERCISES 3B

Level 1 Multiple-
Choice Questions

Level 2 Multiple-
Choice Questions

I. Diagram the following arguments using the techniques described in this chapter. (The first fifteen arguments are from Exercises 1B I. If you worked out answers for that set, then you have already identified the premises and the conclusions.)

1. Exercise helps strengthen your cardiovascular system. It also lowers your cholesterol, increases the blood flow to the brain, and enables you to think longer. Thus, there is no reason for you not to start exercising regularly.

Answer: [1] Exercise helps strengthen your cardiovascular system. [2] It also lowers your cholesterol, [3] increases the blood flow to the brain, and [4] enables you to think longer. [5] There is no reason for you not to start exercising regularly.

2. If you start a strenuous exercise regimen before you know if your body is ready, you can cause serious damage. Therefore, you should always have a physical checkup before you start a rigid exercise program.

3. Since television commercials help pay the cost of programming, and because I can always turn off the sound of the commercials, go to the bathroom, or get something to eat or drink, it follows that commercials are not such a bad thing.

4. Since television commercials disrupt the flow of programs, and given that any disruption impedes the continuity of a show, consequently we can safely say that commercials are a bad thing.

Video Tutorial

★ 5. We should never take our friends for granted. True friends are there when we need them. They suffer with us when we fail, and they are happy when we succeed.

6. They say that "absence makes the heart grow fonder," so my teachers should really love me, since I have been absent for the last 2 weeks.

7. I think, therefore I am.   René Descartes

8. I believe that androids will inherit the Earth because humans will eventually be destroyed by a meteor or pollution. Also, androids will soon be able to think and solve problems far better and faster than us.

Video Tutorial

★ 9. At one time Gary Kasparov had the highest ranking of any chess grandmaster in history. However, he was beaten in a chess tournament by a computer program called Deep Blue, so the computer program should be given a ranking higher than Kasparov.

10. It is true that $1 + 4 = 5$, and it is also true that $2 + 3 = 5$. Thus, we can conclude with certainty that $(1 + 4) = (2 + 3)$.

11. We are experiencing a loss of privacy through CCTV cameras tracking our every move. "Smart" homes and appliances can get us to change our behavior. Our children are manipulated by their toys and gadgets. Thus, humans will soon be stripped of their autonomy.

12. You should buy the digital camera at Cameras Galore. After all, you did say that you wanted the most megapixels you can get for up to $200. The digital camera on sale today at Cameras Galore has 5.0 megapixels and costs $200. But the digital camera on sale at Camera Warehouse has only 4.0 megapixels and it costs $150.

⭐13. The world will end on August 6, 2045. I know this because my guru said it would, and so far everything she predicted has happened exactly as she said it would.

14. You ought to start reading more books. Reading helps you to see other points of view. Reading improves critical thinking skills. Moreover, reading makes you a more interesting person.

15. Carbon dioxide emissions from coal combustion have risen steadily for the last ten years in the United States. Because more and more large coal reserves are being discovered, the cost of coal will continue to fall. This will lead to electric power companies and industries having no incentive to switch to cleaner energy sources. Therefore, we can expect to see an increase in carbon dioxide emissions from coal combustion for at least the next twenty years.

II. Identify and number the premises and conclusions in the following passages, and then diagram the argument. (The passages are taken from Exercises 1B II and 1C.)

1. All living things (plants, animals, humans) have the ability to absorb nourishment, to grow, and to propagate. All "living creatures" (animals and humans) have in addition the ability to perceive the world around them and to move about. Moreover, all humans have the ability to think, or otherwise to order their perceptions into various categories and classes. So there are in reality no sharp boundaries in the natural world.   Jostein Gaarder, *Sophie's World*

Answer: [1] All living things (plants, animals, humans) have the ability to absorb nourishment, to grow, and to propagate. [2] All "living creatures" (animals and humans) have in addition the ability to perceive the world around them and to move about. Moreover, [3] all humans have the ability to think, or otherwise to order their perceptions into various categories and classes. So [4] there are in reality no sharp boundaries in the natural world.

2. For the last 10 years the best picture Oscar has gone to a drama. A comedy has no chance of winning the Oscar for best picture this year.

3. An independent candidate will never win the presidency of the United States. This is because the two-party system of Democrats and Republicans is too powerful to let a third party get any wide base of support among the American voting public.

4. That God cannot lie is no advantage to your argument, because it is no proof that priests can not, or that the Bible does not.   Thomas Paine

⭐ 5. Sue hesitated; and then impulsively told the woman that her husband and herself had been unhappy in their first marriages, after which, terrified at the thought of a second irrevocable union, and lest the conditions of the contract should kill their love, yet wishing to be together, they had literally not found the courage to repeat it, though they had attempted it two or three times. Therefore, though in her own sense of the words she was a married woman, in the land-lady's sense she was not.   Thomas Hardy, *Jude the Obscure*

6. Since there is biological evidence that the genetic characteristics for nonviolence have been selected over time by the species, we should see an overall decrease in violence among humans worldwide in the coming centuries.

7. Project Gutenberg eBooks are often created from several printed editions, all of which are confirmed as Public Domain in the U.S. unless a copyright notice is included. Thus, we do not necessarily keep eBooks in compliance with any particular paper edition.   Project Gutenberg website

8. Stepan Arkadyevitch had learned easily at school, thanks to his excellent abilities, but he had been idle and mischievous, and therefore was one of the lowest in his class.   Leo Tolstoy, *Anna Karenina*

⭐ 9. We are intelligent beings: intelligent beings cannot have been formed by a crude, blind, insensible being: there is certainly some difference between the ideas of Newton and the dung of a mule. Newton's intelligence, therefore, came from another intelligence.   Voltaire, *Philosophical Dictionary*

10. Kedah Health Department employees who smoke will not be eligible for the annual excellence performance awards even if they do well in their work. The Director said, "Thirty percent or 3,900 of our 13,000 department personnel are smokers. As staff representing a health department, they should act as role models. Thus, I hope that they will quit smoking."
                      Embun Majid, "Health Department Snuffs Out Excellence Awards for Smokers"

11. The '80s debaters tended to forget that the teaching of vernacular literature is quite a recent development in the long history of the university. (The same could

be said about the relatively recent invention of art history or music as an academic research discipline.) So it is not surprising that, in such a short time, we
have not yet settled on the right or commonly agreed upon way to go about it.

Robert Pippin, "In Defense of Naïve Reading"

12. The officer shook his head, perplexed. The handprint on the wall had not been
made by the librarian himself; there hadn't been blood on his hands. Besides,
the print did not match his, and it was a strange print, the whorls of the fingers
unusually worn. It would have been easy to match, except that they'd never
recorded one like it.

Elizabeth Kostrova, *The Historian*

13. After supper she got out her book and learned me about Moses and the Bulrushers, and I was in a sweat to find out all about him; but by and by she let it out that
Moses had been dead a considerable long time; so then I didn't care no more
about him, because I don't take no stock in dead people.

Mark Twain, *Huckleberry Finn*

14. To me the similarities between the *Titanic* and *Challenger* tragedies are uncanny.
Both disasters could have been prevented if those in charge had heeded the
warnings of those who knew. In both cases, materials failed due to thermal
effects. For the *Titanic*, the steel of her hull was below its ductile-to-brittle transition temperature; and for the *Challenger*, the rubber of the O-rings lost pliability in sub-freezing temperatures. And both tragedies provoked a worldwide
discussion about the appropriate role for technology.

Mark E. Eberhart, *Why Things Break*

15. Your friends praise your abilities to the skies, submit to you in argument, and
seem to have the greatest deference for you; but, though they may ask it, you
never find them following your advice upon their own affairs; nor allowing you
to manage your own, without thinking that you should follow theirs. Thus, in
fact, they all think themselves wiser than you, whatever they may say.

Viscount William Lamb Melbourne, *Lord Melbourne's Papers*

16. I stated above that I am among those who reject the notion that a full-fledged
human soul comes into being the moment that a human sperm joins a human
ovum to form a human zygote. By contrast, I believe that a human soul—and,
by the way, it is my aim in this book to make clear what I mean by this slippery, shifting word, often rife with religious connotations, but here not having
any—comes slowly into being over the course of years of development. It may
sound crass to put it this way, but I would like to suggest, at least metaphorically, a numerical scale of "degrees of souledness." We can initially imagine it
as running from 0 to 100, and the units of this scale can be called, just for the
fun of it, "hunekers." Thus you and I, dear reader, both possess 100 hunekers of
souledness, or thereabouts.

Douglas Hofstadter, *I Am a Strange Loop*

Video Tutorial

★ 17. It may be no accident that sexual life forms dominate our planet. True, bacteria account for the largest number of individuals, and the greatest biomass. But by any reasonable measures of species diversity, or individual complexity, size, or intelligence, sexual species are paramount. And of the life forms that reproduce sexually, the ones whose reproduction is mediated by mate choice show the greatest biodiversity and the greatest complexity. Without sexual selection, evolution seems limited to the very small, the transient, the parasitic, the bacterial, and the brainless. For this reason, I think that sexual selection may be evolution's most creative force.   Geoffrey Miller, *The Mating Mind*

18. I don't know when children stop dreaming. But I do know when hope starts leaking away, because I've seen it happen. Over the years, I have spent a lot of time talking with school children of all ages. And I have seen the cloud of resignation move across their eyes as they travel through school without making any real progress. They know they are slipping through the net into the huge underclass that our society seems willing to tolerate. We must educate our children. And if we do, I believe that will be enough.

Alan Page, Minnesota Supreme Court Justice, NFL Hall of Fame Induction Speech

19. The Keynesian argument that if the private sector lacks confidence to spend, the government should spend is not wrong. But Keynes did not spell out where the government should spend. Nor did he envisage that lobbyists can influence government spending to be wasteful. Hence, every prophet can be used by his or her successors to prove their own points of view. This is religion, not science.

Andrew Sheng, "Economics Is a Religion, Not a Science"

III. Identify and number the premises and conclusions in the following passages, and then diagram the argument.

1. We will soon get more oil from areas of our country that were once protected by law. However, it has been projected that the amount of oil will be too small to have any serious effect on the overall oil supply. Although coal production will be raised, the amount will not meet the increased amount of energy that will be needed. In addition, new legislation has eliminated the requirement for the automobile industry to increase gas mileage in their new cars. So, it seems that gasoline prices will not go down in the near future.

Answer: [1] We will soon get more oil from areas of our country that were once protected by law. However, [2] it has been projected that the amount of oil will be too small to have any serious effect on the overall oil supply. [3] Although coal production will be raised, [4] the amount will not meet the increased amount of energy that will be needed. In addition, [5] new legislation has eliminated the requirement for the automobile industry to increase gas mileage in their new cars. So, [6] it seems that gasoline prices will not go down in the near future.

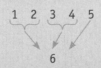

2. Driving a car without a seatbelt is dangerous. Statistics show you are 10 times more likely to be injured in an accident if you are not wearing a seat belt. Besides, in our state you can get fined $100 if you are caught not wearing one. You ought to wear one even if you are driving a short distance.

3. Jean studied at least 10 hours for the exam, and she got an A. Bill studied at least 10 hours for the exam, and he got an A. Sue studied at least 10 hours for the exam, and she got an A. Jim studied at least 10 hours for the exam. Jim probably got an A on the exam.

4. Fathers and mothers have lost the idea that the highest aspiration they might have for their children is for them to be wise—as priests, prophets or philosophers are wise. Specialized competence and success are all that they can imagine.

Allan Bloom, *The Closing of the American Mind*

★ 5. Death is not an event in life: we do not live to experience death. If we take eternity to mean not infinite temporal duration but timelessness, then eternal life belongs to those who live in the present. Our life has no end in just the way in which our visual field has no limits.

Ludwig Wittgenstein, *Tractatus Logico-Philosophicus*

Video Tutorial

6. But while college debt has proven a financial chokehold for some people, a four-year degree is still great insurance, especially in a tough job market: The unemployment rate for people with a bachelor's degree or higher was 4.5 percent in July, compared to 10.1 percent for those with only a high school diploma.

Allison Linn, "Is It Worth It to Go to College?"

7. We measure the success of schools not by the kinds of human beings they promote, but by whatever increases in reading scores they chalk up. We have allowed quantitative standards, so central to the adult economic system, to become the principal yardstick for our definition of our children's worth.

Kenneth Keniston, "The 11-Year-Olds of Today Are the Computer Terminals of Tomorrow"

8. We have discovered dozens and dozens of artfully disguised items that have posed a risk. The threats are real, the stakes are high, and we must prevail. When it comes to the Transportation Security Administration (TSA), we are the last line of defense. Therefore, full-body scanners and enhanced pat-downs are necessary to catch nonmetallic security threats.

John Pistole, Head of the TSA, quoted at Washingtonpost.com

★ 9. Because there is a law such as gravity, the universe can and will create itself from nothing. Spontaneous creation is the reason there is something rather than nothing, why the universe exists, why we exist. It is not necessary to invoke God to light the blue touch paper and set the universe going.

Stephen Hawking and Leonard Mlodinow, *The Grand Design*

Video Tutorial

10. Because robots can stage attacks with little immediate risk to the people who operate them, opponents say that robot warriors lower the barriers to warfare, potentially making nations more trigger-happy and leading to a new

technological arms race. "Wars will be started very easily and with minimal costs" as automation increases, predicted Wendell Wallach, a scholar at the Yale Interdisciplinary Center for Bioethics and chairman of its technology and ethics study group.   John Markoff, "U.S. Military Recruits Robots for Combat"

11. Although we like to think of young children's lives as free of troubles, they are in fact filled with disappointment and frustration. Children wish for so much, but can arrange so little of their own lives, which are so often dominated by adults without sympathy for the children's priorities. That is why children have a much greater need for daydreams than adults do. And because their lives have been relatively limited they have a greater need for material from which to form daydreams.   Bruno Bettelheim, "Children and Television"

12. I know that this world exists. That I am placed in it like my eye in its visual field. That something about it is problematic, which we call its meaning. This meaning does not lie in it but outside of it. That life is the world. That my will penetrates the world. That my will is good or evil. Therefore that good and evil are somehow connected with the meaning of the world.

                        Ludwig Wittgenstein, *Journal*

⬆ 13. The line that I am urging as today's conventional wisdom is not a denial of consciousness. It is often called, with more reason, a repudiation of mind. It is indeed a repudiation of mind as a second substance, over and above body. It can be described less harshly as an identification of mind with some of the faculties, states, and activities of the body. Mental states and events are a special subclass of the states and events of the human or animal body.

                        Willard Van Orman Quine, *Quiddities*

14. During the next few decades, many Haitian species of plants and animals will become extinct because the forests where they live, which originally covered the entire country, are nearly gone. The decline of frogs in particular, because they are especially vulnerable, is a biological early-warning signal of a dangerously deteriorating environment. When frogs start disappearing, other species will follow and the Haitian people will suffer, as well, from this environmental catastrophe.   "Scientists: Haiti's Wildlife Faces Mass Extinction," *Our Amazing Planet*

15. In fact, in a backward way, Vick has been the best thing to happen to pit bulls. "It's very true," says John Goodwin of the Humane Society of the United States. "For the big picture, Michael has been a tipping point. Since his case, there have been 30 new laws enacted all over the country toughening dog fighting penalties. Raids [on dog fighting rings] were up twice as much in 2008—after Vick—as they were in 2006, before him. There's much more awareness. People see it now and call it in."   Rick Reilly, "Time to Forgive Vick Is Here"

16. Institutionalized rejection of difference is an absolute necessity in a profit economy which needs outsiders as surplus people. As members of such an economy,

we have all been programmed to respond to the human differences between us with fear and loathing and to handle that difference in one of three ways: ignore it, and if that is not possible, copy it if we think it is dominant, or destroy it if we think it is subordinate. But we have no patterns for relating across our human differences as equals. As a result, those differences have been misnamed and misused in the service of separation and confusion.

Audre Lorde, "Age, Race, Class, and Sex: Women Redefining Difference"

17. It has only just begun to dawn on us that in our own language alone, not to speak of its many companions, the past history of humanity is spread out in an imperishable map, just as the history of the mineral earth lies embedded in the layers of its outer crust. But there is this difference between the record of the rocks and the secrets which are hidden in language: whereas the former can only give us knowledge of outward dead things—such as forgotten seas and the bodily shapes of prehistoric animals—language has preserved for us the inner living history of man's soul. It reveals the evolution of consciousness.

Owen Barfield, *History in English Words*

18. Logic is not concerned with human behavior in the same sense that physiology, psychology, and social sciences are concerned with it. These sciences formulate laws or universal statements which have as their subject matter human activities as processes in time. Logic, on the contrary, is concerned with relations between factual sentences (or thoughts). If logic ever discusses the truth of factual sentences it does so only conditionally, somewhat as follows: if such-and-such a sentence is true, then such-and-such another sentence is true. Logic itself does not decide whether the first sentence is true, but surrenders that question to one or the other of the empirical sciences. Rudolf Carnap, "Logic"

19. We learned that in addition to the noxious chemicals in our pricey blowouts, there were sketchy ingredients in just about everything we used—from our daily shampooing to our biweekly manicures. We also learned that only 11 percent of the 10,500 ingredients determined by the Food and Drug Administration (FDA) to be in use by the cosmetics industry have been tested for safety by a publicly accountable agency. Of the ones we do know about, some are flat-out dangerous to our health, others are questionable at best, and most are doing almost nothing to improve the quality, feel, and health of our skin and hair. So not only are these products wreaking some unspeakable havoc on our bodies, they're also making us look worse.

Siobhan O'Connor and Alexandra Spunt, *No More Dirty Looks*

20. All logical truth and all truths that logic can warrant must turn upon meaning in the sense of intension. Because logic and the logically certifiable comprise only such facts as are independent of all particular experience and are capable of being known with certainty merely through clear and cogent thinking. The same must hold of any analytic truth: if it is capable of being known by taking

thought about it, then it must be independent of meaning in the sense of extension and turn upon meanings only in the sense of intension.

Clarence Lewis, "The Modes of Meaning"

★ 21. It is a commonplace that all religion expresses itself in mythological or metaphorical terms; it says one thing and means another; it uses imagery to convey truth. But the crucial fact about religion is not that it is metaphor, but that it is unconscious metaphor. No one can express any thought without using metaphors, but this does not reduce all philosophy and science to religion, because the scientist knows that his metaphors are merely metaphors and that the truth is something other than the imagery by which it is expressed, whereas in religion the truth and the imagery are identified. To repeat the Creed as a religious act it is necessary not to add "All this I believe in a symbolical or figurative sense": to make that addition is to convert religion into philosophy.

R. G. Collingwood, "Outlines of a Philosophy of Art"

22. Leprosy is a disease caused by the bacteria *mycobacterium leprae*, which causes damage to the skin and the peripheral nervous system. Unfortunately, the history of leprosy and its interaction with man is one of suffering and misunderstanding. The newest research suggests that at least as early as 4000 B.C. individuals had been infected with the bacteria, while the first known written reference to the disease was found on Egyptian papyrus in about 1550 B.C. The disease was well recognized in ancient China, Egypt, and India, and there are several references to the disease in the Bible. Because the disease was poorly understood, very disfiguring, slow to show symptoms, and had no known treatment, many cultures thought the disease was a curse or punishment from the gods. Consequently, leprosy was left to be "treated" by priests or holy men, not physicians. Adapted from "Leprosy (Hansen's Disease)," MedicineNet, Inc.

23. The biggest misconception when discussing Los Angeles' attractiveness as a market is thinking every NFL owner would salivate at the prospect of having a team in the second biggest media market in the country and the entertainment capital of the world. That is simply not the case in the NFL's egalitarian model, in which all national revenues are equally divided among the 32 teams. In the NFL, the amount of money a team can generate from its stadium with as little risk as possible is what NFL owners are after. So if they can get their state, city, or county to completely subsidize the stadium while giving 100 percent of the revenue to the owner, as is the case in many NFL cities, that's the best possible deal. That would never happen in Los Angeles, and therefore moving an NFL team to L.A. has never made financial sense for an owner with a better deal in a smaller market. Arash Markazi, "A 16-Year Rocky Relationship"

Summary

- Diagramming premises and conclusions displays the relationships between all the parts of an argument.
- The first step in diagramming an argument is to number the statements as they appear in the argument. The next step is to diagram the relationships by connecting the premises to the conclusion with an arrow.
- Simple diagram: A diagram consisting of a single premise and a single conclusion.
- Premises are independent when the falsity of any one would not nullify the support the others give to the conclusion.
- Convergent diagram: Reveals the occurrence of independent premises.
- Dependent premises work together to support a conclusion. In other words, the falsity of one dependent premise weakens the support that the other dependent premises give to the conclusion.
- Linked diagram: Reveals the occurrence of dependent premises.
- Divergent diagram: Shows a single premise used to support independent conclusions.
- Serial diagram: Shows a conclusion from one argument that becomes a premise in a second argument.

Study Materials

KEY TERMS

convergent diagram 114	**independent premises** 114	**serial diagram** 116
dependent premises 114	**linked diagram** 115	**simple diagram** 114
divergent diagram 115		

LOGIC CHALLENGE: THE TRAIN TO VEGAS

You live in Los Angeles and decide to spend New Year's Eve in Las Vegas. You board the nonstop express train and consult the timetable for departures and arrivals. You read that it takes exactly 5 hours to get from Los Angeles to Las Vegas and the same length of time for the return trip. You also read that a train leaves each of the two cities every hour on the hour, and a train arrives in each of the two cities every hour on the hour. Now suppose for the sake of accuracy and precision of reasoning that every train runs perfectly on time. (Yes, this is a fantasy.)

The express trains have their own private set of tracks, so you will only pass those express trains that left Las Vegas. You decide to count the number of trains that you will pass on the trip. Your train leaves at 3:00 PM, and just as you are departing, sure enough a train from Las Vegas arrives. You begin counting with the train that just arrived, so it is train number 1.

How many express trains will you see by the end of your trip?

Chapter 4

Informal Fallacies

A. Why Study Fallacies?
B. Fallacies Based on Personal Attacks or Emotional Appeals
C. Weak Inductive Argument Fallacies
D. Fallacies of Unwarranted Assumption or Diversion
E. Recognizing Fallacies in Ordinary Language

Study Materials

We run into arguments everywhere—even when we are not looking for them. For example, you might be watching television, listening to the news, or watching a sporting event when you hear the following:

> For a number of years, seven-time Tour de France bicycle champion Lance Armstrong has been accused of using performance-enhancing drugs. An article in the French newspaper *L'Equipe* alleged that six of Armstrong's urine samples from the 1999 race were retested and found to contain the drug erythropoietin (EPO). If EPO is injected it can give an athlete a tremendous performance boost; however, it had already been banned by the Tour de France in 1999.
>
> Both the newspaper that published the report and the Tour de France race are owned by Amaury Sport Organization (ASO). In his response to the accusation by the newspaper, Armstrong said, "My question is how ASO can own the paper and the race."
>
> Adapted from Philip Hersh, "Armstrong, Defenders Not Forthright," *Chicago Tribune*

Armstrong's response avoided the question of his possible use of the drug, and shifted any potential wrongdoing to ASO. He deflected our attention away by implying that since the newspaper and the race have the same owner, they have formed a conspiracy against him. We now know that Armstrong finally admitted to using illegal doping techniques, and he has been stripped of all his Tour de France titles. Nevertheless, when asked how he felt about winning the races illegally, Armstrong said, "I feel that I won the races. . . . I know that is not a popular answer, but the reality is that . . . it was just a messy time," referring to widespread doping in cycling. "It was basically an arms race, and we all played ball that way." Armstrong tried to justify his behavior by saying that *because everyone did it*, he still considers himself the winner of the races.

We often encounter arguments that appear to be correct, but on close inspection they lack real merit. Trying to pin down why can be a challenge—or part of the game. Here is an example from a popular television show:

> *Homer*: Not a bear in sight. The Bear Patrol must be working like a charm!
> *Lisa*: That's specious reasoning, Dad.
> *Homer*: Thank you, dear.
> *Lisa*: By your logic I could claim that this rock keeps tigers away.
> *Homer*: Oh, how does it work?
> *Lisa*: It doesn't work.
> *Homer*: Uh-huh.
> *Lisa*: It's just a stupid rock.
> *Homer*: Uh-huh.
> *Lisa*: But I don't see any tigers around, do you?
> *Homer*: Lisa, I want to buy your rock.
>
> From "Much Apu About Nothing," *The Simpsons*

Homer has committed a fallacy, and he is not going to give it up without a fight.

The term "fallacy" derives from a Latin word meaning *to deceive*. (Another label for fallacies is revealing—"*non sequitur*," which literally means *it does not follow*.) Fallacious arguments are often misleading or deceptive, but they can also be unintentional. They can also be intentionally comic, like in *The Simpsons*. Clearly fallacious reasoning is often used in literature, movies, and jokes to point out the irrelevancy or absurdity of a statement or an argument.

Arguments purport to offer evidence for a conclusion, but they can fail, and some special cases of failure are classified as fallacies. A **formal fallacy** is a logical error that occurs in the form or structure of an argument. Formal fallacies are restricted to deductive arguments, and an understanding of deductive analysis and logical form makes it possible to recognize and understand them. (Formal fallacies were introduced in Chapter 1. They are developed in detail in Chapters 6, 7, and 8.) An **informal fallacy** is a mistake in reasoning that occurs in ordinary language and concerns the content of the argument rather than its form. Informal fallacies include mistakes of relevance, assumption, ambiguity, and diversion. In addition, some informal fallacies are persuasive because they involve fear, anger, pity, or even admiration. If we adopt fallacious reasoning, then we reduce our ability to reason properly, and if we accept other people's fallacious reasoning, then we erode our ability to critically assess arguments.

Good arguments have premises that are relevant and establish logical, reasonable ties to the conclusion. However, some informal fallacies use irrelevant premises. Although these fallacies have reasoning flaws, they can be psychologically persuasive. Other kinds of fallacies rely on assumptions that have not been justified. These fallacies assume the truth of a claim that has not been supported. When we uncover the unwarranted assumption, then we show the fallacious nature of the argument.

Formal fallacy A logical error that occurs in the form or structure of an argument; it is restricted to deductive arguments.

Informal fallacy A mistake in reasoning that occurs in ordinary language and concerns the content of the argument rather than its form.

Some fallacies misuse generalizations. The mistakes include making a generalization on the basis of insufficient or biased evidence. Other fallacies misapply the methods of science to make unsubstantiated cause-effect claims. We shall meet them all in this chapter.

The classification of fallacies into small groups is meant to help you recognize similarities among certain fallacies. These groups rely on the concept of "family resemblance," where the members of a group share some common characteristic. However, since this is *not* meant to be a rigid method of categorization, you can expect to see some general concepts, such as relevance, appear in more than one group. For example, we talked earlier about good arguments having *relevant* premises. But fallacies can suffer from an "irrelevancy" in many different ways. Therefore, the use of small groups is meant to help you to recognize a characteristic common to all members of a group, and to distinguish the specific characteristics of each group member.

A. WHY STUDY FALLACIES?

If you are aware of the existence of fallacies, and understand the specific nature of fallacious reasoning, then you can recognize examples in everyday life. Recognition, and the ability to expose the reasoning flaws in fallacies, arms you against the psychological power of persuasion that often accompanies fallacious reasoning.

Fallacies are instances of flawed reasoning whose premises do not offer good grounds for believing the conclusion. Although none of us want to believe what is false, we are all, on occasion, subject to the powers of persuasion. We must guard against such things as deception, the prejudice of stereotypes, and the acceptance of ungrounded beliefs. Unfortunately, it is often relatively easy and common to accept poor reasoning for a strongly held belief. But it is not enough to have strong beliefs; we must also have strong reasons and strong arguments to support our beliefs. By studying fallacies you will be less likely to make these mistakes. Since we are all inundated with information on a daily basis, we need to have critical thinking skills that we can apply naturally and consistently, whether in the area of politics, advertisements, work, school, or even personal relationships.

Each type of fallacy has a specific flaw, yet there are some general aspects that allow us to group related fallacies together. Knowing how to recognize and analyze instances of fallacies protects us from their illogical lure and gives us a better understanding and appreciation of instances of good reasoning.

B. FALLACIES BASED ON PERSONAL ATTACKS OR EMOTIONAL APPEALS

Both the *truth of a statement* and the *strength of an argument* should be judged on objective grounds. We can reject a *statement* if we have credible, objective evidence that contradicts the claim. However, we should *not* reject a statement merely because we have a strong opinion against it. We need to back up our rejection with factual evidence. We can reject an *argument* if we base our criticism on logical analysis and truth value analysis. For example, the argument might be *invalid* (deductive) or *weak* (inductive). On the other hand, the argument might be valid but *unsound*, or else it might be strong but *uncogent*. However, when an argument is rejected based solely on an *attack against the person* making the argument, not on the merits of the argument itself, then a fallacy occurs. We will explore four types of fallacies based on personal attacks and then look at three types of fallacious appeals to emotion that attempt to get us to accept a conclusion. These kinds of arguments employ psychological tactics that draw on group solidarity, or the desire to belong to a group.

Fallacies Based on Personal Attacks

1. AD HOMINEM ABUSIVE

The *ad hominem* **abusive** fallacy is distinguished by an attack on alleged character flaws of a person instead of the person's argument. ("*Ad hominem*" means *against the person*.) Generally speaking, a person's character is irrelevant to the determination of the truth or falsity of her claims, or the strength of her argument. Clear cases of *ad hominem* abusive are not difficult to recognize. They divert attention away from the logical determination of the strength of an argument, and instead denigrate the character of the person making the argument. Here are some examples:

- You should not believe what he says about our economy because he is a left-leaning, card-carrying liberal.
- She is old, out of touch with reality, and belongs in a loony bin. So, you cannot accept her advice on marriage.
- Don't listen to her criticism of our senator. After all, she is too young and probably experimented with drugs when she was in college.

In all these cases, the reason to reject someone's statement or position is based on irrelevant information. In the first example, an economic argument should be judged on the merits of the advice and strength of the argument presented, not by vague labels denigrating a person's character. In the second example, the age of the person offering advice has no bearing on the strength or weakness of her argument. Furthermore, no evidence is given to show that the person has any mental impairment that might affect her reasoning. Finally, in the third example, the criticism of the senator should be judged on the logical strength of the arguments and the factual nature of the claims. The person's age or college experiences are irrelevant to the merits of her argument. All of the fallacies fail because they avoid a logical analysis of whether the opponent's arguments are valid or invalid (deductive), strong or weak (inductive). The fallacies also avoid a truth value analysis of whether the opponent's premises are true or false, and whether the arguments are sound or unsound, cogent or uncogent.

2. AD HOMINEM CIRCUMSTANTIAL

The *ad hominem* **circumstantial** fallacy occurs when someone's argument is rejected based on the circumstances of a person's life. Circumstances are different from

Ad hominem abusive The fallacy is distinguished by an attack on alleged character flaws of a person instead of the person's argument.

Ad hominem circumstantial When someone's argument is rejected based on the circumstances of the person's life.

character. For example, political affiliation, educational institution, place of birth, religious affiliation, and income are circumstances connected to people's lives. When we insinuate that someone's circumstances dictate the truth or falsity of their claims or the strength of their arguments, then we are once again attacking the person rather than the claim. These kinds of attacks also include the use of negative stereotypes, such as racial, sexual, or religious stereotypes, and can be subtle or overtly dismissive. However, they do not advance anyone's cause. A reference to any kind of stereotype is irrelevant to the determination of the strength of an argument. Here is an example:

> Of course Senator Hilltop argues that my administration's tax proposals are bad for the country. But since her party lost the last election, her opinions have no credibility.

The passage clearly shows that Senator Hilltop's reasons for why she is against the tax proposals, whether good or not, are not even being considered. This is an obvious instance of *ad hominem* circumstantial; it attacks the senator's party affiliation instead of her argument.

The following two arguments illustrate the same point:

- You told us why you are against raising taxes. But we know the real reason is that you are a billionaire, and you want to hold on to as much of your money as you can.
- I heard your argument why you are against euthanasia. But you failed to point out the real reason: You are a physician, so you make money only if terminally ill people are kept alive as long as possible.

In the first example, no details of the argument against raising taxes are addressed. Instead, the rejection of the argument rests entirely on the person's wealth. In the second example, the physician's argument is rejected, not by any logical analysis or counterexample, but simply by the circumstances of the person being a physician.

3. POISONING THE WELL

Poisoning the well The fallacy occurs when a person is attacked *before* she has a chance to present her case.

A third version of *ad hominem* argument, called **poisoning the well**, occurs when a person is attacked *before* she has a chance to present her case. The attacker mentions something about the opponent's character or life and uses that information to warn the audience not to believe anything they hear or read. For example:

> Before you read her article "Stop All Wars," you should know that she was arrested six times for protesting in front of the Pentagon and White House. She also has been investigated by the FBI for possible ties to peace movements in other countries, some of which resulted in violence. It is crystal clear that these kinds of people are dangerous and want to destroy our Constitution and take away our basic freedoms. We must not let them.

As illustrated by the passage, the fallacy uses abusive or circumstantial evidence to paint a negative opinion of someone before that person has a chance to make her case. This can be an effective way to influence an audience, but it has no logical credibility.

4. *TU QUOQUE*

The fourth type of *ad hominem* fallacy is known as **tu quoque** (meaning *you too* or *look who's talking*). It is distinguished by the specific attempt of one person to avoid the issue at hand by claiming the other person is a hypocrite. In other words, the fallacy occurs when someone points to the discrepancy between another person's *claim* and *actions* as a basis for discrediting the other person's *claim*. For example:

> You have been lecturing me about not joining a gang. But Dad, you were a gang member, and you never went to jail. So, I'll make my own decision about joining a gang.

The premises are used to imply the following: *Dad, you are a hypocrite.* This result is then used to reject the dad's arguments: *Because you are a hypocrite, I can disregard your lectures.* As we can see from the reconstructed argument, the conclusion is the result of a *tu quoque* fallacy. The fallacy occurs because the argument attacks the dad, not the dad's arguments.

Another example comes from the political world. If a U.S. senator criticizes the human rights failings of China by offering a detailed description of recorded UN inquiries, a Chinese representative might say the following:

> The senator should look in his own backyard. What about the complete disregard of the universal rights of people who the U.S. government incarcerates without any recourse to courts or a lawyer? What about the U.S. policy of spying on its own citizens without a court order? The senator should not throw stones when he lives in a glass house. Let me remind him that "whoever is without sin let him cast the first stone."

Other than stringing together a number of clichés, this response offers no rational rebuttal of the assertions of human rights violations.

Instances of *tu quoque* fallacies occur quite often in personal arguments. For example, a child might say the following:

> Mom, I don't know why you keep pressuring me to give up smoking. You keep showing me statistics proving that smoking is bad for my health, that it will shorten my life, that it costs too much money. But you started smoking at my age and only recently quit. How can you honestly tell me to stop?

Since there are many good reasons to support the conclusion that someone should stop smoking, these reasons must be rationally argued against. To attack the person making the argument rather than the argument is to commit the fallacy.

Ad hominem fallacies follow a similar pattern:

a. Person X presents an argument.
b. Person Y attacks the character or circumstances of person X.
c. Based solely on the attack against person X, person Y rejects person X's argument.

Tu quoque The fallacy is distinguished by the specific attempt of one person to avoid the issue at hand by claiming the other person is a hypocrite.

The general pattern illustrates the importance of recognizing that any criticism of a person's argument should be restricted to their argument and should not be based on *ad hominem* attacks. (The pattern is slightly different for *poisoning the well* fallacies, where the person under attack has yet to make her argument.) All *ad hominem* fallacies rest on the same kind of reasoning errors—the rejection of an opponent's argument by criticizing a person's character or circumstances, and the absence of any logical or factual analysis of the opponent's argument.

When the fallacy does not occur: There are some instances where an argument might appear to commit an *ad hominem* fallacy but it does not. For example, if someone has previously been exposed as a liar based on contradictions in statements given under oath, then there are objective grounds for suspicion about any current or future *statements*. Likewise, if the person presents an argument, we might have reason to question the accuracy of some of his premises. In that case, pointing out specific instances of an untrustworthy character would not be fallacious since there are objective grounds for doubting the person's claims. It is important to acknowledge that by rejecting a known liar's claim we are *not* saying that his claims are in fact false; we are simply saying that we have a good reason not to believe him.

Another exception is when someone's argument is *not* under consideration, but his or her character is being described. For example:

> Bernard Madoff is guilty of one of the most infamous financial frauds in history. The evidence against him was so strong that he pled guilty to eleven felonies, including money laundering, perjury, and wire fraud. It's safe to say he will spend the rest of his life in prison because he would be over 200 years old when he is eligible for release in the year 2139. The perjury charge means that he is a liar. He is also a cheat and a person without conscience, with no sympathy for his victims. By any moral sense, Madoff is a most despicable character.

Although the passage does conclude something about Madoff's character, it *does not* reject any of Madoff's arguments. Thus, it is not an instance of an *ad hominem* argument.

Fallacies Based on Emotional Appeals

Some arguments rely solely on the arousal of a strong emotional state or psychological reaction to get us to accept a conclusion. This fallacious tactic has been used by tyrants and bigots throughout history, with devastating social effects. It often appeals to a mob mentality, an "us against them" attitude, with a fixation on fear or hate. Exposing the fallacy can sometimes be the first step in defeating this potentially harmful social ill.

The first type of appeal to emotion that we will cover relies on the desire to belong to a group that is admired, or appeal to the people. This tactic is used effectively by many advertisements. The next kind of appeal to emotion covered relies exclusively on our sense of pity and mercy. Finally, we will address an appeal to emotion that relies on fear or the heavy hand of force to sway people to agree to a conclusion they might not otherwise accept.

5. APPEAL TO THE PEOPLE

The fallacy of **appeal to the people** occurs when an argument manipulates a psychological need or desire, such as the desire to belong to a popular group, or the need for group solidarity, so that the reader or listener will accept the conclusion. However, the avoidance of objective evidence in favor of an emotional response defeats the goal of a rational investigation of truth. We will look at three forms of the fallacy.

The first form makes an emotional appeal based on the psychological force of *group solidarity*. An arguer who uses an emotional response based on the power of one's connection to a group is also known to be "rallying the troops." Appeals to the people are usually laced with emotionally charged words that arouse strong feelings for or against some deep-seated belief. For example:

> We must not let our country be taken over by illegal aliens. After all, they knowingly and brazenly broke the law by entering illegally, so they are nothing but criminals. They will continue to flout our laws, steal our jobs, and threaten our very way of life.

The passage has a series of emotionally charged phrases: "brazenly broke the law," "nothing but criminals," "flout our laws," and "threaten our very way of life." This kind of emotional appeal can be dangerous because mob psychology is often violent. In groups, people will often do things they would not do alone. The group offers a psychological protective shield that insulates individual members from having to think for themselves. The phrase "to run amok" captures the irrational aspect of mob mentality.

Political pollsters also use the appeal to the people tactic. They can manipulate poll questions so that the appeal to an emotional response overrides the rational grounds for a person's belief. Here is an example of a rhetorical, or loaded, question:

> Public schoolteachers are demanding a pay raise and threaten to strike if they don't get it. A prolonged strike will jeopardize our children's future. In addition, some economists predict that any substantial pay raise will result in an unbalanced budget, which in turn will lead to an increase in taxes. Although the school year lasts only 180 days, the teachers get paid 12 months a year, whether or not school is in session. So are you for or against a pay raise for public schoolteachers?

Although the final sentence is a rhetorical question, it is obvious that it is disguised as a statement: *You should be against a pay raise for public schoolteachers*. The language employed is meant to appeal to the emotions of taxpayers and voters. The terms "demanding," "threaten," "prolonged strike," and "jeopardize" are used to evoke a sense of dire consequences and to provoke anger. The argument offers negative consequences of a teachers' pay raise, but only as possibilities, not as facts. Also, the mention of higher taxes serves to fuel the emotions of voters.

A second form of appeal to the people draws on an individual's desire to belong to a popular group. This form of the fallacy is called the *bandwagon effect*. The fallacy derives its name from the emotions involved in joining a movement merely because it is popular (to "jump on the bandwagon"). Advertisements often prey on the appeal

Appeal to the people
The fallacy occurs when an argument manipulates a psychological need or desire, such as the desire to belong to a popular group, or the need for group solidarity, so that the reader or listener will accept the conclusion.

of being included in a popular fad and the pressure of being left out. Here are some examples of the bandwagon effect fallacy:

- More than 80% of families have given up their old landline phones and switched to cell phones. Don't be the last to make the change. Hurry and get yours now and feel the excitement of calling from anywhere.
- The PlayBox 6 is the number one game console in America. Your friends probably own them. Why wait to use theirs? Ask your parents to get you one today.
- Hard Pink Lemonade has captured the taste of adults. Sales have tripled in the last 6 months. But don't take our word for it. Ask your friends. Better yet, get some and be the life of the next party.

Fallacious bandwagon arguments conclude that you should do something simply because "everyone else is doing it."

The third form of the appeal to the people fallacy occurs as a common thread that runs through some advertising campaigns. The idea rests on the desire of some people to belong to an *exclusive* or *elite group*. For example, many people wish to be rich or famous. This is different from the bandwagon effect, in that the desire is *not* to follow the lead of a large group but a small elite group instead. The fallacy occurs when the argument avoids objective evidence in favor of a direct emotional appeal that activates the desire.

Slick ads are created in order to arouse a desire to attain the product. Such products are often displayed being used by an exclusive group: the rich, the beautiful, the successful—in other words, the lucky few. The obvious implication is that if you use this product, you will be transformed into one of the lucky ones. Such ads push psychological buttons: the need to belong to a group, the desire to be respected, the desire to be successful, and so on. Playing upon emotions is a powerful tool that is understood and effectively used by corporations to sell their products. For example:

> You work hard. You deserve more from life. Don't get stuck in a boring routine. Driving the new turbo-charged Zephyer will have everyone looking at you. Get one and turn heads.

The desire to stand out is also powerful motivation, and it is a desire on which many advertisers design their campaigns. Here is another example:

> Why just watch sports? Why not become the athlete you know you are. Hard-Armour T-shirts. For the athlete deep inside you waiting to get out.

Although the tactics used in appeals to the people can often influence people's behavior, they have no logical credibility.

6. APPEAL TO PITY

Appeal to pity The fallacy results from an exclusive reliance on a sense of pity or mercy for support of a conclusion.

A second type of the fallacious appeal to emotion is the **appeal to pity**, which exclusively relies on a sense of pity or mercy for support of a conclusion. For example, a defense attorney may attempt to get the jury to sympathize with the defendant prior to deliberation. If the defendant is found guilty, then the appeal may be addressed to the judge, asking for a light sentence based on the effects that a harsh sentence would have on the defendant's family. On the other side, the prosecution may appeal to the jury to sympathize with the victim. The prosecutor may also appeal to the judge to consider the emotional devastation inflicted on the victim's family. In this way, she may persuade the judge to sentence the defendant to the maximum penalty allowed by law. However, trials are, ideally, rational decision-making processes whose goals are to weigh evidence objectively. If pity is substituted for evidence and the rule of law, then the judgment is fallacious.

Here is an example:

> Your honor, before you sentence my client for the murder of his parents, I ask you to consider his situation. He is an orphan. Perhaps you can give him the lightest punishment possible.

The premises provide no objective evidence for a light punishment. The argument is ironic since the premises ask the judge to pity the defendant because he is a self-caused orphan.

Many charities arouse a sense of pity, and perhaps even guilt, when they solicit pledges of support. These charities know that people do not always act rationally and in their own best interests. Nevertheless, any cause worthy of support should have rational, legitimate reasons, which, when understood, should be sufficient to get people to give. In addition to evoking our human sense of compassion for those who are suffering, a *legitimate* argument will not have to rely solely on pity to support its conclusion.

7. APPEAL TO FEAR OR FORCE

A third type of the fallacious appeal to emotion relies on fear or the threat of harmful consequences (physical or otherwise) and is called the **appeal to fear or force.** The perceived threat places pressure on a person or group that, when effective, causes the person or group to reluctantly accept a course of action that otherwise would be unacceptable. For example, there are recorded instances where witnesses and jurors have been threatened with physical harm to themselves or to their families if they go against a defendant. In a different setting, it has been revealed that some voters have been pressured into changing their vote by the threat of violence. However, the threat need not be so overt and directly physical. For example, a company may send out the following memo to its employees:

> If the workers of this company do not agree to a 25% cut in salary, then the company may have to shut its doors. Therefore, the workers of this company must agree to a 25% cut in salary.

Appeal to fear or force
A threat of harmful consequences (physical or otherwise) used to force acceptance of a course of action that would otherwise be unacceptable.

The premise is an obvious threat. It does not, by itself, provide objective evidence for the conclusion. If the company is in bad financial shape, then there should be objective evidence to present to the workers that shows that without the pay cut the company would be forced to close. Without this evidence, the threat by the company to close its doors unless its employees take a pay cut results in an instance of the fallacy of appeal to fear or force.

The following example illustrates the same point. A parent may threaten a child with loss of privileges or being grounded in order to achieve desired results:

> You had better get straight A's on your next report card. If you don't, then we will have to punish you. You will not be allowed to go out with your friends for a month.

It is not difficult to imagine perfectly legitimate reasons why students should get good grades. Rational, objective evidence can be used as support for why students should do well in school. However, anytime an overt or implied threat is used to convince someone to make a decision, in the absence of supporting evidence for the conclusion, the rational decision-making process is subverted.

Fallacious appeals to emotion follow a similar pattern:

a. Person A uses psychological methods known to arouse strong emotions: appeals to group solidarity; jumping on the bandwagon; the desire to belong to an admired group; a sense of pity; and fear or the threat of force.

b. Person B is expected to accept the conclusion based solely on the emotional appeal.

The general pattern illustrates the importance of recognizing that when premises are irrelevant they fail to support the conclusion.

Summary of Fallacies Based on Personal Attacks

Fallacies based on personal attacks occur when someone's argument is rejected based solely on an *attack against the person* making the argument, not on the merits of the argument itself.

1. *Ad hominem* **abusive:** The fallacy is distinguished by an attack on alleged character flaws of a person instead of the person's argument.
2. *Ad hominem* **circumstantial:** The fallacy occurs when someone's argument is rejected based on the circumstances of the person's life.
3. **Poisoning the well:** The fallacy occurs when a person is attacked *before* she has a chance to present her case.
4. *Tu quoque***:** The fallacy is distinguished by the specific attempt of one person to avoid the issue at hand by claiming the other person is a hypocrite.

Summary of Fallacies Based on Emotional Appeals

Fallacies based on emotional appeals occur when an argument relies solely on the arousal of a strong emotional state or psychological reaction to get a person to accept the conclusion.

5. **Appeal to the people:** The fallacy occurs when an argument manipulates a psychological need or desire, such as the desire to belong to a popular group,

or the need for group solidarity, so that the reader or listener will accept the conclusion.

6. **Appeal to pity:** The fallacy results from an exclusive reliance on a sense of pity or mercy for support of a conclusion.

7. **Appeal to fear or force:** The fallacy occurs when a threat of harmful consequences (physical or otherwise) is used to force acceptance of a course of action that would otherwise be unacceptable.

EXERCISES 4B

I. Determine whether each statement is true or false.

1. *Tu quoque* is distinguished by the specific attempt of one person to avoid the issue at hand by claiming the other person is a hypocrite.

Answer: True

Level 1 Multiple-Choice Questions

2. *Ad hominem* fallacies occur when an argument uses character flaws or circumstances of people's lives to reject their claims.

3. The appeal to pity occurs when the character flaws of a person are used against him or her.

Level 2 Multiple-Choice Questions

4. The appeal to fear or force uses rational reasons in support of a controversial position.

⭐ 5. An example of the bandwagon effect is when an appeal is made to increase the group solidarity of an elite group.

6. A threat of harmful consequences (physical or otherwise) used to force acceptance of a course of action that would otherwise be unacceptable is called an appeal to pity.

7. An appeal to join an exclusive group is an *ad hominem* fallacy.

8. An *ad hominem* circumstantial fallacy occurs when someone's argument is rejected based on the circumstances of the person's life.

⭐ 9. A poisoning the well fallacy occurs when a person is attacked *before* she has a chance to present her case.

Level 1 Multiple-Choice Questions

10. A fallacious appeal to emotion occurs when an argument relies solely on the arousal of a strong emotional state or psychological reaction to get a person to accept the conclusion.

II. Read the following passages. If an argument commits a fallacy of a personal attack or an emotional appeal, then identify the specific fallacy. If a passage does not contain a fallacy, then answer "No fallacy." Explain your answers.

Level 2 Multiple-Choice Questions

1. You just bought that book, but I recommend that you don't read it. Everything he writes is false. All he does is spend time promoting his book on TV, radio talk shows, and in magazines trying to get people interested so it will become a best seller.

    Answer: Poisoning the well. The fallacy occurs when a person is attacked *before* he has a chance to present his case.

2. She did not vote in the last election. In fact, she is not even registered to vote. It follows that anything she suggests about how our country should be run cannot possibly be of any concern to us.

3. You spend most of your time in your room reading books. When I was your age, I played all types of sports. So, if you don't start joining some teams, then I won't give you any more money to buy books, and I'll tear up your library card.

4. My uncle drinks a six-pack of beer a day, so I couldn't believe it when he lectured me on the dangers of alcohol. He's one to talk! Nothing he says about drinking can be true because he cannot stop drinking himself.

★ 5. My opponent says that he is well qualified for city council. But he failed to tell you that he was arrested twice. Once for protesting the war in Iraq, and once during the Occupy Wall Street demonstrations. It is obvious that he hates our country and is a liar. I urge you, therefore, to reject his candidacy.

6. HD3D TVs have set the new standard in television viewing. All we ask is that you go into any of our stores and look at one yourself. We bet that you will join the millions of others who have switched.

7. Maybe you didn't know that she is an orphan. Her outrageous behavior should be excused because of her background.

8. In the past 3 months, you missed work without calling in five times, and each time you couldn't produce a doctor's note. On two occasions in 1 week, you left work early without notifying your supervisor. You fell asleep at your desk and missed two important calls from clients. Given this poor record, we have decided to let you go.

★ 9. In that newspaper article, she argued that the works of Charles Darwin caused the world's major religions to reconcile their basic beliefs with the results of science. Of course she would say that. After all, she teaches biology, so she must be an atheist.

10. This team beat us 64–0 last year. So we need to go out and give them a taste of their own medicine and see how they like it. Are you ready to fight?

11. My aunt just stopped eating meat, and now she is lecturing everyone to give it up. She cites all this stuff from medical journals and other scientific research showing the harmful long-term effects of eating red meat. But she ate red meat most of her life, so why should I listen to her?

12. Mr. Jenkins has submitted a detailed proposal for our city's revitalization project. I happen to know Mr. Jenkins. In my honest opinion, he is argumentative, inflexible, and highly opinionated. Given these insurmountable obstacles, I must conclude that we should reject his proposal.

⭐13. This administration is proposing lots of dangerous ideas. For example, it wants to raise taxes on the wealthy; it wants to expand Medicare and Medicaid coverage to the poor; it wants to cut military spending; it wants to eliminate many capital gains deductions; and it wants to spend more money on government projects. But all their fancy speech and slick arguments are just a smokescreen to hide their true communist intentions. If we don't vote them out of office we will be slaves to their dictatorial regime.

14. You should forget that she spent both of your savings on losing lottery tickets. After all, she is penniless and unemployed.

15. Macrobiotic diets and gluten-free foods are the hottest trends among today's health-conscious and savvy people. Therefore, you should join the smart set.

16. Tomorrow night you will hear the president's budget proposal. It will be the same old, tired economic arguments as the last 4 years. The president has fooled the public for too long with false promises and unrealistic goals. Therefore, if you listen to her carefully, you will see that I am right.

⭐17. That physician is a male, so he couldn't possibly know anything about female health problems.

18. Your daughter was caught breaking into the school's computer lab. She said that she wanted to copy some expensive software programs to sell to her friends so she could make some money. We have no choice but to suspend her from school, pending a police investigation.

19. I know you don't want to visit your grandparents, but if you don't go, then you can't go to the concert next month. In fact, you won't be able to see your friends, except in school, for the rest of the semester.

20. She did not do well on the exams; nevertheless, you should give her an A for the course. After all, she is taking 18 credits and is holding down a full-time job.

⭐21. Our biology teacher tried to convince us that "creation science" is not an acceptable part of science because it doesn't fit the methods and standards of acceptable science. He is a liar and a bully who likes to see students fail. He tries to intimidate students, so there's no reason to accept his arguments.

22. I know your cousin recommends taking vitamins every day. After all, she's a pharmacist; what do you expect her to tell you?

23. The Snake Charmers have sold out every concert on their latest world tour, and their new single, "Python Mounties," reached No. 1 in the first week of its

release. People everywhere are clamoring to get tickets to the upcoming concert. Don't get shut out. Hurry and get yours before your friends beat you to it.

24. You have successfully completed both the written exam and the motor vehicle operation parts as required by the state. Thus, you are eligible to get your driver's license.

★25. You are about to hear a proposal to clean up the pollution in our local river. The speaker will make some wild claims about health effects, but her evidence is suspect. Of course, she will swear that she is telling you the truth, but don't fall for her stories. It's very important that you reject her proposals.

26. If you don't break off your relationship with him, your mother and I will disinherit you. So, you'd better end the relationship now.

27. You tell me to wear a seat belt when I drive because it will protect me in case I get in an accident. I never see you wear one when you drive, so why should I wear one?

28. Our political party lost the last election, not because of our platform, but because we allowed the opposition to dictate the debate. Now is not the time to be on the defensive. We must not apologize for our beliefs, which, as you will all agree, are based on the core principles of the Founding Fathers, who fought for what they believed was right for the country. Let's not sit back and see liberty destroyed. I expect everyone to take the fight to our opponents.

★29. Fighting pollution is something everyone can do. All it takes is a few minutes of your time. For example, turn off lights that are not being used and use recycle bins. Try not to waste water. None of these simple guidelines require much time or effort.

30. His reasons for believing that humans do not need a religious basis for morality should be rejected. After all, he is an atheist, so he cannot possibly have anything relevant to say on ethical issues.

31. You need to stop wearing those clothes. Just look at some teen magazines and check out the latest fashions at the mall. No one cool wears that style anymore.

32. Of course you should pay us for protection. Here's why. If you don't, we will have to break your arms, wreck your business, and harass your customers.

★33. I'm running for school president. A lot of you know me, but perhaps you don't know my opponent. Soon she will tell you why she deserves your vote. But I want to warn you that she is very argumentative, sharply critical, and finds fault with everyone. In fact, I'll bet you that she objects to everything I say. So, stay on guard and don't fall for her negative remarks.

34. You have received this letter because someone loves you. This chain letter has been around the world fifty times. I urge you to send a copy to five close friends. Some people who have broken the chain suffered tragic consequences. So, if you don't want to suffer unnecessarily, you must not break the chain.

35. The committee to reelect Senator Hatfield is meeting this Wednesday. We will also be taking applications for volunteer projects. Therefore, if you have any fresh ideas that you would like the committee to consider, bring them to the meeting.

36. We need City Hall to fix our neighborhood. Are we just going to sit back and be ignored? Are we nobodies that the power elite can ignore? We all know the answer, so I urge you to sign the petition.

⭐ 37. Jimmy sent us an e-mail laying out the details for starting a club. But Jimmy has been known to cheat on his income tax returns. Given that, how good could his ideas be?

38. I know that Senator Wickhaven has been found guilty of harassment, but did you know that he was twice wounded in the Korean War? Since he has suffered so much for our country, he should not be punished for this crime.

39. Our cars are not for everyone. In order to fully appreciate them, you must enjoy being pampered by the finest custom-made seats, state-of-the-art sound system, and personalized temperature controls. Don't settle for the ordinary.

40. The main character in that movie was vain, superficial, self-centered, and arrogant. So, it's not surprising that his partner left him.

⭐ 41. He is not a psychiatrist, so his arguments and explanations for why some people are addicted to gambling cannot be correct.

42. After lunch today, my assistant football coach gave me some advice. He saw me drinking soda, eating a candy bar, and smoking a cigarette. He said that if I wanted to maximize my potential as an athlete, I need to give up stuff that is bad for my health. Have you ever seen that guy? He is really overweight and smokes cigars. It's obvious that he has nothing to offer to make me a top athlete.

43. Our golf establishment admits only a few new members every year. Our standards are high, but why settle for something that anyone can have? See if you have what it takes to be among a special group.

44. He failed his final exam, so don't blame him for destroying his dorm room.

⭐ 45. Since that sports reporter is a female, her analysis of what caused our team to lose the game is irrelevant.

46. My supervisor said that I should try not to miss any work days during my first 6-month evaluation period. She also said that it would help me stand out to the upper management if I volunteer to work overtime. I've been working for only 1 month, but in that time she has taken three sick days, and she never works overtime. Given her bad example, I'm not going to listen to her career advice.

47. You can't give me an F on the exam. If you do, my mother and father will be so upset they will have to be hospitalized.

48. The reporter cited evidence that alcohol consumption among college students has been steadily declining for the last 20 years. But she used to be a college student, so she will twist the facts to make herself look good.

★ 49. The witness has been twice convicted of perjury. Given this evidence, we should doubt the truth of his testimony.

50. Our competitors have accused us of manipulating market prices. But let me remind you that 10 years ago those very same competitors were fined $2 million for price manipulation. So, why should anyone believe their charges against us?

C. WEAK INDUCTIVE ARGUMENT FALLACIES
Generalization Fallacies

A generalization fallacy occurs when an argument relies on a mistaken use of the principles behind making a generalization. For example, it is not unusual for someone to have a negative experience with members of a group and then quickly stereotype the other members by assigning derogatory characteristics to all or most of the group. On the other hand, a generalization may be mistakenly applied to a case that is an exception to the rule. We will explore several types of generalization fallacies, but first we need to define a few terms to help our analysis.

A *sample* is part of a population. A *population* is any group of objects, not just human groups. A *representative sample* occurs when the characteristics of a sample are correctly identified and matched to the population under investigation. If the premises of an argument rely on an unrepresentative sample, intentionally or unintentionally, then they fail to provide relevant objective evidence for the conclusion. The result is a weak generalization.

8. RIGID APPLICATION OF A GENERALIZATION

Rigid application of a generalization When a generalization or rule is inappropriately applied to the case at hand. The fallacy results from the belief that the generalization or rule is universal (meaning it has no exceptions).

The fallacy of a **rigid application of a generalization** arises when a generalization is inappropriately applied to the case at hand. The fallacy results from the belief that the generalization or rule is universal (meaning it has no exceptions). In fact, many generalizations and rules have exceptions—a special case that does not fall under the general rule. We often make allowances for circumstances that permit breaking a rule. (In fact, *exceptions to the rule* are sometimes called "accidental circumstances," so the fallacy is also called the *fallacy of accident*.) Therefore, to rigidly apply an otherwise acceptable generalization, even in the face of known exceptions, is to commit the fallacy of rigid application of a rule. For example, suppose someone says the following:

> I can't believe the police didn't give the driver of that ambulance any citations. He was speeding, he went through a red light, and the ambulance swerved from lane to lane without using any turn signals.

It is true that under nonemergency circumstances the driver's behavior would be subject to penalties. However, exceptions apply to ambulance drivers, firefighters, and police when they are responding to emergencies. Therefore, the speaker in the foregoing example has rigidly applied an otherwise acceptable generalization in the face of known exceptions. The mistake in this case is the belief that there are no exceptions to the rule.

Here is another example:

> My cousin's illegal drug supply was stolen last week. Luckily, the thief was caught. Therefore, the police have to return my cousin's stolen drug supply to him.

Normally, stolen property is returned to the original owner (usually after it has been presented as evidence in the event of a trial). However, if the stolen property is illegal drugs or counterfeit money, then the property will not be returned. Therefore, the speaker in the foregoing example has rigidly applied an otherwise acceptable generalization in the face of known exceptions. Once again, the mistake is believing that there are no exceptions to the rule.

9. HASTY GENERALIZATION

In order to explore the next type of generalization fallacy, we return to an earlier example. It is common for someone to notice a few negative characteristics of the members of a particular group and, on that basis alone, conclude that the majority of the group has the same negative characteristic. However, it is improbable that such a small sample is representative of the entire group. An argument that relies on a small sample that is unlikely to represent the population commits the fallacy of **hasty generalization**. This fallacy proceeds in the opposite direction from the rigid application of a generalization. Whereas a rigid application of a generalization argues *from the general to the specific*, a hasty generalization argues *from the specific to the general*. (We saw earlier that a rigid application of a generalization is also referred to as "accident." In this regard, a hasty generalization is also referred to as "reverse or converse accident.")

Hasty generalization
An argument that relies on a small sample that is unlikely to represent the population.

Let's analyze the following argument:

> I saw a fraternity guy act rudely to a fast-food employee in the food court. Probably most fraternity and sorority members are rude and arrogant.

The premise reports the observation of a single instance, but the conclusion generalizes the observed behavior to most fraternity *and* sorority members, even though no sorority members were observed. Thus, the conclusion was based on the mistaken belief that a single observation is representative of the entire group. The evidence in this case is not adequate to make such a generalization, so the premise cannot provide a good reason to support the conclusion.

Here is another example:

> The first two students whose exams I graded each got an A. Thus, I expect all fifty students in the class to get A's on the exam.

The teacher is probably being overly optimistic. Although it is possible that all fifty students will get an A on the exam, the fallacy of hasty generalization is apparent in this case. The conclusion was based on the mistaken belief that the grades of two students are a representative sample and can therefore be generalized to all fifty students in the class.

When the fallacy does not occur: Groups of objects, such as human groups, are often quite diverse, so a small sample is unlikely to accurately represent the group. However, some groups of objects include members that are extremely similar to one another, such as certain manufactured products. For example, a flaw in the ignition switch design of certain models of General Motors (GM) cars led to the cars' shutting down all power, thus causing the deaths of at least thirteen people. Based on a small sample of reported defects, GM recalled millions of cars. Since all the ignition switches have the same design and are manufactured using the same process, the switches are all nearly identical. Therefore, this is *not* an instance of a hasty generalization.

This same reasoning process is behind the strategy of relying on quality control experts in most large manufacturing sectors. For example, a company may manufacture hundreds of thousands of a certain item in a week. If a small sample of identically made products is judged to be flawed, it is reasonable to expect that all (or most of) the members of the group are flawed. On the other hand, if a small sample of the items is judged to meet acceptable standards, then the company expects the remaining items to meet the acceptable standards. However, since these are inductive arguments, the conclusions might turn out to be false.

10. COMPOSITION

Composition There are two forms of the fallacy: (1) the mistaken transfer of an attribute of the individual *parts of an object* to the *object as a whole* and (2) the mistaken transfer of an attribute of the individual *members of a class* to the *class itself.*

Let's turn to another type of generalization fallacy. There are two forms of the fallacy of **composition**: (1) the mistaken transfer of an attribute of the individual *parts of an object* to the *object as a whole* and (2) the mistaken transfer of an attribute of the individual *members of a class* to the *class itself.* Let's look at an example of the first form. Suppose someone said the following of a seven-foot-tall basketball player:

All the cells in his body are tiny. Thus, he is tiny.

The mistake is taking an attribute that is true of the cells of the person and erroneously applying it to the whole person. The fallacy can also occur when the conclusion is not necessarily untrue, but merely in doubt:

The bricks in this building are sturdy, so the building must be sturdy.

Even if the individual bricks are sturdy (the premise), the building may not be sturdy (the conclusion). Here are three other examples:

- The thread you are using is easily torn, so the garment you are making will be easily torn.
- Each ingredient you are using tastes delicious. Therefore, the cake has to taste delicious.
- I understand every word in the poem, so I must understand what the poem is about.

All of the examples of the composition fallacy so far have concerned a possible mistaken identity—of parts of an object with the whole object (a body, a building, a garment, a cake, and a poem). However, another form of composition fallacy occurs when the attributes of individual *members of a class* are mistakenly applied to the class itself. This mistake occurs when we confuse the *distributive* and *collective* use of terms. "Distributive" means that an attribute or characteristic is claimed to be true of all or most of the *individual members* of a class of objects. In other words, the attribute is *distributed* to the *members* of the class. For example, in the statement "Motorcycles are noisy," the term "noisy" is being used distributively to refer to individual motorcycles. In contrast to this, "collective" means that an attribute or characteristic of *the individual members* of a class is claimed to be true of the *class itself*. For example, in the statement "Motorcycles make up only 5% of all vehicles on U.S. roadways," the phrase "make up only 5% of all vehicles on U.S. roadways" is being used collectively to refer to the class of motorcycles, not to the individual motorcycles. Given this information, we can now examine the second form of composition fallacy. Consider the following argument:

> More noise is produced by a motorcycle than by a car. Therefore, more noise is produced on U.S. roadways by motorcycles than by cars.

The fallacy results from the mistaken transfer of an attribute of individual motorcycles and cars to their respective classes. It may be true that an individual motorcycle makes more noise than an individual car, but since there are many times more cars than motorcycles, the conclusion does not follow.

Here is an example that clearly illustrates how the fallacy occurs:

> All the *members of my club* are high school seniors. Therefore, *my club* is a high school senior.

Although no one would make this mistake, the point is to expose how the fallacy occurs. The obvious error of applying the attribute "high school senior" to a club illustrates the difference between *distributing* the attribute to the members of the club and applying that attribute *collectively* to the club itself.

Here is one more example:

> A bus uses more gasoline than a car. Therefore, buses use more gasoline in a year than cars.

In the premise, the attribute "uses more gasoline" is claimed to hold for each *member* of the class of buses (the attribute is *distributed* throughout the individual members). However, the conclusion makes a claim about the *class itself* (the attribute is claimed to hold *collectively*).

At this point, it may seem that some composition fallacies resemble hasty generalizations. Let's look closely at the difference by comparing a hasty generalization to a fallacy of composition.

> *Hasty generalization*: Those three buses get fewer than five miles to a gallon of gasoline. Therefore, most buses probably get fewer than five miles to a gallon.

In the premise, the attribute "gets fewer than five miles to a gallon of gasoline" is claimed to hold for the three observed buses. The conclusion then *distributes* the attribute to the remaining *members* of the class, *not* to the *class itself* (collectively). So, this is an instance of hasty generalization, not a fallacy of composition.

Now compare that result with the following:

> *Composition fallacy*: All the parts of that television set are inexpensive, so that television set is inexpensive.

In the premise, the attribute "inexpensive" is claimed to hold for each *part* of the television set. However, the conclusion makes a claim about the television set *as a whole* (the attribute is claimed to hold *collectively*).

When the fallacy does not occur: We must be careful not to misapply the fallacy of composition. Not every argument that reasons from parts to a whole is fallacious. For example:

> Every thread of material of which this shirt is composed is red, so the shirt is red.

This argument does not commit the fallacy of composition; in fact, it is a strong argument.

Here is another example of an argument that does not commit the fallacy of composition:

> Since every piece of my sewing machine is made from steel, it follows that my sewing machine is steel.

Compare the earlier fallacious examples with the two exceptions. The composition fallacies are not mistakes in the structure of the argument. Rather, the context of the argument, together with our knowledge of the world, is usually needed to distinguish fallacious from nonfallacious informal arguments.

11. DIVISION

The next type of generalization fallacy is the reverse of the fallacy of composition. There are two forms of the fallacy of **division**: (1) the mistaken transfer of an attribute of an *object as a whole* to the individual *parts of the object* and (2) the mistaken transfer of an attribute of a *class* to the individual *members of the class*.

For example, suppose someone said the following of a seven-foot-tall basketball player:

> He is huge, so he must have huge cells.

The mistake is taking an attribute that is true of the whole object and erroneously applying it to the parts that make up the object. Here are three other examples of the fallacy:

- She is intelligent, so she must have smart brain cells.
- The garment is strong, so the individual threads must be strong.
- The cake tastes burnt, so you must have used burnt ingredients.

All the examples of the fallacy so far have concerned a possible mistaken identity of an object (a body, a person's intelligence, a garment, and a cake) with its parts. However, a second form of division fallacy is similar to the second form of composition fallacy.

Division There are two forms of the fallacy: (1) the mistaken transfer of an attribute of an *object as a whole* to the individual *parts of the object* and (2) the mistaken transfer of an attribute of a *class* to the individual *members of the class.*

This occurs when an attribute of a class is mistakenly applied to the individual members of that class. As before, the mistake occurs when the distributive and collective uses of terms are confused. For example, in the statement "Bald eagles are disappearing," the term "disappearing" is being used collectively to refer to the class of bald eagles; individual members may still live full lives. This is illustrated by the following argument:

> My teacher said that bald eagles are disappearing. I remember seeing a bald eagle at the zoo. Therefore, we better hurry to see it before it disappears.

Here is another example that clearly illustrates how the fallacy occurs:

> That fraternity celebrated its fiftieth birthday. A guy on my floor is a member of that fraternity, so he must have celebrated his fiftieth birthday.

No one would seriously make this mistake, but it does present a clear example of how the fallacy occurs.

When the fallacy does not occur: As with the fallacy of composition, we must be careful not to misapply the fallacy of division. Not every argument that reasons from the whole object to its parts is fallacious. For example:

> That is a wooden chair, so the legs are made of wood.

This argument does not commit the fallacy of division; in fact, it is a strong argument. Here is another example:

> The book she is reading is made of paper. Therefore, the pages of the book are made of paper.

Compare the earlier fallacious examples with the two exceptions. As with composition fallacies, division fallacies are *not* mistakes in the structure of the argument. Once again, the context of the argument coupled with our general knowledge helps to distinguish fallacious from nonfallacious arguments.

12. BIASED SAMPLE

Let's turn to another type of generalization fallacy. In the fallacy of **biased sample**, an argument uses a nonrepresentative sample as support for a statistical claim about an entire population. A representative sample occurs when the characteristics of a sample are correctly identified and matched to the population under investigation. For example, consider this argument:

Biased sample An argument that uses a nonrepresentative sample as support for a statistical claim about an entire population.

> Recently, a sample of 1000 Catholics in the United States revealed that 85% believe that abortion is morally wrong. Therefore, evidence shows that approximately 85% of all Americans believe that abortion is morally wrong.

The sample is fairly large, so it is not a hasty generalization. However, the sample surveyed only Catholics in the United States, but the conclusion generalizes to *all* Americans. This illustrates how even a large sample may intentionally or unintentionally exclude segments of the entire population. This results in a nonrepresentative sample, and the argument commits the fallacy of biased sample.

Here is another example:

> A survey of 100 seniors at our university showed that 90% do not oppose a parking fee increase that will go into effect next year. Therefore, we can report that almost all students do not oppose a parking fee increase.

The sample surveyed only seniors at the university, but the conclusion generalizes to *all* students. Since seniors are unlikely to be affected by an increase in parking fees next year, the sample intentionally or unintentionally excluded segments of the entire population. The resulting biased sample does not provide good evidence for the conclusion. (Chapter 13 offers more information on statistical arguments.)

False Cause Fallacies

Scientific advances owe much to experiments that verify cause-effect relationships. Science also has methods that confirm the existence of patterns that help us to understand the world and to predict future events. Fallacies of false cause occur when a causal connection is assumed to exist between two events when none actually exists, or when the assumed causal connection is unlikely to exist. Since causal claims require strong evidence, a cause-effect claim based on insufficient evidence commits a fallacy of false cause. We will look at two types of false cause fallacies.

13. POST HOC

It is normal and helpful for us to look for connections between events; that's how we learn about the world. Scientific results are achieved by correctly identifying cause-effect connections. This is how we are able to discover the cause of diseases, how and why things deteriorate over time, how to develop helpful drugs, how certain genes are connected to risk factors, and many other types of knowledge. However, not every connection that we happen to notice reveals a true cause-effect relationship. When unwanted things happen to us, it is reasonable to seek out the cause, but we must recognize that many things we connect in our day-to-day life are just coincidences.

Superstitions develop over time when instances of individual coincidences get passed from one person to another. After a few instances are noticed, it often becomes accepted that a cause-effect relationship exists. However, this is a self-sustaining result: Only positive connections are recognized; negative instances are overlooked. A scientific approach would record the number of positive and negative instances to see if there is truly a causal connection. Instead of this, anecdotal evidence that recognizes only positive instances gets passed on, thus reinforcing the superstition. The type of fallacious reasoning that develops over time from a few coincidences is related to the *post hoc* fallacy, our next topic.

The *post hoc* fallacy occurs from the mistaken assumption that just because one event occurred after another event, the first event *must have caused* the second event. ("*Post hoc*" means *after the fact*. The fallacy is also known as "*post hoc, ergo propter hoc,*" which means *after the fact, therefore because of the fact*.) The fallacious reasoning follows this simple pattern:

X occurred before Y, therefore X caused Y.

Post hoc The fallacy occurs from the mistaken assumption that just because one event occurred before another event, the first event *must have caused* the second event.

The simplest form of the *post hoc* fallacy is a *coincidence* that results from the accidental or chance connection between two events. For example, suppose someone says the following:

> Last week I bought a new car, and today I found out that I am being laid off at work. I shouldn't have bought that car; it brought me bad luck.

The speaker incorrectly infers that buying the new car *caused* him to be laid off. The fallacious reasoning relies on the assumption that because X occurred before Y, therefore X caused Y. However, there is no credible evidence of a cause-effect relationship between buying the new car and getting laid off.

There are more complex forms of the *post hoc* fallacy. For example, it is not unusual for someone to find either a short- or long-term pattern and to make a causal connection between two things. The fallacy lies in mistaking a statistical pattern, or *correlation*, for cause and effect. For example, you might read the following:

> Researchers have discovered that, for over 30 years, there has been a definite pattern connecting the party affiliation of the U.S. president and specific soft drink sales. During the years when a Democrat was president, Morphiacola topped all soft drink sales. When a Republican was president, Opiacola was number one in sales. If you are an investor, we advise you to put your money on the soft drink company based on who is in the White House.

The premises fail to provide the necessary support for a true causal claim. Arguments that use *post hoc* reasoning fall prey to the mistake of confusing a *correlation* with a *cause*. Fallacies of this type can be persuasive, because unlike a mere coincidence, a regular pattern seems to have emerged. Although every cause-effect relationship reveals a strong correlation, not all strong correlations reveal cause-effect relationships. For example, there is a strong correlation between wearing bathing suits and getting wet, but wearing a bathing suit does not cause us to get wet. (For more details on the difference between a *correlation* and a *cause*, see Chapter 14.)

The pattern in the cola argument was between the party in the White House and the type of cola having the most sales. Patterns like these are also referred to as *trends* and are often the basis for gambling purposes. For example, in baseball, the National League may win four straight All-Star games. In football, the American Conference might win three consecutive Super Bowls. In roulette, a red number may come up six times in a row. However, trends are temporary, and unless some definite cause-effect relationship is independently discovered that would *explain* the trend, we should not expect the trend to continue indefinitely.

Another special form of the *post hoc* fallacy is the *common cause* fallacy, which occurs when one event is believed to cause a second event, when in fact both events are the result of a common cause. For example, someone might claim that the falling barometer is the cause of a storm, when in fact both events are caused by a change in atmospheric pressure. The following illustration reveals the common cause fallacy:

Atmospheric Pressure

Falling Barometer ◄———✕———► Storm

The two downward arrows indicate that the atmospheric pressure is the common cause of both the falling barometer and the storm. The arrow with the X through it shows the fallacious cause-effect claim.

Another example of the fallacy occurs when someone mistakenly thinks that a rash is causing a fever. It is quite possible that both the rash and the fever have a common cause: a virus.

There is another important point about cause-effect relationships that we need to consider. In many real-life settings, events occur because of a complex network of causal factors. Demonstrating that a true causal relationship exists requires being able to *isolate one factor* as the cause and *eliminating all other possible explanations* for the effect. This is what a good scientific experiment is able to do. Unfortunately, most people are not in a position to conduct a good experiment, so they fall prey to a mistake in believing that a complex event has a single cause, when, in fact, there might be no good evidence to support that belief.

Here is an example:

> The United States is the most successful country in history. That's why people in most Middle East countries hate us.

The argument assumes that a single factor is the cause of animosity toward the United States. The argument overlooks a complex network of factors: Social, economic, military, governmental, religious, and cultural factors probably have contributed in some degree to the current state of relations. The fallacy results from the mistaken belief that there is a single cause for the phenomenon.

Consider the following argument:

> I told you not to trust her. After all, she was born under the sign of Aquarius in the year of the Rabbit. She can't help herself; the stars dictate her behavior.

Astrology places human behavior under the influence of the planets and stars. It claims that we are causally connected to astral influences that occurred at the time of our birth and continue throughout our lives. These causal claims do not have any credible scientific evidence in their support; they are based mostly on anecdotal evidence. In addition, the general personality traits associated with astrology can be applied to anyone. The argument overlooks the role of genetics; environment; socioeconomic status; child-rearing practices; and cultural, religious, and ethical influences, all of which probably contribute to our behavior.

Here is one final example:

> Public education has been declining in the United States for the last 50 years. Students today do not know as much as their parents. The decline is caused by the steady erosion of classroom discipline ever since teachers were forbidden to punish their students.

The argument assumes that a single factor is the cause of the decline of public education in the United States. Once again, we can see that the argument overlooks a complex network of factors: Social, economic, cultural, and technological issues, as well as class size and testing standards, are only some of the factors that probably have contributed to the current state of education. The argument is another example of the mistaken belief in a single cause for a complex phenomenon.

When the fallacy does not occur: Of course, there are instances in real-life where we can in fact make a good determination that a single factor was the cause of an event. For example, if you throw a rock against someone's window and the window breaks, then, for the purposes of assigning blame, the cause of the broken window is quite apparent.

In a different setting, a medical examiner can sometimes pinpoint a single cause of death, but not always. Similarly, a physician can sometimes isolate a single cause of pain, or determine that a patient is suffering from a specific disease. But this is not always the case. A set of symptoms may be connected to several different diseases, thus making it difficult for physicians to make a definite diagnosis. This is why numerous tests are conducted. The additional tests can help to eliminate some diseases; the goal being to isolate one cause.

14. SLIPPERY SLOPE

Some complex arguments attempt to link events in such a way as to create an alleged, but unsupported, chain reaction. An argument that attempts to connect a series of occurrences such that the first link leads directly to a second link, and so on, until a final unwanted situation is said to be the inevitable result is called a **slippery slope** fallacy. The arguer urges us to stop the chain reaction before it has a chance to begin, by preventing the first act from ever happening. For example, consider the following argument:

> If you start smoking marijuana for pleasure, then you will need more and more to achieve the expected high. You will begin to rely on it whenever you feel depressed. Eventually you will experiment with more powerful drugs that act faster and last longer. Of course, the amount of drug intake will have to increase to achieve the desired results. The addiction will take hold and will lead to a loss of ambition, a loss of self-esteem, the destruction of your health, and the dissolution of all social ties. Therefore, you should not start smoking marijuana.

Slippery slope An argument that attempts to connect a series of occurrences such that the first link in a chain leads directly to a second link, and so on, until a final unwanted situation is said to be the inevitable result.

The argument paints a tragic picture where smoking marijuana for pleasure starts the slide down a slippery slope leading eventually to the dissolution of all social ties. However, the alleged inevitability of the final effect needs to be supported by specific objective evidence for *each step* in the alleged causal network. Each link in the chain requires scientifically accepted evidence of a verified causal connection to the next link in the chain. Until this is established, the argument need not be accepted.

Here is another example:

> If we stop water-boarding enemy combatants, then we will lose the ability to extract important information about terrorists and their future activities. The loss of information will lead to the terrorists plotting attacks with impunity. Since we will not be able to stop or disrupt their planning, we will suffer another tragic attack on United States soil.

The argument constructs a causal chain where the elimination of water-boarding leads to another tragic attack on United States soil. Once again, the alleged inevitability of the final effect has not been supported by any evidence. Each link is asserted to be a cause of the next link in the chain, but no reasons are given to back the assertions. Therefore, without support, each causal claim is unwarranted.

When the fallacy does not occur: Real cases of chain reactions are not hard to find. For example, scientists have discovered how to create nuclear reactions by setting up a series of steps where the result is known to follow. Similarly, causal links can sometimes be found in medicine, where an initial health issue can cause a series of steps leading to the death of a patient. However, each of these kinds of cases has been meticulously researched and is backed by reliable evidence.

Summary of Weak Inductive Argument Fallacies

Generalization fallacies occur when an argument relies on a mistaken use of the principles behind making a generalization. There are five individual fallacies in this group.

8. **Rigid application of a generalization:** When a generalization or rule is inappropriately applied to the case at hand. The fallacy results from the mistaken belief that the generalization or rule is universal (meaning it has no exceptions).

9. **Hasty generalization:** An argument that relies on a small sample that is unlikely to represent the population.

10. **Composition:** There are two forms of the fallacy: (1) the mistaken transfer of an attribute of the individual *parts of an object* to the *object as a whole*; and (2) the mistaken transfer of an attribute of the individual *members of a class* to the *class itself.*

11. **Division:** There are two forms of the fallacy: (1) the mistaken transfer of an attribute of an *object as a whole* to the individual *parts of the object*; and (2) the mistaken transfer of an attribute of a *class* to the individual *members of the class.*

12. **Biased sample:** An argument that uses a nonrepresentative sample as support for a statistical claim about an entire population.

A false cause fallacy occurs when a causal connection is assumed to exist between two events when none actually exists, or when the assumed causal connection is unlikely to exist. There are two individual fallacies in this group.

13. *Post hoc:* The fallacy occurs from the mistaken assumption that just because one event occurred before another event, the first event *must have caused* the second event.

14. **Slippery slope:** An argument that attempts to connect a series of occurrences such that the first link in a chain leads directly to a second link, and so on, until a final unwanted situation is said to be the inevitable result.

EXERCISES 4C

I. Determine whether each statement is true or false.

1. In the fallacy of biased sample, an argument uses a nonrepresentative sample as support for a statistical claim about an entire population.

Answer: True

2. An argument that relies on a small sample that is unlikely to represent the population commits the fallacy of hasty generalization.

3. To rigidly apply an otherwise acceptable generalization, even in the face of known and understood exceptions, is to commit the fallacy of composition.

4. A slippery slope fallacy concerns a long-term pattern that is noticed after the fact.

⭐ 5. One way the fallacy of division can occur is by the mistaken transfer of an attribute of an *object as a whole* to the individual *parts of the object.*

6. A false cause fallacy occurs when a causal connection is assumed to exist between two events when none actually exists.

7. A coincidence results from the accidental or chance connection between two events.

8. An argument that attempts to make a final event the inevitable outcome of an initial act is called *post hoc.*

⭐ 9. A special form of the *post hoc* fallacy is the *common cause* fallacy, which occurs when one event is believed to cause a second event, when in fact both events are the result of a coincidence.

10. Demonstrating that a true causal relationship exists requires being able to *isolate one factor* as the cause and *eliminating all other possible explanations* for the effect.

II. Read the following passages. If an argument commits a weak inductive argument fallacy, then identify the specific fallacy. If a passage does not contain a fallacy, then answer "No fallacy." Explain your answers.

1. Ninety-five percent of a sample of registered Republicans in one state district said that they will vote for the Republican nominee for Congress from their district. So, we can expect that all the Republican nominees in the state will get around 95% of the total votes this fall.

Answer: Biased sample. An argument that uses a nonrepresentative sample as support for a statistical claim about an entire population.

2. That ambulance didn't even stop for the red light. It went zooming right through! And the police didn't even give the driver a citation. If I did that, I would get a citation. Life just isn't fair.

Level 1 Multiple-
Choice Questions

Level 2 Multiple-
Choice Questions

Level 1 Multiple-
Choice Questions

Level 2 Multiple-
Choice Questions

3. My horoscope said I would meet someone new. Today my company hired a really good-looking salesperson and we will be working closely together. Now do you see why I read my horoscope every day?

4. For the last 50 years, whenever the American League won the World Series, there was a recession that year, but when the National League won, stock prices went up. There must be some unknown economic force at work that we don't understand.

5. There were six cases of food poisoning from undercooked burgers at that chain of fast-food restaurants. This caused the company to change its method of cooking burgers.

6. Each grain of sand is hard, so your sand castle will be hard.

Video Tutorial

7. Our experiment tested the effect of multivitamins on the common cold. We studied 1000 people who began to experience the onset of typical cold symptoms. Daily multivitamins were given to 500 randomly selected patients in the group, while the other 500 were told not to take any multivitamins. The results show that there was no statistically significant difference between the two groups in either the severity of the cold symptoms or the length of time for the symptoms to subside. We conclude that multivitamins have no noticeable effect on the common cold.

8. I met two people from that state, and they were both rude. There must be something in the drinking water of that state that makes all the people from there so rude.

9. If you don't clean your room, then the dirt and dust will build up. Before you know it, bacteria will grow. Whatever you touch in your room will then spread bacteria, which will contaminate the entire house. We will all wind up in the hospital, terminally ill.

10. On seven different occasions it rained the day after I washed my car. I washed my car today, so take your umbrella with you tomorrow.

11. When I need to travel to another city I have to buy my own airplane ticket. The president of the United States has Air Force One to take him wherever he wants to go, and he doesn't have to pay a penny. Therefore, I should be afforded the same opportunity.

12. She is very beautiful, so she must have a lovely appendix.

13. All the people in my fraternity think that hazing is not a problem. So, I'm sure that the entire student population agrees with us on this issue.

14. Whenever I step in the shower, either my phone rings or someone knocks on the door. I'll have to change my bathing habits, I suppose.

15. Humans need fresh fruit and raw vegetables in order to get their daily supply of vitamins. So, you should start feeding your newborn baby some fresh fruit and raw vegetables every day.

16. If you drop out of one course this semester, you will have less than a full-time load. It will take you longer to graduate. It will delay your getting a job for another year, meaning that you won't get promoted as fast as others who graduated on time. So, you can expect to lose approximately $100,000 during your lifetime.

⭐ 17. The coroner determined that the cause of death was an overdose of toxic drugs. No evidence of foul play was found. In addition, there was no suicide note. We conclude that the death was an accident.

18. My bill at the restaurant was $4.29. I played the number 429 on the lottery today, and it came up. Therefore, it was my destiny to play that number today and win.

19. I don't recommend that you eat at that restaurant. I did not like the breakfast I had there last week. I'm sure that all of their meals are of poor quality.

20. I know for a fact that the acrylic paints that Vincent van Gogh used to create this portrait were very inexpensive. So even though his painting is hanging in a museum, it can't be very expensive.

⭐ 21. Every football player at Crestfallen High School can run two miles in under 15 minutes, so all the students at that school must be in great physical condition.

22. I had two station wagons, and they were both lemons. Thus, I'm sure that there is something in the design of station wagons that makes them all terrible vehicles.

23. I read that cars in the United States consume more gasoline each year than trucks. I guess that means that my car uses more gasoline each year than that tractor trailer over there.

24. Chicken eggs do not weigh very much. So if I eat an omelet made from fifty eggs, it will not weigh very much.

⭐ 25. A random and representative sample of registered voters shows that 70% are opposed to Proposition 13 that will be on the upcoming ballot. Given this, we project that the proposition will fail to get enough votes to pass.

26. I read that the city's closed circuit video surveillance cameras that are positioned to watch for traffic violations are being stolen. Apparently, the thieves can sell the electronic equipment to unscrupulous companies. The city then had the bright idea to install a second set of cameras to watch the ones observing the traffic. This led to the thieves stealing the second set of cameras so they wouldn't be seen stealing the traffic ones. It's obvious where this is going. Pretty soon the city will have to install a third set, and then a fourth set, and then have someone stationed 24 hours a day watching each camera. In the end, this will bankrupt the city.

27. In one of my dreams last week, I saw a car wreck, but I was not in the car. I just heard that my aunt had a fender-bender in the mall's parking lot. This shows that dreams are videos sent from the future to warn us of dangers in the present.

28. Every time I bet on our team, they lose. And every time I don't bet, they win. It follows that my betting on them causes them to lose.

★29. A large survey of SUV owners revealed that 80% believe that global warming is a hoax intended to get them to give up their vehicles. This shows that the vast majority of Americans don't believe that global warming is real.

30. When I get on a bus, it's usually first come, first served. In other words, if a seat is available, you take it. But they have a sign on the bus that asks people to give up their seats for older people, people with infirmities, or someone who is pregnant. I think it should be the same for everyone. If I'm lucky enough to get a seat, why should I have to give it up?

31. Since the 1950s, our society has become increasingly more violent. It is obvious what has caused this to happen. Check the facts. As the number of television sets bought by consumers rose every year, so did crime.

32. You forgot to water your plants for 3 weeks and now they are dead. Clearly, the lack of water caused their untimely demise.

★33. My car goes from zero to sixty miles an hour in under 5 seconds, so the windshield wipers must be able to clean the front window in under 5 seconds, too.

34. In physics class we learned that elementary particles have little or no mass. My $150 physics textbook is made up of elementary particles, thus it has little or no mass.

35. I waited 30 minutes for a bus to work, and because of that I was late. The bus system in this city is completely unreliable.

36. Sending arms to Middle East militants trying to overthrow their governments is a crazy idea. Those militants will most likely force the collapse of the current regime and then take over power. But the militants are not capable of running a complex society. This will lead to instability in the region, and then a clash of cultures. Soon we will be forced to send in troops. Russia, China, and India will get involved. This will lead to World War III.

★37. She began making $100,000 the year after she graduated from college, and when she took an IQ test, she scored 20 points higher than when she was in high school. See, I told you: Money makes people smarter.

38. Four of us ate at that restaurant last night. Three of us had lasagna, and one had a salad. The three who had lasagna all got severe stomach aches, but not the one

Video Tutorial

who had salad. We all had the same kind of appetizers and dessert. It follows that the lasagna probably caused the stomach aches.

39. Each page of the encyclopedia weighs practically nothing, so the encyclopedia weighs practically nothing.

40. The other day my sister helped an old lady cross the street, and today she won $100 on the lottery. See, I told you that doing good deeds brings you luck.

⭐41. According to the census data, the population of that city is 10% atheists. My Uncle Sam lives there, so he must be 10% atheist.

42. My daughter was listening to some music on her headphones, and I asked her to play it for me. She said it was called "EDM," which means electronic dance music. I heard one song and asked her to stop it because it was repetitive and monotonous. I imagine all EDM sounds the same.

43. If you major in humanities, then you will stop taking math and science courses. By the time you graduate you will be locked out of all the high-paying jobs. You will have to take jobs that you could have gotten with a high-school diploma. You won't be able to contribute to an IRA, and when you finally retire, your Social Security checks will not be enough to survive.

44. Every time the barometer drops below 30, it rains. It has some mysterious power over the weather, I guess.

⭐45. You have chosen great paint colors; therefore, your house will look great.

46. On two different occasions, I saw our next-door neighbor wash his new car and the next day it rained. So, if you want to make sure that it won't rain for your picnic tomorrow, then you'd better hope our neighbor doesn't wash his car today.

47. All it takes is one. If you throw your empty can on the sidewalk, then someone else will either see you do it or else think it is okay. Especially kids. Pretty soon people will throw glass and plastic bottles. Then there will be all kinds of trash. The sanitation department will not be able to keep up with the level of garbage in the streets. The rat population will grow, and when that happens, bubonic plague will not be far behind.

48. A veterinarian found that 70% of the German shepherd dogs she examined had a hip displacement before they reached 10 years of age. Given this, probably 70% of all dogs will have a hip displacement before they reach 10 years of age.

⭐49. The house is poorly constructed, so the material it is made of must be poorly constructed as well.

50. I bought a new car, and a week later I was fired. That proves the car is a jinx, so I'm getting rid of it.

D. FALLACIES OF UNWARRANTED ASSUMPTION OR DIVERSION

Unwarranted Assumption

Fallacies of unwarranted assumption exhibit a special kind of reasoning error: They assume the truth of some unproved or questionable claim. The fallacies become apparent when the assumptions and lack of support are exposed, thus revealing the weak points of the argument.

15. BEGGING THE QUESTION

Begging the question
In one type, the fallacy occurs when a premise is simply reworded in the conclusion. In a second type, called circular reasoning, a set of statements seem to support each other with no clear beginning or end point. In a third type, the argument assumes certain key information that may be controversial or is not supported by facts.

There are several types of the fallacy of **begging the question** (*"petitio principii,"* meaning *assume at the beginning*). In one type, the fallacy occurs when a premise is simply reworded in the conclusion. In a second type, called *circular reasoning*, a set of statements seem to support each other with no clear beginning or end point. In a third type, the argument assumes certain key information that may be controversial or is not supported by facts. Cases of begging the question can go unnoticed because they often sound convincing. This should not be surprising; in some cases, the conclusion is already assumed in the premises, so on the surface it might appear to be a strong argument.

Let's look at an example:

> The Beatles are the greatest band of all time. So it is safe to say that no band has ever been better than the Beatles.

The conclusion is already assumed in the premise; it is merely worded differently. Since both the premise and the conclusion assert the same thing, no new evidence is offered to support the conclusion. Obviously, *if* the claim is true in the premise, it will be true in the conclusion, so it is valid. However, the argument begs the question because it assumes what it intends to prove. We need additional information to answer the question "What evidence is there that the Beatles are the greatest band of all time?"

Here is an example of circular reasoning:

> You can believe her because she never lies. Furthermore, since she always tells the truth, she is someone that you can believe.

Paraphrasing the argument reveals the problem:

> You can believe her. She never lies. She always tells the truth. She is someone that you can believe.

If you look closely, you can see that the second and third statements say the same thing: Saying that someone never lies is the same thing as saying that she always tells the truth. Also, the first and fourth statements say the same thing; they both say that you can believe her. Ultimately, the first statement is used to support the second statement, which in turn, is then used to support the first statement. The argument goes in a circle. But the argument begs the question "What additional evidence is there that she never lies?"

The third type of the fallacy occurs when an argument fails to supply a premise that is needed to support the conclusion. For example, if your argument relies on a controversial or unsubstantiated premise that you leave out, then you are assuming information that could be unacceptable to those you are trying to convince. Consider this argument:

> The murder of a human being is always wrong. Therefore, capital punishment is always wrong.

Most people would probably accept the premise. If clarity is needed, we could offer a definition of "murder" as "the unjustified taking of the life of a human being." Our discussion might exempt cases of self-defense, legitimate police activity while protecting the citizenry, and certain military engagements. However, the conclusion *assumes* that capital punishment is a form of murder. This assumption is often the central point on which opposing positions regarding capital punishment rest. Therefore, someone who disagrees with the conclusion can point out that the assumed premise "begs the question," in that it assumes as a good reason what is in fact an unwarranted assumption: that capital punishment is a form of murder.

As it stands, the original argument (with the single premise) is invalid. However, the reconstructed argument is valid. The fallacious nature of the argument is *not* based on the underlying logic, because *if* both premises are true, then the argument is valid. In other words, if it is true that "the murder of a human being is always wrong," and if it is also true that "capital punishment is a form of murder," then the conclusion is necessarily true. The reconstructed argument may be valid, but its soundness is in question. The fallacy occurs because the truth of the added controversial premise has been assumed. The argument lacks sufficient additional, independent reasons or facts to support the assumed premise. We need additional information to answer the question "What evidence is there that capital punishment is a form of murder?"

Here is another example:

> We are justified in going to war to defend our country from foreign aggression. It follows that we should go to war with Syria.

The premise is probably acceptable to most people. However, the conclusion *assumes* that Syria is actively engaged in aggression toward our country. Thus, someone who disagrees with the conclusion can point out that the assumed premise "begs the question," in that it assumes as a good reason what is in fact an unwarranted assumption: that Syria is actively engaged in aggression toward our country. We need additional information to answer the question "What evidence is there that Syria is actively engaged in aggression toward our country?" The original argument (with the single premise) is invalid, but the reconstructed argument is valid. This illustrates once again that the fallacious nature of the argument is *not* based on the underlying logic, because *if* both premises are true, then the argument is valid.

The fallacy occurs because the truth of the added controversial premise has been assumed. The argument lacks sufficient additional, independent reasons or facts to support the assumed premise.

When the fallacy does not occur: The examples of arguments that beg the question contained information that needed additional support. Assumptions were made that were not backed up by additional evidence. Although the fully fleshed out arguments may be valid, they are either clearly unsound or else their soundness is under question. However, there are arguments that might appear to be instances of begging the question, but they are not. Here is an example:

> Albany is the capital of New York or Sacramento is the capital of California. It follows that Sacramento is the capital of California or Albany is the capital of New York.

The argument may be trivial but it is sound (it is valid and the premise is true). It is not an instance of begging the question because it has not assumed something that needs additional support. Here is another example:

> Buffalo is the capital of New York or San Diego is the capital of California. It follows that San Diego is the capital of California or Buffalo is the capital of New York.

Once again, the argument may be trivial but in this case it is unsound (it is valid but the premise is false). Yet again, it is not an instance of begging the question because it has not assumed something that needs additional support.

16. COMPLEX QUESTION

Complex question The fallacy occurs when a single question actually contains multiple parts and an unestablished hidden assumption.

The fallacy of **complex question** occurs when a single question actually contains multiple parts and an unestablished hidden assumption. The questioner tries to force a single answer that, in turn, is then used against the respondent. As such, the question itself is not a fallacy, but either a "yes" or "no" answer allows the questioner to create an argument that establishes the truth of the hidden assumption. For example, suppose you are asked the following question:

> Do you still cheat on your taxes?

Answering either "yes" or "no" is an admission that you did, in fact, cheat on your taxes. The key words that create the complex question are "still cheat." The unestablished hidden assumption is that you have cheated. If you answer "yes," then you establish the truth of the hidden assumption, and the questioner can then conclude that you currently cheat on your taxes and you have done so in the past. On the other hand, even if you never cheated on your taxes, answering "no" once again establishes the truth of the hidden assumption. In other words, it is an admission that you did cheat on your taxes, but you no longer do. Therefore, the questioner can use this as evidence to support the conclusion that you cheated on your taxes. Here is how the questioner's argument would look:

> I asked you if you still cheat on your taxes. You said "no." Therefore, by your own admission, you did cheat on your taxes.

The premises rely on the fact that the complex question contained two distinct questions and an unestablished hidden assumption. We can eliminate the hidden assumption by separating the two questions:

A. Did you ever cheat on your taxes?
B. If so, are you still cheating on your taxes?

The ability to recognize that there are actually two questions at work here allows us to avoid the trap of the complex question. Once the questions are separated, a person who never cheated on her taxes can answer "no" to question A and, by so doing, eliminate the need to answer question B. This prevents the questioner from drawing an unjustified conclusion.

Complex questions can be used to trap us in many kinds of unacceptable situations. For example, suppose someone asks:

Aren't you going to do something about your child's terrible behavior?

The complex question hides two unestablished assumptions: (1) You agree that your child's behavior needs correcting, and (2) you are going to correct it. Therefore, if you answer "yes" to the complex question, you have admitted the child's behavior needs correcting. However, even if you answer "no" to the complex question, then you have, once again, established the truth of the hidden assumption. In other words, you are admitting that the child's behavior needs correcting. You simply are not going to do anything about it.

When the fallacy does not occur: A question that does *not* try to trap the respondent into establishing the truth of a hidden assumption is not a fallacy of complex question. For example, if you ask your roommate, "Did you see the final episode of *How I Met Your Mother*?" then your question is not hiding any assumptions. In that case, answering "yes" or "no" is a satisfactory answer.

In a legal setting, a lawyer asks many kinds of questions. If she asks a complex question, then the opposing lawyer has a chance to object. If the objection is upheld, the judge might ask that the question be rephrased. On the other hand, a lawyer might ask a witness a *leading question* such as, "Did you see anyone enter the building after the defendant left?" This kind of question is meant to set the groundwork for potential follow-up questions. So, if the witness responds "yes" to the leading question, then the lawyer can ask other questions designed to elaborate on what the witness knows. However, if the witness answers "no," then the lawyer can go on to other topics. Once again, we must pay close attention to the context at hand to determine if the complex question fallacy has occurred.

17. APPEAL TO IGNORANCE

An **appeal to ignorance** (lack of knowledge) argument makes one of two possible mistakes: (1) A claim is made that a statement *must be true* because it has not been proven to be false, or (2) a claim is made that a statement *must be false* because it has not been proven to be true. Both claims are unjustified.

Appeal to ignorance
An argument built on a position of ignorance claims either that (1) a statement must be true because it has not been proven to be false or (2) a statement must be false because it has not been proven to be true.

An example of the first kind of mistake is this:

> UFOs must exist because no one has proven that they don't exist.

Here is an example of the second kind of mistake:

> There is definitely no life anywhere else in the universe. This follows from the fact that we have never received signals from any part of space.

The conclusion in the second example is based on a single factor—the lack of signals from outer space. But our failure to have detected any signals may simply signify our lack of sophisticated methods of detection. Also, the ability to send signals is not a necessary requirement for life to exist. Both examples illustrate that fallacies of ignorance result from a general misunderstanding of science and the role of inductive arguments. For example, for a long time it was believed that an invisible substance called "phlogiston" existed in all objects that burned. When a flame burned, the phlogiston was released until no more existed in the burning object. It was thought that if you placed a candle in a glass container, the candle will eventually go out because the phlogiston was trapped in the confined space, so no more could be released. However, decisive experiments by a scientist named Lavoisier led not only to the demise of the theory of phlogiston, but also to the discovery of oxygen.

Scientists can often make *strong arguments* that something exists or does not exist. Scientists generally use inductive reasoning to shape their arguments, so they are *not* proving the certainty of their conclusions in the sense of a valid deductive argument. Instead,

PROFILES IN LOGIC
Arthur Schopenhauer

Arthur Schopenhauer (1788–1860) is not generally regarded as a logician or a mathematician, but rather as a philosopher who devoted his life to, as he tells us, "debunking charlatans, windbags, and claptrap." Schopenhauer firmly believed that fallacies should be exposed whenever they appear. In *The Art of Controversy*, he remarks that "it would be a very good thing if every trick could receive some short and obviously appropriate name, so that when a man used this or that particular trick, he could be at once reproached for it." Indeed, hundreds of fallacies have been recognized, described, and named.

Schopenhauer is often called the philosopher of pessimism because he thought that human experience is filled with all manner of brutality, pain, and suffering. Humans are compelled to hate, love, and desire, with only temporary escapes—philosophic contemplation, art (especially music), and sympathy for the plight of others.

In addition, Schopenhauer was one of the first Western philosophers to recognize and incorporate ideas from Eastern religions, such as Buddhism. In his system of thought, we are asked to "see ourselves in all existence."

scientists rely on the accumulated evidence of scientific research to make their arguments. Much of science is considered "tentative," because the arguments are not meant to be deductively valid. However, a good scientific argument is inductively strong.

If substantial evidence is available to decide an issue, then the fallacy of ignorance does not arise. For example, if a police investigation results in no credible evidence found linking a suspect to a crime, then no matter how strongly the police might feel about the suspect, the suspect will most likely be released. But this does not mean that we can conclude with certainty that the person is innocent; it just means that the person is *probably* not guilty of the crime. Similarly, if the verdict of a jury is that the defendant is "not guilty," then the jury is saying that the evidence presented by the prosecution was not sufficient to determine guilt *beyond a reasonable doubt*. (It is important to recognize that the legal phrase "not guilty" is not synonymous with "innocent.")

PROFILES IN LOGIC
Francis Bacon

Francis Bacon (1561–1626) held that certain fundamental fallacies prevent us from achieving a correct understanding of nature. Bacon referred to these fallacies as "idols," by which he meant sources of misunderstanding that undermine human knowledge. However, he argued that we can learn to recognize and avoid these idols.

Bacon discussed four types of idols: (1) *Idols of the Tribe*. These are part of basic human nature, so they affect everyone. For example, our sense perceptions are easily tricked, so we need to invent precise and accurate mechanical instruments to help us understand nature. Bacon tells us that "human understanding is like a false mirror, which, receiving rays irregularly, distorts and discolors the nature of things by mingling its own nature with it." We also have the tendency to believe what we *want* to be true, rather than what *is* objectively true. (2) *Idols of the Cave*. These are specific to each individual. In a sense, each one of us is housed in the cave of our mind,

where our thoughts are subject to the accidental nature of our personal experience. Over time, each of us evolves a particular view of the world, by which we judge all things. (3) *Idols of the Marketplace*. These are mistakes based on an uncritical use of language. Although we need to communicate our ideas and beliefs to others, words can be vague or ambiguous, so we must be careful. Inattention to the correct meaning of words leads to fallacious reasoning. (4) *Idols of the Theater*. These are systems of belief that have solidified over time but which rest on a false foundation. They exist in belief systems that have over time insulated themselves from objective scrutiny. They are ruled by elite groups whose authority is unquestioned by masses of followers.

In order to overcome the four idols, knowledge must be based on observation and experimentation. Bacon developed a system of thought based on an objective study of facts of nature by which we can slowly build general theories.

Let's return to the first example: "UFOs must exist because no one has proven that they don't exist." The person making this argument is probably using the phrase "no one has proven" to mean a deductively valid argument. Given this, the person's conclusion, "UFOs must exist," relies on a mistaken interpretation of science and, in that sense, the premise is irrelevant to the conclusion.

18. APPEAL TO AN UNQUALIFIED AUTHORITY

Arguments often rely on the opinions of experts, specialists whose education, experience, and knowledge provide relevant support for a claim. When an argument uses expert testimony that is backed by strong evidence with no hint of impropriety, then the argument is most likely strong (as long as the testimony falls within the realm of the expert's field). On the other hand, arguments that rely on the opinions of people who either have *no* expertise, training, or knowledge relevant to the issue at hand, or whose testimony is not trustworthy, are arguments that **appeal to an unqualified authority**.

A person may have the credentials of an expert, but he may be *biased* toward a certain result. For example, some physicians who worked for insurance companies have testified under oath at congressional hearings that they knowingly denied payment for many patients' treatment even though they knew that they should approve it. The physicians admitted to receiving enormous yearly commissions depending on how much money they saved the insurance company. The reason that they revealed the truth was that they could not live with the consequences of their actions: the fact that their decisions led directly to some people's death. Therefore, when those physicians used their power to deny treatment to otherwise qualified patients, they were biased in their decision making.

One of the most prevalent fallacious uses of inappropriate authority is in advertisements. Athletes, celebrities, and former politicians often endorse products to boost sales. The consumer is expected to respect the famous personalities and trust their opinion. Here is an example:

> I'm Nick Panning, quarterback of the Los Angeles Seals. I've been eating *Oaties* for breakfast since I was a kid. *Oaties* taste great, and they have all the nutrition kids need. You should get some for your kids today.

Merely being famous does not qualify someone to pronounce the merits of a product. An athlete generally has no expertise in the nutritional value of a breakfast cereal. On the other hand, a person with a Ph.D. in nutrition would presumably be in a good position to offer a fair assessment of the breakfast cereal (provided the opinion is not based on monetary compensation).

Turning once again to science, no scientist would conclude that a statement is true merely because Albert Einstein said so. Every scientific statement has to be backed up by objective evidence, and replicable results. Albert Einstein, the famous *physicist*, was asked to be the first *president* of Israel. He humbly declined, stating that he had no idea how to run a country. Such modesty is rare.

Appeal to an unqualified authority
An argument that relies on the opinions of people who either have *no* expertise, training, or knowledge relevant to the issue at hand, or whose testimony is not trustworthy.

19. FALSE DICHOTOMY

The fallacy of **false dichotomy** ("dichotomy" means *to cut in two parts*) occurs when it is assumed that only two choices are possible, when in fact others exist. The argument contains a premise that presents an "either . . . or . . ." choice with the assumption that no other choices are available. For example, suppose that a person defending the Patriot Act and its potential infringement on certain basic freedoms says the following:

> Either we give up some traditional basic freedoms or we lose the war on terror.

The argument is missing a premise and a conclusion. Since the person is defending the Patriot Act, the missing premise might be "No one wants to lose the war on terror," and the missing conclusion is most likely "We must give up some traditional basic freedoms."

Let's reveal the argument form. If we let G = *we give up some traditional basic freedoms*, and L = *we lose the war on terror*, then we get this result:

> G or L.
> Not L.
> _____
> G.

The argument is *valid*: If the premises are assumed to be true, the conclusion is necessarily true. However, the argument is *unsound*. The fallacy occurs because the first premise is false. Since the first premise fails to acknowledge that other possibilities exist, it sets up a false dichotomy. If we are captured by the passionate nature of the assertion and its implications, then we seem to be facing a difficult choice. According to the assertion, there are only two choices. If we don't want to lose the war on terror, then we must conclude that we are willing to give up some traditional basic freedoms. On the other hand, if we are not willing to give up some traditional basic freedoms, then we must conclude that we will lose the war on terror. However, once we see that this is really an instance of the fallacy of false dichotomy, then we can reject the entire notion of having only two choices in the matter. We can argue that it is possible to win the war on terror without giving up traditional basic freedoms.

Here is another example:

> He was born on a Monday or a Thursday. He was not born on a Thursday, so he was born on a Monday.

Although the argument is valid, we can question its soundness. The first premise assumes that there are only two choices, but we are not given any evidence to support that assumption. Since there are five other days of the week on which the person in question might have been born, this is an instance of a false dichotomy.

When the fallacy does not occur: Not all arguments that present two choices in one of the premises are fallacies of false dichotomy. The key determination is whether the dichotomy assumes the two choices that are offered exhaust all the possibilities available. Here is an example:

> Teddy Roosevelt was the twentieth U.S. president, or Fairbanks is the capital of Alaska. Teddy Roosevelt was not the twentieth U.S. president, so Fairbanks is the capital of Alaska.

False dichotomy A fallacy that occurs when it is assumed that only two choices are possible, when in fact others exist.

This is a valid argument: *If* the premises are assumed to be true, then the conclusion is true. However, truth value analysis shows that the first premise and the conclusion are both false (the second premise is true), thus the argument is unsound. But since the first premise does not offer a false dichotomy, this argument, although unsound, is not fallacious.

In order to illustrate a false dichotomy, let's look at a modified example from the philosopher Arthur Schopenhauer:

> Either you agree with our country's policies or you should go live in another country. You don't agree with our country's policies. Therefore, you should go live in another country.

The argument assumes that only two possibilities exist when in fact more than two exist. In the foregoing example, only two choices are given:

(1) You agree with our country's policies.
(2) You should go live in another country.

Surely these are not the only two possibilities. A concerned citizen has the right and obligation to try to change a country's policies if they are illegal, immoral, or at least not in the best interests of the country. Certainly not every political decision will turn out to be the best for a particular country. Hence, a third possibility can be added to the example:

(3) You disagree with the country's policies, and you want to change them peacefully and legally.

Exception: Not all arguments that offer two choices are fallacious. If the two choices are in fact the only two options, then the fallacy does not occur. For example, suppose that you need to make an appointment to see a doctor and she has only 2 days available this week. We might see something like the following:

> The doctor can see you either on Tuesday or Friday. You said that Tuesday will not work for you, so I'll schedule you for Friday.

Since the two choices are in fact your only options, the argument is not an instance of false dichotomy.

Fallacies of Diversion

A fallacy of diversion occurs when the meanings of terms or phrases are changed (intentionally or unintentionally) within the argument, or when our attention is purposely (or accidentally) diverted from the issue at hand. Also known as fallacies of ambiguity, these types of fallacies depend on the fact that words or phrases can have many different meanings, and context is crucial. Ambiguity, vagueness, or any unclear use of a term can seriously affect the understanding, analysis, and evaluation of an argument. On the other hand, an arguer may divert our attention by *changing the subject*, thereby setting up an argument that avoids the actual discussion.

20. EQUIVOCATION

The first fallacy of diversion we will look at, **equivocation**, occurs when the conclusion of an argument relies on an intentional or unintentional shift in the meaning of a term or phrase that was used in the premises. ("Equivocation" means to use different senses of a term or phrase.) For example, someone might say the following:

> My older brother tries hard to be cool. I told him he has the personality of a cucumber. Since a refrigerator is a good place to keep things cool, he should spend some time in there.

The term "cool" has several meanings that tend to sort themselves out in the context of particular sentences. The equivocation in this example is easy to spot, but it does show clearly how the fallacy works. Equivocation can also occur when *relative terms* such as "big" and "small" are misused. Here is another example:

> I was told that he is a big man on campus (BMOC). But big men are at least 6'4" tall. He is no more than 5'7" tall, so he can't be a BMOC.

The equivocation occurs when the relative term "big" is used in two different senses.
  Here are two other examples of the fallacy:

- Judy said she had a hot date last night. Her apartment can get hot unless she uses the air conditioner. Therefore, the air conditioner in her apartment must not have been working.
- That looks like a hard outfit to get into. The factory that made it must have used really hard material. So, perhaps you should wash the outfit in some fabric softener.

The first example equivocates on the term "hot," while the second example uses two different senses of the term "hard." When an argument is an equivocation fallacy, it is most likely invalid, and thus unsound. This stems from the fact that the two different meanings of a key term will not be sufficient, by themselves, to support the conclusion.

  Let's look at some examples where the equivocation is not so obvious. The world of politics offers numerous examples, one of which is the issue of employment. A recent presidential administration had to respond to a huge loss of manufacturing jobs during its time in office. To counteract the statistics showing a loss of jobs, the administration proposed that some fast-food workers should be reclassified from service workers to manufacturing workers. Under the new definition, anyone who cooked a burger, placed it on a bun, added condiments, and put it in a wrapper was engaged in manufacturing a product. There would thus have been a gain in manufacturing jobs during the course of the administration's time in office. Of course, once the opposing political party found out about the idea, it was quickly dropped. The administration's argument that it had cut unemployment rested on a shift in the meaning of the term "manufacturing worker," and thus was an instance of a fallacy of equivocation.

  An earlier administration hatched a similar idea. The federal government normally defines the "unemployed" as only those people who are actively collecting government

Equivocation The fallacy occurs when the conclusion of an argument relies on an intentional or unintentional shift in the meaning of a term or phrase in the premises.

unemployment checks. Under this definition, people who have either exhausted their checks or are on welfare are not considered unemployed. The unemployment rate is then calculated by finding the number of unemployed and comparing this with the total number of those employed. In addition, the entire military was not used to calculate the unemployment rate; military personnel were considered neither employed nor unemployed. However, just before a presidential election, a scheme was considered that proposed that all active military personnel should be considered employed. This would have seriously reduced the unemployment rate, favoring the incumbent administration. Once again, the idea was exposed and abandoned. The administration intentionally used two different meanings of the term "employed" designed to make it appear that their economic policies were working. The argument they tried to present was an instance of the fallacy of equivocation.

21. STRAW MAN

Straw man The fallacy occurs when someone's argument is misrepresented in order to create a new argument that can be easily refuted. The new argument is so weak that it is "made of straw." The arguer then falsely claims that his opponent's real argument has been defeated.

A fallacy can occur when attention is purposely (or accidentally) diverted from the issue at hand. In other words, statements or arguments intending one thing are subtly distorted in order to divert the emphasis to a different issue. A **straw man** fallacy occurs when an argument is misrepresented in order to create a new argument that can be easily refuted. The new argument is so weak that it is "made of straw." The arguer then falsely claims that his opponent's real argument has been defeated. The straw man fallacy relies on an act of diversion, a tactic that is common in the political arena. Candidates often attempt to distort the views of their opponents by clipping a small piece out of a speech or interview and using it out of context, creating an impression directly opposite from that of the original argument. For example, a person running for public office might say the following:

> I oppose the law that requires teaching intelligent design as an alternative to evolutionary theory in public school biology classes. Evolution is an established scientific theory and deserves to be taught in science classes. Intelligent design is not a scientific theory, and it should not be taught in science classes.

An opponent of this candidate might criticize her position this way:

> She is against the new law that mandates teaching intelligent design alongside the theory of evolution. It should be obvious to anyone that she really wants to eliminate religious beliefs. She wants to destroy one of the basic principles of the Constitution of the United States.

The opponent has created a straw man argument by taking the original statement and adding an unjustified premise, "It should be obvious to anyone that she really wants to eliminate religious beliefs." The fallacious argument concludes, "She wants to destroy one of the basic principles of the Constitution of the United States."

The straw man fallacy is often used to create a false impression that a certain group holds an unacceptable position. The argument usually refers to a vague group who supposedly holds an extreme position. Here is an example:

> The Democrats promise that a government health care system will reduce the cost of health care, but as the economist Thomas Sowell has pointed out,

government health care will not reduce the cost; it will simply refuse to pay the cost. And who will suffer the most when they ration care? The sick, the elderly, and the disabled, of course. The America I know and love is not one in which my parents or my baby with Down Syndrome will have to stand in front of Obama's "death panel" so his bureaucrats can decide, based on a subjective judgment of their "level of productivity in society," whether they are worthy of health care. Such a system is downright evil.

Sarah Palin, "Statement on the Current Health Care Debate"

Palin has created a straw man argument about "death panels." In so doing, she takes the hollow defeat of straw man to support her claim that the proposed government health-care plan "is downright evil." Straw man arguments like this are used by most political parties, and are a staple of television programs featuring political pundits (critics or commentators) who argue about domestic and world affairs.

22. RED HERRING

Another fallacy of diversion, the **red herring** fallacy, occurs when someone completely ignores an opponent's position. By changing the subject, the red herring "throws one off the scent," diverting the discussion in a new direction. This type of fallacy differs from the straw man fallacy in that a straw man argument is purposely created to be weak, whereas a red herring argument may in fact be strong. But because a strong red herring argument diverts our attention from the real argument, it has no bearing on an opponent's argument. Here is an example:

> Many people criticize TV as turning America into an illiterate society. How can we criticize the very medium that is the envy of countries all over the world? The entertainment quality and variety of TV programs today are greater than ever before, not to mention the enormous number of cable options available to members of the viewing audience. Thus, the critics are wrong.

Rather than presenting evidence that contradicts the claim that TV is turning America into an illiterate society, the argument diverts our attention to the entertainment value of TV. Although the evidence that is presented may be true, it fails in this case to support the conclusion.

Let's look at another example. A lot of accusations were made that Barack Obama was not born in the United States. If the accusations were true, then perhaps he is not a U.S. citizen. In that case, according to the U.S. Constitution, he is not legally allowed to be president. Critics demanded that he prove his citizenship. Obama eventually produced his birth certificate that showed he was born in Honolulu, Hawaii, and thus was indeed a U.S. citizen.

However, some critics were not satisfied. They argued that this proved nothing because the document listed Obama's father's race as *African*. In other words, if Barack Obama had dual citizenship at birth, then perhaps he does not meet the Constitution's definition of a "natural-born" citizen. The critics claimed that this possibility required a reinterpretation of the intentions of the original framers of the Constitution. The critics shifted the argument from whether Obama could offer evidence that

Red herring A fallacy that occurs when someone completely ignores an opponent's position and changes the subject, diverting the discussion in a new direction.

he was a citizen by diverting the debate to an examination of the intentions of the Founding Fathers.

In this next example we will first look at an argument supporting the claim that nuclear power plants are dangerous. Next, we will see how a red herring argument is created to try to defeat the first argument.

> Nuclear power plants are dangerous. We are all aware of the recent problems with the Fukushima reactor in Japan and the extent of damage and radiation leaks. Also, the 1986 disaster in Chernobyl caused many deaths and thousands of cancer cases. There is also credible evidence linking several nuclear power plants in the United States to unusual rises in leukemia, as well as dramatic increases in birth defects to children born near the facilities.

An opponent of the argument might create a red herring argument that diverts our attention from the main issue regarding the dangers that nuclear power plants pose, and shift the argument to another issue by using words or phrases designed to "push our emotional buttons."

> The dangers of nuclear power plants have been overstated. Don't forget that we are caught in an international economic war over oil controlled by Middle Eastern dictatorial regimes that brutally punish any dissent and refuse to acknowledge democratic principles. Also, because shadowy international oil cartels manipulate oil prices, our economy and our individual rights are violated. If we want to take charge of our lives, we must build more nuclear power plants.

The argument does *not* address the dangers of nuclear power plants. It diverts our attention by talking about "Middle Eastern dictatorial regimes," and how they treat their citizens, as well as "shadowy international oil cartels" that violate individual rights. Perhaps there are strong arguments that show how the United States has access to more state-of-the-art technologies that can reduce the likelihood of future disasters and protect people from harmful radiation; however, the foregoing red herring argument does none of these things.

23. MISLEADING PRECISION

Misleading precision A claim that appears to be statistically significant but is not.

A fallacy of **misleading precision** occurs when a claim appears to be statistically significant but is not. Statistics are often used misleadingly. The following is an example that we might find in an advertisement:

> Our cookies contain 30% less fat, so you should start eating them if you want to lose weight.

Our attention is captured by the seemingly impressive statistic. The idea is to dazzle us with the precise percentage in order to divert our attention from assessing its relevance to the conclusion. However, the argument does not stand up to scrutiny. It is fair to ask, "30% less fat than what?" The asserted percentage is relative to some other item, and we need to know what that is in order to know if this product is really significantly lower in fat than competing products. It might be the case that the cookies have

30% less fat than they did before, but they still might contain more fat than is ideal for someone trying to lose weight.

Here is another example of the kind of claim we might find in an advertisement:

> In order to clear out inventory, we have reduced our used car prices by 20%. These prices won't last forever, so you'd better hurry in and buy one of these cars before the sale ends.

In this example we need to ask, "Reduced by 20% from what?" The car dealership might have used an outdated markup price no longer in effect in order to get an artificial reduction. Another possibility is that the dealer might have recently tried raising the cost of used cars and, if sales were slow, simply returned the prices to their previous level.

The fallacy of misleading precision can even occur in a seemingly straightforward scientific claim. Consider the following:

> The full moon affects people in strange ways. We have found that you have a 100% greater chance of being physically assaulted during a full moon than at any other time of the month.

In order to evaluate the argument, we need to know the average rate of physical assault over an extended period of time. Suppose we find that the average physical assault rate per month is 1 out of every 10,000 persons. According to the argument, the full moon rate would then be 2 out of every 10,000 persons. Although the statistics show that you have a 100% greater chance of being physically assaulted during a full moon, nevertheless the greater chance is not significant. Whenever statistics are used without a reference or comparison group, you should try to determine if this is an instance of misleading precision.

24. MISSING THE POINT

The fallacy of **missing the point** occurs when premises that seem to lead logically to one conclusion are used instead to support an unexpected conclusion. A conclusion "misses the point" when the premises do not adequately prepare us for it. For example:

> I read that it can take years to find the "black boxes" that contain crucial flight information regarding an airplane crash, and sometimes they are never found. Given this, all air travel should be suspended.

The conclusion diverts us from the direction of the premises. In fact, the evidence in the premises regarding the sometimes difficult task of locating the black boxes might be relevant to the following conclusions:

- The airline industry should adopt the latest technology whereby the black boxes can either float in water or have the capacity to send out beacon signals for more than 1 month.
- Airlines need to upgrade their airplanes with the latest GPS devices.
- The search-and-rescue teams that look for missing commercial airplanes should have the same equipment that is available to the military.

Missing the point
When premises that seem to lead logically to one conclusion are used instead to support an unexpected conclusion.

However, since the gap between the premises and conclusion that "all air travel should be suspended" is so great, we say that the argument misses the point.

Here is another example:

> The Affordable Care Act has been difficult to implement. There were system failures in which people could not log on to the government website, and even cases of people's private information being compromised. Therefore, we should never let the government try to solve social problems.

The premises provide evidence regarding the difficulty of putting the law into effect. Given this, we might expect to read conclusions like the following:

- The government should have waited until the systems were thoroughly tested.
- The government should have contracted with major computing companies to ensure that the systems were state of the art.

However, since the gap between the premises and conclusion that "we should never let the government try to solve social problems" is so great, we can say that the argument misses the point and has an irrelevant conclusion.

Summary of Fallacies of Unwarranted Assumption and Diversion

Fallacies of unwarranted assumption are arguments that assume the truth of some unproved or questionable claim.

15. **Begging the question:** In one type, the fallacy occurs when a premise is simply reworded in the conclusion. In a second type, called *circular reasoning*, a set of statements seem to support each other with no clear beginning or end point. In a third type, the argument assumes certain key information that may be controversial or is not supported by facts.

16. **Complex question:** The fallacy occurs when a single question actually contains multiple parts and an unestablished hidden assumption.

17. **Appeal to ignorance:** An argument built on a position of ignorance claims either that (1) a statement must be true because it has not been proven to be false or (2) a statement must be false because it has not been proven to be true.

18. **Appeal to an unqualified authority:** An argument that relies on the opinions of people who either have *no* expertise, training, or knowledge relevant to the issue at hand, or whose testimony is not trustworthy.

19. **False dichotomy:** The fallacy occurs when it is assumed that only two choices are possible, when in fact others exist.

A fallacy of diversion occurs when the meanings of terms or phrases are changed (intentionally or unintentionally) within the argument, or when our attention is purposely (or accidentally) diverted from the issue at hand.

20. **Equivocation:** The fallacy occurs when the conclusion of an argument relies on an intentional or unintentional shift in the meaning of a term or phrase in the premises.

21. **Straw man:** The fallacy occurs when an argument is misrepresented in order to create a new argument that can be easily refuted. The new argument is so weak that it is "made of straw." The arguer then falsely claims that his opponent's real argument has been defeated.

22. **Red herring:** The fallacy occurs when someone completely ignores an opponent's position and changes the subject, diverting the discussion in a new direction.

23. **Misleading precision:** A claim that appears to be statistically significant but is not.

24. **Missing the point:** When premises that seem to lead logically to one conclusion are used instead to support an unexpected conclusion.

EXERCISES 4D

I. Determine whether each statement is true or false.

1. The appeal to an unqualified authority occurs when an argument relies on the experience, training, or knowledge of people who are experts relevant to the issue at hand.

Level 1 Multiple-Choice Questions

Answer: False

2. An appeal to ignorance occurs when a person's character or circumstances are used to reject their claims.

Level 2 Multiple-Choice Questions

3. An argument that claims either (1) a statement must be true because it has not been proven to be false or (2) a statement must be false because it has not been proven to be true is called *ad hominem*.

4. A complex question is a single question that contains multiple hidden parts.

⭐ 5. An argument that offers only two alternatives when in fact more exist is an example of a biased sample.

6. An argument that assumes as evidence the very thing that it attempts to prove in the conclusion begs the question.

7. A false dichotomy fallacy is an argument that attacks a person rather than a person's argument.

8. The fallacy of missing the point occurs in an argument where premises that seem to lead logically to one conclusion are used instead to support an unexpected conclusion.

⭐ 9. A fallacy of equivocation mistakenly transfers an attribute of the individual parts of an object to the entire object.

10. When a claim is made that appears to be statistically significant but which, upon analysis, is not, is an example of the fallacy of misleading precision.

11. The red herring fallacy occurs when someone's words are taken out of context to create an argument that distorts the person's position.

12. A fallacy of equivocation can happen only if the argument intentionally uses different meanings of words or phrases.

⭐ 13. A straw man fallacy is a misapplication of statistics.

14. A claim that appears to be statistically significant, but which upon analysis is not, is the fallacy of accident.

15. A fallacy of equivocation occurs when a term has a different meaning in the premises than it has in the conclusion.

II. Read the following passages. If an argument commits a fallacy of unwarranted assumption or diversion, then identify the specific fallacy. If a passage does not contain a fallacy, then answer "No fallacy." Explain your answers.

1. She argued that we should raise taxes on people who make more than $250,000 a year. But she failed to mention that the government has a duty to protect all of its citizens, especially when we are constantly under threat of terrorists who want to see us destroyed. We can't let our guard down for a minute, so there is no reason to seriously consider her position at this time.

Answer: Straw man. The fallacy occurs when an argument is misrepresented in order to create a new argument that can be easily refuted. The new argument is so weak that it is "made of straw." The arguer then falsely claims that his opponent's real argument has been defeated.

2. Either you love your country or you are a traitor. I'm sure you are not a traitor. Therefore, you must love your country.

3. George Soros is famous because he broke the Bank of England. It follows that the Bank of England must have spent a lot of money on construction costs to fix all the broken parts of the bank.

4. Biology 1 was easy for me. Physics 1 was no problem. I think I'm going to change my major to social work.

⭐ 5. This car combines top engineering with classic styling. You can't buy a better engineered or classically styled car at any cost.

6. I believe that we are reincarnated. No one has ever been able to prove that after death our spirits don't move on to another baby.

7. The producer presented his budget for the movie. However, a lot of newspapers are going bankrupt, and so are many magazines. The cost of printing presses, newsprint, and ink is rising. Thus, we should reject his budget proposal.

8. Last week's poll showed the incumbent senator lost 10% in his overall approval rating. So, we can safely say that the incumbent senator has the lowest approval rating of any senator from this state in the last 50 years.

Level 1 Multiple-
Choice Questions

Level 2 Multiple-
Choice Questions

Video Tutorial

9. We verified your employment history and did a credit check. I assume that you have read our repayment terms, since you signed the loan agreement form. Therefore, I am going to approve your application for a loan.

10. Do you still plagiarize your research papers from the Internet?

11. The sign says that there is no mass on Sunday. But my science teacher said that mass is the same as energy. So I guess there is no energy on Sunday either.

12. That must be a great product for men since a former senator and presidential candidate endorsed it.

13. My boss caught me playing video games on my office computer during work hours. She said that it was a violation of office policies, and she warned me to stop or I would be fired. However, there are government protections to prevent employers from any discrimination on the basis of race, religion, or sexual orientation. Do we want to give up these protections? No. So we must fight to change the office policies.

Video Tutorial

14. I told my daughter that either she must stop listening to rock and roll music or she is a devil worshiper. She says that there is nothing wrong with rock and roll music. That proves it. Only a devil worshiper would say that.

15. That guy plays a doctor on my favorite TV show. I saw him in a commercial where he said that Asperalinol was great for migraine headaches. It must really work, so the next time you go to a drugstore pick me up a bottle.

16. All I know is that no one has proven that the Abominable Snowman does not exist. So, that, in itself, proves that he exists.

17. Have you stopped stealing money from your parents' wallets?

18. Your mother said that you can't afford a new car with your current income. But you said that your girlfriend is ashamed of riding in your car, and she doesn't like its color. Also, think how a new car will impress the guys at work. Given this, you should definitely buy a new car.

19. Mr. Crabhouse is a hard grader. Not only that, he forces you to attend class, participate in discussions, and do homework. He actually expects us to think about the material outside of class. So you can believe that his class teaches students nothing about real life.

20. Our hot dogs are made from 100% natural meat, so they taste better.

21. You scored at least 93% on all three exams, and you did all the homework. Your class participation was excellent. In addition, the only time you missed class, you provided a doctor's excuse. Given this level of performance, you will receive an A for the course.

22. That is the type of movie you don't like, so I'm sure you will hate it.

23.   There is no record of how the Egyptian pyramids were actually constructed. So, the only possible explanation is that aliens from another planet must have built them.

24.   Do you still look for discarded food in dumpsters?

★25.   You said that I don't spend enough time with you and that I ignore you when we are together. Do you want me to be like the guy next door? He doesn't work, so he spends all day at home with his wife. But he is constantly screaming at her and putting her down, even in public. So, if that's what you want, then I'll do it.

26.   Everything written in that book is 100% accurate. It has to be, since nothing in it is false.

27.   Statistics show that people with a college degree earn 50% more during their lifetime than those without a degree. So, you should begin investing in blue chip stocks.

28.   The label on that cheesecake says that it has 40% fewer calories. If I eat that cheesecake regularly, then I should lose some weight.

★29.   My mother wants me to take piano lessons because studies show that early music training helps students in math. But pianos cost a lot of money, and even if we could afford one, our apartment is too small.

30.   The missing Malaysian airplane was either hijacked by space aliens or it was sucked into a worm hole. But NASA didn't report any recent space-time continuum anomalies, so it must have been space aliens.

31.   I am going to vote for the incumbent, Senator Loweman, because my chemistry teacher said he is the best candidate.

32.   I know you like chocolate ice cream and you like cake. We're about to have dessert, so I'll make you a chili dog.

★33.   Even though neither of us was at home when it happened, the dog must have broken the window by jumping on it. You have not shown me any other way that it could have happened.

34.   He is a very honest individual because he is not dishonest.

35.   The advertisement shows the latest Nobel Prize winner in literature drinking that new wine, Chateau Rouge. So, it must taste divine.

36.   Scientific experiments have never proved conclusively that there are not any ghosts; therefore, I firmly believe that they do exist.

★37.   Either we cut school funding or we raise taxes. Nobody wants to cut school funding, so we must raise taxes.

38. The advertisement for that DVD player claims that it has 50% fewer moving parts. You should buy it; it is less likely to break down in the future.

39. That politician never tells the truth because every time he tries to explain why he did something wrong, he fabricates a story.

40. Dad, you told me why I should help more around the house, especially in the evenings. But don't you know the law? I did some research regarding the federal child labor laws and found that "14- and 15-year-olds may not be employed before 7 a.m. or after 7 p.m., except from June 1 through Labor Day when the evening hour is extended to 9 p.m. (time is based on local standards; i.e., whether the locality has adopted daylight savings time)." I think the law is clear, so you can't expect me to comply with your demands.

41. She is a chess grand master, so when she says that Russia is manipulating the internal affairs of countries that were once part of the old Soviet Union, you should believe her.

42. I hear that Walter is handling some hot stocks right now. The new asbestos gloves I bought protect your hands from hot objects. Maybe I should give them to Walter for protection.

43. If you buy two lottery tickets, then you double your chances of hitting the jackpot. Knowing that, why would you buy just one?

44. When high school students graduate, they have a choice to make: They can either go to college or become bums. My niece decided not to go to college, so, mark my words, she will certainly become a bum.

45. You want a raise because you have been here 2 years, your evaluations have been consistently high, you rarely miss work, and the company has experienced its highest stock dividends in the last 10 years. All of that is true, but have you forgotten that there are hundreds of thousands of people who are unemployed in this country? Any of them would be thrilled to have your job. In fact, most of them would even take less than you are making now. Given these facts, we can't justify giving you a raise.

46. Look, the picture of the Olympic basketball team is on this cereal. That proves it must be good for athletes.

47. The government's spending of our income tax money on public education without asking our permission is wrong; therefore, the government's actions are a violation of our human rights. Furthermore, since the government's actions are a violation of our human rights, it follows that the government's spending of our income tax money on public education without asking our permission is wrong.

48. The flight attendant said that the only two choices for the main entrée are chicken or fish. I don't like fish, so I'm getting the chicken.

⭐ 49. Evolution is a biological law of nature. All civilized people should obey the law. Therefore, all civilized people should obey the law of evolution.

50. You said that you don't believe in God. But here's something you overlooked. It is estimated that from 1975 to 1979, the Khmer Rouge, under the leadership of Pol Pot, killed roughly 25% of the population of Cambodia. The figure is believed to be between one and three million people out of a population of eight million. The Khmer Rouge were godless people, so ending their reign of terror was a good thing.

E. RECOGNIZING FALLACIES IN ORDINARY LANGUAGE

The examples of informal fallacies analyzed so far have been constructed to clearly reveal the mistake in reasoning. They were meant to be fairly easy to recognize—once you understand the underlying techniques. However, when you read something or hear someone talk, detecting informal fallacies may be a bit more challenging. A writer who has a fluid prose style can sometimes produce a persuasive passage merely by dazzling you with her brilliant writing. A great speaker can mesmerize his audience with the mere sound of his voice, so much so that we overlook the substance of what is being said.

For example, the great actor Laurence Olivier once gave an emotional acceptance speech at the Academy Awards:

> Mr. President and Governors of the Academy, Committee Members, fellows, my very noble and approved good masters, my colleagues, my friends, my fellow-students. In the great wealth, the great firmament of your nation's generosity, this particular choice may perhaps be found by future generations as a trifle eccentric, but the mere fact of it—the prodigal, pure, human kindness of it—must be seen as a beautiful star in that firmament which shines upon me at this moment, dazzling me a little, but filling me with warmth and the extraordinary elation, the euphoria that happens to so many of us at the first breath of the majestic glow of a new tomorrow. From the top of this moment, in the solace, in the kindly emotion that is charging my soul and my heart at this moment, I thank you for this great gift which lends me such a very splendid part in this, your glorious occasion.

This short speech left most of the audience in awe, in part because Olivier was considered perhaps the greatest Shakespearian actor and in part because of his dramatic delivery. Few people went back to read the words, which, although poetic and emotional, do not contain much of substance. The moral of the story is that we have to be careful when we encounter either impressive-sounding speech or beautifully crafted written material. This is especially true if the passages contain arguments.

Some fallacies occur because the emotional attachment to a belief overrides the demands of a clear, rational, well-supported argument. Here is one example:

> Our acceptance of abortion does not end with the killing of unborn human life; it continues on to affect our attitude toward all aspects of human life. This is most obvious in how quickly, once we accept abortion, then comes the acceptance of infanticide, the killing of babies who after birth do not come up to someone's standard of life worthy to be lived, and then on to euthanasia of the aged. If human life can be taken before birth, there is no logical reason why human life cannot be taken after birth.   Francis Schaeffer, *Who Is for Life?*

The author's position about abortion is clear. However, the attempt to discredit any acceptance of abortion leads the author to commit the slippery slope fallacy. No evidence is offered in the passage to support the (assumed) link in the chain of reasoning that "once we accept abortion, then comes the acceptance of infanticide." Similarly, the author provides no support for the next (assumed) link in the chain, namely the claim that "and then on to euthanasia of the aged." This example points out the importance of separating a belief from the possible reasons in support of a belief. It also illustrates the need to guard against the quick acceptance (or rejection) of a position based solely on our emotional attachment to a position.

The next passage contains another example of a slippery slope argument.

> Health care providers, researchers, and advocates around the country were alarmed to learn that POPLINE (POPulation information onLINE) had rendered the search term "abortion" a stopword—which directs the database to ignore the term when used in a search . . . self-censorship of a specific term like "abortion" in a scientific setting sets a dangerous precedent. . . . It's scary enough to consider the possibility that ideological searches are being performed by anonymous government employees who troll our scientific databases for the word "abortion." [The terms] "contraception," "sexuality," and "reproductive health" are the next stopwords, unless we remain vigilant and protest loudly.
> Pablo Rodriguez, M.D., Jennifer Aulwes, and Wayne C. Shields, "Abortion and the Slippery Slope," Scienceprogress.org

The authors argue that the website was directed to ignore the stopword "abortion" so the database would ignore it as a search term. The authors conclude that this form of censorship will lead to other terms being designated as stopwords. However, no evidence is offered to support their dire predictions. The argument fails to support the (assumed) links in the chain of reasoning that the terms "'contraception,' 'sexuality,' and 'reproductive health' are the next stopwords." Therefore, the argument commits the slippery slope fallacy.

Fallacies are not just the result of an emotional attachment to a moral question or to a controversial political viewpoint. In fact, they can occur in a scientific study:

> Winning the Nobel Prize adds nearly two years to your lifespan, and it's not because of the cash that goes with it. The status alone conferred on a scientist by the world's most famous prize is enough to prolong his life; in fact, the status seems to work a *health-giving magic*. The study compared Nobel Prize winners with scientists who were nominated, but did not win. The average lifespan for the winners was just over 76 years, while those who had merely been nominated lived on average for 75.8 years. The researchers found that since the amount of actual prize money won had no effect on longevity, therefore the sheer status of the award is the important factor in extending lifespan.   Donald MacLeod, "Nobel Prize Winners Live Longer," *Education Guardian*

Quite often, a single piece of research gets widespread coverage because it seems to indicate some new and exciting discovery. However, advances in science occur through repeated and exhaustive trials in which many groups of researchers try to eliminate every possible explanation for an effect, leaving only one answer. Therefore, preliminary results, or studies with limited data, need to be carefully weighed. In this example, a correlation has been found, but the difference in longevity between the two groups is small. The argument to support the claim that "status causes the Nobel Prize winners to live longer" could be an instance of the *post hoc* fallacy—or simple coincidence.

Although emotional appeals are a powerful way to sway public opinion, unfortunately some of those appeals are fallacious. Most of us try to balance our feelings with reason, but it is not always easy. Strong emotions can sometimes override rational thinking and lead to disastrous results. This can be seen in the increase in political anger in the United States and the way it is broadcast over the airwaves. Incivility is on view almost daily, and rudeness, discourteous behavior, and disrespect can escalate into violence.

Many people have begun pleading for a less heated and less passionate climate in the public arena. The call is for a reduction in unhelpful rhetoric—in thinly veiled acts of retaliation, in blatant threats, in the exaggeration of apocalyptic social and political consequences, in direct insults, in misinformation and outright lies, and in an unhealthy disregard of intellectual thought and the role of reason. We can replace the negative and destructive tone with constructive and reasonable debate. Issues can be discussed based on facts and the merits of the arguments, without resorting to emotionally charged language that does nothing to advance the correctness of a position.

The call for a reduction in highly charged political discourse reached a high point following the shooting of a member of Congress in 2011. However, another member of Congress objected:

> We can't use this as a moment to try to stifle one side or the other. We can't use this as a moment to say, one side doesn't have a right to talk about the issues they are passionate about.

The response sets up a *straw man* argument by claiming that the advocates for a reduction in emotional rhetoric are saying that "one side doesn't have a right to talk about the issues they are passionate about." The speaker is arguing against a position that no one holds.

The principles of reason, intellectual honesty, and analysis that we applied to short examples can be adapted to longer passages as well. In fact, the next set of exercises allows you to apply those principles to recent events and to historically important cases, many of which are examples of extended arguments.

EXERCISES 4E

The following passages were taken from various sources. Use your understanding of all the fallacies that were presented in this chapter to determine which fallacy best fits the passage. In some cases a passage may contain more than one fallacy. If a passage does not contain a fallacy, then answer "No fallacy." Explain your answers.

Level 1 Multiple-
Choice Questions

Level 2 Multiple-
Choice Questions

1. You can't speak French. Petey Bellows can't speak French. I must therefore conclude that nobody at the University of Minnesota can speak French.

    Max Shulman, "Love Is a Fallacy"

    Answer: Hasty generalization. The conclusion about the entire university is based on two instances.

2. It's a mistake because it is in error.

    William Safire, "On Language: Take My Question Please!"

3. Over and over, they're saying something like this: "We don't know what the noise in the old house was, or the white shape in the photo. So it must be a ghost."   Alan Boyle, "Sleuth Finds the Truth in Ghost Stories," Cosmiclog.nbcnews.com

4. Either man was created just as the Bible tells us, or man evolved from inanimate chemicals and random chance.   Skeptic.org

5. People for the Ethical Treatment of Animals has filed multiple complaints—including alleged animal abuse, the misuse of drugs on horses, and fraud—against trainer Steve Asmussen and his top assistant, Scott Blasi. . . . Clark Brewster, the attorney representing Asmussen and Blasi, said that he had not seen any of the complaints. . . . "Until I see the materials, it's hard to comment. It's obviously a piece completely out of context slanted for the purposes of the organization that caused somebody to deceptively be hired by the Asmussen stable."

    David Grening, "PETA Accuses Asmussen Stable of Mistreating Its Horses," *Daily Racing Form*

6. "The fact that we received so much feedback to the Wolfe-Simon paper suggests to us that science is proceeding as it should," the editors said in a statement. "The study involved multiple techniques and lines of evidence, and the authors felt their conclusion was the most plausible explanation for these results when

considered as a whole. We hope that the study and the subsequent exchange being published today will stimulate further experiments—whether they support or overturn this conclusion."

Alan Boyle, "Arsenic-Life Debate Hits a New Level," NBC News

7. It is the case that either the nobility of this country appear to be wealthy, in which case they can be taxed, or else they appear to be poor, in which case they are living frugally and must have immense savings, which can be taxed.

"Morton's Fork," *Encyclopedia Britannica*

8. I don't like spinach, and I'm glad I don't, because if I liked it I'd eat it, and I just hate it.

Clarence Darrow, in *Clarence Darrow: A One-Man Play*

Video Tutorial

9. I often read the Mexico enablers justify the 800,000 Mexicans illegally crossing the U.S. border each year, rationalizing this with a statement such as, "well it is either they stay in Mexico and starve, or risk their lives crossing the border."

"The Fulano Files," at Fulanofiles.blogspot.com

10. To be an atheist, you have to believe with absolute certainty that there is no God. In order to convince yourself with absolute certainty, you must examine all the Universe and all the places where God could possibly be. Since you obviously haven't, your position is indefensible.

Infidels.org

11. Near-perfect correlations exist between the death rate in Hyderabad, India, from 1911 to 1919, and variations in the membership of the International Association of Machinists during the same period.

David Hackett Fischer, *Historians' Fallacies*

12. I hardly think that 58 is the right age at which to talk about a retirement home unless there are some serious health concerns. My 85-year-old mother power-walks two miles each day, drives her car safely, climbs stairs, does crosswords, and reads the daily paper.

Letter to the editor, *Time*

13. For the natives, they are near all dead of the smallpox, so as the Lord hath cleared our title to what we possess.

John Winthrop, governor, Massachusetts Colony, 1634

14. Information is what you need to make money short term. Knowledge is the deeper understanding of how things work. It's obtained only by long and inefficient study. It's gained by those who set aside the profit motive and instead possess an intrinsic desire just to know.

David Brooks, "The Moral Power of Curiosity," *The New York Times*

15. He's not a moron at all, he's a friend. My personal relations with the president are extremely good.

Canadian prime minister Jean Chrétien, quoted in the *Canadian Press*

16. Why opium produces sleep: Because there is in it a dormitive power.

Molière, *The Imaginary Invalid*

17. My opponent wants to sever the Danish church from the state for his own personal sake. His motion is an attempt to take over the church and further his ecumenical theology by his usual mafia methods.

Charlotte Jorgensen, "Hostility in Public Debate"

18. I do not have much information on this case except the general statement of the agency that there is nothing in the files to disprove his Communist connections.

Richard H. Rovere, *Senator Joe McCarthy*

19. We took the Bible and prayer out of public schools, and now we're having weekly shootings practically. We had the '60s sexual revolution, and now people are dying of AIDS.

Christine O'Donnell, quoted in the *New Statesman*

20. In many ways, the process reflects the history of the Capitol and the nation, said Mr. Ritchie, the historian. "The Capitol building is an interesting conglomeration," he said. "It is a whole series of buildings put together at different times, and in that way it is a nice reflection of American democracy, which was put together piecemeal from a lot of different materials. It reflects one motto of our nation, '*E pluribus unum*,' Latin for 'Out of many, one.'"

Jennifer Steinhauer, "Leaky Capitol Dome Imperiled by 1,300 Cracks, Partisan Rift," *The New York Times*

21. How is education supposed to make me feel smarter? Besides, every time I learn something new, it pushes some old stuff out of my brain. Remember when I took that home winemaking course, and I forgot how to drive?

Homer Simpson, "Secrets of a Successful Marriage," *The Simpsons*

22. The community of Pacific Palisades is extremely wealthy. Therefore, every person living there is extremely wealthy.

Peter A. Angeles, *Dictionary of Philosophy*

23. Dear Friend, a man who has studied law to its highest degree is a brilliant lawyer, for a brilliant lawyer has studied law to its highest degree.

Oscar Wilde, *De Profundis*

24. The most stringent protection of free speech would not protect a man in falsely shouting fire in a theater and causing a panic.

Oliver Wendell Homes, Supreme Court Opinion, *Schenk v. United States*

25. Musical chills are known as aesthetic chills, thrills, shivers, and involve a seconds-long feeling of goose bumps and tingling . . . the emotions evoked by beautiful music stimulate the hypothalamus, which controls primal drives such as hunger, sex and rage and also involuntary responses like blushing and goosebumps.

Brian Alexander, "*Messiah* Give You Chills? That's a Clue to Your Personality," MSNBC.com

26. Twenty-seven years ago, Luis Alvarez first proposed that the Cretaceous–Tertiary extinction event was caused by an asteroid that struck the earth 65.5 million years earlier. This means the dinosaurs died out 65,500,027 years ago.

Worldlingo.com

27. Should we not assume that just as the eye, hand, the foot, and in general each part of the body clearly has its own proper function, so man too has some function over and above the function of his parts?   Aristotle, *Nicomachean Ethics*

28. We will starve terrorists of funding, turn them one against another, drive them from place to place, until there is no refuge or rest. And we will pursue nations that provide aid or safe haven to terrorism. Every nation, in every region, now has a decision to make. Either you are with us, or you are with the terrorists.   George W. Bush, Sept. 20, 2001, in an address to Congress

⭐ 29. You may be interested to know that global warming, earthquakes, hurricanes, and other natural disasters are a direct effect of the shrinking numbers of Pirates since the 1800s. For your interest, I have included a graph of the approximate number of pirates versus the average global temperature over the last 200 years. As you can see, there is a statistically significant inverse relationship between pirates and global temperature.   Bobby Henderson, "Open Letter to Kansas School Board"

30. Why should farmers and plant owners expect people to take a back-breaking seasonal job with low pay and no benefits just because they happen to be offering it? If no one wants an available job—especially in extreme times—maybe the fault doesn't rest entirely with the people turning it down. Maybe the market is inefficient.

Elizabeth Dwoskin, "Why Americans Won't Do Dirty Jobs," *Bloomberg Businessweek*

31. Gerda Reith is convinced that superstition can be a positive force. "It gives you a sense of control by making you think you can work out what's going to happen next," she says. "And it also makes you feel lucky. And to take a risk or to enter into a chancy situation, you really have to believe in your own luck. In that sense, it's a very useful way of thinking, because the alternative is fatalism, which is to say, 'Oh, there's nothing I can do.' At least superstition makes people do things."   David Newnham, "Hostages to Fortune"

32. We can't change the present or the future. . . . We can only change the past, and we do it all the time.   Interview with Bob Dylan in *Rolling Stone*

⭐ 33. Morality in this nation has worsened at the same time that adherence to traditional Christian beliefs has declined. Obviously, the latter has caused the former, so encouraging Christianity will ensure a return to traditional moral standards.   About.com

34. Whether deconstruction is an art or a science, a malady or a Catch-22, it would seem to belong at honours level in university degrees. School is for basics and knowledge, certainly accompanied by critical thinking, but not in a milieu where all is relative and there are no absolutes for young people who do not have the intellectual maturity to cope with the somewhat morbid rigour of constant criticism and questioning of motives. If you go on deconstructing for long enough you will become a marshmallow or a jelly.

Kenneth Wiltshire, "In Defense of the True Values of Learning"

35. It's our job to make college basketball players realize that getting an education is something that's important, because life after basketball is a real long time.

Larry Brown, Southern Methodist University basketball coach

36. *Dan Quayle:* I have far more experience than many others that sought the office of vice president of this country. I have as much experience in Congress as Jack Kennedy did when he sought the presidency. I will be prepared to deal with the people in the Bush administration, if that unfortunate event would ever occur. *Lloyd Bentsen:* I served with Jack Kennedy; I knew Jack Kennedy; Jack Kennedy was a friend of mine. Senator, you're no Jack Kennedy.

The 1988 U.S. vice presidential debates

37. I call this the "Advertiser's Fallacy" because it's so prevalent in commercials, such as the one where a famous baseball slugger gives medical advice on erectile dysfunction (that should pick up the hit count!). No. See a properly qualified doctor for ED, see Rafael Palmiero only if you want to improve your baseball swing.

Joe McFaul, "Law, Evolution, Science, and Junk Science"

38. Recently, we highlighted a British journalist's story about the underside of Dubai's startling ascent. Some in Dubai called foul, including one writer who wants to remind Britons that their own country has a dark side. After all, what to think of a country in which one fifth of the population lives in poverty?

Freakonomics.com, "Dubai's Rebuttal"

39. The anti-stem-cell argument goes like this: If you permit scientists to destroy human embryos for the purpose of research, [then it goes] from there to killing human fetuses in order to harvest tissue, and from there to euthanizing disabled or terminally ill people to harvest their organs, and from there to human cloning and human-animal hybrids, and if making chimeras is okay, well then Dr. Frankenstein must also be okay, and Dr. Mengele, too, and before you know it, it's one long hapless inevitable slide from high-minded medicine to the Nazis.

Marty Kaplan, in an article at Huffingtonpost.com

40. In Aesop's fable, "the crow and the pitcher," a thirsty crow dropped stones in a pitcher to raise the water level and quench its thirst. Past experiments have shown that crows and their relatives—altogether known as corvids—are indeed "remarkably intelligent, and in many ways rival the great apes in their physical intelligence and ability to solve problems," said researcher Christopher Bird at the University of Cambridge in England.

Charles Q. Choi, "Bird's Tool Use Called 'Amazing,'" Livescience.com

41. These are the times that try men's souls. The summer soldier and the sunshine patriot will in this crisis shrink from the service of his country; but he that stands it now deserves the love and thanks for man and woman. Tyranny, like hell, is not easily conquered; yet we have this consolation with us, that the harder the conflict, the more glorious the triumph. What we obtain too cheap, we esteem too lightly; 'tis dearness only that gives everything its value. Heaven

knows how to put a proper price upon its goods; and it would be strange indeed, if so celestial an article as freedom should not be highly rated. Britain, with an army to enforce her tyranny, has declared that she has a right (not only to tax) but "to bind us in all cases whatsoever," and if being bound in that manner is not slavery, then there is no such thing as slavery upon earth.

Thomas Paine, The Crisis

42. Once one is caught up into the material world not one person in ten thousand finds the time to form literary taste, to examine the validity of philosophic concepts for himself, or to form what, for lack of a better phrase, I might call the wise and tragic sense of life. F. Scott Fitzgerald

43. If the Iraqi regime is able to produce, buy, or steal an amount of highly-enriched uranium a little larger than a single softball, it could have a nuclear weapon in less than a year. And if we allow that to happen, a terrible line would be crossed. Saddam Hussein would be in a position to blackmail anyone who opposes his aggression. He would be in a position to dominate the Middle East. He would be in a position to threaten America. And Saddam Hussein would be in a position to pass nuclear technology to terrorists. Knowing these realities, America must not ignore the threat gathering against us. Facing clear evidence of peril, we cannot wait for the final proof—the smoking gun—that could come in the form of a mushroom cloud. President George W. Bush, October 8, 2002

44. A person apparently hopelessly ill may be allowed to take his own life. Then he may be permitted to deputize others to do it for him should he no longer be able to act. The judgment of others then becomes the ruling factor. Already at this point euthanasia is not personal and voluntary, for others are acting on behalf of the patient as they see fit. This may well incline them to act on behalf of other patients who have not authorized them to exercise their judgment. It is only a short step, then, from voluntary euthanasia (self-inflicted or authorized), to directed euthanasia administered to a patient who has given no authorization, to involuntary euthanasia conducted as a part of a social policy.

J. Gay Williams, "The Wrongfulness of Euthanasia"

★45. The Supreme Court sided with the video game industry today, declaring a victor in the six-year legal match between the industry and the California lawmakers who wanted to make it a crime for anyone in the state to sell extremely violent games to kids. . . . "The basic principles of freedom of speech . . . do not vary with a new and different communication medium," [Justice] Scalia wrote in the Court's opinion.

Stephen Totilo, "1st Amendment Beats Ban in Video Game Battle," MSNBC.MSN.com

46. Once, many National Football League (NFL) teams played on Thanksgiving; to this day, high school teams play championship or rivalry games on Thanksgiving. In the 1950s, the old NFL began a tradition of having only one game on turkey day, always at Detroit. In the 1960s, a Cowboys' home date was added

on Thanksgiving, to help the Dallas expansion franchise become established. Detroit and Dallas have been the traditional hosts since.

Gregg Easterbrook, ESPN.com's Page 2

47. If I were to suggest that between the Earth and Mars there is a china teapot revolving about the sun in an elliptical orbit, nobody would be able to disprove my assertion provided I were careful to add that the teapot is too small to be revealed even by our most powerful telescopes. But if I were to go on to say that, since my assertion cannot be disproved, it is an intolerable presumption on the part of human reason to doubt it, I should rightly be thought to be talking nonsense. If, however, the existence of such a teapot were affirmed in ancient books, taught as the sacred truth every Sunday, and instilled into the minds of children at school, hesitation to believe in its existence would become a mark of eccentricity and entitle the doubter to the attentions of the psychiatrist in an enlightened age or of the Inquisitor in an earlier time.

Bertrand Russell, "Is There a God?"

48. *Dorothy:* Are you doing that on purpose, or can't you make up your mind?
Scarecrow: That's the trouble. I can't make up my mind. I haven't got a brain—just straw.
Dorothy: How can you talk if you haven't got a brain?
Scarecrow: I don't know. But some people without brains do an awful lot of talking, don't they?
Dorothy: I guess you're right.

From the movie *The Wizard of Oz*

49. Great college football rivalries engage the healthy, activate the disturbed, fascinate the thoughtful, amaze the detached, mystify the rational, horrify the scholarly, encourage the immature, enrich the greedy, and terrify the faint of heart.

Bill Curry, "Stoops, Brown Legacies Entangled in Red River Rivalry," ESPN.com

50. A rabid debate about security and privacy has begun. As the Edward Snowden affair enters its second month, Americans don't seem to have much appetite for the subtlety of such a debate. The Prism leak discussion has been framed repeatedly as a zero-sum game, pitting privacy on one side and security on the other. "You can't have 100 percent security and also have 100 percent privacy," President Obama said on June 7, in his principal public statement in the issue, suggesting there is some dial which forces government officials to pick one over the other.

Bob Sullivan, "Privacy vs. Security: 'False Choice' Poisons Debate on NSA Leaks," NBC News

Summary

- Formal fallacy: A logical error that occurs in the form or structure of an argument and is restricted to deductive arguments.
- Informal fallacy: A mistake in reasoning that occurs in ordinary language and concerns the content of the argument rather than its form.

Study Materials

- *Ad hominem* abusive: The fallacy is distinguished by an attack on alleged character flaws of a person instead of the person's argument.
- *Ad hominem* circumstantial: When someone's argument is rejected based on the circumstances of the person's life.
- Poisoning the well: The fallacy occurs when a person is attacked *before* she has a chance to present her case.
- *Tu quoque*: The fallacy is distinguished by the specific attempt of one person to avoid the issue at hand by claiming the other person is a hypocrite.
- Fallacious appeal to emotion: When an argument relies solely on the arousal of a strong emotional state or psychological reaction to get us to accept the conclusion.
- Appeal to the people: The fallacy occurs when an argument manipulates a psychological need or desire, such as the desire to belong to a popular group, or the need for group solidarity, so that the reader or listener will accept the conclusion.
- Appeal to pity: The fallacy results from an exclusive reliance on a sense of pity or mercy for support of a conclusion.
- Appeal to fear or force: A threat of harmful consequences (physical or otherwise) used to force acceptance of a course of action that would otherwise be unacceptable.
- Generalization fallacy: A fallacy that occurs when an argument relies on a mistaken use of the principles behind making a generalization.
- Rigid application of a generalization: When a generalization or rule is inappropriately applied to the case at hand. The fallacy results from the belief that the generalization or rule is universal (meaning it has no exceptions).
- Hasty generalization: An argument that relies on a small sample that is unlikely to represent the population.
- Composition: There are two forms of the fallacy: (1) the mistaken transfer of an attribute of the individual *parts of an object* to the *object as a whole* and (2) the mistaken transfer of an attribute of the individual *members of a class* to the *class itself*.
- Division: There are two forms of the fallacy: (1) the mistaken transfer of an attribute of an *object as a whole* to the individual *parts of the object* and (2) the mistaken transfer of an attribute of a *class* to the individual *members of the class*.
- Biased sample: An argument that uses a nonrepresentative sample as support for a statistical claim about an entire population.
- False cause fallacy: A fallacy that occurs when a causal connection is assumed to exist between two events when none actually exists, or when the assumed causal connection is unlikely to exist.

- *Post hoc*: The fallacy occurs from the mistaken assumption that just because one event occurred before another event, the first event *must have caused* the second event.
- Slippery slope: An argument that attempts to connect a series of occurrences such that the first link in a chain leads directly to a second link, and so on, until a final unwanted situation is said to be the inevitable result.
- Fallacies of unwarranted assumption: Arguments that assume the truth of some unproved or questionable claim.
- Begging the question: In one type, the fallacy occurs when a premise is simply reworded in the conclusion. In a second type, called *circular reasoning*, a set of statements seem to support each other with no clear beginning or end point. In a third type, the argument assumes certain key information that may be controversial or is not supported by facts.
- Complex question: The fallacy occurs when a single question actually contains multiple parts and an unestablished hidden assumption.
- Appeal to ignorance: An argument built on a position of ignorance claims either that (1) a statement must be true because it has not been proven to be false or (2) a statement must be false because it has not been proven to be true.
- Appeal to an unqualified authority: An argument that relies on the opinions of people who either have *no* expertise, training, or knowledge relevant to the issue at hand, or whose testimony is not trustworthy.
- False dichotomy: A fallacy that occurs when it is assumed that only two choices are possible, when in fact others exist.
- Fallacy of diversion: A fallacy that occurs when the meanings of terms or phrases are changed (intentionally or unintentionally) within the argument, or when our attention is purposely (or accidentally) diverted from the issue at hand.
- Equivocation: The fallacy occurs when the conclusion of an argument relies on an intentional or unintentional shift in the meaning of a term or phrase in the premises.
- Straw man: The fallacy occurs when someone's argument is misrepresented in order to create a new argument that can be easily refuted. The new argument is so weak that it is "made of straw." The arguer then falsely claims that his opponent's real argument has been defeated.
- Red herring: A fallacy that occurs when someone completely ignores an opponent's position and changes the subject, diverting the discussion in a new direction.
- Misleading precision: A claim that appears to be statistically significant but is not.
- Missing the point: When premises that seem to lead logically to one conclusion are used instead to support an unexpected conclusion.

KEY TERMS

ad hominem abusive   131
ad hominem
    circumstantial   131
appeal to an unqualified
    authority   166
appeal to fear or force   137
appeal to ignorance   163
appeal to pity   136
appeal to the people   135
begging the question   160

biased sample   149
complex question   162
composition   146
division   148
equivocation   169
false dichotomy   167
formal fallacy   129
hasty generalization   145
informal fallacy   129
misleading precision   172

missing the point   173
poisoning the well   132
post hoc   150
red herring   171
rigid application of a
    generalization   144
slippery slope   153
straw man   170
tu quoque   133

LOGIC CHALLENGE: A CLEVER PROBLEM

In a certain faraway country (long, long, ago), prisoners to be executed were either shot or hanged. Prisoners were allowed to make one statement. If their statement turned out to be true, then they were hanged. If their statement turned out to be false, then they were shot. That is, until one clever prisoner put an end to the practice of execution. The prisoner made her one statement, upon which the judge was forced to set her free. What statement did she make?

PART IV

INDUCTIVE LOGIC

Chapter 10

Analogical Arguments

A. *The Framework of Analogical Arguments*
B. *Analyzing Analogical Arguments*
C. *Strategies of Evaluation*

Study Materials

A good analogy opens up new ways of thinking. It offers us an unexpected connection between things that arouse our imagination.

> A nation wearing atomic armor is like a knight whose armor has grown so heavy he is immobilized; he can hardly walk, hardly sit his horse, hardly think, hardly breathe. The H-bomb is an extremely effective deterrent to war, but it has little virtue as a weapon of war, because it would leave the world unin-habitable.
>
> E. B. White, "Sootfall and Fallout"

Analogy To draw an analogy is simply to indicate that there are similarities between two or more things.

To draw an **analogy** is simply to indicate that there are similarities between two or more things. You might be more inclined to buy a particular car if you had good experience with a similar model. On the other hand, you might decide *not* to buy that model because of the poor performance of the last car you owned. In each case, we reason that, because two cars share some relevant characteristics, they might also share others.

Analogical reasoning One of the most fundamental tools used in creating an argument. It can be analyzed as a type of inductive argument—it is a matter of probability, based on experience, and it can be quite persuasive.

Analogical reasoning is one of the most fundamental tools used in creating an argument, and it can be quite persuasive. It can be analyzed as a type of inductive argument: It is a matter of probability, based on experience. For example, another car of the same model may not perform the same as yours. However, if an analogical argument is strong, then the probability that the conclusion is true is high.

Analogical reasoning plays a major part in legal decisions. Suppose a court has ruled that college students may not be restrained from speaking out about cuts in scholarships. A different court may conclude, by analogical reasoning, that the same group cannot be stopped from holding a peaceful rally because a rally is similar to speaking. An argument from an older legal decision, like this one, is said to appeal to *precedent*. When spelled out in detail, the analogy will identify those respects in which the older decision and the current one are alike. (We will return to legal arguments in the next chapter.) This chapter explores how analogical arguments work and how they can be evaluated.

A. THE FRAMEWORK OF ANALOGICAL ARGUMENTS

We know that ordinary language arguments often require rewriting, and that in turn requires a close reading to determine the premises and conclusion. We will construct a general framework that can guide our analysis and evaluation of analogical reasoning.

Every analogical argument has three defining features. First, it must refer to characteristics that two (or more) things have in common. Second, it must identify a new characteristic in one of the things being compared. Finally, it concludes that the other thing in the comparison probably has the new characteristic as well. (In analogical arguments, the things being compared are also referred to as *analogues*.) The framework for an **analogical argument** translates these features into premises and a conclusion:

> ### ANALOGICAL ARGUMENTS: A FRAMEWORK
> Premise 1: X and Y have characteristics $a, b, c \ldots$ in common.
> Premise 2: X has characteristic k.
> Therefore, *probably* Y has characteristic k.

Analogical argument
The argument lists the characteristics that two (or more) things have in common and concludes that the things being compared probably have some other characteristic in common.

Example 1
A father buys his son, Mike, a shirt that (naturally) the son does not like. The father justifies his decision:

> I bought the shirt for you because your friend Steve has one like it, and you guys wear your hair the same, wear the same kind of pants and shoes, and like the same music and television programs. Since Steve must like his shirt, I thought that you would like the shirt, too.

If we let S = *Steve*, M = *Mike*, a = *you guys wear your hair the same*, b = *wear the same kind of pants*, c = *shoes*, d = *the same music*, e = *television programs*, and f = *the shirt*, then the father's analogical reasoning can be displayed as follows:

> Premise 1: S and M have $a, b, c, d,$ and e in common.
> Premise 2: S likes f.
> Therefore, *probably* M will like f.

The force of an analogical argument works through the two premises, and each plays a specific role. Premise 1 takes two different objects (in this case, people) and shows how they are similar by listing certain characteristics that the two objects have in common. If premise 1 does its job effectively, then we should begin to see that the two objects share certain characteristics:

Premise 1

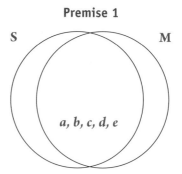

The circles represent the two people referred to in the argument (Steve and Mike). The lowercase letters stand for the five characteristics that they have in common, and these are placed in the area where the two circles overlap.

At this point, premise 2 is introduced to make a claim regarding one of the two objects: S has a new characteristic that was not listed in premise 1. In other words, the two premises work together. Premise 1 shows that S and M have several characteristics in common (*a, b, c, d,* and *e*). Premise 2 points out that S has an additional characteristic, namely *f*, which is somewhere in the S circle. The conclusion is that M very probably has characteristic *f*, too.

Premise 1, if effective, persuades us that S and M share certain characteristics. Premise 2 places the *f* inside S, as a matter of objective fact. The conclusion asserts that *f* should be applied to M as well. The goal is for us to accept this picture:

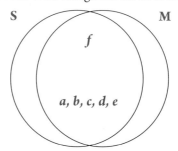

According to the picture, the conclusion is true. However, we can show that it is *possible* for the conclusion to be false because *f* could actually be placed in at least two different locations:

What Premise 2 Really Says

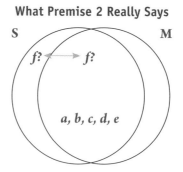

Always remember that an analogical argument does *not* claim that S and M are identical, but only that they are similar. Premise 2 merely states that *f* is in S, but it is possible that characteristic *f* is not in M. Given this, the conclusion might be false, even if the premises are assumed to be true, as indicated by the next picture:

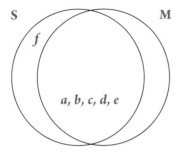

In sum, an analogical argument can claim, at best, only that it is *probable* that *f* is in M, and this probability rests heavily on the first premise and its relevance to the conclusion. *The way to assess the strength of an analogical argument is to determine the degree of support that the first premise provides for the conclusion*, as we will see in the rest of this chapter. For now, though, we will continue applying the general framework to reveal the reasoning behind analogical arguments.

Example 2
Analogical arguments can be about people, places, times, and animate or inanimate objects. Let's look at an example involving defective tires.

> *Premise 1*: The steel-belted tires that have been involved in blowouts (T) and the steel-belted tires on your automobile (Y) have the following attributes in common: *a*, same size; *b*, same tread design; *c*, same manufacturer; *d*, same place of manufacture; *e*, on same type of vehicle; and *f*, same recommended tire pressure.
> *Premise 2*: The steel-belted tires involved in blowouts (T) have been determined to be *g*, defective.
> *Conclusion*: Therefore, *probably* the steel-belted tires on your automobile (Y) are *g*, defective.

First, we use the framework for analogical arguments to extract the relevant information:

> Premise 1: T and Y have *a, b, c, d, e,* and *f,* in common.
> Premise 2: T has *g*.
> Therefore, *probably* Y has g.

The force of the analogical argument works through the two premises. The idea is to get us to agree that the two things being compared share several characteristics. The first premise can be depicted as follows:

Premise 1

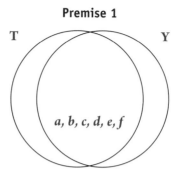

Premise 2 introduces a new characteristic attached to T. As in our earlier example, we can actually draw two different pictures of the argument:

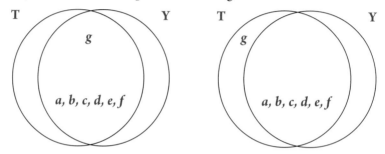

Premise 1, if effective, persuades us that T and Y share certain characteristics. Premise 2 places the *g* inside T (objective fact). However, it is possible for the conclusion to be false, even if the premises are assumed to be true. Since premise 2 merely states that *g* is in T, it could turn out that *g* is not in Y. How likely is it that *g* is in Y? In other words, how strong is the analogical argument? The rest of this chapter will concentrate on specific techniques for determining the strength of analogical arguments.

EXERCISES 10A

Level 1 Multiple-
Choice Questions

Level 2 Multiple-
Choice Questions

I. Reveal the framework of the analogical argument in each example by determining what would go in the premises and the conclusion.

1. We know that humans are capable of highly abstract thinking by their ability to understand and use complex concepts. Recent research on dolphins has revealed that dolphins have brains almost identical in size to humans. Dolphins have a body size nearly identical to humans. Experiments have shown that dolphins can understand verbal commands and sign language instructions, which humans can do quite easily. Like humans, dolphins have a strong sense of self-identity, because it has been shown that dolphins can recognize themselves in mirrors and when shown their image on a TV screen. Therefore, it is highly probable that dolphins are capable of highly abstract thinking.

Answer:

> **Premise 1:** X, humans, and Y, dolphins, have the following attributes in common: *a*, dolphins have brains almost identical in size to humans; *b*, dolphins have a body size nearly identical to humans; *c*, dolphins can understand verbal commands and sign language instructions, which humans can do quite easily; *d*, like humans, dolphins have a strong sense of self-identity, because it has been shown that dolphins can recognize themselves in mirrors and when shown their image on a TV screen.
>
> **Premise 2:** We know that X, humans, are *e*, capable of highly abstract thinking by their ability to understand and use complex concepts.
>
> **Conclusion:** Therefore, it is highly probable that Y, dolphins, are *e*, capable of highly abstract thinking.

The structure of the argument can now be displayed:

> X and Y have *a*, *b*, *c*, and *d* in common.
> X has *e*.
> Therefore, *probably* Y has *e*.

2. Chimpanzees are certainly capable of feeling pain. They will avoid negative feedback (electrical shocks) in a laboratory setting when given the opportunity to do so. When one chimpanzee is injured, others will recognize the pain behavior and try to comfort and help the injured member of the group. Chimpanzees that have been given pain-relief medicine soon after an injury connect the medicine to the relief from pain, because when injured again they will give the sign for the medicine. Humans display all of these behaviors as well. There are legal and ethical constraints that protect humans from experimentation without their consent. Therefore, chimpanzees should be afforded the same protections.

3. When a dog has killed or severely injured a human for no apparent reason, we feel justified in killing the dog in order to stop it from doing more damage. We don't try to figure out the psychological reasons for its violent behavior, we just figure it is part of its genetic makeup and it cannot be changed. We don't lock the dog up for 5 years to life with the possibility of parole. Humans who kill or injure other humans for no apparent reason are like those dogs. We should feel justified in killing them in order to stop them from doing more damage.

4. England and Japan have much lower overall crime rates than the United States. The United States has 20 times more homicides than England and 30 times more than Japan. All three countries have large populations, are highly industrialized, and are in the top five in terms of economic strength among the world's countries. In addition, all three countries are democracies, have separate branches of government, and a large prison system. But England and Japan have strict gun control legislation. If the United States wants to lower its homicide rate, then it has to pass strict gun control legislation.

Video Tutorial

★ 5. I am a junior at Lincoln Heights High School. My parents make me do all the housework, like taking out the trash, laundry, dishes, vacuuming, washing the car, and cleaning up the rooms. My kid brother, who is in fifth grade, doesn't have to do anything. But he eats the same food as me, has his own bedroom like me, and gets the same amount of allowance as me. If I have to do so much work, then he should, too.

6. The recent unearthing of some bones in central China has been the source of much controversy. Some experts are claiming that it is the oldest evidence of a human ever discovered, because it predates the next earliest fossil by 20,000 years. The experts claim that the cranial area is the same as the earliest agreed upon fossil of a human. The jawbone matches human fossils of a later date. Crude tools were found near the bones. The teeth match the later human fossils. If the oldest recognized bones have been declared to be human, then these must be human as well.

7. The government gives billions of dollars to big farming companies *not* to grow crops, in order to keep prices stable. Thus consumers are protected—at least so say the farmers. I run a business. I have a small area where I raise worms. Like big businesses, I too have expenses. I pay for help, buy equipment, purchase supplies, suffer losses, pay taxes, pay utilities, and am subject to the laws of supply and demand. If they can get money for not growing crops, then I would be more than willing to get money from the government, so I can stop growing those slimy worms!

Video Tutorial

8. A computer program developed by professors at Carnegie-Mellon University beat Garry Kasparov when he was the world chess champion. Computer programs are used to help diagnose diseases and predict economic trends, the winners in horse races, and other sports. They can calculate and analyze, in a few seconds, problems that no human could do in a lifetime. Advanced computer programs have demonstrated the ability to learn from experience and adapt to new situations. They can understand language and communicate concepts and ideas. Any human who can do these things is considered to possess consciousness. Some computer programs should be given the same designation.

★ 9. Fruit has many attributes that are good for your health. Fruit provides energy, roughage, sugars, citric acid, vitamins, and minerals. The new candy bar, Chocolate Peanut Gooies, provides energy, roughage, sugar, citric acid, vitamins, and minerals. How can it not be good for your health too?

10. *Planet X24: Our Last Hope*, the new movie by director Billy Kuberg, has just been released. It's his fourth sci-fi film. His other three had newcomers in the starring roles, were based on novels by Joel Francis Hitchmann, opened in the summer, and had huge marketing tie-ins. This new movie has an unknown actor in the lead role, is based on a novel by Joel Francis Hitchmann, is opening in the summer, and has huge marketing tie-ins. Each of Kuberg's first three sci-fi films grossed over $550 million. I predict this new film will gross about the same amount.

11. I already ate apples, oranges, peaches, and cherries from her fruit stand, and I enjoyed all of them. I am going to try her pears. I am sure I will enjoy them.

12. I took Philosophy 101, 102, 103, and 104 and got an A in each course. I am going to take Philosophy 105, so I expect to get an A in that course as well.

⭐ 13. Evidence indicates that adding fertilizer helps fruit trees and vegetable plants to grow better. Seaweed is a plant. Therefore, adding fertilizer should help seaweed grow better.

▷

Video Tutorial

II. Reveal the framework of the analogical argument in each example by determining what would go in the premises and the conclusion.

1. A study by U.S. and Korean researchers, including Harvard Business School's Jordan Siegel, found that if you operate in a sexist country full of educated, talented women, it makes good business sense to tap them for management roles. . . . It's depressing how governments don't realize that failing to harness half of populations holds back growth. Planes that need two engines to fly don't take off when one isn't working, so why do nations think they can thrive in our madly competitive world with one engine?

William Pesek, "Sexism That Irks Goldman Is Boon for Savvy CEOs"

Answer:

Premise 1: X, planes with two engines, and Y, nations, have the following attributes in common: *a*, they both have two crucial components.
Premise 2: We know that X, planes with two engines, *e*, do not take off when one engine isn't working.
Conclusion: Therefore, probably Y, nations, are *e*, not capable of taking off economically in a competitive world without utilizing the talent of women.

The structure of the argument is:

X and Y have *a* in common.
X has *e*.
Therefore, probably Y has *e*.

2. You expect far too much of a first sentence. Think of it as analogous to a good country breakfast: what we want is something simple, but nourishing to the imagination. Hold the philosophy; hold the adjectives; just give us a plain subject and verb and perhaps a wholesome, nonfattening adverb or two.

Larry McMurtry, *Some Can Whistle*

3. Students should be allowed to look at their textbooks during examinations. After all, surgeons have X-rays to guide them during an operation, lawyers have briefs to guide them during a trial, carpenters have blueprints to guide them when they are building a house. Why, then, shouldn't students be allowed to look at their textbooks during an examination?   Max Shulman, "Love Is a Fallacy"

4. Like other colonial peoples, adolescents are economically dependent on the dominant society, and appear in its accounts as the beneficiaries of its philanthropy. Like them also, adolescents are partly dependent because of their immature stage of development, but even more because of restrictions placed upon them by the dominant society. . . . Nevertheless, "teen-agers" do have money. . . . They scrounge it from home or earn it at odd times, and this, too, contributes to their colonial status. The "teen-age" market is big business. We all share an economic interest in the dependency of the "teen-ager." The school is interested in keeping him off the streets and in custody. Labor is interested in keeping him off the labor market. Business and industry are interested in seeing that his tastes become fads and in selling him specialized junk that a more mature taste would reject. Like a dependent native, the "teen-ager" is encouraged to be economically irresponsible because his sources of income are undependable and do not derive from his personal qualities.

Edgar Z. Friedenberg, *Coming of Age in America*

⋆ 5. Many orthodox people speak as though it were the business of sceptics to disprove received dogmas rather than of dogmatists to prove them. This is, of course, a mistake. If I were to suggest that between the Earth and Mars there is a china teapot revolving about the sun in an elliptical orbit, nobody would be able to disprove my assertion provided I were careful to add that the teapot is too small to be revealed even by our most powerful telescopes. But if I were to go on to say that, since my assertion cannot be disproved, it is an intolerable presumption on the part of human reason to doubt it, I should rightly be thought to be talking nonsense. If, however, the existence of such a teapot were affirmed in ancient books, taught as the sacred truth every Sunday, and instilled into the minds of children at school, hesitation to believe in its existence would become a mark of eccentricity and entitle the doubter to the attentions of the psychiatrist in an enlightened age or of the Inquisitor in an earlier time. It is customary to suppose that, if a belief is widespread, there must be something reasonable about it. I do not think this view can be held by anyone who has studied history.   Bertrand Russell, "Is There a God?"

B. ANALYZING ANALOGICAL ARGUMENTS

Four criteria can be used to analyze the strength of an analogical argument. Each involves looking specifically at the first premise. We look at the *number of things* referred to in the premise, the *variety* of those things, the *number of characteristics* claimed to be similar, and the *relevance* of those characteristics.

First, the strength of an analogical argument is related to the *number of things* referred to in the first premise. A large number of examples of the same kind, with the same item, will serve to establish the conclusion with a much higher degree of probability than if the conclusion were based on one instance alone. In example 1 before, if the father had compared his son to a number of friends rather than just to Steve, and if all the friends had worn the same shirt, then this would increase the probability that the conclusion is true. In example 2 before, presumably an adequate number of instances of defective tires have been examined to make the conclusion probably true.

There is rarely a simple numerical ratio between the number of instances and the probability of the conclusion. For example, if one analogical argument refers to two instances, and a second refers to ten instances, we *cannot* claim that the conclusion in the second is exactly five times as probable as the first.

Second, the strength of an analogical argument is related to the *variety of things* referred to in the first premise. In example 1, if the father could show that a lot of people of different ages seem to be wearing the shirt in question, then this would seem to make the shirt desirable to more people, and it might raise the probability that Mike would like the shirt. In example 2, if it can be shown that defective tires were made in many locations and at different times, then this variety in the place and time of manufacture would increase the likelihood that defective tires are on your automobile. This additional evidence would increase the probability that the conclusion is true.

Third, the strength of an analogical argument is related to the *number of characteristics* that are claimed to be similar between the things being compared. All things being equal, the greater the number of characteristics listed in the first premise the more probable the conclusion will be. In example 1, premise 1 lists five characteristics. Example 2 lists six characteristics in its first premise. This does not mean that the conclusion of the second argument is 20% more likely to be true. There is no simple mathematical formula for judging the probability of the conclusion based on the number of characteristics in the first premise.

Fourth, the strength of an analogical argument is related to the *relevance of the characteristics* referred to in the first premise. Some characteristics may have no real bearing on the analogy, and the weight of each characteristic has to be determined on its own merits. In fact, relevance is the single most important criterion on which to judge the strength of an analogical argument. An argument based on a single *relevant* characteristic between two things will be far more convincing than an argument based on ten *irrelevant* characteristics between ten things. However, determining relevance is not always easy. This is why it is important to make arguments by analogy strong enough to withstand scrutiny.

The relevance of any particular characteristic in the premises depends on how it is related to the conclusion of an argument. Take, for example, the color of a car:

A. My Ford Fusion Hybrid and your Hummer are the same color. My vehicle averages 40 miles per gallon of gasoline. Therefore, your vehicle will probably average 40 miles per gallon of gasoline.

B. My Toyota Camry and your Hyundai Sonata are the same color. My daughter likes the color of my car. Therefore, my daughter will probably like the color of your car, too.

In A, the characteristic that the two vehicles have in common (the color) is not relevant to gas mileage, so it does not offer support for the conclusion. However, in B, the characteristic that the two cars have in common (the color) *is* relevant to whether the daughter will like the color, so it does offer support for the conclusion.

Relevance is often the most crucial factor, even when the things being compared have several things in common. Here are two more examples:

C. My sister's Chevrolet Volt Hybrid and her boyfriend's Dodge Ram pickup truck are the same color, they were both bought on the same day, and they have the same kind of financing deal. My sister's car averages 50 miles per gallon of gasoline. Therefore, her boyfriend's truck will probably average 50 miles per gallon of gasoline.

D. My father's Toyota Prius and my mother's Honda Civic Hybrid have the same engine size. My father's car averages 48 miles per gallon of gasoline. Therefore, my mother's car will probably average 48 miles per gallon of gasoline.

In C, three characteristics are listed in the first premise, while only one characteristic is referred to in the first premise of D. But since none of the three characteristics in C are relevant to gas mileage, together they offer no support for the conclusion. However, in D, the single characteristic referred to in the first premise is relevant to gas mileage, so by itself it offers some support for the conclusion.

Of course, in another argument engine size may not be relevant. This is why we must be careful to assess each characteristic in its relationship to a particular argument. Note, too, that some characteristics might be relevant and others might not. Again, each characteristic has to be evaluated in relation to the argument in which it appears.

Criteria for Analyzing Analogical Arguments

1. The strength of an analogical argument is related to the *number of things* referred to in the first premise. A large number of examples of the same kind, with the same item, establish the conclusion with a much higher degree of probability than would be the case if the conclusion were based on one instance alone.

2. The strength of an analogical argument is related to the *variety of things* referred to in the first premise. If the first premise shows some variety among the things being compared, then it might make the conclusion more likely.

3. The strength of an analogical argument is related to the *number of characteristics* that are claimed to be similar between the things being compared. All things being equal, the greater the number of characteristics listed in the first premise, the more probable the conclusion.

4. The strength of an analogical argument is related to the *relevance of the characteristics* referred to in the first premise. These characteristics must carry weight when it comes to deciding the probability of the conclusion.

EXERCISES 10B

I. You have already revealed the framework of the analogical arguments in Exercises 10A. Now analyze those same arguments by applying the four criteria for the strength of the argument: (a) Determine the number of things referred to in the first premise; (b) assess the variety of things referred to in the first premise; (c) list the number of characteristics that are claimed to be similar between the things being compared; (d) determine the relevance of the characteristics.

Level 1 Multiple-Choice Questions

Level 2 Multiple-Choice Questions

Video Tutorial

Refer back to Exercises 10A I for the exercises. The first exercise and a solution are provided here:

1. We know that humans are capable of highly abstract thinking by their ability to understand and use complex concepts. Recent research on dolphins has revealed that dolphins have brains almost identical in size to humans. Dolphins have a body size nearly identical to humans. Experiments have shown that dolphins can understand verbal commands and sign language instructions, which humans can do quite easily. Like humans, dolphins have a strong sense of self-identity, because it has been shown that dolphins can recognize themselves in mirrors and when shown their image on a TV screen. Therefore, it is highly probable that dolphins are capable of highly abstract thinking.

Answer:

1. (a) *Number of entities:* Dolphins and humans (we are not told how many dolphins were studied).
   (b) *Variety of instances:* We are not given specific information on the age, sex, or species of the dolphins studied.
   (c) *Number of characteristics:* Brain size; body size; ability to understand verbal commands; ability to understand sign language; strong sense of self-identity.
   (d) *Relevancy:* Of all the characteristics referred to, body size seems the least relevant to the question of highly abstract thinking.

II. Analyze the arguments from Part II of Exercises 10A by applying the four criteria introduced in this section: (a) Determine the number of things referred to in the first premise; (b) assess the variety of things referred to in the first premise; (c) list the number of characteristics that are claimed to be similar between the things being compared; and (d) determine the relevance of the characteristics.

Refer back to Exercises 10A II for the exercises. The first exercise and a solution are provided here:

1. A study by U.S. and Korean researchers including Harvard Business School's Jordan Siegel found that if you operate in a sexist country full of educated, talented women, it makes good business sense to tap them for management roles. . . . It's depressing how governments don't realize that failing to harness

half of populations holds back growth. Planes that need two engines to fly don't take off when one isn't working, so why do nations think they can thrive in our madly competitive world with one engine?

William Pesek, "Sexism That Irks Goldman Is Boon for Savvy CEOs"

Answer:

1. (a) *Number of entities:* Planes with two engines; nations.
   (b) *Variety of instances:* Planes differ in size, structure and use; nations differ in size, economies, cultures, and languages.
   (c) *Number of characteristics:* Planes operating with one engine; countries that do not employ educated, talented women.
   (d) *Relevancy:* The characteristic of a plane needing two engines to operate effectively, and a nation needing to use all its qualified workers to compete in the world's marketplace is probably related to both instances.

III. For the following argument by analogy, consider alternative scenarios. For each of these, decide whether it *strengthens, weakens,* or *is irrelevant to* the original argument. Do each one independently of the others.

Imagine that an auto mechanic says the following:

> Your car has ABS brakes manufactured by Skidmore Brake Company. Unfortunately, that company is no longer in business. Research has shown that the brakes made by that company failed to work in at least 1000 cases. The brakes failed in cars, trucks, and SUVs. Therefore, I recommend that you replace your ABS brake system.

1. What if there had been only 10 recorded cases of brake failure with those particular brakes?

Answer: Weakens the argument. The number of entities in the premises is now decreased substantially.

2. What if the recorded cases of failure had all been in cars and you have a truck?

3. What if the majority of the recorded cases of brake failure involved red cars, but your car is blue?

4. What if none of the recorded cases of failure involved SUVs, and you have an SUV?

⬆ 5. What if the brakes in your car are only 1 month old?

C. STRATEGIES OF EVALUATION

Three strategies can further help determine the strength of analogical arguments. We look in turn at *disanalogies, counteranalogies,* and the *unintended consequences* of analogies.

Disanalogies

The first strategy involves the obvious fact that any two distinct things have differences between them. These differences can be exploited and, if significant, can severely weaken any analogical argument. To point out differences between two things is to reveal **disanalogies**.

Disanalogies To point out differences between two things.

As we saw earlier, the function of premise 1 of an analogical argument is to point out similarities between the two things. Disanalogies can affect the degree of overlap between the two things in question by acknowledging significant and relevant differences between them. If effective, this strategy lowers the probability that the characteristic attached to the thing referred to in premise 2 is also attached to the thing referred to in the conclusion. In example 1, the son Mike could point out differences between himself and Steve. These differences might include the following: *p*, the color of shirts they wear; *q*, the logos (or lack of logos) on the shirts they typically wear; *r*, the food they like; and *v*, the movies they like. Pointing out the disanalogies (differences) deemphasizes the overlap between the two, as illustrated here:

Disanalogies and Overlap

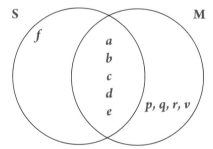

Notice that the strategy of pointing out disanalogies does not directly affect the original characteristics (*a* through *e*) listed in premise 1. Those characteristics remain in the area where S and M overlap. Rather, the new picture reveals that, *if* we can effectively point out relevant differences between S and M, then even if Steve likes his shirt, *f*, the probability, according to our new picture, is that *f* is *not* in M (Mike does not like the shirt). If we look back at the overlap *without* disanalogies, we can see how disanalogies can reduce the likelihood that the conclusion is true.

Overlap Without Disanalogies

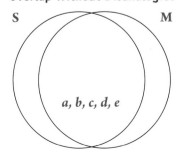

Counteranalogy

Counteranalogy A new, competing argument—one that compares the thing in question to something else.

A second type of evaluation relies on a **counteranalogy**—a new, competing argument—one that compares the thing in question to *something else*. This new argument may lead to a conclusion that contradicts the conclusion of the original argument. In example 1, for instance, suppose that Mike's mother insists she predicted all along that Mike would *not* like the shirt his father bought. Her reasoning might run like this:

> Mike (M) is more like Nick (N) because they both wear the same kind of pants (*a*); like the same music (*b*); like the same television programs (*c*); like the same colors (*d*); wear the same kinds of logos (*e*); like the same kinds of food (*f*); and like the same movies (*g*). Nick does *not* like that kind of shirt (*h*); therefore, probably Mike will not like it.

PROFILES IN LOGIC
David Hume

The ideas of David Hume (1711–76) echo throughout modern philosophy, but one of his most memorable contributions to logic concerns reasoning by analogy. In his *Dialogues Concerning Natural Religion*, Hume dissects a famous analogical argument. The *design argument*—which many people still use today—starts with the idea that objects like watches could not have randomly assembled themselves. Anything so orderly and intricate had to be designed and built for a specific purpose by an intelligent creature. In the same way, observation of the universe reveals an orderly design and purpose. It follows by analogy that it was designed and built for a specific purpose by an intelligent creature, namely God.

Hume provides several criticisms of the design argument. First, he points out, watches and other man-made objects are very different from much of the universe, which in fact exhibits great disorder and randomness. These flaws in the analogy (relevant disanalogies) weaken the analogical argument.

Second, Hume offered a counteranalogy. He points out that some forms of animal life and vegetation do reveal order, but they are still the result of natural processes without any intentional intelligent design or purpose.

Third, Hume notes, the argument by design has unintended consequences. Since we human designers of watches are finite creatures, then probably God is finite; since we are imperfect, then perhaps God is imperfect; since groups of designers and builders create watches, then many gods were needed to create our universe. Since humans can create imperfect products, perhaps our universe "is a botched creation of an inferior deity who afterwards abandoned it, ashamed of the poor quality of the product."

This completely new, competing analogical argument is pictured here:

The Counteranalogy

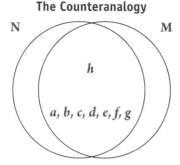

A counteranalogy, appropriately enough, *counters* the original analogical argument. In fact, there is no limit to the number of counteranalogies we can create from a given analogy. Of course, we are still faced with the prospect of weighing, judging, and evaluating the competing strengths of two analogies. And all the counteranalogies, as well as the original analogy, are subject to disanalogies as well.

Unintended Consequences

The third strategy of evaluating an analogy is the discovery of **unintended consequences**: If you can show that something unacceptable to a person presenting an analogy follows from that analogy, then you put that person in a difficult position. We say that the person has "painted himself into a corner." The discovery forces the person either to accept the unintended consequence or to weaken the original analogy. For example, suppose Mike says the following:

> O.K., Dad, you are correct; Steve and I are very much alike. But since Steve likes smoking cigarettes, you won't mind if I start smoking, too, right?

The father might respond by saying the following:

> Steve's parents don't seem to care what he does, but I care what you do. Besides, Steve's parents are rich and can give him more spending money than we can give you. Also, Steve doesn't seem too interested in personal grooming and the odor associated with smoking cigarettes, but you are very particular about the scent you give off. Therefore, I do mind if you smoke.

Mike's father sounds reasonable, but he is really pointing out disanalogies. He is thus effectively weakening his own original analogical argument by admitting there are relevant differences between Steve and Mike.

Combining Strategies

Let's see how disanalogies, counteranalogies, and unintended consequences can affect our analysis of a more extended analogical argument—the kind that appear in the media nearly everyday. Suppose a political commentator makes the following argument:

Unintended consequences If you can show that something unacceptable to a person presenting an analogy follows from that analogy, then you put that person in a difficult position.

The United States has the right to defeat and to destroy the Islamic State of Iraq and Syria (ISIS). If your neighbors threatened your property, stockpiled dangerous weapons, disparaged our form of government and our social customs, threatened our very way of life, and killed innocent people, then our government is justified in going into their house and stopping them—by force, if necessary. The ISIS terrorists have threatened several countries, stockpiled dangerous weapons, disparaged our form of government and our social customs, threatened our very way of life, and killed innocent people, including some of our citizens. Therefore, we are justified in going into Syria and eliminating ISIS by force.

Let X = *a family living in the United States*, I = *Islamic State of Iraq and Syria*, a = *threatened their neighbor's property*, b = *stockpiled dangerous weapons*, c = *disparaged our form of government*, d = *disparaged our social customs*, e = *threatened our very way of life*, f = *killed innocent people*, and g = *we would feel justified in going in and stopping them by force*. We can then reconstruct the argument:

X and I have *a, b, c, d, e,* and *f* in common.
<u>In the case of X, *g*.</u>
Therefore, in the case of I, *probably g*.

We can now draw the analogical argument:

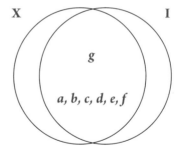

On the same TV program, another talking head might respond by saying this:

You are comparing apples to oranges. A family living in the United States is subject to the laws of this country; this is not the case with foreign countries. We have no right to impose, nor can we enforce, our laws on another country. A threat by one U.S. citizen on another is grounds for immediate action by our government, so if your neighbor threatens your property, you are afforded the protection of our government. Although a threat or an action by a terrorist group should cause us to be ready for any eventuality, it does not give us the right to invade a sovereign nation such as Syria.

This commentator is pointing out differences and is using disanalogies to weaken the original analogy. Of course, we should pay close attention to the relevance of the characteristics in both the original analogy and the disanalogy to see how much weight we should give to each. We can then determine for ourselves the strength of the original analogy.

A different commentator might respond like this:

> Syria is more like Vietnam when we first got involved. Vietnam was a divided country, at war with itself, with one side asking for our help and the other side telling us to keep out. North Vietnam received military and financial assistance from the Soviet Union, while Russia has argued that we have no right to invade Syria today. We suffered too many deaths and wounded in Vietnam. We already know how costly the war in Iraq has been, and any invasion of Syria will result in many more deaths and wounded. We stayed too long in Vietnam and Iraq and, in the end, the results were not what we had hoped for. This will happen again in Syria. Many people felt that we should not have gone into Vietnam in the first place. Therefore, we are not justified in invading Syria.

This commentator is using a counteranalogy to show that a completely different conclusion can be reached. As we have seen, a counteranalogy is subject to the three strategies of evaluation: (1) its strength can be questioned by pointing out disanalogies between Vietnam and Syria; (2) unintended consequences of the analogy might be discovered; and (3) a new counteranalogy could also be constructed.

A final commentator might have this to say:

> I agree that we are justified in invading Syria to eliminate ISIS by force. Of course, this means that countries such as Russia and China will not join in any coalition to help us defeat ISIS. Some countries may even sever economic and diplomatic ties with us, as they have forcefully repeated. In turn, this will make our economy suffer. But that's the price we have to be willing to pay for protecting ourselves.

This illustrates the strategy of pointing out some unintended consequences of the analogy. Of course the original talking head might find these results acceptable; but if the last commentator is wise enough, and knows the opponent well, then she is sure to think of consequences that she knows her opponent will find unacceptable.

STRATEGIES FOR EVALUATING ANALOGICAL ARGUMENTS
Disanalogy: To point out the *differences* between the two (or more) things referred to in the first premise of an analogical argument.
Counteranalogy: To create a completely new, competing, analogical argument.
Unintended consequences of an analogy: To point to something that is a direct result of the original analogy, but that is unacceptable to the person presenting that analogy.

EXERCISES 10C

Level 1 Multiple-
Choice Questions

Level 2 Multiple-
Choice Questions

Video Tutorial

I. You revealed the framework of the analogical arguments in Exercises 10A. Next, you analyzed those arguments in Exercises 10B. Now, you are in position to conclude your evaluation of those arguments by using the three strategies illustrated in this section: (a) point out any relevant disanalogies between the things being compared; (b) construct a counteranalogy; and (c) determine any unintended consequences of the analogy.

Refer back to Exercises 10A I for the exercises. The first exercise and a solution are provided here:

1. We know that humans are capable of highly abstract thinking by their ability to understand and use complex concepts. Recent research on dolphins has revealed that dolphins have brains almost identical in size to humans. Dolphins have a body size nearly identical to humans. Experiments have shown that dolphins can understand verbal commands and sign language instructions, which humans can do quite easily. Like humans, dolphins have a strong sense of self-identity, because it has been shown that dolphins can recognize themselves in mirrors and when shown their image on a TV screen. Therefore, it is highly probable that dolphins are capable of highly abstract thinking.

Answer:

(a) *Disanalogies:* Humans display complex speech patterns and can create completely new forms. Mathematical skills, which are taken as a hallmark of abstract thinking, are not mentioned as one of the dolphins' abilities; poetry, art, music and other aesthetic abilities have not been shown to exist in dolphins.
(b) *Counteranalogy:* Dolphins are more like dogs. They both have highly sensitive senses of smell; they both have extraordinary sensitivity to sounds that humans cannot detect; they both can learn to react correctly to certain signs or verbal commands; they both seem to bond well with humans; they both are able to learn tricks of performance. Since there is no evidence that dogs are capable of highly abstract thinking, dolphins probably do not have that ability either.
(c) *Unintended consequences:* If dolphins are capable of highly abstract thinking, then perhaps they should be afforded rights similar to humans. They should not be kept and raised in captivity and be subject to experiments like those mentioned in the article. The researchers should obtain informed consent agreements from the dolphins before embarking on any further experiments.

II. Analyze the arguments from Part II of Exercises 10A by applying the criteria introduced in this section. For each of the following arguments, (a) point out any

relevant disanalogies between the things being compared; (b) construct a counteranalogy; and (c) determine any unintended consequences of the analogy.

Refer back to Exercises 10A II for the exercises. The first exercise and a solution are provided here:

1. A study by U.S. and Korean researchers including Harvard Business School's Jordan Siegel found that if you operate in a sexist country full of educated, talented women, it makes good business sense to tap them for management roles. . . . It's depressing how governments don't realize that failing to harness half of populations holds back growth. Planes that need two engines to fly don't take off when one isn't working, so why do nations think they can thrive in our madly competitive world with one engine?

William Pesek, "Sexism That Irks Goldman Is Boon for Savvy CEOs"

Answer:

(a) *Disanalogies:* Airplane engines and humans are quite different—in size, function, structure, and motivation in the case of humans. Airplane engines are mechanical; humans are organic.

(b) *Counteranalogy:* Nations are like genes. The dominant gene wins out and the recessive gene is not used. So, only one aspect of a nation is needed to compete.

(c) *Unintended consequences:* When engines fail, they are discarded or put on the scrap heap. So, if humans fail, do we discard them?

Summary

Study Materials

- To draw an analogy is simply to indicate that there are similarities between two or more things.
- Analogical reasoning is one of the most fundamental tools used in creating an argument. It can be analyzed as a type of inductive argument—it is a matter of probability, based on experience, and it can be quite persuasive.
- An analogical argument is analyzed by revealing the general framework of the argument. The argument lists the characteristics that two (or more) things have in common and concludes that the things being compared probably have some other characteristic in common.
- If an analogical argument is strong, then it raises the probability that the conclusion is true.
- Four criteria are used to analyze the first premise of an analogical argument: (*a*) the strength of an analogical argument is related to the number of things referred to in the first premise. (*b*) The strength of an analogical argument is related to the variety of things referred to in the first premise. (*c*) The strength of an analogical argument is related to the number of characteristics that are

claimed to be similar between the things being compared. (*d*) The strength of an analogical argument is related to the relevance of the characteristics referred to in the first premise.

- Disanalogies: To point out differences between two or more things.
- Counteranalogy: A new, competing argument—one that compares the thing in question to something else.
- Unintended consequences: If you can show that something unacceptable to a person presenting an analogy follows from that analogy, then you put that person in a difficult position.

KEY TERMS

analogical argument 535	counteranalogy 548	unintended
analogical reasoning 534	disanalogies 547	consequences 549
analogy 534		

LOGIC CHALLENGE: BEAT THE CHEAT

While walking downtown, you come across a very excited group of people. They have gathered around a loud man who is challenging them to a bet. You watch as the man holds up two cards; one is blank, and the other has an X written on it. He then quickly places them face down on a small table and shuffles their positions many times. He is willing to bet $10 that no one can locate the card with the X. Another man steps forward and puts $10 down on the table and chooses one of the cards. He turns it over, reveals that it is blank, and promptly loses $10. Three other people try and they each fail, too.

By now you are convinced that the game is a scam. The man is obviously palming or hiding the card with the X and putting two blank cards down on the table. Suddenly, you realize that you can beat the cheat. You ask the crowd how many people lost $10, and then you challenge the cheat to bet that amount for one game.

You win the bet and return everyone's lost $10. How did you do it?

Chapter 11

Legal Arguments

Study Materials

You have probably seen the old image of *Justice* wearing a blindfold and holding a balancing scale. The image is meant to evoke an ideal. Justice, it says, has nothing to do with stereotypes or emotional appeals. The law should be blind to any sort of prejudice. Yet legal debates often involve politically and emotionally charged issues, such as gay marriage, crime, or abortion. When civil rights protesters were met with violence, the courts were called to decide legal arguments. When fears of terrorism led to imprisonment without trial and, some say, even torture, the courts again had to decide what must be done. And when citizens then protest court decisions, they are exercising a right protected by law.

In fact, disputes like these help explain the ideal of blind justice. The process of making legal decisions has evolved to emphasize rationality and impartiality, which we depend on for our everyday safety, security, and well-being. Although legal debates often involve emotional issues, legal discourse has evolved patterns and conventions that we can recognize. Legal arguments can be understood once you are able to grasp the underlying logic, and our reasoning skills can complement our understanding of the practical demands of the law.

This chapter looks at the logical foundation of legal arguments. We will explore the use of *conditional statements, sufficient and necessary conditions, disjunction, conjunction,* and the role of *analogies.* We will see how inductive analysis helps explain legal reasoning.

A. DEDUCTIVE AND INDUCTIVE REASONING

The logical basis of legal arguments has a long history. According to Aristotle, writing in the 4th century BCE, "The law is reason free from passion." The defining documents of the United States describe the rights of citizens, and the duties and responsibilities of government. The Constitution spells out in detail guidelines for many legal issues and their remedies in Amendment 5:

> No person shall be held to answer for a capital, or otherwise infamous crime, unless on a presentment or indictment of a Grand Jury, except in cases arising in the land or naval forces, or in the Militia, when in actual service in time of War or public danger; nor shall any person be subject for the same offense to be twice put in jeopardy of life or limb; nor shall be compelled in any criminal case to be a witness against himself, nor be deprived of life, liberty, or property, without due process of law; nor shall private property be taken for public use, without just compensation.

Legislative bodies usually enact laws, which then get expressed in formal documents. Federal laws are also referred to as *statutes*. In charging individuals with crimes, for example, federal prosecutors must make a judgment that a statute is applicable to the case at hand. An average reader may not find that judgment so easy. Take this example:

Crimes and Criminal Procedure
US Code—Section 111: Assaulting, resisting, or impeding certain officers or employees.
 (a) In General—Whoever
  (1) forcibly assaults, resists, opposes, impedes, intimidates, or interferes with any person designated in section 1114 of this title while engaged in or on account of the performance of official duties; or . . .

And that's just the first clause. Fortunately, the ability to recognize a few basics will let you engage in reasoned debates about the meaning and intent of laws like these. **Appellate courts** are courts of appeal that review the decisions of lower courts. Legal briefs to these courts may also look complicated, but they, too, rely on the same kind of reasoning.

Appellate courts Courts of appeal that review the decisions of lower courts.

In law, the term "deductive reasoning" generally means going from the *general* to the *specific*—that is, from the statement of a *rule* to its application to a particular legal case. Although this definition is too narrow to capture all the varieties of deductive reasoning in logic, for legal purposes it serves the intended goal. On the other hand, many law textbooks define "inductive reasoning" as the process of going from the *specific* to the *general*. It comes into play whenever we move from a *specific case* or legal opinion to a *general rule*. Again, although this legal use, too, is narrow, it is a legitimate part of the larger class of inductive reasoning in logic.

B. CONDITIONAL STATEMENTS

Rule-based reasoning Legal reasoning is also referred to as "rule-based reasoning."

Conditional statements play a major role in *legal reasoning*, which is also referred to as **rule-based reasoning**. Once you recognize a conditional statement, you have a powerful tool for assessing the strengths or weaknesses of the legal argument quickly and precisely. (Conditional statements were introduced in Chapter 1 and further developed in Chapter 7.)

When legal terminology contains the words "if" or "only if," then the application of sufficient and necessary conditions can often assist in unraveling the legal issues. Let's work through some examples to sharpen our skills:

> A judge may admit evidence of a prior conviction, if it falls within either of two categories.

Although we do not yet know the "two categories" mentioned in the statement, the key word is "if"; it alerts us that we are dealing with a conditional statement. Since the "if" always precedes the antecedent, it must be placed first when we reconstruct the given sentence. In our example, we could rewrite the sentence as follows:

> If evidence of a prior conviction falls within either of two categories, then it may be admitted.

Here is another example:

> If the judge has refused to admit into evidence a piece of evidence, that information cannot be considered when deciding a case.

Although the word "then" is absent, you should recognize that this is a conditional statement. We can easily reconstruct the sentence by placing the word "then" in the appropriate place.

In examples of rule-based legal reasoning, you should pay attention to the possibility of the existence of conditional statements. We already know that the word "if" is a good indicator. We also know that certain statements in ordinary language can be translated into a conditional statement using the word "if." The phrases *every time*, *whenever, all cases where, given that*, and *in the event of* all indicate a conditional statement. If we encounter, say, the statement "*Whenever* the judge has refused to admit into evidence a piece of evidence, that information cannot be considered when deciding a case," we can recognize this as an instance of a conditional statement.

C. SUFFICIENT AND NECESSARY CONDITIONS

Before we see how conditional statements relate to legal concerns, we need to review two kinds of conditions. A **sufficient condition** occurs whenever one event ensures that another event is realized. Another way of saying that something is a sufficient condition is to think of the phrases "is enough for" or "it guarantees." Now suppose that the law of the state in which you are driving states that anyone caught driving with a blood alcohol level above 0.08% will be subject to a citation for *driving while intoxicated* (DWI) or, in some states, *driving under the influence* (DUI). If you are stopped by the police and agree to take a breath-analyzer test, then the following indicates a sufficient condition.

> If your blood alcohol level exceeds 0.08%, then you are cited for DWI.

Sufficient condition
Whenever one event ensures that another event is realized.

In other words, anyone caught driving with a blood alcohol level above 0.08% has met a *sufficient condition* for being issued a citation for DWI. Compare these results with a new case:

If you are cited for DWI, then your blood alcohol level exceeds 0.08%.

Even though it might be true that you were cited for a DWI, this is *not sufficient* information to determine that your blood alcohol level exceeds 0.08%. You might have refused to take a breath-analyzer test, so your blood alcohol level was not determined. Or you might have been given a variety of field sobriety tests, such as walking a straight line and turning, standing on one foot, or closing your eyes and touching the tip of your nose. If, in the officer's opinion, you failed the field sobriety test, then you may have been cited for DWI.

PROFILES IN LOGIC
Cesare Beccaria

Cesare Beccaria (1738–94) wrote a short but influential book, *On Crimes and Punishments*, to provide a clear foundation for the criminal justice system. Theoretical justifications for the punishment of criminals have a long history: *retribution* (revenge, or "an eye for an eye"); *rehabilitation* (reforming the offender into a productive member of society); *incapacitation* (simply removing the offender from society); and *deterrence* (discouraging others from committing crimes). Since Beccaria thought that the only justification for punishment was to create a better society, he advocated deterrence as the fundamental justification for punishment.

For Beccaria, two basic principles must be rigorously followed for deterrence to work effectively—*certainty* and *celerity*. "Certainty" means that everyone in the society must see that laws will be strictly enforced and that punishment will be consistent. In other words, identical punishments must follow identical crimes. For

that reason, Beccaria argued, judges should not have the power to alter any punishment. "Celerity" means that punishment should occur swiftly. People need to connect a specific punishment to a specific crime (*certainty*)—and to connect it immediately (*celerity*). "A punishment may not be an act of violence, of one, or of many, against a private member of society; it should be public, immediate, and necessary, the least possible in the case given, proportioned to the crime, and determined by the laws."

Beccaria argued that the most damaging crimes are committed by those who have gained the greatest benefits from society. In today's terms, this means that white-collar crimes are the most damaging. In support of this idea, Beccaria argued that most people are not likely to imitate violent crimes. However, seeing wealthy criminals abusing their positions in society for personal gain, and often getting light punishment for it, tears the fabric of society.

On the other hand, a **necessary condition** means that one thing is *essential, manda-tory,* or *required* in order for another thing to be realized. Here is a simple example of a necessary condition:

> If you are allowed to vote in the presidential election, then you are at least 18 years old.

Necessary condition
Whenever one thing is *essential, mandatory,* or *required* in order for another thing to be realized.

According to the law, you must be at least 18 years of age in order to be able to vote in a presidential election. Therefore, being at least 18 years of age is a *necessary condition* to vote. In other words, if you are *not* at least 18 years of age, then you are *not* allowed to vote in the presidential election. Compare the foregoing results with a new example:

> If you are not allowed to vote in the presidential election, then you are not at least 18 years old.

Even if you are *not* allowed to vote in the presidential election, we *cannot* say for sure that you are *not* at least 18 years old. There are many other reasons why you might not be allowed to vote as well. Perhaps you missed the deadline for registering, or you were convicted of a certain felony.

D. DISJUNCTION AND CONJUNCTION

The legal use of *disjunction* is illustrated by an "either/or" test, in which at least one component must be satisfied. Here is one possible example:

> A lawyer is not permitted to get a contingent fee in child custody cases or divorce cases.

If we let C = *child custody cases*, and D = *divorce cases*, then we can write:

> A lawyer is *not* permitted to get a contingent fee for C *or* D.

C or D is a *sufficient* condition for the lawyer *not* to be allowed to get a contingent fee. Thus, the rule sets the condition that a particular result will occur *if* a case falls within one of two possibilities. The word "if" is essential here. It alerts us that we are dealing with sufficient conditions and a conditional statement. If we let "L" stand for the phrase "A lawyer is *not* permitted to get a contingent fee," we then reconstruct the statement:

> If (C or D), then L.

This is a compound statement and it contains three simple statements (represented by the letters "C," "D," and "L"). We can now picture the rule:

This picture can also be interpreted as indicating that we have an *exclusive* disjunction (where C and D cannot both occur at the same time), because C and D do not overlap.

(As an exercise in legal thinking, do you think that this is correct when it comes to our hypothetical lawyer? Does the rule clearly indicate that we are dealing with exclusive disjunction? Why or why not?)

On the other hand, a *rule* containing a *conjunction* specifies a test for *necessary conditions* that must be met for the rule to apply. Suppose a rule defines "burglary" as having five components, *all of which must be met* for a case to fall under the definition. If even one of the five parts is not met, then the burglary rule should not be applied. Necessary conditions and conjunctions specify logical, and in this case legal, commitments that are specific and comprehensive.

E. ANALYZING A COMPLEX RULE

We now have the logical tools to analyze a complex legal rule. For example, Rule 609(a) of the Federal Rules of Evidence deals with questioning the character of a witness for truthfulness. We will paraphrase the rule to highlight the grounds for the possible impeachment of a witness by evidence of a conviction of a crime:

> Evidence that a witness has been convicted of a crime shall be admitted if either (1) the crime was punishable by death or imprisonment in excess of one year under the law under which he/she was convicted, and its **probative value** of admitting this evidence outweighs its **prejudicial effect** to the accused, or (2) that establishing the elements of the crime required proof or admission of an act of dishonesty or false statement by the witness, regardless of punishment.

Probative value
Evidence that can be used during a trial to advance the facts of the case.

Prejudicial effect
Evidence that might cause some jurors to be negatively biased toward a defendant.

The term "probative value" refers to evidence that can be used during a trial to advance the facts of the case. The term "prejudicial effect" describes evidence that might cause some jurors to be negatively biased toward a defendant. For example, the defendant might belong to a religious group that is not popular.

A complete analysis will, of necessity, take many steps. However, at the end we will have revealed the logic behind this complex rule. We start by highlighting in italics all the logical operators at work:

> Evidence that a witness has been convicted of a crime shall be admitted *if* either (1) the crime was punishable by death *or* imprisonment in excess of one year under the law under which he/she was convicted, *and* its probative value of admitting this evidence outweighs its prejudicial effect to the accused, *or* (2) that establishing the elements of the crime required proof *or* admission of an act of dishonesty *or* false statement by the witness, regardless of punishment.

We can use the logical operators to outline the rule:

> Evidence that a witness has been convicted of a crime shall be admitted (E) *if* it meets *either* criterion A *or* B:

> **Criterion A:** The evidence shall be admitted *if* both A1 *and* A2 are true:
> A1. The prior conviction was punishable by either a or b:
> a. Death

   b. Imprisonment in excess of one year
A2. Its probative value outweighs its prejudicial effect.

Criterion B: The evidence shall be admitted *if* it involved either of the following:
   B1. Establishing the elements of the crime required *proof* of either a or b, as follows:
      a. An act of dishonesty by the witness
      b. A false statement by the witness
   B2. Establishing the elements of the crime required an *admission* of either a or b:
      a. An act of dishonesty by the witness
      b. A false statement by the witness

Given this, the overall logical structure of this rule is simple: If either A or B, then E. From this basic structure we can recognize that this rule designates both A and B as *sufficient conditions* for E. This means that the antecedent of the conditional statement will be satisfied if either A or B is true.

Our next step is to analyze both A and B into their components. Criterion A is very complex, but we can see that three logical operators are involved (*if; and; or*). We are told that A is realized whenever two further conditions are true at the same time: A1 and A2. Thus, *if* both A1 *and* A2 are true, then A will be true (we already know that if A is true, then E will be true).

On closer inspection, we see that A1 is itself complex: It contains "or." This tells us that A1 can be realized in either of two ways—when either A1a is true or A1b is true. A2 is a bit more complicated, because it asks us to gauge the relative value of two things. We are told that the court must be able to determine that A2a, the probative value, outweighs A2b, the prejudicial effect. Of course, we would need to know the facts of the case before we could determine the actual value of each component; a judge would have to decide. However, we can still understand the logic behind this requirement. In order for A2 to hold, A2a must be greater than A2b.

We can now combine our analysis into one result for criterion A:

> *If* [(A1a, the prior conviction was punishable by death, *or* A1b, by imprisonment in excess of one year), *and* (A2a, its probative value outweighs A2b, its prejudicial effect)], *then* E, evidence of a prior conviction shall be admitted.

As we have outlined, we must acknowledge that E can be realized even if A does not occur, because the rule asserts that B is sufficient to bring about E. As before, let E = *evidence of a prior conviction shall be admitted*. We notice that B can be realized if either B1 or B2 is the case. So either B1 or B2 is sufficient for B to occur. However, for a complete analysis we need to explore B1 and B2. It turns out that B1 can occur if either B1a is the case (*proof* of an act of dishonesty by the witness), *or* B1b is the case (*proof* of a false statement by the witness). Similarly, B2 can occur if either B2a is the case (*admission* of an act of dishonesty by the witness), *or* B2b is the case (*admission* of a false statement by the witness). This analysis results in the following conditional statement:

If [(B1a, *proof* of an act of dishonesty by the witness, *or* B1b, *proof* of a false statement by the witness), *or* (B2a, *admission* of an act of dishonesty by the witness, *or* B2b, *admission* of a false statement by the witness)], *then* E, evidence of a prior conviction shall be admitted.

Our analysis of a complex rule is complete. It has revealed the existence of sufficient and necessary conditions, the use of conjunction, disjunction, and conditional statements. It has shown what must occur in order for the rule to be applied. Taking apart legal rules this way allows us to see how the rules work by showing the logical foundation of the legal reasoning. We can then see both the strengths and weaknesses of a legal position by asking whether the facts at hand fit the rule. As we move back and forth between the statements and the logical operators, we become more sensitive to the subtleties of legal language and its logical structure.

EXERCISES 11E

Level 1 Multiple-
Choice Questions

Level 2 Multiple-
Choice Questions

For each exercise you are to explain the logical apparatus used in a particular rule of evidence. Follow the method of analysis that we did for Rule 609(a) of the Federal Rules of Evidence. Highlight any logical operators when available. Rewrite and reconstruct the statements whenever necessary in order to reveal the logic of the rule. (All the exercises are adapted from the Federal Rules of Evidence.)

1. RULE 603. OATH OR AFFIRMATION.
Before testifying, every witness shall be required to declare that the witness will testify truthfully, by oath or affirmation administered in a form calculated to awaken the witness' conscience and impress the witness' mind with the duty to do so.
Answer:

Highlight logical operators:

Before testifying, every witness shall be required to declare that the witness will testify truthfully, by oath **or** affirmation administered in a form calculated to awaken the witness' conscience **and** impress the witness' mind with the duty to do so.

Reconstruct the statements in order to reveal the logic of the rule:

If (T) testifying, then either (O) a witness shall be required to declare that the witness will testify truthfully by oath or (A) a witness shall be required to declare that the witness will testify truthfully by affirmation, and (C) administered in a form calculated to awaken the witness' conscience and (D) administered in a form calculated to impress the witness' mind with the duty to do so.

If T, then (0 or A) and (C and D)

2. RULE 605. COMPETENCY OF JUDGE AS WITNESS.
The judge presiding at the trial may not testify in that trial as a witness.

3. RULE 606(A). COMPETENCY OF JUROR AS WITNESS—AT THE TRIAL.

A member of the jury may not testify as a witness before that jury in the trial of the case in which the juror is sitting. If the juror is called so to testify, the opposing party shall be afforded an opportunity to object out of the presence of the jury.

4. RULE 606(B). COMPETENCY OF JUROR AS WITNESS—INQUIRY INTO VALIDITY OF VERDICT OR INDICTMENT.

Upon an inquiry into the validity of a verdict or **indictment** (a formal accusation presented by a grand jury), a juror may not testify as to any matter or statement occurring during the course of the jury's deliberations or to the effect of anything upon that or any other juror's mind or emotions as influencing the juror to assent to or dissent from the verdict or indictment or concerning the juror's mental processes in connection therewith. But a juror may testify about (1) whether extraneous prejudicial information was improperly brought to the jury's attention, (2) whether any outside influence was improperly brought to bear upon any juror, or (3) whether there was a mistake in entering the verdict onto the verdict form. A juror's **affidavit** (a written statement signed before an authorized official), or evidence of any statement by the juror may not be received on a matter about which the juror would be precluded from testifying.

> **Indictment** A formal accusation presented by a grand jury.

> **Affidavit** A written statement signed before an authorized official.

5. RULE 608(A). EVIDENCE OF CHARACTER AND CONDUCT OF WITNESS—OPINION AND REPUTATION EVIDENCE OF CHARACTER.

The credibility of a witness may be attacked or supported by evidence in the form of opinion or reputation, but subject to these limitations: (1) the evidence may refer only to character for truthfulness or untruthfulness, and (2) evidence of truthful character is admissible only after the character of the witness for truthfulness has been attacked by opinion or reputation evidence or otherwise.

Video Tutorial

6. RULE 608(B). EVIDENCE OF CHARACTER AND CONDUCT OF WITNESS—SPECIFIC INSTANCES OF CONDUCT.

Specific instances of the conduct of a witness, for the purpose of attacking or supporting the witness' character for truthfulness, other than conviction of crime as provided in Rule 609, may not be proved by extrinsic evidence. They may, however, in the discretion of the court, if probative of truthfulness or untruthfulness, be inquired into on cross-examination of the witness (1) concerning the witness' character for truthfulness or untruthfulness, or (2) concerning the character for truthfulness or untruthfulness of another witness as to which character the witness being cross-examined has testified. The giving of testimony, whether by an accused or by any other witness, does not operate as a waiver of the accused's or the witness' privilege against self-incrimination when examined with respect to matters that relate only to character for truthfulness.

7. RULE 609(B). IMPEACHMENT BY EVIDENCE OF CONVICTION OF CRIME—TIME LIMIT.

Evidence of a conviction under this rule is not admissible if a period of more than 10 years has elapsed since the date of the conviction or of the release of the witness from the confinement imposed for that conviction, whichever is the later date, unless the court determines, in the interests of justice, that the probative value of the conviction supported by specific facts and circumstances substantially outweighs its prejudicial effect. However, evidence of a conviction more than 10 years old as calculated herein, is not admissible unless the proponent gives to the adverse party sufficient advance written notice of intent to use such evidence to provide the adverse party with a fair opportunity to contest the use of such evidence.

8. RULE 609(C). IMPEACHMENT BY EVIDENCE OF CONVICTION OF CRIME— EFFECT OF PARDON, ANNULMENT, OR CERTIFICATE OF REHABILITATION.

Evidence of a conviction is not admissible under this rule if (1) the conviction has been the subject of a pardon, annulment, certificate of rehabilitation, or other equivalent procedure based on a finding of the rehabilitation of the person convicted, and that person has not been convicted of a subsequent crime which was punishable by death or imprisonment in excess of one year, or (2) the conviction has been the subject of a pardon, annulment, or other equivalent procedure based on a finding of innocence.

9. RULE 609(D). IMPEACHMENT BY EVIDENCE OF CONVICTION OF CRIME— JUVENILE ADJUDICATIONS.

Evidence of juvenile adjudications is generally not admissible under this rule. The court may, however, in a criminal case allow evidence of a juvenile adjudication of a witness other than the accused if conviction of the offense would be admissible to attack the credibility of an adult and the court is satisfied that admission in evidence is necessary for a fair determination of the issue of guilt or innocence.

10. RULE 609(E). IMPEACHMENT BY EVIDENCE OF CONVICTION OF CRIME— PENDENCY OF APPEAL.

The pendency of an appeal therefrom does not render evidence of a conviction inadmissible. Evidence of the pendency of an appeal is admissible.

11. RULE 610. RELIGIOUS BELIEFS OR OPINIONS.

Evidence of the beliefs or opinions of a witness on matters of religion is not admissible for the purpose of showing that by reason of their nature the witness' credibility is impaired or enhanced.

12. RULE 611(A). MODE AND ORDER OF INTERROGATION AND PRESENTATION—CONTROL BY COURT.

The court shall exercise reasonable control over the mode and order of interrogating witnesses and presenting evidence so as to (1) make the interrogation and presentation effective for the ascertainment of the truth, (2) avoid needless consumption of time, and (3) protect witnesses from harassment or undue embarrassment.

13. RULE 611(B). MODE AND ORDER OF INTERROGATION AND PRESENTATION—SCOPE OF CROSS-EXAMINATION.

Cross-examination should be limited to the subject matter of the direct examination and matters affecting the credibility of the witness. The court may, in the exercise of discretion, permit inquiry into additional matters as if on direct examination.

Video Tutorial

14. RULE 611(C). MODE AND ORDER OF INTERROGATION AND PRESENTATION—LEADING QUESTIONS.

Leading questions should not be used on the direct examination of a witness except as may be necessary to develop the witness' testimony. Ordinarily leading questions should be permitted on cross-examination. When a party calls a hostile witness, an adverse party, or a witness identified with an adverse party, interrogation may be by leading questions.

15. RULE 612. WRITING USED TO REFRESH MEMORY.

Except as otherwise provided in criminal proceedings by section 3500 of title 18, United States Code, if a witness uses a writing to refresh memory for the purpose of testifying, either (1) while testifying, or (2) before testifying, if the court in its discretion determines it is necessary in the interests of justice, an adverse party is entitled to have the writing produced at the hearing, to inspect it, to cross-examine the witness thereon, and to introduce in evidence those portions which relate to the testimony of the witness.

16. RULE 613(A). PRIOR STATEMENTS OF WITNESSES—EXAMINING WITNESS CONCERNING PRIOR STATEMENT.

In examining a witness concerning a prior statement made by the witness, whether written or not, the statement need not be shown nor its contents disclosed to the witness at that time, but on request the same shall be shown or disclosed to opposing counsel.

17. RULE 613(B). PRIOR STATEMENTS OF WITNESSES—EXTRINSIC EVIDENCE OF PRIOR INCONSISTENT STATEMENT OF WITNESS.

Extrinsic evidence of a prior inconsistent statement by a witness is not admissible unless the witness is afforded an opportunity to explain or deny the same and the opposite party is afforded an opportunity to interrogate the witness thereon, or the interests of justice otherwise require. This provision does not apply to admissions of a party-opponent as defined in rule 801(d)(2).

18. RULE 614(A). CALLING AND INTERROGATION OF WITNESSES BY COURT—CALLING BY COURT.

The court may, on its own motion or at the suggestion of a party, call witnesses, and all parties are entitled to cross-examine witnesses thus called.

19. RULE 614(B). CALLING AND INTERROGATION OF WITNESSES BY COURT—INTERROGATION BY COURT.

The court may interrogate witnesses, whether called by itself or by a party.

20. RULE 614(C). CALLING AND INTERROGATION OF WITNESSES BY COURT—OBJECTIONS.

Objections to the calling of witnesses by the court or to interrogation by it may be made at the time or at the next available opportunity when the jury is not present.

🔺 21. RULE 615. EXCLUSION OF WITNESSES.

At the request of a party the court shall order witnesses excluded so that they cannot hear the testimony of other witnesses, and it may make the order of its own motion. This rule does not authorize exclusion of (1) a party who is a natural person, or (2) an officer or employee of a party which is not a natural person designated as its representative by its attorney, or (3) a person whose presence is shown by a party to be essential to the presentation of the party's cause, or (4) a person authorized by statute to be present.

F. ANALOGIES

Precedent A judicial decision that can be applied to later cases.

Legal reasoning probably could not work without using analogies. It relies on **precedent** (a judicial decision that can be applied to later cases), and the use of similar cases. Lawyers' arguments and judges' written opinions usually contain reasoning by analogy as an essential component. (Chapter 10 introduced analogical reasoning.)

Once you know where and how a legal argument uses analogies, you gain a foothold to start your analysis of the case at hand. You should always look for the logical components involved in legal reasoning, because the more you begin to see them, the more quickly you can apply them.

Rules of law The legal principles that have been applied to historical cases.

Analogical reasoning is one of the most fundamental tools used in the legal profession. Lawyers try to find **rules of law**, or legal principles that have been applied to historical cases. Along with this, the lawyers must show that the facts of the current case are sufficiently similar to the precedent. Because they share relevant characteristics, they should share the same legal outcome. Therefore, the lawyers argue, the judge should make the same decision as laid down in the precedent.

A rational decision will choose a course of action that has the highest probability of being correct. If an analogical argument is strong, then it raises the probability that the conclusion is true. For example, once a court has decided that members of a group may not be restrained from *speaking*, another court is likely to conclude, by analogical reasoning, that the same group cannot be stopped from *parading*. In other words, the court holds that parading and speaking share relevant characteristics. Arguments like this, from precedent, will identify those respects in which the older cases and the current case are closely alike.

Knowing how to reconstruct the analogy's structure allows you to uncover the mechanisms at work in legal reasoning. Let's imagine that lawyers are arguing a case about that parade, which we will designate as case A. One of the lawyers might argue that case B, a case previously decided by the courts about free speech, and case A, the present case, have many points in common. She would have to illustrate clearly the common points to the court by referring to the facts in A and B. She then shows that case B has already been decided by having rule Z applied to it. She then concludes that rule Z should be applied to the present case A. Therefore, she has argued by analogy that case B should be used as a precedent in deciding case A.

However, the argument is strong only if cases A and B are judged to be similar enough for the rule to apply. Of course, an opposing lawyer will try to show that cases A and B contain substantial differences. He will argue that rule Z *should not* be applied to the present case, because the two cases are *not* similar enough for the rule to be applied. He must point out relevant differences (disanalogies) between case authority (the prior case) and the case being currently adjudicated in order to justify a different result.

Of course, it is not always easy to identify the *relevant* characteristics in a particular legal case. Ultimately, a judge (or an appeals court) will have to decide what kinds of similarities and differences are legally significant. A lawyer argues that significant relevant *similarities* exist, and the opposing lawyer argues that significant relevant *differences* exist. Even then, however, there still remain the *logical* issues regarding the uses of analogies. We can engage in a logical assessment of the legal analogies and offer a reasonable, informed opinion.

Let's examine a fictional case, *Judy B. v. Quickoilz*:

> Judy B. had the oil in her car changed at a company called Quickoilz. While driving home, the oil light came on and the engine temperature gauge began to rapidly rise. She quickly stopped the car, looked underneath, and saw that the screw in the oil pan was missing. All the oil had been lost and the car was overheating. She lived in a rural area outside Las Vegas, and it was 117 degrees outside. She had a baby with her, and instead of trying to walk the five miles to her home, with no water, she decided to keep driving the car. She managed to get the car to within 100 yards of her house before the engine seized up. The engine was ruined, so she sued Quickoilz.

Judy B. is the **plaintiff**, or person initiating the lawsuit, and Quickoilz is the defendant in the case. During the hearing, Judy's lawyer argues that Quickoilz is fully responsible for the damage to the engine, since they must have improperly replaced the oil pan screw. Therefore, Quickoilz should be required to pay the entire bill for a new engine replacement.

Plaintiff The person who initiates a lawsuit.

Quickoilz's lawyer argues that Judy B. is ultimately responsible for the engine failure. He claims that if she had turned off the car as soon as the oil light came on and the temperature gauge began rising, then the engine would not have been damaged. Since she willingly and knowingly kept driving, she assumed responsibility for the consequences. Quickoilz's lawyer then cites a rule of law, which we shall call "AR-1: Assumption of Risk":

> A plaintiff has voluntarily accepted or exposed him or herself to a risk of damage, injury, or loss, whenever he or she understands that the condition or situation is clearly dangerous, but nevertheless makes the decision to act. In all such cases, the defendant in the case may raise the issue of the plaintiff's knowledge and appreciation of the danger as an affirmative defense. If successful, the application of the assumption of risk as an affirmative defense shall result in either a reduction or complete elimination of the damages assessed against the defendant.

Quickoilz's lawyer then refers the court to a past case, *The Spyder v. Kaufman Brothers*:

> A man calling himself *The Spyder* attempted to climb to the top of a fifty-story office building owned by the Kaufman brothers. The plaintiff did this without the permission of the owners of the building. He managed to get thirty feet off the ground when he stepped on a ledge that collapsed under him. He fell to the ground and broke his pelvis. He sued the building's owners for damages, and argued that they were responsible for letting a defective ledge go unrepaired.

The defendant's lawyer argued that Rule AR-1 should be applied because the man had voluntarily accepted and exposed himself to a risk of injury; he clearly understood that the situation was dangerous, but nevertheless he made the decision to climb the building. The court agreed with the defendant's argument that Rule AR-1 was applicable to this case and found in favor of the defendant.

Quickoilz's lawyer then argues that *The Spyder v. Kaufman Brothers* case should be applied to the present case. Applying the language of Rule AR-1, "Judy B. voluntarily accepted and exposed herself to damage or loss; she clearly understood that the situation was dangerous, but nevertheless she made the decision to drive the car." Therefore, since she voluntarily assumed the risk, she bears responsibility for the engine damage. Thus, Rule AR-1 is applicable, and the court should decide in favor of the defendant.

In response, the plaintiff's lawyer argues that Judy B. was caught in a dilemma—a decision that had to be made between two choices, either of which would lead to an unwanted result.

> *The Spyder v. Kaufman Brothers* does *not* apply to the present case, because the facts of the two cases are substantially different. In *The Spyder v. Kaufman Brothers* the plaintiff voluntarily placed himself in the dangerous situation. But Judy B.'s decision was not made voluntarily. It was the defendant's negligence that put her between a rock and a hard place. She could either keep driving the car and expose the engine to damage, or walk in 117 degrees heat with no water and expose herself and her baby to serious physical harm. Her decision was *not* voluntary, because she was caught in a dilemma not of her own making. The two choices were forced on her by Quickoilz's negligence; they were not initiated by Judy B.

The plaintiff's lawyer then refers the court to another past case, which we will call *Elsa W. v. Ian R.*:

> Elsa W. jumped in front of a swerving car in order to get her child out of harm's way. The parent was injured and sued the driver to recover medical bills. The defendant in the case, Ian R., invoked AR-1 (the assumption of risk rule as described above), claiming that the parent voluntarily chose the action that led to the injury. The court rejected the defendant's argument that the parent had voluntarily assumed the risk, and held instead that the action of the driver forced the parent to save the child, as any parent would naturally do; therefore, the parent's actions were not voluntary.

Judy B.' s lawyer argues that the court's decision in *Elsa W. v. Ian R.* should be used in the present case. Rule AR-1 is not applicable to this case; therefore, the court should decide in favor of the plaintiff.

Both the defendant and the plaintiff use analogical reasoning. Both sides refer to a rule of law, and both sides cite cases that could be used as precedent. Let's diagram the arguments:

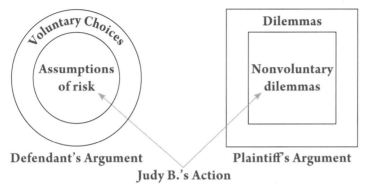

The defendant's argument is illustrated by the large circle representing the class of human actions called "voluntary choices" and the smaller circle representing the class of human actions called "assumptions of risk." We can see that every instance of an assumption of risk falls within the larger class of voluntary choices. This follows because many everyday voluntary choices assume *no* risk—such as which book to read or what to have for dinner. So, although every assumption of risk is also a voluntary choice, not every voluntary choice is an assumption of risk. The defendant concludes that Judy B.' s action should be placed inside the class of "assumptions of risk."

Judy B.' s lawyer has argued that her decision was not voluntary. This is seen in the right side of the diagram, which illustrates the difference between *assumption of risk* (which requires a *voluntary choice*), and a *dilemma* forced upon the plaintiff (which absolves her of voluntary choice).

The plaintiff's argument is illustrated by the large rectangle representing the class of situations called "dilemmas" and the smaller rectangle representing the class of situations called "nonvoluntary dilemmas." We can see that every instance of a nonvoluntary dilemma falls within the larger class of dilemmas. Many dilemmas are self-imposed— for example, asking two people out on a date at the same time. Whoever you choose, someone will be hurt by your action. So, although every nonvoluntary dilemma is a dilemma, not every dilemma is a nonvoluntary dilemma. The plaintiff concludes that Judy B.' s action should be placed inside the class of "nonvoluntary dilemmas."

G. THE ROLE OF PRECEDENT

State and federal appeals courts, state supreme courts, and the Supreme Court of the United States all render decisions and opinions that we can analyze with our logical tools. We look for instances of analogical reasoning, sufficient and necessary conditions, and logical operators such as conjunction, disjunction, negation, and conditional statements.

The use of a prior court decision as a precedent can be understood as a species of analogical reasoning. Arguing that a prior case should be applied to a present case requires pointing out the relevant similarities of the two cases. The legal use of analogical reasoning is subject to all the same constraints as in everyday use. It can be analyzed and evaluated for its strengths and weaknesses using the criteria for judging analogical arguments.

We will look next at an actual U.S. Supreme Court decision. The case involved an Oregon jury that determined that Honda had to pay $5 million to plaintiffs who had suffered injuries while driving an ATV. That sounds like a lot of money, but there were horrible injuries. The case raised important legal questions: Are "punitive damages" in the millions crucial to protecting consumers? Is there such a thing as "excessive damages"? It was up to the Supreme Court to decide. First, we provide a summary of the case. This is not an official part of either the actual court opinion or the dissenting opinion. It is the abstract, or *syllabus*, offered by the court's Reporter of Decisions. It names the justice who wrote the opinion of court, as well as those who joined the opinion. It also mentions who wrote the dissenting opinion and who joined in the dissent.

Second, we give the opening sections of the Opinion of the Court. This introduces the court's reasoning, along with important legal and historical background.

Third, we leave an edited version of the remainder of the Opinion of the Court to the exercises, so that you can practice applying what you know. Each exercise contains only part of a complex court opinion. However, when you are finished, you will have analyzed the entire decision.

Fourth, the dissenting opinion provides the material for another set of exercises. You will see the entire legal procedure as it unfolds. Since the dissenting opinion offers criticism of the opinion, you will see how courts wrestle with difficult decisions.

SUPREME COURT OF THE UNITED STATES

HONDA MOTOR CO., LTD. V. OBERG
Argued April 20, 1994—Decided June 24, 1994

Syllabus

After finding petitioner Honda Motor Co., Ltd., liable for injuries that respondent Oberg received while driving a three-wheeled all-terrain-vehicle manufactured and sold by Honda, an Oregon jury awarded Oberg $5 million in punitive damages, over five times the amount of his compensatory damages award. In affirming, both the Oregon State Court of Appeals and the Oregon State Supreme Court rejected Honda's argument that the punitive damages award violated due process because it was excessive and because Oregon courts have no power to correct excessive verdicts under a 1910 Amendment to the State Constitution, which prohibits judicial review of the amount of punitive damages awarded by a jury "unless the court can affirmatively say there is no evidence to support the verdict."

The decision of Supreme Court of the United States: "The judgment is reversed, and the case is remanded to the Oregon Supreme Court for further proceedings not inconsistent with this opinion. *It is so ordered.*"

Justice *Stevens, J.,* delivered the opinion of the Court, in which *Blackmun, O'Connor, Scalia, Kennedy, Souter,* and *Thomas, J.J.,* joined. *Scalia, J.,* filed a concurring opinion. Justice *Ginsburg, J.,* filed a dissenting opinion, in which *Rehnquist, C. J.,* joined.

OPINION OF THE COURT

An amendment to the Oregon Constitution prohibits judicial review of the amount of punitive damages awarded by a jury, "unless the court can affirmatively say there is no evidence to support the verdict." The question presented is whether that prohibition is consistent with the Due Process Clause of the Fourteenth Amendment. We hold that it is not.

Petitioner Honda Motor Co. manufactured and sold the three-wheeled all-terrain vehicle that overturned while respondent was driving it, causing him severe and permanent injuries. Respondent brought suit alleging that petitioner knew or should have known that the vehicle had an inherently and unreasonably dangerous design. The jury found petitioner liable and awarded respondent $919,390.39 in compensatory damages and punitive damages of $5 million. The compensatory damages, however, were reduced by 20% to $735,512.31, because respondent's own negligence contributed to the accident. On appeal, relying on our then recent decision in *Pacific Mut. Life Ins. Co.* v. *Haslip,* 499 U. S. 1 (1991), petitioner argued that the award of punitive damages violated the Due Process Clause of the Fourteenth Amendment, because the punitive damages were excessive and because Oregon courts lacked the power to correct excessive verdicts.

The Oregon Court of Appeals affirmed, as did the Oregon Supreme Court. The latter court relied heavily on the fact that the Oregon statute governing the award of punitive damages in product liability actions and the jury instructions in this case contain substantive criteria that provide at least as much guidance to the factfinders as the Alabama statute and jury instructions that we upheld in *Haslip.* The Oregon Supreme Court also noted that Oregon law provides an additional protection by requiring the plaintiff to prove entitlement to punitive damages by clear and convincing evidence rather than a mere preponderance. Recognizing that other state courts had interpreted *Haslip* as including a "clear constitutional mandate for meaningful judicial scrutiny of punitive damage awards," the Court nevertheless declined to "interpret *Haslip* to hold that an award of punitive damages, to comport with the requirements of the Due Process Clause, always must be subject to a form of postverdict or appellate review that includes the possibility of remittitur." It also noted that trial and appellate courts were "not entirely powerless" because a judgment may be vacated if "there is no evidence to support the jury's decision," and because "appellate review is available to test the sufficiency of the jury instructions."

We granted *certiorari,* to consider whether Oregon's limited judicial review of the size of punitive damage awards is consistent with our decision in *Haslip.* Our recent cases have recognized that the Constitution imposes a substantive limit on the size of punitive damage awards. *Pacific Mut. Life Ins. Co. v. Haslip; TXO Production Corp. v. Alliance Resources, Corp.* Although they fail to "draw a mathematical bright line between the constitutionally acceptable and the constitutionally unacceptable," a majority of the Justices agreed that the Due Process Clause imposes a limit on punitive damage awards. A plurality assented to the proposition that "grossly excessive" punitive damages would violate due process, while Justice O'Connor, who dissented because she favored more rigorous standards, noted that "it is thus common ground that an award may be so excessive as to violate due process." In the case before us today we are not directly concerned with the character of the standard that will identify unconstitutionally excessive awards; rather we are confronted with the question of what procedures are necessary to ensure that punitive damages are not imposed in an arbitrary manner. More specifically, the question is whether the Due Process Clause requires judicial review of the amount of punitive damage awards.

The opinions in both *Haslip* and *TXO* strongly emphasized the importance of the procedural component of the Due Process Clause. In *Haslip*, the Court held that the common law method of assessing punitive damages did not violate procedural due process. In so holding, the Court stressed the availability of both "meaningful and adequate review by the trial court" and subsequent appellate review. Similarly, in *TXO*, the plurality opinion found that the fact that the "award was reviewed and upheld by the trial judge" and unanimously affirmed on appeal gave rise "to a strong presumption of validity." Concurring in the judgment, Justice Scalia (joined by Justice Thomas) considered it sufficient that traditional common law procedures were followed. In particular, he noted that "'procedural due process' requires judicial review of punitive damages awards for reasonableness. . . ."

All of those opinions suggest that our analysis in this case should focus on Oregon's departure from traditional procedures. We therefore first contrast the relevant common law practice with Oregon's procedure, which that State's Supreme Court once described as "a system of trial by jury in which the judge is reduced to the status of a mere monitor." We then examine the constitutional implications of Oregon's deviation from established common law procedures.

Judicial review of the size of punitive damage awards has been a safeguard against excessive verdicts for as long as punitive damages have been awarded. One of the earliest reported cases involving exemplary damages, *Huckle v. Money*, (1763), arose out of King George III's attempt to punish the publishers of the allegedly seditious *North Briton*, No. 45. The King's agents arrested the plaintiff, a journeyman printer, in his home and detained him for six hours. Although the defendants treated the plaintiff rather well, feeding him "beef steaks and beer, so that he suffered very little or no damages," the jury awarded him £300, an enormous sum almost three hundred times the plaintiff's weekly wage. The defendant's lawyer requested a new trial, arguing that the jury's award was excessive. Plaintiff's counsel, on the other hand, argued that "in cases of tort . . . the Court will never interpose in setting aside verdicts for excessive damages." While the court denied the motion for new trial, the Chief Justice explicitly rejected plaintiff's absolute rule against review of damages amounts. Instead, he noted that when the damages are "outrageous" and "all mankind at first blush must think so," a court may grant a new trial "for excessive damages." In accord with his view that the amount of an award was relevant to the motion for a new trial, the Chief Justice noted that "[u]pon the whole, I am of opinion the damages are not excessive."

Subsequent English cases, while generally deferring to the jury's determination of damages, steadfastly upheld the court's power to order new trials solely on the basis that the damages were too high. *Fabrigas v. Mostyn*, (1773): Damages "may be so monstrous and excessive, as to be in themselves an evidence of passion or partiality in the jury"; *Sharpe v. Brice*, (1774): "It has never been laid down, that the Court will not grant a new trial for excessive damages in any cases of tort"; *Leith v. Pope*, (1779): "[I]n cases of tort the Court will not interpose on account of the largeness of damages, unless they are so flagrantly excessive as to afford an internal evidence of the prejudice and partiality of the jury"; *Hewlett v. Cruchley*, (1813): "[I]t is now well acknowledged in all the Courts of *Westminster-hall,* that whether in actions for criminal conversation, malicious prosecutions, words, or any other matter, if the damages are clearly too large, the Courts will send the inquiry to another jury."

EXERCISES 11G

I. The following passages are from the *Opinion of the Court.* They continue the Court's opinion and lay out the reasons for the majority decision. Some of the passages have been edited to simplify the task at hand. In many instances we have omitted reference to case numbers (e.g., *Hurtado v. California*, 110 U.S. 516, 538 is reduced to *Hurtado v. California*). On the one hand, we have tried to keep as much of the legal arguments and apparatus intact; on the other hand, we tried to emphasize the logic at play.

Your job is to describe the reasoning involved in each passage. You can do this by illustrating the logic involved. You should look for uses of logical operators such as conjunction, disjunction, negation, and conditional statements; sufficient and necessary conditions; and the analogical reasoning involved in the Court's arguments.

Level 1 Multiple-Choice Questions

Level 2 Multiple-Choice Questions

1. Respondent calls to our attention the case of *Beardmore v. Carrington*, in which the court asserted that "there is not one single case, (that is law), in all the books to be found, where the Court has granted a new trial for excessive damages in actions for torts." Respondent would infer from that statement that 18th century common law did not provide for judicial review of damages. Respondent's argument overlooks several crucial facts. First, the *Beardmore* case antedates all but one of the cases cited in the previous paragraph. Even if respondent's interpretation of the case were correct, it would be an interpretation the English courts rejected soon thereafter.

Answer:

Three items can be used to get started: first, the passage uses analogical reasoning (*Beardmore v. Carrington*); second, it uses the logical operators "not" and "if"; third, it contains the word "infer."

The respondent argued that the case of *Beardmore v. Carrington* offers a precedent for the court not to grant a new trial. The court in *Beardmore* asserted that "there is **not** one single case, (that is law), in all the books to be found, where the Court has granted *a new trial* for excessive damages in actions for torts." However, in its opinion the U.S. Supreme Court argued that the respondent's inference "that 18th century common law did **not** provide for *judicial review of damages*" was faulty. The opinion pointed out that the "respondent's *argument overlooks several crucial facts*": First, *Beardmore* came before (antedates) *all but one of the cases* cited. Second, "even **if** respondent's interpretation of the case were correct, [then] it would be an interpretation the English courts rejected soon thereafter." In other words, although the respondent's interpretation of the court's assertion in *Beardmore* might be correct, the assertion was rejected by later courts.

2.   Second, *Beardmore* itself cites at least one case which it concedes granted a new trial for excessive damages, *Chambers v. Robinson*, although it characterizes the case as wrongly decided.

3.   Third, to say that "there is not one single case . . . in all the books" is to say very little, because then, much more so than now, only a small proportion of decided cases was reported. For example, the year *Beardmore* was decided only 16 Common Pleas cases are recorded in the standard reporter.

4.   Finally, the argument respondent would draw, that 18th century English common law did not permit a judge to order new trials for excessive damages, is explicitly rejected by *Beardmore* itself, which cautioned against that very argument: "We desire to be understood that this Court does not say, or lay down any rule that there never can happen a case of such excessive damages in tort where the Court may not grant a new trial."

Video Tutorial

5.   Common law courts in the United States followed their English predecessors in providing judicial review of the size of damage awards. They too emphasized the deference ordinarily afforded jury verdicts, but they recognized that juries sometimes awarded damages so high as to require correction. In 1822, Justice Story ordered a new trial unless the plaintiff agreed to a reduction in his damages. In explaining his ruling, he noted: "As to the question of excessive damages, I agree, that the court may grant a new trial for excessive damages. . . . It is indeed an exercise of discretion full of delicacy and difficulty. But if it should clearly appear that the jury have committed a gross error, or have acted from improper motives, or have given damages excessive in relation to the person or the injury, it is as much the duty of the court to interfere, to prevent the wrong, as in any other case." *Blunt v. Little*.

6.   In the 19th century, both before and after the ratification of the Fourteenth Amendment, many American courts reviewed damages for "partiality" or "passion and prejudice." Nevertheless, because of the difficulty of probing juror reasoning, passion and prejudice review was, in fact, review of the amount of awards. Judges would infer passion, prejudice, or partiality from the size of the award. *Taylor v. Giger*: "In actions of tort . . . a new trial ought not to be granted for excessiveness of damages, unless the damages found are so enormous as to

shew that the jury were under some improper influence, or were led astray by the violence of prejudice or passion."

7. Nineteenth century treatises similarly recognized judges' authority to award new trials on the basis of the size of damage awards. "[E]ven in personal torts, where the jury find *outrageous damages*, clearly evincing partiality, prejudice and passion, the court will interfere for the relief of the defendant, and order a new trial"); "The court again holds itself at liberty to set aside verdicts and grant new trials . . . whenever the damages are so excessive as to create the belief that the jury have been misled either by passion, prejudice, or ignorance"); When punitive damages are submitted to the jury, "the amount which they may think proper to allow will be accepted by the court, unless so exorbitant as to indicate that they have been influenced by passion, prejudice or a perverted judgment."

8. Modern practice is consistent with these earlier authorities. In the federal courts and in every State, except Oregon, judges review the size of damage awards. See *Dagnello v. Long Island R. Co.*, citing cases from all 50 States except Alaska, Maryland, and Oregon.

9. There is a dramatic difference between the judicial review of punitive damages awards under the common law and the scope of review available in Oregon. An Oregon trial judge, or an Oregon Appellate Court, may order a new trial if the jury was not properly instructed, if error occurred during the trial, or if there is no evidence to support any punitive damages at all. But if the defendant's only basis for relief is the *amount* of punitive damages the jury awarded, Oregon provides no procedure for reducing or setting aside that award. This has been the law in Oregon at least since 1949 when the State Supreme Court announced its opinion in *Van Lom v. Schneiderman*, definitively construing the 1910 amendment to the Oregon Constitution. In that case the court held that it had no power to reduce or set aside an award of both compensatory and punitive damages that was admittedly excessive.

10. Respondent argues that Oregon's procedures do not deviate from common law practice, because Oregon judges have the power to examine the size of the award to determine whether the jury was influenced by passion and prejudice. This is simply incorrect. The earliest Oregon cases interpreting the 1910 amendment squarely held that Oregon courts lack precisely that power. No Oregon court for more than half a century has inferred passion and prejudice from the size of a damages award, and no court in more than a decade has even hinted that courts might possess the power to do so.

11. Finally, if Oregon courts could evaluate the excessiveness of punitive damage awards through passion and prejudice review, the Oregon Supreme Court would have mentioned that power in this very case. Petitioner argued that Oregon procedures were unconstitutional precisely because they failed to provide judicial review of the size of punitive damage awards.

12. Respondent also argues that Oregon provides adequate review, because the trial judge can overturn a punitive damage award if there is no substantial evidence to support an award of punitive damages. This argument is unconvincing, because the review provided by Oregon courts ensures only that there is evidence to support *some* punitive damages, not that there is evidence to support the amount actually awarded. While Oregon's judicial review ensures that punitive damages are not awarded against defendants entirely innocent of conduct warranting exemplary damages, Oregon, unlike the common law, provides no assurance that those whose conduct is sanctionable by punitive damages are not subjected to punitive damages of arbitrary amounts. What we are concerned with is the possibility that a guilty defendant may be unjustly punished; evidence of guilt warranting some punishment is not a substitute for evidence providing at least a rational basis for the particular deprivation of property imposed by the State to deter future wrongdoing.

13. Oregon's abrogation of a well-established common law protection against arbitrary deprivations of property raises a presumption that its procedures violate the Due Process Clause. As this Court has stated from its first Due Process cases, traditional practice provides a touchstone for constitutional analysis. Because the basic procedural protections of the common law have been regarded as so fundamental, very few cases have arisen in which a party has complained of their denial. In fact, most of our Due Process decisions involve arguments that traditional procedures provide too little protection and that additional safeguards are necessary to ensure compliance with the Constitution. Nevertheless, there are a handful of cases in which a party has been deprived of liberty or property without the safeguards of common law procedure. When the absent procedures would have provided protection against arbitrary and inaccurate adjudication, this Court has not hesitated to find the proceedings violative of Due Process.

14. Of course, not all deviations from established procedures result in constitutional infirmity. As the Court noted in *Hurtado*, to hold all procedural change unconstitutional "would be to deny every quality of the law but its age, and to render it incapable of progress or improvement." A review of the cases, however, suggests that the case before us is unlike those in which abrogations of common law procedures have been upheld.

    In *Hurtado*, for example, examination by a neutral magistrate provided criminal defendants with nearly the same protection as the abrogated common law grand jury procedure. Oregon, by contrast, has provided no similar substitute for the protection provided by judicial review of the amount awarded by the jury in punitive damages. . . . If anything, the rise of large, interstate and multinational corporations has aggravated the problem of arbitrary awards and potentially biased juries.

15. Punitive damages pose an acute danger of arbitrary deprivation of property. Jury instructions typically leave the jury with wide discretion in choosing amounts, and the presentation of evidence of a defendant's net worth creates the potential that juries will use their verdicts to express biases against big businesses, particularly those without strong local presences. Judicial review of the amount awarded was one of the few procedural safeguards which the common law provided against that danger. Oregon has removed that safeguard without providing any substitute procedure and without any indication that the danger of arbitrary awards has in any way subsided over time. For these reasons, we hold that Oregon's denial of judicial review of the size of punitive damage awards violates the Due Process Clause of the Fourteenth Amendment.

16. Respondent argues that Oregon has provided other safeguards against arbitrary awards and that, in any event, the exercise of this unreviewable power by the jury is consistent with the jury's historic role in our judicial system.

    Respondent points to four safeguards provided in the Oregon courts: the limitation of punitive damages to the amount specified in the complaint, the clear and convincing standard of proof, pre-verdict determination of maximum allowable punitive damages, and detailed jury instructions.

⭐ 17. The first, limitation of punitive damages to the amount specified, is hardly a constraint at all, because there is no limit to the amount the plaintiff can request, and it is unclear whether an award exceeding the amount requested could be set aside. See *Tenold v. Weyerhaeuser Co:* Oregon Constitution bars court from examining jury award to ensure compliance with $500,000 statutory limit on noneconomic damages.

18. The second safeguard, the clear and convincing standard of proof, is an important check against unwarranted imposition of punitive damages, but, like the "no substantial evidence" review discussed above, it provides no assurance that those whose conduct is sanctionable by punitive damages are not subjected to punitive damages of arbitrary amounts.

19. Regarding the third purported constraint, respondent cites no cases to support the idea that Oregon courts do or can set maximum punitive damage awards in advance of the verdict. Nor are we aware of any court which implements that procedure.

20. Respondent's final safeguard, proper jury instruction, is a well-established and, of course, important check against excessive awards. The problem that concerns us, however, is the possibility that a jury will not follow those instructions and may return a lawless, biased, or arbitrary verdict.

    In support of his argument that there is a historic basis for making the jury the final arbiter of the amount of punitive damages, respondent calls our attention to early civil and criminal cases in which the jury was allowed to judge the law as well as the facts. As we have already explained, in civil cases, the jury's discretion to determine the amount of damages was constrained by judicial review. The criminal cases do establish—as does our practice today—that a jury's arbitrary decision to acquit a defendant charged with a crime is completely unreviewable. There is, however, a vast difference between arbitrary grants of freedom and arbitrary deprivations of liberty or property. The Due Process Clause has nothing to say about the former, but its whole purpose is to prevent the latter. A decision to punish a tortfeasor by means of an exaction of exemplary damages is an exercise of state power that must comply with the Due Process Clause of the Fourteenth Amendment. The common law practice, the procedures applied by every other State, the strong presumption favoring judicial review that we have applied in other areas of the law, and elementary considerations of justice, all support the conclusion that such a decision should not be committed to the unreviewable discretion of a jury.

II. **The next set of passages is from the** *footnotes* **to the** *Opinion of the Court.* **They offer additional examples of the majority's decision-making process. Once again, you are to describe the reasoning involved in each passage. Illustrate the logical apparatus involved (the uses of logical operators), and the analogical reasoning that constitutes the Supreme Court's arguments.**

1. The jury instructions in the original Oregon trial, in relevant part, read: "Punitive damages may be awarded to the plaintiff in addition to general damages to punish wrongdoers and to discourage wanton misconduct. In order for plaintiff to recover punitive damages against the defendant[s], the plaintiff must prove by clear and convincing evidence that defendant[s have] shown wanton disregard for the health, safety, and welfare of others. . . . If you decide this issue against the defendant[s], you may award punitive damages, although you are not required to do so, because punitive damages are discretionary. In the exercise of that discretion, you shall consider evidence, if any, of the following: First, the likelihood at the time of the sale [of the three-wheeled vehicle] that serious harm would arise from defendants' misconduct. Second, the degree of the defendants' awareness of that likelihood. Third, the duration of the misconduct. Fourth, the attitude and conduct of the defendant[s] upon notice of the alleged condition of the vehicle. Fifth, the financial condition of the defendant[s]. And the amount of punitive damages may not exceed the sum of $5 million."

Answer:

The passage presents a series of rules that must be followed for two issues: (1) "In order for plaintiff to recover punitive damages against the defendant," and (2) the jury's exercise of discretion if they decide against the defendant.

(A) In order for plaintiff to recover punitive damages against the defendant[s], (B) the plaintiff must prove by clear and convincing evidence that defendant[s have] shown wanton disregard for the health, safety, and welfare of others. . . . If (C) you decide this issue against the defendant[s], [**then**] (D) you may award punitive damages, although you are **not** required to do so, **because** punitive damages are discretionary. In the exercise of that discretion, you shall consider evidence, **if** any, of the following: (E) First, the likelihood at the time of the sale [of the three-wheeled vehicle] that serious harm would arise from defendants' misconduct. (F) Second, the degree of the defendants' awareness of that likelihood. (G) Third, the duration of the misconduct. (H) Fourth, the attitude and conduct of the defendant[s] upon notice of the alleged condition of the vehicle. (I) Fifth, the financial condition of the defendant[s]. **And** (J) the amount of punitive damages may not exceed the sum of $5 million.

> A only if B.
> If C, then (D or not D).
> If C, then [(E or F or G or H or I) and J].

2. As in many early cases, it is unclear whether this case (*Fabrigas v. Mostyn*) specifically concerns punitive damages or merely ordinary compensatory damages. Since there is no suggestion that different standards of judicial review were applied for punitive and compensatory damages before the twentieth century, no effort has been made to separate out the two classes of case.

3. The amended Article VII, §3, of the Oregon Constitution provides: "In actions at law, where the value in controversy shall exceed twenty dollars, the right of trial by jury shall be preserved, and no fact tried by a jury shall be otherwise re-examined in any court of this State, unless the court can affirmatively say there is no evidence to support the verdict."

4. The Oregon Supreme Court in *Van Lom v. Schneiderman* stated the following: "The court is of the opinion that the verdict of $10,000.00 is excessive. Some members of the court think that only the award of punitive damages is excessive; others that both the awards of compensatory and punitive damages are excessive. Since a majority are of the opinion that this court has no power to disturb the verdict, it is not deemed necessary to discuss the grounds for these divergent views."

⭐ 5. The Oregon Supreme Court in *Van Lom v. Schneiderman* stated the following: "The guaranty of the right to jury trial in suits at common law, incorporated in the Bill of Rights as one of the first ten amendments of the Constitution of the United States, was interpreted by the Supreme Court of the United States to refer to jury trial as it had been theretofore known in England; and so it is that the federal judges, like the English judges, have always exercised the prerogative of granting a new trial when the verdict was clearly against the weight of the evidence, whether it be because excessive damages were awarded or for any other reason."

6. Respondent cites as support for its argument *Chicago, R. I. & P. R. Co. v. Cole*. In that case, the Court upheld a provision of the Oklahoma Constitution providing that "the defense of contributory negligence . . . shall . . . be left to the jury." *Chicago, R. I.* provides little support for respondent's case. Justice Holmes'

reasoning relied on the fact that a State could completely abolish the defense of contributory negligence. This case, however, is different, because the *TXO* and *Haslip* opinions establish that States cannot abolish limits on the award of punitive damages.

7. Respondent also argues that empirical evidence supports the effectiveness of these safeguards. It points to the analysis of an *amicus* showing that the average punitive damage award in a products liability case in Oregon is less than the national average. While we welcome respondent's introduction of empirical evidence on the effectiveness of Oregon's legal rules, its statistics are undermined by the fact that the Oregon average is computed from only two punitive damage awards. It is well known that one cannot draw valid statistical arguments from such a small number of observations.

    Empirical evidence, in fact, supports the importance of judicial review of the size of punitive damage awards. The most exhaustive study of punitive damages establishes that over half of punitive damage awards were appealed, and that more than half of those appealed resulted in reductions or reversals of the punitive damages. In over 10 percent of the cases appealed, the judge found the damages to be excessive.

8. Judicial deference to jury verdicts may have been stronger in 18th century America than in England, and judges' power to order new trials for excessive damages more contested. Nevertheless, because this case concerns the Due Process Clause of the Fourteenth Amendment, 19th century American practice is the "crucial time for present purposes." As demonstrated above, by the time the Fourteenth Amendment was ratified in 1868, the power of judges to order new trials for excessive damages was well established in American courts. In addition, the idea that jurors can find law as well as fact is not inconsistent with judicial review for excessive damages.

III. The next set of passages is from the *dissenting opinion* by Justice Ginsberg. They offer examples of the reasons for dissenting from the majority opinion. Once again, some of the passages have been edited to simplify the task at hand. As before, you are to describe the reasoning involved in each passage. Illustrate the logical apparatus involved (the uses of logical operators) and the analogical reasoning that constitutes the dissenting opinion.

1. Where the factfinder is a jury, its decision is subject to judicial review to this extent: The trial court, or an appellate court, may nullify the verdict if reversible error occurred during the trial, if the jury was improperly or inadequately instructed, or if there is no evidence to support the verdict. Absent trial error, and if there is evidence to support the award of punitive damages, however, Oregon's Constitution, Article VII, §3, provides that a properly instructed jury's verdict shall not be reexamined. Oregon's procedures, I conclude, are adequate to pass the Constitution's due process threshold. I therefore dissent from the Court's judgment upsetting Oregon's disposition in this case.

Answer:

(A) Where the factfinder is a jury, its decision is subject to judicial review to this extent: (B) The trial court, **or** an appellate court, may nullify the verdict **if** (C) reversible error occurred during the trial, **if** (D) the jury was improperly **or** inadequately instructed, **or if** (E) there is no evidence to support the verdict. (F) Absent trial error, **and if** (G) there is evidence to support the award of punitive damages, however, [**then**] (H) Oregon's Constitution, Article VII, §3, provides that a properly instructed jury's verdict shall **not** be reexamined. (I) Oregon's procedures, I **conclude**, are adequate to pass the Constitution's due process threshold. (J) I **therefore** dissent from the Court's judgment upsetting Oregon's disposition in this case.

> If A, then [if (C or D or E), then B].
> If (F and G), then H.
> Therefore I.
> Therefore J.

2. To assess the constitutionality of Oregon's scheme, I turn first to this Court's recent opinions in *Haslip*, and *TXO*. The Court upheld punitive damage awards in both cases, but indicated that due process imposes an outer limit on remedies of this type. Significantly, neither decision declared any specific procedures or substantive criteria essential to satisfy due process. In *Haslip*, the Court expressed concerns about "unlimited jury discretion, or unlimited judicial discretion for that matter, in the fixing of punitive damages," but refused to "draw a mathematical bright line between the constitutionally acceptable and the constitutionally unacceptable. . . ." And in *TXO*, a majority agreed that a punitive damage award may be so grossly excessive as to violate the Due Process Clause. In the plurality's view, however, "a judgment that is a product" of "fair procedures . . . is entitled to a strong presumption of validity."

3. The procedures Oregon's courts followed in this case satisfy the due process limits indicated in *Haslip* and *TXO*; the jurors were adequately guided by the trial court's instructions, and Honda has not maintained, in its full presentation to this Court, that the award in question was "so 'grossly excessive' as to violate the Federal Constitution."

4. Several preverdict mechanisms channeled the jury's discretion more tightly in this case than in either *Haslip* or *TXO*. First, providing at least some protection against unguided, utterly arbitrary jury awards, respondent Oberg was permitted to recover no more than the amounts specified in the complaint, $919,390.39 in compensatory damages and $5 million in punitive damages. The trial court properly instructed the jury on this damage cap. No provision of Oregon law appears to preclude the defendant from seeking an instruction setting a lower cap, if the evidence at trial cannot support an award in the amount demanded. Additionally, if the trial judge relates the incorrect maximum amount, a defendant who timely objects may gain modification or nullification of the verdict.

⭐ 5.   Second, Oberg was not allowed to introduce evidence regarding Honda's wealth until he "presented evidence sufficient to justify to the court a prima facie claim of punitive damages. During the course of trial, evidence of the defendant's ability to pay shall not be admitted unless and until the party entitled to recover establishes a prima facie right to recover [punitive damages]." This evidentiary rule is designed to lessen the risk "that juries will use their verdicts to express biases against big businesses," to take into account "[t]he total deterrent effect of other punishment imposed upon the defendant as a result of the misconduct."

6.   Third, and more significant, as the trial court instructed the jury, Honda could not be found liable for punitive damages unless Oberg established by "clear and convincing evidence" that Honda "show[ed] wanton disregard for the health, safety and welfare of others." [Governing product liability actions, see §41.315(1): "Except as otherwise specifically provided by law, a claim for punitive damages shall be established by clear and convincing evidence."] "[T]he clear and convincing evidence requirement," which is considerably more rigorous than the standards applied by Alabama in *Haslip* and West Virginia in *TXO*, "constrain[s] the jury's discretion, limiting punitive damages to the more egregious cases." Nothing in Oregon law appears to preclude a new trial order if the trial judge, informed by the jury's verdict, determines that his charge did not adequately explain what the "clear and convincing" standard means.

7.   Fourth, and perhaps most important, in product liability cases, Oregon requires that punitive damages, if any, be awarded based on seven substantive criteria: "(a) The likelihood at the time that serious harm would arise from the defendant's misconduct; (b) [t]he degree of the defendant's awareness of that likelihood; (c) [t]he profitability of the defendant's misconduct; (d) [t]he duration of the misconduct and any concealment of it; (e) [t]he attitude and conduct of the defendant upon discovery of the misconduct; (f) [t]he financial condition of the defendant; and (g) [t]he total deterrent effect of other punishment imposed upon the defendant as a result of the misconduct, including, but not limited to, punitive damage awards to persons in situations similar to the claimant's and the severity of criminal penalties to which the defendant has been or may be subjected."

8.   These substantive criteria (*a* through *g* in question 7), and the precise instructions detailing them, gave the jurors "adequate guidance" in making their award, far more guidance than their counterparts in *Haslip* and *TXO* received. In *Haslip*, for example, the jury was told only the purpose of punitive damages (punishment and deterrence) and that an award was discretionary, not compulsory. We deemed those instructions, notable for their generality, constitutionally sufficient.

⭐ 9. The Court's opinion in *Haslip* went on to describe the checks Alabama places on the jury's discretion *postverdict*—through excessiveness review by the trial court, and appellate review, which tests the award against specific substantive criteria. While postverdict review of that character is not available in Oregon, the seven factors against which Alabama's Supreme Court tests punitive awards strongly resemble the statutory criteria Oregon's juries are instructed to apply. And this Court has often acknowledged, and generally respected, the presumption that juries follow the instructions they are given. As the Supreme Court of Oregon observed, *Haslip* "determined only that the Alabama procedure, as a whole and in its net effect, did not violate the Due Process Clause."

10. The Oregon court also observed, correctly, that the Due Process Clause does not require States to subject punitive damage awards to a form of postverdict review "that includes the possibility of remittitur." Because Oregon requires the factfinder to apply objective criteria, moreover, its procedures are perhaps more likely to prompt rational and fair punitive damage decisions than are the *post hoc* checks employed in jurisdictions following Alabama's pattern.

11. The Supreme Court of Oregon's conclusions are buttressed by the availability of at least some postverdict judicial review of punitive damage awards. Oregon's courts ensure that there is evidence to support the verdict: "If there is no evidence to support the jury's decision—in this context, no evidence that the statutory prerequisites for the award of punitive damages were met—then the trial court or the appellate courts can intervene to vacate the award."

12. The State's courts have shown no reluctance to strike punitive damage awards in cases where punitive liability is not established, so that defendant qualifies for judgment on that issue as a matter of law. In addition, punitive damage awards may be set aside because of flaws in jury instructions. See *Honeywell v. Sterling Furniture Co*: setting aside punitive damage award because it was prejudicial error to instruct jury that a portion of any award would be used to pay plaintiff's attorney fees and that another portion would go to State's common injury fund. As the Court acknowledges, "proper jury instructio[n] is a well established and, of course, important check against excessive awards."

⭐ 13. In short, Oregon has enacted legal standards confining punitive damage awards in product liability cases. These state standards are judicially enforced by means of comparatively comprehensive preverdict procedures but markedly limited postverdict review, for Oregon has elected to make fact-finding, once supporting evidence is produced, the province of the jury.... The Court today invalidates this choice, largely because it concludes that English and early American courts generally provided judicial review of the size of punitive damage awards. The Court's account of the relevant history is not compelling.

14. I am not as confident as the Court about either the clarity of early American common law, or its import. Tellingly, the Court barely acknowledges the large authority exercised by American juries in the 18th and 19th centuries. In the early years of our Nation, juries "usually possessed the power to determine both law and fact." *Georgia v. Brailsford*: Chief Justice John Jay, trying a case in which State was party, instructed jury it had authority "to determine the law as well as the fact in controversy." And at the time trial by jury was recognized as the constitutional right of parties "[i]n [s]uits at common law," U.S. Constitution, Amendment 7, the assessment of "uncertain damages" was regarded, generally, as exclusively a jury function.

15. More revealing, the Court notably contracts the scope of its inquiry. It asks: Did common law judges claim the power to overturn jury verdicts they viewed as excessive? But full and fair historical inquiry ought to be wider. The Court should inspect, comprehensively and comparatively, the procedures employed—at trial *and* on appeal—to fix the amount of punitive damages. Evaluated in this manner, Oregon's scheme affords defendants like Honda *more* procedural safeguards than 19th century law provided.

16. Oregon instructs juries to decide punitive damage issues based on seven substantive factors and a clear and convincing evidence standard. When the Fourteenth Amendment was adopted in 1868, in contrast (see *Haslip*), "no particular procedures were deemed necessary to circumscribe a jury's discretion regarding the award of [punitive] damages, or their amount." The responsibility entrusted to the jury surely was not guided by instructions of the kind Oregon has enacted.

17. Furthermore, common law courts reviewed punitive damage verdicts extremely deferentially, if at all. See *Day v. Woodworth*: assessment of "exemplary, punitive, or vindictive damages . . . has been always left to the discretion of the jury, as the degree of punishment to be thus inflicted must depend on the peculiar circumstances of each case"; *Missouri Pacific R. Co. v. Humes*: "[t]he discretion of the jury in such cases is not controlled by any very definite rules"; *Barry v. Edmunds*: in "actions for torts where no precise rule of law fixes the recoverable damages, it is the peculiar function of the jury to determine the amount by their verdict." True, 19th century judges occasionally asserted that they had authority to overturn damage awards upon concluding, from the size of an award, that the jury's decision must have been based on "partiality" or "passion and prejudice." But courts rarely *exercised* this authority.

18. Because Oregon's procedures assure "adequate guidance from the court when the case is tried to a jury," (*Haslip*), this Court has no cause to disturb the judgment in this instance, for Honda presses here only a *procedural* due process claim. True, in a footnote to its petition for *certiorari*, not repeated in its briefs,

Honda attributed to this Court an "assumption that procedural due process requires [judicial] review of *both* federal substantive due process and state law excessiveness challenges to the size of an award." But the assertion regarding "state law excessiveness challenges" is extraordinary, for this Court has never held that the Due Process Clause requires a State's courts to police jury fact-findings to ensure their conformity with state law. And, as earlier observed, the plurality opinion in *TXO* disavowed the suggestion that a defendant has a federal due process right to a correct determination under state law of the "reasonableness" of a punitive damages award.

19. Honda further asserted in its *certiorari* petition footnote: "Surely . . . due process (not to mention Supremacy Clause principles) requires, at a minimum, that state courts entertain and pass on the federal law contention that a particular punitive verdict is so grossly excessive as to violate substantive due process. Oregon's refusal to provide even that limited form of review is particularly indefensible." But Honda points to no definitive Oregon pronouncement post-dating this Court's precedent setting decisions in *Haslip* and *TXO* demonstrating the hypothesized refusal to pass on a federal law contention.

20. It may be that Oregon's procedures guide juries so well that the "grossly excessive" verdict Honda projects in its *certiorari* petition footnote never materializes. [Between 1965 and the present, awards of punitive damages in Oregon have been reported in only two products liability cases, including this one.] If, however, in some future case, a plea is plausibly made that a particular punitive damage award is not merely excessive, but "so 'grossly excessive' as to violate the Federal Constitution," *TXO*, and Oregon's judiciary nevertheless insists that it is powerless to consider the plea, this Court might have cause to grant review. No such case is before us today, nor does Honda, in this Court, maintain otherwise (size of award against Honda does not appear to be out of line with awards upheld in *Haslip* and *TXO*).

⭐ 21. To summarize: Oregon's procedures adequately guide the jury charged with the responsibility to determine a plaintiff's qualification for, and the amount of, punitive damages, and on that account do not deny defendants procedural due process; Oregon's Supreme Court correctly refused to rule that "an award of punitive damages, to comport with the requirements of the Due Process Clause, *always* must be subject to a form of postverdict or appellate review" for excessiveness; the verdict in this particular case, considered in light of this Court's decisions in *Haslip* and *TXO*, hardly appears "so 'grossly excessive' as to violate the substantive component of the Due Process Clause," *TXO*. Accordingly, the Court's procedural directive to the state court is neither necessary nor proper. The Supreme Court of Oregon has not refused to enforce federal law, and I would affirm its judgment.

IV. The next set of passages is from the *footnotes* to the *dissenting opinion*. They offer additional examples of the dissenting opinion's decision-making process. Once again, you are to describe the reasoning involved in each passage. Illustrate the logical apparatus involved (the uses of logical operators) and the analogical reasoning that constitutes the Supreme Court's arguments.

1. The *Haslip* jury was told that it could award punitive damages if "reasonably satisfied from the evidence" that the defendant committed fraud.

Answer:

(A) The *Haslip* jury was told that it could award punitive damages **if** (B) "reasonably satisfied from the evidence" that the defendant committed fraud.

If B, then A.

No argument is put forward in this passage. The statement is meant to help clarify the facts of the case.

2. The trial court in the Oregon case instructed the jury as follows: "Punitive damages: If you have found that plaintiff is entitled to general damages, you must then consider whether to award punitive damages. Punitive damages may be awarded to the plaintiff in addition to general damages to punish wrong-doers and to discourage wanton misconduct."

3. The trial judge did not instruct the jury on the following factors: (1) The "profit-ability of [Honda's] misconduct," or (2) the "total deterrent effect of other punishment" to which Honda was subject. Honda objected to an instruction on factor (1), which it argued was phrased "to assume the existence of misconduct," and expressly waived an instruction on factor (2), on the ground that it had not previously been subject to punitive damages. In its argument before the Supreme Court of Oregon, Honda did not contend that the trial court failed to instruct the jury concerning the criteria, or "that the jury did not properly apply those criteria."

4. The trial judge in *Haslip* instructed the jury as follows:

"Now, if you find that fraud was perpetrated then in addition to compensatory damages you may in your discretion, when I use the word discretion, I say you don't have to even find fraud, you wouldn't have to, but you may, the law says you may award an amount of money known as punitive damages.

"This amount of money is awarded to the plaintiff but it is not to compensate the plaintiff for any injury. It is to punish the defendant. Punitive means to punish or it is also called exemplary damages, which means to make an example. So, if you feel or not feel, but if you are reasonably satisfied from the evidence that the plaintiff[s] . . . ha[ve] had a fraud perpetrated upon them and as a direct result they were injured [then] in addition to compensatory damages you may in your discretion award punitive damages. . . .

"Should you award punitive damages, in fixing the amount, you must take into consideration the character and the degree of the wrong as shown by the evidence and necessity of preventing similar wrong."

Study Materials

Summary

- Legal arguments can be appreciated and understood when you are able to grasp the underlying logic. Legal discourse has evolved patterns and conventions that we can recognize and apply to specific legal cases.
- Appellate courts: Courts of appeal that review the decisions of lower courts.
- A rule that specifies a test with mandatory elements lists all the necessary conditions that must be met in order for the rule to be applicable.
- In law, the term "deductive reasoning" generally means as going from the *general* to the *specific*—that is, from the statement of a *rule* to its application to a particular legal case.
- Many law textbooks define "inductive reasoning" as the process of going from the *specific* to the *general*. It comes into play whenever we move from a specific case or legal opinion to a general rule.
- Legal reasoning is also called "rule-based reasoning."
- Sufficient condition: Whenever one event ensures that another event is realized.
- Necessary condition: Whenever one thing is *essential, mandatory,* or *required* in order for another thing to be realized.
- Probative value: Evidence that can be used during a trial to advance the facts of the case.
- Prejudicial effect: Evidence that might cause some jurors to be negatively biased toward a defendant.
- Indictment: A formal accusation presented by a grand jury.
- Affidavit: A written statement signed before an authorized official.
- Legal reasoning, relying as it does on precedent (a judicial decision that can be applied to later cases) and similar cases, often relies on analogies.
- Rules of law: The legal principles that have been applied to historical cases.
- Plaintiff: The person who initiates a lawsuit.

KEY TERMS

affidavit   563
appellate courts   556
indictment   563
necessary condition   559

plaintiff   567
precedent   566
prejudicial effect   560
probative value   560

rule-based reasoning   556
rules of law   566
sufficient condition   557

LOGIC CHALLENGE: A GUILTY PROBLEM

Imagine that you are a private investigator specializing in determining the truth value of suspects' statements to the police. You are shown a videotape of four suspects accused of robbing a quick-loan store. The four suspects happen to know each other. When you view the videotape, you are allowed to hear each suspect make only one statement.

Alice: Benny did it.
Benny: David did it.
Connie: I did not do it.
David: What Benny said about me is false.

Assume that only one person did it and only one of the four statements is true. If so, determine the following two things:

1.   Who committed the crime?
2.   Which one of the statements is true?

Chapter 12

Moral Arguments

Study Materials

On a gut level, moral arguments are about right and wrong, and they can quickly become demanding, commanding, and heated. "Thou shalt not kill." "Abortion is wrong." "Leave your sister alone." However, value judgments enter a lot of what we do and say—and so does the word "should." "You should remember to wash your hands before eating." "I should really be studying for that test tomorrow." "I should never have bought that stupid car."

To make things more complicated, some arguments rely solely on *factual claims* for support, some arguments rely solely on *value judgments* for support, and some arguments rely on a mixture of the two. "You take one more step, and you're in deep trouble." "You should stop lying, because you will quickly lose your credibility." "Without affordable health care, thousands of Americans will die." Where exactly do the factual claims end and the value judgments begin?

Since logic is the systematic use of methods and principles to analyze, evaluate, and construct arguments, logic provides many skills that you can apply to moral reasoning. For example, you can reconstruct someone's moral argument, adding missing premises if needed. You can also use analogical reasoning or evaluate a moral argument for inconsistencies.

As usual, the first step in analyzing an argument is clarifying the premises and conclusion. Imagine that you want to take a vacation to Los Angeles from your home in New York. You discuss it with two friends, who offer their advice. One friend mentions the fact that you can fly from the East Coast of the United States to the West Coast nonstop in about 6 hours. He then adds another piece of information by citing the fact that it would take about 4 days to drive the same distance across the United States (factoring in time needed to eat and sleep). From this, he concludes that you *should* fly rather than drive to Los Angeles. Here is the argument:

> You can fly from New York to Los Angeles in about 6 hours. It takes about 4 days to drive the same distance. You *should* fly rather than drive.

However, the second friend might agree with the two premises just described, but she comes to the opposite conclusion—that you *should* drive instead of fly.

> You can fly from New York to Los Angeles in about 6 hours. It takes about 4 days to drive the same distance. You *should* drive rather than fly.

Can these differences be explained by just the facts involved? Obviously, both arguments use the same factual claims in the premises. However, the word "should" appears in both conclusions, but it is found nowhere in the premises. What is the justification for its introduction? The exploration of the difference between facts and values, as well as words such as "should" and "ought," starts our discussion of moral arguments. Let's begin.

A. VALUE JUDGMENTS

Value judgment A claim that a particular human action or object has some degree of importance, worth, or desirability.

A **value judgment** is a claim that a particular human action or object has some degree of importance, worth, or desirability. Let's see how value judgments enter into our discussion of your travel plans.

Justifying "Should"

Justifying the use of the word "should" in the conclusion of both arguments requires an introduction of new information in the premises. Since both arguments are missing this important ingredient, we can treat them as enthymemes (Chapter 1 introduced enthymemes and missing information). For the first argument, a possible implied premise is that *you probably want to make the trip as quickly as possible*. Adding this as a new premise would make the first argument strong. On the other hand, for the second argument, a possible implied premise is that *you probably want to see as much of the country as possible*. Adding this new information would make the second argument strong.

Both argument reconstructions deliberately supplied a premise designed to make each argument strong. When you have the time to reflect more thoroughly about the available options, then you might decide that you do want to see as much of the country as possible. In that case, the added premise in the first argument would be false, so the argument would not be cogent. However, the added premise in the second argument would be true, so that would yield a cogent argument.

In these two examples, the word "should" in the conclusion was justified as following from a *desired goal*. The intent of each argument was to offer good reasons why you should choose one method of transportation over another. The evaluation of the arguments hinged on how well the arguments match the intended goal. Notice that *if* you had decided that you wanted to make the trip as quickly as possible, then the added premise in the first argument would be true and the argument would be cogent. It would also follow that the added premise in the second argument would be false and the argument would not be cogent.

But what happens if we eliminate the intended goal of the trip? What if, instead, you and your friends were just talking about travel in general? Now suppose that one of your friends remarked that he hated driving long distances, while another friend remarked that she loved taking long road trips. These would be instances of value judgments.

Types of Value Judgments

There are many types of value judgments. For example, moral value judgments place emphasis on human actions or behaviors by asserting that they are *good, bad, right,* or *wrong.* Here are some examples of moral claims:

1. Murder is wrong.
2. You should always tell the truth.
3. Torturing prisoners is an immoral act.
4. Extracting information by torture in order to save lives is the morally right thing to do.

A second type of value judgment concerns matters of personal taste or value. For example, one person might say "Anchovies taste great" while another might say "Anchovies taste terrible." *Neither of these two statements asserts any facts about anchovies.* At best, they are an assertion of a person's feelings about the taste of anchovies. Examine the following three sentences:

5. Anchovies taste great.
6. Anchovies taste terrible.
7. Anchovies are small fish belonging to the herring family.

Sentence 7 is the only one of the three that *asserts something factual* about anchovies. If they are members of the herring family, then the statement is true; otherwise the statement is false. The first two sentences may appear to assert something about anchovies, but they do not. If you hate the taste of anchovies you might imagine that everyone else does too, and are amazed that anyone would find the taste desirable. On the other hand, if you love the taste of a certain kind of ice cream you might be surprised that other people do not share your personal value judgment. We would like our personal value judgments to be *universally shared* and are often surprised when they are not. So, for example, when you introduce your favorite ice cream to a friend and she says that "it is just OK," you might ask her to take another bite, hoping that she will change her mind and agree with your value judgment.

Another way of describing the set of three sentences regarding anchovies is to label the first two *subjective* and the third *objective.* In other words, the first two sentences *refer to the person* making the claim about anchovies and are, therefore, *subjective* claims. As such, these claims can be rewritten to bring out this point:

8. Anchovies taste great *to me.*
9. Anchovies taste terrible *to me.*

Now, these two statements can be considered either true or false, but their truth value cannot be determined by an examination of the facts concerning anchovies. These *subjective* statements are true if the persons uttering the statements are accurately describing how anchovies taste *to them*, otherwise they are false. Contrast those two statements with the third statement whose *objective* truth value can be determined by the facts concerning anchovies.

Now look closely at the next statement:

> Killing another human being is always wrong.

It is fair to say that when most people make this claim they intend it to be an objective assertion. It is not likely that they would think that it was comparable to the assertions regarding the taste of anchovies. Nevertheless, it is a value judgment; more specifically, a *moral value judgment*. It is typically used in the following way:

> You *should not* kill a human being.

Here we have another instance of the word "should." It is being used as a directive for how you *ought to* act toward other humans. When the words *should* and *ought* are used in a moral setting, the resulting statements are also referred to as *prescriptive* or *normative*. **Prescriptive statements** offer advice. In a medical setting, a physician may prescribe medicine or a course of treatment. In a moral setting, advice may be offered either by specifying a particular action that ought to be performed or by providing general moral rules, principles, or guidelines that should be followed.

Normative statements establish standards for correct moral behavior, determining norms or rules of conduct. Given this, we can see that the statement "You *should not* kill a human being" has a different function from the earlier example "You *should* drive across the United States." There, the emphasis was not in any way connected to a moral decision. Therefore, different types of value judgments play decidedly different roles in the construction and analysis of arguments. Since we are interested in moral reasoning we need to explore how moral value judgments function in the construction, analysis, and evaluation of moral arguments.

Prescriptive statement
A statement that offers advice either by specifying a particular action that ought to be performed or by providing general moral rules, principles, or guidelines that should be followed.

Normative statement
A statement that establishes standards for correct moral behavior, determining norms or rules of conduct.

Taste and Value

Let's imagine that someone is trying to persuade you that incest is morally wrong. She might resort to empirical research that indicates nearly all cultures view incest as morally wrong. This evidence is then used to conclude that "You should not commit incest." Now compare this result with the following scenario. Imagine that someone is trying to persuade you that anchovies taste terrible. She might resort to surveys that show that most people do not like the taste of anchovies. This evidence is then used to conclude that "You should not like anchovies."

Most people agree that there is a substantial difference between the incest and anchovies examples, because they believe there is a fundamental difference between a moral value judgment and one involving personal taste. Of course, both arguments are classified as value judgments, and both arguments have the word "should" in the conclusion. But suppose a close friend claims that the two cases are *not* fundamentally different; in other words, he thinks that *all value judgments are the same*. In fact, he believes that since empirical evidence is irrelevant in the anchovy argument, then it is also irrelevant in the incest argument. Therefore, we need to think seriously about two questions:

A. Are the two uses of "should" really that different?

B. If so, in what fundamental ways are they different?

We can start out by assessing the use of the empirical data. In the anchovy example, no matter if you were the only person on earth who liked the taste of anchovies, we would think it foolish for anyone to claim that *you should not like them*. Since personal taste concerning foods is subjective, any supposed "objective" evidence regarding other humans is actually just a tally of their personal tastes.

On the other hand, the use of empirical data regarding cultural attitudes toward incest seems to appeal to an *objective fact* and not just a tally of personal feelings. Those holding this position argue that there are "moral facts" that support moral beliefs. The challenge is then to determine the "objective" nature of certain moral judgments. In other words, if they are objective, then how do we come to that determination? To help us gain insight into the nature and complexity of moral claims, we need to look at some moral theories, the subject of the next section.

EXERCISES 12A

Determine whether the following statements are factual claims or value claims. If a statement makes a value claim, then determine if it is a moral value claim or a personal value claim.

Level 1 Multiple-Choice Questions

1. Capital punishment is wrong.

Answer: Moral value claim

2. Your answer to the homework problem is wrong.

Level 2 Multiple-Choice Questions

3. Pizza is the most delicious kind of food on the planet.

4. Euthanasia is an acceptable act.

⭐ 5. The movie *Inception* won four Academy Awards.

6. The movie *Inception* was confusing and difficult to follow.

7. Venison is deer meat.

8. Eating meat is wrong.

⭐ 9. Air travel is boring.

10. Air travel is the safest way to travel.

11. Anyone afraid of flying is irrational.

Video Tutorial

12.   Tax evasion is a criminal offense.

🖋 13.   Not paying taxes is a justified form of protest.

14.   Giving big corporations tax breaks is welfare for millionaires.

15.   Microsoft employs the most workers of any software company in the United States.

B. MORAL THEORIES

There are many different kinds of moral theories. We can distinguish *normative ethical theories* from *meta-ethical theories*. Normative ethical theories focus on what is right and wrong. They concentrate directly on clarifying criteria for judging how we ought to act or the kind of person we should be. In contrast, meta-ethical theories focus on the nature of moral judgments through an analysis of moral language. In other words, a meta-ethical theory is not directly concerned with articulating which actions are right or wrong; instead, the focus is on what it means to say that an action is right or wrong. The focus is thus on the logical analysis of moral concepts and how they are used.

Some ethical theories offer ways of determining whether a human action is morally right or wrong by placing emphasis on the outcome of the action. These theories look to the ultimate consequences of our actions as the focal point for moral deliberations. On the other hand, some theories reject any consideration of the outcome of an action and instead hold that moral acts are right or wrong in themselves. In addition, some moral theories try to combine these two types of approaches. There are even theories that hold that *all* moral judgments are relative to individuals, cultures, and societies. Although there are numerous normative and meta-ethical theories, we will examine only a few in this section.

Emotivism

Consider the following claims:

- Murder is morally wrong.
- You ought always to tell the truth.
- You ought not to steal.

To most people, these seem like perfectly understandable and meaningful *moral statements*. It would be easy to take a survey and get people's responses to each statement. But it is unlikely that you will find many people who say that they do not understand the statements at all. Now compare the three foregoing claims with three different statements:

- Harrisburg is the capital of Pennsylvania.
- The Eiffel Tower is in Paris, France.
- Mount Everest is the fourth tallest mountain in the world.

Once again, most people would think these to be perfectly understandable and meaningful *factual statements*. Also, it would be easy to take a survey and get people's responses to each of these statements. And again, it is unlikely that you will find many people who say that they do not understand the statements at all. Now suppose we ask people how they would *verify* the truth or falsity of the *factual* statements. It should be an easy task, because each of the statements refers to objective facts about the world. Therefore, appropriate and uncontroversial empirical support would be readily available.

But suppose we ask people how they would *verify* the truth or falsity of the *moral statements*. This would not be as easy, because it is not obvious that each of the moral statements refers to any kind of objective facts about the world. Therefore, appropriate and uncontroversial empirical support would not be readily available.

Difficulties such as these are addressed by **emotivism**, a theory that asserts that moral value judgments are merely expressions of our attitudes or emotions. Emotivism thus bypasses the problem of objectively verifying the truth or falsity of moral value judgments. If a moral judgment is an expression of one's personal emotions, then it is not an assertion of fact in the objective sense. Supporters of emotivism often point out that we currently have no reliable means of verifying the accuracy of anyone's subjective statements. The important thing to remember is that emotivism rejects any notion that moral value judgments are in any way descriptions of objective moral facts. Therefore, moral value judgments are no different from other personal value judgments, for example, expressions of taste, such as the utterance "Apples taste delicious (*to me*)."

Thus, for emotivism, moral statements are nothing but expressions of what we personally like and dislike, or of what we approve and disapprove of. As such, they can be used to persuade others to have the same moral feelings that we have. So, according to emotivism, when you say "Murder is wrong," you are not referring to anything objective; this and all other moral value judgments assert nothing factual about the world.

However, emotivism raises some important practical considerations. How do we talk about related moral and legal issues, such as blame, responsibility, and praise? How do we decide when there is a legitimate moral dispute? Since emotivism holds that moral judgments are merely pronouncements of personal taste, then a dispute about a case of child negligence, for example, would be reduced to assertions about each individual's personal feelings. If emotivism is correct, there would be no objective moral aspect to consider in the case.

Consequentialism

Consequentialism refers to a *class* of moral theories in which the moral value of any human action or behavior is determined exclusively by its outcomes. In other words, consequentialist theories hold that a human action is judged morally right or wrong, good or bad, solely on the end result of the action. Similarly, people are judged to be morally good or bad strictly by the consequences of their actions.

Emotivism A theory that asserts that moral value judgments are merely expressions of our attitudes or emotions.

Consequentialism A class of moral theories in which the moral value of any human action or behavior is determined exclusively by its outcomes.

Teleology The philosophical belief that the value of an action or object can be determined by looking at the purpose or the end of the action or object.

Consequentialist theories are based on **teleology**, the philosophical belief that the value of an action or object can be determined by looking at the purpose or the end of the action or object. (The term "teleology" comes from "*telos*," meaning *end*, so it is the study of the end, purpose, or design of an object or human action.) We will look at two consequentialist theories: *egoism* and *utilitarianism*.

Egoism

Egoism The basic principle that everyone should act in order to maximize his or her own individual pleasure or happiness.

As the name indicates, **egoism** is the basic principle that everyone should act in order to maximize his or her own individual pleasure or happiness. Egoism reduces the moral value of an act to the outcome of its consequences to one person, the acting agent. (Since "ego" means *the self*, the moral theory is really just *self-ism*.) Egoism's moral directive is quite simple: *All humans ought to pursue their own personal pleasure.*

It is interesting to consider whether an unintended, but potentially positive consequence of egoism is possible. If everyone consistently followed the directive of egoism, could this increase the overall happiness of society as a whole? Some argue that since we cannot know with certainty how our actions will affect other people, we should not even attempt to consider them. By consistently pursuing our own pleasure or happiness, we are doing our best to maximize the overall happiness of society. As evidence for this position, quite often the best intentions go in vain. As a consequence, if we give up the chance to pursue our own pleasure, then we risk the possibility that no happiness will be achieved. How often has it happened that a seemingly good deed has failed to achieve its goal? (There is a popular paraphrase of a line in Robert Burns's poem "To a Mouse": "The best laid plans of mice and men often go astray.") Therefore, we *ought* always to pursue our own happiness.

Of course, since we cannot know precisely all the future consequences of our actions, we cannot be certain that our own pursuit of pleasure or happiness will end in a good result. An action may result in a short-term pleasure, but if repeated often enough, it might lead to long-term unhappiness and pain. Think of alcohol and drug addiction.

These considerations point to two challenges to most ethical theories. First, how do we *define* what would be *happiness* or *pleasure* for everyone (or for egoism, my own happiness or pleasure)? And second, how do we *measure* or quantify amounts or degrees of *happiness* or *pleasure*? For example, is the happiness or the pleasure of a child comparable to that of an adult? In other words, the challenge is to develop measuring devices, scales, or charts that we can consult to determine the level, degree, or extent of happiness or pleasure in an individual (for egoism), or for society as a whole, or even between cultures.

Utilitarianism

Another specific and important example of a consequentialist moral theory (and therefore, teleological) is *utilitarianism*. Although there are many varieties of utilitarianism, they all agree on a few fundamental principles. The most important principle for **utilitarianism** can be summed up in the famous dictum "the greatest good for the greatest number." Any action or human behavior is to be judged by its outcomes—specifically, whether it brought about the greatest good to the greatest number of people. (The name *utilitarianism* is derived from the term "utility," which means *usefulness*.) Since utilitarianism is a moral theory, it concentrates on the usefulness of human actions and behaviors and asks how they affect the overall good or happiness of a society. (Compare this with the term "public utilities," which typically refers to organizations that supply water or electricity, which are useful and beneficial to society.)

Utilitarianism (like egoism, for that matter) is grounded on the psychological assumption that the great driving force of human behavior is the *avoidance of pain* and the *seeking of pleasure*. So, from the psychological evidence supporting this view of human nature, utilitarianism derives its moral directive: *All humans ought to act in order to maximize the greatest pleasure or happiness for the greatest number of people.*

According to utilitarianism, every human action demonstrates **universalizability**, meaning that the same principles hold for all people at all times. More simply, "What if everyone did that?" The underlying sentiment is utilitarian because it appeals to the outcome of our actions. Generally speaking, the question is mostly used in a rhetorical way, in that it appeals to the possible *negative* effects of certain actions. For example, you throw a piece of litter on the ground and are asked, "What would happen if everyone littered?" Since the end result of everyone performing that action would be an unwanted situation, we are then instructed not to litter.

Jeremy Bentham, one of the foremost defenders of utilitarianism, thought that we could measure or quantify the results of our actions. Bentham counseled us to do the following:

1. Determine the possible actions available to you in any given situation.
2. List all the people your action will affect. (Be sure to include yourself in the list.)
3. Calculate the total amount of pleasure derived as the outcome of each possible action.
4. Calculate the total amount of pain derived as the outcome of each possible action.
5. Subtract the amount of pain from the amount of pleasure derived as the outcome of each possible action.
6. You ought to choose the action whose outcome results in the greatest amount of pleasure.

However, the same challenges associated with consequentialist theories are relevant to Bentham's six-step procedure. First, we need clear definitions of "happiness" and "pleasure," definitions that cut across individuals, cultures, and societies. Second, we need to develop ways to *measure* or *quantify* the amount of pleasure and pain as a result of our possible actions.

Nevertheless, many people do try to apply Bentham's ideas, even if they are not familiar with the specifics of his theory. People often attempt to weigh the pros and

Utilitarianism It can be summed up in the famous dictum "the greatest good for the greatest number."

Universalizability The notion that the same principles hold for all people at all times.

cons of their actions. We sometimes try to gauge the extent of the pain and pleasure that will result, even though we do not have a clear-cut system of quantifying them. We often use our decidedly nonquantitative "calculations" to justify our actions, and we do often try to maximize the greatest happiness for the greatest number.

Deontology

A deontological moral theory is radically different from a consequentialist theory. We know that consequentialist theories emphasize the results of our actions. A deontological theory rejects any emphasis on the results or outcomes of an action, and instead recognizes the *role of duty*. **Deontology** holds that duty to others is the first and foremost moral consideration, and it lays the groundwork for discovering those duties. (The root word "deon" means *duty* or *obligation*, so *deontology* is the study of duties.)

An important distinction for deontology is that performing a particular duty does not have to have any immediate positive consequence. In this sense, a recognized duty (for example, telling the truth) is an instance of what Immanuel Kant called a **categorical imperative**. The basic idea is that your actions or behavior toward others should always be such that *you would want everyone to act in the same manner*. In this context, "categorical" means *absolute* and *unconditional*, and "imperative" means

Deontology The theory that duty to others is the first and foremost moral consideration.

Categorical imperative The basic idea is that your actions or behavior toward others should always be such that you would want everyone to act in the same manner.

PROFILES IN LOGIC
Jeremy Bentham

Happiness, for Jeremy Bentham (1748–1832), is achieved by maximizing pleasure and minimizing pain. Bentham was influenced by the social upheavals of the Industrial Revolution. Although qualified to practice law, he chose not to; instead, he tried to influence society by his writings. His *Introduction to the Principles of Morals and Legislation* contains the details of "the greatest happiness principle."

Bentham's thinking combined the clarification of concepts with rigorous deductive argument. He chose reason over tradition, and rationality over authority. He also championed a scientific description of human nature. His emphasis on "pleasure and pain" as the prime motivations for human behavior anticipated

the modern approach to modifying that behavior, through *positive* and *negative feedback*—in other words, rewards and punishment. "Nature has placed mankind under the governance of two sovereign masters, *pain* and *pleasure*. It is for them alone to point out what we ought to do, as well as to determine what we shall do."

Upon his death, Bentham had tens of thousands of unpublished pages of material that he hoped would eventually be published. He left the bulk of his considerable fortune to help support University College, London. According to his instructions, his body was to be preserved and displayed sitting in a chair. In fact, you can visit Bentham at the university today.

command or *obligation*. In other words, a categorical imperative is an absolute and universal moral law. For example, telling the truth would be a categorical imperative, because it is something that each individual would want everyone to do. However, even if it is a universal moral law to always tell the truth, we cannot expect that good consequences will result every time we apply the moral law. This is illustrated by the saying "the truth often hurts." Therefore, a deontological theory is quite different from a consequentialist moral theory that is based on the outcomes of our actions.

Deontology and consequentialism can also be distinguished by exploring two moral uses of the word "ought." Consequentialist theories rely on a *conditional ought*. For example, the statement "You ought to tell the truth" would be correct only if this would result in the best possible outcome in a given situation. Therefore, consequentialist theories place *conditions* on the use of *ought*. On the other hand, deontological theories rely on an *unconditional ought*. For example, the statement "You ought to tell the truth" would *always* be applicable, *with no exceptions no matter what the outcome*. For deontology, all moral rules are universal, they have no exceptions, and they are absolutely binding to all people. In other words, it is your unconditional duty to always tell the truth.

Relativism

Relativism makes two claims:

1. All moral value judgments are determined by a society's beliefs toward actions or behavior.
2. There are no objective or universal moral value judgments.

This means that all moral judgments are *intersubjective*. For example, the statement "Stealing is wrong" means that the community in general disapproves of stealing. Moral judgments are therefore reduced to a society's attitudes toward a particular behavior.

Adherents of relativism point to profound cultural and ethical differences among societies. For example, some cultures developed in the difficult terrain of the arctic. Those people survived the yearlong harsh conditions and became meat eaters, simply because there was no vegetation. By the relativist light, it would be absurd to expect them to be vegetarians and to hold that they are somehow morally deficient. Similarly, some nomadic cultures found it impossible to raise too many children at the same time, or to raise children who would not be able to quickly survive on their own. Consequently, infanticide was a regularly practiced way of life. Again, the relativist concludes that we cannot judge their actions and behaviors by our ethical standards that were developed over centuries in far different environments and under completely different circumstances.

Relativists also point out that most people's moral beliefs were conditioned by some combination of their immediate family and the society in which they were raised. Therefore, your individual moral beliefs are determined for the most part by where and when you were raised, just like the language you learned. In addition, relativists

Relativism First, all moral value judgments are determined by a society's beliefs toward actions or behavior. Second, there are no objective or universal moral value judgments.

emphasize the difficult (and they think impossible) problem of judging between two competing moral systems. Relativists point out that every set of moral beliefs is judged by its adherents to be superior to all other sets of moral beliefs. Thus, relativists stress the point that there are no objective criteria that we could apply to decide which moral system is "correct."

Situation ethics The idea that we should not rigidly apply moral rules to every possible situation.

A special version of relativism, called **situation ethics**, holds that we should not rigidly apply moral rules to every possible situation. This is similar to the legal principle that reminds us to distinguish the letter of the law from the spirit of the law. Although laws are designed to help prevent unwanted behavior, it is also true that most laws have exceptions. For example, suppose someone is rushing to the hospital with an injured relative. The driver might slow down at a red light (just enough to make sure there is no oncoming traffic) and then proceed through the intersection without having come to a full stop. The letter of the law has been broken, but the spirit of the law has not. The law is meant to deter flagrant violations of running through red lights, and as such is meant to make driving safe for all concerned. But the violation in question was clearly not flagrant; in fact, the driver made sure no one was coming before continuing on.

Situation ethics asks us to acknowledge that each situation has some unique characteristics. Because of this obvious fact, we must learn to balance the letter and the spirit of any moral rule that might be applicable to the present situation. Therefore, situation ethics calls for flexibility when making moral decisions.

Contrasting Moral Theories

The many different moral theories can be illustrated by analyzing a hypothetical situation. A large cruise ship sinks and twenty people manage to make it to a small lifeboat. However, there are only enough provisions to keep ten people alive for at most a few days. Also, the lifeboat will capsize if all twenty people are allowed to enter it. The officer in charge decides that ten adult males will have to swim away from the lifeboat in order to give the remaining ten people a chance to survive.

A consequentialist might agree that the decision was morally justified based on a calculation of the best possible outcome for the most people. On the other hand, a deontologist might disagree with the decision. The deontologist could invoke the categorical imperative that our actions or decisions should never purposely or consciously harm innocent people. Finally, a relativist would argue that there is no one right answer.

EXERCISES 12B

Answer "true" or "false" to the following statements.

1. A utilitarian argument for capital punishment might be that it benefits society by eliminating dangerous individuals.

   Answer: True

2. Every moral theory is based on the determination of how a person's act either produces pleasure or avoids pain.

3. An ethical theory is teleological if it relies on duties and responsibilities to others.

4. The fact that pleasure, pain, and happiness are different for each person is a problem for deontological theories.

⭐ 5. Consequentialist moral theories are based on our duties to others.

6. Deontological theories hold that one should always act so as to produce the greatest happiness for the greatest number of people.

7. Utilitarianism holds that moral values are relative to individuals and cultures; therefore, there can be no universal moral principles.

8. Emotivism holds that moral judgments must be based on the consequences of our acts.

⭐ 9. A categorical imperative is a rule relative to a particular culture or religion.

10. Egoism holds that every rule should be obeyed without exception and without regard for any possible negative consequences of the act.

11. Situation ethics holds that all value judgments are merely expressions of our feelings about certain human behaviors.

12. Relativism holds that universal ethical principles do not exist.

⭐ 13. A criticism of utilitarianism is that we can never know all the consequences of our actions.

14. A criticism of deontology is that we do not have a way to measure pleasure and pain.

15. An important factor for teleological moral theories is the motive behind a particular act or behavior.

Level 2 Multiple-Choice Questions

Video Tutorial

C. THE NATURALISTIC FALLACY

As we saw earlier, some moral theories use facts about human nature as the basis for moral value judgments. They rely on psychological and biological evidence to argue that human behavior can be reduced to two forces: the desire for pleasure (or happiness) and the avoidance of pain. The basic principle for all *naturalistic* moral theories, such as egoism and utilitarianism, is captured by the **naturalistic moral principle**:

> Since it is *natural* for humans to desire pleasure (or happiness) and to avoid pain, we can conclude that human behavior *ought* to be directed to these two ends.

The argument has been criticized for falling prey to the **naturalistic fallacy**: *Value judgments cannot be logically derived from statements of fact.* This line of criticism (also

Naturalistic moral principle Since it is natural for humans to desire pleasure (or happiness) and to avoid pain, human behavior ought to be directed to these two ends.

Naturalistic fallacy Value judgments cannot be logically derived from statements of fact.

known as the "is-ought" distinction) was originally presented by David Hume, but the name *naturalistic fallacy* was coined by G. E. Moore. The criticism begins by drawing a line between factual statements and value judgments. On one side of the line are the factual statements, and on the other side of the line are value judgments. In other words, an ethical pronouncement that you *ought to do* something *cannot* be logically deduced from statements that assert only *what is the case*.

The fallacious use of the naturalistic moral principle can be illustrated by a few examples. We know that *factual statements* assert that something is or is not the case, and they are decided by empirical investigations. For example, we could gather data about human eating habits and determine the following fact: Most humans get pleasure from eating ice cream. Since we have discovered a fact about humans, we can apply the naturalistic moral principle to create this argument:

> It *is* true that most humans get pleasure from eating ice cream. Therefore, humans *ought* to eat ice cream.

Our data gathering about human eating habits might also reveal this fact: Most humans do not like the taste of anchovies. Once again, if we have discovered a fact about humans, then we can apply the naturalistic moral principle:

PROFILES IN LOGIC
G. E. Moore

G. E. Moore (1873–1958), a British philosopher, preferred to use the initials "G. E." instead of his given names "George Edward." Moore was a well-respected teacher at the University of Cambridge who treated his students "as responsible thinkers."

Moore's approach to philosophical problems is often called "common sense realism," by which he hoped to refute skepticism. For example, Moore argued that a statement such as "The earth has existed for many years before I was born" is a truism that he knows for certain. But Moore argues that we must be careful to separate the *truism* from the subsequent *analysis of the truism*.

One of Moore's major contributions is his influential work in the area of ethics.

For Moore, the property of *goodness* is simple, and it cannot be analyzed by non-moral terms. In other words, the property cannot be analyzed by empirical research. For example, Moore held that we cannot define "goodness" in terms of pleasure or the evolution of certain human habits, traits, or desires. Any attempt to apply scientific results to moral arguments falls prey to the "naturalistic fallacy." However, Moore argued that we can avoid the naturalistic fallacy by accepting that ethical questions must be answered by invoking ethical beliefs. Any ethical question—for example, Should we use human embryos for stem cell research?—can be answered only by the application of ethical concepts.

It *is* the case that most humans do not like the taste of anchovies. Therefore, humans *ought not* to eat anchovies.

Once we recognize that these are two instances of the *naturalistic fallacy*, then we can assert that the "ought" in the two conclusions does not follow logically from the "is" in the premises. To avoid the fallacy, the factual premise (the "is") has to be combined with a *moral principle* in order to derive the ethical "ought" in the conclusion. This is the subject of the next section.

D. THE STRUCTURE OF MORAL ARGUMENTS

Moral arguments generally have conclusions that assert some moral position or action, such as "You ought to do X" or "It is wrong to do Y." In its simplest form, these are the requirements for a moral argument:

1. There is at least one premise describing a particular situation where a decision to act will be made by someone (this is a nonmoral statement).
2. There is at least one premise that supplies a moral rule, principle, or command.
3. The conclusion asserts that a specific action should be performed.

Of course, not all moral arguments come in complete packages. Some have missing premises or conclusions, but these are generally easily filled in by those familiar with the context in which the moral argument occurs. The moral premise is necessary for two reasons:

1. It fills in the gap described by the "is-ought" problem.
2. It supplies the general moral rule or principle needed to derive a specific moral action or behavior. In other words, it provides the moral grounds for *why you ought to do X*.

In order to see how the moral and nonmoral premises work, consider these four arguments:

A. Some prisoners of war have been tortured while in U.S. custody. Therefore, the United States should stop torturing prisoners of war.

B. Some prisoners of war have been tortured while in U.S. custody. Therefore, the United States should not stop torturing prisoners of war.

C. Some prisoners of war have been tortured while in U.S. custody. The United States has signed an agreement to abide by the Geneva Convention. The United States is violating the Geneva Convention, which prohibits the torture of prisoners of war. Therefore, the United States should stop torturing prisoners of war.

D. Some prisoners of war have been tortured while in U.S. custody. The United States is gaining valuable information from the torture of prisoners of war. Anything the United States can do to fight the war on terror should be permitted. Therefore, the United States should not stop torturing prisoners of war.

In arguments A and B the single nonmoral premise describes a reported fact about U.S. treatment of prisoners of war. It is easily seen that neither the conclusion in argument A, nor the conclusion in B, follows from the single premise. However, arguments C and D have premises that attempt to provide the necessary moral justification for their respective conclusions. As with most moral arguments, the moral premises are generally the point of departure for further argumentation and analysis. Nevertheless, many times nonmoral issues drive the force of analysis. For example:

> Our mother has been in a coma for several months and is being kept alive by life-sustaining equipment. The attending physician's opinion is that the coma is irreversible. There appears to be little or no brain activity in our mother. Therefore, we should ask the physician to take our mother off the life-sustaining equipment.

It is possible that other relatives might disagree with the conclusion for a variety of moral and nonmoral reasons. For example, they might point out that the physician cannot be certain that the patient will never come out of the coma. They might argue that little or no brain activity is a measure of what is occurring in the patient's brain, but not in her mind. Also, the equipment to measure brain activity is only our best guide today as to what is happening in a person's brain. They might point out that more powerful equipment will be developed in the future that will give us a better picture of what is occurring in the brain. In other words, the argument against taking the patient off the life-sustaining equipment may be over the factual or empirical nature of the status of the coma, and not a moral debate over "pulling the plug." In fact, it is possible that all the relatives will agree to the decision to let the mother die if they can agree on the nature and extent of the coma.

When starting to analyze moral arguments it often helps to see them as deductive. This simplifies the logical analysis into *valid*, *invalid*, *sound*, and *unsound*. For example, many moral arguments have this structure:

> X is Y.
> Anything Y is morally wrong.
> X is morally wrong.

For example, let X = *killing an innocent human*, and Y = *murder*:

> Killing an innocent human is murder.
> Murder is morally wrong.
> Killing an innocent human is morally wrong.

To see another example, this time let X = *stealing*, and Y = *taking other people's property without their consent*:

> Stealing is taking other people's property without their consent.
> Taking other people's property without their consent is morally wrong.
> Stealing is morally wrong.

Since both examples result in valid arguments, the remaining question is one of soundness. The first premise in both arguments is considered by most people to be merely definitional. One premise defines "killing," and the other defines "stealing." As such, their truth value would probably not be debated. But in order to determine soundness, we must be able to decide the truth value of the second premise of each argument. Here is where we run into problems. The second premise of each of the two arguments is a moral value judgment. We already discussed the problems with determining the truth value of this kind of statement. The statement is not merely definitional; nor does it seem to assert a fact of the world. Therefore, the soundness issue will usually be a difficult hurdle to overcome.

So, should we treat some moral arguments as deductive? One reason to do this is that many people feel strongly that moral rules or principles are universal. Hence, the logical intent of an argument using a general moral rule as a premise must be to have the moral action prescribed in the conclusion to follow with necessity. And this indeed is how many people perceive or intend their moral arguments to be interpreted.

Of course, we can also classify some moral arguments as inductive, instead of deductive. Let's see how the logical analysis and evaluation would proceed. For example, suppose you come across a research survey that asked a large number of Christians, chosen at random, to state their beliefs concerning several social issues. You might read the following statistic: "Ninety percent of Christians believe that stem cell research is morally wrong." Now, perhaps you know someone who is a Christian; if so, you might create this argument:

> **E.** Ninety percent of Christians believe that stem cell research is morally wrong. Gerry is a Christian. Therefore, Gerry *probably* believes that stem cell research is wrong.

This is a straightforward inductive argument. If the premises are assumed to be true, then we can classify it as a strong argument. In addition, if the research was well conducted and we have reason to believe that the evidence in the first premise is factually true, then we can also classify the argument as cogent. But now look at the next argument:

> **F.** Ninety percent of Christians believe that stem cell research is morally wrong. Gerry is a Christian. Therefore, Gerry *ought* to believe that stem cell research is wrong.

This is a not a straightforward inductive argument. The "ought" in the conclusion of argument F is quite different from the word "probably" in the conclusion of argument E. The conclusion of E merely asserts that a high statistical probability can be attached to the claim that "Gerry believes that stem cell research is wrong." Of course, the conclusion is not necessarily true, but that is not a requirement of a strong inductive argument. The premises in argument E, if true, do provide strong statistical evidence for the conclusion.

On the other hand, the conclusion of F does *not* assert anything about a statistical probability that can be attached to the claim that "Gerry believes that stem cell research is wrong." Instead, the conclusion of F offers a *moral prescription* of what

Gerry *ought* to do. Here again we see an *ought statement* derived from an *is statement*. But perhaps the argument is missing some key information, and we can provide the missing moral link:

> **G.** Ninety percent of Christians believe that stem cell research is morally wrong. Gerry is a Christian. Every Christian ought to believe what the vast majority of Christians believe. Therefore, Gerry *ought* to believe that stem cell research is wrong.

The added premise seems to fill in the missing gap between the "is" in the premises and the "ought" in the conclusion. However, now the argument is no longer inductive, it is deductive. Thus, we are back to determining its validity and soundness.

Let's add one more twist to the argument. Suppose we change the conclusion:

> **H.** Ninety percent of Christians believe that stem cell research is morally wrong. Gerry is a Christian. Every Christian ought to believe what the vast majority of Christians believe. Therefore, Gerry *probably ought* to believe that stem cell research is wrong.

This would have the appearance of making the argument inductive once again. Nevertheless, there is something odd about the phrase "probably ought." Moral prescriptions about what we ought to do are not generally couched in terms of what we *probably ought to do*, but rather of what we *ought to do*, with no added qualifications.

You can apply the discussion thus far to two last examples, to deepen your understanding:

> **I.** Seventy-five percent of Americans believe that abortions are sometimes morally justified. Maxine is an American. Therefore, Maxine *probably* believes that abortions are sometimes morally justified.
>
> **J.** Seventy-five percent of Americans believe that abortions are sometimes morally justified. Maxine is an American. Therefore, Maxine *ought* to believe that abortions are sometimes morally justified.

E. ANALOGIES AND MORAL ARGUMENTS

Analogies are often used in moral arguments as a way to support a moral prescription in the conclusion. Like all analogical reasoning, the premises of an analogical moral argument try to link two or more situations that call for a moral decision or determination to be made. The idea is to persuade others that they should (or should not) perform a certain action (or hold a certain belief), because the present case is similar to a previously determined moral situation. Thus, analogical moral arguments are attempts to point out that our moral actions (or beliefs) should be consistent. The following is an analogical moral argument:

> You believe that every human embryo or fetus is a human being. You believe that abortion is wrong, because it is the murder of an innocent human being. Yet you also believe that abortion is morally permissible in cases of rape and incest. But a human embryo or fetus conceived by an act of rape or incest is

no less an innocent human being than one conceived by an act of consensual sex. Therefore, you *ought* to believe that abortion is *not* morally permissible in cases of rape and incest.

The point of the premises is to force someone into recognizing the inconsistency of holding (1) that *every* human embryo or fetus is a human being and (2) that an embryo or fetus conceived by incest or rape is *not* an innocent human being. In other words, people who hold (1) and (2) would need to explain why and how a fetus conceived by rape or incest is different from a fetus that was conceived through consensual sex. They would have to explain how the act of conception in the case of rape or incest causes the resulting fetus to be excluded from the class of innocent human beings.

Let's look at another example of an analogical moral argument:

> You told me that you think that using marijuana is morally wrong, not because it is illegal, but because it is addictive and physically harmful after long-term use. But you regularly drink alcohol, even though you are aware of studies that show that it is addictive and physically harmful after long-term use. Therefore, you *ought* not to drink alcohol, because it is morally wrong.

As in the previous example, the intent of the premises is to force others into recognizing that they hold inconsistent positions. (1) They believe that using marijuana is morally wrong, because it is addictive and physically harmful after long-term use. (2) They regularly drink alcohol, even though they are aware of studies that show that it is addictive and physically harmful after long-term use. Hence, they would have to explain how regularly drinking alcohol is different from using marijuana in order to justify its continued use on moral grounds. Furthermore, the first premise precludes them from replying that the illegality of marijuana is the relevant moral difference.

In sum, we can reconstruct, analyze, and evaluate analogical moral arguments by using the same techniques as for nonmoral analogical arguments. We can evaluate the strengths and weaknesses of analogical moral arguments by assessing the relevant instances in the premises. We can also apply the familiar techniques of looking for disanalogies, counteranalogies, and any unintended consequences of the analogy. These logical analysis techniques allow us to understand how analogical moral arguments function—and how they can be evaluated for degrees of strength.

EXERCISES 12E

I. Discuss the following moral issues in light of the ideas put forward in this chapter. Use the moral theories described in this chapter to construct arguments regarding the following issues. Choose a moral theory and construct an argument by applying it to an issue. Then take a different moral theory and apply it to a different issue. Discuss the strength of the arguments you construct in light of the discussions regarding each particular theory you use. Try to use each moral theory at least twice.

Level 1 Multiple-Choice Questions

Level 2 Multiple-Choice Questions

1. downloading music illegally
2. gambling
3. state-run lotteries
4. rehabilitation of criminals
⭐ 5. stealing
6. murder

7. welfare
8. giving to charities
⭐ 9. animal rights
10. abortion
11. capital punishment
12. affirmative action

⭐ 13. freedom of speech
14. smokers' rights
15. prostitution
16. cheating on exams
⭐ 17. birth control
18. telemarketing

Answer to #1: downloading music illegally

Your answers will depend on the particular moral theory you choose for each issue. Here is an example that applies *utilitarianism*:

Argument: *Downloading music illegally* denies artists (music composers, lyricists, and musicians) a fair share of any royalties for their original work. It also reduces the sales of the companies that produced and marketed the music. Without royalties, artists lose incentive to create new music, and without sales, music companies cannot afford to produce new music. The immediate pleasure derived from those listening to illegally downloaded music does not outweigh the pain of the artists and company employees who will not be able to survive a continued economic loss. The long-term effect is that artists and music companies will no longer produce new music.

Discussion of the argument: Not everyone downloads music illegally. Enough people are willing to buy music to ensure that artists get some royalties and to keep music companies in business. Also, with the explosion of the Internet, some artists now self-publish their work or even offer it for free. The idea is to gain a following of loyal fans willing to pay a small fee directly to the artist, instead of buying music from a company at a higher cost. In some cases this income will match the artist's royalty derived from a contract in which the music company keeps the lion's share of the profits.

II. The following passages are taken from various sources. Identify the moral arguments in each passage, and use any of the theories discussed in this chapter in your analysis of the arguments.

1. But across action sports, where individuality is prized, many are uncomfortable with rules or restrictions. "I respect that everyone should wear a helmet, like I wear a helmet," professional snowboarder Keir Dillon says. "But I don't think it should be mandated. For me, I always get worried about mandating or having governing bodies over our sport."   Matt Higgins, "Head Games"

Answer:

Argument: Everyone should wear a helmet, [just as] I wear a helmet. [However,] I always get worried about mandating or having governing bodies over our sport. [Therefore,] I don't think it [wearing a helmet] should be mandated.

Discussion: *Situation ethics* holds that we should not rigidly apply rules to every possible situation. Although wearing a helmet reduces the likelihood of injuries, we should allow individual riders the freedom to choose for themselves. The governing bodies of the sport can strongly suggest that riders use helmets, but should not mandate their use; we should allow for exceptions.

2. With over 1 billion people, China should have a greater voice on the issue of world peace. Norway is only a small country, but it must be in the minority concerning the conception of freedom and democracy. Hence, the selection of the "Nobel Peace Prize" should be open to the people in the world.

      Ed Flanagan, "Big PR Goof? China's Confusing Confucius Prize," *NBC News*

3. "Never did get you for stealing that money?"
    "I didn't consider it stealing."
    "It didn't belong to you."
    "I needed a road stake. Like that bank in New Mexico. I needed a road stake, and there it was. I never robbed no citizen or took a man's watch!"
    "It's all stealing."   From the screenplay of the 1969 movie *True Grit*

4. While most people took Internet access for granted as a constant, the suddenness of Egypt's Internet shutdown raises the question: Is access to the Internet a human right? "There are certain technological advances that are such leaps forward in human evolution that they do, in fact, become human rights. Vaccines, for example. Potable water. I believe the Internet has become one as well," said John Addis.   Wilson Rothman, "Is Internet Access a Human Right?" *Technolog*

Video Tutorial

5. After more than three years of pressure from shareholders, religious groups and blacks, the Colgate-Palmolive Company announced yesterday that it would rename Darkie, a popular toothpaste that it sells in Asia, and redesign its logotype, a minstrel in blackface. "It's just plain wrong," Reuben Mark, chairman and chief executive of Colgate-Palmolive, said about the toothpaste's name and logotype. "It's just offensive. The morally right thing dictated that we must change."

      Douglas C. McGill, "Colgate to Rename a Toothpaste," *The New York Times*

6. It is frequently stated that illicit drugs are "bad, dangerous, destructive," or "addictive," and that society has an obligation to keep them from the public. But nowhere can be found reliable, objective scientific evidence that they are any more harmful than other substances and activities that are legal. In view of the enormous expense, the carnage and the obvious futility of the "drug war," resulting in massive criminalization of society, it is high time to examine the supposed justification for keeping certain substances illegal.

      Benson B. Roe, M.D., "Why We Should Legalize Drugs"

7. The violent behavior caused by drugs won't magically stop because the drugs are legal. Legal PCP isn't going to make a person less violent than illegally purchased PCP. So, crimes committed because of drugs will increase as the number of drug users will increase with the legalization of drugs. The psychopathic behavior that drugs cause will not somehow magically stop because drugs are legal.   Carolyn C. Gargaro, "Drugs"

8. And yet, while young men's failures in life are not penalizing them in the bed-room, their sexual success may, ironically, be hindering their drive to achieve in life. Don't forget your Freud: Civilization is built on blocked, redirected, and channeled sexual impulse, because men will work for sex. Today's young men, however, seldom have to. As the authors of last year's book *Sex at Dawn: The Prehistoric Origins of Modern Sexuality* put it, "Societies in which women have lots of autonomy and authority tend to be decidedly male-friendly, relaxed, tol-erant, and plenty sexy." They're right. But then try getting men to do anything.

Mark Regnerus, "Sex Is Cheap," *Slate*

⭐ 9. "It's interesting because different cultures have different views on concussions and different views on identifying concussions, or even what the symptoms are that may suggest concussion," Dr. Ruben Echemendia recently told reporters. "So we know from our research, for example, that the reporting of symptoms varies by language of origin." Echemendia's group has determined that play-ers from different nationalities and cultural backgrounds report concussions in different manners. Different cultures also put more or less importance around different symptoms, Echemendia explained. One culture may not consider a headache to be important and won't report it, but they will report dizziness. Meanwhile, headaches can be one of the indicators for post-concussion syn-drome.   Pierre LeBrun, "National Hockey League Has Unique Off-Ice Concussion Foe"

10. The list of growing jobs is heavy on nurturing professions, in which women, ironically, seem to benefit from old stereotypes and habits. Theoretically, there is no reason men should not be qualified. But they have proved remarkably unable to adapt. Over the course of the past century, feminism has pushed women to do things once considered against their nature—first enter the workforce as singles, then continue to work while married, then work even with small children at home. Many professions that started out as the province of men are now filled mostly with women—secretary and teacher come to mind. Yet I'm not aware of any that have gone the opposite way. Nursing schools have tried hard to recruit men in the past few years, with minimal success. Teaching schools, eager to recruit male role models, are having a similarly hard time. The range of acceptable masculine roles has changed comparatively little, and has perhaps even narrowed as men have shied away from some careers women have entered. And with each passing day, they lag further behind.

Hanna Rosin, "The End of Men," *Atlantic*

11. Let me make my somewhat seditious proposal explicit: We should not call our-selves "atheists." We should not call ourselves "secularists." We should not call ourselves "humanists," or "secular humanists," or "naturalists," or "skeptics," or "anti-theists," or "rationalists," or "freethinkers," or "brights." We should not call ourselves anything. We should go under the radar—for the rest of our

lives. And while there, we should be decent, responsible people who destroy bad ideas wherever we find them. Now, it just so happens that religion has more than its fair share of bad ideas. And it remains the only system of thought, where the process of maintaining bad ideas in perpetual immunity from criticism is considered a sacred act. This is the act of faith. And I remain convinced that religious faith is one of the most perverse misuses of intelligence we have ever devised. So we will, inevitably, continue to criticize religious thinking. But we should not define ourselves and name ourselves in opposition to such thinking. So what does this all mean in practical terms? Well, rather than declare ourselves "atheists" in opposition to all religion, I think we should do nothing more than advocate reason and intellectual honesty—and where this advocacy causes us to collide with religion, as it inevitably will, we should observe that the points of impact are always with specific religious beliefs—not with religion in general. There is no religion in general.

Sam Harris, "The Problem with Atheism," Washington Post

12. *Lotteries Bilk the Poor*: Last week, the Mega Millions lotto paid what was described in media reports as a "$380 million" jackpot. Actually the number reflects an annuity that pays $380 million over 26 years. The present value of the annuity, the only figure that matters, is $240 million—heady enough. Any money sum can be made to appear to roughly twice as great by expressing the number as a long-term annuity. If your employer offered you $50,000 this year, or $80,000 conveyed as one payment of $3,000 annually for each of the next 26 years—the same proportion as the Mega Millions markup—which would you choose? The media should not sensationalize lottery numbers by using the phony figures the lotto companies promote. But that's the least of the problems with lotteries, whose financial structure—spectacularly low chances of winning for players, combined with riches for those administering the lottos—make them, as a wag once said, "a tax on the stupid." As TMQ wrote two years ago of state-sponsored lotteries, "There is almost no chance you will win, while total assurance you will lose the average of $190 annually that Americans throw away on government-run roulette. Worse, public lotteries, with their glitzy false promises of instant wealth, are a tax on poverty—as David Brooks of *The New York Times* has noted, households with an income of less than $13,000 spend an average of $645 annually on scratch-off tickets, meaning the poor are the main group throwing away cash at government lotto sites." Government, which ought to aid the poor, instead cynically markets lottos to the poor—with false promises of instant wealth, plus a high concentration of lotto sales outlets in low-income neighborhoods. The goal of this cynicism? Wealth for lotto companies and kickbacks—excuse me, consulting fees—for the politicians and government bureaucrats involved.

Gregg Easterbrook, "The Next Step"

Study Materials

Summary

- Some arguments rely solely on factual claims for support, some arguments rely solely on value judgments for support, and some arguments rely on a mixture of the two.
- Value judgment: A claim that a particular human action or object has some degree of importance, worth, or desirability.
- Prescriptive statement: In a moral setting, a statement that offers advice either by specifying a particular action that ought to be performed or by providing general moral rules, principles, or guidelines that should be followed.
- Normative statement: A statement that establishes standards for correct moral behavior, determining norms or rules of conduct.
- Emotivism: A theory that asserts that moral value judgments are merely expressions of our attitudes or emotions.
- Consequentialism: A class of moral theories in which the moral value of any human action or behavior is determined exclusively by its outcomes.
- Teleology: The philosophical belief that the value of an action or object can be determined by looking at the purpose or the end of the action or object.
- Egoism: The basic principle that everyone should act in order to maximize his or her own individual pleasure or happiness.
- The most important principle for utilitarianism can be summed up in the famous dictum "the greatest good for the greatest number."
- According to utilitarianism, every human action demonstrates "universalizability," meaning that the same principles hold for all people at all times.
- Deontology: The theory that duty to others is the first and foremost moral consideration; it lays the groundwork for discovering those duties.
- The basic idea of a categorical imperative is that your actions or behavior toward others should always be such that you would want everyone to act in the same manner.
- Relativism makes two claims: First, all moral value judgments are determined by a society's beliefs toward actions or behavior. Second, there are no objective or universal moral value judgments.
- Situation ethics: The idea that we should not rigidly apply moral rules to every possible situation.
- Naturalistic moral principle: Since it is natural for humans to desire pleasure (or happiness) and to avoid pain, human behavior ought to be directed to these two ends.
- Naturalistic fallacy: Value judgments cannot be logically derived from statements of fact.

KEY TERMS

LOGIC CHALLENGE: DANGEROUS CARGO

You own a small resort on a tropical island where the only way on and off is by boat. Three of your guests, Leo, Aries, and Aquarius, had a bad weekend and they are standing by the boat dock with their luggage demanding to get off the island as quickly as possible. Leo, Aries, and Aquarius are all relatives who came together in one car, which is parked on the mainland. Over the last few days, old childhood squabbles surfaced, which threaten to escalate into violence.

To make things worse, a further difficulty arises. Your large boat is broken, and the small boat can hold only you and one passenger. As soon as the three guests hear this, they make more demands. Leo says, "Don't leave me alone either here or at the car with Aries." Upon hearing this, Aquarius says, "Well, you'd better not leave me alone either here or at the car with Leo." How can you get the three relatives to their car while meeting their demands?

Chapter 13

Statistical Arguments and Probability

A. *Samples and Populations*
B. *Statistical Averages*
C. *Standard Deviation*
D. *What If the Results Are Skewed?*
E. *The Misuse of Statistics*
F. *Probability Theories*
G. *Probability Calculus*
H. *True Odds in Games of Chance*
I. *Bayesian Theory*

Study Materials

Television commercials are fond of claims like this:

- Four out of five dentists recommend the ingredient found in our toothpaste.
- Our diet cola has 30% fewer calories.
- Get up to 70% off our previously low prices on selected items.
- American children watch an average of five hours of television a day. That means that they have watched an average of 5000 hours of television before entering first grade. Our *Early Reading Program* DVDs are fun and educational at the same time. So why not let your child's television viewing help prepare them for their first days in school? Don't let your children fall behind. Give them the right head start.

After the commercials end, a short news update might announce this: "A recent survey reveals that the incumbent mayor, who is running for reelection and who is being investigated for alleged ties to a securities fraud scandal, trails his opponent: 34% of those surveyed said they will vote for the mayor; 62% said they will vote for his opponent; and 4% said that they haven't made up their minds."

Evaluating arguments that rely on statistical evidence requires us to interpret correctly the statistical evidence as it is presented. However, in many everyday arguments the words "average" and "percentage" are ambiguous because we are not told how the average or percentage was derived. (Chapter 4 examined the *fallacy of misleading precision*.) Information as to how statistical figures are computed is just as crucial for evaluating many statistical arguments. This chapter supplies the tools we need to make those evaluations and then introduces probability.

A. SAMPLES AND POPULATIONS

Suppose a criminal justice researcher wants to know the conviction rate in felony cases in the state where she teaches. She compiles this statistic: 70% of a sample of defendants in criminal cases were found guilty. Let's look at how this statistic might be used in an argument:

> Seventy percent of a *sample* of defendants in criminal cases were found guilty.
> Therefore, probably 70% of *all* defendants in criminal cases are found guilty.

But how was the sample gathered? How large was the sample? Was it a random sample? Is there any evidence that the sample is not representative of the population of all defendants? Our answers to these questions will help determine the strength of the argument. Therefore, we need to know as much as we can about the research that was conducted.

Population refers to any group of objects, not just a human population. A **sample** is a subset, or part, of a population. If the population in question is the student body of a large university (say, 10,000 students), then a sample would be any portion of that population. A **representative sample** accurately reflects the characteristics of the population as a whole. Let's see what that takes.

Imagine that a senior class in sociology is told to determine the student population's opinion on a proposed tuition increase. Two members of this class decide to work together. They each interview two students in the remaining three classes that day, for a total of twelve students. They discover that ten students are opposed to the tuition increase. Armed with this data, they make a bold generalization:

> Eighty-three percent of a *sample* of students is opposed to a tuition increase.
> Therefore, probably 83% of the student *population* is opposed to a tuition increase.

The teacher points out that they have based their generalization on a small sample. A sample size of twelve, relative to a student body of 10,000, is small and extremely unlikely to be representative of the population. This is an example of the *fallacy of hasty generalization* (see Chapter 4).

There is no simple formula for calculating the ratio of sample size to population to ensure a representative sample. However, when a sample size is small relative to the size of the population, other factors (which we will soon discuss) can help ensure that a representative sample has been achieved. Without the necessary equipment to strengthen it, however, a small sample weakens the argument.

Our intrepid students go back to work and this time they gather a large sample. They begin polling more students in their classes, and they poll students from their dormitory. Their sample size swells to over 300 students. Analyzing the data prompts them to make a new argument:

> Seventy-six percent of a *sample* of 300 students is opposed to a tuition increase.
> Therefore, probably 76% of the student *population* is opposed to a tuition increase.

Population Any group of objects, not just human populations.

Sample A subset of a population.

Representative sample A sample that accurately reflects the characteristics of the population as a whole.

Their teacher does not question the sample size, but does inquire into which students were polled. The researchers admit that the vast majority of those polled in their upper-level classes are probably either juniors or seniors. Also, they live in a dorm reserved for juniors, seniors, and graduate students. These admissions weaken the argument, because the sample is not representative of all students: It is *biased* toward upperclassmen. This is an example of the *fallacy of biased sample* (see Chapter 4) because both freshmen and sophomores are underrepresented in the sample. If the researchers had restricted their conclusion to upperclassmen, then their argument would be stronger. Since the researchers wanted to make a generalization about the entire student population, their sample was biased because it excluded certain subsets of that population.

The researchers go back to work and supplement their data by polling an appropriate number of freshmen and sophomores. Their new data yields a new argument:

> Seventy-two percent of a *sample* of 500 students is opposed to a tuition increase. Therefore, probably 72% of the student *population* is opposed to a tuition increase.

Random sample
A sample in which every member of the population has an equal chance of getting in.

The teacher remarks that both the sample size and the distribution of students' year in school strengthen the argument. However, this is not a *random sample*. The researchers polled only students they had easy access to. To get a **random sample**, you must ensure that *every member of the population has an equal chance of getting in*. A random sample strengthens the likelihood that the sample represents the population.

EXERCISES 13A

Level 1 Multiple-Choice Questions

Level 2 Multiple-Choice Questions

For the following passages, first identify the *sample* and *population* in the passages. Next, discuss whether the sample is representative of the population referred to in the conclusion. Analyze for sample size, potential bias, and randomness. Determine how your answers to these questions affect the strength of the arguments.

1. I am never going to buy another Hinckley car again. I had one and so did my sister. Both our cars were constantly in the shop. They had electrical and carburetor problems that caused them to stall all the time with no warning. Then we would have to get them towed, because they wouldn't start again. I am sure that all Hinckley cars have the same kinds of problems; that's why I won't buy one no matter what the price.

Answer:

Sample: Two Hinckley cars.
Population: All Hinckley cars.
Sample size: Two cars are a very small sample when we are discussing potentially millions of cars. This reduces the likelihood that the sample is representative of the population.
Potential bias: The sample excludes any cars that other owners might praise. It doesn't allow for the possibility of evidence that would go against its

claims. This reduces the likelihood that the sample is representative of the population.

Randomness: This is not a random sample because not every Hinckley car had an equal chance of getting into the sample. This reduces the likelihood that the sample is representative of the population.

2. For 1 year, a veterinarian kept track of all the dogs brought in for testing after they had bitten someone. Out of 132 dogs brought in, pit bulls accounted for 67% of all attacks resulting in bite wounds to people. The veterinarian concluded that pit bulls are twice as likely to bite someone as all other dog breeds combined.

3. A study of psychiatric outpatients at a major hospital in Chicago showed that patients given counseling, plus some form of drug therapy, stayed in the program only one-third as long as those given just counseling. For 3 years the researchers followed 1,600 patients; half were given only counseling and the other half were given counseling and drug treatment. The group given counseling and drugs felt confident that they could now cope with their problems and left the program, while the group given just counseling stayed in the program three times longer.

Video Tutorial

4. There have been over 4000 UFO sightings around the world in the past five years. Our analysis of these cases shows that 78% of the sightings have never been adequately explained by any government agency in any country where the sightings occurred. The number of sightings that appear to be hoaxes, or where the credibility of the eyewitnesses is under question, is insignificant. Given this information, we can confidently say that UFOs are real and the sightings are unequivocally of extraterrestrial spaceships manned by organisms far more advanced than earthlings.

5. A random study of 6000 urban public high school seniors throughout the United States has confirmed what many have long suspected. The students were given the same verbal, mathematical, perceptual, and manual dexterity test that was given 20 years ago to high school seniors. The Bincaid-Forbush test had not been used for over 15 years, so the researchers thought that it could be a good way of comparing the results of the preceding generation (many of whom are probably the parents of today's seniors) with the current crop of students. As expected, verbal and math scores have declined by 20% in today's students.

    Surprisingly, the perceptual and manual dexterity scores of today's students are 34% higher than their parents' generation. The researchers speculate that the rise of computers and arcade video games can explain both results. They hypothesize that verbal and math skills have deteriorated because video games require very little reading or calculating. However, these games require superior perceptual and manual dexterity skills, and thus give today's students much more exposure to this kind of skill development.

6. I have closely examined ninety-three wars that took place within the last 200 years. I use the word "war" to include both external conflicts (between two or more countries) and internal or civil wars. In 84% of those cases the wars were precipitated by a recent change in the government. Specifically, those 84% occurred soon after a conservative leader of that country took over from someone who was more liberal. The terms "conservative" and "liberal" are applied after examining and rating the leader on a scale from one to ten for variables related to economic beliefs, religious pronouncements, social welfare programs, military buildup, judicial appointments, immigration laws, and the treatment of criminals. From these results, we can safely conclude that approximately four out of every five future wars around the world will occur after a conservative leader replaces a liberal leader.

7. Eight out of ten people surveyed chose Slacker Soda over the next four most popular brands of soft drink. It is clear that America has spoken. Eighty percent of all Americans can't be wrong. Don't you think that you should start drinking Slacker Soda?

8. Research on people's dreams shows that they are not visions of the future. A group of psychologists monitored thirty volunteers for 1 year. The volunteers were told to keep a daily log only of the dreams they could clearly recall. They were also told to record anything that happened within a few days of the dream that they felt corresponded to the dream (to determine if they thought the dream was a premonition). On average, the volunteers recorded three dreams a night. In 1 year the researchers had over 25,000 dreams to analyze. They found that less than 1% of the dreams could be accurately correlated with a subsequent event in the dreamer's life (and these were usually trivial events). They concluded that humans' dreams do not come from the future, they do not offer a glimpse of some inevitable occurrence, nor do they act as a warning so we can avoid unpleasant events.

9. From 1903 to 2008, whenever the American League won the World Series, cigarette sales rose 20% over the previous year. But when the National League won the World Series, liquor sales rose 25% for the next year. Stock buyers pay heed! Watch who wins the World Series, and then buy or sell accordingly.

10. A study of college majors has revealed some interesting results. The study looked at more than 20,000 students who were accepted to U.S. law schools and medical schools for the past 20 years. The highest *percentage* of any major to be accepted to both law and medical schools was philosophy majors. The researchers speculate that this can be partially explained by the fact that philosophy majors have to take numerous logic courses and to write critical papers using logical reasoning. Since both the LSAT and MCAT (the law school and medical school standardized tests required of all applicants) have a *logical reasoning* section, philosophy majors are better prepared and tend to score higher on that section. The researchers encourage those planning to apply to law or medical school to take as many philosophy courses as they can.

B. STATISTICAL AVERAGES

Imagine that in class one day, your instructor tells you that a slide will appear on screen, showing a room with people whose average age is 45. Now, if you are around 20 years of age, you might anticipate that the people on the slide will look somewhat like your parents. To your surprise, you see five very young children and six people who look to be your grandparents' age. To you, none of the people appear even close to 45 years of age; everyone is either much too young or much too old. One of your classmates is equally puzzled and complains to the teacher: The class was misled. You were told that the average age in the slide would be 45, so it should depict a middle-aged person, right? Yet not even one person looks middle-aged.

The average age given was correct. Your teacher lists the ages of the people in the picture:

The Ages of the Five Younger People	The Ages of the Six Older People
5	76
5	77
4	78
3	79
2	80
	86

If we add the ages in the first column, we get 19. The second column adds up to 476. Together they add up to 495, which is the total age of the eleven people. We now divide the *total age* by the *number of people* to get the *average age*; this gives us $495 \div 11 = 45$. The average age of the eleven people in the slide is indeed 45.

This type of statistical average, called the *mean*, is one way to describe a set of data. The **mean** is determined by adding the numerical values in the data for the objects examined, then dividing by the number of objects. When newspapers, magazines, and other nontechnical sources refer to the "average" of a set of numerical data, they usually intend the *mean*. You have probably run into claims like these (whether or not they are true):

- The average yearly salary of a National Basketball Association (NBA) player is $5 million.
- The top ten movie stars average $20 million per movie.
- High school teachers in the United States average $30,000 a year.
- The top fifteen corporation CEOs in the United States averaged $50 million in stock compensation last year.
- The average yearly income for U.S. teenagers is $2000.

Since calculating the mean uses simple arithmetic (adding and dividing), it is normally the first kind of average that we are taught in school. (In fact, it is also referred to as the *arithmetical mean*.) As we saw in the slide example, the *mean* can be psychologically misleading, even when it is perfectly accurate. If you, too, felt misled, you can appreciate how easily statistics can be used to manipulate our ideas. For most people, "average" easily calls up an *image* rather than data. And the image that you have of a

Mean A statistical average that is determined by adding the numerical values in the data concerning the examined objects, then dividing by the number of objects that were measured.

45-year-old depends partly on your own age. A teenager's conception of someone who is 45 will surely differ from the perspective of a person who really is 45. People around 85 years of age will probably envision someone who is 45 as quite young. Very young children may not have a clear picture of a 45-year-old at all.

To see this more fully, imagine that your teacher promises another slide, and it, too, will have eleven people whose average age is 45. At this point, you might try to avoid picturing in your mind what the people will look like, since your first guess was way off the mark. As soon as the slide appears, however, you see that all of the people look around the same age and not unlike your parents. Your teacher lists the ages of the people in the new picture:

The Ages of the Eleven People in the Second Slide

41	46
42	47
43	47
43	47
44	47
	48

To calculate the mean of this second set of values, we once again add all eleven ages, and once again the result is 495. We now divide 495 by the total number of people to get $495 \div 11 = 45$. Sure enough, the mean age of the eleven people in the second slide is 45. As far as this one "average" is concerned, there is no difference between the two sets of people on the two slides. Of course, there is still a great gap between the ages of the younger and older people in the first slide, while the people in the second slide differ very little in age. That is why knowing the *mean* can tell us only so much.

Fortunately, additional kinds of *average* can add to our understanding of the data. The **median**, for one, is determined by locating the value that breaks the entire set of data in half. In other words, 50% of the data is above the median, and 50% is below it. For the people in the first slide, the *median* age is 76. Exactly five values are smaller than 76 (5, 5, 4, 3, 2), and exactly five values are greater than 76 (77, 78, 79, 80, 86). In contrast, for the people in the second slide, the *median* age is 46. You can easily check for yourself that half the values are smaller than 46 (41, 42, 43, 43, 44), and half are larger (47, 47, 47, 47, 48).

Let's put what we know about the ages of the two sets of people together:

Slide 1: Mean = 45; Median = 76
Slide 2: Mean = 45; Median = 46

Having information about the median age often greatly expands our understanding. To see why, suppose you discuss what happened in class with your roommates later that night. If you give them only the *mean* age (45), then they would have no way to differentiate between the two groups of people. However, let's see what happens when you provide them with the *median* age of the groups. Since the median age is 76 for the people on slide 1, half are older than 76 and half younger than 76. Thus, the younger people must be very young in order for the mean age to be 45. Although your

Median A statistical average that is determined by locating the value that separates the entire set of data in half.

roommates would not know the exact ages of the eleven people involved, they can correctly infer that the slide includes children.

However, the results for slide 2 are not as informative. If you tell your roommates that the mean is 45 and the median is 46, then what can they conclude? Remember, they did not see the slides, and you did not tell them what you saw. Can they conclude that all the people are in their 40s? No, they could not do this. The ages might be clustered in the 40s, or they might instead be more like the ages in the first slide—sharply divided between older people and children. Take the following set of numbers:

1, 2, 3, 4, 5, 46, 84, 86, 87, 88, 89

Here, the numbers again total 495, and the *mean* is again 495 ÷ 11 = 45. But what about the median age? Well, since there are exactly five values smaller than 46 (1, 2, 3, 4, 5) and exactly five values larger than 46 (84, 86, 87, 88, 89), the median is exactly the same as for slide 2.

For an odd number of items like these, it is easy to find the median; you simply find the number in the middle of the set. However, an even number of items requires two more quick steps. Suppose a data set consists of these six numbers:

8, 11, 17, 33, 36, 40

The first step is to locate the *two values* that together make up the middle of the set. Here 17 and 33 make up the middle, because there are two values to the left of them (8, 11) and two to the right (36, 40). The second step is to *add* the two middle values; in this case we get 17 + 33 = 50. The final step is to *divide* this number by two (the number of items we added together). The result is 50 ÷ 2 = 25. Hence, the median for these six numbers is 25. (For practice, how does the median compare to the mean for those six numbers?)

There is one more type of average that you should know. The **mode** is the value that occurs most. For example, for slide 1 the mode is 5, because that value occurs twice and no other value occurs more than once. For slide 2 the mode is 47, because it occurs four times (43 occurs twice, but this time it is not the mode).

If two values have the same number of instances, then we call the data *bimodal*, like this set:

4, 6, 10, 10, 22, 35, 35, 56

The numbers 10 and 35 each occur twice, and all the other values occur only once. In much the same way, if three different values occur the most, the set is *trimodal*. Let's look at all three measures of average age for the two slides:

Slide 1: Mean = 45; Median = 76; Mode = 5
Slide 2: Mean = 45; Median = 46; Mode = 47

Once again, let's see how the new information regarding the *mode* affects your roommates' understanding. (Remember: They do not have access to the slides or to the actual ages for each group.) Your roommates were able to infer from the mean and median that group 1 had five very young children; in fact, from the mode, they can

Mode A statistical average that is determined by locating the value that occurs most.

infer that *at least two* are 5 years old. However, your roommates could not infer very much before about group 2. Now, thanks to the mode, they know that *at least two* are 47 years old. They can begin to suspect that the ages are somewhat close together.

Unfortunately, they cannot know just *how* close. Knowing the mean, median, and mode still often gives a limited picture. To understand the *amount of diversity* within a group, we need a more powerful statistical tool, as we will see in the next section.

EXERCISES 13B

Level 1 Multiple-
Choice Questions

Level 2 Multiple-
Choice Questions

I. Determine the *mean*, *median*, and *mode* for the following sets of values:

1. [2, 3, 4, 4, 8, 10]
Answer: Mean: 5.17; Median: 4; Mode: 4

2. [3, 5, 7, 9, 11, 11, 11]

3. [1, 2, 3, 3, 5, 7, 11, 13, 13]

4. [10, 20, 30, 40]

5. [100, 110, 200, 200, 210, 300]

II. Determine the *mean*, *median*, and *mode* for the following sets of incomes:

1. [$6,000, $42,000, $42,000, $120,000]
Answer: Mean: $52,500; Median: $42,000; Mode: $42,000

2. [$100,000, $100,000, $100,000, $3 million, $5 million]

3. [$10, $10, $10, $10]

4. [$7, $77, $777, $7777]

5. [50 cents, $1, $1000, $1000, $4000]

Video Tutorial

III. Determine the *mean*, *median*, and *mode* for the following sets of grade point averages (GPAs):

1. [2.14, 2.49, 3.26, 3.26, 3.78, 3.99]
Answer: Mean: 3.15; Median: 3.26; Mode: 3.26

2. [1.88, 2.03, 2.56, 2.89, 3.64, 3.89]

3. [3.25, 3.25, 3.25, 3.75, 3.75]

4. [1.00, 2.00, 3.00, 4.00]

5. [2.86, 2.96, 3.16, 3.16, 3.26, 3.36]

IV. Determine the *mean*, *median*, and *mode* for the following sets of heights (in inches):

1. $[37", 45", 48", 67", 67", 78", 86"]$

Answer: Mean: 61.14"; Median: 67"; Mode: 67"

2. $[38", 40", 44", 45", 49", 52"]$

3. $[23", 27", 27", 27", 29", 29"]$

4. $[30", 31", 32", 33", 34", 35", 36"]$

5. $[24", 27", 28", 74", 74", 80", 80"]$

C. STANDARD DEVIATION

The **standard deviation** is a measure of the *amount of diversity* in a set of numerical values. Consider a bell-shaped, or *normal*, curve. Although the numerical values are spread throughout the curve, the majority of the values are clustered around the *mean*:

Standard deviation A measure of the amount of diversity in a set of numerical values.

A Bell Curve

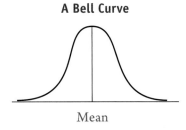

Mean

We call that spread or clustering the *distribution*. Let's see how to interpret the standard deviation to understand that distribution for a normal curve.

Dividing the Curve

As you can see, an equal number of values are found on both sides of the mean; this gives the curve its bell shape. Statisticians have developed a way of dividing the area under the curve into equal parts:

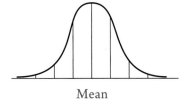

Mean

The areas to the *right* of the mean represent values that are *larger* than the mean, and the areas to the *left* represent values that are *smaller* than the mean. Each of the areas constitutes one standard deviation from the mean. Thus, the area directly to the right of the mean is designated as +1 SD (standard deviation), the next area to the right is +2 SD, and the third area is +3 SD. Similarly, the area directly to the left of the mean is designated as −1 SD, the next area to the left is −2 SD, and the third area is −3 SD:

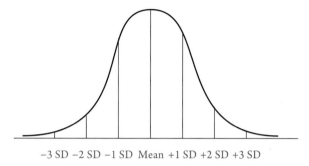

−3 SD −2 SD −1 SD Mean +1 SD +2 SD +3 SD

If you look closely, you can observe that the area from +1 SD to −1 SD makes up the largest portion of the bell curve. In fact, this area contains approximately 68% of all the data. This means that approximately 34% of the data is in the +1 SD area, and approximately 34% is in the −1 SD area. The next two areas, +2 SD and −2 SD, each contain approximately 13.5% of the data, for a total of 27%. Therefore, the four areas from +2 SD to −2 SD contain approximately 95% of all the data. The +3 SD and the −3 SD areas each contain approximately 2.3% of the data, for a total of 4.6%. The grand total of all six areas is *approximately* 99.6%. The remaining 0.4% lie at the extreme ends:

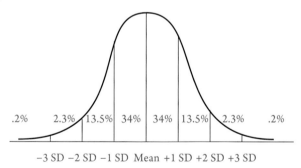

.2%   2.3% 13.5% 34%   34% 13.5% 2.3%   .2%

−3 SD −2 SD −1 SD Mean +1 SD +2 SD +3 SD

Apparently, a bell curve has few values indeed at the extremes. We can see this easily by adding color, to illustrate the total area captured by each SD:

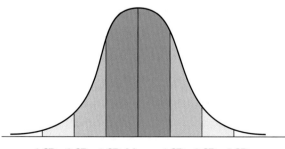

−3 SD −2 SD −1 SD Mean +1 SD +2 SD +3 SD

The two dark areas contain the data for +1 SD and −1 SD; the next two areas contain the data for +2 SD and −2 SD; the next two areas contain the data for +3 SD and −3 SD; and the two small areas at each end of the curve contain the fewest members—the extreme limits.

The Size of the Standard Deviation

Another way to look at the diversity is to ask how far from the mean we need to go to get a given percentage of the values. For example, you take a test for which the possible scores range anywhere from 0 to 100 (in whole numbers). You learn later that a graph of the scores takes the form of a normal curve, so the scores are spread equally on both sides of the mean. Let's imagine that the mean score was 50. You would then know that approximately 34% of the scores were within +1 SD from the mean, and approximately 34% of the scores were within −1 SD from the mean. Therefore, approximately 68% of all the scores fell within these two areas. *But how far from the mean do we have to go to get that 68%?*

The answer lies in the *size* of the standard deviation—in our picture, the width of each vertical slice in the bell curve. Suppose you are told that the standard deviation was 15 points. This tells us how far we have to go from the mean to get each area of the curve. *The larger the size of the standard deviation, the larger the diversity; the smaller the size of the standard deviation, the smaller the diversity.*

In our example, the mean was 50, and to get the value for +1 SD, you simply *add* 15 points to the mean: 50 + 15 = 65. To get the value for −1 SD you must *subtract* 15 points from the mean: 50 − 15 = 35. Therefore, approximately 68% of the scores fell within the range of 35–65.

The range of scores in the next two areas is calculated in much the same way. Since the standard deviation is 15, to get +2 SD means that we have to go 15 × 2 = 30 points away from the mean. This time, you *add* 30 to the mean: 50 + 30 = 80. To get the value for −2 SD you must *subtract* 30 points from the mean: 50 − 30 = 20. Therefore, approximately 95% of the scores fell within the range of 20–80.

What about the range of scores in the 3 SD range? To get +3 SD, we have to go 15 × 3 = 45 points away from the mean: 50 + 45 = 95. To get −3 SD, we have to subtract 45 points from the mean: 50 − 45 = 5. We now know that approximately 99.6% of the scores fell within the range of 5–95. If you scored 100, you were very special.

Let's compare these results with another example. Suppose the same test is given to another class. A graph of the scores once again takes the form of a normal curve, with a mean of 50. But now suppose that the standard deviation for the second group was 3. Since *the smaller the size of the standard deviation, the smaller the diversity,* you can immediately infer that the second class has very little difference in its scores. In that group, you would have been very special if you had come even close to 100.

We can calculate the SD ranges to verify our inference. To get the value for +1 SD, you *add* 3 to the mean: 50 + 3 = 53. To get the value for −1 SD, you *subtract* 3 points from the mean: 50 − 3 = 47. Therefore, approximately 68% of the scores fell within the range of 47–53. This means that 68% of the scores were separated by only 6 points (47–53). Compare this to your own class, in which 68% of the scores were separated by 30 points (35–65).

The range of scores in the next two areas is easily calculated. To get the value for +2 SD, you *add* 6 to the mean: $50 + 6 = 56$. To get the value for −2 SD, you *subtract* 6 points from the mean: $50 - 6 = 44$. Therefore, approximately 95% of the scores fell within the range of 44–56. This means that 95% of the scores were separated by only 12 points (44–56). In contrast, in your class, 95% of the scores were separated by 60 points (20–80).

Finally, let's determine the range of scores in the 3 SD area. To get the value for +3 SD, you *add* 9 to the mean: $50 + 9 = 59$. To get the value for −3, SD you *subtract* 9 points from the mean: $50 - 9 = 41$. Therefore, approximately 99.6% of the scores fell within the range of 41–59. This means that 99.6% of the scores were separated by only 18 points (41–59). Again, compare this to your class, in which 99.6% of the scores were separated by 90 points (5–95).

The graph of the second group is a normal curve, but its shape has to reflect its lack of diversity. It must show that scores are relatively close to the mean. That means the curve is very narrow, *because the size of the deviation is small*:

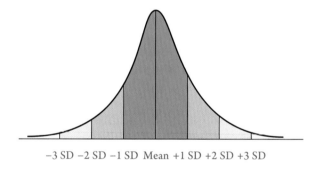

−3 SD −2 SD −1 SD Mean +1 SD +2 SD +3 SD

Since the range of scores for each SD was quite small, the sides of the curve slope down very sharply from the top—once again indicating the small diversity in the group.

How to Calculate the Standard Deviation

In real-life research, the amount of data can be enormous, but computers can do the calculations quickly, efficiently, and with little chance of error. (Handheld calculators programmed to do statistical calculations can handle smaller data sets.) Still, finding the standard deviation has just six steps. Let's do a simple calculation ourselves to see how it works. We will use the following small set of values as our reference.

[1, 3, 8, 17, 22, 33, 42]

STEP 1: Calculate the mean value. The sum of the seven numbers in our set is 126. We divide this by the number of items in the set to get the mean: $126 \div 7 = 18$.

STEP 2: Calculate the difference between each value in the set and the mean value. A value that is smaller than the mean will result in a negative difference; a value greater than the mean will result in a positive difference; a value that is identical to the mean will result in a 0. Here are the results for our set (the boldface numbers are the values in our data set):

1 $- 18 = -17$	**17** $- 18 = -1$	**42** $- 18 = 24$
3 $- 18 = -15$	**22** $- 18 = 4$	
8 $- 18 = -10$	**33** $- 18 = 15$	

STEP 3: Multiply each difference by itself. This means that we are *squaring the differences.*

Why is squaring necessary to get the amount of variation? Why not just add the differences? To see why, take a worst-case scenario. Suppose that there were only four values in a set of data, and the mean was 20. If the values of the four members of the set were 18, 19, 21, and 22, then the differences would be −2, −1, 1, and 2. Adding these four numbers gives us a result of 0—but there is some small variation nonetheless. To get a meaningful result, we must change a negative value into a positive value by squaring, so all the results will be positive numbers.

In our problem, squaring the differences (−17, −15, −10, −1, 4, 15, 24) gives 289, 225, 100, 1, 16, 225, and 576.

STEP 4: Add the results of the squaring process in step 3. The sum of the seven numbers (289, 225, 100, 1, 16, 225, 576) is 1432.

STEP 5: Divide the result of step 4 by *one fewer* than the number of members in the set. This gives us the following result: $1432 \div 6 = 238.7$. This result is called the *total variance.*

STEP 6: The square root of the total variance is the standard deviation. The square root of 238.7 is 15.4. Therefore, the set of values [1, 3, 8, 17, 22, 33, 42] has a standard deviation of 15.4.

THE SIX STEPS TO THE STANDARD DEVIATION

Step 1: Calculate the mean value.
Step 2: Calculate the difference between each value in the set and the mean value.
Step 3: Multiply each difference by itself (square each difference).
Step 4: Add the results of the squaring process in step 3.
Step 5: Divide the result of step 4 by one fewer than the number of members in the set.
Step 6: The square root of the total variance is the standard deviation.

EXERCISES 13C

Level 1 Multiple-
Choice Questions

Level 2 Multiple-
Choice Questions

Video Tutorial

Since you have already calculated the mean value of each set of data in Exercises 13B, you have already finished step 1 of calculating the standard deviation. Now perform steps 2–6 and determine the standard deviation for each set of data. Refer back to Exercises 13B for the exercises. The first exercise and a solution are provided here:

1. $[2, 3, 4, 4, 8, 10]$

Answer: The standard deviation is 3.13.

Step 1: 5.17

Step 2: $2 - 5.17 = -3.17$ $4 - 5.17 = -1.17$

$3 - 5.17 = -2.17$ $8 - 5.17 = 2.83$

$4 - 5.17 = -1.17$ $10 - 5.17 = 4.83$

Step 3: 10.05; 4.71; 1.37; 1.37; 8.01; 23.33

Step 4: 48.84

Step 5: 9.77

Step 6: 3.13

D. WHAT IF THE RESULTS ARE SKEWED?

So far we have looked at normal curves. While real-life data do not always fit perfectly bell-shaped curves, the same basic principles apply in calculating the standard deviation. The problem lies in interpreting and applying the unexpected results.

Many measurements involve "objective" criteria for some "naturally occurring" phenomenon. For example, you can measure the height of every student in class and determine the mean, median, mode, and standard deviation. A ruler or tape measure is equally objective, whether it is in inches or centimeters. But not all measuring devices are objective—especially when it comes to human capabilities. For example, many people have challenged whether I.Q. exams truly measure intelligence. Perhaps intelligence is not even quantifiable or not just one simple thing. For many children, the results of some verbal and mathematical I.Q. exams give substantially different results from tests that do not rely on the same verbal skills.

At least some physical skills lend themselves to objective measurement. For example, we can measure the amount of time it takes each class member to run 100 yards, to swim 50 meters, or to throw a baseball. We can measure how much weight each student can lift, or even many types of hand and finger dexterity. We can then determine the amount of variation.

However, when it comes to nonphysical skills, things can get more difficult. Teachers try very hard to create tests that will accurately determine the level of understanding. But we all know from experience that something can go very wrong. For example, suppose a teacher decides on the following scale for determining grades on an upcoming exam:

A: 90–100
B: 80–89
C: 70–79
D: 60–69
F: 0–59

After the exam, the teacher calculates the mean and the standard deviation. Here is one possible distribution of grades:

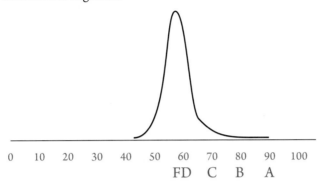

The mean appears to be around 58, and we can see that most of the class got an F. Only a very small percentage of the class received an A, B, or C grade. (F and D are right next to each other at the bottom of the graph, because 59 starts the F range and 60 is the lowest possible score for a D.)

If the class results reflected a normal curve, the *mean* would instead be somewhere over the C range. There would then be a smaller number of D and B grades, followed by an even smaller number of F and A grades. The actual results lean far to the left of what we had anticipated, and they are said to be *skewed*. How should we understand the outcome? On one hand, the students might interpret the graph to mean that the exam was *too hard*. On the other hand, the teacher might conclude that the class had not prepared adequately for the exam. Either way, the teacher might decide to *curve* the results of the exam by simply sliding the existing curve to the right:

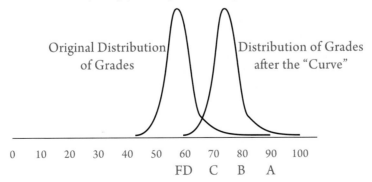

This places the mean over the C range. The teacher can then adjust the original grading scale to get an appropriate number of A, B, D, and F grades.

What if, however, the results of the exam had produced this graph?

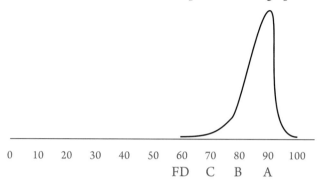

Here the mean appears to be around 91, and we can see that most of the class got an A. Only a very small percentage received an F, D, or C. If we expected a normal curve, we instead find a curve that is *skewed* far to the right. On one hand, the students might explain the results as the outcome of their having studied diligently for the exam. On the other hand, the teacher might conclude that the test was *too easy*. This time, the teacher might decide to curve the results by sliding the existing curve to the left:

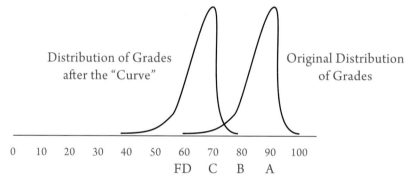

This movement of the curve places the mean over the C range. The teacher can then easily adjust the original grading scale to get an appropriate number of A, B, D, and F grades.

As you can see, data analysis often leads to new questions—and disagreement about the answers. In our two examples, did the original results accurately measure what the class knew? Have the new curves produced more accurate pictures? How can we best decide?

These kinds of questions need to be asked and debated whenever we have to interpret complex statistical data. Social policy, such as federal funding for early childhood education, often depends on the results of statistical studies. For some administrations, statistical data justified an increase in the amount of money for preschools. Other administrations have used statistical data to justify a decrease in the amount of money available. They relied on different data as well as different interpretations of that data.

E. THE MISUSE OF STATISTICS

Statistics can mislead us either intentionally or unintentionally. Statements containing quantitative terms are often interpreted differently than those containing qualitative terms. For example:

1. The latest album by the Green Biscuits is number one in sales this year.
2. The latest album by the Green Biscuits is the best album this year.

Most people would accept statement 1 at face value because they assume that the statistics were compiled objectively and accurately. However, the word "best" in statement 2 is vague. Even when an album wins awards people often argue about the subjective nature of the voting process.

As explained in Chapter 4, the fallacy of misleading precision occurs when a claim appears to be statistically significant but is not. Statistics can be accurate, but they can also be easily misinterpreted. For example, suppose you read the following:

> Since we began advertising on the Internet, sales of our Premium Widgets have increased 400% over the first quarter. Stock options will be offered only for a limited time, so this might be your best chance to invest in our growing company.

Put your checkbook away. More information is needed to evaluate the claim. For example, suppose we find that the company sold a total of two Premium Widgets during the first quarter (at $10 each), and the company lost a million dollars. A 400% increase in sales means that they sold eight Premium Widgets during the second quarter (for a whopping $80 in sales), and they still lost a lot of money. The statistics are accurate, but if you misinterpret the information, then you might make a bad investment.

Statistics can mislead in other ways as well. In the article "Skipping Breakfast and Heart Disease: Not So Simple," author Madelyn Fernstrom raises some important questions concerning a large research study. The researchers examined surveys designed to estimate food intake of 26,902 male health professionals from 1992 to 2008 (16 years). At the start of the surveys, the subjects were between 45 and 82 years old.

The researchers determined that men who skipped breakfast had a 27% higher risk of heart attack or death from coronary heart disease than those who ate breakfast. After reading this statistic, it may be tempting to conclude two things: (1) Males who regularly skip breakfast are increasing their risk of heart disease, and (2) eating breakfast can lower the risk of heart disease in males. But before we accept these conclusions we should carefully analyze the information in the study.

Several key problems stand out that reduce the generalizability of the findings:

- The study used only male subjects who were health professionals.
  Weakness: This is not representative of all occupations.

- The subjects were between 45 and 82 years old.
  Weakness: This is not representative of all age categories.

- Only 3400 of the more than 26,000 were self-reported breakfast skippers.
  Weakness: Only approximately 13% of the subjects were self-reported breakfast skippers.

- The subjects were asked only once, at the start of the study, if they were breakfast eaters.
  Weakness: It assumes that the subjects' eating habits did not change over the 16-year study period.

As Fernstrom correctly points out, "It's important to note that simply grabbing breakfast—any breakfast at all, even if it's something unhealthy like a doughnut—is not enough to protect your heart health." In addition, breakfast may be one factor in maintaining a healthy heart, but there are many others of equal importance, such as exercise, smoking, alcohol intake, and the kinds of food eaten, to name only a few. Fernstrom adds, "The important health message is that it's not just when you eat, but *what* you eat.... Grabbing a high calorie, low nutrient breakfast, on the other hand, is not a health plus."

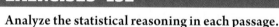

EXERCISES 13E

Level 1 Multiple-
Choice Questions

Level 2 Multiple-
Choice Questions

Analyze the statistical reasoning in each passage.

1. In general, however, the financial odds still greatly favor a person with a college degree. The Bureau of Labor Statistics estimates that median weekly earnings for a person with a bachelor's degree was $1,025 in 2009, compared with just $626 for those with only a high school diploma.

    Allison Linn, "Is It Worth It to Go to College?"

Answer:

Since the Bureau of Labor Statistics has access to large amounts of data, we can assume that the size of the data set is adequate. The *median* weekly income for persons with a bachelor's degree was $1025 (in 2009); therefore we know that 50% of that data set made more than that amount and 50% made less. For those with only a high school diploma, 50% of that data set made more than $626 a week and 50% made less.

On the surface, the difference between $1025 and $626 is substantial. However, we are not told either the *mean* or the *standard deviation* in the two sets of data. Without that information, we cannot determine the amount of diversity in the sets. In addition, people with bachelor's degrees in engineering and computer science average three to four times the yearly salary of many social science majors. The article does not distinguish between majors. It therefore may misleadingly suggest that any kind of bachelor's degree puts you in a position to make substantially more than a person with only a high school diploma.

2. A study finds that Best Actress Oscar winners have a 63% chance of their marriages ending sooner than nonwinners. The median marriage duration was 4.30 years; 9.51 for nonwinners.   Ken McGuffin, "The Oscar Curse?"

3. Reuters Legal compiled a tally of reported decisions in which judges granted a new trial, denied a request for a new trial, or overturned a verdict, in whole or in part, because of juror actions related to the Internet. The data show that since 1999 at least 90 verdicts have been the subject of challenges, because of alleged Internet-related juror misconduct. More than half of the cases occurred in the last two years. Judges granted new trials or overturned verdicts in 28 criminal and civil cases—21 since January 2009. In three-quarters of the cases in which judges declined to declare mistrials, they nevertheless found Internet-related misconduct on the part of jurors. These figures do not include the many incidents that escape judicial notice.   "As Jurors Go Online, U.S. Trials Go Off Track," Reuters

Video Tutorial

4. Alberto Contador might face a one-year doping suspension and be stripped of his 2010 Tour de France title. . . . Contador, whose sample contained 50 picograms (trillionths of a gram) of a banned substance, is being diagnosed as a little bit pregnant in a context where there shouldn't be any ambiguity. When Contador offered the explanation that he had consumed tainted beef purchased in Spain, . . . statistics about Clenbuterol contamination in the food and water supply were debated. One authority didn't swallow the steak story. Christiane Ayotte, longtime director of the WADA-accredited lab in Montreal, was blunt with reporters in an informal media briefing in mid-October. "You'll never find a ton of [Clenbuterol] because the doses are really small," Ayotte said then, calling the beef excuse implausible. "Most of the samples are below 1 nanogram—a billionth of a gram."   Bonnie D. Ford, "Why Contador Case Sets Bad Precedent"

⭐ 5. It's possible to see procrastination as the quintessential modern problem. It's also a surprisingly costly one. Each year, Americans waste hundreds of millions of dollars because they don't file their taxes on time. The Harvard economist David Laibson has shown that American workers have forgone huge amounts of money in matching 401(k) contributions because they never got around to signing up for a retirement plan. Seventy percent of patients suffering from glaucoma risk blindness because they don't use their eyedrops regularly. Procrastination also inflicts major costs on businesses and governments. The recent crisis of the euro was exacerbated by the German government's dithering, and the decline of the American auto industry, exemplified by the bankruptcy of General Motors was due in part to executives' penchant for delaying tough decisions.
          James Surowiecki, "Later: What Does Procrastination Tell Us About Ourselves?"

6. Another argument for Zenyatta is that she brought more mainstream coverage to the Sport. . . . The numbers simply do not support that. In 2004, Smarty Jones was attempting to join Seattle Slew as the only undefeated Triple Crown winners in history; a record crowd of 120,139 showed up to see his Belmont. Compare that to the 72,739 who came to Churchill Downs on Nov. 6 to see if Zenyatta would retire undefeated. . . . A search of news archives shows far more was written about Smarty Jones throughout the course of 2004 than Zenyatta in 2010: 7,350 articles for Smarty Jones; 2,260 articles for Zenyatta.

    Amanda Duckworth, "Facts vs. Feelings"

7. There's been a lot of misinformation thrown around during Michigan's rather hastily arranged price tag debate. The governor cited research offered up by a group called the Coalition for Retail Pricing Modernization saying price tag application cost Michigan stores $2.2 billion annually. The governor cited the cost as a cause of Michigan's downtrodden economy. The questionable research extrapolates from a 2007 economics paper, which found that prices in an area of New York that then required price tags were about 10 percent higher than stores in nearby New Jersey, which didn't. It ignored other factors which make New York stores pricier. Then, the group calculated 10 percent of Michigan store sales to arrive at the $2.2 billion. The back-of-the-envelope calculation was cited by the governor in his arguments, but derided by consumer advocates. "The true cost of placing price stickers on Michigan groceries is a small fraction of $2 billion," said Edgar Dworsky.

    Bob Sullivan, "Another Nail in the Coffin of Price Tags"

Summary

Study Materials

- Evaluating arguments that rely on statistical evidence requires that we can correctly interpret the statistical evidence as it is presented.
- Population: Any group of objects, not just human populations.
- Sample: A subset of a population.
- Representative sample: A sample that accurately reflects the characteristics of the population as a whole.
- Random sample: A sample in which every member of the population has an equal chance of getting in.
- Mean: A statistical average that is determined by adding the numerical values in the data concerning the examined objects, then dividing by the number of objects that were measured.
- Median: A statistical average that is determined by locating the value that separates the entire set of data in half.
- Mode: A statistical average that is determined by locating the value that occurs most.
- Standard deviation: A measure of the amount of diversity in a set of numerical values.

- Probability calculations using the *a priori* theory rely on hypothetical reasoning based on two major assumptions. The first is that all the possible outcomes can be determined, and the second is that each of the possible outcomes has an equal probability of occurring (equiprobable).
- In the relative frequency theory, some probabilities can be computed by dividing the number of favorable cases by the total number of observed cases.
- Reliance on statistical, historical data is not the same as relative frequency applications. Calculations of this kind fall under the subjective theory of probability, where determinations are based on the lack of total knowledge regarding an event.
- Probability calculus: The rules for calculating the probability of compound events from the probability of simple events. The results can be displayed as fractions, percentages, ratios, or a decimal between 0 and 1.
- The restricted conjunction method is used in situations dealing with two or more independent events, where the occurrence of one event has no bearing whatsoever on the occurrence or nonoccurrence of the other event.
- The general conjunction method is used for calculating the probability of two or more events occurring together, regardless of whether the events are independent.
- Conditional probability: The calculation of the probability that one event will occur given the knowledge that another event has already occurred. For example, *Pr (B, if A)* is read as the *probability of B given A*.
- The restricted disjunction method is used to calculate the probability when two (or more) events are independent of each other, and the events are mutually exclusive (if one event occurs, then the other cannot).
- The general disjunction method is used for calculating the probability of occurrence of two or more events that are not mutually exclusive.
- The negation method is used once the probability of an event occurring is known; it is then easy to calculate the probability of the event not occurring.

KEY TERMS

LOGIC CHALLENGE: THE SECOND CHILD

You are at a playground and happen to strike up a conversation with a stranger. You are told that he is there to watch his daughter play basketball. When you ask if he has any other children, he tells you that he has one more child. What is the probability that the second child is a female?

Chapter 14

Causality and Scientific Arguments

A. *Sufficient and Necessary Conditions*
B. *Causality*
C. *Mill's Methods*
D. *Limitations of Mill's Methods*
E. *Theoretical and Experimental Science*
F. *Inference to the Best Explanation*
G. *Hypothesis Testing, Experiments, and Predictions*
H. *Science and Superstition*

Medical research has uncovered the cause of many diseases and how to treat them. In fact, the news is filled with the latest discoveries—but not all the claims you meet are unambiguous or true. Here are some items that you might have come across:

> Electronic cigarettes, which are increasingly used worldwide, are said to be unsafe and pose health risks, a new study suggests.
>
> "Electronic Cigarettes Pose Health Risks," Bernama.com

> It might be the potlucks, it might be those long hours sitting in pews, but whatever the cause, a new study presented this week shows a link between religious activity and weight gain.
>
> Diane Mapes, "Praise the Lard? Religion Linked to Obesity in Young Adults," Msnbc.com

> Girls, but not boys, who walk or bike to school instead of getting a ride perform better in tests of verbal and math skills, according to a new study of teens living in Spanish cities. And the longer the commute, the higher the test scores. "Girls Who Walk, Bike to School Do Better in Tests," Reuters

> A new report from British scientists suggests that long-term, low-dose aspirin use may modestly reduce the risk of dying of certain cancers, though experts warn the study isn't strong enough to recommend healthy people start taking a pill that can cause bleeding and other problems.
>
> "Aspirin May Cut Cancer Deaths, but Caution Urged," Associated Press

The search for causes is a large part of science, medicine, as well as everyday life. Cause-effect relationships are at the heart of physics, chemistry, biology, and many other fields. In everyday life you might look for reasons as to why your car is stalling in traffic, why your computer suddenly stopped working, or why your stomach is aching. We begin by discussing cause-effect relationships. We will see how John

Stuart Mill developed basic principles of causality and scientific investigation. The rest of the chapter will focus on scientific theories and hypotheses, how they are tested in experiments, how they differ from superstition—and why they provide the best, and generally most reliable, way to understand the physical world.

A. SUFFICIENT AND NECESSARY CONDITIONS

The word "cause" has several meanings, and in everyday situations the possibility of ambiguity arises. For example, parents often tell their children that they must take vitamins because vitamins will help them grow. The claim is not that vitamins alone will cause children to grow; it is that vitamins are a *necessary condition* for children's growth. In another situation a child might complain of a stomachache. The parent could suggest that the child stop drinking so much soda. Of course, the parent could also give the child some medicine to ease the pain. The parent relies on an understanding that several methods of reducing or eliminating the stomachache are possible. In other words, the parent is offering a *sufficient condition* to bring about a desired effect. A basic knowledge of sufficient and necessary conditions can help in the overall understanding of scientific arguments. To begin our discussion, consider this statement:

If you live in New Jersey, then you live in the United States.

Sufficient condition
Whenever one event ensures that another event is realized.

A **sufficient condition** occurs whenever one event ensures that another event is realized. Another way of saying that something is a sufficient condition is to think of the phrases "is enough for" or "it guarantees." In the foregoing statement, living in New Jersey is *sufficient* for living in the United States. Of course, if you live in any of the other forty-nine states, then you also live in the United States. Nevertheless, living in New Jersey is sufficient (is enough) to guarantee that you live in the United States.

Necessary condition
Whenever one thing is *essential, mandatory,* or *required* in order for another thing to be realized.

On the other hand, a **necessary condition** means that one thing is *essential, mandatory,* or *required* in order for another thing to be realized. Given this, in the foregoing statement, living in the United States is necessary for living in New Jersey. In other words, if you *do not* live in the United States, then you *do not* live in New Jersey.

These ideas can also be expressed in the following ways:

Sufficient condition: If you live in New Jersey, then you live in the United States.

Necessary condition: If you do not live in the United States, then you do not live in New Jersey.

Here are some more examples of sufficient and necessary conditions:

Sufficient condition: If you have a gerbil for a pet, then you have an animal for a pet.

Necessary condition: If you do not have an animal for a pet, then you do not have a gerbil for a pet.

Sufficient condition: If there is a fire in the room, then there is oxygen in the room.

Necessary condition: If there is no oxygen in the room, then there is not a fire in the room.

There are instances where *both* sufficient and necessary conditions are present. For example, the ideal gas law holds that as the pressure of a gas rises (or falls), so does its temperature. In other words, the rising (or falling) pressure is both a sufficient and a necessary condition for the rising (or falling) temperature of the gas. Here is another example:

A. If today is Friday, then tomorrow is Saturday.
B. If today is not Friday, then tomorrow is not Saturday.

Upon analysis, we see that today's being Friday is *both* sufficient and necessary for tomorrow being Saturday. The days of the week follow each other in a standard, accepted, and stipulated pattern. Therefore, if today is Friday, then of course tomorrow must be Saturday. In addition, if today is not Friday, then tomorrow cannot possibly be Saturday.

Let's analyze two more statements:

C. If today is Friday, then I am six feet tall.
D. If today is not Friday, then I am not six feet tall.

Upon analysis we see that today's being Friday is *neither* sufficient *nor* necessary for my being six feet tall. These results should not be surprising if we look at the relationship between the things talked about in C and D. There is no connection between the two that would make the truth or falsity of one somehow dependent on the other.

Let's examine a situation that has several sufficient and necessary ingredients. Universities and colleges have specific requirements that must be met in order to get a bachelor's degree, so let's consider a hypothetical situation where the following four requirements need to be fulfilled:

1. A recognized major
2. A recognized minor (must be different from the major)
3. An overall grade point average (GPA) of at least 2.00
4. A passing grade in at least 125 credits

Furthermore, the university stipulates that each of these four requirements is *necessary* (you cannot get a bachelor's degree unless you fulfill all four requirements). The university also lists the options that are available to satisfy each of the four requirements. For example, the university lists twenty recognized majors, such as psychology, history, physics, economics, and English. Therefore, majoring in psychology is sufficient to fulfill requirement 1. The university also lists the recognized minors (we can use the same list as the majors for our purposes). Therefore, minoring in history is sufficient to fulfill requirement 2. An overall GPA of 2.75 (or higher) is sufficient to fulfill requirement 3. Finally, a total of 128 credits with a passing grade is sufficient to fulfill requirement 4. This combination of fulfilled requirements is referred to as a *set of necessary and sufficient conditions* (in this example, to get a bachelor's degree). The following diagram provides an illustration of the relationship between the sufficient and necessary conditions in this example:

Sufficient Conditions	Psychology	Psychology	2.00	125	
	History	History	2.50	126	
	Physics	Physics	3.23	130	
	Economics	Economics	3.40	132	
	(Etc.)	(Etc.)	(Etc.)	(Etc.)	
Necessary Conditions	Major +	Minor +	Minimum 2.00 GPA +	Minimum 125 credits =	Bachelor's degree

EXERCISES 14A

Level 1 Multiple-Choice Questions

Level 2 Multiple-Choice Questions

I. In each exercise, determine whether the intended *sufficient condition* does in fact guarantee that the other event is realized.

1. If Ed is a bachelor, then Ed is an adult male.

Answer: Sufficient condition. A bachelor is defined as being an unmarried adult male. Given this, if Ed is a bachelor, then Ed is an adult male.

2. If Ed is an adult male, then Ed is a bachelor.

3. If there is oxygen in the room, then there is a fire in the room.

4. If there is a fire in the room, then there is oxygen in the room.

★ 5. If this is the month of June, then this month has exactly 30 days.

6. If this month has exactly 30 days, then this is the month of June.

7. If I live in the White House, then I am the president of the United States.

8. If I am the president of the United States, then I live in the White House.

★ 9. If I have exactly 100 pennies, then I have at least the equivalent of $1.

10. If I have at least the equivalent of $1, then I have exactly 100 pennies.

11. If I am over 21 years of age, then I am over 10 years of age.

12. If I am over 10 years of age, then I am over 21 years of age.

★ 13. If I am eating a banana, then I am eating a fruit.

14. If I am eating a fruit, then I am eating a banana.

15. If I hurt a human, then I hurt a mammal.

16. If I hurt a mammal, then I hurt a human.

II. In each exercise, determine whether the intended *necessary condition* is in fact required in order for the other event to be realized.

1. If Ed is not an adult male, then Ed is not a bachelor.

Answer: Necessary condition. A bachelor is defined as being an unmarried adult male. Given this, if Ed is *not* an adult male, then Ed is *not* a bachelor.

2. If Ed is not a bachelor, then Ed is not an adult male.

3. If there is not a fire in the room, then there is not oxygen in the room.

4. If there is not oxygen in the room, then there is not a fire in the room.

★ 5. If this month does not have exactly 30 days, then this is not the month of June.

6. If this is not the month of June, then this month does not have exactly 30 days.

7. If I am not the president of the United States, then I do not live in the White House.

8. If I do not live in the White House, then I am not the president of the United States.

★ 9. If I do not have at least the equivalent of $1, then I do not have exactly 100 pennies.

10. If I do not have exactly 100 pennies, then I do not have at least the equivalent of $1.

11. If I am not over 10 years of age, then I am not over 21 years of age.

12. If I am not over 21 years of age, then I am not over 10 years of age.

★ 13. If I am not eating a fruit, then I am not eating a banana.

14. If I am not eating a banana, then I am not eating a fruit.

15. If I do not hurt a mammal, then I do not hurt a human.

16. If I do not hurt a human, then I do not hurt a mammal.

B. CAUSALITY

A *cause* is a set of conditions that bring about an effect. For example, imagine that a window in your house breaks. If we saw a rock hit the window, we probably would claim that the rock was *the cause* of the broken window. For practical purposes, for assigning blame perhaps, this is a normal claim to make. However, for a deeper understanding of causality, we need to consider some alternatives.

If we take the same rock and strike a similar window, we would expect to get similar results. That already tells us something about what we expect of a cause-effect relationship: *same cause, same effect*. However, if we throw the rock so that it barely grazes the window, then the window might not break. Alternatively, we could keep the rock the same and the angle at which it strikes the window the same, but change the velocity with which it strikes the window. In other words, we throw the rock more softly. Again, it might not break the window. The weight of the rock, the angle of incidence, and the velocity are all parts of the event, and all of them can vary. In a scientific experiment, they are the *variables*.

Causal network A set of conditions that bring about an effect.

What we originally called *the cause* (the rock) has evolved into a **causal network**, a *set of conditions* that bring about an effect. By changing the parts of the event, the variables, we can achieve different results. For example, by varying the velocity of the rock, or by varying the angle of incidence of the rock, or by using rocks of various densities, we can discover the set of conditions that are involved in cause-effect relationships. This holds for the window itself, which is surely part of the event. By conducting experiments, we can find the necessary range of glass density and strength needed to bring about a desired effect—if it is our house, to keep the window from breaking. However, we must be sure to eliminate factors that are *not* necessary for the effect to have happened, such as the time of day, the color of the window frame, or the color of the rock. This is how we establish the set of *necessary and sufficient conditions* that constitute the cause of the event in question.

Normal state The historical information regarding an object.

We single out the rock as the cause because we are able to establish the **normal state** of a system. If the window has been in an unbroken state for some time, then that is its normal state. As soon as it breaks, an **abnormal state** is established. Any change from the normal state requires explanation, typically a causal one.

Abnormal state A drastic change in the normal state regarding an object.

A **precipitating cause** is the object or event directly involved in bringing about an effect. In our example, it would be safe to call the rock the precipitating cause of the broken window. We then add to the precipitating cause the causal network in order to have a complete scientific explanation of the cause-effect relationship.

Precipitating cause The object or event directly involved in bringing about an effect.

On the other hand, a **remote cause** is something that is connected to the precipitating cause by a chain of events. We can trace the chain of events back in time depending on our needs. For example, we might not be interested in determining how the rock came to hit the window if we are scientists or engineers developing stronger windows. However, we may very much want to know the remote cause in order to assign blame and recover the cost of repairs. Let's imagine that some children had been playing baseball. Without thinking, and for no real reason other than curiosity and a dare from another player, the pitcher picked up a rock and tossed it at the batter. The batter hit the rock, which then hit the window. If we were interested in assigning blame for legal purposes, we could charge the batter, the pitcher, and perhaps the player who instigated the dare.

Remote cause Something that is connected to the precipitating cause by a chain of events.

A legal test to determine the cause of an event is not the same as a scientific one. For scientific purposes, to determine the *physical cause* of the broken window, we need consider only the precipitating cause and the causal network, not the remote causes. Of course, a trial often calls on scientific testimony. However, for legal purposes, the remote causes would probably be emphasized—in our example, the chain of events that led to the rock hitting the window. In a trial, too, we would have to show that we suffered a loss (the broken window). A scientific investigation would focus simply on what happened when the rock hit the window.

These same issues appear in other cases. If someone is found dead under suspicious circumstances, the police will probably have an autopsy performed. The medical expert performing the autopsy seeks the physical cause of death—the precipitating cause and its effects on the body. So far, there need be no legal or moral issues involved. However, if it is determined that death was by poison, then the police will have to investigate if it was self-administered or was left by someone else. They will also ask if the poison was administered accidentally or deliberately. If there is evidence of a crime, then the police and district attorney will look for the remote causes of the death.

C. MILL'S METHODS

Is there a best way to discover causes? And if we found the right method, would it be what we call science? Many scientists and philosophers have suggested what they thought would be the most efficient and reliable way to conduct experiments. John Stuart Mill proposed one influential program in his book *A System of Logic*. We will look at five methods of experimental inquiry (also called "canons," which means general principles) that are discussed in Mill's book. They are the *method of agreement*, the *method of difference*, the *joint method of agreement and difference*, the *method of residues*, and the *method of concomitant variations*. As you will see, Mill's principles are the basis for many of the causal inductive arguments people make in everyday life.

Method of Agreement

The **method of agreement** looks at two or more instances of an event to see what they have in common. For example, if four people eat at a restaurant, but only three get food poisoning, then the method of agreement tells us to investigate what the three instances have in common. We can create a chart to display the data:

Method of agreement
The method that looks at two or more instances of an event to see what they have in common.

Instances of the **Effect**	Possible Causes							
	Fish	Spaghetti	Ham	Bread	Appetizer	Soda	Beer	Wine
John: Food poisoning		√		√	√		√	
Robert: Food poisoning	√				√	√		
Christina: Food poisoning			√	√	√			√

The check marks indicate when a condition has been met. A blank space under an item indicates that a condition has not been met. For example, the chart indicates that John had the spaghetti, bread, appetizer, and beer. We also know from the chart that he did *not* have fish, ham, soda, or wine. We see that all three cases of food poisoning have just one thing in common: the appetizer. Therefore, of the eight conditions under investigation, the appetizer is the probable cause of the food poisoning.

Whenever a series of similar, but unexplained events occur, we are likely to wonder what they have in common. However, the method of agreement does not provide conclusive proof that we have found the cause. It can offer only partial, tentative inductive evidence. For example, the three people who came down with food poisoning might have had other features in common, and we simply overlooked them. All three victims might have had water (tap or bottled), or they might have grabbed a mint at the cash register before leaving. Maybe the three ate something even before going to the restaurant. Or perhaps their utensils were not washed properly.

The method of agreement may also run into trouble because it depends on how we decide to list things. Consider the possibility that two *different* items on our chart caused the food poisoning. For example, what if both the fish and the bread were contaminated, but not the appetizer? Could this explain why the three got sick? Since Robert ate the fish, this explains one instance. And since John and Christina both ate the bread, this would explain the remaining two instances of food poisoning. This is why experimental data can offer evidence to support a claim that something is a cause, but still leave a measure of uncertainty.

Let's look at another example. Suppose a mechanic has four cars towed to her garage in less than 1 hour, and the car owners all complain that their car just began sputtering and then stalled. Once again, we can draw a chart to see the results:

Instances of the **Effect**	Spark Plugs	Generator	Water in Gasoline	Alternator	Carburetor
Car 1: Stopped running	✓		✓		
Car 2: Stopped running			✓		
Car 3: Stopped running	✓		✓		
Car 4: Stopped running			✓		

We can now interpret the results. In two instances, the spark plugs had to be replaced (car 1 and car 3). There were no instances in which the generator, alternator, or carburetor showed signs of being defective. But in all four cases water was found in the gasoline. The mechanic can use this information to do follow-up research. For example, she might find that all four drivers had recently bought gas from the same nearby gas station. She could then refill the tanks with good gas and see the result. The mechanic could also replace the two sets of old spark plugs to see if the cars start. Here the method of agreement adds something to our investigation: It allows the mechanic to follow up on the initial results. It helps narrow the search, once we have the right background information to know which of the hundreds of possible variables are relevant. However, if an event is truly novel, then background knowledge will not be much help.

Method of Difference

Method of difference
The method that looks for what all the instances of an event do not have in common.

The **method of difference** looks instead for what all the instances of an event do *not* have in common. If they have everything in common except one item, then that item is a likely cause.

Let's examine that unfortunate group of diners at a different meal. This time we need to investigate all four people to locate the *difference* between the three who got food poisoning and the one person who did not get it. We are really looking at the *absence* of food poisoning. Once again, we can create a chart to display the data:

Instances of the **Effect**	Possible Causes			
	Hamburger	French Fries	Tea	Pie
John: Food poisoning	✓	✓	✓	✓
Robert: Food poisoning	✓	✓	✓	✓
Christina: Food poisoning	✓	✓	✓	✓
Kristin: No food poisoning	✓		✓	✓

We look for a single condition that was present when the effect occurred and that was absent when the effect did not occur. We see that there is only one circumstance that differentiates Kristin, who does not have food poisoning, from the three other people—the French fries. We conclude that, of the four circumstances under investigation, the French fries are the probable cause of the food poisoning.

The method identifies a *sufficient condition* as the probable cause. However, it still does not provide conclusive proof. Once again, we might have disregarded or overlooked other variables that differ among the four people. Those other possibilities have still not been ruled out.

Joint Method of Agreement and Difference

The **joint method of agreement and difference** combines our first two approaches. If two or more instances of an event have only one thing in common, while the instances in which it does *not* occur all share the absence of that thing, then the item is a likely cause.

Adding the results of the method of agreement and the method of difference into one analysis strengthens our claim. We can highlight the results to illustrate how each method is to be applied:

Joint method of agreement and difference If two or more instances of an event have only one thing in common, while the instances in which it does not occur all share the absence of that thing, then the item is a likely cause.

Instances of the **Effect**	Possible Cause							
	Fish	Spaghetti	Ham	Bread	Appetizer	Soda	Beer	Wine
John: Food poisoning		✓		✓	✓		✓	
Robert: Food poisoning	✓				✓	✓		
Christina: Food poisoning			✓	✓	✓			✓
Kristin: No food poisoning	✓			✓				✓

The three white rows (John, Robert, and Christina) show the results of the method of agreement, while the shaded row (Kristin) shows the results of the method of difference. First, *the effect must always be present when the cause is present*. In each instance in white, the cause, the appetizer, is present. Second, *the effect must always be absent when the cause is absent*. The shaded box shows that food poisoning is absent when the cause, the appetizer, is absent.

Our conclusion has a higher probability of being correct than if we had used either of the first two methods alone. The method of agreement by itself could not rule out the possibility that two different items listed on our chart caused the food poisoning. Perhaps both the fish and the bread were contaminated, but not the appetizer. The joint method eliminates this possibility. In the shaded row, Kristin ate the fish and the bread and did not get food poisoning. Therefore, neither of those items could be a cause of the illness.

The joint method allows us to assert that the appetizer was a *sufficient condition* for food poisoning. The joint method also allows us to assert that the appetizer was a *necessary condition*.

The same principles apply to our example of stalled cars:

Instances of the **Effect**	Possible Causes				
	Spark Plugs	Generator	Water in Gasoline	Alternator	Carburetor
Car 1: Stopped running	✓		✓		
Car 2: Stopped running			✓		
Car 3: Stopped running	✓		✓		
Car 4: Stopped running			✓		
Car 5: Did not stop running					

Again, the four white rows show the results of the method of agreement, while the shaded row shows the results of the method of difference. First, *the method of agreement requires that the effect must always be present when the cause is present*. In each case in white, the cause, water in the gasoline, is present whenever the car stopped running. Second, *the method of difference requires that the effect must always be absent when the cause is absent*. In the shaded row, the effect (the car stopping) is absent when the cause, water in the gasoline, is absent.

Again our conclusion has a higher probability than with each of the first two methods considered alone. The joint method allows us to assert that water in the gasoline was probably both a *sufficient condition* and a *necessary condition* for the effect.

Method of Residues

Method of residues
The method that subtracts from a complex set of events those parts that already have known causes.

The **method of residues** subtracts from a complex set of events those parts that already have known causes. Whatever remains (the "residue") is a likely cause of the remaining effect.

Suppose your roommate returns from a party with a stomachache, headache, and a rash. You piece together the food and drinks that your roommate consumed and form this list: hot dogs, pizza, chips, pretzels, macadamia nuts, and soda. Soda always gives him a headache, so that explains one symptom. He sometimes gets a stomachache from hot dogs, so that could account for another symptom. He does not remember ever having had a reaction to pizza, chips, or pretzels. That leaves just two things—the nuts and the rash. Sure enough, this was the first time he had eaten macadamia nuts, so the rash was probably caused by an allergic reaction to them. He plans on visiting the campus medical clinic to get tested for allergies to verify his conclusion.

We can again follow the reasoning by drawing a chart:

Symptoms	Possible Causes of the Symptoms					
	Hot Dogs	Pizza	Chips	Pretzels	Macadamia Nuts	Soda
Stomachache	√	x	x	x	x	x
Headache	x	x	x	x	x	√
Rash	x	x	x	x	√	x

However, we need to interpret this chart differently from the previous examples. With the method of residues, we are actively drawing on our background knowledge. For example, we concluded from past experience that hot dogs were the probable cause of the stomachache, so we placed a check mark to indicate that cause-effect relationship. Similarly, the two x's in the hot dogs column indicate that hot dogs had not been connected before to either a headache or rash.

We also concluded from past experience that soda was the probable cause of the headache, so we placed a check mark to indicate a causal connection. The two x's in the soda column indicate that soda has not been connected previously to either a stomachache or rash. In the columns for pizza, chips, and pretzels we find only x's because they have not been connected before to any of the symptoms.

The method of residues tells us to subtract from a complex set of events those parts that are already understood. We have done just that for the stomachache and headache. We also eliminate items that have no previous connection to any of the symptoms. Whatever remains, we conclude, is the most likely cause of the remaining effect. In this case, the macadamia nuts are the probable cause of the rash. We placed the check mark in a shaded box to indicate that this causal connection is newly discovered.

Method of Concomitant Variations

The **method of concomitant variations** looks for two factors that vary together. If a variation of one part of an event accompanies a variation in another part of the event, then the two parts are probably causally connected. (The word "concomitant" means *accompanying*.)

This method looks for a **correlation**, or correspondence between two sets of objects, events, or data. For example, suppose a car company wants to determine the speed at which a particular car gets the best gas mileage. Many automatic transmissions have three gears that shift up and down, depending on the car's speed and the engine's revolutions per minute (RPM). In a simple experiment, a test car is equipped with a special one-gallon gasoline tank. The car will go around a test track and maintain a

Method of concomitant variations The method that looks for two factors that vary together.

Correlation A correspondence between two sets of objects, events, or data.

fixed speed until it uses up that single gallon of gasoline. The number of miles traveled will determine the car's mileage at that speed, in miles per gallon (MPG). The engineers then repeat the test run at different speeds to see which gives the best mileage.

This example involves isolating one variable, *speed*. The engineers thus make sure to keep tire size, tire pressure, the weather, road conditions, and other factors constant throughout the experiment, in order to see how speed affects the gas mileage of this one car model. Of course, many variables affect gas mileage, and the same method could test for those as well. The engineers could increase or decrease the tire size, for example, while keeping other variables constant. Regardless, in each case they are looking for a *correlation*—between a given variable and gas mileage.

Focusing for now on speed and mileage, suppose we make a chart of the results for the company's most popular subcompact car:

	Miles per Hour (MPH)								
	0	10	20	30	40	50	60	70	80
Miles per gallon of gasoline (MPG)	0	12	18	25	35	37	29	25	21

The first column indicates the worst possible driving situation, just sitting with the car idling. When the gallon of gasoline is used up, the car will have traveled exactly 0 miles at 0 MPH, so its MPG will also be 0. You can see that the MPG increases steadily until it reaches its peak at 37 MPG, when the car's speed is 50 MPH. It then decreases steadily for speeds over 50 MPH.

The method of concomitant variations looks for correlations, but the correlation can be either positive or negative. In other words, the two variables must change together, but they may change in the same direction or in opposite directions. In this example, in the range from 0 to 50 MPH we observe a positive correlation between speed and MPG. From 50 to 80 MPH, we see a negative correlation.

Once the method has found a correlation, it can help reveal a cause-effect relationship. Here we observe a complex relationship between speed and gas mileage, but why? Perhaps the explanation lies in the car's three gears. Because the lowest two gears are used to accelerate from a standing position, a lower MPG is found from 10 to 40 MPH. The engine needs the most power to get moving, so it consumes a lot of gasoline. If you ever rode a ten-speed bicycle, you know that when you start out at the lowest gears, you need a lot of energy to turn the pedals. As your speed increases, and you shift through higher gears, the power needed to turn the pedals decreases, and you reach a "sweet spot." The same principle holds true for cars, too. With the results in hand, the engineers can do further tests to confirm that causal relationship.

All cars have a "sweet spot," the speed at which the car runs most efficiently, which varies considerably from car to car, especially with engine size and car weight. The "sweet spot" typically occurs soon after the car shifts into its highest gear. After that, further acceleration will usually cause a decrease in MPG. We can see just that in the chart for the range from 50 to 80 MPH.

As we can already see, the method of concomitant variations has its limits. It can point to a causal relationship, but that still leaves work to be done to discover why. The results can even be misleading, because neither variable may prove to be the cause of the other. A basic principle of science holds that *every cause-effect relationship is a case of correlation, but not every correlation is a cause-effect relationship.* In other words, causality requires correlation, but correlation does not require causality. For example, there is a high correlation between Sundays and Mondays: One always follows directly after the other. But Sundays do not cause Mondays to occur. There is a high correlation between a person's weight and pants size. But your weight does not cause your pants size to be what it is, nor does your pants size cause you to weigh a certain amount. Of course, the *reason* you buy a certain pants size is your weight. Nevertheless there is no direct cause-effect relationship between your weight and the pants.

EXERCISES 14C

I. Answer "true" or "false" to the following:

1. A causal network is the degree of probability that we assign to an event occurring.

Answer: False

Level 1 Multiple-Choice Questions

2. A remote cause is something that is connected to the precipitating cause by a chain of events.

3. A correlation is a sufficient condition for making a causal claim.

4. The method of residues tells us that if two or more instances in which an event occurs have only one thing in common, while the two or more instances in which it does not occur all have the absence of that thing, then the item in which the two sets of instances differ is causally connected to the event.

Level 2 Multiple-Choice Questions

5. The method of agreement tells us that if all the instances in which the event under investigation occurs, and an instance in which it does not occur, have everything in common except one item, then that item is causally connected to the event.

6. The method of difference tells us that if two or more instances of an event under investigation have only one thing in common, then the circumstance in which all the instances agree is causally connected to the given event.

7. The method of concomitant variations tells us that if a variation of one part of an event accompanies a variation in another part of the event, either in direct or inverse proportion, then the two parts are causally connected.

8. The joint method of agreement and difference tells us that if you subtract from any complex set of events those parts that are already understood to be the effects of known causes, then what remains is causally connected to the remaining effect.

⭐ 9. Since the word "cause" has several meanings, when it is used in everyday situations the possibility of ambiguity arises.

10. Mill's methods provide conclusive proof of causality.

II. Determine which of Mill's methods matches the descriptions that follow:

1. If you subtract from any complex set of events those parts that are already understood to be the effects of known causes, then what remains is causally connected to the remaining effect.

Answer: The method of residues

2. If all the instances in which the event under investigation occurs, and an instance in which it does not occur, have everything in common except one item, then that item is causally connected to the event.

3. If a variation of one part of an event accompanies a variation in another part of the event, either in direct or inverse proportion, then the two parts are causally connected.

4. If two or more instances of an event under investigation have only one thing in common, then the circumstance in which all the instances agree is causally connected to the given event.

⭐ 5. If two or more instances in which an event occurs have only one thing in common, while the two or more instances in which it does not occur all have the absence of that thing, then the item in which the two sets of instances differ is causally connected to the event.

III. For each of the following cases, do three things. First, construct a chart based on the information given for each case. Second, determine which of Mill's methods apply to each case. Third, determine the conclusion that can be derived from the method.

1. Tom and Marsha both bought new cars. They chose the same make and model, with the same size engine, automatic transmission, and same tire size. They both buy the same octane gas at the same gas station. Tom drives his car exclusively in the city, while Marsha does mainly highway driving. However, when they compared gas mileage, Marsha's car averages 35 miles per gallon (MPG), but Tom's car averages only 26 MPG.

Answer:

	Possible Causes								
The **Effect**	Make	Model	Engine Size	Automatic Transmission	Tire Size	Gas Station	Gas Octane	City Driving	Highway Driving
Tom: 26 MPG	√	√	√	√	√	√	√	√	
Marsha: 35 MPG	√	√	√	√	√	√	√		√

The chart displays the *method of difference*. We can conclude that city driving is the probable cause of Tom's car averaging 26 MPG, and highway driving is the probable cause of Marsha's car averaging 35 MPG.

2. A student majoring in physics wanted to see if a relationship exists between height above or below sea level and the boiling point of water. Her experiments result in the following data: At sea level, water boils at approximately 212° F; at 500 feet above sea level, water boils at approximately 211° F; at 1000 feet above sea level, water boils at approximately 210° F; at 500 feet below sea level, water boils at approximately 213° F; and at 1000 feet below sea level, water boils at approximately 214° F.

3. Lois received at least a score of 90 on all four math exams this semester. She tried to determine why she did so well. She had different meals the night before the exams; she studied a different number of hours; two times she studied with friends and two times she didn't. The only thing that she remembered doing before all four exams was getting at least 8 hours of sleep the night before.

4. Judy's electric bill averaged $200 a month for 3 months. She noticed that she used the air conditioner in the bedroom all night. For the next 2 months she decided to try to sleep without using the air conditioner. The electric bill for those 2 months averaged $75 a month.

5. Suzie had $250 in her wallet on Friday afternoon. By Sunday night she had only $10 left. She recalled spending $60 on a dinner and a date Friday night. Then she spent $70 on groceries, $40 on gas for her car, and lent $50 to a friend. She didn't recall spending any more money, so the only thing she could think of was that she must have lost $20 somewhere.

6. Frank's three dogs suddenly started having fleas. They get baths at different times, and he uses different dog shampoos on them since they have very different hair types. They eat different kinds of food and like different doggie snacks. But last week a neighbor's dog got into the backyard and all three dogs played with it. The flea problem occurred soon after.

7. Two students who share the same dorm room received coupons in the mail for a free meal at a restaurant that recently opened near campus. However, the two students across the hall in the same dorm did not get any coupons. All four are juniors, they all have cafeteria passes, and they have lived in the same dorm for two years. The two students who received coupons in the mail remember participating in a survey at the student union the previous month. The other two students did not fill out the survey forms.

8. Linda's house was quite hot in the summer. She tried adding insulation to the attic, and it helped some the next summer. She added sunscreens to the windows, and that helped too. She planted six large shade trees, and the house was even somewhat cooler. She added aluminum siding to the house, but it didn't get any cooler.

9. Two tomato plants were started from the same batch of seeds. They were all placed in the same kind of soil, given the same watering schedule and same amount of water, and had the same access to sun. Only one of the plants was sprayed with a fertilizer once a week; the other plant never received the fertilizer. The plant that received the fertilizer produced twice as many pounds of tomatoes as the nonfertilized plant.

10. After Luke washes his T-shirts, it takes them 25 minutes to dry in a heavy-duty dryer. Whenever he adds his underwear and socks to the T-shirts load, it takes 50 minutes to dry. If he adds his jeans to the underwear, socks, and T-shirts load, it takes an hour and a half to dry.

11. Marcie heard a buzzing sound that sounded like it came from an electronic source. She switched off the TV, but the sound did not go away. She turned off her computer, but the sound persisted. She switched off the lights in the room, but she still heard the sound. She decided that the sound must be coming from the next-door apartment.

12. Chris noticed that for the entire spring semester she had a backache on Tuesdays and Thursdays, but not on the other three school days. On all 5 days she walked the same route to school and back home, and she spent the same amount of hours on campus. She ate similar meals each day and did similar exercise routines. She got the same amount of sleep each night and slept in the same bed each night. But she did note that on Tuesdays and Thursdays she had to carry four heavy textbooks in her backpack instead of only two small books on the other 3 school days.

13. TreShawn boiled an egg for 3 minutes. Opening it, he found that it was quite runny. He tried boiling another egg for 4 minutes; it was a little thicker, but still not what he wanted. He boiled another egg for 5 minutes, and it was exactly what he wanted. He then decided to try to get a hard-boiled egg. After adding an additional minute of boiling to each subsequent egg, he determined that the hard-boiled egg he liked took 10 minutes of boiling.

14. Leslie wanted to try to spend less money, so she gathered information about her spending habits. According to her bank records she averaged ten ATM withdraws amounting to $200 a month. She decided to keep the ATM card at home except for Saturdays. For the next 3 months she averaged four withdrawals amounting to $80 a month.

15. Five friends (let's call them 1, 2, 3, 4, and 5) each lost approximately six pounds in the last month. Friends 2, 4, and 5 eat meat; friends 1 and 3 are vegetarians; 1, 3, 4, and 5 drink coffee regularly; 2 drinks nothing but tea; 2, 3, and 5 work full time; 1 and 4 work part time; 1, 3, 4, and 5 take night classes; 2 does not take any classes. They have all been meeting three times a week at a gym where they do intense aerobic routines.

Video Tutorial

D. LIMITATIONS OF MILL'S METHODS

Mill's basic principles can be adapted to a variety of settings in both science and every-day life. In fact, we shall see how they help understand the process of science. However, the methods all have their limitations, especially if they are applied in a simplistic way. Suppose a person woke up three mornings in a row with a terrible hangover. He care-fully lists what he had the three previous nights: gin and tonic water, vodka and tonic water, and whisky and tonic water. Applying the method of agreement, he concludes that the tonic water caused the hangovers.

Similar mistakes can be made using the method of difference. For example, suppose someone drove to work each day for a year; but with the price of gas getting so high, she decided to start walking to work to save some money. At the end of the workday the manager announces that, because of the economic downturn, everyone will have to take a 10% pay cut. On the way home she reconstructs the evidence. For 1 year, she drove her car to work, and each day there was no pay cut. She walked to work for 1 day, and her pay was cut 10%. She concludes that walking to work caused the pay cut. (For a related discussion, see the *false cause fallacies* section in Chapter 4.)

Although Mill's methods do not provide conclusive proof of causality, they are helpful in discovering correlations and potential causes. However, they still rely heav-ily on background knowledge in order to get started. Experimenters must list what they think are *relevant* similarities or differences among sets of objects or events. The methods are thus not very helpful in discovering new cause-effect relationships. After all, if we have never encountered a factor before, or have never seen it as a cause, we can easily overlook or reject it. Finally, Mill's methods can show only a correlation, but correlation does not guarantee causation. At best, a correlation reveals a probable case of causality. Mill's methods can help reveal a *necessary* ingredient in causation (a *correlation*), but they do not by themselves provide *sufficient* evidence of causation.

The ability to discover causes is a powerful tool. When we know how part of the world works, we can often create things that will benefit us, such as vaccines, antibi-otics, and cures for diseases. Discovering the cause of malaria enabled scientists to create drugs to fight the disease. Scientists are trying other new approaches as well:

> Scientists working on malaria have found a way of genetically manipulating large populations of mosquitoes that could dramatically reduce the spread of the deadly disease . . . making genetic changes to a few mosquitoes and then allowing them to breed; genetic alterations could spread through large mosquito populations in just a few generations.
>
> Kate Kelland, "Scientists Tweak Mosquito Genes to Fight Malaria," Reuters

Knowing that certain types of mosquitoes carry the disease to humans has not yet enabled us to eradicate the disease. A complex, worldwide problem like malaria requires a multipronged solution. However, without knowing the cause, we could not even think of rational ways to combat the disease.

Discovering causes also expands our ability to predict correctly the future. If we know what causes things to break, collapse, or burn, then we can often predict their life span. Although we cannot predict with perfect accuracy when any water heater will break, for example, we can use statistical data on similar models to predict the average life expectancy. This information helps you determine when to purchase a new water heater.

Similarly, physicians can often predict with great accuracy how a disease will run its course. This knowledge allows decisive action by targeting the cause and administering potential remedies. Of course, many phenomena are very complex, and our knowledge of the underlying causes may not yet allow accurate predictions. This is especially true for many social issues, such as poverty, crime, and domestic and international conflicts:

> Predictions usually deal with events—who will win an election, whether or not a country will go to war, the specification of a new invention; they center on decisions. Yet such predictions, while possible, cannot be formalized, i.e., made subject to rules. The prediction of events is inherently difficult. Events are the intersect of social vectors (interests, forces, pressures, and the like). While one can to some extent assess the strength of these vectors individually, one would need a "social physics" to predict the exact crosspoints where

PROFILES IN LOGIC
John Stuart Mill

John Stuart Mill (1806–73) believed that the advance of knowledge went hand in hand with advances in human freedom and equality. For Mill, logic played a crucial role in that advancement. Deductive logic tells us if our reasoning is correct, and inductive logic is our best guide to discovering new truths. Since our inductive inferences are a combination of our current experiences and our memory, the conclusions do not follow with necessity. Although our inductive reasoning is subject to error, Mill argued that a scientific approach to knowledge, however fallible, is superior to superstitious beliefs that direct observation shows to be false.

Mill argued that our ability to recognize patterns existing in nature is the foundation of our discovering the "laws of nature," which in turn are shown to be accurate through our ability to explain and predict. Science advances by assuming that *causes* exist and that we can discover them.

Mill believed that we will find the best ways to live by carefully observing the way the world is. "Few human creatures would consent to be changed into any other lower animals, for a promise of the fullest allowance of a beast's pleasures; no intelligent human being would consent to be a fool, no instructed person would be an ignoramus, no person of feeling and conscience would be selfish and base, even though they should be persuaded that the fool, the dunce, or the rascal is better satisfied with his lot than they are with theirs."

decisions and forces combine. . . . Forecasting is possible where there are regularities and recurrences of phenomena (these are rare), of where there are persisting trends whose direction, if not an exact trajectory, can be plotted with statistical time-series or be formulated as historical tendencies. Necessarily, therefore, one deals with probabilities and an array of possible projections. But the limitations of forecasting are also evident. The further one reaches ahead in time with a set of forecasts, the greater the margin for error, since the fan of the projections widens.

Daniel Bell, *The Coming of the Post-Industrial Society*

As we saw, Mill's methods can only reveal evidence of probable causes; they provide no real explanatory power. Discovering instances of causation is an important step in understanding the world—but it is only part of what we need. We also need to understand *how* and *why* particular instances of causation function as they do. Answers to these questions take us beyond being able to identify cause-effect relationships. We must develop theories and hypotheses—the basis of scientific reasoning.

E. THEORETICAL AND EXPERIMENTAL SCIENCE

We sometimes need an explanation that not only captures certain facts, but also gives us a way of discovering new ones. This is what a good **hypothesis** does. It provides an explanation for known facts and a way to test our explanation. In addition, a good hypothesis can foster new technologies, which in turn create new ways of exploring the world. These inventions allow us to make more precise observations and to discover new facts.

Hypothesis Provides an explanation for known facts and a way to test an explanation.

The interplay of science and technology is a complex process, but it follows a repeating pattern:

Fact ➤ Hypothesis ➤ Technology ➤ New facts ➤ New hypothesis. . . .

For example, the creation of better and stronger telescope lenses allowed Galileo to see clearly the surface of our moon, and to discover some moons of Jupiter. The new information that Galileo gathered by using the improved telescopes helped refute the then generally accepted view of the universe and Earth's place in it. More recently, advances in artificial intelligence and animal sensation provide new information that can lead to new hypotheses about the nature of consciousness. For example, evidence about the nervous systems of certain animals can be used to discuss the theoretical frameworks that argue for or against animal consciousness.

There are two aspects of science—*theoretical* and *experimental*—and each has an important role to play in our knowledge of the physical world. **Theoretical science** proposes explanations for observations of natural phenomena, while **experimental science** tests those explanations. Both theoretical science and experimental science are involved in the development of new inventions and technologies that may allow us to gather new data and new facts about the physical world.

Theoretical science Proposes explanations for natural phenomena.

Experimental science Tests the explanations proposed by theoretical science.

The impact of experimental science and theoretical science that occurred during Galileo's time can be seen throughout the ensuing centuries. For example, recent advances in technology are forcing us to rethink our theories of mind and consciousness; this is especially true in the role that genetics plays in human behavior. We are achieving greater insight into the physiology and chemistry of the brain thanks to such advancements as magnetic resonance imaging (MRI) and computerized axial tomography (CAT) scans. These reveal structures and processes never before seen, which forces us to create new hypotheses of the mind.

Theoretical science, in turn, can have sweeping consequences as well. The *theoretical* breakthrough regarding the structure of DNA, made by James Watson and Francis Crick, provided *experimental* scientists with clues about where to look, what to look for, and what could be predicted based on consequences of the theoretical work. The early twentieth century saw the rise of Albert Einstein's theories of space-time, as well as quantum theory (the physics of subatomic particles). These theories led to many unexpected and unique predictions about the world. When experimental results verified both Einstein's theories and quantum physics, they opened new horizons for understanding the world and our place in it.

Chapter 2 explained how theoretical definitions assign a meaning to a term and assist in understanding how a term fits into a general theory. For example, Mendel's theory of inheritance contains a set of definitions of key terms, such as "trait," "dominant," and "recessive." A theory is scientific if it generates hypotheses that can be tested. A theory that produces untestable hypotheses is not a scientific theory. A fruitful scientific theory is one that generates multiple *confirmed* hypotheses. In contrast, a theory that repeatedly generates *refuted* hypotheses is not useful. The words "confirmed" and "refuted" are not identical to "true" and "false" when they are used to describe hypotheses. Instead, they mean that we have some evidence that *supports* one hypothesis and *denies* the other hypothesis.

An important factor for any theory is its ability to let the physical world decide. A controlled experiment opens the possibility of letting the physical world answer unambiguously "yes" or "no" to our hypotheses. A successful scientific theory also provides fertile ground for invention and experimentation. For example, recently the most precise measurements of an electron ever made suggest that it's nearly perfectly spherical. The laser experiments conducted by researchers at Imperial College London took ten years to design and complete. One of the researchers made the point well:

> We're really pleased that we've been able to improve our knowledge of one of the basic building blocks of matter. It's been a very difficult measurement to make, but this knowledge will let us improve our theories of fundamental physics. People are often surprised to hear that our theories of physics aren't "finished," but in truth they get constantly refined and improved by making ever more accurate measurements.   ScienceDaily.com

A scientific theory functions like an abstract tool. Physical tools often come with manuals that tell you how to operate the tool safely and effectively. The manuals speak in general terms to let you know which tasks are appropriate. Physical tools can be useful for some tasks and useless for others. For example, a hammer is good for driving nails into wood, but it's not good for delicate brain surgery. Through trial and error we learn the limits of tools.

Just as we do not expect any physical tool to solve all our problems, we should not expect a scientific theory to answer every possible question. For example, because Mendel's theory of inheritance failed to correctly predict a few outcomes for a small set of inherited traits in humans, it was abandoned. However, several decades later scientists realized that Mendel's theory was indeed useful for explaining and predicting many kinds of inheritance problems, but of course not all. In fact, Mendel's theory offers a simple and accurate explanation for why some diseases reappear after a few generations. In many cases the theory can accurately predict the probability that a child will inherit a disease based on the genetic profile of the parents.

Over time we have learned where Mendel's theory works, and where it doesn't. We are able to learn something about the world because the hypotheses it generates are testable, which is why experimentation is so important. Scientific experiments and repeated testing under strict controls provide the best method for determining the success, failure, or limitations of a theory. We learn from success, but also from failure.

F. INFERENCE TO THE BEST EXPLANATION

The logician Charles S. Peirce argued that it is a common human trait to infer explanations for our experience, especially for events with recurring patterns. He called this process **abduction**. But what happens when people infer different explanations for the same facts? How do we decide which explanation is correct? In **inference to the best explanation**, we reason from the premise that a hypothesis would explain certain facts to the conclusion that the hypothesis is the best explanation for those facts. For scientists, the term "best explanation" means *the most plausible explanation* based on our *background knowledge*, which is everything we know to be true. It includes all facts and hypotheses that have already been confirmed or refuted through observation and experiment. Science is an interrelated set of elements, all of which support each other in the quest to understand the physical world. Together, they make up the scientific method.

Peirce's ideas apply to a recent tragedy. Many explanations for the earthquake and the devastating tsunami that struck Japan in 2011 have been proposed. Here are three:

- The disasters are God's way of punishing the Japanese for their attack on Pearl Harbor.
- The Japanese built the nuclear plants too close to the ocean.
- Japan is located on the Pacific "rim of fire," which is one of the world's major geological fault lines. It has a long history of powerful earthquakes and massive tsunamis, and similar disasters have been documented for centuries.

The first hypothesis does nothing to explain the dozens of earthquakes and tsunamis that have occurred in the same places in Japan going back several centuries—long before the attack on Pearl Harbor. The second hypothesis might help explain why the nuclear power plants were damaged by the earthquake and tsunami. They were built

Abduction The process that occurs when we infer explanations for certain facts.

Inference to the best explanation Reasoning from the premise that a hypothesis would explain certain facts to the conclusion that the hypothesis is the best explanation for those facts.

too close to the ocean. However, it does nothing to explain the cause of the earthquake and the tsunami. The third hypothesis provides a causal explanation based on historical data, contemporary knowledge of the causes of earthquakes and tsunamis, and their probability.

In cases like this, perhaps we can pay attention to Peirce's advice: "Facts cannot be explained by a hypothesis more extraordinary than these facts themselves; and of various hypotheses the least extraordinary must be adopted" (quoted in *The Play of Musement* by Thomas Sebeok).

Let's look at another example. Suppose there was no snow in your yard when you went to sleep, but when you woke up there was snow in the yard. This is a fact, and one explanation is that it snowed last night. A second explanation is that your friends have executed an elaborate prank by placing artificial snow in your yard. How do we decide which explanation is best? We had better gather more evidence.

The idea is to force the explanation to predict something else that we do not know yet. For example, we might look around the neighborhood to see if there is snow anywhere besides your yard. If there is snow everywhere in the neighborhood, then it is unlikely that your friends would have been able to get hold of that much artificial snow. If snow is everywhere in the neighborhood, then we say that the snow hypothesis has been *confirmed* and the prank hypothesis has been *refuted*. Gathering additional evidence is an ongoing process. Only in exceptional cases can a single confirmation or refutation establish a definitive answer. Instead, the accumulation of evidence after repeated experiments points us in the right direction.

PROFILES IN LOGIC
Charles S. Peirce

Charles S. Peirce (1839–1914) is recognized as the greatest American philosopher-mathematician. He did outstanding work in both logic and mathematics, creating many of the notations used today. According to Peirce, the conclusions of mathematics follow by necessity, but logic is broader still, because it investigates any and all kinds of arguments.

In philosophy he founded *pragmatism*, the application of scientific methods and results to philosophical problems. Peirce coined the term "abduction" to an all-encompassing activity—generating hypotheses in order to explain facts and to deduce predictions. Deduction and induction alone, he believed, are not sufficient to complete logic.

Peirce stressed the use of truth tables as a way to reveal the logic behind truth-functional operators. Although it took the work of others, most notably the philosopher Ludwig Wittgenstein (1889–1951), before truth tables were fully accepted, this system became the perfect tool for something else as well: It helped in creating computers. The system of truth values (true and false) is a foundation of computer languages and hardware applications.

To see why we cannot determine the best explanation based solely on what we already know, take the two hypotheses to explain the snow in your yard. The reasoning might go as follows:

- If it snowed last night, then there is snow in your yard. There is snow in your yard. Therefore, it snowed last night.
- If your friends played a prank on you last night, then there is snow in your yard. There is snow in your yard. Therefore, your friends played a prank on you last night.

Both arguments commit the fallacy of affirming the consequent; they are, therefore, both invalid. This is why we need evidence that goes beyond the known facts. We need to think of things that we can do that will allow us to gather new facts, and this additional information will help us decide which explanation is better.

The same process can be seen in a criminal trial. The prosecution needs to gather important and relevant incriminating evidence in order to convince the jury of the guilt of the defendant. But what determines guilt "beyond a reasonable doubt"? It may take several additional pieces of evidence. Of course, the defense will do its best to discredit the prosecution's evidence.

In biology, Charles Darwin's reasoning was partly based on his inference that, although natural selection was not the only explanation for the diversity of species, as far as he could determine, it was the best explanation. In fiction, Sherlock Holmes remarked, "Once you eliminate the impossible, whatever remains, no matter how improbable, must be the truth." The private detective started his reasoning process with a set of facts. Next, he devised various hypotheses—his possible suspects. Holmes's subsequent investigations and research led him to a series of new facts that, one by one, allowed him to eliminate hypotheses until one remained—the best explanation. (Holmes referred to his method as "deduction," but he repeatedly used the process of abduction.)

Our hypotheses are only as good as our imagination. We might fail to think of the correct hypothesis. In this sense, abduction has many of the drawbacks that we saw with Mill's methods. Whether we hit on the correct hypothesis often depends on our background knowledge and our imagination. This is why breakthroughs in science and other fields often take so long. It sometimes takes several generations for someone to think of the correct hypothesis or to devise a new way of gathering evidence—a novel experiment—that will point us in the right direction.

G. HYPOTHESIS TESTING, EXPERIMENTS, AND PREDICTIONS

Hypotheses are sometimes easy to propose but difficult to test. Exploring this idea will allow us to see how experiments and predictions help us understand the world. This, in turn, will enable us to analyze scientific reasoning in greater detail.

Controlled Experiments

Controlled experiment
One in which multiple experimental setups differ by only one variable.

The best way to test a hypothesis is with a **controlled experiment**—an experiment in which multiple experimental setups differ by only one variable. You might have recognized that the principle behind this kind of research is Mill's method of difference. In fact, many of Mill's methods have been adapted for modern scientific research. This should not be surprising, since we know that the methods are useful for revealing instances of correlation and uncovering potential causes.

In everyday life, many variables affect the outcome of a given situation, often making strong cause-effect claims very difficult. But a laboratory setting can reduce the number of variables. For example, suppose we want to see the effect of a new fertilizer on plant growth. The idea is to make things as similar as possible—except for one variable. The researchers need to control the plant seeds, growing areas, soil, amount of water, and available sunlight, making sure that these items are as similar as possible for every plant in the experiment. One group of plants, the **experimental group**, is given a precise amount of a fertilizer, which the other group, the **control group**, does not get. At the end of the experiment, the plants in the two groups are compared. Any statistical difference between the groups—for example, size or crop yield—might then be ascribed to the fertilizer. Further tests must then replicate all the experimental factors. These *repeated trials* are necessary before the effects of the fertilizer, positive or negative, can be accepted as definitive.

Experimental group
The group that gets the variable being tested.

Control group The group in which the variable being tested is withheld.

Through this painstaking attention to detail and methodical procedure, controlled laboratory experiments help scientists to uncover causal relationships. A scientific theory must stand up to the severest testing we can devise. It must provide coherent and effective explanations. It must provide correct predictions repeatedly, and help us to discover new facts about the world. When opponents of Darwin's theory of evolution by natural selection call it "only a theory," they ignore what a theory means in science. They ignore how much it predicts, the repeated success of its predictions, and the breadth of causal relationships that it has helped biologists to discover.

Determining Causality

Of course, many things can affect the results of an experiment, forcing scientists to go to great lengths to ensure that nothing disrupts the experimental setting. In addition, since a controlled experiment is by definition "artificial," the results may not match real life. For example, quite often laboratory experiments that test new drugs are conducted on animals whose physiology does not match that of humans. Consequently, positive (or negative) results with the laboratory animals may not match what we would find if the drug were given to humans. This is why taking the results of controlled laboratory experiments and proclaiming that similar connections exist in the outside world is so problematic. Most scientists candidly admit that their promising lab results may not fit the world at large. Unfortunately, popularized versions of laboratory results are sometimes disseminated mistakenly to the public. This is why we often see claims that a cure for a disease has been found, or that scientists have isolated the cause of a disease, only to be disappointed later on.

In understanding the complex nature of causality, we can point to five criteria:

CRITERIA FOR DETERMINING CAUSALITY
1. There should be a *correlation* between the *cause* and the *effect*.
2. The cause should precede the effect.
3. The cause should be in the *proximity* of the effect.
4. A set of *sufficient* and *necessary* conditions should exist.
5. *Alternative explanations* should be ruled out.

None of the five criteria alone is sufficient to establish a cause-effect relationship. Instead, it is the weight of the answers to all five criteria that together support our determination of a cause-effect relationship.

As we saw earlier, a correlation alone cannot establish a causal relationship. For example, there is a strong correlation between a barometer falling and a storm. There is also a strong correlation between people putting on swimsuits and getting wet. In neither case do we have a causal relationship.

The second criterion cautions us to consider the time lag between the cause and the effect. The longer the time between the cause and the effect, the more the situation can be interrupted by other variables that might have brought about the effect. This same note of caution is realized in the third criterion. The greater the spatial distance between the cause and the effect the greater the chance of other variables interfering.

The fourth criterion derives its meaning from the results of our discussion of sufficient and necessary conditions. In other words, the criterion requires that a claim that "X caused Y" must be backed by two things: (1) X was *sufficient* to bring about Y; and (2) X was *necessary* for Y (without X, Y would *not* have occurred).

The fifth criterion, the ability to rule out plausible alternative explanations, is the glue that unifies the set. Any causal claim can be challenged by suggestions of alternative potential causes. (We saw this earlier in the example of the two competing hypotheses for the snow in your yard.) Therefore, a strong causal claim should be backed up by evidence that confirms the hypothesis, and evidence that refutes (or disconfirms) rival, alternative causal claims.

Each of these five criteria has its place in science. They can also help us see how scientific explanations are vastly different from superstitious beliefs.

H. SCIENCE AND SUPERSTITION

Even in science, a causal hypothesis is often extremely difficult to test directly. Although it may say something about the world that is either true or false (for example, "The disease was caused by a parasite"), we cannot simply look at a hypothesis and directly determine its truth or falsity. We must force the hypothesis to do something—to put itself out on a limb, so to speak. This is accomplished by getting the hypothesis to make a *prediction*.

The Need for a Fair Test

A proposed experiment is simply another way of asking the question "What if we do this?" For example, if your car does not start, someone might suggest that you have a dead battery. Although the suggestion (which is a hypothesis or conjecture) is either true or false, we cannot discover the answer by looking at the battery. What we can do is propose a simple experiment: What if we try the headlights? The person who hypothesized that we have a dead battery would be forced to predict that the headlights would not work (in most cars the headlights need power from the battery). If the headlights come on as normal, then the prediction is false, and we would have evidence to refute the hypothesis. However, if the headlights do not come on as normal, then the prediction is true and we would have evidence to support (confirm) the hypothesis.

We can try different experiments in order to get different predictions. For example, if we disconnect the battery, take it to a garage, and hook it up to a battery tester (the experiment), the dead-battery hypothesis would predict that the battery would have little or no power. Again, this prediction is either true or false, and the results can be used to confirm or disconfirm the hypothesis. Another possible experiment would be to try to start the car using jumper cables that are attached to another car's battery. If the dead-battery hypothesis is correct, the car should then start. The truth or falsity of this prediction will again be the indirect evidence that confirms or refutes the hypothesis.

Predictions are crucial to our understanding of the truth of hypotheses. In fact, even a hypothesis that does not make an explicit causal claim should be tested. Since predictions are generally specific statements that are testable, they provide the means for determining, *indirectly*, the truth or falsity of the hypothesis. After an experiment is completed, we can take the truth value of the prediction and trace it back to its source, the hypothesis. Therefore, the fate of the hypothesis rests on the fate of the prediction.

When considering scientific results, we must make decisions about the relevance of the available evidence. We need to have criteria that will eliminate evidence that is misleading or irrelevant. These criteria must also help us to decide how much weight to give each piece of evidence. This is required if we are to judge accurately the strength of a causal argument. Here are three requirements for acceptable predictions that ensure that a fair test of a causal hypothesis has been conducted:

REQUIREMENTS FOR A FAIR TEST OF A CAUSAL HYPOTHESIS
1. The prediction should be *verifiable*.
2. The prediction should *not* be *trivial*.
3. The prediction should have a *logical connection* to the hypothesis.

Verifiable Predictions

Verifiable prediction
A prediction that, if true, must include an observable event.

A **verifiable prediction** is a prediction that, if it is true, includes an observable event. Suppose there is a house where all the people living there got sick for no apparent reason. Two causal hypotheses are put forward:

Hypothesis 1: A high degree of radioactivity in the house is causing the illness.

Hypothesis 2: A disease-causing ghost is haunting this house.

The two hypotheses are statements that could be either true or false. Also, neither hypothesis can be tested directly by simply looking around the house, because both of the conjectured entities are things that are invisible to the unaided human eye (radioactivity and ghosts). But are both hypotheses equally testable and verifiable?

An advocate of hypothesis 1 might predict that if we take a Geiger counter and go around the house (the experiment), then we will find a high reading of radioactivity. If the Geiger counter is operating correctly, and we do get a high reading, then we can safely say that the prediction is true; therefore, the hypothesis has some evidence to support, or to confirm it. However, if there is no sign of radioactivity, then the prediction is false, and we would have evidence to refute the hypothesis. A verifiable prediction does not have to be true, only verifiable. In other words, there must be a method for deciding, clearly and objectively, the truth or falsity of the prediction.

We would accept the evidence for or against hypothesis 1 because Geiger counters are an established source of scientific evidence. Their reliability has been repeatedly confirmed. Geiger counters provide one source of empirical evidence in the complex field of subatomic particles and quantum physics. We understand how Geiger counters work, and we trust them to be a good source of objective evidence. There is also a well-established theoretical framework that secures their place in the scientific community.

Let's turn now to hypothesis 2. What would function as a device that is comparable to the Geiger counter? Short of a *Ghostbusters*-type gadget, there seems to be no comparable method of gathering evidence for the ghost hypothesis. A ghost hypothesis defender might say "But of course the ghost is invisible, so it is impossible to detect." Yet exactly the same challenge confronted hypothesis 1, since we cannot see radioactivity either. Nevertheless, we are able to gather indirect physical evidence to decide if the radioactivity is actually there. In addition, although radioactivity is invisible, we know that it is a part of the physical world and is therefore subject to detection.

Our knowledge of the physical reality of radioactivity also allows us to determine how it causes illness. We have learned how radioactivity affects human tissue and alters human cells, often leading to tragic results. The ghost hypothesis provides no comparable understanding. For example, if ghosts are not only invisible, but also immaterial (not part of the physical world), as many ghost hypotheses allege, then it would be extremely difficult to explain how ghosts could physically affect us. Quite often ghost stories are filled with inconsistencies. For example, a movie might depict a ghost walking unimpeded through doors or walls, but in the next instant the ghost is seen climbing stairs. If the ghost is truly immaterial, then it should not be able to interact with any material objects.

We can assert, then, that a prediction does not meet the first requirement whenever there is no acceptable method to check objectively the truth value of the prediction. Therefore, we need not accept as evidence someone's subjective claim that he can see ghosts.

Nontrivial Predictions

The first requirement for a fair test of a causal hypothesis turns on predictions of future observations and future experiments. The second requirement turns on what we already know and wish to explain. A **nontrivial prediction** requires reference to background knowledge, which is everything we know to be true. Of course, background knowledge changes over time. Therefore, to decide if a prediction satisfies the second requirement, it is necessary to judge it in the light of what we know at the time it is put forth.

Nontrivial prediction A prediction that requires reference to background knowledge, which is everything we know to be true.

Suppose I claim to have the power to see the future (hypothesis). Of course, my claim is either true or false. Now, having understood and accepted the first requirement for a fair test of a hypothesis, you correctly ask me to provide some evidence. That is easy enough for me to do. If all you want is a prediction that is verifiable, then I predict that tomorrow the sun will come up. If you have only the first requirement to use, then you are forced to accept my prediction as being a fair test of the hypothesis. Therefore, the claim that I have the power to see the future will most probably turn out to be true. However, this should *not* be acceptable. We want to avoid situations such as this; we want to be able to eliminate predictions like this one, ones that are highly likely to be true. This is just what the second requirement effectively does. It provides a way of handling predictions that should not be used as evidence. Without the second requirement, we would be forced to accept almost anything as evidence, as long as it is merely verifiable (as long as it satisfied the first requirement). Although the first requirement is a necessary condition, by itself it is not a sufficient condition to ensure a fair test of a hypothesis.

Let's get back to the hypothesis that I have the power to see the future. The second requirement for predictions allows us to eliminate predictions that we consider trivial, and hence carry no weight. This new requirement forces me to revise my original prediction ("The sun will come up tomorrow") because as it stands, even if it turns out true (which is a near certainty), it will carry no weight in support of my hypothesis. Accepting this criticism now forces me to be more specific. I offer this prediction as evidence of my power to see the future:

> Tomorrow, at exactly 1:35 PM, it will start raining on the steps of the U.S. Capitol building. Then it will stop raining at exactly 1:57 PM. But it will rain only on the steps of the Capitol building; it will not rain anywhere else in Washington, D.C.

Would you accept this as a good test? Is this prediction trivial? What we know about the weather should lead us to say that the prediction, being so specific about something that is as unpredictable as the weather in a specific part of a city, is nontrivial. This is all that the second requirement asks of a prediction. Furthermore, the prediction meets the first requirement, because it is easily verifiable. Therefore, according to the first two requirements, this would be a fair test of the hypothesis. Of course, when my prediction turns out to be false, then you would have good evidence that refutes my hypothesis.

The history of Halley's Comet illustrates the principles we have been describing. Applying part of Isaac Newton's theories, Edmund Halley hypothesized that comets reappear in regular cycles. In 1705, Halley predicted that a comet would appear in the year 1758 in a precise location of the sky. In order to judge whether his prediction was trivial, we have to consider not what we know to be true today, but rather what the background knowledge was in 1705. Halley's hypothesis was not yet part of what was known to be true. Therefore, his prediction was considered, at that time, unlikely to be true.

If Halley had predicted that a comet would appear *somewhere* in the sky *sometime* in the 1750s, this would have been a trivial prediction, because many comets had been observed throughout recorded history. The phrase *"somewhere* in the sky," is vague, and the range of dates—*"sometime* in the 1750s"—is too long to offer any precision to the prediction. Therefore, when Halley's specific, and unlikely, prediction did in fact turn out to be true (in the location and time predicted), scientists had good justification for claiming that his hypothesis was also true (based on the confirming evidence).

Halley's hypothesis then became part of the background knowledge, something scientists knew to be true. Therefore, after 1758, if anyone predicted that Halley's Comet would reappear in another 76 years, this would have been considered likely to be true. Therefore, future predictions regarding the return of Halley's Comet do not carry the same weight as the initial one. Each correct prediction confirms the hypothesis to some extent, but the weight diminishes with each subsequent confirmation. When background knowledge changes, then our decisions regarding the second requirement often change as well.

Connecting the Hypothesis and Prediction

The third requirement for an acceptable prediction ensures that there is a connection between the hypothesis and the prediction. This is necessary because we want to use the prediction's truth value as evidence to confirm or refute the hypothesis. We therefore need a direct link.

To derive a prediction from a hypothesis, we must first develop an experiment that will test the hypothesis. We cannot simply take a hypothesis and deduce a prediction straight away. For example, Halley's hypothesis simply stated that comets are part of Newtonian particle systems. From this claim nothing much can be predicted. However, Halley consulted the information about comets that had been gathered over many centuries. He noticed a pattern: A comet appeared in a specific place in the sky in 1682, 1606, and 1530. Halley conjectured that they were instances of the same comet. In other words, from the available data and his hypothesis that comets return, he was able to calculate the next return of the comet. This process enabled Halley to make a specific prediction. Of course, the prediction could have turned out to be false. However, when the prediction turned out to be true, then the truth value could be transferred back to the hypothesis as confirmation. (Unfortunately, Halley did not live long enough to see his hypothesis confirmed.)

Science and Superstition

These examples illustrate the vast difference between science and superstition. Our knowledge of the world has allowed us to shed some beliefs that were based on a general lack of understanding of the physical world. For example, although we do not yet know everything about human diseases, we do know enough to say that they are caused by physical processes.

Of course, some individuals refuse to accept medical and scientific advances. These people often stubbornly refuse to allow medical treatment for their children, for example. The result is that sometimes society has to step in and provide the medical assistance that might cure the disease, or at least reduce the symptoms, and needless pain and suffering. Still others refuse to accept evolution or global warming. Their beliefs have practical and political consequences.

Evolutionary theory faces an ongoing battle. Based on the standards that we have been discussing in this chapter, there should be no question that evolutionary theory is scientific. It is highly testable, it has been tested repeatedly, and it has been tremendously successful and fruitful in explaining a large part of the world. Neither creationism nor "intelligent design" can make the same claims. They do not generate testable hypotheses, and they are not fruitful in explaining anything new about the physical world. They do not meet the basic criteria for a scientific theory as set forth in this chapter.

Physical tools and inventions are usually put through rigorous tests in order to learn the conditions under which they are likely to fail. When, how, and why they fail unlocks part of nature's secrets. This knowledge provides the basis for improving our inventions. The same holds for scientific theories. Our scientific knowledge of the world advances by confronting our theories with new problems. If the theory fails, then we can improve it. However, a nonscientific theory insulates itself from failure—it does not help us learn anything new about the world.

Applying the criteria for testing hypotheses can help expose false beliefs. For example, some people have claimed to be able to perform *mental telepathy*, the act of sending and receiving thoughts. A few believers have accepted the challenge of displaying their "powers" in controlled scientific experiments. One simple test is to place two people in separate rooms and show one of them a series of cards. The cards might be pictures of animals, they might have numbers written on them, or they can be ordinary playing cards. If experimental subjects can perform mental telepathy, then they should score higher on their responses than non-telepathists.

Suppose you were told that someone in another room is going to turn over a random series of ten cards. Your job is to guess what is written on each card. You are told that each card has one number written on it. To make it easy, the numbers run from 1 to 10, and no number occurs twice. Using simple probability, we can see that you should guess correctly approximately 10% of the time. Repeated experiments have shown this to be the case.

The self-proclaimed mental telepathists who agreed to be tested under strict experimental conditions scored no higher than other subjects. When confronted with the results, some subjects refused to accept the outcome. They resorted to *ad hoc* rescue of their belief (*ad hoc* means *for this specific purpose*), which is an attempt to save a belief that has been confronted with refuting evidence. For example, subjects might say that skeptics (like the experimenters) give off "negative waves" that interfere with the positive telepathic waves—in other words, that there is something about a scientific experiment that causes the failure. And, yes, there is indeed something about a well-controlled scientific experiment: It reveals the truth.

A rational and scientific approach can reveal the utter foolishness of many nonscientific beliefs. For example, based on his cryptic calculations and reading of the Bible, Harold Camping predicted that the "rapture" would occur on May 21, 2011. We were told that all good Christians would ascend to heaven that day, while everyone else would be left behind to suffer until the end of the world. Camping predicted that God would completely destroy Earth (and presumably the entire universe) after 5 months, on October 21, 2011. Needless to say, Camping was wrong.

Camping had a history of failed predictions about the end of the world. He previously predicted that it would occur on May 21, 1988. When that day came and went he then predicted that it would end on September 7, 1994. After each of his first two failed predictions, Camping resorted to *ad hoc* rescue. He proclaimed that he had miscalculated, but that his basic system was correct. It just needed some fine-tuning. (To be fair, Camping was not the only one to fail miserably in his predictions; failed predictions of the end of the world litter the pages of history.)

Although Camping's system of calculations and predictions based on his interpretations of the Bible are scientifically bankrupt, they are not economic failures. His Family Radio and ministry have generated more than $100 million in donations, some of it from people who sold everything they had because of their fervent belief in Camping's predictions. This is an example in which an understanding of sound reasoning and sound claims can have enormous practical consequences.

The Allure of Superstition

The allure of superstitions and their psychological hold on humans are not difficult to understand. Here is one explanation of why superstitions are so easily formed, and why they are so difficult to remove:

> It was in 1947 that a dozen pigeons gave researchers at the University of Indiana what was to prove the most fundamental insight into the roots of superstition and magic—even, many would argue, of religion itself. These birds were put on restricted rations, so that before long their body weight had fallen by 25% and they were permanently hungry. When each bird had, in the words of Professor Burrhus Frederic (B.F.) Skinner, been "brought to a stable state of hunger," it found itself spending several minutes every day in a special cage. At one end of the cage was an automatic food hopper, linked to a timer so that it would swing into place every 15 seconds, and remain in place for five seconds before disappearing.

Crucial to the set-up was the fact that, no matter what the pigeon did, the food came and went at set intervals. For the purpose of the experiment was to observe what affect its comings and goings had on the pigeons. And, sad to say, it made them—and, by extension, us—look somewhat foolish.

Before long, one of the pigeons had begun making strange counterclockwise turns in the intervals between the hopper's arrivals. Others indulged in repetitive head movements, while two birds developed a complicated pendulum motion of the head and body. By the end of the experiment, six of the eight subjects were performing elaborate routines, clearly with the intention of hastening the return of the food. In each case, the routine grew out of some action that the bird had just happened to be performing when the hopper appeared.

Describing what is now regarded as a classic experiment, Skinner was in no doubt as to the mechanism involved: "The bird behaves as if there were a causal relation between its behavior and the presentation of food, although such a relation is lacking." . . . "The experiment," he said, "might be said to demonstrate a sort of superstition."

David Newnham, "Hostages to Fortune," Guardian

It is the interplay of theories, hypotheses, data, experiments, and predictions that establishes authentic scientific understanding of the world. We cannot deduce a prediction only from a hypothesis; we cannot make a prediction only from data; and we cannot get a prediction only from an experiment. A scientific prediction is the offspring of hypotheses, data, and experiments; it is a direct logical consequence that may or may not actually fit the real world. If the prediction turns out to be true, then the hypothesis is confirmed (to some degree). If the prediction turns out to be false, then the hypothesis is refuted.

Notice that in this process we transfer the truth value to the hypothesis. (It is said to be *confirmed* or *refuted*.) But what about the experiment's role in the process? Could something have gone wrong with the experimental setup? These are very important questions. If the prediction is a product of the hypothesis, data, and the experiment, then why is the hypothesis saddled with the results? Part of the answer lies in our ability to check directly the experimental setup and the data. This is another reason that the results of a single experiment are never taken as a final proof. Scientific experiments must be repeated and the results must be replicated. It is the cumulative aspect of scientific research in the light of repeated and rigorous testing over long periods of time and under varying conditions that makes science our best guide to understanding the physical world.

It is important to remember that the application of the scientific method attempts to confirm or refute a hypothesis. As such, this process should always be considered partial and tentative. The weight we give to a confirmation or refutation is never all or nothing. We must accumulate evidence over a long time. If we make mistakes, they will be revealed by the results of repeated experiments.

EXERCISES 14H

I. Answer "true" or "false" to the following:

1. Inference to the best explanation produces a valid argument.

Answer: False

2. Experimental science proposes explanations for observations of natural phenomena.

3. The process of abduction occurs when we infer explanations for certain facts.

4. A good hypothesis provides an explanation of facts and gives us a way of discovering new facts.

⭐ 5. The results of experiments are used to confirm (support) or disconfirm (refute) a hypothesis.

6. A controlled experiment tries to establish a causal link between several variables at once.

7. A prediction must be unlikely to be true based on our background knowledge.

8. The control group is the group that gets the variable being tested.

⭐ 9. Each of the five criteria for establishing causality is a sufficient condition for supporting a causal claim.

10. A verifiable prediction must be true.

II. Create two different hypotheses to explain the circumstances in each of the following situations. For each hypothesis, think of an experiment that would result in additional evidence that could be used to either confirm or refute the hypothesis. (*Note:* It is often possible to devise a single experiment to test more than one hypothesis at the same time, but it is not required.)

1. You come home to find that the lights in your apartment do not work. You then determine that nothing that requires electricity works in your apartment.

Answer:

  Hypothesis 1: The circuit breaker in your fuse box tripped off.
  Experiment 1: Check the fuse box settings.
  Hypothesis 2: There is no electricity in other apartments on your floor due to a main circuit malfunction.
  Experiment 2: Call the building superintendent to see if other apartments are affected.

2. A credit card company calls to tell you that your payment is overdue. However, you know that you sent them a check by mail more than a week ago.

3. You turn the key in the ignition of your car and the car does not start. In fact, there is just a small clicking sound when you turn the key.

Video Tutorial

4. After washing your clothes at the laundromat, you place everything in a dryer and put in enough money for 1 hour of drying time. You return in 1 hour to find that your clothes are still as wet as when you first put them in the dryer.

★ 5. You go away for a 2-week vacation and ask your friend to water your house-plants. When you return you see that the plants are dying.

6. You are a salesclerk in a clothing store. A customer comes in and complains that you did not give her the correct change when she purchased a few items less than half an hour ago.

7. You are driving your car when suddenly you notice that the gas gauge is almost at empty. However, you know that you just filled up the gas tank yesterday and you have not driven the car since then.

8. You had a soft-boiled egg and a coffee with milk, but no sugar, for breakfast; then you had a cheeseburger and yogurt shake for lunch. On your way home your stomach begins to ache.

★ 9. You are using your cell phone to talk to your mother when the connection suddenly ends. You try dialing your mother's number, but you cannot get a dial tone on the phone.

10. Arrangements have been made for you to meet your friend at a certain movie theater. Before leaving your house, you verified the time and place, and your friend said that he was taking a taxi to meet you. The movie is about to start in 5 minutes and your friend has not arrived. Neither one of you has a cell phone.

III. Analyze the following *fictional* case studies by picking out the hypothesis, experiment, and prediction. Does the evidence offered in the case study confirm or disconfirm the hypothesis? How much weight would you give to the evidence? If a causal claim is being put forward, then analyze the strength of the argument by checking for any reasonable alternative explanations or other possible facts which, if uncovered, would weaken the causal claim.

1. There have been reports from around the world of some extraordinary "operations." It seems that people with cancerous tumors have been "cured" without any incisions made. When captured on film, the "doctor" seems to be pressing on the patient's body where the tumor is located. Suddenly, blood begins to ooze and the tumor appears to be removed. When cleaned, the patient shows no sign of having been cut. Skeptical researchers did some checking. They performed two simple experiments. First, they tested the material supposedly taken from the patient's body. The patients and their "doctors" claimed that they were cancerous tumors. Results of laboratory analysis showed that the material and blood were from a pig. The second experiment was to take the patients back to the clinic or hospital where the tumors were first noticed, and where records and X-rays were available, in order to see if the tumors had been removed. In all cases, the tumors were exactly where they had originally been; none had been removed.

Answer:

Hypothesis: Cancerous tumors can be physically removed by "surgery," but without any incision.

Experiment: There are two experiments. (A) Test the material (supposedly) taken from the patient to determine its composition. (B) Check the patients to see if the tumors had been removed.

Prediction: The "doctors" and the believing patients (those putting forth the hypothesis) should predict the following: (a) the material will be human cancerous tissue; (b) the tumors will no longer be in the patient.

Confirm/Disconfirm: Since both predictions were false, the evidence gathered from the experiments disconfirms the hypothesis. The evidence carries a lot of weight, because the scientific results are objective and can be accepted as a clear refutation of the hypothesis.

Alternative Explanations: A reasonable explanation is that the "doctors" were scam artists or sleight-of-hand tricksters preying on desperate people.

2. Recently, some physiological psychologists have hypothesized that something in the blood of schizophrenics causes their abnormal behavior. In order to test their conjecture they took some blood from a patient who had been receiving treatment for acute schizophrenia. The researchers then took two groups of spiders that regularly spin uniformly geometrical webs. One group of spiders was given a small injection of the blood, while the other group was left untouched. For the next 2 weeks, the spiders given the blood produced bizarre, asymmetrical webs, which one researcher called *surreal.* The other group spun their normal webs. The researchers are claiming that this supports their contention that there is some, as yet unknown, factor in the schizophrenic's blood that caused the spider's unusual behavior, and is causing the abnormal behavior in the human subject.

3. I decided to revisit the "executive monkey syndrome" hypothesis. Many years ago some researchers stumbled onto what they thought was evidence that the psychological pressure of "command decisions" caused illness. They restrained two monkeys in chairs. One monkey was provided with a button that, if pressed at the right time, would stop an electrical shock given to both monkeys at the same time. This was the "executive monkey." The other monkey had no way to stop the shock. The executive monkey learned quickly that it could stop the shock from occurring, and it seemed preoccupied with timing the button pressing. This went on for some weeks. Once the experiment was completed, autopsies on the two monkeys revealed that the "executive" had stomach ulcers while the other monkey had none. However, subsequent research has failed to duplicate these results.

4. If you bought a condo in the wrong tower, you were unlucky. It has been revealed that tenants living in one of the two *Sublime Inn* towers are suffering from a mysterious disease. It is believed that the disease is linked to a fungus growing

in the air-conditioning system of the tower. The towers are both 5 years old and were built by the same contractor, yet there is no sign of the fungus in the other tower. Engineers, medical personnel, and others are looking for any other difference between the two towers, or between the tenants themselves, that could explain what is happening.

★ 5. Joe's car would not start. He wondered why. His friend said the battery was dead. Joe replaced the battery. The car started. The friend said that this proved he was right.

6. Joe's car would not start. He wondered why. His friend said the battery was dead. Joe turned on the car's headlights. They came on with normal intensity. Joe knew that it was not the battery.

7. "The garlic is what does it," says Ralph. He was referring to his dog, Balboa, now 14 years of age. "I started mixing a clove of garlic into his dog food ever since he was a puppy. There were six puppies in the litter when he was born. I've kept track of Balboa's sisters and brothers and all of them died before they were 10 years old. He's the last one left. The garlic's what has done it."

8. The study of twins separated at birth confirms that genetics controls your destiny. Researchers tracked down a set of twins, now 25 years old, and checked for similarities. Both males eat the same brand of cereal, smoke the same brand of cigarettes, have each married a nurse, work as auto mechanics, and are registered Democrats, and yet neither twin has ever come in contact with the other. The only possible cause of these remarkable similarities is that they have identical genetic makeup.

Video Tutorial

★ 9. For the past 2 weeks, every time Becky's cat, Melanie, sat on her lap, Becky started sneezing uncontrollably. Thinking that she was becoming allergic to her cat, Becky tried an experiment. She gave the cat to her neighbor for a day; during that time, she did not sneeze. As soon as the cat returned and sat on Becky's lap, she began sneezing. Becky started taking some over-the-counter allergy medicine, and the sneezing stopped. What Becky did not know was that the bottle of a new kind of flea powder her husband started using a few weeks earlier had broken, and so he bought the powder they had always used before. Becky continues to take the allergy medicine.

10. Pete was videotaping his sister Nancy while she was walking toward the line of people waiting to go on a roller-coaster ride. Nancy fell hard on the concrete and broke her arm. After getting the arm set and placed in a cast, Pete watched the video to see if he could determine why Nancy fell. Nancy maintained that someone had pushed her from behind. However, when Pete replayed the video recording of the event, he could not see anyone near her. The next day he decided to go back to the park to see if he could find something that might have made Nancy trip and fall. Using the video as a guide, he located the spot where she fell; however, he could not find a hole in the ground or any uneven surface

that might have caused her to fall. Pete concluded that Nancy must have lost her balance as she was walking.

Summary

Study Materials

- The word "cause" has several meanings, and in everyday situations the possibility of ambiguity arises.
- Sufficient condition: Whenever one event ensures that another event is realized.
- Necessary condition: Whenever one thing is *essential*, *mandatory*, or *required* in order for another thing to be realized.
- Causal network: A set of conditions that bring about an effect.
- Normal state: The historical information regarding an object.
- Abnormal state: A drastic change in the normal state. Any change from the normal state requires an explanation, typically a causal one.
- Precipitating cause: The object or event directly involved in bringing about an effect.
- Remote cause: Something that is connected to the precipitating cause by a chain of events.
- Method of agreement: The method that looks at two or more instances of an event to see what they have in common.
- Method of difference: The method that looks for what all the instances of an event do not have in common.
- Joint method of agreement and difference: If two or more instances of an event have only one thing in common, while the instances in which it does *not* occur all share the absence of that thing, then the item is a likely cause.
- Method of residues: The method that subtracts from a complex set of events those parts that already have known causes.
- Method of concomitant variations: The method that looks for two factors that vary together.
- Correlation: A correspondence between two sets of objects, events, or data.
- Although Mill's methods do not provide conclusive proof of causality, the five methods are helpful in discovering correlations and potential causes.
- A good hypothesis provides an explanation for known facts and a way to test an explanation.
- Theoretical science proposes explanations for natural phenomena, while experimental science tests those explanations.
- The process of abduction occurs when we infer explanations for certain facts.
- Inference to the best explanation: Reasoning from the premise that a hypothesis would explain certain facts to the conclusion that the hypothesis is the best explanation for those facts.
- Controlled experiment: One in which multiple experimental setups differ by only one variable.
- Experimental group: The group that gets the variable being tested.

- Control group: The group in which the variable being tested is withheld.
- Five criteria need to be considered to fully appreciate the complexity of causality: (1) There should be a correlation between the cause and the effect. (2) The cause should precede the effect. (3) The cause should be in the proximity of the effect. (4) A set of necessary and sufficient conditions should exist. (5) Alternative explanations should be ruled out.
- The weight of our answers to all five criteria together establishes the grounds for a satisfactory cause-effect relationship.
- We can test a hypothesis by getting it to make a prediction. Predictions are either true or false; the results are used to confirm (support) or disconfirm (refute) the hypothesis.
- Three requirements ensure a fair test of the causal hypothesis: (1) The prediction should be something that is verifiable. (2) The prediction should be unlikely to be true based on our background knowledge. (3) There should be a connection between the hypothesis and the prediction.
- Verifiable prediction: A prediction that, if true, must include an observable event.
- Nontrivial prediction: A prediction that requires reference to background knowledge, which is everything we know to be true.
- The weight we give to a confirmation or refutation is never all-or-nothing. We need to accumulate evidence over a long time.

KEY TERMS

abduction 671	hypothesis 669	method of residues 660
abnormal state 656	inference to the best	necessary condition 652
causal network 656	explanation 671	nontrivial prediction 678
control group 674	joint method of agreement	normal state 656
controlled	and difference 659	precipitating cause 656
experiment 674	method of agreement 657	remote cause 656
correlation 661	method of concomitant	sufficient condition 652
experimental group 674	variations 661	theoretical science 669
experimental science 669	method of difference 658	verifiable prediction 676

LOGIC CHALLENGE: THE SCALE AND THE COINS

You are given ten large canvas bags of identical-looking coins. Nine of the bags contain coins that weigh 1 ounce each, and one bag contains coins that weigh 1.1 ounces each. Because of the small difference in weight, you cannot distinguish the 1-ounce coin from the 1.1-ounce coin just by holding them in your hands. And since they look identical in shape and size, they cannot be distinguished that way either.

You are given a scale. You can place on the scale as much or as little of the contents of the bags that you wish, and it will display the total weight placed on it. However, you are permitted to use the scale only once. You will get only one chance to figure out which bag has the 1.1-ounce coins. How would you solve the problem?

Appendix A
THE LSAT AND LOGICAL REASONING

INTRODUCTION

The Law School Admission Council describes the Law School Admission Test (LSAT) as follows:

> The test consists of five 35-minute sections of multiple-choice questions. Four of the five sections contribute to the test taker's score. These sections include one Reading Comprehension section, one Analytical Reasoning section, and two Logical Reasoning sections. The unscored section, commonly referred to as the variable section, typically is used to pretest new test questions or to preequate new test forms. The placement of this section will vary. Identification of the unscored section is not available until you receive your score report. A 35-minute, unscored writing sample is administered at the end of the test. Copies of your writing sample are sent to all law schools to which you apply. (https://www.lsac.org/jd/lsat/about-the-lsat)

Since law schools require you to take the LSAT, you should practice taking past exams, which are available for purchase or through your school and local libraries. Doing so will familiarize you with several key points:

a. the number of minutes allowed for each section;
b. the directions for each section;
c. typical terminology used;
d. how well you respond to the pressure of taking an actual LSAT exam, especially if you adhere to real-time scenarios for each section; and
e. the answers and explanations for the questions.

An old joke captures this nicely: A world-famous violinist was walking in New York City when a young person asked her, "How do I get to Carnegie Hall?" The violinist replied, "Practice, practice, practice!"

Because getting a law degree requires the ability to comprehend and analyze complex material, it is not surprising that the LSAT asks you to do two things: *read* and *analyze*. And because the LSAT is a timed test, you need to *read efficiently* and *analyze with precision*. Your ability to work *efficiently* is crucial because you have 35 minutes to answer approximately twenty-five questions, meaning you have roughly a minute and a half for each question. This fact reinforces the need for you to practice as much as you can. Your ability to *analyze with precision* can be strengthened by using this book because many of the techniques presented apply directly to the skills required to do well on the LSAT. The chapters in *Logic* provide precise definitions, explanations, examples, and exercises for the logical terms and types of reasoning tasks you will encounter in the LSAT. A thorough knowledge of this content will give you a firm foothold by allowing you to zero in on the logical issues at play in each question.

We will point out how various chapters in *Logic* teach skills that are applicable specifically to the two *logical reasoning* sections, which, as the Law School Admission Council points out, contain questions that "assess the ability to analyze, critically evaluate, and complete arguments as they occur in ordinary language." If you have already worked through the relevant chapters in *Logic*, you can use this guide as a refresher and revisit the exercise sets with an eye toward the specific needs of LSAT questions. If you have not yet worked through these chapters, you can use this guide as a bridge to each chapter's exercise sets and the types of questions asked in the LSAT.

The LSAT has evolved over the years. Today, *most of the LSAT logical reasoning questions involve inductive arguments.* There are many kinds of inductive arguments, such as analogical arguments, statistical arguments, causal arguments, legal arguments, moral arguments, and scientific arguments. *Analogical arguments* (see Chapter 10) are based on the idea that when two things share some relevant characteristics, they probably share other characteristics as well. *Statistical arguments* (see Chapter 13) are based on our ability to generalize. When we observe a pattern, we often create an argument that relies on a statistical regularity. *Causal arguments* (see Chapter 14) are arguments based on knowledge of either causes or effects. For example, a team of medical scientists may conduct experiments to determine if a new drug (the potential cause) will have a desired effect on a particular disease.

As we proceed, we will look at several specific examples of inductive and deductive arguments. We will analyze the arguments in many ways to identify the conclusion and premises, what additional information would strengthen (or weaken) the argument, what assumptions are being made by the person making the argument, specific reasoning flaws, and argument patterns. *You should try analyzing the examples before you look at the answers.* This will give you valuable experience and practice to see how you are doing. You can then compare your answers with the ones we provide.

1. LOGICAL REASONING

A typical logical reasoning section contains around 25 multiple-choice questions. A short *argument* is often given consisting of three or four *statements*. Recall the following definitions from Chapter 1:

- An **argument** is a group of *statements* in which the *conclusion* is claimed to follow from the *premise(s)*.
- A **statement** is a sentence that is either true or false.
- A **premise** is the information intended to provide support for the *conclusion*.
- A **conclusion** is a statement that is claimed to follow from the *premises* of an argument; the *main point* of an argument.

Argument A group of statements in which the conclusion is claimed to follow from the premise(s).

Statement A sentence that is either true or false.

Premise The information intended to provide support for a conclusion.

Conclusion The statement that is claimed to follow from the premises of an argument; the main point of an argument.

The most important thing to remember is that *statements are true or false but arguments are neither true nor false*.

Each LSAT *logical reasoning question* is followed by five possible answers. Your job is *not* to determine whether the *statements* that make up the *argument* are true or false. Instead, your job is to *identify* the *conclusion* and to *assume* that the *premises* are true. Why? Because the LSAT is not a test about facts, it is a test of *logical reasoning*. In other words, what follows from a set of *premises* that are *assumed to be true*?

As most study guides will tell you, *read the question before you read the argument*. The reason is that the LSAT uses several common question types, so if you know what type of question you are required to answer, you can then read the argument with that in mind. Here are some of the most common question types:

- Which one of the following *most accurately expresses* the *main conclusion* of the argument?
- If the *statements* in the argument are *true*, then which one of the following *must also* be true?
- Which one of the following is an *assumption* that is required by the argument?
- Which one of the following, *if true, most weakens* the argument?
- Which one of the following, *if true, most strengthens* the argument?
- Which one of the following is a *reasoning flaw* in the argument?
- Which one of the following exhibits a *reasoning pattern* that is *most like* the one exhibited in the argument?

Notice that many of the question types previously listed use the term "most" (*most accurately expresses; most weakens; most strengthens; most like*). This means that although several of the answer choices might, for example, strengthen the argument, your job is to choose the answer that *strengthens it the most*. In multiple-choice questions, the wrong answers are appropriately called *distractors* because their purpose is to distract you from the correct answer. They will often sound reasonable, but that shouldn't be surprising. The LSAT questions ask you to choose the best answer over the several possibly good answers.

2. DEDUCTIVE AND INDUCTIVE ARGUMENTS

Earlier we said that arguments are *neither true nor false*. Some of the ways logicians classify arguments are *strong, weak, valid,* or *invalid*. We can now further define arguments as being deductive or inductive. A **valid deductive argument** is one in which it is *impossible* for the conclusion to be false, assuming the premises are true. In other words, the conclusion follows necessarily from the premises. On the other hand, an **invalid deductive argument** is one in which it is *possible* for the conclusion to be false, assuming the premises are true. In other words, the conclusion does not follow necessarily from the premises (see Chapter 1, section 1F).

In contrast, a **strong inductive argument** is such that if the premises are *assumed* to be true, then the conclusion is *probably* true. In other words, the probable truth of the

Valid deductive argument An argument in which, assuming the premises are true, it is *impossible* for the conclusion to be false. In other words, the conclusion follows necessarily from the premises.

Invalid deductive argument An argument in which, assuming the premises are true, it is *possible* for the conclusion to be false. In other words, the conclusion does not follow necessarily from the premises.

Strong inductive argument An argument such that if the premises are *assumed* to be true, then the conclusion is *probably* true. In other words, the probable truth of the conclusion *follows from* the truth of the premises.

Weak inductive argument An argument such that either (a) if the premises are *assumed* to be true, then the conclusion is *probably not true*, or (b) a probably true conclusion *does not follow from the premises.*

conclusion *follows from* the truth of the premises. On the other hand, a **weak inductive argument** is such that either (a) if the premises are *assumed* to be true, then the conclusion is *probably not true*, or (b) a probably true conclusion *does not follow from the premises* (see Chapter 1, section 1G).

Let's look at some arguments:

A. All Y are Z.
All X are Y.
All X are Z.

B. All Z are Y.
All X are Y.
All X are Z.

Upon analysis, no matter what terms we substitute for X, Y, and Z in example A, it will always turn out to be a valid argument. In other words, if we *assume* the two premises are true, then *necessarily* the conclusion is true. However, the same doesn't hold for argument B. Even if we *assume* that all Z's and all X's are Y's, it *does not necessarily follow* that all X's are Z's; thus argument B is invalid. For example, although it is true that all whales are mammals, and it is also true that all humans are mammals, it is false that all humans are whales. This is a counterexample to argument B. A **counterexample** to an argument shows the possibility that premises assumed to be true do not make the conclusion necessarily true. A single counterexample to a deductive argument is enough to show that the argument is invalid. Since argument A is valid, it has no counterexamples. If we look once again at argument A, then we can see that the conclusion *does not* amplify or expand the scope of the information in the premises. The first premise states that *every* Y is a Z; the second premise states that every X is a Y. Therefore, under the *assumption* that the premises are true, the conclusion *does not go beyond* what is already contained in the premises. (Exercises 1F.I can be used for practice.)

Counterexample A counterexample to a statement is evidence that shows the statement is false. A counterexample to an argument shows the possibility that premises assumed to be true do not make the conclusion necessarily true. A single counterexample to a deductive argument is enough to show that the argument is invalid.

Let's now look at two different kinds of arguments:

C. Most X are Y.
I have an X.
Probably I have a Y.

D. Some X are Y.
I have an X.
Probably I have a Y.

Upon analysis, if we *assume* the two *premises* in argument C are *true*, then the conclusion is *probably true*; thus, it is a *strong* argument. This is very different from a *valid* argument. A *valid* argument *guarantees* that *if the premises are true*, then the conclusion is true. A *strong inductive argument* cannot offer that guarantee. In other words, the conclusion of a strong inductive argument might be false even if the premises are true.

Analysis also shows that argument D is weak. The key difference is that the term "some" does not carry the same weight as the term "most" did in argument C. Even if we *assume* that both *premises* are *true*, then the conclusion is *not probably true*.

Inductive arguments *amplify* the scope of the information in the premises. For example, the first premise in argument C provides information about *most* X's, but it *does not* make a claim about *every* X. The second premise picks out my X. It is in this sense that we say that the conclusion regarding my X *goes beyond* the information in the premises; thus, it is *possible* that the *conclusion is false* even under the *assumption* that the *premises are true*. (Exercises 1G can be used for practice.)

In all four previous examples, the *logical analysis* focused on the *relationship* between the premises and the conclusion. We simply had to *assume* the premises were true, then analyze either (a) whether the conclusion was *guaranteed* to be true (valid or invalid argument), or (b) whether the conclusion was *probably* true (strong or weak argument).

3. IDENTIFYING CONCLUSIONS AND PREMISES

Every argument has a conclusion, so it helps to identify that first. Here are some **conclusion indicator** words and phrases that may appear in the argument: *therefore, thus, so, consequently, suggests that, it follows that, implies that, hence.* If you are not sure which sentence is the conclusion, you can simply place the word "therefore" in front of each of them to see which works best. On the other hand, the argument might have some **premise indicator** words and phrases: *because, since, as shown by, given that, it follows from.* If you are not sure which sentences are the premises, you can simply place the word "because" in front of each of them to see which works best (see Chapter 1, section 1B). Here is an example of an argument without any indicator words:

> We should boycott that company. They have been found guilty of producing widgets that they knew were faulty, and that caused numerous injuries.

In this case, the first sentence seems to be the point of the argument, and the second sentence seems to offer reasons in support of the conclusion. In other words, *because* the company has been found guilty of producing widgets that they knew were faulty, and that caused numerous injuries, *therefore* we should boycott the company. (Exercises 1B can be used for practice.)

A. Identifying the Conclusion

LSAT questions might ask you to identify the conclusion in a passage. Alternatively, you might have to identify *missing* premises or conclusions (this is covered in Chapter 1, section 1H). Here is a simple example where all you have to do is identify the conclusion:

> There is no reason for you not to start exercising regularly. Exercise helps strengthen your cardiovascular system. It also lowers your cholesterol, increases the blood flow to the brain, and enables you to think longer.

The conclusion is the first sentence. The other two sentences are the premises (support, evidence) offered as *reasons* to accept the conclusion. If you place the word "therefore" in front of each of the three sentences, then the first sentence stands out as the most logical choice. Another way to get the same result is to see that the second and third sentences *work together.* The second sentence states a benefit of exercise, and the third sentence adds three more benefits. (Another tipoff: The third sentence starts out by stating that "It [exercise] also . . . ," which indicates that it is another *reason* that is being put forward.) Let's analyze another argument, but this time we will provide

Conclusion indicators
Words and phrases that indicate the presence of a conclusion (the statement claimed to follow from premises).

Premise indicators
Words and phrases that help us recognize arguments by indicating the presence of premises (statements being offered in support of a conclusion).

five answer choices. As we pointed out earlier, you should approach each example as if it were an actual LSAT test question. If you try analyzing each example before you look at the answer, then you gain valuable experience and practice.

> I don't like movies that rely on computer-generated graphics to take the place of intelligent dialogue, interesting characters, and an intricate plot. After watching the ads on TV, I have the feeling that the new movie *Bad Blood and Good Vibes* is not very good. I predict that it will not win any Academy Awards.

Which of the following is the main point of the argument?

> **A.** The author claims that only movies that have intelligent dialogue, interesting characters, and an intricate plot win Academy Awards.
> **B.** The author does not like movies that rely on computer-generated graphics.
> **C.** The author feels that the new movie is not very good.
> **D.** The author predicts that the movie will not win any Academy Awards.
> **E.** The author obviously watches a lot of movies.

Did you read the question before you read the argument? Doing so would have alerted you that your task is to identify the *main point* (the conclusion) of the argument. It is common to forget this advice; however, with enough practice it will become second nature, so when you start taking practice LSAT exams you will have trained yourself *to read the question first.*

Let's go through the five choices one by one. Although the author does predict that the movie will not win any Academy Awards, nowhere in the argument does the author claim that *only* movies that have intelligent dialogue, interesting characters, and an intricate plot win Academy Awards. Thus, we can eliminate choice (A). Although choice (B) is a statement made by the author, it is a premise, not the conclusion of the argument; thus, we can eliminate it. This is a very important point to remember. An answer choice might be true, but that alone doesn't make it correct. What counts is that it is the *best choice for a particular task*, which in this case is the identification of the main point of the argument. Notice that choice (C) is also a statement made by the author, but it, too, is a premise, not the conclusion of the argument; thus, we can eliminate it. Choice (D) seems to be the conclusion, especially if we add the word "therefore" in front of it. Nevertheless, we should still look at choice (E). Although the statement may be true, there is no evidence that supports this claim as being the main point of the argument. Therefore, choice (D) is the correct answer. Let's analyze another example.

> Wild hogs often damage newly planted seedlings and food crops by rooting, and that also causes soil erosion. In addition, hogs compete with other animals that also forage, usually crowding them out. Lastly, hogs are vectors for diseases communicable to humans and livestock. Farmers should always take vigorous action to reduce wild hog populations near their land.

Which of the following is the main point of the argument?

> **A.** Wild hogs offer farmers a great return on investment.
> **B.** Wild hogs compete with other foraging animals.

C. Wild hogs spread disease to humans and livestock.
D. Farmers need to take action to reduce wild hog populations.
E. Farmers should take the advice of government funded scientific studies.

The key to solving this question is to recognize that the first three sentences offer support for the conclusion, which can be seen if we add the word "because" in front of them and the word "therefore" in front of the last sentence. All we need to do is locate the answer that most closely mirrors the conclusion: *Farmers should always take vigorous action to reduce wild hog populations near their land.* Choice (A) does not reflect the conclusion, so it is eliminated. Choices (B) and (C) are premises, so they are eliminated. Choice (D) restates the conclusion, making it the best choice so far. Choice (E) refers to government studies, but that was not part of the argument, so it is eliminated. Therefore, choice (D) is the correct answer.

B. Choosing the Best Missing Conclusion

Another type of question has a passage containing premises but no conclusion, requiring you to choose the answer that offers the best conclusion given the stated premises. *Don't waste time* trying to decide whether the premises are *actually true or false*—for the purposes of the LSAT just *assume* that the premises are true. Here is an example of a simple argument with a *missing conclusion*:

Banks lend money. We're a bank.

If we *assume* it is true that "Banks lend money," and we *assume* it is also true that "We're a bank," then the *conclusion* is "We lend money."

Another type of question might ask you to choose the conclusion that is *most strongly supported* by the given premises. These kinds of question rely on your ability to analyze subtle uses of everyday words, as illustrated in the next example:

I have a headache. I just took two aspirins. Aspirins can relieve headaches.

The key to solving this is to understand the force of the third sentence. The word "can" implies that aspirin has the ability to relieve a headache, but it *does not* imply that aspirin will always relieve a headache. Therefore, the conclusion that is most strongly supported by the given premises is "My headache will probably be relieved." Here is another example for analysis:

He set three new world record times in the 100-meter sprint this year alone. In almost all cases, when someone has done something remarkable like that in the history of track and field they have later been found guilty of doping.

Which one of the following is the most logical conclusion for this passage?

A. If someone is doping, then they set world records.
B. He is definitely guilty of doping.
C. He is probably guilty of doping.
D. Doping is becoming the major problem in all athletics.
E. Anyone caught doping should be stripped of his or her world record performances.

The key to solving this question is to recognize that the conclusion needs to connect the *person who set the three records* to *people who have later been found guilty of doping*. With this in mind, choice (A) reverses the connection between setting records and doping, so it is eliminated. Choice (B) goes too far; the term "definitely" does not conform with the premise that states "In almost all cases," so it is eliminated. Choice (C) uses the term "probably," which conforms with the premise that states "In almost all cases," making it the best answer so far. Choice (D) does not make the connection that we want, so it is eliminated. Choice (E) makes an assertion about anyone who has already been caught doping, going beyond what the premises tell us, so it is eliminated. Therefore, choice (C) is the correct answer. Let's analyze another example.

> My phone isn't an iPhone, nor is it an Android, and those are the only phones that have state-of-the-art voice recognition personal assistant programs. I can't just ask my phone to find stuff for me, but I need that capability for my research.

Which one of the following is the most logical conclusion for this passage?

- **A.** iPhones and Androids are the most user-friendly phones available.
- **B.** I should get either an iPhone or Android.
- **C.** No other phones offer state-of-the-art voice recognition personal assistant programs.
- **D.** I cannot ask my phone to find stuff.
- **E.** I'm sure other companies will start competing in the personal assistant program market.

The key to solving this question is seeing how the premises work together. The first sentence states that there are only two kinds of phones that offer state-of-the-art voice recognition personal assistant programs (it *doesn't matter* whether this or any other premise is true or false). The next sentence states two important things: (1) The person can't just ask her/his phone to find stuff, and (2) she/he needs that capability for research. The conclusion should be a statement that follows from all the information in the premises; in this case, it should be something that states an action that the speaker will most likely do. With this in mind, choice (A) doesn't offer any course of action, so it is eliminated. Choice (B) seems to offer what we need, so we can keep it for now. Choices (C) and (D) simply restate a premise, so they are eliminated. Choice (E) might be something that will happen in the future; however, it doesn't state an action that the *speaker* will most likely do, so it is eliminated. Therefore, choice (B) is the correct answer.

C. Assumptions: Choosing the Best Missing Premise

Some questions provide stated premises and a conclusion but leave out important information that is needed to support the conclusion. Your job is to determine the *missing assumption*. Here is a simple example:

> Judy must be an honest person because she has an advanced degree.

The premise indicator word "because" lets us know that the statement "she (Judy) has an advanced degree" is used to support the conclusion "Judy must be an honest person." However, in order to connect the given premise to the conclusion we need to supply some missing information. Since the conclusion makes a strong claim, the missing premise is "Every person who has an advanced degree is honest." (Alternatively, "All people who have an advanced degree are honest.") We are *not* concerned with whether the missing premise is actually true; we simply need to determine what needs to be *assumed* in order to derive the conclusion. What would happen if the argument had been slightly different?

Judy is probably an honest person because she has an advanced degree.

The word "probably" indicates the conclusion might be false, so we don't need the strong words "every" or "all" in the missing premise. This will work: "Most people with an advanced degree are honest." The term "most" means more than 50%. Once again, we are *not* concerned with whether the missing premise is actually true; thus, if we *assume* both *premises* are true, then they make the conclusion *likely to be true*.

Why can't the missing premise be "Some people with an advanced degree are honest"? The term "some" is defined as at least one, but the upper limit is unspecified. Since the term allows for the possibility of less than 50%, it does *not* make the *conclusion* likely to be true. The following is an example that requires you to fill in a *missing assumption*:

A. Every dog is a mammal. Therefore, every dog is an animal.

In order for the conclusion to logically follow, we need to connect *mammals* to *animals* such that there can be no doubt that the conclusion follows. This will work: Every mammal is an animal. In other words, the conclusion needs information that connects *every* mammal to the class of animals, and that is what the missing assumption does.

On the other hand, an argument may not need such a strong connection. Here is an example:

B. I have a new car. Therefore, my car probably uses gasoline.

The conclusion needs additional information that, if assumed to be true, makes the conclusion *likely to be true* because the conclusion contains the key word "probably." We need to connect *new cars* to *uses gasoline* such that the conclusion is likely to be true. This will work: Most new cars use gasoline. The missing assumption uses the word "most" to make the connection. As stated earlier, the word "some" would not work because it is too weak (it can mean less than 50%, whereas "most" means more than 50%).

Compare argument B with the following:

C. I have a new car. Therefore, my car definitely uses gasoline.

The term "definitely" implies a much stronger claim than the term "probably" in argument B. Given this, we need to find a missing assumption that supports the stronger conclusion: Every new car uses gasoline. If we assume the original premise and the missing assumption are both true, then the conclusion follows.

You might be thinking, "But that missing assumption is factually false—not every new car uses gasoline." Although your intuition is correct, it is misplaced here. Remember, the LSAT is *not* asking you questions about what is factually true or false. All the questions are artificial; they are *not* designed to assess what you *know*, they are designed to assess how well you can *reason*. Here is an argument and five choices for you to analyze:

> Earmarks are provisions in congressional legislation that direct federal funds to specific projects. Earmarks are meant to benefit all the residents of a particular state. My investigation thus shows that earmarks really benefit only those who make the largest campaign contributions.

Which one of the following, if assumed, enables the argument's conclusion to be properly inferred?

- **A.** Recent congressional legislation takes entirely too long to enact.
- **B.** I have evidence that shows that earmarks are actually written by congressional aides.
- **C.** I have evidence that shows a direct correlation between campaign contributions and earmark benefits to rich donors.
- **D.** I have evidence that shows the largest states get the most earmarks.
- **E.** Congressional legislation can be vetoed by the president.

Did you read the question before you read the argument? Let's go through the five choices. Even though the information in choice (A) may be true, it does not support the conclusion that "earmarks really benefit only those who make the largest campaign contributions," so we can eliminate it. We can apply the same analysis to choice (B), thus eliminating it. Choice (C) does offer evidence, *if it is assumed to be true*, that supports the conclusion, so we can keep it for now. Even if choice (D) were true, that the largest states get the most earmarks, it can simply indicate that the states with the largest populations need more money to help with infrastructure, among other things, than states with smaller populations; this does not add the missing support for the conclusion, so we can eliminate it. Finally, choice (E) states a fact about legislation but it does not support the conclusion. Therefore, choice (C) is the correct answer. Here is another argument for analysis:

> Eating meat is natural, so it's unobjectionable to eat meat.

On which one of the following assumptions does the argument rely?

- **A.** Some people are vegetarians.
- **B.** Human beings have teeth that help chew meat so it can be easily digested.
- **C.** Eating uncooked meat is dangerous.
- **D.** Natural activities are unobjectionable.
- **E.** Meat is a good source of usable protein.

To solve this question, we must recognize that a missing premise (assumption) is needed to connect the natural part of eating meat with its being unobjectionable.

Keeping that in mind, choice (A) does not make the needed connection (it does *not* help support the conclusion), so it is eliminated. The information provided in choice (B) does not make the needed connection either, so it is eliminated. Choice (C) does not help make the needed connection, so it is eliminated. Choice (D) connects *natural* to *unobjectionable*, making it the best choice so far. Choice (E) offers a reason to eat meat, but does not make the needed connection, so it is eliminated. Therefore, choice (D) is the correct answer. (Exercises 1H can be used for practice for missing conclusions and missing premises.)

4. ADDITIONAL INFORMATION THAT STRENGTHENS OR WEAKENS AN ARGUMENT

Some questions will ask you to determine whether additional evidence, *if assumed to be true*, either *strengthens* or *weakens* a given argument (see Chapter 1, "The Role of New Information"). Sometimes adding an additional premise to a weak argument can create a strong argument. For example, consider the following:

> There are green and black marbles in a box. Thus, a marble picked at random will probably be green.

Since we do not know how many marbles of each color are in the box, the premise *does not* make the conclusion likely to be true; thus, it is a weak argument. However, suppose we are given some additional information:

> There are green and black marbles in the box. *Eight of the marbles are green and two are black.* Thus, a marble picked at random will probably be green.

If the additional information is *assumed to be true*, then there is an 80% (8/10) chance of picking a green marble. Since the conclusion is now highly likely to be true, the assumed evidence *strengthens* the original argument. Here is another example for analysis:

> The gas pump stopped pumping gas into Jane's car; therefore, her car's gas tank is full.

Which one of the following, if true, would most strengthen the argument?

- **A.** Jane prepaid $10 for gas.
- **B.** Jane usually buys gas every 3 days.
- **C.** The electricity that runs the gas pump housing stopped working.
- **D.** Jane unknowingly bumped the dispenser, which shut off the gas being pumped.
- **E.** Jane's gas tank holds twenty gallons, and nineteen gallons was pumped into the gas tank.

Choice (A) can explain why the gas pump automatically stopped pumping gas (once it reached $10), but it does *not* help strengthen the conclusion because it is unlikely that Jane would have known that exactly $10 would fill the gas tank, so it is eliminated. Choice (B) tells us when Jane buys gas but it doesn't add support to the conclusion, so it is eliminated. Choices (C) and D actually weaken the argument as to why the pump stopped, so they are eliminated. Choice (E) tells us that nineteen gallons was administered into a twenty-gallon tank, which is enough to fill Jane's gas tank in most normal cases; since this offers the *most strength* of all the answers, it is the correct answer.

On the other hand, it is also possible that additional information will *weaken* an argument. For example, consider the following:

> I just drank a bottle of Sunrise Spring Mineral Water. Since it has been shown that most bottled water is safe, I can conclude, with some confidence, that the water was safe.

Assuming the premises are true, this is a strong argument. However, suppose we are given this additional evidence:

> Happy Sunshine Manufacturing Corporation has announced that it is recalling all of its Sunrise Spring Mineral Water due to a suspected contamination at one of its bottling facilities.

If we assume that this additional information is true, then the original conclusion is unlikely to be true; thus its addition weakens the original argument. Here is another example for analysis:

> The large box of cereal I bought says that it contains twenty-four ounces. But when I opened it, there was at least three inches of empty space instead of it being full to the top of the inner bag. The manufacturers are obviously guilty of false labeling.

Which one of the following, if true, would most weaken the argument?

- **A.** The cereal is number one in sales in the United States.
- **B.** Some cereals are lighter in weight than others.
- **C.** The box says that the contents might settle as a result of shipping.
- **D.** Cereals are boxed by an automatic dispenser.
- **E.** Empty space in packaging usually means contents do not meet specifications.

Choice (A) does nothing to weaken the argument, so we can eliminate it. Choice (B) sounds promising until we realize that it does not affect the argument's conclusion, so it is eliminated. Choice (C) provides evidence to explain the empty space, which weakens the conclusion, so we can keep it while we analyze the rest of the choices. Choice (D) does not help us understand why the empty space is there and it doesn't weaken the argument, so it can be eliminated. Choice (E) actually strengthens the argument, so it can't be correct. Therefore, choice (C) is the correct answer.

Of course, not all additional information will affect an argument. Thus, you must also be able to rule out additional evidence that is *irrelevant to the strength of the conclusion.* Eliminating wrong choices makes your final decision much easier. For example, consider the earlier argument:

> I just drank a bottle of Sunrise Spring Mineral Water. Since it has been shown that most bottled water is safe, I can conclude, with some confidence, that the water was safe.

We already know that this is a strong argument. Now suppose we are given this additional evidence:

> The bottle of water I just drank contained sixteen ounces.

If we assume that this additional information is true, then the original conclusion is unaffected because the additional evidence is *irrelevant* to the strength of the conclusion. Of course, in another context this additional information might be relevant. For example, if further information states that only the sixteen-ounce bottles of the water are contaminated, then this would be relevant to the strength of the argument. (Exercises 1G can be used for practice.)

5. ARGUMENTS THAT USE EITHER ANALOGICAL, STATISTICAL, OR CAUSAL REASONING

A. Analogical Reasoning

Some questions that ask which piece of evidence, if true, would most weaken (or strengthen) a given argument rely on *analogical reasoning*, the subject of Chapter 10. To draw an analogy is simply to indicate that there are similarities between two or more things. Analogical reasoning can be analyzed as a type of inductive argument; it is a matter of probability, based on experience.

If a question asks you to choose the answer that most *strengthens* a given analogical argument, then the correct answer will provide additional evidence of *similarities* between the items mentioned. In contrast, if a question asks you to choose the answer that most *weakens* a given analogical argument, then the correct answer will provide additional evidence of *differences* between the items mentioned. Let's look at a few examples.

> **A.** We both bought new vehicles. My vehicle averages 40 miles per gallon of gasoline. Therefore, your vehicle will probably average 40 miles per gallon of gasoline.

Suppose you are given this new information:

> We both bought the same make and model car with identical engine size.

This information, if true, *strengthens* the original analogical argument because the two cars share some additional *similar* characteristics that are relevant to gas mileage.

However, suppose you are given this new information:

> I bought a hybrid car, and you bought a heavy-duty pickup truck.

This information, if true, *weakens* the original analogical argument because the two vehicles have some additional *different* characteristics that are relevant to gas mileage.

Questions that rely on analogical reasoning can be asked in different ways. Here is an example:

> The new *Batman* movie set a box-office record. The last movie that set a box-office record won the Oscar for Best Picture. So, the new *Batman* movie is probably going to win the Oscar for Best Picture.

Which one of the following, if true, would most support the argument?

- **A.** The *Batman* movie is rated PG-13.
- **B.** The last movie to set a box-office record was based on a comic book hero.
- **C.** The previous Best Picture movie was made in England; the *Batman* movie was made in the United States.
- **D.** No movie based on a comic book character has ever won Best Picture.
- **E.** No movie that runs for more than 2 hours has ever won the Best Picture award.

The argument relies on an analogy between the *Batman* movie and a past Best Picture winner. It offers one common characteristic between the two movies—namely, the fact that they both set a box-office record. Since you are asked to locate the answer that would most support the argument, you need to find an additional relevant characteristic that the two movies have in common.

Choice (A) does not connect the *Batman* movie to the previous Best Picture movie, so it can be eliminated. Choice (B) provides an additional characteristic that both movies have in common, so it is the best choice so far. Choice (C) weakens the argument because it shows how the two movies differ; it can be eliminated. Choice (D) weakens the argument because it makes it unlikely that such a movie will win the Best Picture award; it can be eliminated. Choice (E) is irrelevant in this context because we don't know the running time of the *Batman* movie, so it can be eliminated. Therefore, choice (B) is the correct answer. Let's analyze another example:

> If you like the taste of Russ's Steaks, then you'll like the taste of Mutt's Burgers. Mutt gets his burger meat from the same supplier that Russ gets his steaks. Russ gets his meat fresh daily. So does Mutt. Russ grills his steaks. Mutt grills his burgers.

Which one of the following, if true, would most weaken the argument?

- **A.** Both restaurants are well within your price range for eating out.
- **B.** Russ's Steaks is closer to your apartment than Mutt's Burgers.
- **C.** At Russ's Steaks you can buy beer, but not at Mutt's Burgers.
- **D.** Neither of the two restaurants has won any awards.
- **E.** Russ uses a special sauce on the steaks that is not available to Mutt.

The argument relies on an analogy between Russ's Steaks and Mutt's Burgers and offers three common characteristics (same supplier; fresh meat daily; grilled). Since you are asked to locate the answer that most weakens the argument, you need to find a relevant characteristic that the restaurants *do not share*. Choice (A) strengthens the argument, so it can be eliminated. Choice (B) provides a difference between the two restaurants, but the difference is *irrelevant* to whether you will like the taste of the food, which is what the conclusion claims, so it can be eliminated. Choice (C) offers a difference between the two restaurants, but it doesn't speak to the taste of the steaks and burgers; let's see if we can locate a better answer. Choice (D) tells us something that the two restaurants have in common, so it doesn't weaken the argument; it can be eliminated. Choice (E) shows a relevant difference between the two restaurants—the sauce—which can directly affect the taste of the steaks but which is lacking in the burgers. Since the two restaurants *do not share this relevant characteristic*, this information, if true, most weakens the argument. Therefore, choice (E) is the correct answer. (Exercises 10A, 10B, and 10C can be used for practice.)

B. Statistical Reasoning

Some questions that ask which piece of evidence, if assumed to be true, would most weaken (or strengthen) a given argument rely on *statistical reasoning*, the subject of Chapter 13. Evaluating arguments that rely on statistical evidence requires the correct interpretation of the statistical evidence as it relates to the conclusion of the argument.

The most important items to consider in an analysis of a statistical argument concern the population and sample. *Population* refers to any group of objects, not just human populations. A *sample* is a subset, or part, of a population. For example, if the *population* in question were the student body of a large university, say, 10,000 students, then a *sample* would be any portion of that population. A *representative sample* accurately reflects the characteristics of the population as a whole. Let's look at an example.

> Nearly 90% of a sample of registered voters said that they will vote for the Democratic nominee for mayor. Therefore, we can confidently predict that the Democratic nominee will be elected mayor.

Suppose you are given this new information:

> The sample was large, random, and had an equal number of registered Democrats, Republicans, and Independents.

This information, if true, *strengthens* the original statistical argument because the sample gave equal representation to Democrats, Republicans, and Independents. However, suppose you are given this new information:

> The sample included only registered Democrats.

This information, if true, *weakens* the original statistical argument because it is a biased sample; it only surveyed registered Democratic voters.

Questions that rely on statistical reasoning can be asked in different ways. For example:

> Nine out of 10 students surveyed claimed the graduation requirements for a baccalaureate degree were too stringent. Therefore, graduation requirements at colleges nationwide are too stringent.

Which one of the following, if true, would most weaken the argument?

A. The students surveyed were from one small community college in Iowa.
B. The students surveyed had at least twenty-four credits.
C. The survey consisted of 10,000 students from all across the United States.
D. College students can choose from a wider variety of courses than ever before.
E. Today's graduates have an average college debt of $24,000.

The argument relies on the results of a single survey (the *sample*) to support a claim about colleges nationwide (the *population*). Since you are asked to locate the answer that most weakens the argument, the answer must demonstrate that the sample is *not* representative of the population. Choice (A), if true, clearly shows that the sample (one community college in Iowa) is unlikely to be representative of the population (all colleges in the United States), so it may be the answer we are looking for. Let's examine the other choices to be sure. Choice (B) tells us that the sample did not include students with fewer than twenty-four credits, so it does weaken the argument somewhat; however, it does not tell us the size of the sample or where it was conducted, so it is not as good an answer as choice (A). Choice (C) strengthens the argument, so it can be eliminated. Choices (D) and (E) do *not* discuss the issue of whether graduation requirements for a baccalaureate degree are too stringent, so these choices can be eliminated. Therefore, choice (A) is the correct answer. Let's analyze another example:

> Last year, more than 5000 people in the northeastern United States contracted a rare and sometimes fatal tick disease called babesiosis. The microscopic organism infects red blood cells, and symptoms take anywhere from 1 to 8 weeks to manifest. Thus, we can conclude that people with autoimmune problems are especially vulnerable to this tick-borne disease.

Which one of the following, if true, would most strengthen the argument?

A. Babesiosis is fatal only if medical treatment is not started within 48 hours after the tick bite.
B. Researchers found that 80% of the 5000 people infected with babesiosis were over 12 years old.
C. Researchers found that 72% of the 5000 people infected with babesiosis had preexisting autoimmune disorders.
D. Babesiosis occurs in people of all ages.
E. Very few cases of babesiosis occur in other parts of the United States.

The argument relies on statistics regarding 5000 people in the northeastern United States to conclude that people with autoimmune problems are especially vulnerable to a disease. Since you are asked to locate the answer that most strengthens the argument, the answer must connect autoimmune problems to the disease. Choices (A) and (B), although interesting, do not directly connect autoimmune problems to the disease; therefore, they can be eliminated. Choice (C) tells us that 72% of the 5000 people infected with babesiosis had preexisting autoimmune disorders, making it the best answer so far. Choices (D) and (E) do not connect autoimmune problems to the disease, so they are eliminated. Therefore, choice (C) is the correct answer. (Exercises 13A and 13E can be used for practice.)

C. Causal Reasoning

Some questions that ask which piece of evidence, if assumed to be true, would most weaken (or strengthen) a given argument rely on *causal reasoning*, the subject of Chapter 14. Simply put, a *cause* is a set of conditions that bring about an effect. A common error is to confuse a *correlation* with *causation*. For example, it is a fact that most people who go swimming wear swimsuits. Also, people tend to put on their swimsuits *before* they go swimming, so there is a strong correlation between the two things. Nevertheless, *correlation does not guarantee causation*. In our example, merely putting on a swimsuit does not cause you to go swimming (you might simply be trying on a new swimsuit in a store). In other words, just because one thing happens before another thing does not guarantee that the first thing caused the second thing. At best, a correlation reveals a *possible* case of causality. Let's look at a few simple examples:

The lamp in your room does not work. Therefore, the light bulb is defective.

Determine whether the following new information strengthens or weakens the argument.

A. The ceiling light works.

If we assume this information is true, then there is electricity available in the room; thus, the new information *strengthens* the argument. However, suppose we were given this new information instead:

B. The ceiling light does not work.

If we assume this information is true, then perhaps there is no electricity available anywhere in the room; thus, the new information *weakens* the argument.

An LSAT question regarding causality will contain an argument based on some cause-and-effect scenario. If you are asked to pick an answer that will *weaken* the argument, then you are expected to locate an *alternative explanation*—some other cause that could have brought about the effect. Any causal claim can be challenged by suggestions of alternative potential causes. On the other hand, you might be asked to pick an answer that will *strengthen* the argument. If so, then you are expected to locate the answer that either (a) most supports the causal claim offered in the given argument, or (b) best eliminates other alternative explanations.

Questions that rely on causal reasoning can be asked in different ways. Here is an example:

Shortly after purchasing a new synthetic scarf, Carolyn developed a rash around her neck. She decided to stop wearing the scarf. In a few days, the rash went away. She concluded that she is allergic to the synthetic material used to make the scarf.

Which one of the following, if true, would most weaken the argument?

A. Carolyn had a similar allergic reaction to a sweater that contained synthetic material.
B. On the same day she purchased the scarf, Carolyn ate a new brand of bread that contained an allergen.
C. The scarf manufacturer recommends that you wash the scarf before wearing.
D. Carolyn often wears scarves, especially when it is cold outside.
E. Research has shown that some synthetic materials can cause allergic reactions.

The argument relies on a *conjectured* causal connection between the synthetic material in a new scarf and a rash (an allergic reaction). It offers a correlation—the rash occurred *after* she wore the scarf. Since you are asked to locate the answer that most weakens the argument, the answer must provide an *alternative explanation*—some other cause that could have brought about the effect. Choice (A) *supports* the conclusion, so it cannot be the correct answer. Choice (B) provides an alternative explanation (cause) for the rash—the bread contains an allergen that could have brought about the effect. This is the best answer so far. Choice (C) would be relevant if we knew whether Carolyn washed the scarf before she wore it. Without this additional information, the answer, by itself, doesn't weaken the argument. Choice (D) does not provide an alternative explanation for the rash, so it can be eliminated. Choice (E) *supports* the conclusion, so it cannot be the correct answer. Therefore, choice (B) is the correct answer. Let's analyze another example:

> Jill claims that her longevity (she is 85 years old) is the result of a rigorous exercise program and a healthy diet. Jill had two siblings who died before they reached 50 years of age.

Which one of the following, if true, would most strengthen the argument?

A. Jill and her siblings all lived in different cities throughout their adult lives.
B. All of Jill's siblings liked the same kinds of food as Jill.
C. Jill and her siblings got married before they were 24 years old.
D. Jill's two siblings died from different causes.
E. None of Jill's siblings exercised.

The argument relies on a *conjectured* causal connection between a rigorous exercise program and a healthy diet and Jill's longevity. Since you are asked to locate the answer that most strengthens the argument, the answer must either (a) most support the causal claim offered in the given argument, or (b) best eliminate other alternative explanations. Choice (A) offers an alternative explanation for Jill's longevity (life expectancy is often different for many cities), which weakens the argument. You can eliminate it. Choice (B) also weakens the argument since it offers evidence that all the siblings ate similar food; it can be eliminated. Choice (C) offers a similarity between the siblings, so it doesn't offer an alternative explanation for Jill's longevity; it can be eliminated. Choice (D) does not provide additional support for Jill's causal claim, and it doesn't tell us how the siblings died (perhaps as the result of accidents), so it can be eliminated. Choice (E) shows how Jill differed from her siblings in one important way—the rigorous exercise program. Although it doesn't mention anything about a healthy diet, it is the best choice available. Therefore, choice (E) is the correct answer. (Exercises 14H can be used for practice.)

6. EXPLAINING OR RESOLVING GIVEN INFORMATION

Some questions will *not* contain an argument. Instead, you will be given a few pieces of information that appear to conflict with each other, but which you must assume to be true. Your job is to pick an answer that *explains* or *resolves* the apparent discrepancy between the pieces of information. Let's analyze an example:

> Upon responding to a burglary, Jacob's fingerprints were found at the scene of a crime. However, Jacob's sister testified that Jacob was at her house fifty miles away at the time of the burglary.

Which one of the following, if true, most helps to resolve the apparent discrepancy in the passage?

- **A.** Jacob has never been arrested before for a crime.
- **B.** Jacob's sister is lying to protect Jacob.
- **C.** The burglary took place at a gated community.
- **D.** The police responded to the burglary within 15 minutes of the report.
- **E.** Jacob owns several pairs of gloves.

Remember that you must *assume* that two pieces of information are true: (1) Jacob's fingerprints were found at the scene of a crime, and (2) Jacob's sister testified that Jacob was at her house fifty miles away at the time of the burglary. Your job is to locate the answer that, *if true*, best explains or reconciles (1) and (2). Choice (A) doesn't explain why Jacob's fingerprints were found at the crime scene, so we can eliminate it. Choice (B) explains why Jacob's sister's *testified* as she did—*she lied*—and it explains why Jacob's fingerprints were found at the crime scene (he was not fifty miles away), so this is possibly the best answer. Choice (C) does not explain why Jacob's fingerprints were found at the crime scene, so it is eliminated. Although Choice (D) seems to support the sister's claim that Jacob was fifty miles away (it would be quite difficult for Jacob to travel fifty miles in 15 minutes), nevertheless, it doesn't explain why Jacob's fingerprints were found at the crime scene, nor does choice (E). Thus, choice (B) is the correct answer. Let's analyze another example:

> People whose income places them within the government's guidelines for "living in poverty," are, by definition, those who have the lowest income. However, studies show that this group spends more proportionally on state-run lottery tickets than any other socioeconomic group.

Which one of the following, if true, most helps to resolve the apparent discrepancy in the passage?

A. The federal government should make state-run lotteries unconstitutional.
B. Playing the lottery is a good way to have fun.
C. Many of those living in poverty view winning the lottery as their only hope of getting out of poverty.
D. You have a greater chance of being struck by lightning than winning the lottery.
E. A lot of money is spent on television advertisements for state lotteries.

To solve this problem, we need something that can *reconcile* the (assumed) facts that those in poverty have the lowest incomes, *but* they spend the most (proportionally) on lottery tickets. The answer must explain *why* they spend the little money that they have on lottery tickets. Choice (A) offers a recommendation but it doesn't explain the actions of people living in poverty, so it is eliminated. Choice (B) seems to apply to all socioeconomic groups, not just those living in poverty; however, let's leave it for now. Choice (C) offers an explanation that directly focuses on the actions of those living in poverty, so it is the best choice so far. Choice (D) also doesn't explain the actions of people living in poverty, so it is eliminated. Choice (E) can be eliminated because television advertisements are accessible to all socioeconomic groups. Thus, choice (C) is the correct answer.

7. ARGUMENT FLAWS

Some questions require you to expose the *reasoning flaw* in an argument. These kinds of questions *do not* ask you to determine any factual issues. You simply need to figure out *why the argument is weak*, which is a logical issue, not a factual one. This is different from questions that ask you to choose an answer that would *weaken* an argument. A *flawed-argument* question asks you to choose the answer that correctly describes why the argument is weak.

Some of these questions involve informal fallacies, the subject of Chapter 4, which presents twenty-four fallacies. An *informal fallacy* is a mistake in reasoning that occurs in ordinary language and concerns the content of the argument rather than its form. Informal fallacies include mistakes of relevance, assumption, ambiguity, and diversion. We will mention only a few fallacies here, so you should work through the chapter and answer all the exercise sets; this will give you a good foundation for these types of LSAT questions.

A. Fallacies Based on Personal Attacks or Emotional Appeals

The strength of an argument should be judged on objective grounds. If an argument is based solely on an attack against the person making the argument, not on the merits of the argument itself, then a reasoning flaw occurs and the argument is weak.

The *ad hominem abusive fallacy* is distinguished by an attack on alleged character flaws of a person instead of the person's argument. Generally speaking, a person's character is irrelevant to the determination of the truth or falsity of her claims or the strength of her argument. Here is an example:

> You should not believe what she says about our economy because she is a left-leaning, card-carrying liberal.

An economic argument should be judged on the merits of the advice and strength of the argument presented, not by vague labels denigrating a person's character. The fallacy occurs because it avoids a logical analysis of whether the opponent's arguments are strong or weak. Let's analyze another example:

> You can be sure the senator's tax plan is not going to benefit the country as a whole because he's a multimillionaire and stands to benefit from extending the current tax cuts.

Which of the following most accurately describes a flaw in the argument?

A. Tax increases generally result in a recession.
B. The senator has recently been divorced.
C. The senator is the highest ranking member of his party.
D. Whether someone stands to benefit from his own tax plan does not give a reason why that tax plan will or will not benefit the country as a whole.
E. Most proposed legislation never makes it out of committee.

The key to solving this problem is to see if the *conclusion* (the senator's tax plan is not going to benefit the country as a whole) is supported by the *single premise* (he's a multimillionaire and stands to benefit from extending the current tax cuts). To identify a *reasoning flaw* requires showing *why* the evidence (the premise) *does not* strongly support the conclusion. The argument talks about tax cuts, not tax increases, so choice (A) is irrelevant to the discussion of an argument flaw. Choice (B) does not pertain to an argument flaw either, so it can be eliminated. Choice (C) does not directly connect to the conclusion, so it can be eliminated. Choice (D) shows that the reasoning is flawed; the *premise*, even if true, does not support the *conclusion* because the tax plan may still benefit the country as a whole. Choice (E) also does not talk about the connection of the premise to the conclusion, so it can be eliminated. Thus, choice (D) is the correct answer. (Exercises 4B can be used for practice.)

B. Weak Inductive Argument Fallacies

A *generalization* fallacy occurs when an argument relies on a mistaken use of the principles behind making a generalization. For example, it is not unusual for someone to have a negative experience with members of a group and then quickly stereotype the other members by assigning derogatory characteristics to all or most of the group. An argument that relies on a small sample that is unlikely to represent the population commits the *fallacy of hasty generalization*. Here is an example:

> I saw a fraternity guy act rudely to a fast-food employee in the food court. Probably most fraternity and sorority members are rude and arrogant.

The premise reports the observation of a single instance, but the conclusion generalizes the observed behavior to most fraternity *and* sorority members, even though no sorority members were observed. Thus, the conclusion was based on the mistaken belief that a single observation is representative of the entire group. The evidence in this case is not adequate to make such a generalization, so the premise cannot provide a good reason to support the conclusion.

Scientific advances owe much to experiments that verify cause-effect relationships. Science also has methods that confirm the existence of patterns that help us to understand the world and to predict future events. *Fallacies of false cause* occur when a causal connection is assumed to exist between two events when none actually exists, or when the assumed causal connection is unlikely to exist. Since causal claims require strong evidence, a cause-effect claim based on insufficient evidence commits the fallacy of false cause. Here is an example:

> Last week I bought a new car, and today I found out that I am being laid off at work. I shouldn't have bought that car; it brought me bad luck.

The person *incorrectly infers* that buying the new car caused him to be laid off. The fallacious reasoning relies on the *mistaken causal assumption* that simply because X occurred *before* Y, therefore X *caused* Y. Let's analyze an example:

> The Dow Jones Industrial Average surged by 200 points this afternoon. This proves my theory that the stock market is sensitive to solar activity, because there was a substantial solar flare this morning.

Which of the following most accurately describes a flaw in the argument?

    A. The argument uses the sun as an analogy to explain the Dow surge.
    B. The argument is based on the authority of the stock market.
    C. No mechanism is offered for a causal link between the sun and the stock market, so this is best classified as a coincidence.
    D. The argument begs the question because the evidence for the conclusion is already smuggled into the premises.
    E. Since the argument uses terms that change in the premises and the conclusion, the argument suffers from the fallacy of equivocation.

The answer to this problem must demonstrate that the *conclusion* ("This proves my theory that the stock market is sensitive to solar activity") is supported by the *premises* ("The Dow Jones Industrial Average surged by 200 points this afternoon"; "there was a substantial solar flare this morning"). Since the argument makes a *causal claim* (the solar flare caused the Dow to surge) the answer must hit on this point. Choice (A) claims the flaw is based on an *analogy*, but the argument involves a cause-effect claim, so this choice is incorrect. Choice (B) claims the argument is based on *authority*, but again, the argument involves a cause-effect claim, thus eliminating this choice. Choice (C) identifies that the argument does not offer a plausible mechanism for the conjectured causal link, making it the best choice so far. Choice (D) claims the argument *begs the question*, while choice (E) claims the argument is flawed because of *equivocation*, but since we know the argument involves a cause-effect claim, both choices can be eliminated. Thus, choice (C) is the correct answer. (Exercises 4C can be used for practice.)

C. Fallacies of Unwarranted Assumption or Diversion

Fallacies of unwarranted assumption exhibit a special kind of reasoning error: They assume the truth of some unproved or questionable claim. The fallacies become apparent when the assumptions and lack of support are exposed, thus revealing the weak points of the argument.

Arguments often rely on the opinions of experts, specialists whose education, experience, and knowledge provide relevant support for a claim. When an argument uses expert testimony that is backed by strong evidence with no hint of impropriety, then the argument is most likely strong (as long as the testimony falls within the realm of the expert's field). On the other hand, arguments that rely on the opinions of people who either have *no* expertise, training, or knowledge relevant to the issue at hand, or whose testimony is not trustworthy, are arguments that *appeal to an unqualified authority*. Here is an example:

> I'm Nick Panning, quarterback of the Los Angeles Seals. I've been eating *Oaties* for breakfast since I was a kid. *Oaties* taste great, and they have all the nutrition kids need. You should get some for your kids today.

Merely being famous does not qualify someone to pronounce the merits of a product. An athlete generally has no expertise in the nutritional value of a breakfast cereal. On the other hand, a person with a Ph.D. in nutrition would presumably be in a good position to offer a fair assessment of the breakfast cereal (provided the opinion is not based on monetary compensation). Let's analyze the following example:

> Given its voracious appetite, a great white shark eats more than any person does. Additionally, great white sharks are more massive than adult humans. Therefore, it follows that great white sharks as a whole consume more food than human beings do.

Which of the following most accurately describes a flaw in the argument?

- **A.** The argument assumes a causal link between shark size and how much food it consumes.
- **B.** Just because individual sharks eat more than people do, it does not mean sharks as a whole eat more than humans do. There are many more people than there are sharks.
- **C.** The argument relies on a false analogy between sharks and humans.
- **D.** The argument generalizes from one shark to all sharks; it overlooks the possibility that some sharks eat less than some humans.
- **E.** A red herring is smuggled into the premises; this results in attention being diverted from the apparent false conclusion.

The key to solving this problem is to see if the *conclusion* ("great white sharks *as a whole* consume more food than human beings do") is supported by the *premises* ("a great white shark eats more than any person"; "great white sharks are more massive than adult humans"). From evidence about the *individual members of two groups*, the argument concludes with a statement about the *groups as a whole*. In other words, it assumes that the two groups in question have the same number of members. Choice (A) claims the flaw is based on a faulty causal link, but it is not a causal argument so it can be eliminated. Choice (B) correctly points out that although an individual shark eats more than an individual person, there are many more people than there are sharks, making it the best answer so far. Choice (C) claims the flaw is based on a false analogy, but it is not an analogical argument so it can be eliminated. Choice (D) misses the point of the conclusion, which talks about two groups, sharks and humans, so it can be eliminated. Choice (E) claims the argument is flawed because of a red herring fallacy, but because this is not what occurs in the argument, it is eliminated. Thus, choice (B) is the correct answer. (Exercises 4D can be used for practice.)

8. RECOGNIZING REASONING PATTERNS

Some questions will ask you to choose the answer that *mirrors* the reasoning pattern of a given argument. To do so, you must know how to *identify* reasoning patterns. Learning to symbolize the *logical form* (structure) of the argument by substituting capital letters for either *class terms* or *statements* in the argument can help you answer these types of questions. The techniques required for these skills are presented in Chapters 1, 5, and 7.

A. Class Terms

Here are two examples that use class terms:

A. All *dogs* are *mammals*.   **B.** All *mammals* are *dogs*.
All *beagles* are *dogs*.   All *beagles* are *dogs*.
All *beagles* are *mammals*.   All *beagles* are *mammals*.

For the purposes of our analysis, we italicized the *class terms* in the argument. Remember that when taking the LSAT, you will *not* be asked to determine whether the statements are true or false. Any time spent thinking about this shortens the time you have to identify the correct answer. Additionally, *it does not matter whether either argument A or B is valid or invalid*. All you need to do is identify the reasoning pattern. To do this, use capital letters to represent *class terms*; for example, D = *dogs*, M = *mammals*, and B = *beagles*.

A. All D are M.   **B.** All M are D.
All B are D.   All B are D.
All B are M.   All B are M.

Once you reveal the given argument's pattern, you simply have to identify which of the five choices mirrors that reasoning pattern. Let's analyze an example.

Some ingredients in soap are known to cause cancer. Some ingredients in hair shampoo are known to cause cancer. It follows that some ingredients in soap are the same as some ingredients in hair shampoo.

Which of the following exhibits a reasoning pattern that is most similar to the argument?

- **A.** Some vegetables are low-calorie foods. Most low-calorie foods are organic plants. It follows that most vegetables are organic plants.
- **B.** Some vegetables are low-calorie foods. All low-calorie foods are organic plants. Thus, most vegetables are organic plants.
- **C.** Nearly all vegetables are organic plants. That's because some vegetables are low-calorie foods, and some organic plants are low-calorie foods.
- **D.** Some vegetables are low-calorie foods, and some organic plants are low-calorie foods. So, no vegetables are organic plants.
- **E.** Some vegetables are organic plants. That's because some vegetables are low-calorie foods, and some organic plants are low-calorie foods.

To solve this problem, we must identify the reasoning pattern in the given argument. Let's start by substituting letters for the terms: S = *ingredients in soap*, C = *known to cause cancer*, and H = *ingredients in hair shampoo*:

Some S are C. Some H are C. *It follows that* some S are H.

We italicized "It follows that" to emphasize that it is a *conclusion indicator phrase*. It is important to note that the answer *may have* a different conclusion indicator word or phrase, such as "thus" or "therefore," which will *not* affect the overall reasoning pattern. Also, the answer *may have* the conclusion appear first instead of last. Again, this will *not* affect the overall reasoning pattern because it doesn't matter where the conclusion appears. However, to make it easier to find the correct answer you could reconstruct the arguments in the five answers so the conclusion occurs last as it does in the given argument.

Choice (A) uses the word "most," which means more than 50%, instead of the word "some," which means "at least one," making this a crucial difference; thus, this choice is eliminated. Choice (B) uses the word "all" instead of the word "some" which is also a crucial difference; thus, this choice is eliminated. Choice (C) uses the phrase "nearly all" instead of the word "some" and Choice (D) uses the word "no," both of which make a crucial difference, so these choices are eliminated. In choice (E), the conclusion comes first, but if we reconstruct the argument, then we can see that it has the same reasoning pattern as the given argument. Therefore, choice (E) is the correct answer. (Exercises 1F.I can be used for practice.)

B. Conditional Statements

So far, we have been using letters to represent class terms (for example, D = *dogs*). We can now expand this technique to different types of statements. Let's compare the following two examples:

- **H.** All *pizza toppings* are *delicious morsels*.
- **I.** If *Sherry lives in Los Angeles,* then *Sherry lives in California*.

In example H, the two italicized words are *class terms*, which *by themselves* are neither true nor false. However, the two italicized parts of example I are *statements* that are either true or false (we call them *simple statements*). In addition, example I contains the logical vocabulary words "if" and "then." Taken as a whole, example I is a *compound statement* and it, too, is either true or false. We can use letters to represent the simple statements in example I while keeping the logical vocabulary in place. For example, if we let *L = Sherry lives in Los Angeles* and *C = Sherry lives in California*, then we get the following for example I: If *L*, then *C*.

C. Translating Conditional Statements

A thorough grasp of conditional statements can help you navigate many LSAT questions. As we discussed, it is important to avoid thinking about whether LSAT question statements are true or false, and having a technique for translating conditional statements using simple symbols can help. We use the horseshoe symbol ($\supset$) to translate conditional statements. For example, the ordinary language statement "If you smoke two packs of cigarettes a day, then you have a high risk of getting lung cancer" can be translated as $S \supset L$, with *S = you smoke two packs of cigarettes a day*, and *L = you have a high risk of getting lung cancer*. When you read the ordinary language statement, the *meaning* of the statement might tempt you to think about whether it is true or false. However, when you read the symbolic translation consisting of only two letters and a symbol, the meaning of the statement or whether it is true or false does not distract you.

The statement that follows "if" is the *antecedent*, and the statement that follows "then" is the *consequent*. Therefore, whatever phrase follows "if" must be placed *first* in the translation. Here are two examples to illustrate this point:

- If you wash the car, then you can go to the movies. $W \supset M$
- You can go to the movies, if you wash the car. $W \supset M$

The word "if" immediately reveals the existence of a conditional statement, making it a clear indicator word. There are additional English words and phrases that can indicate a conditional statement. For example, consider this statement: "Whenever it snows, my water pipes freeze," which can be translated as $S \supset F$. (Chapter 7 presents more words and phrases that indicate conditionals.) Learning to recognize conditional statements makes the task of translation easier.

Another important technique that can help you analyze some LSAT questions is to understand that two kinds of statements that use *class terms* can be translated as *conditional statements*. The first type of *categorical* statement uses the word "all" (see Chapter 5 for more details regarding categorical statements). For example, the statement "*All* scientists *are* people trained in mathematics" can be translated as "*If* a person is a scientist, *then* that person is trained in mathematics." Likewise, the statement "*All* unicorns *are* mammals" can be translated as "*If* something is a unicorn, *then* that thing is a mammal." The second type of *categorical* statement uses the word "no." For example, the statement "*No* slackers *are* reliable workers" is translated as "*If* a person is a slacker, *then* that person is not a reliable worker." (We will see these types of translations in action later in section F.)

D. Distinguishing "If" from "Only If"

As discussed in Chapter 7, section 7A, the word "if" precedes the *antecedent* of a conditional, while "only if" precedes the *consequent* of a conditional. Here are some examples:

- You will get the bonus only if you finish by noon. $B \supset F$
  (B = *You will get the bonus*, and F = *you finish by noon*.)
- Only if she has a 10% down payment will she get a mortgage. $M \supset P$
  (M = *she will get a mortgage*, and P = *she has a 10% down payment*.)

E. Conditionals and Arguments

We can apply the translating techniques to understand and analyze arguments that use conditional statements. For example:

Argument J: **Argument Form:**

If *Sherry lives in Los Angeles*, then *Sherry lives in California*.	$L \supset C$
Sherry lives in California.	C
Sherry lives in Los Angeles.	L

At this stage, the most important thing to recognize is that a conditional statement *does not assert* that either the antecedent or the consequent is true. What is asserted is that *if* the antecedent is true, *then* the consequent is true. Given this understanding of a conditional statement, we can start by assuming that the first premise is true. Why? Because it *does not assert* that Sherry actually lives in Los Angeles, it just asserts that *if* she lives in Los Angeles, then she lives in California. Next, let's assume that the second premise is also true (Sherry lives in California). We can now ask: Is the conclusion *necessarily* true? No, because it is *possible* that Sherry lives in San Francisco. Thus, argument J is invalid. The *argument form* for argument J is referred to as the *fallacy of affirming the consequent*. It is a *formal fallacy*, a logical error that occurs in the form of an argument. Formal fallacies are restricted to *deductive* arguments. (Formal fallacies are discussed in Chapters 1, and 6–8.) Let's look at another argument.

Argument K: **Argument Form:**

If Sherry lives in Los Angeles, then Sherry lives in California.	$L \supset C$
Sherry lives in Los Angeles.	L
Sherry lives in California.	C

Relying on our understanding of a conditional statement, we can analyze argument K. As with argument J, we can start by assuming that the first premise is true. Now, *if* the second premise is true, then the conclusion is *necessarily true*. Thus, argument K is valid. The *argument form* for argument K is referred to as *modus ponens*. In order to fully appreciate this result, we need to understand that since argument K is valid, no counterexample exists. This is an important claim, and we will explain it with the apparatus we currently have.

We were able to create a counterexample to Argument J by recognizing that even if both premises were true, it is possible that the conclusion is false (that Sherry lives in

San Francisco). Let's try that with argument K. As before, we can assume that the first premise is true. Now if we assume that the second premise is true, then the conclusion follows necessarily. (You can learn about different methods for demonstrating validity, as well as other methods for showing invalidity, in Part III, "Formal Logic.")

Let's look at a few more examples. To do this, we need to introduce a new symbol, "~" which stands for "not" or "it is not the case that." We use this when we want to negate a given statement. For example, we can symbolize the statement "Today is Monday" as M, and its negation, "Today is not Monday" as $\sim M$.

Argument M:	**Argument Form:**
If Sherry lives in Los Angeles, then Sherry lives in California.	$L \supset C$
Sherry does not live in Los Angeles.	$\sim L$
Sherry does not live in California.	$\sim C$

We have been using "L" to represent the simple statement "Sherry lives in Los Angeles." In order to represent the statement "Sherry does *not* live in Los Angeles," we place the phrase "It is not the case that" in front of "L." Similarly, we have been using "C" to represent the simple statement "Sherry lives in California." In order to represent the statement "Sherry does *not* live in California," we place the phrase "It is not the case that" in front of "C."

Let's analyze argument M. We can start by assuming that the two premises are true. Is the conclusion necessarily true? No, because it is possible that Sherry lives in San Francisco. Thus, argument M is invalid. The *argument form* for argument M is referred to as the *fallacy of denying the antecedent,* and it is a *formal fallacy.* Here is another example:

Argument N:	**Argument Form:**
If Sherry lives in Los Angeles, then Sherry lives in California.	$L \supset C$
Sherry does not live in California.	$\sim C$
Sherry does not live in Los Angeles.	$\sim L$

Let's analyze argument N. We can start by assuming that the premises are true. Given this, the conclusion is necessarily true. Thus, argument N is valid. The *argument form* for argument N is referred to as *modus tollens.* Since argument N is valid, no counterexample exists. Let's look at one more example.

Argument P:	**Argument Form:**
If Sherry lives in Los Angeles, then Sherry lives in California.	$L \supset C$
If Sherry lives in California, then Sherry lives in the United States.	$C \supset U$
If Sherry lives in Los Angeles, then Sherry lives in the United States.	$L \supset U$

Let's analyze argument P. We start by assuming that the premises are true. Given this, the conclusion is necessarily true. Thus, argument P is valid. The *argument form* for argument P is referred to as *hypothetical syllogism.* Since argument P is valid, no counterexample exists.

Let's see if you can determine whether the following argument (a) has a flaw (invalid) or (b) has no flaw (valid). Try translating the argument using symbols, then refer back to the different argument forms that we discussed. Work out your answer before reading the analysis that follows. Here is the argument:

Argument Q

I will buy you dinner if you clean my room. You did not clean my room, so I will not buy you dinner.

The first step is the translation. If we let C = *you clean my room* and D = *I'll buy you dinner*, then here is the argument form:

$$C \supset D$$
$$\underline{\sim C}$$
$$\sim D$$

You might have recognized this as an instance of the *fallacy of denying the antecedent*. If so, then you know that it is an invalid argument. (Exercises 1F.II can be used for practice.) However, we can add to our understanding of the argument flaw by introducing some new logical concepts, the subject of the next section.

F. Sufficient and Necessary Conditions

The first premise of the previous argument Q , "I will buy you dinner if you clean my room," claims that cleaning the room will lead to dinner. But what the premise *does not* claim is that cleaning the room is the *only way* to get dinner. This is a crucial difference. If the premise had been "I will buy you dinner *only if* you clean my room," then it would be translated as "$D \supset C$" instead of "$C \supset D$." If so, then the argument would have been valid (it would be an instance of *modus tollens*). This illustrates how apparently simple differences can dramatically change the strength of an argument.

We can now use our basic understanding of conditional statements to explore two important concepts: *sufficient and necessary conditions* (see Chapters 7, 11, and 14.) To begin our discussion, consider this statement:

A. If you live in New Jersey, then you live in the United States. $N \supset U$

Let's look at the relationship between the antecedent and the consequent in the foregoing statement. If it is true that you live in New Jersey, then it is true that you live in the United States. In other words, living in New Jersey is *sufficient* for living in the United States. Of course, if you live in any of the other forty-nine states, then you also live in the United States. A *sufficient condition* occurs whenever one event ensures that another event is realized. In other words, the truth of the antecedent guarantees the truth of the consequent. The principle behind a sufficient condition can be captured by the phrases "is enough for" or "guarantees." Here is another example of a sufficient condition:

B. If my car engine starts, then I have gasoline. $S \supset G$

Of course, we must stipulate that it is not an electric car (the car needs gasoline to start and run). Given this stipulation, if the antecedent is true, then the consequent is true. Consider the next example:

C. If my dog is a poodle, then today is Monday. $P \supset M$

If the antecedent is true, it would *not* guarantee that the consequent is true. Therefore, this is not an example of a sufficient condition.

Suppose that the law of the state in which you are driving states that anyone caught driving with a blood alcohol level above 0.08% will be subject to a citation for driving while intoxicated (DWI) or, in some states, driving under the influence (DUI). If you are stopped by the police and agree to take a breath-analyzer test, then the following indicates a sufficient condition:

If your blood alcohol level exceeds 0.08%, then you are cited for DWI.

In other words, anyone caught driving with a blood alcohol level above 0.08% has met a *sufficient condition* for being issued a citation for DWI. Compare these results with a new case:

If you are cited for DWI, then your blood alcohol level exceeds 0.08%.

Even though it might be true that you were cited for a DWI, this is *not sufficient* information to determine that your blood alcohol level exceeds 0.08%. You might have refused to take a breath-analyzer test, so your blood alcohol level was not determined. Or you might have been given a variety of field sobriety tests, such as walking a straight line and turning, standing on one foot, or closing your eyes and touching the tip of your nose. If in the officer's opinion you failed the field sobriety test, then you may have been cited for DWI.

In contrast, a *necessary condition* means that one thing is *essential, mandatory,* or *required* in order for another thing to be realized. Consider this statement from earlier:

A. If you live in New Jersey, then you live in the United States. $N \supset U$

You cannot live in New Jersey unless you live in the United States. Given this, we can say that living in the United States is a *necessary condition* for living in New Jersey. If you *do not* live in the United States, then you *do not* live in New Jersey. This can also be written using the phrase "only if":

D. You live in New Jersey *only if* you live in the United States. $N \supset U$

It is important to remember that a necessary condition exists when the falsity of the consequent ensures the falsity of the antecedent. Here is another example of a necessary condition:

E. My car engine starts only if I have gasoline. $S \supset G$

Once again, we stipulate that my car needs gasoline to start and run. Given this, we can see that having gasoline is a necessary condition for my car engine to start. Of course, there are many other things that are necessary for my car engine to start, such as a battery, spark plugs, and ignition wires, to name only a few. So, although gasoline is not the only necessary condition for my car engine to start, it is definitely required. This example also illustrates the fact that in many real-life circumstances multiple necessary conditions are required to bring something about. The principle behind a necessary condition can be captured by the words "mandatory," "essential," and the phrase "is required for." Let's look at one more example:

G. If my dog is a poodle, then today is Monday. $P \supset M$

If the consequent is false, then the antecedent might be true or false. Therefore, this is *not* an example of a necessary condition.

The word "cause" has several meanings, and in everyday situations the possibility of ambiguity arises. For example, parents often tell their children that they must take vitamins because vitamins will help them grow. The claim is not that vitamins alone will cause children to grow; it is that vitamins are a *necessary condition* for children's growth. In another situation, a child might complain of a stomachache. The parent could suggest that the child stop drinking so much soda. Of course, the parent could also give the child some medicine to ease the pain. The parent relies on an understanding that several methods of reducing or eliminating the stomachache are possible. In other words, the parent is offering a *sufficient condition* to bring about a desired effect. A basic knowledge of sufficient and necessary conditions can help in the overall understanding and analysis of causal arguments. Here is an example for analysis:

> All acids are carbon-based compounds. Stignoric is a carbon-based compound, so it is an acid.

It doesn't matter whether you know if any of the statements that make up the argument are true or false. All you need to do is determine the *reasoning process*, which you can do if you translate the statements using symbols. The first premise, "All acids are carbon-based compounds" can be translated as a conditional: If A then C. The second premise, "Stignoric is a carbon-based compound" can be translated as: S is a C. The conclusion, "it (Stignoric) is an acid," can be translated as: S is an A.

The flaw is in mistaking a necessary condition for a sufficient condition. The first premise, if true, tells us that being a carbon-based compound is a necessary condition for being an acid; in other words, something cannot be an acid unless it is carbon-based. What the first premise *does not assert* is that all carbon-based compounds are acids. But that is exactly what the conclusion asserts, so that is where the flaw occurs.

Let's put all this together and analyze another example. Suppose you were given this argument question on the LSAT:

> John deposited a check for $1 million into his bank account. Thus, he won the lottery.

The conclusion follows logically if which one of the following is assumed?

A. If anyone wins the lottery, then he deposits a check for $1 million into his bank account.

B. All millionaires make bank deposits.

C. You must have a bank account in order to make a deposit of $1 million.

D. John has always been a lucky person.

E. If anyone deposits a check for $1 million into his bank account, then he won the lottery.

The key to solving this problem is to recognize that the missing information has to connect two things: (1) depositing a check for $1 million and (2) winning the lottery. It is also important to suspend your judgment as to whether any of the information is actually true. Choice (A) sounds appealing. However, if we symbolize the argument using this choice we get the following: L = *anyone wins the lottery* and D = *he deposits a check for $1 million into his bank account.* Given this, the argument form is $L \supset D, D$, thus L. Since this is an invalid argument form (*affirming the consequent*), the conclusion *does not follow logically,* so it can't be the correct answer. Choices (B), (C), and (D) cannot be correct because they fail to connect the bank deposit to winning the lottery. Choice (E) is a conditional statement that has what we need. The *antecedent* connects depositing a check for $1 million to the *consequent* winning the lottery. It creates the valid argument form *modus ponens,* so the conclusion follows logically. (Exercises 7A.II and 7A.III can be used for practice.)

9. CONTINUING THE PROCESS

In order to continue the process begun with this short guide, you should go through the relevant chapters of *Logic* mentioned along the way. The text of each chapter will provide clear definitions, explanations, and examples of the kinds of skills needed for the LSAT *logical reasoning* sections. You should also do as many of the exercise sets as possible. Although the chapter exercise sets were not created to mirror the way LSAT questions are written, they do apply the basic *reasoning principles* on which the logical reasoning sections of the LSAT rely. The exercises also provide direct application of the important logical skills, which will sharpen and focus your ability to analyze LSAT questions.

Appendix B
THE TRUTH ABOUT PHILOSOPHY MAJORS*

Here's the inaccurate, old-school way of thinking:
- Philosophy majors have no marketable skills; they are unemployable.
- They are unprepared for professional careers in anything but teaching philosophy.
- They are useless in an economy built on exploding tech, speed-of-light innovation, and market-wrenching globalization.
- They are destined to earn low salaries.

Here's the new reality: All these assumptions are FALSE.

CAREERS

A wide range of data suggest that philosophy majors are not just highly employable; they are thriving in many careers that used to be considered unsuitable for those holding "impractical" philosophy degrees. The unemployment rate for recent BA philosophy graduates is 4.3 percent, lower than the national average and lower than that for majors in biology, chemical engineering, graphic design, mathematics, and economics.[1]

Nowadays most philosophy majors don't get PhDs in philosophy; they instead land jobs in many fields outside academia. They work in business consulting firms, guide investors on Wall Street, lead teams of innovators in Silicon Valley, do humanitarian work for nongovernment organizations, go into politics, and cover the world as journalists. They teach, write, design, publish, create. They go to medical school, law school, and graduate school in everything from art and architecture to education, business, and computer science. (Of course, besides majoring in philosophy, students can also minor in it, combining a philosophy BA with other BA programs, or take philosophy courses to round out other majors or minors.)

Many successful companies—especially those in the tech world—don't see a philosophy degree as impractical at all. To be competitive, they want more than just engineers, scientists, and mathematicians. They also want people with broader, big-picture skills—people who can think critically, question assumptions, formulate and defend ideas, develop unique perspectives, devise and evaluate arguments, write effectively, and analyze and simplify complicated problems. And these competencies are abundant in people with a philosophy background.

Photo 1: Carly Fiorina, businessperson and political figure
Photo 2: Stewart Butterfield, cofounder of Flickr and Slack
Photo 3: Sheila Bair, nineteenth chair of the FDIC
Photo 4: Katy Tur, author and broadcast journalist for NBC News
Photo 5: Damon Horowitz, entrepreneur and in-house philosopher at Google

Plenty of successful business and tech leaders say so. Speaking of her undergraduate studies, Carly Fiorina, philosophy major and eventual chief executive of Hewlett-Packard, says, "I learned how to separate the wheat from the chaff, essential from just interesting, and I think that's a particularly critical skill now when there is a ton of interesting but ultimately irrelevant information floating around."[2]

Flickr and Slack cofounder Stewart Butterfield, who has both bachelor's and master's degrees in philosophy, says, "I think if you have a good background in what it is to be human, an understanding of life, culture and society, it gives you a good perspective on starting a business, instead of an education purely in business. You can always pick up how to read a balance sheet and how to figure out profit and loss, but it's harder to pick up the other stuff on the fly."[3]

Sheila Bair got her philosophy degree from the University of Kansas and went on to become chair of the Federal Deposit Insurance Corporation from 2006 to 2011. She says that philosophy "helps you break things down to their simplest elements. My

Philosophy: A Natural Segue to Law and Medicine

Law schools will tell you that a major in philosophy provides excellent preparation for law school and a career in law. Philosophy excels as a pre-law major because it teaches you the very proficiencies that law schools require: developing and evaluating arguments, writing carefully and clearly, applying principles and rules to specific cases, sorting out evidence, and understanding ethical and political norms. Philosophy majors do very well on the LSAT (Law School Admission Test), typically scoring higher than the vast majority of other majors.

Philosophy has also proven itself to be good preparation for medical school. Critical reasoning is as important in medicine as it is in law, but the study and practice of medicine requires something else—expertise in grappling with the vast array of moral questions that now confront doctors, nurses, medical scientists, administrators, and government officials. These are, at their core, philosophy questions.

David Silbersweig, a Harvard Medical School professor, makes a good case for philosophy (and all the liberal arts) as an essential part of a well-rounded medical education. As he says,

If you can get through a one-sentence paragraph of Kant, holding all of its ideas and clauses in juxtaposition in your mind, you can think through most anything. . . . I discovered that a philosophical stance and approach could identify and inform core issues associated with everything from scientific advances to healing and biomedical ethics.[4]

philosophy training really helps me with that intellectual rigor of simplifying things and finding out what's important."[5]

Philosophy major and NBC journalist Katy Tur says, "I would argue that for the vast majority of people, an education of teaching you to think critically about the world you are in and what you know and what you don't know is useful for absolutely everything that you could possibly do in the future."[6]

It's little wonder, then, that the top ranks of leaders and innovators in business and technology have their share of philosophy majors, a fair number of whom credit their success to their philosophy background. The list is long, and it includes:[7]

> Patrick Byrne, entrepreneur, e-commerce pioneer, founder and CEO of Overstock.com
> Damon Horowitz, entrepreneur, in-house philosopher at Google
> Carl Icahn, businessman, investor, philanthropist. . . .
> Larry Sanger, Internet project developer, cofounder of Wikipedia
> George Soros, investor, business magnate, philanthropist
> Peter Thiel, entrepreneur, venture capitalist, cofounder of PayPal
> Jeff Weiner, CEO of LinkedIn

Of course, there are also many with a philosophy background who are famous for their achievements outside the business world. This list is even longer and includes:

> Wes Anderson, filmmaker, screenwriter (*The Royal Tenenbaums*, *The Grand Budapest Hotel*)
> Stephen Breyer, Supreme Court justice
> Mary Higgins Clark, novelist (*All By Myself, Alone*)
> Ethan Coen, filmmaker, director
> Stephen Colbert, comedian, TV host
> Angela Davis, social activist
> Lana Del Rey, singer, songwriter
> Dessa, rapper, singer, poet
> Ken Follett, author (*Eye of the Needle*, *Pillars of the Earth*)
> Harrison Ford, actor
> Ricky Gervais, comedian, creator of *The Office*
> Philip Glass, composer
> Rebecca Newberger Goldstein, author (*Plato at the Googleplex*)
> Matt Groening, creator of *The Simpsons* and *Futurama*
> Chris Hayes, MSNBC host
> Kazuo Ishiguro, Nobel Prize–winning author (*The Remains of the Day*)
> Phil Jackson, NBA coach
> Thomas Jefferson, U.S. president
> Charles R. Johnson, novelist (*Middle Passage*)
> Rashida Jones, actor

Photo 6: Larry Sanger, Internet project developer, cofounder of Wikipedia
Photo 7: Stephen Breyer, Supreme Court justice
Photo 8: Stephen Colbert, comedian, TV host
Photo 9: Angela Davis, social activist
Photo 10: Lana Del Rey, singer and songwriter
Photo 11: Chris Hayes, MSNBC host

Martin Luther King Jr., civil rights leader
John Lewis, civil rights activist, congressman
Terrence Malick, filmmaker, director (*The Thin Red Line*)
Yann Martel, author (*Life of Pi*)
Deepa Mehta, director, screenwriter (*Fire, Water*)
Iris Murdoch, author (*Under the Net*)
Robert Parris Moses, educator, civil rights leader
Stone Phillips, broadcaster
Susan Sarandon, actor
Susan Sontag, author, (*Against Interpretation*) MacArthur Fellow
David Souter, Supreme Court justice
Alex Trebek, host of *Jeopardy!*
George F. Will, journalist, author (*Men at Work: The Craft of Baseball*)
Juan Williams, journalist

Philosophy Majors and the GRE

Philosophy majors score higher than *all other majors* on the Verbal Reasoning and Analytical Writing sections of the GRE (Graduate Record Examinations).

	Verbal Reasoning	Quantitative Reasoning	Analytic Writing
Philosophy	160	154	4.3
Average	149.97	152.57	3.48

Educational Testing Service, 2017 GRE Scores, between July 1, 2013 and June 30, 2016.

Photo 12: Rashida Jones, actor
Photo 13: Martin Luther King Jr., civil rights leader
Photo 14: John Lewis, civil rights activist, congressman
Photo 15: Terrence Malick, filmmaker, director
Photo 16: Yann Martel, author (Life of Pi)
Photo 17: Deepa Mehta, director, screenwriter (Fire)
Photo 18: Susan Sontag, author, MacArthur Fellow

SALARIES

According to recent surveys by PayScale, a major source of college salary information, philosophy majors can expect to earn a median starting salary of $44,800 and a median mid-career salary of $85,100. As you might expect, most of the higher salaries go to STEM graduates (those with degrees in science, technology, engineering, or mathematics). But in a surprising number of cases, salaries for philosophy majors are comparable to those of STEM graduates. For example, while the philosophy graduate earns $85,100 at mid-career, the mid-career salary for biotechnology is $82,500; for civil engineering, $83,700; for chemistry, $88,000; for industrial technology, $86,600; and for applied computer science, $88,800. Median end-of-career salaries for philosophy majors (10–19 years' experience) is $92,665—not the highest pay among college graduates, but far higher than many philosophy-is-useless critics would expect.[8]

Another factor to consider is the increase in salaries over time. On this score, philosophy majors rank in the top ten of all majors with the highest salary increase from start to mid-career at 101 percent. The major with the highest increase: government, at 118 percent. Molecular biology is the fifth highest at 105 percent.[9]

Salary Potential for Bachelor's Degrees

Major	Median Early Pay (0–5 yrs. work experience)	Median Mid-Career Pay (10+ yrs. work experience)
Mechanical Engineering	$58,000	$90,000
Applied Computer Science	$53,100	$88,800
Information Technology	$52,300	$86,300
Civil Engineering	$51,300	$83,700
Business and Finance	$48,800	$91,100
Biotechnology	$46,100	$82,500
Business Marketing	$45,700	$78,700
Philosophy	**$44,800**	**$85,100**
History	$42,200	$75,700
Advertising	$41,800	$84,200
General Science	$41,600	$75,200
Telecommunications	$41,500	$83,700
English Literature	$41,400	$76,300
Marine Biology	$37,200	$76,000

PayScale, "Highest Paying Bachelor Degrees by Salary Potential," *2017–2018 College Salary Report*, https://www.payscale.com/college-salary-report/majors-that-pay-you-back/bachelors.

And among liberal arts majors, philosophy salaries are near the top of the list. All liberal arts majors except economics earn lower starting and mid-career pay than philosophy does.

Salary Potential for Liberal Arts Bachelor Degrees

Major	Median Early Pay (0–5 yrs. work experience)	Median Mid-Career Pay (10+ yrs. work experience)
Economics	$54,100	$103,200
Philosophy	**$44,800**	**$85,100**
Political Science	$44,600	$82,000
Modern Languages	$43,900	$77,400
Geography	$43,600	$72,700
History	$42,200	$75,700
English Literature	$41,400	$76,300
Anthropology	$40,500	$63,200
Creative Writing	$40,200	$68,500
Theatre	$39,700	$63,500
Psychology	$38,700	$65,300
Fine Art	$38,200	$62,200

PayScale, "Highest Paying Bachelor Degrees by Salary Potential," *2017–2018 College Salary Report*, https://www.payscale.com/college-salary-report/majors-that-pay-you-back/bachelors.

MEANING

In all this talk about careers, salaries, and superior test scores, we should not forget that for many students, the most important reason for majoring in philosophy is the meaning it can add to their lives. They know that philosophy, after two-and-one-half millennia, is still alive and relevant and influential. It is not only for studying but also for living—for guiding our lives toward what's true and real and valuable. They would insist that philosophy, even with its ancient lineage and seemingly remote concerns, applies to your life and your times and your world. The world is full of students and teachers who can attest to these claims. Perhaps you will eventually decide to join them.

RESOURCES

American Philosophical Association, "Who Studies Philosophy?" http://www.apaonline.org/?whostudiesphilosophy.

BestColleges.com, "Best Careers for Philosophy Majors," 2017, http://www.bestcolleges.com/careers/philosophy-majors/.

The University of North Carolina at Chapel Hill, Department of Philosophy, "Why Major in Philosophy?" http://philosophy.unc.edu/undergraduate/the-major/why-major-in-philosophy/.

University of California, San Diego, Department of Philosophy, "What Can I Do with a Philosophy Degree?" https://philosophy.ucsd.edu/undergraduate/careers.html.

University of Maryland, Department of Philosophy, "Careers for Philosophy Majors," http://www.philosophy.umd.edu/undergraduate/careers.

George Anders, "That 'Useless' Liberal Arts Degree Has Become Tech's Hottest Ticket," *Forbes*, July 29, 2015, https://www.forbes.com/sites/georgeanders/2015/07/29/liberal-arts-degree-tech/#5fb6d740745d.

Laura Tucker, "What Can I Do with a Philosophy Degree?" TopUniversities.com, March 2, 2015, https://www.topuniversities.com/student-info/careers-advice/what-can-you-do-philosophy-degree.

NOTES

[1] Federal Reserve Bank of New York, "The Labor Market for Recent College Graduates," January 11, 2017, https://www.newyorkfed.org/research/college-labor-market/college-labor-market_compare-majors.html.

[2] T. Rees Shapiro, "For Philosophy Majors, the Question after Graduation Is: What Next?" *Washington Post*, June 20, 2017.

[3] Carolyn Gregoire, "The Unexpected Way Philosophy Majors Are Changing the World of Business," *Huffpost*, March 5, 2014, https://www.huffingtonpost.com/2014/03/05/why-philosophy-majors-rule_n_4891404.html.

[4] David Silbersweig, "A Harvard Medical School Professor Makes a Case for the Liberal Arts and Philosophy," *Washington Post*, December 24, 2015.

[5] Shapiro, "For Philosophy Majors."

[6] Shapiro.

[7] American Philosophical Association, "Who Studies Philosophy?" (accessed November 14, 2017), http://www.apaonline.org/?whostudiesphilosophy.

[8] PayScale, "Highest Paying Bachelor Degrees by Salary Potential," *2017–2018 College Salary Report*, https://www.payscale.com/college-salary-report/majors-that-pay-you-back/bachelors.

[9] PayScale; reported by Rachel Gillett and Jacquelyn Smith, "People with These College Majors Get the Biggest Raises," *Business Insider*, January 6, 2016, http://www.businessinsider.com/college-majors-that-lead-to-the-biggest-pay-raises-2016-1/#20-physics-1.

Glossary

A

A *priori* theory of probability: Ascribes to a simple event a fraction between 0 and 1.

A-proposition: A categorical proposition having the form "All S are P."

Abduction: The process that occurs when we infer explanations for certain facts.

Abnormal state: A drastic change in the normal state regarding an object.

Ad hominem abusive: The fallacy is distinguished by an attack on alleged character flaws of a person instead of the person's argument.

Ad hominem circumstantial: When someone's argument is rejected based on the circumstances of the person's life.

Addition (Add): A rule of inference (implication rule).

Affidavit: A written statement signed before an authorized official.

Affirmative conclusion/negative premise: A formal fallacy that occurs when a categorical syllogism has a negative premise and an affirmative conclusion.

Analogical argument: The argument lists the characteristics that two (or more) things have in common and concludes that the things being compared probably have some other characteristic in common.

Analogical reasoning: One of the most fundamental tools used in creating an argument. It can be analyzed as a type of inductive argument—it is a matter of probability, based on experience, and it can be quite persuasive.

Analogy: To draw an analogy is simply to indicate that there are similarities between two or more things.

Appeal to an unqualified authority: An argument that relies on the opinions of people who either have *no* expertise, training, or knowledge relevant to the issue at hand, or whose testimony is not trustworthy.

Appeal to fear or force: A threat of harmful consequences (physical or otherwise) used to force acceptance of a course of action that would otherwise be unacceptable.

Appeal to ignorance: An argument built on a position of ignorance claims either that (1) a statement must be true because it has not been proven to be false or (2) a statement must be false because it has not been proven to be true.

Appeal to pity: The fallacy results from an exclusive reliance on a sense of pity or mercy for support of a conclusion.

Appeal to the people: The fallacy occurs when an argument manipulates a psychological need or desire, such as the desire to belong to a popular group, or the need for group solidarity, so that the reader or listener will accept the conclusion.

Appellate courts: Courts of appeal that review the decisions of lower courts.

Argument: A group of statements in which the conclusion is claimed to follow from the premise(s).

Argument form: (1) In categorical logic, an argument form is an arrangement of logical vocabulary and letters that stand for class terms such that a uniform substitution of class terms for the letters results in an argument. (2) In propositional logic, an argument form is an arrangement of logical operators and statement variables.

Association (Assoc): A rule of inference (replacement rule).

Asymmetrical relationship: Illustrated by the following: If A is the father of B, then B is not the father of A.

B

Begging the question: In one type, the fallacy occurs when a premise is simply reworded in the conclusion. In a second type, called circular reasoning, a set of statements seem to support each other with no clear beginning or end point. In a third type, the argument assumes certain key information that may be controversial or is not supported by facts.

Biased sample: An argument that uses a nonrepresentative sample as support for a statistical claim about an entire population.

Biconditional: A compound statement consisting of two conditionals—one indicated by the word "if" and the other indicated by the phrase "only if." The triple bar symbol is used to translate a biconditional statement.

Bound variables: Variables governed by a quantifier.

C

Categorical imperative: The basic idea is that your actions or behavior toward others should always be such that you would want everyone to act in the same manner.

Categorical proposition: A proposition that relates two classes of objects. It either affirms or denies total class inclusion, or else it affirms or denies partial class inclusion.

Categorical syllogism: A syllogism constructed entirely of categorical propositions.

Causal network: A set of conditions that bring about an effect.

Change of quantifier (CQ): The rule allows the removal or introduction of negation signs. (The rule is a set of four logical equivalences.)

Class: A group of objects.

Cogent argument: An inductive argument is cogent when the argument is strong and the premises are true.

Cognitive meaning: Language that is used to convey information has cognitive meaning.

Commutation (Com): A rule of inference (replacement rule).

Complement: The set of objects that do not belong to a given class.

Complex question: The fallacy occurs when a single question actually contains multiple parts and an unestablished hidden assumption.

Composition: There are two forms of the fallacy: (1) the mistaken transfer of an attribute of the individual *parts of an object* to the *object as a whole* and (2) the mistaken transfer of an attribute of the individual *members of a class* to the *class itself.*

Compound statement: A statement that has at least one simple statement and at least one logical operator as components.

Conclusion: The statement that is claimed to follow from the premises of an argument; the main point of an argument.

Conclusion indicators: Words and phrases that indicate the presence of a conclusion (the statement claimed to follow from premises).

Conditional probability: The calculation of the probability that one event will occur given the knowledge that another event has already occurred.

Conditional proof (CP): A method that starts by assuming the antecedent of a conditional statement on a separate line and then proceeds to validly derive the consequent on a separate line.

Conditional statement: In ordinary language, the word "if" typically precedes the *antecedent* of a conditional, and the statement that follows the word "then" is referred to as the *consequent.*

Conjunction: A compound statement that has two distinct statements (called *conjuncts*) connected by the dot symbol.

Conjunction (Conj): A rule of inference (implication rule).

Consequentialism: A class of moral theories in which the moral value of any human action or behavior is determined exclusively by its outcomes.

Consistent statements: Two (or more) statements that have at least one line on their respective truth tables where the main operators are true.

Constructive dilemma (CD): A rule of inference (implication rule).

Contingent statements: Statements that are neither necessarily true nor necessarily false (they are sometimes true, sometimes false).

Contradictories: In categorical logic, pairs of propositions in which one is the negation of the other.

Contradictory statements: Two statements that have opposite truth values under the main operator on every line of their respective truth tables.

Contraposition: An immediate argument formed by replacing the subject term of a given proposition with the complement of its predicate term, and then replacing the predicate term of the given proposition with the complement of its subject term.

Contraposition by limitation: Subalternation is used to change a universal E-proposition into its corresponding particular O-proposition. We then apply the regular process of forming a contrapositive to this O-proposition.

Contraries: Pairs of propositions that cannot both be true at the same time, but can both be false at the same time.

Control group: The group in which the variable being tested is withheld.

Controlled experiment: One in which multiple experimental setups differ by only one variable.

Convergent diagram: A diagram that reveals the occurrence of independent premises.

Conversion: An immediate argument formed by interchanging the subject and predicate terms of a given categorical proposition.

Conversion by limitation: We first change a universal A-proposition into its corresponding particular I-proposition, and then we use the process of conversion on the I-proposition.

Copula: The words "are" and "are not" are referred to as copula; they are simply forms of "to be" and serve to link (to "couple") the subject class with the predicate class.

Correlation: A correspondence between two sets of objects, events, or data.

Counteranalogy: A new, competing argument—one that compares the thing in question to something else.

Counterexample: A counterexample to a statement is evidence that shows the statement is false. A counterexample to an argument shows the possibility that premises assumed to be true do not make the conclusion necessarily true. A single counterexample to a deductive argument is enough to show that the argument is invalid.

D

De Morgan (DM): A rule of inference (replacement rule).

Decreasing extension: A sequence of terms in which each term after the first denotes a set of objects with fewer members than the previous term.

Decreasing intension: A sequence of terms in which each term after the first connotes fewer attributes than the previous term.

Deductive argument: An argument in which the inferential claim is that the conclusion follows *necessarily* from the premises. In other words, under the *assumption* that the premises are true it is *impossible* for the conclusion to be false.

Definiendum: Refers to that which is being defined.

Definiens: Refers to that which does the defining.

Definite description: Describes an individual person, place, or thing.

Definition: A definition assigns a meaning to a word, phrase, or symbol.

Definition by genus and difference: Assigns a meaning to a term (the species) by establishing a genus and combining it with the attribute that distinguishes the members of that species.

Definition by subclass: Assigns meaning to a term by naming subclasses (species) of the class denoted by the term.

Deontology: The theory that duty to others is the first and foremost moral consideration.

Dependent premises: Premises are dependent when they work together to support a conclusion. In other words, the falsity of one dependent premise weakens the support that the other dependent premises give to the conclusion.

Disanalogies: To point out differences between two things.

Disjunction: A compound statement that has two distinct statements (called *disjuncts*) connected by the wedge symbol.

Disjunctive syllogism (DS): A rule of inference (implication rule).

Distributed: If a categorical proposition asserts something about every member of a class, then the term designating that class is said to be distributed.

Distribution (Dist): A rule of inference (replacement rule).

Divergent diagram: A diagram that shows a single premise supporting independent conclusions.

Division: There are two forms of the fallacy: (1) the mistaken transfer of an attribute of an *object as a whole* to the individual *parts of the object* and (2) the mistaken transfer of an attribute of a *class* to the individual *members of the class.*

Domain of discourse: The set of individuals over which a quantifier ranges.

Double negation (DN): A rule of inference (replacement rule).

E

E-proposition: A categorical proposition having the form "No S are P."

Egoism: The basic principle that everyone should act in order to maximize his or her own individual pleasure or happiness.

Emotive meaning: Language that is used to express emotion or feelings has emotive meaning.

Emotivism: A theory that asserts that moral value judgments are merely expressions of our attitudes or emotions.

Empty class: A class that has zero members.

Enthymemes: Arguments with missing premises, missing conclusions, or both.

Enumerative definition: Assigns meaning to a term by naming the individual members of the class denoted by the term.

Equiprobable: When each of the possible outcomes has an equal probability of occurring.

Equivocation: The fallacy occurs when the conclusion of an argument relies on an intentional or unintentional shift in the meaning of a term or phrase in the premises.

Exceptive propositions: Statements that need to be translated into compound statements containing the word "and" (for example, propositions that take the form "All except S are P" and "All but S are P").

Exclusive disjunction: When we assert that *at least one* disjunct is true, but *not* both. In other words, we assert that the truth of one *excludes* the truth of the other. Given this, an exclusive disjunction is true when only one of the disjuncts is true, otherwise it is false.

Exclusive premises: A formal fallacy that occurs when both premises in a categorical syllogism are negative.

Existential fallacy: A formal fallacy that occurs when a categorical syllogism has a particular conclusion and two universal premises.

Existential generalization (EG): A rule that permits the valid introduction of an existential quantifier from either a constant or a variable.

Existential import: A proposition has existential import if it presupposes the existence of certain kinds of objects.

Existential instantiation (EI): A rule that permits giving a name to a thing that exists. The name can then be represented by a constant.

Existential quantifier: Formed by putting a backward E in front of a variable, and then placing them both in parentheses.

Experimental group: The group that gets the variable being tested.

Experimental science: Tests the explanations proposed by theoretical science.

Explanation: An explanation provides reasons for why or how an event occurred. By themselves, explanations are not arguments; however, they can form part of an argument.

Exportation (Exp): A rule of inference (replacement rule).

Extension: The class or collection of objects to which the term applies. In other words, what the term denotes (its reference).

Extensional definition: Assigns meaning to a term by indicating the class members denoted by the term.

F

Factual dispute: Occurs when people disagree on a matter that involves facts.

Fallacy of affirming the consequent: An invalid argument form; it is a formal fallacy.

Fallacy of denying the antecedent: An invalid argument form; it is a formal fallacy.

False dichotomy: A fallacy that occurs when it is assumed that only two choices are possible, when in fact others exist.

Figure: The middle term can be arranged in the two premises in four different ways. These placements determine the figure of the categorical syllogism.

Finite universe method: The method of demonstrating invalidity that assumes a universe, containing at least one individual, to show the possibility of true premises and a false conclusion.

Formal fallacy: A logical error that occurs in the form or structure of an argument; it is restricted to deductive arguments.

Free variables: Variables that are not governed by any quantifier.

Functional definition: Specifies the purpose or use of the objects denoted by the term.

G

General conjunction method: The method that is used for calculating the probability of two or more events occurring together, regardless of whether the events are independent.

General disjunction method: The method that is used for calculating the probability when two or more events are not mutually exclusive.

H

Hasty generalization: An argument that relies on a small sample that is unlikely to represent the population.

Hypothesis: Provides an explanation for known facts and a way to test an explanation.

Hypothetical syllogism (HS): A rule of inference (implication rule).

I

I-proposition: A categorical proposition having the form "Some S are P."

Identity relation: A binary relation that holds between a thing and itself.

Illicit major: A formal fallacy that occurs when the major term in a categorical syllogism is distributed in the conclusion but not in the major premise.

Illicit minor: A formal fallacy that occurs when the minor term in a categorical syllogism is distributed in the conclusion but not in the minor premise.

Immediate argument: An argument that has only one premise.

Implication rules: Valid argument forms that are validly applied only to an entire line.

Inclusive disjunction: When we assert that *at least one* disjunct is true, and *possibly both* disjuncts are true. Given this, an inclusive disjunction is false when both disjuncts are false, otherwise it is true.

Inconsistent statements: Two (or more) statements that do not have even one line on their respective truth tables where the main operators are true (but they can be false) at the same time.

Increasing extension: A sequence of terms in which each term after the first denotes a set of objects with more members than the previous term.

Increasing intension: A sequence of terms in which each term after the first connotes more attributes than the previous term.

Independent premises: Premises are independent when the falsity of one does not nullify any support the others would give to the conclusion.

Indictment: A formal accusation presented by a grand jury.

Indirect proof (IP): A method that starts by assuming the negation of the required statement and then validly deriving a contradiction on a subsequent line.

Individual constants: The subject of a singular statement is translated using lowercase letters. The lowercase letters act as names of individuals.

Individual variables: The three lowercase letters x, y, and z.

Inductive argument: An argument in which the inferential claim is that the conclusion is *probably true* if the premises are true. In other words, under the *assumption* that the premises are true it is *improbable* for the conclusion to be false.

Inference: A term used by logicians to refer to the reasoning process that is expressed by an argument.

Inference to the best explanation: Reasoning from the premise that a hypothesis would explain certain facts to the conclusion that the hypothesis is the best explanation for those facts.

Inferential claim: If a passage expresses a reasoning process—that the conclusion follows from the premises—then we say that it makes an inferential claim.

Informal fallacy: A mistake in reasoning that occurs in ordinary language and concerns the content of the argument rather than its form.

Instantial letter: The letter (either a variable or a constant) that is introduced by universal instantiaton or existential instantiation.

Instantiation: When instantiation is applied to a quantified statement, the quantifier is removed, and every variable that was bound by the quantifier is replaced by the same instantial letter.

Intension: The intension of a term is specified by listing the properties or attributes that the term connotes—in other words, its sense.

Intensional definition: Assigns a meaning to a term by listing the properties or attributes shared by all the objects that are denoted by the term.

Intransitive relationship: Illustrated by the following: If A is the mother of B, and B is the mother of C, then A is not the mother of C.

Invalid deductive argument: An argument in which, assuming the premises are true, it is *possible* for the conclusion to be false. In other words, the conclusion does not follow necessarily from the premises.

Irreflexive relationship: An example of an irreflexive relationship is expressed by the statement "Nothing can be taller than itself."

J

Joint method of agreement and difference: If two or more instances of an event have only one thing in common, while the instances in which it does not occur all share the absence of that thing, then the item is a likely cause.

Justification: Refers to the rule of inference that is applied to every validly derived step in a proof.

L

Lexical definition: A definition based on the common use of a word, term, or symbol.

Linked diagram: A diagram that reveals the occurrence of dependent premises.

Logic: The systematic use of methods and principles to analyze, evaluate, and construct arguments.

Logical analysis: Determines the strength with which the premises support the conclusion.

Logical operators: Special symbols that can be used as part of ordinary language statement translations.

Logical truth: A statement that is necessarily true; a tautology.

Logically equivalent statements: Two truth-functional statements that have identical truth tables under the main operator.

M

Main operator: The operator that has the *entire* well-formed formula in its scope.

Major premise: The first premise of a categorical syllogism (it contains the major term).

Major term: The predicate of the conclusion of a categorical syllogism.

Material equivalence (Equiv): A rule of inference (replacement rule).

Material implication (Impl): A rule of inference (replacement rule).

Mean: A statistical average that is determined by adding the numerical values in the data concerning the examined objects, then dividing by the number of objects that were measured.

Median: A statistical average that is determined by locating the value that separates the entire set of data in half.

Mediate argument: An argument that has more than one premise.

Method of agreement: The method that looks at two or more instances of an event to see what they have in common.

Method of concomitant variations: The method that looks for two factors that vary together.

Method of difference: The method that looks for what all the instances of an event do not have in common.

Method of residues: The method that subtracts from a complex set of events those parts that already have known causes.

Middle term: The term that occurs only in the premises of a categorical syllogism.

Minor premise: The second premise of a categorical syllogism (it contains the minor term).

Minor term: The subject of the conclusion of a categorical syllogism.

Misleading precision: A claim that appears to be statistically significant but is not.

Missing the point: When premises that seem to lead logically to one conclusion are used instead to support an unexpected conclusion.

Mode: A statistical average that is determined by locating the value that occurs most.

Modus ponens (MP): A rule of inference (implication rule). A valid argument form (also referred to as *affirming the antecedent*).

Modus tollens (MT): A rule of inference (implication rule). A valid argument form (also referred to as *denying the consequent*).

Monadic predicate: A one-place predicate that assigns a characteristic to an individual.

Mood: The mood of a categorical syllogism consists of the type of categorical propositions involved (**A**, **E**, **I**, or **O**) and the order in which they occur.

Mutually exclusive: Two events, such that if one event occurs, then the other cannot.

N

Natural deduction: A proof procedure by which the conclusion of an argument is validly derived from the premises through the use of rules of inference.

Naturalistic fallacy: Value judgments cannot be logically derived from statements of fact.

Naturalistic moral principle: Since it is natural for humans to desire pleasure (or happiness) and to avoid pain, human behavior ought to be directed to these two ends.

Necessary condition: Whenever one thing is *essential*, *mandatory*, or *required* in order for another thing to be realized. In other words, the falsity of the consequent ensures the falsity of the antecedent.

Negation: The word "not" and the phrase "it is not the case that" are used to deny the statement that follows them, and we refer to their use as negation.

Negation method: The method that is used once the probability of an event occurring is known; it is then easy to calculate the probability of the event not occurring.

Negative conclusion/affirmative premises: A formal fallacy that occurs when a categorical syllogism has a negative conclusion and two affirmative premises.

Noncontingent statements: Statements such that the truth values in the main operator column do not depend on the truth values of the component parts.

Nonreflexive relationship: A relationship that is neither reflexive nor irreflexive.

Nonsymmetrical relationship: When a relationship is neither symmetrical nor asymmetrical, then it is nonsymmetrical. Illustrated by the following: If Kris loves Morgan, then Morgan may or may not love Kris.

Nontransitive relationship: Illustrated by the following: If Kris loves Morgan and Morgan loves Terry, then Kris may or may not love Terry.

Nontrivial prediction: A prediction that requires reference to background knowledge, which is everything we know to be true.

Normal state: The historical information regarding an object.

Normative statement: A statement that establishes standards for correct moral behavior, determining norms or rules of conduct.

O

O-proposition: A categorical proposition having the form "Some S are not P."

Obversion: An immediate argument formed by changing the quality of the given proposition, and then replacing the predicate term with its complement.

Operational definition: Defines a term by specifying a measurement procedure.

Opposition: When two standard-form categorical propositions refer to the same subject and predicate classes but differ in quality, quantity, or both.

Order of operations: The order of handling the logical operators within a proposition; it is a step-by-step method of generating a complete truth table.

Ostensive definition: Involves demonstrating the term—for example, by pointing to a member of the class that the term denotes.

P

Particular affirmative: An I-proposition. It asserts that at least one member of the subject class is a member of the predicate class.

Particular negative: An O-proposition. It asserts that at least one member of the subject class is not a member of the predicate class.

Persuasive definition: Assigns a meaning to a term with the direct purpose of influencing attitudes or opinions.

Plaintiff: The person who initiates a lawsuit.

Poisoning the well: The fallacy occurs when a person is attacked *before* she has a chance to present her case.

Population: Any group of objects, not just human populations.

Post hoc: The fallacy occurs from the mistaken assumption that just because one event occurred before another event, the first event *must have caused* the second event.

Precedent: A judicial decision that can be applied to later cases.

Precipitating cause: The object or event directly involved in bringing about an effect.

Precising definition: Reduces the vagueness and ambiguity of a term by providing a sharp focus, often a technical meaning, for a term.

Predicate logic: Integrates many of the features of categorical and propositional logic. It combines the symbols associated with propositional logic with special symbols that are used to translate predicates.

Predicate symbols: Predicates are the fundamental units in predicate logic. Uppercase letters are used to symbolize the units.

Predicate term: The term that comes second in a standard-form categorical proposition.

Prejudicial effect: Evidence that might cause some jurors to be negatively biased toward a defendant.

Premise: The information intended to provide support for a conclusion.

Premise indicators: Words and phrases that help us recognize arguments by indicating the presence of premises (statements being offered in support of a conclusion).

Prescriptive statement: A statement that offers advice either by specifying a particular action that ought to be performed or by providing general moral rules, principles, or guidelines that should be followed.

Principle of charity: We should choose the reconstructed argument that gives the benefit of the doubt to the person presenting the argument.

Principle of replacement: Logically equivalent expressions may replace each other within the context of a proof.

Probability calculus: The rules for calculating the probability of compound events from the probability of simple events. The results can be displayed as fractions, percentages, ratios, or a decimal between 0 and 1.

Probative value: Evidence that can be used during a trial to advance the facts of the case.

Proof: A sequence of steps (also called a deduction or a derivation) in which each step either is a premise or follows from earlier steps in the sequence according to the rules of inference.

Proposition: The information content imparted by a statement, or, simply put, its meaning.

Propositional logic: The basic components in propositional logic are statements.

Q

Quality: When we classify a categorical proposition as either affirmative or negative, we are referring to its quality.

Quantifier: The words "all," "no," and "some" are quantifiers. They tell us the extent of the class inclusion or exclusion.

Quantity: When we classify a categorical proposition as either universal or particular, we are referring to its quantity.

R

Random sample: A sample in which every member of the population has an equal chance of getting in.

Red herring: A fallacy that occurs when someone completely ignores an opponent's position and changes the subject, diverting the discussion in a new direction.

Reflexive property: The idea that *anything is identical to itself* is expressed by the reflexive property.

Relational predicate: Establishes a connection between individuals.

Relative frequency theory of probability: The theory that some probabilities can be computed by dividing the number of favorable cases by the total number of observed cases.

Relativism: First, all moral value judgments are determined by a society's beliefs toward actions or behavior. Second, there are no objective or universal moral value judgments.

Remote cause: Something that is connected to the precipitating cause by a chain of events.

Replacement rules: Pairs of logically equivalent statement forms.

Representative sample: A sample that accurately reflects the characteristics of the population as a whole.

Restricted conjunction method: The method that is used in situations dealing with two or more independent events, where the occurrence of one event has no bearing whatsoever on the occurrence or nonoccurrence of the other event.

Restricted disjunction method: The method that is used to calculate probability when two (or more) events are independent of each other, and the events are mutually exclusive.

Rigid application of a generalization: When a generalization or rule is inappropriately applied to the case at hand. The fallacy results from the belief that the generalization or rule is universal (meaning it has no exceptions).

Rule-based reasoning: Legal reasoning is also referred to as "rule-based reasoning."

Rules of inference: The function of rules of inference is to justify the steps of a proof.

Rules of law: The legal principles that have been applied to historical cases.

S

Sample: A subset of a population.

Scope: The statement or statements that a logical operator connects.

Self-contradiction: A statement that is necessarily false.

Serial diagram: A diagram that shows that a conclusion from one argument is a premise in a second argument.

Simple diagram: A diagram consisting of a single premise and a single conclusion.

Simple statement: One that does not have any other statement or logical operator as a component.

Simplification (Simp): A rule of inference (implication rule).

Singular proposition: A proposition that asserts something about a specific person, place, or thing.

Situation ethics: The idea that we should not rigidly apply moral rules to every possible situation.

Slippery slope: An argument that attempts to connect a series of occurrences such that the first link in a chain leads directly to a second link, and so on, until a final unwanted situation is said to be the inevitable result.

Sorites: A special type of enthymeme that is a chain of arguments. The missing parts are intermediate conclusions, each of which, in turn, becomes a premise in the next link in the chain.

Sound argument: A deductive argument is sound when the argument is valid, and the premises are true.

Standard-form categorical proposition: A proposition that has one of the following forms: "All S are P," "Some S are P," "No S are P," "Some S are not P."

Standard-form categorical syllogism: A categorical syllogism that meets three requirements: (1) All three statements must be standard-form categorical propositions. (2) The two occurrences of each term must be identical and have the same sense. (3) The major premise must occur first, the minor premise second, and the conclusion last.

Standard deviation: A measure of the amount of diversity in a set of numerical values.

Statement: A sentence that is either true or false.

Statement form: (1) In categorical logic, a statement form is an arrangement of logical vocabulary and letters that stand for class terms such that a uniform substitution of class terms for the letters results in a statement. (2) In propositional logic, an arrangement of logical operators and statement variables such that a uniform substitution of statements for the variables results in a statement.

Statement function: A pattern for a statement. It does not make any universal or particular assertion about anything, and it has no truth value.

Statement variable: A statement variable can stand for any statement, simple or compound.

Stipulative definition: Introduces a new meaning to a term or symbol.

Strategy: Referring to a greater, overall goal.

Straw man: The fallacy occurs when someone's argument is misrepresented in order to create a new argument that can be easily refuted. The new argument is so weak that it is "made of straw." The arguer then falsely claims that his opponent's real argument has been defeated.

Strong inductive argument: An argument such that if the premises are *assumed* to be true, then the conclusion is *probably* true. In other words, the probable truth of the conclusion *follows from* the truth of the premises.

Subalternation: The relationship between a universal proposition (referred to as the *superaltern*) and its corresponding particular proposition (referred to as the *subaltern*).

Subcontraries: Pairs of propositions that cannot both be false at the same time, but can both be true; also, if one is false, then the other must be true.

Subject term: The term that comes first in a standard-form categorical proposition.

Subjectivist theory of probability: The theory that some probability determinations are based on the lack of total knowledge regarding an event.

Substitution instance: (1) In categorical logic, a substitution instance of a *statement* occurs when a uniform substitution of class terms for the letters results in a statement. A *substitution instance* of an *argument* occurs when a uniform substitution of class terms for the letters results in an argument. (2) In propositional logic, a substitution instance of a *statement* occurs when a uniform substitution of statements for the variables results in a statement. A substitution instance of an *argument* occurs when a uniform substitution of statements for the variables results in an argument.

Sufficient condition: Whenever one event ensures that another event is realized. In other words, the truth of the antecedent guarantees the truth of the consequent.

Syllogism: A deductive argument that has exactly two premises and a conclusion.

Symmetrical relationship: Illustrated by the following: If A is married to B, then B is married to A.

Synonymous definition: Assigns a meaning to a term by providing another term with the same meaning; in other words, by providing a synonym.

T

Tactics: The use of small-scale maneuvers or devices.

Tautology: A statement that is necessarily true.

Tautology (Taut): A rule of inference (replacement rule).

Teleology: The philosophical belief that the value of an action or object can be determined by looking at the purpose or the end of the action or object.

Term: A single word or a group of words that can be the subject of a statement; it can be a common name, a proper name, or even a descriptive phrase.

Theoretical definition: Assigns a meaning to a term by providing an understanding of how the term fits into a general theory.

Theoretical science: Proposes explanations for natural phenomena.

Transitive relationship: Illustrated by the following: If A is taller than B, and B is taller than C, then A is taller than C.

Transposition (Trans): A rule of inference (replacement rule).

Truth-functional proposition: The truth value of any compound proposition using one or more of the five logical operators is a function of (that is, uniquely determined by) the truth values of its component propositions.

Truth table: An arrangement of truth values for a truth-functional compound proposition that displays for every possible case how the truth value of the proposition is determined by the truth values of its simple components.

Truth value: Every statement is either true or false; these two possibilities are called *truth values*.

Truth value analysis: Determines if the information in the premises is accurate, correct, or true.

Tu quoque: The fallacy is distinguished by the specific attempt of one person to avoid the issue at hand by claiming the other person is a hypocrite.

U

Uncogent argument: An inductive argument is uncogent if either or both of the following conditions hold: The argument is weak, or the argument has at least one false premise.

Undistributed: If a proposition does not assert something about every member of a class, then the term designating that class is said to be undistributed.

Undistributed middle: A formal fallacy that occurs when the middle term in a categorical syllogism is undistributed in both premises of a categorical syllogism.

Unintended consequences: If you can show that something unacceptable to a person presenting an analogy follows from that analogy, then you put that person in a difficult position.

Universal affirmative: An A-proposition. It affirms that every member of the subject class is a member of the predicate class.

Universal generalization (UG): A rule by which we can validly deduce the universal quantification of a statement function from a substitution instance with respect to the name of any arbitrarily selected individual (subject to restrictions).

Universal instantiation (UI): The rule by which we can validly deduce the substitution instance of a statement function from a universally quantified statement.

Universal negative: An E-proposition. It asserts that no members of the subject class are members of the predicate class.

Universal quantifier: The symbol used to capture the idea that universal statements assert something about every member of the subject class.

Universalizability: The notion that the same principles hold for all people at all times.

Unsound argument: A deductive argument is unsound when the argument is invalid, or when at least one of the premises is false.

Utilitarianism: It can be summed up in the famous dictum "the greatest good for the greatest number."

V

Valid deductive argument: An argument in which, assuming the premises are true, it is *impossible* for the conclusion to be false. In other words, the conclusion follows necessarily from the premises.

Value judgment: A claim that a particular human action or object has some degree of importance, worth, or desirability.

Venn diagram: A diagram that uses circles to represent categorical proposition forms.

Verbal dispute: Occurs when a vague or ambiguous term results in a linguistic misunderstanding.

Verifiable prediction: A prediction that, if true, must include an observable event.

W

Weak inductive argument: An argument such that either (a) if the premises are *assumed* to be true, then the conclusion is *probably not true,* or (b) a probably true conclusion *does not follow from the premises.*

Well-formed formula: Any statement letter standing alone, or a compound statement such that an arrangement of operator symbols and statement letters results in a grammatically correct symbolic expression.

Word origin definition: Assigns a meaning to a term by investigating its origin. The study of the history, development, and sources of words is called *etymology.*

Answers to Selected Exercises

CHAPTER 1

Exercises 1B

I.

5. **Premises:**
   (a) True friends are there when we need them.
   (b) They suffer with us when we fail.
   (c) They are happy when we succeed.
   Conclusion: We should never take our friends for granted.
   Although there are no indicator words, the first statement is the conclusion, the point of the passage, for which the other statements offer support.

9. **Premises:**
   (a) At one time Gary Kasparov had the highest ranking of any chess grand master in history.
   (b) He was beaten in a chess tournament by a computer program called Deep Blue.
   Conclusion: The computer program should be given a ranking higher than Kasparov.
   The indicator word "So" identifies the conclusion. The other statements are offered as support.

13. **Premises:**
    (a) My guru said the world will end on August 6, 2045.
    (b) So far everything she predicted has happened exactly as she said it would.
    Conclusion: The world will end on August 6, 2045.
    The indicator word "because" identifies the premises, so the first statement is the conclusion.

II.

5. Argument. The phrase "It follows that" identifies the premise, which is offered as support for the conclusion "she must be a vegetarian."

9. Not an argument. The statements do not act as either premises or conclusions; they simply convey information.

13. Argument. The conclusion is "The handprint on the wall had not been made by the librarian himself." The premises are "there hadn't been blood on his hands" and "the print did not match his [the librarian's]."

17. Not an argument.

21. Argument. The conclusion (as indicated by the word "Thus") is "we do not necessarily keep eBooks in compliance with any particular paper edition."

25. Not an argument. The passage provides a definition of "authoritarian governments" and a definition of "democratic governments." Although there is no direct conclusion, the author's choice of definitions indicates his point of view.

29. Not an argument

33. Not an argument; the information is offered as advice.

37. Not an argument

41. Not an argument

45. Not an argument

49. Not an argument

Exercises 1C

5. Argument. The term "clearly" is used as a conclusion indicator.

9. Argument. A reason is given to support the claim "texting discourages thoughtful discussion or any level of detail."

13. Explanation. The information is offered to explain why "the iPhone and Android are popular."

17. Explanation. The information is offered to explain why Twain "gave up the idea" of making a lecturing trip through the antipodes and the borders of the Orient.

Exercises 1E

5. Deductive. The first premise tells us something about *all* fires. If both premises are assumed to be true, then the conclusion is necessarily true.

9. Deductive. The first premise tells us something about *all* elements with atomic weights greater than 64. If both premises are assumed to be true, then the conclusion is necessarily true.

13. Deductive. The first premise specifies the minimum age when someone can legally play the slot machines in Las Vegas. The second premise tells us Sam is 33 years old. If both premises are true, then the conclusion is necessarily true.

17. Inductive. We are told something about *most* Doberman dogs. Also, the use of the word "probably" in the conclusion indicates that it is best classified as an inductive argument.

21. Inductive. The conclusion is *not* meant to follow necessarily from the premise.
25. Inductive. The use of the phrase "you're more likely" in the conclusion indicates that it is best classified as an inductive argument.
29. Deductive. The decision is intended to follow necessarily from the Supreme Court's arguments for the unconstitutionality of the law in question.

Exercises 1F

I.

5. If we let C = *computers*, E = *electronic devices*, and A = *things that require an AC adapter*, then the argument form is the following:

All C are E.
All A are E.
All C are A.

The following substitutions create a counterexample: let C = *cats*, E = *mammals*, and A = *dogs*.

All cats are mammals.
All dogs are mammals.
All cats are dogs.

Both premises are true, and the conclusion is false. Therefore, the counterexample shows that the argument is invalid.

9. If we let U = *unicorns*, I = *immortal creatures*, and C = *centaurs*, then the argument form is the following:

No U are I.
No C are I.
No U are C.

The following substitutions create a counterexample: let U = *cats*, I = *snakes*, and C = *mammals*.

No cats are snakes.
No mammals are snakes.
No cats are mammals.

Both premises are true, and the conclusion is false. Therefore, the counterexample shows that the argument is invalid.

13. We must make sure that whatever birth dates we assign to Fidelix and Gil the premises must turn out to be *true*. Suppose Fidelix was born in 1989 and Gil was born in 1988. Both premises are then true. However, the conclusion is then *false*.

17. If we let S = *strawberries*, F = *fruit*, and P = *plants*, then the argument form is the following:

All S are F.
All S are P.
All F are P.

The following substitutions create a counterexample: let S = *puppies*, F = *mammals*, and P = *dogs*.

All puppies are mammals.
All puppies are dogs.
All mammals are dogs.

Both premises are true, and the conclusion is false. Therefore, the counterexample shows that the argument is invalid.

II.

5. If we let S = *birds can swim*, and A = *birds are aquatic animals*, then the argument form is the following:

If S, then A.
It is not the case that A.
It is not the case that S.   *Modus tollens*. The argument is valid.

9. If we let L = *you are lost*, and C = *you are confused*, then the argument form is the following:

L or C.
It is not the case that L.
C.   Disjunctive syllogism. The argument is valid.

13. If we let S = *I can save $1000*, and C = *I can buy a car*, then the argument form is the following:

If S, then C.
S.
C.   *Modus ponens*. The argument is valid.

Exercises 1G

I.

5. Weak. The fact that it came up heads ten times in a row has no bearing on the next toss; each coin toss is an independent event, each having a 50-50 chance of heads or tails.
9. Strong. If we assume the premises are true, then the conclusion is probably true.

II.

5. *Weakens the argument.* If the lamp is not plugged in correctly, then electricity is probably not getting to the lamp.
9. *Strengthens the argument.* If every other electrical fixture in the room works, then electricity is probably getting to the lamp.
13. *Strengthens the argument.* Since the battery is so old, it is likely to be defective or worn out; therefore, we can determine that this new evidence strengthens the argument.
17. *Weakens the argument.* The loose terminal clamps are probably not relaying the battery power; therefore, we can determine that this new evidence weakens the argument.

Exercises 1H

I.

5. *Missing conclusion:* My headache will be relieved.

This makes the argument valid, provided the third premise means that in *all instances* taking aspirin relieves a headache. However, since this interpretation is false, this reconstruction is an unsound argument.

Missing conclusion: My headache will probably be relieved. This makes the argument strong, provided we interpret the third premise as asserting that *in most cases* taking aspirin relieves a headache. However, we would have to gather data to see if this assertion is true or false. If it is true, then the argument is cogent; if it is false, then the argument is uncogent.

9. *Missing conclusion:* The penicillin pills Jill took will have no effect on her viral infection.
This makes the argument valid. The argument is unsound if any premise is false.
Missing conclusion: The penicillin pills Jill took will probably have no effect on her viral infection.
This makes the argument strong. The argument is uncogent if any premise is false.

13. *Missing premise:* All safe drivers have low insurance rates.
This makes the argument valid.
Missing premise: Most safe drivers have low insurance rates.
This makes the argument strong.

17. In the passage "urban dwellers with little access to green spaces have a higher incidence of psychological problems than people living near parks," the term "higher incidence" indicates a statistical result. Given this, a charitable reconstruction of the missing conclusion would make the argument inductive rather than deductive. Something like the following is appropriate:
Missing conclusion: The results strongly suggest that getting out into natural environments could be an easy and almost immediate way to improve moods for city dwellers.
This makes the argument strong. If the premises are true, then the argument is cogent.

II.

5. [He suddenly gained forty pounds of muscle.]
[He doubled his average home run total.]
[He has taken steroids.]

The rhetorical forces are the two assertions "he suddenly gained forty pounds of muscle" and "he doubled his average home run total." Given this, it seems to be indicating that the conclusion should be that he has taken steroids.

9. [There is no trace of gunpowder on her hands.]
[She did not commit suicide by shooting herself.]

The rhetorical force behind the assertion "there is no trace of gunpowder on her hands" seems to be indicating that the conclusion should be negative in tone.

13. *Rhetorical conditional*
[You want to get rich quick.]
[You should buy more lottery tickets.]

CHAPTER 2

Exercises 2A

I.
5. head of state, executive officer, elected official, commander-in-chief
9. produces food from photosynthesis, multicellular, rigid cell walls, manufacturing business

II.
5. Socrates, Plato, Aristotle
9. Lake Superior, Lake Tanganyika, Lake Erie

III.
5. Great Pyramid of Giza, Colossus of Rhodes, Lighthouse of Alexandria, Hanging Gardens of Babylon, Statue of Zeus at Olympia, Mausoleum at Halicarnassus, Temple of Artemis at Ephesus
9. January, March, May, July, August, October, December

IV.
5. robin, thrush, bird, flying animal, animal
9. Cherry Jell-O, Jell-O, chilled dessert, dessert, food

Exercises 2C
5. Synonymous
9. Enumerative
13. Subclass
17. Subclass
21. Operational
25. Enumerative
29. Ostensive
33. Synonymous

Exercises 2D
5. Theoretical
9. Lexical
13. Precising
17. Stipulative
21. Precising
25. Precising
29. Stipulative
33. Functional
37. Lexical
41. Precising
45. Functional
49. Theoretical

Exercises 2E
5. The definition uses figurative language (Guideline 7). In addition, it fails to provide the essential meaning of the term (Guideline 2).
9. We can use Guideline 1 to add quotation marks: "Grade point average."

13. We can add quotation marks (Guideline 1): "Romanticism."
17. The definitions use ambiguous and vague language (Guideline 6).

Exercises 2F

5. Cognitive meaning
9. Both cognitive meaning and emotive meaning. The claims about the wealth of some players provide cognitive meaning. However, an emotional twinge is provided by the claim "I don't feel we owe anybody anything monetarily. Some of these players are wealthier than their bosses."
13. Emotive meaning

Exercises 2G

5. Verbal dispute
9. Verbal dispute
13. Verbal dispute
17. Verbal dispute

CHAPTER 3

Exercises 3B

I.

5. [1]We should never take our friends for granted. [2]True friends are there when we need them. [3]They suffer with us when we fail, and [4]they are happy when we succeed.

9. [1]At one time Gary Kasparov had the highest ranking of any chess grandmaster in history. However, [2]he was beaten in a chess tournament by a computer program called Deep Blue, so [3]the computer program should be given a ranking higher than Kasparov.

13. [1]The world will end on August 6, 2045. I know this because [2]my guru said it would, and [3]so far everything she predicted has happened exactly as she said it would.

II.

5. Sue hesitated; and then impulsively told the woman that [1]her husband and herself had been unhappy in their first marriages, [2]after which, terrified at the thought of a second irrevocable union, and lest the conditions of the contract should kill their love, yet wishing to be together, they had literally not found the courage to repeat it, [3]though they had attempted it two or three times. Therefore, [4]though in her own sense of the words she was a married woman, in the landlady's sense she was not.

9. [1]We are intelligent beings: [2]intelligent beings cannot have been formed by a crude, blind, insensible being: [3]there is certainly some difference between the ideas of Newton and the dung of a mule. [4]Newton's intelligence, therefore, came from another intelligence.

13. [1]After supper she got out her book and learned me about Moses and the Bulrushers, and [2]I was in a sweat to find out all about him; but by and by [3]she let it out that Moses had been dead a considerable long time; so then [4]I didn't care no more about him, because [5]I don't take no stock in dead people.

17. [1]It may be no accident that sexual life forms dominate our planet. True, [2]bacteria account for the largest number of individuals, and the greatest biomass. But [3]by any reasonable measures of species diversity, or individual complexity, size, or intelligence, sexual species are paramount. And [4]of the life forms that reproduce sexually, the ones whose reproduction is mediated by mate choice show the greatest biodiversity and the greatest complexity. [5]Without sexual selection, evolution seems limited to the very small, the transient, the parasitic, the bacterial, and the brainless. For

this reason, [6]I think that sexual selection may be evolution's most creative force.

III.

5. [1]Death is not an event in life: we do not live to experience death. [2]If we take eternity to mean not infinite temporal duration but timelessness, then eternal life belongs to those who live in the present. [3]Our life has no end in just the way in which our visual field has no limits.

9. Because [1]there is a law such as gravity, [2]the universe can and will create itself from nothing. [3]Spontaneous creation is the reason [4]there is something rather than nothing, [5]why the universe exists, [6]why we exist. [7]It is not necessary to invoke God to light the blue touch paper and set the universe going.

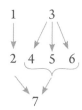

13. [1]The line that I am urging as today's conventional wisdom is not a denial of consciousness. [2]It is often called, with more reason, a repudiation of mind. [3]It is indeed a repudiation of mind as a second substance, over and above body. [4]It can be described less harshly as an identification of mind with some of the faculties, states, and activities of the body. [5]Mental states and events are a special subclass of the states and events of the human or animal body.

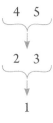

17. [1]It has only just begun to dawn on us that in our own language alone, not to speak of its many companions, the past history of humanity is spread out in an imperishable map, just as the history of the mineral earth lies embedded in the layers of its outer crust. But [2]there is this difference between the record of the rocks and the secrets which are hidden in language: [3]whereas the former can only give us knowledge of outward dead things—such as forgotten seas and the bodily shapes of prehistoric animals—[4]language has preserved for us the inner living history of man's soul. [5]It reveals the evolution of consciousness.

```
   1 2 3 4
      ↓
      5
```

21. [1]It is a commonplace that all religion expresses itself in mythological or metaphorical terms; [2]it says one thing and means another; [3]it uses imagery to convey truth. But [4]the crucial fact about religion is not that it is metaphor, but [5]that it is unconscious metaphor. [6]No one can express any thought without using metaphors, but [7]this does not reduce all philosophy and science to religion, because [8]the scientist knows that his metaphors are merely metaphors and [9]that the truth is something other than the imagery by which it is expressed, whereas [10]in religion the truth and the imagery are identified. [11]To repeat the Creed as a religious act it is necessary not to add "All this I believe in a symbolical or figurative sense": [12]to make that addition is to convert religion into philosophy.

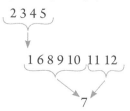

CHAPTER 4

Exercises 4B

I.
5. False
9. True

II.
5. *Ad hominem* abusive
9. *Ad hominem* circumstantial
13. Appeal to the people

17. *Ad hominem* circumstantial
21. *Ad hominem* abusive
25. Poisoning the well
29. No fallacy
33. Poisoning the well
37. *Ad hominem* abusive
41. *Ad hominem* circumstantial
45. *Ad hominem* circumstantial
49. No fallacy

Exercises 4C

I.
5. True
9. False

II.
5. No fallacy
9. Slippery slope
13. Biased sample
17. No fallacy
21. Biased sample
25. No fallacy
29. Biased sample
33. Division
37. *Post hoc* fallacy
41. Division
45. Composition
49. Division

Exercises 4D

I.
5. False
9. False
13. False

II.
5. Begging the question
9. No fallacy
13. Straw man fallacy
17. Complex question
21. No fallacy
25. Straw man
29. Red herring
33. Appeal to ignorance
37. False dichotomy
41. Appeal to an unqualified authority
45. Straw man
49. Equivocation

Exercises 4E

5. Red herring fallacy. Notice that Brewster does not deny the allegations. Also, he says, "Until I see the materials, it's hard

to comment." But he does offer comments: "It's obviously a piece completely out of context slanted for the purposes of the organization that caused somebody to deceptively be hired by the Asmussen stable."

9. False dichotomy. The disjunction offers two choices, but it neglects to acknowledge that other possibilities exist.
13. *Post hoc* (coincidence). The fallacy occurs from the mistaken assumption that just because one event occurred before another event, the first event *must have caused* the second event.
17. *Ad hominem* abusive. The argument uses purported character flaws of people's lives to reject their claims.
21. Hasty generalization. The generalization is created on the basis of one instance.
25. No fallacy
29. *Post hoc*. A fallacy involving either a short-term or long-term pattern that is noticed *after the fact*.
33. Two possibilities. (1) *Post hoc* (coincidence). The fallacy occurs from the mistaken assumption that just because one event occurred before another event, the first event *must have caused* the second event. (2) *Post hoc* (common cause). The mistake occurs when the writer thinks that one event causes another when both events are the result of a common cause (perhaps the rise of economies).
37. Appeal to an unqualified authority. The argument relies on the opinions of people who have no expertise, training, or knowledge relevant to the issue at hand.
41. Appeal to the people. The avoidance of objective evidence in favor of an emotional response.
45. No fallacy
49. No fallacy

CHAPTER 10

Exercises 10A

I.
5. **Premise 1:** X, the junior, and Y, the fifth grader, have the following attributes in common: *a*, eat the same food; *b*, have their own bedrooms; *c*, get the same amount of allowance.
   Premise 2: X has *d*: has to do housework.
   Conclusion: Therefore, *probably* Y should have *d*: has to do housework.

The structure of the argument:

X and Y have *a, b, c,* in common.
X has *d*.
Therefore, probably Y should have *d*.

9. *Premise 1:* X, fruit, and Y, Chocolate Peanut Goo-ies, have the following attributes in common: *a*, provides energy; *b*, roughage; *c*, sugar; *d*, citric acid; *e*, vitamins; *f*, minerals.

    Premise 2: X has *g*: is good for your health.

    Conclusion: Therefore, *probably* Y has *g*: is good for your health.

    The structure of the argument:

    X and Y have *a, b, c, d, e, f,* in common.
    <u>X has *g*.</u>
    Therefore, probably Y has *g*.

13. *Premise 1:* X, fruit trees and vegetables, and Y, seaweed, have the following attribute in com-mon: *a*, they are plants.

    Premise 2: X has *b*: adding fertilizer helps them to grow better.

    Conclusion: Adding fertilizer should help sea-weed grow better.

    The structure of the argument:

    X and Y have *a* in common.
    <u>X has *b*.</u>
    Therefore, probably Y has *b*.

II.

5. *Premise 1:* X, my assertion and belief that be-tween the Earth and Mars there is a china teapot revolving about the sun in an elliptical orbit, and Y, received dogmas, have the following attributes in common: *a*, they are purposely devised to be incapable of disproof by physical and scientific methods; *b*, based on pure belief without any physical evidence to support them; *c*, since the assertions cannot be disproved it is an intoler-able presumption on the part of human reason to doubt them.

    Premise 2: We know that for X, *d*, I should rightly be thought to be talking nonsense.

    Conclusion: Therefore, it is probable that for Y, a received dogma, *d*, it should rightly be thought to be talking nonsense.

    The structure of the argument:

    X and Y have *a, b, c,* in common.
    <u>X has *d*.</u>
    Therefore, probably Y has *d*.

Exercises 10B

I.

5. (a) *Number of entities:* The high school student and the fifth grader.
    (b) *Variety of instances:* Just two people are being compared.
    (c) *Number of characteristics:* Food; bedroom; allowance.
    (d) *Relevancy:* They seem relevant to the question of chores.

9. (a) *Number of entities:* Fruit and Chocolate Peanut Gooies.
    (b) *Variety of instances:* It is assumed that many kinds of fruit are referred to in the example.
    (c) *Number of characteristics:* Providing energy; roughage; sugars; citric acid; vitamins; minerals.
    (d) *Relevancy:* The characteristics listed are relevant to the issue of health.

13. (a) *Number of entities:* Fruit trees, vegetables plants, and seaweed.
    (b) *Variety of instances:* Some are grown on land and some in water.
    (c) *Number of characteristics:* All are plants.
    (d) *Relevancy:* This characteristic is probably related to plant growth.

II.

5. (a) *Number of entities:* Many received dogmas and one contrived assertion.
    (b) *Variety of instances:* Received dogmas differ in their age and popularity.
    (c) *Number of characteristics:* Three are mentioned.
    (d) *Relevancy:* All the characteristics are relevant to the point being made.

III.

5. Since we are not offered any information regarding the av-erage time it took for the brakes to fail, this does not weaken the argument. The evidence is strong enough to warrant having your brakes replaced.

Exercises 10C

I.

5. (a) *Disanalogies:* The age difference is considerable when one factors in the probable difference in size, strength, capabilities, stamina, and level of responsibility.
    (b) *Counteranalogy:* The high school student is more like the parents. The high school student is nearly an adult, and adults are expected to accept responsibility. They are expected to take care of a house and everything in it. They are expected to relieve children of the burdens of adulthood and let the children be children.
    (c) *Unintended consequences:* Since the high school stu-dent wants equal treatment, then perhaps the parents

should make both children go to bed or be in the house at the same time at night. Since the fifth grader is not permitted to drive the car, then the high school student should not have that privilege either.

9. (a) *Disanalogies*: The candy bar probably contains numerous artificial ingredients whose health benefits may be questioned. Fruit contains no artificial ingredients. The sugar that grows in fruit is not the same as that put in most candy bars.

(b) *Counteranalogy*: The candy bar is like cotton candy. They both taste good to most people, usually because they contain so much sugar (or artificial sugar substitute). They both provide a quick burst of energy. This kind of energy causes a backlash when its effects wear off. The person usually feels lethargic, and his or her attention and focus are disrupted. Both foods are artificial and not organic, natural products. If cotton candy is not healthy, then neither are Chocolate Peanut Gooies.

(c) *Unintended consequences*: Since the candy bar is just as good as fruit, we can eliminate the need for fruit in our diets and substitute the candy bar to meet our minimum daily requirements.

13. (a) *Disanalogies*: All the plants that the fertilizer worked on were grown on land. Fertilizer has not yet been tried on plants grown in water.

(b) *Counteranalogy*: Seaweed grows in saltwater. It has been shown that the fertilizer does not work in saltwater. So, adding the fertilizer will probably not help the seaweed to grow better.

(c) *Unintended consequences*: The fertilizer alters the genetic structure of the plants. If you alter the genetic structure of seaweed, it might disrupt the ecosystem in the sea and prove harmful.

II.

5. (a) *Disanalogies*: The assertion and belief that between the Earth and Mars there is a china teapot revolving about the sun in an elliptical orbit and received dogmas are different in the main sense that the received dogmas have long histories of being believed; also, received dogmas are usually classified as "religions" and are established beliefs that are protected by many democratic societies. Many received dogmas are a source of comfort and hope for the followers.

(b) *Counteranalogy*: The teapot belief offers no hope of an afterlife and provides no moral guides to acting as a human. Therefore, it will not offer hope or comfort to people.

(c) *Unintended consequences*: At most times in history there were scientific hypotheses that could not be tested because the technology was not available. Given this, if we are to discard any belief that cannot be disproved, then some of theoretical science will have to be discarded; for example, if string theory is not testable, then physicists should abandon it.

CHAPTER 11

Exercises 11E

5. (A) The credibility of a witness may be attacked **or** (B) supported by evidence in the form of opinion **or** (C) reputation, **but** subject to these limitations: (D) the evidence may refer **only** to (E) character for truthfulness **or** (F) untruthfulness, **and** (G) evidence of truthful character is admissible **only** after (H) the character of the witness for truthfulness has been attacked by opinion **or** (I) reputation evidence **or** (J) otherwise.

[A or (B or C)] and [If D, then (E or F)] and
[If G, then (H or I or J)].

9. (A) Evidence of juvenile adjudications is generally **not** admissible under this rule. (B) The court may **however**, in a criminal case allow evidence of a juvenile adjudication of a witness other than the accused **if** (C) conviction of the offense would be admissible to attack the credibility of an adult **and** (D) the court is satisfied that admission in evidence is necessary for a fair determination of the issue of guilt **or** (E) innocence.

A or [If C and (D or E), then B].

13. (A) Cross-examination should be limited to the subject matter of the direct examination **and** (B) matters affecting the credibility of the witness. (C) The court may, in the exercise of discretion, permit inquiry into additional matters as if on direct examination.

The information in C gives the court the option to allow "inquiry into additional matters" by referring to those matters "as if" they were being conducted on direct examination. In other words, the "additional matters" are to be understood as being *similar to* those under direct examination.

(A and B) and C.

17. (A) Extrinsic evidence of a prior inconsistent statement by a witness is **not** admissible **unless** (B) the witness is afforded an opportunity to explain **or** (C) deny the same **and** (E) the opposite party is afforded an opportunity to interrogate the witness thereon, **or** (F) the interests of justice otherwise require. (G) This provision does **not** apply to admissions of a party-opponent as defined in rule 801(d)(2).

{If not [(B or C) and (E or F)], then A} and G.

21. (A) At the request of a party (B) the court shall order witnesses excluded so that they cannot hear the testimony of other witnesses, **and** (C) it may make the order of its own motion. This rule does **not** authorize exclusion of (1) (E) a party

who is a natural person, **or** (2) (F) an officer **or** (G) employee of a party which is **not** a natural person designated as its representative by its attorney, **or** (3) (H) a person whose presence is shown by a party to be essential to the presentation of the party's cause, **or** (4) (I) a person authorized by statute to be present.

The use of the word "and" in the phrase "**and** it may make the order of its own motion" is being used to indicate another way that "the court shall order witnesses excluded." In other words, the rule is *not* stating that "the court shall order witnesses excluded" if both A and C occur at the same time; only one of them needs to occur.

[If (A or C), then B] and
[If (E or F or G or H or I), then not B].

Exercises 11G

I.

5. (1) U.S. Common law courts also provided judicial review of the size of damage awards. They deferred to jury verdicts, **but** *they recognized that juries sometimes awarded damages so high as to require correction.*
(2) If the plaintiff did *not* agree to a reduction in his damages, then Justice Story ordered a new trial.
(3) The court may grant a new trial for excessive damages; however, it *is indeed an exercise of discretion full of delicacy and difficulty.*
(4) [**if**] (A) it should clearly appear that the jury have committed a gross error, **or** (B) have acted from improper motives, **or** (C) have given damages excessive in relation to the person **or** (D) the injury, [**then**] (E) it is as much the duty of the court to interfere, to prevent the wrong, as in any other case:

If (A or B or C or D), then E.

9. (A) An Oregon trial judge, **or** (B) an Oregon Appellate Court, may order a new trial **if** (C) the jury was **not** properly instructed, [**or**] **if** (D) error occurred during the trial, **or if** (E) there is no evidence to support any punitive damages at all:

If (C or D or E), then (A or B).

But **if** (F) the defendant's only basis for relief is the *amount* of punitive damages the jury awarded, [**then**] (G) Oregon provides no procedure for reducing **or** (H) setting aside that award:

If F, then (G or H).

The precedent evidence is then added to: "This has been the law in Oregon at least since 1949 when the State Supreme Court announced its opinion in *Van Lom v. Schneiderman*, definitively construing the 1910 amendment to the Oregon Constitution. In that case the court held that it had *no power to reduce or set aside an award* of both compensatory and punitive damages that was admittedly excessive."

13. (A) Oregon's abrogation of a well-established common law protection against arbitrary deprivations of property raises a presumption that its procedures violate the Due Process Clause. (B) As this Court has stated from its first Due Process cases, traditional practice provides a touchstone for constitutional analysis. **Because** (C) the basic procedural protections of the common law have been regarded as so fundamental, [**therefore**] (D) very few cases have arisen in which a party has complained of their denial:

(B and C), therefore D.

In fact, (E) most of our Due Process decisions involve arguments that traditional procedures provide too little protection **and** (F) that additional safeguards are necessary to ensure compliance with the Constitution. **Nevertheless**, (G) there are a handful of cases in which a party has been deprived of liberty **or** property without the safeguards of common law procedure:

(E and F) and G.

(H) When the absent procedures would have provided protection against arbitrary **and** inaccurate adjudication, (I) this Court has **not** hesitated to find the proceedings violative of Due Process:

If H, then I.

17. The Court then begins its response to the argument in 16: (A) The first, limitation of punitive damages to the amount specified, is hardly a constraint at all, **because** (B) there is no limit to the amount the plaintiff can request, **and** (C) it is unclear whether an award exceeding the amount requested could be set aside. (D) See *Tenold v. Weyerhaeuser Co*: Oregon Constitution bars court from examining jury award to ensure compliance with $500,000 statutory limit on noneconomic damages:

(B, C, D), therefore A.

II.

5. Precedent case example: (A) "The guaranty of the right to jury trial in suits at common law, incorporated in the Bill of Rights as one of the first ten amendments of the Constitution of the United States, was interpreted by the Supreme Court of the United States to refer to jury trial as it had been theretofore known in England; **and so** (B) it is that the federal judges, like the English judges, have always exercised the prerogative of granting a new trial when the verdict was clearly against the weight of the evidence, whether it be **because** (C) excessive damages were awarded **or** (D) for any other reason."

[A and (C or D)], therefore B.

III.

5. Second, (A) Oberg was **not** allowed to introduce evidence regarding Honda's wealth until he "presented evidence sufficient to justify to the court a prima facie claim of punitive damages. (B) During the course of trial, evidence of the

defendant's ability to pay shall **not** be admitted **unless and until** (C) the party entitled to recover establishes a prima facie right to recover [punitive damages]." (D) This evidentiary rule is designed to lessen the risk "that juries will use their verdicts to express biases against big businesses," to take into account "[t]he total deterrent effect of other punishment imposed upon the defendant as a result of the misconduct":

A and (B only if C).

9. The passage lays out the facts and issues, but the direct conclusion needs to be added:

(A) The Court's opinion in *Haslip* went on to describe the checks Alabama places on the jury's discretion *postverdict*—through excessiveness review by the trial court, **and** appellate review, which tests the award against specific substantive criteria. (B) While postverdict review of that character is **not** available in Oregon, (C) the seven factors against which Alabama's Supreme Court tests punitive awards strongly resemble the statutory criteria Oregon's juries are instructed to apply. **And** (D) this Court has often acknowledged, **and** generally respected, the presumption that juries follow the instructions they are given. (E) As the Supreme Court of Oregon observed, *Haslip* "determined only that the Alabama procedure, as a whole and in its net effect, did **not** violate the Due Process Clause."

A, B, C, D, E.

Therefore, [The Honda decision did **not** violate the Due Process Clause].

13. In short, (A) Oregon has enacted legal standards confining punitive damage awards in product liability cases. (B) These state standards are judicially enforced by means of comparatively comprehensive preverdict procedures but markedly limited postverdict review, (C) for Oregon has elected to make fact-finding, once supporting evidence is produced, the province of the jury.... (D) The Court today invalidates this choice, largely **because** (E) it concludes that English and early American courts generally provided judicial review of the size of punitive damage awards. (F) The Court's account of the relevant history is **not** compelling.

A and B and C.
E and F.
Therefore D.

17. **Furthermore**, (A) common law courts reviewed punitive damage verdicts extremely deferentially, if at all. (B) See *Day* v. *Woodworth*: assessment of "exemplary, punitive, **or** vindictive damages ... has been always left to the discretion of the jury, as the degree of punishment to be thus inflicted must depend on the peculiar circumstances of each case"; (C) *Missouri Pacific R. Co.* v. *Humes*: "[t]he discretion of the jury in such cases is **not** controlled by any very definite rules"; (D) *Barry* v. *Edmunds*: in "actions for torts where no precise rule of law fixes the recoverable damages, it is

the peculiar function of the jury to determine the amount by their verdict." (E) True, 19th century judges occasionally asserted that they had authority to overturn damage awards upon concluding, from the size of an award, that the jury's decision must have been based on "partiality" **or** "passion and prejudice." **But** (F) courts rarely *exercised* this authority.

B, C, D, E, F.
Therefore A.

21. (A) Oregon's procedures adequately guide the jury charged with the responsibility to determine a plaintiff's qualification for, **and** (B) the amount of, punitive damages, **and on that account** (C) do **not** deny defendants procedural due process; (D) Oregon's Supreme Court correctly refused to rule that "an award of punitive damages, to comport with the requirements of the Due Process Clause, *always* must be subject to a form of postverdict or appellate review" for excessiveness; (E) the verdict in this particular case, considered in light of this Court's decisions in *Haslip* and *TXO*, hardly appears "so 'grossly excessive' as to violate the substantive component of the Due Process Clause," *TXO*. **Accordingly**, (F) the Court's procedural directive to the state court is neither necessary nor proper. (G) The Supreme Court of Oregon has **not** refused to enforce federal law, **and** (H) I would affirm its judgment.

(A and B), therefore C.
Therefore D.
E, therefore (G and H).
Therefore F.

CHAPTER 12

Exercises 12A

5. Factual claim
9. Personal value claim
13. Moral value claim

Exercises 12B

5. False
9. False
13. True

Exercises 12E

I.

5. stealing

Argument: *Situation ethics:* Stealing is sometimes justified. For example, if a society is corrupt and the economy is such that survival is difficult, then stealing from those who have amassed their wealth through corrupt means is morally justified. **Discussion of the argument:** Stealing is never justified. If a society is corrupt, then all citizens must do their best to change it by moral means. That includes protest and civil disobedience. Stealing simply copies a behavior that is unjustified, no matter who does it and for whatever purpose.

9. animal rights

Argument: *Relativism:* Since there are no universal objective rights even for humans, it stands to reason that animals do not have any rights either. Besides, any "right" is provided by a collective agreement among people with free will, those capable of making rational decisions. There is no evidence that animals act on anything other than instinct; therefore, any talk of "animal rights" is misguided.

Discussion of the argument: Even if there are no universal objective rights, we can still agree to establish certain basic rights for others. For example, most people agree that humans have basic rights regardless of their physical or mental capabilities. Likewise, we can choose to designate certain basic rights to animals.

13. freedom of speech

Argument: *Emotivism:* Even though most people believe that freedom of speech is a fundamental right of all humans, that "social fact" does not make it objective. In other words, people have a strong *emotional* attachment to the idea of freedom of speech, but that in no way makes it an objective fact of the world.

Discussion of the argument: The "social fact" aspect of freedom of speech is important for people to be able to recognize repressive and dictatorial regimes, and to take steps to remedy the situations. The ability to criticize a government through freedom of speech is a sign of a healthy and mature society.

17. birth control

Argument: *Situation ethics:* Birth control is an effective way to control overpopulation, especially in undeveloped countries where children have no real hope of long-term survival. It takes pressure off individual families who may not be able to feed another mouth. It allows people to decide when and if they want to have children, and thereby take better control over their lives.

Discussion of the argument: Birth control can also mean stopping pregnancies for any reason whatsoever. There are many countries where female children are not wanted, so couples take it upon themselves to abort female fetuses. In the future, people might decide to eliminate any fetus if it doesn't conform to their expectations.

II.

5. **Argument:** After more than three years of pressure from shareholders, religious groups and blacks, the Colgate-Palmolive Company announced yesterday that it would rename Darkie, a popular toothpaste that it sells in Asia, and redesign its logotype, a minstrel in blackface. It is plain wrong, and it is offensive. Therefore, the morally right thing dictated that we must change. **Discussion:** *Deontology* holds that we have a duty to not offend others. If the toothpaste design and logo offends a group of people, and according to all accounts even shareholders in the company agreed that it is offensive, then the company has the responsibility to change the design.

9. **Argument:** Different cultures have different views on concussions and different views on identifying concussions, or even what the symptoms are that may suggest concussion. We know from research, for example, that the reporting of symptoms varies by language of origin. We have determined that players from different nationalities and cultural backgrounds report concussions in different manners. Different cultures also put more or less importance around different symptoms. One culture may not consider a headache to be important and won't report it, but they will report dizziness. Meanwhile, headaches can be one of the indicators for post-concussion syndrome. [Therefore, we should be more cautious and explore different ways of identifying possible concussion cases.]

Discussion: According to *relativism*, we should not expect people from different cultures, people with different languages and different nationalities, to agree on when a concussion occurred. But since a concussion can be medically defined with some degree of precision, we should apply those medical standards and the appropriate tests to determine the objective aspect of a concussion, instead of relying on people's subjective opinions on whether they think they have suffered a concussion.

CHAPTER 13

Exercises 13A

5. *Sample:* 6000 urban public high school seniors throughout the United States
Population: All U.S. high school seniors
Sample size: The sample is large and taken from throughout the United States. This raises the likelihood that the sample is representative of the population.
Potential bias: The sample excludes private high schools. This reduces the likelihood that the sample is representative of the population, because there may be a significant difference between the two groups' test scores. Their exclusion from the study may bias the results in one direction or another.
Randomness: This is a random sample. This raises the likelihood that the sample is representative of the population. However, it would be better for the researchers to generalize to public school seniors because that is what they studied.

9. *Sample:* The results of the World Series from 1903 to 2008 and the correlation to sales
Population: Future World Series winners
Sample size: The sample includes the results from 105 years. The sample is certainly large enough to be representative of the past winners, since it includes nearly the entire past population. However, since the researchers are projecting into the future, there may be reasons to think that future society may not be the same as that represented in the sample.

Potential bias: The sample clearly shows a past trend. However, since we know that cigarette and liquor sales are affected by many social factors, the extended trend may be a simple correlation and not an indication of any real connection (the issue of *correlation* will be explored further in the next chapter). This allows us to question the likelihood that the sample is representative of the population. *Randomness:* In a sense, randomness is not an issue here. If all the World Series results are included, then no data are missing regarding other World Series.

Exercises 13B

I.
5. Mean: 186.7; Median: 200; Mode: 200

II.
5. Mean: $1200.30; Median: $1000; Mode: $1000

III.
5. Mean: 3.13; Median: 3.16; Mode: 3.16

IV.
5. Mean: 55.29″; Median: 74″; Modes: 74″, 80″

Exercises 13C

I.
5. The standard deviation is 73.67.
   Step 1: 186.7
   Step 2: −86.7; −76.7; 13.3; 13.3; 23.3; 113.3
   Step 3: 7516.9; 5882.9; 176.9; 176.9; 542.9; 12,836.9
   Step 4: 27,133.4
   Step 5: 5426.68
   Step 6: 73.67

II.
5. The standard deviation is 1642.90.
   Step 1: 1200.30
   Step 2: −1199.80; −1199.30; −200.30; −200.30; 2799.70
   Step 3: 1,439,520.04; 1,438,320.49; 40,120.09; 40,120.09; 7,838,320.09
   Step 4: 10,796,400.80
   Step 5: 2,699,100.20
   Step 6: 1642.90

III.

5. The standard deviation is 0.17.

Step 1: 3.13

Step 2: −0.27; −0.17; 0.03; 0.03; 0.13; 0.23

Step 3: 0.07; 0.03; 0.00; 0.00; 0.02; 0.05

Step 4: 0.17

Step 5: 0.03

Step 6: 0.17

IV.

5. The standard deviation is 27.22.

Step 1: 55.29

Step 2: −31.29; −28.29; −27.29; 18.71; 18.71; 24.71; 24.71

Step 3: 979.06; 800.32; 744.74; 350.06; 350.06; 610.58; 610.58

Step 4: 4445.40

Step 5: 740.90

Step 6: 27.22

Exercises 13E

5. First, we are told that the "hundreds of millions of dollars" are wasted, presumably because of late penalties incurred with the IRS. Second, "workers have forgone huge amounts of money in matching 401(k) contributions because they never got around to signing up for a retirement plan." However, no accurate figures are given to support this claim. Third, we are told that "Seventy percent of patients suffering from glaucoma risk blindness because they don't use their eyedrops regularly." However, no information is given to show how this figure was arrived at; we are not told the kind of study, the sample size, or whether it was random. Fourth, the claim that "Procrastination also inflicts major costs on businesses and governments" has no supporting evidence. Also, the term "major costs" is vague. Finally, the claim that "the bankruptcy of General Motors was due in part to executives' penchant for delaying tough decisions" has no supporting evidence.

CHAPTER 14

Exercises 14A

I.

5. Sufficient condition. Since June has exactly 30 days, if the antecedent is true, then the consequent will be true as well.

9. Sufficient condition. Since 100 pennies is the equivalent of $1, if the antecedent is true, then the consequent will be true as well.

13. Sufficient condition. *If* it is true that I am eating a banana, then it must be true that I am eating a fruit.

II.

5. Necessary condition. June has exactly 30 days. Given this, if this month does *not* have exactly 30 days, then this month is *not* June.

9. Necessary condition. If I do *not* have *at least* the equivalent of $1, then I have *at most* 99 cents. Given this, I do *not* have exactly 100 pennies.

13. Necessary condition. If I am *not* eating a fruit, then I am *not* eating a banana.

Exercises 14C

I.

5. False

9. True

II.

5. The joint method of agreement and difference

III.

5.

Possible Causes

The **Effect**	Dinner	Groceries	Gas	Lent to Friend	Lost the Money
Missing $20					✓

The chart displays the *method of agreement*. We can conclude that losing the money is probably causally connected to the missing $20.

9.

Possible Causes

Instances of the **Effect**	Batch of Seeds	Soil	Watering Schedule	Amount of Water	Sun	Fertilizer
Plant 1: Twice the pounds as plant 2.	✓	✓	✓	✓	✓	✓
Plant 2: Half the pounds as plant 1.	✓	✓	✓	✓	✓	

The chart displays the *method of difference*. We can conclude that spraying the plant with a fertilizer once a week is probably causally connected to producing twice as many pounds of tomatoes.

13.

Minutes Boiling an Egg

	3	4	5	6	7	8	9	10
Hardness of Egg	Runny	Thicker	Perfect	Harder	Harder	Harder	Harder	Perfect

The chart displays the *method of concomitant variations*. We can conclude that the number of minutes boiling an egg is probably causally connected to the hardness of the egg.

Exercises 14H

I.

5. True
9. False

II.

5. *Hypothesis 1:* Your friend forgot to water the plants.
   Experiment 1: Check for moisture in the dirt.
   Hypothesis 2: Your plants have contracted a disease.
   Experiment 2: Check with a plant nursery.

9. *Hypothesis 1:* The service was interrupted and you are both calling at the same time.
   Hypothesis 2: Your mother took another call and accidentally disconnected your call.
   Experiment: Wait for a few minutes and try dialing again.

III.

5. *Hypothesis:* The battery in Joe's car is dead.
   Experiment: Replace the battery.
   Prediction: If the hypothesis is correct, then the car will start.
   Confirm/Disconfirm: The prediction was true, and the evidence confirms the hypothesis.
   Alternative Explanations: The clamps on either the positive or negative terminal heads might have been loose. If so, the battery might not have been dead or defective. The battery could have (and should have) been tested. It may have simply needed recharging. Without having evidence to rule out these possibilities, we must be careful not to assign too much weight to the existing evidence.

9. *Hypothesis:* Becky is allergic to her cat.
   Experiment: Two experiments: (A) Becky will give the cat to a neighbor for a day, during which time Becky will see if she stops sneezing. (B) Becky will take allergy medicine to control the sneezing.
   Prediction: For the first experiment, if the hypothesis is correct, then Becky should stop sneezing. For the second experiment, provided the medicine is effective, Becky should stop sneezing.
   Confirm/Disconfirm: Both predictions turned out true, and Becky was convinced that the evidence confirmed her hypothesis.
   Alternative Explanations: We are told that the sneezing started about the same time as Becky's husband started using a new flea powder, and the sneezing stopped when he started using the old brand of flea powder. This evidence certainly weakens Becky's hypothesis, but it does not mean that her hypothesis cannot be true. We would have to do additional experiments with combinations of old and new flea powder and the allergy medicine to be able to gather the strongest possible evidence to confirm or disconfirm either Becky's hypothesis or the alternative flea powder hypothesis.

Index

Notes: Index entries preceded by an asterisk (*) may also be found in the glossary. Page numbers followed by *b* refer to text boxes.

SIX STEPS FOR
CALCULATING STANDARD DEVIATION

Step 1:   Calculate the mean value.

Step 2:   Calculate the difference between each value in the set and the mean value.

Step 3:   Multiply each difference by itself (square each difference).

Step 4:   Add the results of the squaring process in step 3.

Step 5:   Divide the result of step 4 by one fewer than the number of members in the set.

Step 6:   The square root of the total variance is the standard deviation.

PROBABILITY METHODS

Restricted conjunction method: $Pr\,(A\;and\;B) = Pr\,(A) \times Pr\,(B)$

General conjunction method: $Pr\,(A\;and\;B) = Pr\,(A) \times Pr\,(B,\;if\;A)$

Restricted disjunction method: $Pr\,(A\;or\;B) = Pr\,(A) + Pr\,(B)$

General disjunction method: $Pr\,(A\;or\;B) = [Pr\,(A) + Pr\,(B)] - [Pr\,(A) \times Pr\,(B)]$

Negation method: $Pr\,(\sim\!A) = 1 - Pr\,(A)$

Bayes's Theorem: $Pr\,(A,\;if\;B) = \dfrac{Pr\,(B,\;if\;A)\; \times\; Pr\,(A)}{Pr\,(B)}$

MILL'S METHODS

Method of agreement: The method that looks at two or more instances of an event to see what they have in common.

Method of difference: The method that looks for what all the instances of an event do not have in common.

Joint method of agreement and difference: If two or more instances of an event have only one thing in common, while the instances in which it does *not* occur all share the absence of that thing, then the item is a likely cause.

Method of residues: The method that subtracts from a complex set of events those parts that already have known causes.

Method of concomitant variations: The method that looks for two factors that vary together.

TYPES OF DEFINITIONS

Intensional definition: Assigns a meaning to a term by listing the properties or attributes shared by all the objects that are denoted by the term.

Synonymous definition: Assigns a meaning to a term by providing another term with the same meaning; in other words, by providing a synonym.

Word origin definition: A meaning can be assigned to a term by investigating its origin. The study of the history, development, and sources of words is called *etymology*.

Operational definition: Defines a term by specifying a measurement procedure.

Definition by genus and difference: Assigns a meaning to a term (the species) by establishing a genus and combining it with the attribute that distinguishes the members of that species.

Extensional definition: Assigns meaning to a term by indicating the class members denoted by the term.

Ostensive definition: Involves demonstrating the term—for example, by pointing to a member of the class that the term denotes.

Enumerative definition: Assigns meaning to a term by naming the individual members of the class denoted by the term.

Definition by subclass: Assigns meaning to a term by naming subclasses (species) of the class denoted by the term.

Stipulative definition: Introduces a new meaning to a term or symbol.

Lexical definition: A definition based on the common use of a word, term, or symbol.

Functional definition: Specifies the purpose or use of the objects denoted by the term.

Precising definition: Reduces the vagueness and ambiguity of a term by providing a sharp focus, often a technical meaning, for a term.

Theoretical definition: Assigns a meaning to a term by providing an understanding of how the term fits into a general theory.

Persuasive definition: Assigns a meaning to a term with the direct purpose of influencing attitudes or opinions.

INFORMAL FALLACIES

1. **_Ad hominem_ abusive:** The fallacy is distinguished by an attack on alleged character flaws of a person instead of the person's argument.

2. **_Ad hominem_ circumstantial:** The fallacy occurs when someone's argument is rejected based on the circumstances of the person's life.

3. **Poisoning the well:** The fallacy occurs when a person is attacked _before_ she has a chance to present her case.

4. **_Tu quoque:_** The fallacy is distinguished by the specific attempt of one person to avoid the issue at hand by claiming the other person is a hypocrite.

5. **Appeal to the people:** The fallacy occurs when an argument manipulates a psychological need or desire, such as the desire to belong to a popular group, or the need for group solidarity, so that the reader or listener will accept the conclusion.

6. **Appeal to pity:** The fallacy results from an exclusive reliance on a sense of pity or mercy for support of a conclusion.

7. **Appeal to fear or force:** The fallacy occurs when a threat of harmful consequences (physical or otherwise) is used to force acceptance of a course of action that would otherwise be unacceptable.

8. **Rigid application of a generalization:** When a generalization or rule is inappropriately applied to the case at hand. The fallacy results from the mistaken belief that a generalization or a rule is universal (meaning it has no exceptions).

9. **Hasty generalization:** An argument that relies on a small sample that is unlikely to represent the population.

10. **Composition:** There are two forms of the fallacy: (1) The mistaken transfer of an attribute of the individual _parts of an object_ to the _object as a whole_. (2) The mistaken transfer of an attribute of the individual _members of a class_ to the _class itself_.

11. **Division:** There are two forms of the fallacy: (1) The mistaken transfer of an attribute of an _object as a whole_ to the individual _parts of the object_. (2) The mistaken transfer of an attribute of a _class_ to the individual _members of the class_.

12. **Biased sample:** An argument that uses a nonrepresentative sample as support for a statistical claim about an entire population.

13. **_Post hoc_:** The fallacy occurs from the mistaken assumption that just because one event occurred before another event, the first event _must have caused_ the second event.

14. **Slippery slope:** An argument that attempts to connect a series of occurrences such that the first link in a chain leads directly to a second link, and so on, until a final unwanted situation is said to be the inevitable result.

15. **Begging the question:** In one type, the fallacy occurs when a premise is simply reworded in the conclusion. In a second type, called circular reasoning, a set of statements seem to support each other with no clear beginning or end point. In a third type, the argument assumes certain key information that may be controversial or is not supported by facts.

16. **Complex question:** The fallacy occurs when a single question actually contains multiple parts and an unestablished hidden assumption.

17. **Appeal to ignorance:** An argument built on a position of ignorance claims either that (1) a statement must be true because it has not been proven to be false or (2) a statement must be false because it has not been proven to be true.

18. **Appeal to an unqualified authority:** An argument that relies on the opinions of people who either have _no_ expertise, training, or knowledge relevant to the issue at hand, or whose testimony is not trustworthy.

19. **False dichotomy:** The fallacy occurs when it is assumed that only two choices are possible, when in fact others exist.

20. **Equivocation:** The fallacy occurs when the conclusion of an argument relies on an intentional or unintentional shift in the meaning of a term or phrase in the premises.

21. **Straw man:** The fallacy occurs when an argument is misrepresented in order to create a new argument that can be easily refuted. The new argument is so weak that it is "made of straw." The arguer then falsely claims that his opponent's real argument has been defeated.

22. **Red herring:** The fallacy occurs when someone completely ignores an opponent's position and changes the subject, diverting the discussion in a new direction.

23. **Misleading precision:** A claim that appears to be statistically significant but is not.

24. **Missing the point:** When premises that seem to lead logically to one conclusion are used instead to support an unexpected conclusion.

INFERENCE RULES FOR PREDICATE LOGIC

Universal instantiation (UI)

$$\frac{(x)\mathcal{S}x}{\mathcal{S}y} \qquad\qquad \frac{(x)\mathcal{S}x}{\mathcal{S}a}$$

Universal generalization (UG)

Not Permitted

$$\frac{\mathcal{S}y}{(x)\mathcal{S}x} \qquad\qquad \frac{\mathcal{S}a}{(x)\mathcal{S}x}$$

Restrictions on UG:

1. *Universal generalization cannot be used within an indented proof sequence, if the instantial variable is free in the first line of the sequence.*
2. *Universal generalization cannot be used if the instantial variable y is free in any line that was obtained by existential instantiation (EI).*

Existential instantiation (EI)

Not Permitted

$$\frac{(\exists x)\mathcal{S}x}{\mathcal{S}a} \qquad\qquad \frac{(\exists x)\mathcal{S}x}{\mathcal{S}y}$$

Restriction on EI: The existential name (a) cannot be a name that appears in any previous line of the proof, and it cannot appear in the line that indicates the conclusion to be derived.

Existential generalization (EG)

$$\frac{\mathcal{S}a}{(\exists x)\mathcal{S}x} \qquad\qquad \frac{\mathcal{S}y}{(\exists x)\mathcal{S}x}$$

Change of quantifier (CQ)

$$(x)\mathcal{S}x \; :: \; \sim(\exists x)\sim\mathcal{S}x$$
$$\sim(x)\mathcal{S}x \; :: \; (\exists x)\sim\mathcal{S}x$$
$$(\exists x)\mathcal{S}x \; :: \; \sim(x)\sim\mathcal{S}x$$
$$\sim(\exists x)\mathcal{S}x \; :: \; (x)\sim\mathcal{S}x$$

Identity rules (Id)

1. $\underline{\text{Premise}}$ 2. $\Phi = \Psi \; :: \; \Psi = \Phi$ 3. $\mathcal{S}\Phi$

$\Phi = \Phi$ $\dfrac{\Phi = \Psi}{\mathcal{S}\Psi}$

*Φ, Ψ are any individual *variables* or individual *constants*

QUANTITY, QUALITY, AND DISTRIBUTION

A: All S are P.
Universal
Affirmative
Subject term distributed
Predicate term undistributed

E: No S are P.
Universal
Negative
Subject term distributed
Predicate term distributed

I: Some S are P.
Particular
Affirmative
Subject term undistributed
Predicate term undistributed

O: Some S are not P.
Particular
Negative
Subject term undistributed
Predicate term distributed

LOGICALLY EQUIVALENT STATEMENT FORMS

CONVERSION

E: No S are P.   **E:** No P are S.

I: Some S are P.   **I:** Some P are S.

OBVERSION

A: All S are P.   **E:** No S are non-P.

E: No S are P.   **A:** All S are non-P.

I: Some S are P.   **O:** Some S are not non-P.

O: Some S are not P.   **I:** Some S are non-P.

CONTRAPOSITION

A: All S are P.   **A:** All non-P are non-S.

O: Some S are not P.   **O:** Some non-P are not non-S.

FOUR FIGURES OF CATEGORICAL SYLLOGISMS

M P
S M
S P
Figure 1

P M
S M
S P
Figure 2

M P
M S
S P
Figure 3

P M
M S
S P
Figure 4

RULES FOR CATEGORICAL SYLLOGISMS

Rule 1: The middle term must be distributed in at least one premise.
Rule 2: If a term is distributed in the conclusion, then it must be distributed in a premise.
Rule 3: A categorical syllogism cannot have two negative premises.
Rule 4: A negative premise must have a negative conclusion.
Rule 5: A negative conclusion must have a negative premise.
Rule 6: Two universal premises cannot have a particular conclusion.

TRUTH TABLES FOR PROPOSITIONAL OPERATORS

Negation	
p	$\sim p$
T	F
F	T

Conjunction		
p	q	$p \cdot q$
T	T	T
T	F	F
F	T	F
F	F	F

Disjunction		
p	q	$p \vee q$
T	T	T
T	F	T
F	T	T
F	F	F

Conditional		
p	q	$p \supset q$
T	T	T
T	F	F
F	T	T
F	F	T

Biconditional		
p	q	$p \equiv q$
T	T	T
T	F	F
F	T	F
F	F	T

THE EIGHT IMPLICATION RULES

Modus Ponens (MP)

$p \supset q$
$\dfrac{p}{q}$

Modus Tollens (MT)

$p \supset q$
$\dfrac{\sim q}{\sim p}$

Hypothetical Syllogism (HS)

$p \supset q$
$\dfrac{q \supset r}{p \supset r}$

Disjunctive Syllogism (DS)

$p \vee q \qquad p \vee q$
$\dfrac{\sim p}{q} \qquad \dfrac{\sim q}{p}$

Simplification (Simp)

$\dfrac{p \cdot q}{p} \qquad \dfrac{p \cdot q}{q}$

Conjunction (Conj)

p
$\dfrac{q}{p \cdot q}$

Addition (Add)

$\dfrac{p}{p \vee q}$

Constructive Dilemma (CD)

$(p \supset q) \cdot (r \supset s)$
$\dfrac{p \vee r}{q \vee s}$

THE TEN REPLACEMENT RULES

De Morgan (DM)

$\sim(p \cdot q) :: \sim p \vee \sim q$
$\sim(p \vee q) :: \sim p \cdot \sim q$

Double negation (DN)

$p :: \sim\sim p$

Commutation (Com)

$p \vee q :: q \vee p$
$p \cdot q :: q \cdot p$

Association (Assoc)

$p \vee (q \vee r) :: (p \vee q) \vee r$
$p \cdot (q \cdot r) :: (p \cdot q) \cdot r$

Distribution (Dist)

$p \cdot (q \vee r) :: (p \cdot q) \vee (p \cdot r)$
$p \vee (q \cdot r) :: (p \vee q) \cdot (p \vee r)$

Transposition (Trans)

$p \supset q :: \sim q \supset \sim p$

Material implication (Impl)

$p \supset q :: \sim p \vee q$

Material equivalence (Equiv)

$p \equiv q :: (p \supset q) \cdot (q \supset p)$
$p \equiv q :: (p \cdot q) \vee (\sim p \cdot \sim q)$

Exportation (Exp)

$(p \cdot q) \supset r :: p \supset (q \supset r)$

Tautology (Taut)

$p :: p \vee p$
$p :: p \cdot p$